MW00851805

WALT WHITMAN IN CONTEXT

Walt Whitman is a poet of contexts. His poetic practice was one of observing, absorbing, and then reflecting the world around him. *Walt Whitman in Context* provides brief, provocative explorations of thirty-eight different contexts – geographic, literary, cultural, and political – through which to engage Whitman's life and work. Written by distinguished scholars of Whitman and nineteenth-century American literature and culture, this collection synthesizes scholarly and historical sources and brings together new readings and original research.

JOANNA LEVIN is Associate Professor and Chair of the English Department at Chapman University. She is the author of *Bohemia in America, 1858–1920* (2010) and coeditor, with Edward Whitley, of *Whitman among the Bohemians* (2014).

EDWARD WHITLEY is Associate Professor in the English Department at Lehigh University. He is the author of *American Bards: Walt Whitman and Other Unlikely Candidates for National Poet* (2010) and coeditor, with Joanna Levin, of *Whitman among the Bohemians* (2014).

WALT WHITMAN IN CONTEXT

EDITED BY

JOANNA LEVIN

Chapman University

EDWARD WHITLEY

Lehigh University

CAMBRIDGE
UNIVERSITY PRESS

CAMBRIDGE
UNIVERSITY PRESS

University Printing House, Cambridge CB2 8BS, United Kingdom

One Liberty Plaza, 20th Floor, New York, NY 10006, USA

477 Williamstown Road, Port Melbourne, VIC 3207, Australia

314–321, 3rd Floor, Plot 3, Splendor Forum, Jasola District Centre, New Delhi – 110025, India

79 Anson Road, #06–04/06, Singapore 079906

Cambridge University Press is part of the University of Cambridge.

It furthers the University's mission by disseminating knowledge in the pursuit of education, learning, and research at the highest international levels of excellence.

www.cambridge.org
Information on this title: www.cambridge.org/9781108418959
DOI: 10.1017/9781108292443

First published 2018

Printed in the United States of America by Sheridan Books, Inc.

A catalogue record for this publication is available from the British Library.

Library of Congress Cataloging-in-Publication Data
NAMES: Levin, Joanna, editor. | Whitley, Edward.
TITLE: Walt Whitman in context / edited by Joanna Levin, Edward Whitley.
DESCRIPTION: Cambridge ; New York, NY : Cambridge University Press, 2018. | Series: Literature in context | Includes bibliographical references and index.
IDENTIFIERS: LCCN 2017057918 | ISBN 9781108418959 (hardback)
SUBJECTS: LCSH: Whitman, Walt, 1819–1892 – Criticism and interpretation.
CLASSIFICATION: LCC PS3238 .W3666 2018 | DDC 811/.3–dc23
LC record available at https://lccn.loc.gov/2017057918

ISBN 978-1-108-41895-9 Hardback

Contents

Illustrations

Notes on Contributors

DAVID HAVEN BLAKE teaches at The College of New Jersey. He is the author of *Walt Whitman and the Culture of American Celebrity* (2006) and the coeditor of *Walt Whitman, Where the Future Becomes Present* (2008). His most recent book is *Liking Ike: Eisenhower, Advertising, and the Rise of Celebrity Politics* (2016), winner of the 2017 PROSE award for Media & Cultural Studies.

STEPHANIE M. BLALOCK is Digital Humanities Librarian in the Digital Scholarship and Publishing Studio at the University of Iowa Libraries. She is an associate editor of *The Vault at Pfaff's*, an associate editor of the *Walt Whitman Archive*, and coeditor of a digital edition of Whitman's fiction for the *Archive*. She is the author of *Go to Pfaff's: The History of a Restaurant and Lager Beer Saloon* (2014), and her research focuses on Whitman's fiction.

RUTH L. BOHAN is the author of *Looking into Walt Whitman: American Art 1850–1920* (2006). Her essays on Whitman and the visual arts have appeared in *Whitman among the Bohemians* (2014), *The Cambridge Companion to Walt Whitman* (1995), *Word & Image*, *Walt Whitman Quarterly Review*, and *Mickle Street Review*. She is Professor of Art History at the University of Missouri–St. Louis.

ADAM BRADFORD is Associate Professor of English at Florida Atlantic University where he researches and teaches nineteenth-century American literature. His research relating to Whitman has appeared in *Walt Whitman Quarterly Review*, *Mickle Street Review*, and *Sentimentalism in Nineteenth-Century America: Literary and Cultural Practices* (2013). He is also the author of *Communities of Death: Whitman, Poe, and the American Culture of Mourning* (2014).

MARTIN T. BUINICKI is the Friedrich Professor of American Literature at Valparaiso University and author of *Negotiating Copyright: Authorship and the Discourse of Literary Property Rights in Nineteenth-Century America* (2003) and *Walt Whitman's Reconstruction: Poetry and Publishing between Memory and History* (2011). He has published essays in a number of books and journals, including Cambridge's *A History of American Civil War Literature* (2015), *American Literary History*, *American Literary Realism*, the *Walt Whitman Quarterly Review*, and *The Journal of Popular Culture*.

MATT COHEN teaches at the University of Nebraska–Lincoln. He is a contributing editor at the *Walt Whitman Archive* and the author of *Whitman's Drift: Imagining Literary Distribution* (2017).

MICHAEL C. COHEN is Associate Professor of English at the University of California–Los Angeles (UCLA). He is the author of *The Social Lives of Poems in Nineteenth-Century America* (2015) and coeditor of *The Poetry of Charles Brockden Brown* (2018) in addition to other essays on nineteenth-century American poetry and culture. His current project examines the role of poetry in the development of American public education between 1830 and 1940.

PETER COVIELLO is Professor of English at the University of Illinois–Chicago, specializing in American literature and queer studies. He is the editor of Walt Whitman's *Memoranda During the War* (2004) and the author, most recently, of *Tomorrow's Parties: Sex and the Untimely in Nineteenth-Century America* (2013), a finalist for a 2014 Lambda Literary Award in LGBT Studies.

EDWARD S. CUTLER is the Donald R. & Jean S. Marshall Professor of Humanities at Brigham Young University and the author of *Recovering the New: Transatlantic Roots of Modernism* (2003). He has published articles on Whitman in the *Walt Whitman Quarterly Review* and *American Literary Realism*. He is currently completing a monograph on Whitman and romantic philosophy.

JESSICA DESPAIN is Associate Professor of English at Southern Illinois University Edwardsville (SIUE) and codirects SIUE's IRIS Center for the Digital Humanities. She is the author of *Nineteenth-Century Transatlantic Reprinting and the Embodied Book* (2014) and the lead editor of *The Wide, Wide World Digital Edition*, an exploration of the more than 170 reprints of Susan Warner's bestselling nineteenth-century novel. She has published articles on transatlantic studies, book history, and the digital humanities.

DAVID O. DOWLING is Associate Professor and Director of Undergraduate Studies at the University of Iowa School of Journalism and Mass Communication where he specializes in publishing industries and the culture of media production. The author of six books including *Emerson's Protégés: Mentoring and Marketing Transcendentalism's Future* (2014), his articles have appeared in such journals as *Convergence, Genre: Forms of Discourse and Culture, Leviathan: A Journal of Melville Studies, Digital Humanities Quarterly*, and *American Journalism*.

LESLIE ELIZABETH ECKEL is Associate Professor of English at Suffolk University in Boston. She is the author of *Atlantic Citizens: Nineteenth-Century American Writers at Work in the World* (2013), and editor, with Clare Frances Elliott, of *The Edinburgh Companion to Literary Studies* (2016). Her current book project focuses on utopian networks in the long nineteenth century.

PAUL ERICKSON is the Director of the Programs in Arts, Humanities, and Culture and in American Institutions, Society, and the Public Good at the American Academy of Arts and Sciences. From 2007 to 2016 he was the Director of Academic Programs at the American Antiquarian Society. He has written widely on the history of the book and popular antebellum print culture.

ED FOLSOM is the Roy J. Carver Professor of English at The University of Iowa, the editor of the *Walt Whitman Quarterly Review*, codirector of the online *Whitman Archive*, and editor of the Whitman Series at the University of Iowa Press. He is the author or editor of numerous books and essays on Whitman and other American writers. He has been awarded a Guggenheim Fellowship and multiple grants from the National Endowment for the Humanities.

CHRISTINE GERHARDT is Professor of American Studies at the University of Bamberg, Germany. She is the author of *A Place for Humility: Whitman, Dickinson, and the Natural World* (2014) and of a monograph on the Reconstruction period in American novels, *Rituale des Scheiterns: Die Reconstruction-Periode im amerikanischen Roman* (2002). She edited the *Handbook of the American Novel of the Nineteenth Century* (2018), coedited *Religion in the United States* (2011), and has published essays on

Whitman, Dickinson, contemporary American poetry, and ecocriticism in various journals.

NICOLE GRAY is Research Assistant Professor in the English Department at the University of Nebraska–Lincoln and an associate editor of the *Walt Whitman Archive*. She has coedited a range of documents for the *Whitman Archive* including *Franklin Evans*, Whitman's short fiction, and Spanish translations of "Poets to Come." Her articles on American literature and book history have appeared in *Rhetoric Society Quarterly*, *Nineteenth-Century Literature*, *The Papers of the Bibliographical Society of America*, and *PMLA*.

JAY GROSSMAN teaches eighteenth- and nineteenth-century American literature and culture, the history of the book, and the history of sexuality at Northwestern University. He is the author of *Reconstituting the American Renaissance: Emerson, Whitman, and the Politics of Representation* (2003) and is at work on a cultural biography of the literary scholar and political activist F. O. Matthiessen.

WALTER GRÜNZWEIG teaches American Studies at TU Dortmund University, Germany. A native of Graz, Austria, he received his BA in English at Ohio University and his MA in English, American, and German literatures at Karl-Franzens-Universität-Graz. His research focuses on the international Whitman, Emerson's cultural criticism, and international education. In 2010 he received the national prize for excellence in university teaching awarded by the German Rectors Conference. He has taught in Berlin, Binghamton (New York), Dakar, Dresden, Graz, Iowa City, Izmir, Klagenfurt, Maribor, Rome, and Trieste.

KAREN KARBIENER teaches at New York University and is an active public scholar in the city. The recipient of Fulbright and Library of Congress Kluge fellowships, she has published an edition of *Leaves of Grass* (2004), two audiobooks on Whitman's influence on modern American poetry, and a book introducing children to Whitman (*Poetry for Kids: Walt Whitman*, 2017). Karbiener is completing a book entitled *New York's Walt Whitman*.

KERRY LARSON is Professor of English at the University of Michigan. He is the author of *Whitman's Drama of Consensus* (1988) and *Imagining Equality in Nineteenth-Century American Literature* (2008). He has also edited *The Cambridge Companion to Nineteenth-Century American*

Poetry (2011) and is currently at work on a book on poetry written in the United States between the American Revolution and the Civil War.

JOANNA LEVIN is Associate Professor and Chair of the English Department at Chapman University. She is the author of *Bohemia in America, 1858–1920* (2010) and coeditor, with Edward Whitley, of *Whitman among the Bohemians* (2014).

JEROME LOVING is Distinguished Professor Emeritus of English at Texas A&M University–College Station. A recipient of a Guggenheim Fellowship and grants from the National Endowment for the Humanities, Loving is the author of numerous books and articles including *Walt Whitman: The Song of Himself* (1999), as well as biographies of Theodore Dreiser and Mark Twain. His *Jack and Norman: A State-Raised Convict and the Legacy of Norman Mailer's "The Executioner's Song"* (2017) is part literary criticism, part social commentary, and part true-crime story.

STEPHEN JOHN MACK is Associate Teaching Professor at the University of Southern California where he teaches classes in advanced writing specializing in the law, political discourse, and social sciences. His research interests include nineteenth-century American literature, democratic theory and culture, and digital literacy. He is the author of *The Pragmatic Whitman: Reimagining American Democracy* (2002) as well as numerous articles on Whitman.

MATT MILLER is Assistant Professor of English at Yeshiva University in Manhattan where he teaches nineteenth- and twentieth-century American literature and creative writing. He is the author of *Collage of Myself: Walt Whitman and the Making of Leaves of Grass* (2010) and is currently completing a manuscript relating Whitman to some surprising twentieth-century influences, including Gertrude Stein and George Oppen.

MAIRE MULLINS is Professor of English at Pepperdine University. She has recently completed a digital humanities project titled *The Selected Letters of Hannah Whitman Heyde*, available on the website *Scholarly Editing: The Annual of the Association for Documentary Editing* (2016). Her essays on Whitman have appeared in *A Companion to Walt Whitman* (2006), *Tulsa Studies in Women's Literature*, the *Walt Whitman Quarterly Review*, *The Walt Whitman Encyclopedia* (1998), *The Tohoku Journal of*

American Studies (Sendai, Japan), *Renascence*, and *The American Transcendental Quarterly*.

WILLIAM PANNAPACKER is the DuMez Professor of English at Hope College and the author of *Revised Lives: Walt Whitman and Nineteenth-Century Authorship* (2004). He has contributed to *Walt Whitman: An Encyclopedia* (1998), *A Companion to Walt Whitman* (2006), and *Leaves of Grass: The Sesquicentennial Essays* (2007). For a half-decade he reviewed publications on Whitman for *American Literary Scholarship* (2005–09).

SASCHA PÖHLMANN is Associate Professor in American Literary History at Ludwig Maximilian University of Munich, Germany. He is the author of *Future-Founding Poetry: Topographies of Beginnings from Whitman to the Twenty-First Century* (2015) and has written essays on Whitman's poetry and prose, as well as on their relation to Washington, DC, Mark Z. Danielewski's novel *Only Revolutions*, Cascadian Black Metal, and the video game *Everything*.

KENNETH M. PRICE is the Hillegass University Professor and codirects the Center for Digital Research at the University of Nebraska–Lincoln. Since 1995 Price has codirected the *Walt Whitman Archive*. He is the author of *To Walt Whitman, America* (2004) and coauthor, with Ed Folsom, of *Re-Scripting Walt Whitman* (2005). A recipient of a Digital Innovation Award from the American Council of Learned Societies (ACLS), he edited, with Ray Siemens, *Literary Studies in the Digital Age: An Evolving Anthology* (2013).

MICHAEL ROBERTSON is Professor of English at The College of New Jersey and author of the award-winning *Worshipping Walt: The Whitman Disciples* (2008). He is a member of the editorial board of the *Walt Whitman Quarterly Review*, coeditor of *Walt Whitman, Where the Future Becomes Present* (2008), and the author of numerous articles on Whitman and religion. His most recent book is *The Last Utopians: Four Late Nineteenth-Century Visionaries and Their Legacy* (2018).

RACHEL RUBINSTEIN is Associate Professor of American Literature and Jewish Studies at Hampshire College. She is the author of *Members of the Tribe: Native America in the Jewish Imagination* (2010). Her current project examines sites of translation, immigration, racial formation, and nationalism across the Americas.

INGRID I. SATELMAJER teaches English and humanities courses at the University of Maryland, College Park. She has published articles on nineteenth-century poetry and periodicals in *Book History*, *American Periodicals*, and *Textual Cultures*, among other places. Her essay "Publishing Pfaff's: Henry Clapp and Poetry in the *Saturday Press*" appeared in *Whitman among the Bohemians* (2014).

REGINA SCHOBER is Assistant Professor at the American Studies Department of Mannheim University, Germany. Her current book project, *Networks and Emerging Knowledge in American Literature and Culture*, examines the network as an epistemological paradigm in American literature and culture from the nineteenth to the twenty-first century. She is coeditor of the special issue *Network Theory and American Culture* of *Amerikastudien* (with Ulfried Reichardt and Heike Schäfer, 2015), of the special issue *Data Fiction: Naturalism, Narrative, Numbers* of *Studies in American Naturalism* (with James Dorson, 2017), as well as of the essay collection *The Failed Individual: Amid Exclusion, Resistance, and the Pleasure of Non-Conformity* (with Katharina Motyl, 2017).

CARMEN TRAMMELL SKAGGS is Associate Professor of English and Associate Dean for Academic Support at Kennesaw State University. She is the author of *Overtones of Opera in American Literature from Whitman to Wharton* (2010).

JASON STACY is Associate Professor of History at Southern Illinois University Edwardsville. He is the author of *Walt Whitman's Multitudes: Labor Reform and Persona in Whitman's Journalism and the First Leaves of Grass, 1840–1855* (2008), editor of *Leaves of Grass 1860: The 150th Anniversary Facsimile Edition* (2009), and coeditor, with Douglas Noverr, of *Walt Whitman's Selected Journalism* (2015). He has published articles on Walt Whitman in the *Mickle Street Review* and the *Walt Whitman Quarterly Review*. He is also a contributing editor to the *Walt Whitman Archive* where he helps edit Whitman's journalism.

LINDSAY TUGGLE is a Research Associate with the Writing and Society Research Center at Western Sydney University, where she also teaches literature. She is the author of *The Afterlives of Specimens: Medicine, Mourning, and Whitman's Civil War* (2017) and a collection of poetry, *Calenture* (2018). She has been a fellow at the Library of Congress, the Mütter Museum and Historical Medical Library, and the Australian Academy of the Humanities.

WILLIAM T. WALTER is President of the Walt Whitman Birthplace Association (WWBA). He began serving on the Board of Directors of the WWBA in the 1980s and was the point monitor during the construction of the Interpretative Center in the 1990s. He holds a PhD in physics from the Massachusetts Institute of Technology. He has been an associate research professor at the Polytechnic Institute of Brooklyn and was involved in the early development of lasers.

EDWARD WHITLEY is Associate Professor of English at Lehigh University and Director of the Mellon Digital Humanities Initiative. He is the author of *American Bards: Walt Whitman and Other Unlikely Candidates for National Poet* (2010). He is coeditor, with Joanna Levin, of *Whitman among the Bohemians* (2014) and codirector, with Robert Weidman, of *The Vault at Pfaff's: An Archive of Art and Literature by the Bohemians of Antebellum New York*.

IVY G. WILSON is Associate Professor of English and Art, Theory, and Practice and Director of the Program in American Studies at Northwestern University. He teaches courses on the comparative literatures of the black diaspora and US literary studies with a particular focus on African American culture. He has published a number of books on nineteenth-century American literary studies, including *Specters of Democracy: Blackness and the Aesthetics of Politics* (2011) and, more recently, the essay collection *Unsettled States* (2014) with Dana Luciano.

BRIAN YOTHERS is the Frances Spatz Leighton Endowed Distinguished Professor of English at the University of Texas–El Paso. He is the author of *Reading Abolition: The Critical Reception of Harriet Beecher Stowe and Frederick Douglass* (2016), *Sacred Uncertainty: Religious Difference and the Shape of Melville's Career* (2015), *Melville's Mirrors: Literary Criticism and America's Most Elusive Author* (2011), and *The Romance of the Holy Land in American Travel Writing, 1790–1876* (2007).

Preface

Walt Whitman is a poet of contexts. Toward the end of his life, Whitman reflected on the cultural and historical contexts that had been at his elbow as he composed the six major editions of his magnum opus, *Leaves of Grass*, between 1855 and 1881. "My Book and I – what a period we have presumed to span!" he wrote. "Those thirty years from 1850 to '80 – and America in them! Proud, proud indeed may we be, if we have cull'd enough of that period in its own spirit to worthily waft a few live breaths of it to the future!" (LG, 565). But rather than take all the credit himself for having captured the zeitgeist of the United States during the decades before, during, and after the Civil War, Whitman instead claimed that "first-class literature does not shine by any luminosity of its own; nor do its poems. They grow of circumstances, and are evolutionary. The actual living light is always curiously from elsewhere" (LG, 565). It should come as a shock to readers familiar with Whitman that the same poet who anonymously reviewed his own work and tirelessly promoted his personal brand would insist that what shone through most powerfully in his poetry was not necessarily his own efforts, but rather the "living light" of his cultural "circumstances." From the first edition of *Leaves of Grass*, however, Whitman had defined his poetic practice as a process of absorbing and reflecting back the "luminosity" of the world around him. A great poet should "flood himself with the immediate age as with vast oceanic tides" he wrote in the Preface to the 1855 edition, maintaining that the poet should be "himself the age transfigured" (LG55, xi).

One of the poems from this first edition – an untitled work that eventually bore the name "There Was a Child Went Forth" – illustrates this principle through the figure of an endlessly curious child whose engagement with the world feels very much like the "transfigured" poet Whitman described in his Preface:

There was a child went forth every day,
And the first object he looked upon and received with wonder or pity
    or love or dread, that object he became,
And that object became part of him for the day or a certain part of the
    day . . . or for many years or stretching cycles of years.
The early lilacs became part of this child,
And grass, and white and red morningglories, and white and red
    clover, and the song of the phœbe-bird,
[. . .]
The streets themselves, and the facades of houses . . . . the goods in the
    windows,
Vehicles . . teams . . the tiered wharves, and the huge crossing at the
    ferries;
The village and the highland seen from afar at sunset . . . . the river
    between.   (LG55, 90–91)

The poem includes an extensive catalog of the people, places, and things that the child enthusiastically embraces in the course of his journey, all linked together by the idiosyncratic ellipses Whitman used throughout the 1855 *Leaves of Grass*. The poem closes, "These became part of that child who went forth every day, and who now goes and will always go forth every day, / And these become of him or her that peruses them now" (LG55, 91). With this parting comment that anyone who "peruses" his poetry becomes part of a collective poetic experience, Whitman confirms that his poems come most spectacularly to life when taken in context – both the contexts of their original composition and the multiple contexts of their reception throughout time and space. As such, our goal with *Walt Whitman in Context* has been to explore the poetry, fiction, notebooks, journalism, government records, and non-fiction prose of one the world's great writers through brief and provocative essays that place Whitman within the geographic, literary, cultural, and political contexts of his life. It is worth noting that the present volume is not *Contexts for Walt Whitman*; that is, it is not a primer on the history and culture of the nineteenth-century United States. Rather, *Walt Whitman in Context* provides readings, interpretations, and explorations of Whitman *in* the many contexts through which he charted his life and wrote his texts.

There is a longstanding tradition in Whitman scholarship to contextualize the poet and his work according to the places he lived, the art and literature he experienced, the cultural and political upheavals he witnessed, and the legacy he created. Some of the foundational texts in Whitman scholarship have taken this approach, from Roger Asselineau's *The*

Evolution of Walt Whitman (1954), which took seriously the idea that each new edition of *Leaves of Grass* represented a discrete iteration of Whitman's ongoing response to the world around him, to Betsy Erkkila's *Whitman the Political Poet* (1989), which follows Whitman's life and work through the major political events of the century. Similarly, when Joseph Jay Rubin published *The Historic Whitman* in 1973, he offered a template for the deep archival research that scholars could perform as they sought out the long cultural foregrounds of Whitman's texts; this methodology has since been mastered by Ed Folsom in works of scholarship such as *Walt Whitman's Native Representations* (1994) and Kenneth M. Price in *To Walt Whitman, America* (2004), among other publications. In *Calamus Lovers: Walt Whitman's Working-Class Camerados* (1987), Charley Shively made a compelling argument for the poet's homosexuality through close attention to contextual documents (specifically, Whitman's correspondence with male lovers) as well as to broader historical trends and the poems themselves. Similarly, Sherry Ceniza's *Walt Whitman and Nineteenth-Century Women Reformers* (1998) and the essays in Ivy G. Wilson's *Whitman Noir: Black America and the Good Gray Poet* (2014) engage with Whitman's work from within the contexts of gender and race, respectively.

Walt Whitman in Context builds upon this tradition in Whitman scholarship with thirty-eight short essays divided into four major parts: Locations; Literary and Artistic Contexts; Cultural and Political Contexts; and Reception and Legacy. For a poet who wrote about every corner of the globe and virtually every state in the Union, Whitman spent most of his life in relatively few places: Long Island; Brooklyn and Manhattan; New Orleans; Camden, NJ, and neighboring Philadelphia; and Washington, DC. After leaving his birthplace and childhood home on Long Island (as described in Chapter 1 by William T. Walter) Whitman lived in cities that experienced tremendous growth and development during the tenure of his residence, giving him the opportunity to witness firsthand both the rapid industrialization of the United States and the emergence of a truly global economy. Wherever Whitman lived he sought out like-minded men and women with whom he could discuss art, politics, and culture – from the journalists and bohemians of antebellum New York to the artists of post-Civil War Philadelphia (Chapters 2 and 3 by Karen Karbiener and William Pannapacker). These creative communities nurtured Whitman's development as a writer and exposed him to new ideas, practices, and opportunities. The time that Whitman spent south of the Mason–Dixon line – as a young reporter in New Orleans or as an aid in the hospitals of Civil War Washington – had a similarly transformative effect on him, both in his understanding of the fractured nation that he would seek to heal through his poetry and in his sense of the diverse geography and population of the United States (see Chapter 4 on Washington, DC by Kenneth M. Price and Chapter 5 on the American South by Matt Cohen).

The second part of *Walt Whitman in Context* focuses on the literary and artistic contexts of Whitman's life. First as a journalist and then as a poet, Whitman became an expert at absorbing the literary and artistic developments of his time. While working for a variety of newspapers in Brooklyn, Long Island, New Orleans, and Manhattan – as Jason Stacy details in Chapter 9 – Whitman was regularly assigned to write about new fiction, poetry, music, art, theater, and public lectures. He made no effort to hide the impact that such art forms made on his own work but rather celebrated their presence in *Leaves of Grass*, which includes poems written in the declamatory style of public oratory (Chapter 10 by Leslie Elizabeth Eckel) and the aria-and-recitative form of the opera (Chapter 11 by Carmen Trammell Skaggs), along with poems that channel the visual spectacle of early photography (Chapter 13 by Ruth L. Bohan) and the explicit sexuality of nineteenth-century erotica (Chapter 14 by Paul Erickson). In addition to his appreciation for the artistic culture of the nineteenth century, Whitman was also intimately familiar with the workings of the publishing industry both in the United States and abroad: chapters by Nicole Gray on "Bookmaking" (Chapter 16), David O. Dowling on "The Literary Marketplace" (Chapter 17), and Jessica DeSpain on "Transatlantic Book Distribution" (Chapter 18) situate Whitman within a world that he had experienced not only as a writer, but also as a printer, book reviewer, and newspaper editor.

Whitman's early careers as journalist and printer shaped his understanding of the media forms through which the nineteenth century's culture of print would receive him. Chapters by Ingrid I. Satelmajer on "Periodical Poetry" and Stephanie M. Blalock on "Periodical Fiction" (Chapters 7 and 8), explore how periodical publication made literature an integral part of the social life of the nineteenth-century United States. Such trends made Whitman acutely aware of the culture of performance and celebrity that was escalating throughout the United States (see Chapter 12 by David Haven Blake) and how popular poets, such as Henry Wadsworth Longfellow, approached their verse forms with an eye toward readers' expectations (see Chapter 6 by Michael C. Cohen). Despite his almost complete immersion in nineteenth-century print culture, however, Whitman also understood the distinctive capabilities of the manuscript form, as Matt Miller describes in Chapter 15 on "Notebooks and Manuscripts."

The chapters in part three explore a range of cultural and political movements that found their way into Whitman's oeuvre. Whitman lived through a transformative period in US history. The defining moment in his personal life, as well as the life of his nation, was unquestionably the Civil War, the aftermath of which led Whitman to move away from his public persona as "one of the roughs" and to present himself instead as the United States' "good gray poet," a grandfatherly figure dedicated to healing the wounds of a mourning nation, as described in Chapter 27 on the "Civil War" by Peter Coviello, Chapter 28 on "Reconstruction" by Martin T. Buinicki, and Chapter 29 on "Death and Mourning" by Adam Bradford. The war and its aftermath, as these essays demonstrate, also served to expand Whitman's understanding of race, sexuality, and the body politic. The questions that preoccupied Whitman during the antebellum years followed the poet through the crucible of the Civil War, resulting in increasingly complex meditations on the relationship between art and politics – a relationship that, as Kerry Larson argues in Chapter 24, puts Whitman very much at home with the major political philosophers of the past two centuries. Whitman wrote about slavery (see Chapter 30 by Ivy G. Wilson), labor and the rights of working people (Chapter 32 by Jerome Loving), the treatment of Native Americans during the era of Indian Removal, and the United States' relationship to (and involvement in) the imperial ventures of European powers (see Chapter 31 on "Native American and Immigrant Cultures" by Rachel Rubinstein and Chapter 25 on "Imperialism and Globalization" by Walter Grünzweig).

Whitman kept himself abreast of developments in the natural sciences (see Chapter 34 on "The Natural World" by Christine Gerhardt and Chapter 35 on "Science and Medicine" by Lindsay Tuggle) and he was a curious student of both philosophy and religion (Chapters 20 and 26 by Stephen John Mack and Brian Yothers), with German romanticism capturing his attention in a particularly transformative way (see Chapter 33 by Edward S. Cutler). And while the Transcendentalist authors of New England may have been the United States' most direct descendants of Kantian metaphysics (see Chapter 19 by Regina Schober), Whitman felt more at home among the ideologically inconsistent bohemian writers and artists of antebellum New York City than he did among the sages of Boston and Concord (Chapter 21 by Joanna Levin and Edward Whitley). The bohemians' relationship with changing attitudes toward gender and sexuality were also more in line with Whitman's own. Maire Mullins demonstrates in Chapter 22 how Whitman toyed with gender norms in both his life and his writings, and Jay Grossman's discussion of sexuality in Chapter 23 places Whitman's capacious understanding of sexual desire alongside nineteenth-century discourses surrounding sexual activity – discourses that Whitman himself helped to shape in ways that not only contributed to twentieth-century definitions of sexual identity, but that also continue to inform sexual politics in the twenty-first.

The final group of essays on "Reception and Legacy" demonstrates just how transformative a figure Whitman has been – and continues to be – within both national and global contexts. Chapter 36 by Michael Robertson focuses on those readers of Whitman whose devotion to both the man and his poems would better be described as discipleship than readership; while Sascha Pöhlmann's account of Whitman's influence on US culture and Ed Folsom's description of Whitman's impact on writers across the globe (Chapters 37 and 38) point us toward an ongoing feedback loop, wherein Whitman's legacy in the present also reshapes our understanding of his nineteenth-century past and the contexts that appear most relevant and ready for exploration.

Finally, we note that this collection of essays is dedicated to the directors and project staff of the *Walt Whitman Archive*. For over twenty years the *Whitman Archive* has been an indispensable resource for scholars, teachers, and students. The contributors to this volume express our heartfelt gratitude to Ed, Ken, and the many staff members who have logged countless hours into creating Whitman's online home.

Abbreviations

Corr.	*The Correspondence*, vols. 1–6, ed. Edwin Haviland Miller (New York, NY: New York University Press, 1961–77); vol. 7, ed. Ted Genoways (Iowa City, IA: University of Iowa Press, 2004).
Journ.	*The Journalism*, 2 vols., eds. Herbert Bergman, Douglas A. Noverr, and Edward J. Recchia (New York, NY: Peter Lang, 1998–2003).
LG	*Leaves of Grass, Comprehensive Reader's Edition*, eds. Harold W. Blodgett and Sculley Bradley (New York, NY: New York University Press, 1965).
LG55	*Leaves of Grass* (Brooklyn, NY, 1855). Available in facsimile as *Leaves of Grass: A Facsimile of the First Edition* (San Francisco, CA: Chandler, 1968) and as a digital edition on the *Walt Whitman Archive*.
LG56	*Leave of Grass* (Brooklyn, NY: Fowler & Wells, 1856). Available in facsimile as *Leaves of Grass: Facsimile of the 1856 Edition* (Norwood, PA: Norwood Editions, 1976), *Leaves of Grass: 1856 Facsimile Edition* (Ann Arbor, MI: Microfilm International, 1980), and as a digital edition on the *Walt Whitman Archive*.
LG60	*Leaves of Grass* (Boston, MA: Thayer and Eldridge, 1860–61). Available in facsimile as *Leaves of Grass: Facsimile Edition of the 1860 Text* (Ithaca, NY: Cornell University Press, 1961), *Leaves of Grass, 1860: The 150th Anniversary Facsimile Edition*, ed. Jason Stacy (Iowa City, IA: University of Iowa Press, 2009), and as a digital edition on the *Walt Whitman Archive*.
Loving	Jerome Loving, *Walt Whitman: The Song of Himself* (Berkeley, CA: University of California Press, 1999).

NUPM   *Notebooks and Unpublished Prose Manuscripts*, 6 vols., ed. Edward F. Grier (New York, NY: New York University Press, 1984).

PW   *Prose Works, 1892*, 2 vols., ed. Floyd Stovall (New York, NY: New York University Press, 1963–64).

Reynolds   David S. Reynolds, *Walt Whitman's America: A Cultural Biography* (New York, NY: Vintage Books, 1996).

WWA   The *Walt Whitman Archive,* eds. Ed Folsom and Kenneth M. Price, www.whitmanarchive.org.

WWC   Horace Traubel, *With Walt Whitman in Camden*, vol. 1 (Boston, MA: Small, Maynard, 1906); vols. 2–3 (New York, NY: Rowman and Littlefield, 1961); vol. 4 (Philadelphia, PA: University of Pennsylvania Press, 1953); vols. 5–7 (Carbondale, IL: Southern Illinois University Press, 1964–92); vols. 8–9 (Oregon House, CA: W. L. Bentley, 1996). Available as a digital edition on the *Walt Whitman Archive.*

PART I

Locations

CHAPTER I

Long Island

William T. Walter

In his autobiographical account *Specimen Days* (1882) Whitman acknowledged the claims of both nature and nurture, identifying three "formative stamps to my own character, now solidified for good or bad." The first was the "maternal nativity-stock brought hither from far-away Netherlands"; the second was "the subterranean tenacity and central bony structure [. . .] which I get from my paternal English elements"; and the third was environmental, beginning with "the combination of my Long Island birth-spot, sea-shores, childhood's scenes, absorptions, with teeming Brooklyn and New York" (PW, 1:22–23). This essay follows Whitman's lead elaborating on the family histories and formative settings that, as Whitman noted, "are woven all through L. of G." (PW, 1:11). "The successive growth-stages of my infancy, childhood, youth and manhood were all pass'd on Long Island, which I sometimes feel as if I had incorporated," Whitman reflected; he thus linked his personal and poetic development to his birthplace and, by extension, the larger nation (PW, 1:10).

Whitman's childhood

As David Reynolds has noted, Whitman's fusion of "personal ancestry and national history" on Long Island helped the poet to cultivate "the representative 'I' who embraced all America" (Reynolds, 8, 18). Whitman's ancestors were among the early European settlers in the town of Huntington on Long Island in New York. The Whitman line in America began when Englishman John Whitman arrived in Weymouth, Massachusetts in 1640. John's brother Zechariah settled in Milford, Connecticut, and in 1657 Zechariah's son Joseph, at about seventeen years old, crossed the Long Island Sound to Huntington (Reynolds, 9–10). The history of European settlement on Huntington dates to 1653, when three English settlers acquired six square miles of land from the Matinecoc.[1] On April 1, 1668, Walt's great-great-great-grandfather, Joseph

3

Whitman, is listed in the record of a Huntington town meeting as follows: "it was voted and agreed the same Daie that Joseph Whitman shall take up ten or twelve acars of land on the west sid of the south path on the hether side of Samuell Ketchams hollow, it being toward his second division."[2] This parcel of land in the West Hills section of Huntington, according to Walt, grew to "500 acres, all good soil, gently sloping east and south, about one-tenth woods, plenty of grand old trees" (PW, 1:5–6). When Walt later wrote about "Far-swooping elbow'd earth – rich apple-blossom'd earth" in "Song of Myself," this ancestral land could have provided an accompanying visual (LG, 49). This was the farm of Nehemiah Whitman, Joseph's grandson and Walt's great-grandfather. This large tract of land, cultivated in part with the labor of African American slaves, brought prosperity to the Whitmans.[3] Nehemiah, his wife Phoebe White Whitman, and their son Jesse W. Whitman were the last of the substantial Whitman landowners in West Hills. When Jesse died in 1802, the estate was then left to his young children – Jesse, Walter, Tredwell, and Sarah. Walt's father, Walter, born on Bastille Day in 1789, was fifteen when he was sent for an apprenticeship in carpentry under his cousin Jacob Whitman, who was a carpenter and woodworker in Brooklyn. After spending three years in New York City Walter Whitman Sr. returned to Huntington, built a house for his own family in 1810, and a second similar house, most likely in 1819, on nearby land that was originally a farm of 80 acres acquired by Richard Colyer from Tredwell Whitman. Walter married Louisa Van Velsor in 1816. Their first three children – Jesse in 1818, Walt on May 31, 1819, and Mary Elizabeth in 1821 – were born in the Huntington house their father built.[4]

Far less is known about the ancestry of Walt's mother, Louisa Van Velsor. Louisa's mother, Walt's maternal grandmother, was Naomi Williams Van Velsor. Walt called her Amy. She was one of seven girls in a Quaker family named Williams who were of Welsh descent. Many were sailors. Her father and only brother were lost at sea. Walt's maternal grandfather, Cornelius Van Velsor, carried the title of "Major" and was a descendant of the early Dutch settlers on Long Island. The family had been horse breeders. Walt said that his mother, in her youth, was a "daily and daring rider" of horses (PW, 1:6–8). Like the Whitmans, the Van Velsors had lived for many generations on the same farm. As a boy Walt often visited his Van Velsor cousins in Cold Spring Harbor, which was not much more than a mile from his grandfather Jesse's farm. Walt never knew his grandfather Jesse, who died in 1789. His grandmother, Hannah Brush Whitman, who lived in the ancestral Whitman homestead, had been a school mistress and was a strong character fond of telling stories that had been passed on from one generation to the next, including tales of oppression and terror during the British occupation of Huntington. She died when Walt was about sixteen (Reynolds, 10–11).

Walt began his life on an international boundary. In the 1600s, English colonial settlements had moved west from Plymouth into Western Massachusetts into Connecticut and across the Long Island Sound to Southhold (the south holdings of Connecticut settlers) on Long Island.[5] The Dutch began Fort Amsterdam on the island of Manhattan, which was purchased from the Lenape Indians, then crossed the East River to start what became a city called Brooklyn and moved further east on Long Island to establish farms and ports to supply land crops and seafood. The English took over New Netherland in 1664, without firing a shot. All that changed was that the Dutch rules were changed to English rules. The hills furthest west on Long Island occupied by the English settlers were called West Hills, while the hills furthest east reached by the Dutch were called East Hills. Today this provides Long Islanders with the amusing fact that West Hills is east of East Hills. To Walt Whitman it provided diversity, for the Dutch were accompanied by many other nationalities and ethnicities including Portuguese, Spanish, French, Germans, and Jews.[6]

By the year 1643 there were thirteen different tribes of indigenous peoples living on Long Island, but by 1658 a smallpox epidemic reportedly killed two-thirds of the tribes in the area. The influx of white settlers and the resulting expansion of farmland drove animals away, and the Native Americans who were hunters migrated to the mainland in pursuit of game. By 1741 it was estimated that only 400 Natives remained on the island. By the time of the American Revolution in 1775 Native Americans were a rare sight on the island. During the first decades of the nineteenth century Walt's mother, Louisa, had an encounter with a young indigenous woman on Long Island that left such an impact on her that she later shared it with her son, who then recounted the experience in section six of the poem "The Sleepers":

A red squaw came one breakfast-time to the old homestead,
On her back she carried a bundle of rushes for rush-bottoming chairs,
Her hair, straight, shiny, coarse, black, profuse, half-envelop'd her face,
Her step was free and elastic, and her voice sounded exquisitely as she spoke.

My mother look'd in delight and amazement at the stranger,
She look'd at the freshness of her tall-borne face and full and pliant limbs,
The more she look'd upon her she loved her,
Never before had she seen such wonderful beauty and purity,

She made her sit on a bench by the jamb of the fireplace, she cook'd food
  for her,
She had no work to give her, but she gave her remembrance and fondness.

The red squaw staid all the forenoon, and toward the middle of the after-
  noon she went away,
O my mother was loth to have her go away,
All the week she thought of her, she watch'd for her many a month,
She remember'd her many a winter and many a summer,
But the red squaw never came nor was heard of there again.   (LG, 429–30)

This account of Louisa's experience with an indigenous woman on Long
Island carries with it the mix of racism ("squaw" is a derogatory term for
Native women) and exoticism (the woman speaks "exquisitely" and is an
object of "wonderful beauty and purity") that nineteenth-century Americans
had come to expect from representations of Native peoples; the account also
captures Walt's longing for the "old homestead" on Long Island (LG, 429),
and the mythic status it had achieved among the Whitmans as a place of
romanticized wonder after the family had moved inland to Brooklyn. Walt
would continue to associate his nostalgic memories of life on Long Island
with Native American culture. He insisted on calling Long Island by its
Lenape name – "Paumanok," meaning "land of tribute" – and even used the
pseudonym "Paumanok" to identify the authorship of some of his early
work.[7] Beginning with the third edition of *Leaves of Grass* in 1860, Walt
added a poem towards the beginning of the book that carries the lines:
"Starting from fish-shape Paumanok where I was born, / Well-begotten, and
raised by a perfect mother," paying homage both to the indigenous heritage
of his birthplace and to the Whitman family's history there (LG, 15).

  Walt spent his early years in West Hills with an active, large, and busy
family. The 1820 census lists ten persons in the Whitman household:
Walter Sr., his wife Louisa, and their children Jessie, Walt, and Mary
Elizabeth; Louisa's mother, Naomi Van Velsor, was also present, having
moved temporarily from Cold Spring Harbor to help with her grand-
children; Uncle Treadwell Whitman (Walter Sr.'s brother), his wife Maria
Mc Cunne, and daughter Mahatta were also living in the new house; Uncle
Jessie Whitman (Walter Sr.'s bachelor older brother) and Grandmother
Hannah Brush Whitman were also counted as part of the Whitman
household in the census, despite living up the road in the ancestral
home.[8] Furniture inside the house was rude, but substantial. No carpets
or stoves were known, and clothes were mainly homespun. Food also was
plain – no coffee, and tea or sugar was only for the women, with the men
commonly drinking cider. Rousing wood fires gave both warmth and light

on winter nights. Books were scarce. The annual copy of the almanac was a treat, and was pored over through the long winter evenings.[9]

Although Walter Sr. built houses and called himself a carpenter, he also had responsibility of a 30-acre farm and an additional interest in contiguous acreage to the north from the traditional Whitman homestead. He probably continued with his brothers to follow the time-honored planting of crops typical to Long Island: oats, buckwheat, flint corn, winter wheat, and rye. Adjacent to the farmhouse were an apple orchard and a cornfield, while a fenced-in kitchen garden fronted the south side of the house. The barnyard – the setting for the daily routine of milking cows, feeding and watering the animals, mucking out stalls, and grooming animals – was defined by a group of buildings that included a carriage shed, henhouse, smokehouse, and corn crib. While the men were out in the fields from before sunrise, the women were active in the house, kitchen, and yard providing warm water and preparing breakfast. A wood fire was started in the bake oven located in the out kitchen, and while the fire heated the bricks members of the household prepared pies, cakes, stews, and bread for the evening meals. At midday they would rake the ashes out of the bake oven and place earthen-ware vessels filled with foods such as pork, poultry, beef, vegetables, and grains inside the oven to be slow-cooked by the heat of the bricks. Hot coals would also be raked from the fireplace and moved underneath the laundry kettle in the out kitchen to ensure a clean wash. Walt Whitman, in later years, would remember these formative years as ones of security and prosperity (PW, 1:9–11).

After his family had relocated to Brooklyn, Walt was able to return to Long Island during some of the succeeding summers. Reminiscing in *Specimen Days*, he noted that, "The whole experience comes back to me after the lapse of forty and more years – the soothing rustle of the waves, and the saline smell – boyhood's times, the clam digging, bare-foot, and with trowsers roll'd up – hauling down the creek – the perfume of the sedge-meadows – the hayboat, and the chowder and fishing excursions" (PW, 1:12). These childhood joys on Long Island – and the sense of wonder that they instilled in the poet – are nowhere more evident than in an 1855 poem that would later be titled "There Was a Child Went Forth." The poem features a curious child who is utterly transformed by his experiences with the natural world: "There was a child went forth every day, / And the first object he look'd upon, that object he became, / And that object became part of him" (LG, 364). The surroundings explored by the poem's titular child sound very much like the Whitman homestead on Long Island, not to mention the use of the terms "fourth-month" and "fifth-month" (for the months of April and May) that the Whitmans would have adopted from their Quaker neighbors:

The field-sprouts of Fourth-month and Fifth-month became part of him,
Winter-grain sprouts and those of the light-yellow corn, and the esculent
    roots of the garden,
And the apple-trees cover'd with blossoms and the fruit afterward, and
    wood-berries, and the commonest weeds by the road,
And the old drunkard staggering home from the outhouse of the tavern
    whence he had lately risen,
And the schoolmistress that pass'd on her way to the school,
And the friendly boys that pass'd, and the quarrelsome boys,
And the tidy and fresh-cheek'd girls, and the barefoot negro boy and girl,
And all the changes of city and country wherever he went.   (LG, 364–65)

The major work of Walt's career – the poem "Song of Myself" – is
characterized by a mutual absorption between the poet and his surroundings: "And what I assume you shall assume. / For every atom
belonging to me as good belongs to you" (LG, 28). The Long Island
child who made the natural world "part of him" was already moving
toward the complete absorption of both the nation and the globe that is
on full display in "Song of Myself": "In me the caresser of life wherever
moving, backward as well as forward sluing, / To niches aside and junior
bending, not a person or object missing, / Absorbing all to myself and
for this song" (LG, 40).

Long Island also provides the setting for an 1859 poem describing the
moment from Walt's childhood when he claimed to have received the
calling to be a poet. Taking place on the island of "Paumanok, / When the
lilac-scent was in the air and Fifth-month grass was growing" (LG, 247),
Walt hears the plaintive cry of a mockingbird pining for its lost love and
resolves himself to be from that day onward a singer of songs:

> [H]e sang to me in the moonlight on Paumanok's gray beach,
> With the thousand responsive songs at random,
> My own songs awaked from that hour,
> And with them the key, the word up from the waves,
> The word of the sweetest song and all songs.   (LG, 253)

As Jerome Loving has observed, Walt

> was a seashore poet, the poet of "Paumanok" who envisioned some of his
> greatest themes in terms of the land and the sea, between life and death. [. . .]
> We see this relationship most clearly in the poem "Out of the Cradle
> Endlessly Rocking," where he describes the island's lock on his imagination
> as the man-child wakes up to the call of "a thousand singers, a thousand
> songs." (Loving, 26)

Brooklyn and a return to Paumanok

On May 27, 1823 (four days before Walt's fourth birthday), Walter Whitman Sr. took his pregnant wife and three young children from West Hills to seek his fortune in Brooklyn. He did not want to be a farmer, as four generations of Whitmans had been before him. Walter expected success as a builder of small frame houses in Brooklyn since it was in an early phase of an expansion from a rural village to a major American city. However, Brooklyn did not treat Walter Sr. well, and finances were not his forte. Mortgages, speculation, and the aftermath of the 1819 panic all negatively impacted the family's financial health, leading young Walt to drop out of school and begin his employment first as an office boy and then a printer's apprentice. Walter Sr. moved the family back to Long Island in 1833 (Reynolds, 25–26, 53).

Walt remained in Brooklyn to continue working as a printer's devil for the *Long Island Star*. In the summer of 1835 Walt completed his printing apprenticeship and became a journeyman printer; in August, however, a huge fire wiped out many of the printing establishments and printing jobs disappeared. In May of 1836 Walt accepted a four-week teaching position in Norwich near his grandfather's farm in Cold Spring and a short journey to the Whitman family home in Hempstead. In the fall of the same year he accepted a three-month teaching position in Babylon, Long Island, on the Great South Bay, also near to where his family was living. In the spring of 1837 Walt taught in Long Swamp (Huntington) close to his birthplace in West Hills and by the fall he began his most successful teaching assignment in Smithtown, which continued through the winter and spring terms. Whitman's story "The Shadow and Light of a Young Man's Soul" (1848) provides a semi-fictive account of this period in his life. Like Whitman, the protagonist, Archibald Dean leaves the city as a result of the "destructive New-York fire of '35" and "take[s] charge of a little district school"; it is probable that Whitman also shared Archibald Dean's sense of despair at this change in fortune, a feeling that "the last float-plank which buoyed him up on hope and happiness, was sinking, and he with it."[10]

Walt was seventeen when he began teaching. He did not want to be tied down in the endless cycle of farm work and never spent a significant amount of time working as a farm laborer. Teaching positions appeared to offer a new adventure. Long Island towns would construct a one-room schoolhouse and then seek a contract schoolteacher whose low salary was often supplemented by free room and board in the homes of their pupils, termed "boarding round" – that is, living two or three days with one family and perhaps a week with another and so on. Walt said the experience "gives a first-rate opportunity for the study of human nature."[11] Walt loved to roam through the villages interacting with the farmers, bay fishermen, keepers of general stores, blacksmiths, millers, and local officeholders. According to records in Smithtown, Walt was paid $72.20 for approximately five months of teaching reading, writing, arithmetic, spelling, and geography. At one time he had eighty-five pupils from ages five to fifteen (Reynolds, 59). Normally the teaching methodology was rote repetition in which a single teacher handled large classes through a network of student monitors. Walt, however, preferred a teaching method more like twenty questions (Reynolds, 62). Reflecting on Whitman's pedagogical approaches, one former student, Charles A. Roe later recalled that "His ways of teaching were peculiar. He did not confine himself to books, as most of the teachers then did, but taught orally – yes, had some original ideas, all his own. [. . .] The plans he adopted were wholly of his conception, and most successful."[12]

Walt joined the local debating society in Smithtown – which included two judges, a congressman, a justice of the peace, doctors, businessmen, and farmers – and was appointed secretary. His minutes have been preserved by the descendants of one of the members. Debating society records show that Walt took part in eleven debates during his stay in Smithtown, his side winning six with two judged to be ties. Walt's Smithtown experience – where he arranged his own living quarters, won recognition through his skill as a debater and felt comfortable in the company of the town's elite – made him feel that this was the time to move on to accomplish a dream he had since he was a printer's apprentice.[13]

In the spring of 1838 Walt left Smithtown and moved back to his home town of Huntington to start his own weekly newspaper, the *Long-Islander*. Walt was publisher, editor, compositor, pressman, and distributor. Each week Walt mounted his horse, Nina, and made a thirty-mile circuit delivering his paper and picking up news and stories for the next issue.[14] Whitman ran the *Long-Islander* for ten months and then sold it in the spring of 1839 to E. O. Crowell, who revived the paper on July 12 promising readers to faithfully "continue it regularly and permanently."[15] Apparently the appearance of Walt's papers had not been following any fixed schedule. Unfortunately, none of the issues under Walt's ownership have survived.

After leaving the *Long-Islander* Walt found work during the summer of 1839 in Jamaica, Long Island with the *Long Island Democrat* as a typesetter.

In December 1839 he began teaching at Little Bay Side near Jamaica. In the spring of 1840 Walt taught in Trimming Square (about two miles from Hempstead), then in Woodbury (near West Hills) during the summer. His mood darkened in Woodbury and he wrote in 1840 to his friend, Abraham Paul Leech, that Woodbury with its "ignorance, vulgarity, rudeness, conceit, and dulness [*sic*]" was a "deuced sink of despair" (Corr., 7:3). This note of darkness also predominates in Whitman's first-known story, one that as its title indicates takes a school-room as its setting: "Death in the School-Room" (1841). While promoting educational reform ("We are waxing toward the consummation when one of the old-fashion'd schoolmasters, with his cowhide, his heavy birch-rod, and his many ingenious methods of child-torture, will be gazed upon as a scoron'd memento of an ignorant, cruel, and exploded doctrine"[16]) the story nonetheless engages in what David Reynolds has called "dark-reform," namely "the description of vice so vivid that the vice itself predominates over the ostensible moral" (Reynolds, 75). His final teaching post was in Whitestone (near Jamaica) during the fall, and by May 1841 Walt appears to have abandoned school teaching, left Long Island, and returned to Manhattan where he went to work at the weekly paper the *New World*. While still employed as a teacher, Whitman published a series of essays titled "Sun-Down Papers, From the Desk of a Schoolmaster" in three Long Island newspapers: the *Hempstead Inquirer*, the *Long-Island Democrat*, and the *Long-Island Farmer*.[17] Adopting the "Schoolmaster" persona, Whitman promoted various moral reforms and took aim at such habits as tobacco chewing and excessive alcohol consumption. He also looked toward the future, imagining that one day he would "compose a wonderful and ponderous book. [. . .] Yes: I *would* write a book!"[18]

Walt's Paumanok visits

Even though Walt had now moved to New York City, he did make trips out to Long Island. In either 1853 or 1854 Walt had taken his ailing father to visit West Hills for a final three-day visit. They probably took the train as far as Hicksville and then a stage to Woodbury, where they proceeded on foot along the turnpike and across lots to the Colyer Homestead built by Walt's father probably in 1819. The farm had originally belonged to Jesse Whitman, Walt's grandfather. The house is still standing on Mount Misery Road in excellent repair. "I pumped in the kitchen door," wrote Walt, noting that "Aunt S., father's sister, was standing there – I knew her at once, although it is many years since I saw her, and she looked very old and bent."[19] Later, Walt and his father walked down Chichester Road past weathered grey farm buildings and the Peace & Plenty Inn to the earlier house his father had built and where Walt was born. Then they slowly climbed up the shady, myrtle-edged path to the family burial ground on the hill behind the house that was originally that of Nehemiah Whitman, Jesse's father and Walt's great-grandfather.

In July 1881, as his father had done before him, Walt returned to West Hills, with his Canadian friend Dr. Maurice Bucke, and visited the family cemetery. Walt wrote,

> I now write these lines seated on an old grave (doubtless of a century since at least) on the burial hill of the Whitmans of many generations. Fifty and more graves are quite plainly traceable, and as many more decay'd out of all form – depress'd mounds, crumbled and broken stones, cover'd with moss – [...]. My whole family history, with its succession of links, from the first settlement down to date, told here – three centuries concentrate on this sterile acre. (PW, 1:6)

Walt Whitman on Long Island today

Walt Whitman has become Huntington's most famous resident. His name is on roads, a park, a high school, a major shopping mall, and many businesses and commercial establishments. The newspaper Walt began in 1838 continues to be published and today is Huntington's major weekly newspaper. In 1949 Walt's birthplace was placed for sale and a group of his admirers organized and received a charter from New York State to preserve and protect it as a historic landmark. As the Walt Whitman Birthplace Association this group acquired the site and donated it to New York State in 1957. A cooperative agreement was formed between New York State and the Association for the restoration, preservation, interpretation, and use of the Walt Whitman House. The Association maintains a website at waltwhitman.org, publishes the newsletter *Starting from Paumanok*, and runs programs including Walking With Whitman. Each year it selects a Poet-in-Residence for a celebration close to May 31 (Walt's birthday), honors a Champion of Literacy, and designates a Long Island Poet of the Year all in accordance with the Association's mission: "Walt Whitman Birthplace Association is Walt Whitman's voice today, celebrating the poet's vision of democracy, diversity, and creativity. Our programs and exhibits educate the public on Whitman's life and times, explore his contribution to our nation's rich cultural heritage, and inspire young poets and writers."[20]

Notes

1. "The Early Years," *Town of Huntington, Long Island, New York*, http://huntingtonny.gov.
2. Charles R. Street, *Huntington Town Records: Including Babylon, Long Island, N.Y., 1653–1688*, vol. 1 (Huntington and Babylon, NY, 1887), 117. Joseph married Sarah Ketchum about 1660 and the two had six sons together; they established the Whitmans as a family of prominence on Long Island.
3. Slavery was introduced to Long Island in 1660 and not abolished until 1828. As was generally true throughout Long Island, the Whitman and Van Velsor slaves generally stayed in the kitchens of the homesteads (PW, 1:8–9). David Reynolds has argued that Whitman "always maintained a lurking sympathy for the South" in part because of his "nostalgia for his ancestors' ways" (Reynolds, 20). Walt recalled that one of his closest companions during his youth was a liberated West Hills slave named Old Mose: "He was very genial, correct, manly, and cute, and a great friend of my childhood" (PW, 2:580).
4. Bliss Perry, *Walt Whitman: His Life and Work* (New York, NY: Houghton, Mifflin, and Company, 1906), 4–8. See also Reynolds, 10–11.
5. Edwin G. Burrows and Mike Wallace, *Gotham: A History of New York City to 1898* (New York, NY: Oxford University Press, 2000), 14–19.
6. Ibid., 56–72.
7. Ed Folsom, *Walt Whitman's Native Representations* (New York, NY: Cambridge University Press, 1997), 85–87.
8. "Residence 278 Huntington Township," *Fourth Census of the United States (1820)*, 1820, Microfilm Roll 74 (Suffolk County), National Archives and Records Administration, http://archives.gov.
9. Richard Ryan (Curator at the Walt Whitman Birthplace and Old Bethpage Restoration Village) in discussion with the author, February–March 2017.
10. Walt Whitman, "The Shadow and Light of a Young Man's Soul," *The Union Magazine of Literature and Art* 2 (June 1848), 280–81, WWA.
11. Walt Whitman, *The Uncollected Poetry and Prose of Walt Whitman*, vol. 2, ed. Emory Holloway (Garden City, NY: Doubleday, Page, and Co., 1921), 13.
12. Horace L. Traubel, "Walt Whitman, Schoolmaster: Notes of a Conversation with Charles A. Roe," *Walt Whitman Fellowship Papers* 14 (1895), 81–87, quoted in *Whitman in His Own Time*, ed. Joel Myerson (Iowa City, IA: University of Iowa Press, 1991), 110.
13. Bertha H. Funnell, *Walt Whitman on Long Island* (Port Washington, NY: Kennikat, 1971), 42.
14. David S. Reynolds, *Walt Whitman* (New York, NY: Oxford University Press, 2005), 8.
15. Karen Karbiener, "*Long Islander*," in *Walt Whitman: An Encyclopedia*, eds. J. R. LeMaster and Donald D. Kummings (New York, NY: Garland Publishing, 1998), WWA.
16. Walt Whitman, "Death in the School-Room," *The United States Magazine and Democratic Review* 9 (August 1841), 177, WWA.

17. Jason Stacy, "The Sun-Down Papers," WWA.
18. Walt Whitman, "The Sun-Down Papers-No. 7," *Long-Island Democrat* (Long Island, NY), September 29, 1840, 3, WWA.
19. *Papers of Walt Whitman* (MS 3829), Clifton Waller Barrett Library of American Literature, Albert H. Small Special Collections Library, University of Virginia; Trent Collection of Whitmaniana, David M. Rubenstein Rare Book & Manuscript Library, Duke University, WWA.
20. "Our Mission Statement," *Walt Whitman Birthplace Association*, http://walt whitman.org/.

CHAPTER 2

Brooklyn and Manhattan

Karen Karbiener

Walt Whitman was not the first to write about New York. But he was the first of many to let New York write him. By age forty-three, Whitman had composed most of his best poetry, published three editions of *Leaves of Grass*, and left New York only twice. He described his deep connection to Brooklyn and Manhattan[1] as one of three "sources and formative stamps to my own character [. . .] and its subsequent literary and other outgrowth," telling his first biographer Richard Maurice Bucke that *Leaves of Grass* "arose out of my life in Brooklyn and New York from 1838 to 1853, absorbing a million people, for fifteen years, with an intimacy, an eagerness, and an abandon, probably never equaled."[2] If the sprawling, neighborly city of Brooklyn provided the bedrock and materials for Whitman's literary experiments, Manhattan was their inspiration. Not only did the city's dramatic growth exemplify the transformation that the outsetting bard wished for himself; in its size, scope, and singularity, it was a perfect model for *Leaves of Grass*.

"I was of old Brooklyn"

Whitman arrived in Brooklyn with his family from his birthplace on Long Island when he was just turning four; he ended up living there from 1823 to 1836 and again from 1845 to 1862 – longer than he lived in any other place. The village of about 8,000 that first greeted the Whitman family in the 1820s became a city of 24,310 by 1835. By the time he turned forty and completed the third edition of *Leaves of Grass*, 256,714 Brooklynites swelled the city.[3] The accompanying building boom encouraged his father to sell the long-held Whitman farmlands and take up the carpenter's trade. The Whitman family followed Walter Sr. through Brooklyn Heights and Downtown Brooklyn, the neighborhoods experiencing the most rapid growth, as his building projects kept them on the move nearly every year from 1823 to 1833. When the Whitmans fled a cholera epidemic and resettled temporarily on Long Island, Walter Jr. stayed on until the Great Fire of 1835 and an ensuing financial crisis encouraged his search for employment beyond city limits. Returning to Brooklyn after five years on Long Island (1836–41) and four in Manhattan (1841–45) he again roomed with his family, steering their residences towards the eastern edges of the city, today's neighborhoods of Fort Greene, Clinton Hill, and Bedford–Stuyvesant.[4] Though Brooklyn is only referred to by name nine times in *Leaves of Grass* (as opposed to forty-six references to Manhattan), it remains Whitman's spiritual hometown; it was where he conceived, wrote, designed, and printed the landmark 1855 *Leaves of Grass*; it is also the subject of his largest (if incomplete) prose project, a local history that was partially published as the serial "Brooklyniana."[5]

Whitman's passion for books and love affair with language were less products of his few years of schooling than his experiences in Brooklyn's libraries, print shops, and newspaper offices. Attending Brooklyn's first public school until age eleven, perhaps as a charity student, Whitman dropped out and went to work to help with the family's finances (Loving, 31). His first employer gave him a subscription to one of Brooklyn's circulating libraries, which he called the "signal event of my life up to that time," probably because "books were scarce" during his youth (PW, 1:9, 13). He fondly remembered attending the dedication of the Brooklyn Apprentice's Library in 1825; a decade later his name was recorded as "acting librarian."[6] Apprenticed in quick succession at the Jacksonian *Long Island Patriot* and the opposing Whig newspaper the *Long Island Star*, he recounted his first lessons in setting type as a process of discovering the "pleasing mystery of the different letters."[7] Whitman's teacher, the *Patriot*'s foreman printer William Hartshorne, was so in and of Brooklyn that Whitman found it difficult to write a tribute to him "instead of running off into a chronicle of our city" in 1859.[8] Whitman's year at the *Patriot* marked the start of his lifelong interest in typography as well as his first taste of authorship in writing "sentimental bits" for local papers (PW, 1:286–87).

Whitman encountered editor Alden Spooner's strong opinions at the *Star*, which contrasted starkly with those of the *Patriot* and introduced him to political activism. With an eye on national politics he maintained an influential local presence as editor of the Democratic Party organ, the *Brooklyn Daily Eagle*, from March 1846 to February 1848. A vigorous writer of editorials, Whitman also served as secretary of the General Committee of the Kings County Democrats in 1846. When he was fired from the *Eagle* for his attacks on the increasingly divisive Democratic Party and support of the Free Soil position on slavery, Whitman threw his energy behind this party – serving as a Brooklyn delegate at the Free Soil national convention in August 1848, and founding the Free Soil newspaper the *Brooklyn Freeman* in September.[9] In the later 1850s, as the disorganized remnants of the Free Soil party became absorbed into the newly formed Republican Party, Whitman began writing for the Republican-leaning *Brooklyn Daily Times*.[10]

Even as Brooklyn provided a lively forum for his political interests, the city also inspired his active engagement in the arts. He wrote glowing reports of Manhattan's status as the country's premier art market, but at home, he penned his support for establishing a permanent venue for artists and publicly declared that "every mechanic and laboring man and woman of Brooklyn, would have *some* such adornment to his or her abode – however humble that abode may be."[11] Whitman was an outspoken advocate of the newly founded Brooklyn Art Union: in 1850, he wrote three articles on the Union, gave a keynote address, and was elected president.[12] The Union facilitated connections between art lovers like William Cullen Bryant and local artists including the multitalented Gabriel Harrison, who also taught there. A frequent visitor to Harrison's Fulton Street studio, Whitman chose a lithograph of a daguerreotype taken by Harrison as the frontispiece of the 1855 *Leaves of Grass*. For him, Harrison was a model of the "engaged artist-innovator," as committed to advancing the arts in Brooklyn as he was.[13]

"Plumb in the uprights, well entretied, braced in the beams" (LG55, 14), Walter Whitman Jr. was not only a pillar of his community; he helped build Brooklyn in the most literal sense. Whitman's interest in following his father's footsteps into carpentry picked up when he returned from New Orleans in 1848. By 1853, real estate advertisements Whitman placed suggest that "W. Whitman" was literally a household word, which may have encouraged him to leave this tagged name off of his first book of poems in 1855.[14] Constructing homes for Brooklyn's working masses served as a field study of his intended audience and provided the funds as well as the mental freedom to work on his writing project. John Townsend Trowbridge, an American author and one of Whitman's earliest admirers, recalls Walt's own story of the *Leaves'* "seed-time" years:

> He was at work as a carpenter (his father's trade before him) in Brooklyn, building with his own hands and on his own account small and very plain houses for laboring men [. . .]. This was in 1854; he was then thirty five years old. He lived at home with his mother; going off to his work in the morning and returning at night, carrying his dinner pail like any common laborer.

Figure 2.1 Francis Guy, *Winter Scene in Brooklyn* (c. 1819–20). Courtesy of the Brooklyn Museum.

Along with his pail he usually carried a book, between which and his solitary meal he would divide his nooning.[15]

Brooklyn may have been America's third largest city by midcentury, but it remained rural in appearance and character (Figure 2.1). The first feature a visitor to Whitman's Ryerson Street home recalled was "a single window looking out on the barren solitudes of the island."[16] At least where the Whitmans lived through the 1850s, the city was almost indistinguishable from Long Island and encompassed a variety of natural ecosystems. From the salt marshes of calamus around Wallabout Bay to the "ample hills" of Brooklyn Heights where hawks still swoop, the city was remarkably green. Indeed, the very title of *Leaves of Grass* may have been inspired by the grassy meadows of what is now Fort Greene Park – the end result of Whitman's editorializing for a "lung" for his city, and where Walt was found loafing on hot summer days.[17]

Now deemed the "grandfather of literary Brooklyn," Walt Whitman has become a mascot for the borough that has become America's most bookish.[18] From the first release of *Leaves of Grass*, the poet has brought the attention of literary America to Brooklyn. "I shall never forget the first visit [Emerson] paid me – the call, the first call: it was in Brooklyn," Whitman gushed to Traubel (WWC, 2:130). Henry Thoreau and Bronson Alcott made their first journeys to "the very suburbs of the city of Brooklyn"[19] to visit Whitman in 1856; when Thoreau complained, Whitman reportedly chided him, "I do not like my Brooklyn spoken of in this way."[20] If Whitman helped make Brooklyn America's literary capital, Brooklyn must also be credited as an author of *Leaves of Grass* – as he suggests by naming Brooklyn, and not himself, on the first edition's title page.

"Walt Whitman, a kosmos, of Manhattan the son"

We see the world in *Leaves of Grass* because Manhattan was Whitman's "city of the world."[21] The population of New York grew from two hundred thousand in 1830 to half a million in 1850, the steepest growth rate of its time.[22] By 1845 immigrants accounted for 36 percent of the city's residents, while in the years between 1820 and 1860 the immigrant population between the ages of sixteen and forty-five rose to 57 percent.[23] Such immensity and diversity motivated opportunities and possibilities; here, perhaps more than anywhere else on earth during Whitman's day, residents were driven to possess a global awareness, challenged to recognize and tolerate difference, and tested to the limits of their humanity. In 1852, Whitman pronounced it "the most radical city in America at the moment" (Corr., 1:40); three decades later, he saw in New York "the directest proof yet of successful democracy" (PW, 1:172). Though he never owned a home on the island and only boarded there for limited periods (perhaps for a year or two around 1835–36, and then again from 1841–45), this "Brooklyn boy" also declared himself a "Manhattanese, free, friendly, and proud" (LG56, 217).

Whitman first became adventurous about exploring Manhattan after his family left Brooklyn for Long Island around 1833 (his four-year stint in the city also occurred while the Whitmans remained out of town). In *Specimen Days* (1882), he claimed that he started working as a compositor in New York City around this time (PW, 1:15). He also contributed "a piece or two" in the *New York Mirror*, a popular weekly that published the likes of Bryant and Poe and boasted in 1835 that "no literary periodical published in this country has ever attained such an extended circulation."[24] In 1882, Whitman recalled waiting "with half-suppressed excitement" for the delivery of "the then celebrated and fashionable 'Mirror' [. . .]. How it made my

heart double-beat to see my piece on the pretty white paper, in nice type"
(PW, 1:286–87). And so the Brooklyn apprentice was drawn to the faster-
paced, swiftly growing, superlatively ambitious print industry centered
around Manhattan's Park Row.

Perhaps it was at this moment that the teenager sensed the synchronicity
of his life with the city's: Walt Whitman and New York were coming of age
together. The three decades leading up to the publication of *Leaves of Grass*
saw the transformation of a grammar school dropout into America's greatest poet and a sprawling seaport town into a world-class metropolis.[25]
Of particular interest to Whitman was the revolution in popular culture
enlivening city life beginning in the 1830s (Reynolds, 81): dramatic changes
in what America read, wore, ate, heard, saw, believed, and experienced
were available for immediate consumption. The theater was the first of the
city's vast cultural offerings to capture Whitman's imagination (PW, 1:15).
It remained a lifelong passion, though he recalled the shows he enjoyed
"from the time I was fourteen till seventeen or eighteen" as highlights:
"electric" performances by Junius Brutus Booth and Edwin Forrest may
well have influenced the shape-shifting persona of his poetry.[26] In the
following decades, Whitman explored Manhattan's musical offerings –
first favoring folk singers like George Foster and eventually becoming
obsessed with opera (Reynolds, 180–81, 189). At an early age, then,
Whitman began cultivating a cultured urban existence that made it problematic to settle back into the rural lifestyle that the Whitmans had
known for five generations.

Returning to Long Island in the aftermath of one of Manhattan's
most devastating fires, Whitman complained about his five years of
school teaching as a "purgatory" amid "country bumpkins" (Corr., 7:1–
2). But he also gained an outsider's perspective on city life. A common
theme of his prose writings of the 1840s can be summarized by one
article title: "Dangers to Country Youth in the City."[27] His temperance
novel *Franklin Evans* (1842) depicts a Long Island boy who is nearly
ruined by the "great emporium of our western world."[28] When
Whitman moved back to Manhattan in 1841, he was one of
a growing number of men and women leaving country towns for city
jobs.[29] These native migrants had the advantage of speaking the language, but faced the same confusion, diseases, temptations, and corruption as did newcomers from other lands. Whitman's cautionary
tales and essays on the subject mark the beginning of his social
activism, and they indicate how his attempts to heal the country
began at a local and personal level.

If the city was the breeding-ground of such villains as *Franklin Evans's* Colby and Adam Covert of *The Life and Adventures of Jack Engle*,[30] its ubiquitous boarding houses and drinking establishments encouraged camaraderie and introduced opportunities rarely offered beyond city limits. As he began pursuing a writing career in earnest, Whitman became a boarder in Manhattan, where "half the inhabitants of the city hire accommodations" (Journ., 1:60).[31] He stayed at Mrs. Chipman's on Centre Street from May 1841 to at least June 1842, a comparatively long stay in these itinerant years, and six more establishments before May 1845 (NUPM, 1:217, 211). This was nothing like the "boarding round" Whitman had experienced as a rural schoolteacher; as David Faflik notes, "urban America's boarding houses effectively replicated in miniature the multiplicity of the very cities whose existence they foretold and confirmed."[32] Jerome Loving suggests that Whitman's accounts of boarding-house patrons were among his first catalogs (Loving, 61):

> Married men and single men; old women and pretty girls; milliners and masons; cobblers and colonels, and counter jumpers; tailors and teachers; lieutenants, loafers, ladies, lackbrains, and lawyers; printers and parsons – "black spirits and white, blue spirits and gray" – all "go out to board." (Journ., 1:60)

Notably absent from Whitman's description are family members, friends, and neighbors. On Long Island and even in Brooklyn, Whitman lived among faces that not only recognized but resembled his own; boarding in Manhattan, he interacted with an incredible diversity of social, economic, ethnic, and age groups on the streets as well as behind closed doors. Exposure to different types of people and relationships was accompanied by absolute personal freedom. If there was ever a time to question and experiment with his identity, it was this moment, as confirmed in the 1867 volume *Notes on Walt Whitman as Poet and Person* written by John Burroughs and, quite possibly, anonymously cowritten by Whitman himself:

> Through this period – from 1837 to 1848 – without entering into particulars, it is enough to say that he sounded all experiences of life, with all their passions, pleasures, and abandonments. He was young, in perfect bodily condition, and had the city of New York and all its ample opportunities around him. I trace this period in some of the poems in the *Children of Adam*, and occasionally in other parts of his book, including *Calamus*.[33]

Whitman's published tours of Manhattan's "physiognomy" record his transformation into the first great walker in the city.[34] He enthusiastically

Figure 2.2 Photograph of a parade honoring George Washington, Broadway, New York City, on February 23, 1861. The Coleman House Hotel and Pfaff's Restaurant appear in the lower left-hand corner. Photographer unknown. From the private collection of Luther S. Harris.

documented Manhattan's "unspeakable show and lesson"[35] from Castle Garden to the Crystal Palace, Five Points to Fifth Avenue, photography studios to fish markets to Barnum's freak shows; but his urban affection was rooted in the humanity of its crowds – in "Manhattan faces and eyes forever for me"[36] (Figure 2.2). His personal style evolved in response to the street life around him, from the dandyish flâneur of the early 1840s to the bohemian of the late 1850s. The fireman's undershirt Whitman dons on his 1855 frontispiece is a nod at the youthful cult of the Bowery b'hoy, and even liberal-minded Bronson Alcott raised an eyebrow at Whitman's bloomers, a symbol of women's rights in the 1850s.[37] This self-curation of his body was integrally tied to Whitman's curation of his body of work, forming a single powerful aesthetic that was foundational to his development and fame as an artist. By the time he became a regular at Pfaff's Cellar, "the new American poet" had become such a distinct figure on the streets of New York that his portrait was featured on the front page of the *New York Illustrated News* on June 2, 1860.

Whitman's propagation of his own myth as a self-made poet has downplayed the role of Brooklyn artistic circles in his development, including sculptor Henry Kirk Brown's studio around 1849 and Abby Hills Price's coterie that began gathering in 1856.[38] In Manhattan, too, he found community, patronage, and even love in such gatherings, the most famous of which met at Pfaff's Cellar near the corner of Broadway and Bleecker. From about 1857 through 1862, Whitman visited its subterranean vaults "nearly every night."[39] Thanks to its open-minded impresario Charles Pfaff and "King of Bohemia" Henry Clapp, Pfaff's became the birthplace of American bohemian culture – a permissive, open space attracting actors, progressive journalists, and liberal thinkers. Walt gathered just as much inspiration from its workaday patrons like Fred Vaughan, a stagecoach driver who may have been his first serious love interest.[40] Pfaff's enabled Whitman to voice his most intimate expressions of self in *Leaves of Grass* (1860). Even after moving to Camden, Whitman returned to Manhattan for financial and physical comforts that helped him complete the sixth edition of *Leaves of Grass* and his prose memoir *Specimen Days*.[41] Walt stayed for weeks, even months at a time at John H. Johnston's Manhattan residences and his summer home in Mott Haven (now the South Bronx) from 1877 to 1881, where he first experienced uptown, well-heeled New York; the friends he made there, particularly Johnston himself, continued to support him to his death.[42]

"Proud and passionate city! mettlesome, mad, extravagant city!" sang Whitman in one of his several love poems to Manhattan. "Incarnate me as I have incarnated you!"[43] Early in his writing career Whitman began constructing a myth of Manhattan or Mannahatta, alternately using male and female constructions of the island's aboriginal name (as he himself shuttled between male and female personas in his poems). The city possessed such distinct force and character for Whitman that he anthropomorphized his "superb-faced" and "million-footed Manhattan,"[44] endowing it with a living presence and even claiming a familial bond. The proud, passionate, mettlesome, mad, extravagant poet indeed fell heir to his progenitor's most notorious qualities; in turn, Whitman's heartbeat helps drive the pulse of twenty-first century Mannahatta, from its new AIDS Memorial to the "All Are Welcome Here" posters currently proliferating on doors and windows.

Notes

1. New York is now an umbrella term for a city of five boroughs: Manhattan, Brooklyn, Queens, Staten Island, and the Bronx. Before 1898, New York City (or Manhattan) and Brooklyn were sister cities of distinctly different characters, connected only by ferry until the completion of the Brooklyn Bridge in 1883.
2. Richard Maurice Bucke, *Walt Whitman* (Philadelphia, PA: David McKay, 1883), 67.
3. William G. Bishop, *Manual of the Common Council of the City of Brooklyn* (Brooklyn, NY: George C. Bennett, 1861), 474.
4. Whitman's most complete accounts of his movements in Brooklyn and Manhattan from 1823 through 1861 can be found in NUPM (1:8–11) and Emory Holloway, ed., *The Uncollected Poetry and Prose of Walt Whitman* (Garden City, NY: Doubleday, 1921), 2, 86–88.
5. An Exhibition of the Works of Walt Whitman Commemorating the 100th Anniversary of the Printing of His *Leaves of Grass* (Detroit, MI: Friends of the Detroit Public Library, 1955), 1–3.
6. Jennifer Neal, "In Honor of NYU Archives Week," *Brooklyn Museum of Art*, October 2014, http://brooklynmuseum.tumblr.com.
7. Walt Whitman, "Brooklyniana No.6," *Brooklyn Daily Standard* (Brooklyn, NY), January 11, 1862, 1.
8. William White, "A Tribute to William Hartshorne: Unrecorded Whitman," *American Literature* 42.4 (1971), 556.
9. Betsy Erkkila, *Whitman the Political Poet* (New York, NY: Oxford University Press, 1989), 51–52.
10. Karen Karbiener, "Bridging Brooklyn and Bohemia: How the *Brooklyn Daily Times* Brought Whitman Closer to Pfaff's," in *Whitman among the Bohemians*, eds. Joanna Levin and Edward Whitley (Iowa City, IA: University of Iowa Press, 2014), 5–8.
11. Whitman quoted in Ruth L. Bohan, *Looking into Walt Whitman: American Art, 1850–1920* (University Park, PA: Penn State University Press, 2006), 19.
12. Ibid., 19–20.
13. Ibid., 15.
14. See, for example, Whitman's advertisement "$2000–$750 Down – W. Whitman [...] two genteel houses for sale," which ran for two weeks in February 1853 in the *New York Daily Times*, and for February and March 1853 in the *New Yorker Staats-Zeitung*.

15. John Townsend Trowbridge, *My Own Story: With Recollections of Noted Persons* (Boston, MA: Houghton, Mifflin, and Company, 1903), 365–66.

16. Moncure Conway, "Walt Whitman," *Fortnightly Review*, October 15, 1866, 543, WWA.

17. Walt Whitman, "Brooklyn Lungs – Washington Park," *Brooklyn Daily Eagle* (Brooklyn, NY), June 11, 1846, 2; Conway, "Walt Whitman," 542.

18. Evan Hughes, *Literary Brooklyn* (New York, NY: Henry Holt, 2011), 7.

19. "Bronson Alcott on Whitman," in *Walt Whitman: The Critical Heritage*, ed. Milton Hindus (London: Routledge, 1971), 65.

20. Whitman's words as reported by Herbert Gilchrist, in Gay Wilson Allen, *The Solitary Singer* (New York, NY: New York University Press, 1967), 206.

21. Walt Whitman, *Drum-Taps* (New York, NY: 1865), 41, WWA.

22. Richard Briggs Stott, *Workers in the Metropolis: Class, Ethnicity, and Youth in Antebellum New York City* (Ithaca, NY: Cornell University Press, 1990), 111.

23. Ibid., 72–74.

24. Frank Luther Mott, *A History of American Literary Magazines, 1741–1930* (Cambridge, MA: Belknap, 1970), 326.

25. Historian Eric Homberger designates 1825–60 as "the age of 'go ahead'" in Manhattan's history. See his *Historical Atlas of New York City* (New York, NY: Henry Holt, 1994), 70.

26. Walt Whitman, "City Photographs – No.VI," *New York Leader* (New York, NY), May 3, 1862, 2–3, WWA.

27. This is the title of an article Whitman published in the *New York Sun* on December 1, 1842.

28. Walt Whitman, *Franklin Evans, or The Inebriate. A Tale of the Times*, eds. Christopher Castiglia and Glenn Hendler (Durham, NC: Duke University Press, 2007), 5.

29. Edwin Burrows and Mike Wallace, *Gotham: A History of New York City to 1898* (New York: Oxford, 1999), 736–37.

30. Colby encourages Franklin Evans's alcoholism in city saloons; Adam Covert is the villainous lawyer of "Revenge and Requital: A Tale of a Murderer Escaped," *The United States Magazine and Democratic Review* ([New York, NY], July–August, 1845) and *The Life and Adventures of Jack Engle*, *New York Sunday Dispatch* ([New York, NY], March 14–April 18, 1852).

31. In his "Introduction" to Thomas Butler Gunn's *The Physiology of New York Boarding Houses* (New Brunswick, NJ: Rutgers University Press, [1857] 2008), David Faflik notes that Whitman's figures, though "marginally inflated," "did not exaggerate boarding's broad implications" (xii).

32. David Faflik, *Boarding Out: Inhabiting the American Urban Literary Imagination, 1840–1860* (Chicago, IL: Northwestern University Press, 2012), 6.

33. John Burroughs, *Notes on Walt Whitman as Poet and Person* (New York, NY: American News, 1867), 81. According to Carmine Sarracino, *Notes on Walt Whitman as Poet and Person* was "so extensively revised and rewritten by

Whitman himself that it should properly be considered a collaborative effort" ("John Burroughs," in *Walt Whitman: An Encyclopedia*, eds. J. R. LeMaster and Donald D. Kummings [New York, NY: Garland, 1998], 90).

34. Whitman uses this word to describe Manhattan's topography in "City Photographs – No. V," *New York Leader* (New York, NY), April 19, 1862, 1, WWA. Such "walking tours" were first published in the *New York Aurora* (the earliest is "Our City" [New York, NY], March 8, 1842, 2, WWA) and appear with regularity in his antebellum journalism.

35. Walt Whitman, "Broadway," *New York Herald* (New York, NY), April 10, 1888, 6, WWA.

36. Whitman, *Drum-Taps*, 49.

37. "Bronson Alcott on Whitman," 64.

38. Bohan, *Looking into Whitman*, 21; Sherry Ceniza, *Walt Whitman and Nineteenth-Century Women Reformers* (Tuscaloosa, AL: University of Alabama Press, 1998), 50.

39. F. B. S., "A Visit to Walt Whitman," *Brooklyn Daily Eagle* (Brooklyn, NY), July 11, 1888, 10.

40. Ed Folsom and Kenneth M. Price, "Walt Whitman," WWA.

41. Alma Calder Johnston, "Personal Memories of Walt Whitman," in *Whitman in His Own Time*, ed. Joel Myerson (Iowa City, IA: University of Iowa Press, 2000), 263, 267.

42. John H. Johnston, "In Re Walt Whitman," in *Walt Whitman as Man, Poet, and Friend*, ed. Charles N. Elliot (Boston, MA: Richard Badger, 1915), 147–72.

43. Whitman, *Drum-Taps*, 41.

44. Ibid., 51–52.

CHAPTER 3

Camden and Philadelphia

William Pannapacker

In May 1873, Walt Whitman traveled from Washington, DC, to Camden, New Jersey, to see his mother, Louisa Van Velsor Whitman, who was dying at the house of his brother, George Washington Whitman, and sister-in-law, Louisa Orr Haslam Whitman. It probably was the worst year of the poet's life. Walt had suffered a stroke in January that left him paralyzed on his left side. His sister-in-law, Martha "Mattie" Whitman, had died in February in Saint Louis, Missouri, but he was unable to attend her funeral. Whitman's mother died within three days of his arrival in Camden, and observers remember Walt keeping vigil by her bedside through the night, thumping his cane, and weeping. Unable to resume his government work in Washington, DC, and stunned emotionally, Whitman stayed with George and Louisa at 322 Stevens Street, taking his mother's room. A few months later they moved to 431 Stevens Street, where Walt resided until 1884. During those years he spent a lot of time away from the house, traveling, recuperating with the Stafford Family at nearby Timber Creek, and staying as a guest in the houses of other friends in Philadelphia. Drawing on contributions, as well as income from writing and speaking, Whitman eventually bought a small, wood-frame house at 328 Mickle Street. He continued to revise and expand his body of work, gave lectures on Abraham Lincoln, and achieved a higher level of celebrity than he had previously experienced, attracting disciples, patrons, and some famous guests. After a prolonged illness, Whitman died on March 26, 1892, and was interred, with several family members, in a monumental tomb of his own design in Camden's Harleigh Cemetery.

In the second half of the nineteenth century, Camden was a rapidly growing, working-class community, located a short ferry-ride across the Delaware River from Philadelphia, Pennsylvania. The city was, at that time, among the nation's three largest with a population about to exceed one million.[1] The former capital of the United States, Philadelphia was strongly identified with the American Revolution, the Declaration of

Independence, and the Constitution. It had a long tradition of literary societies, a large printing and publishing industry, numerous colleges and professional schools, including the University of Pennsylvania, and prestigious institutions of music and the arts; it also had become the leading American city for the study of medicine. Philadelphia's Quaker heritage, history of religious toleration, and idealized identity as the "City of Brotherly Love" all should have resonated with a freethinking poet of Quaker descent who saw comradeship as the means of forging a stronger national union. A crossroads of the North and South, Philadelphia had played a major role in the Civil War; it was the home of the Union League and had associations with Lincoln, whom Whitman greatly admired. In 1861, Lincoln declared at Independence Hall that he would rather be assassinated than surrender the Union, and his funeral cortege had passed through the city in 1865. Perhaps most important for Whitman, the relationship between Camden and Philadelphia was reminiscent of what he had known in earlier life, living in Brooklyn across the East River from Manhattan. Whitman's long-term residence in Camden may have started as an accident, but it provided him with the support of his family and affordable housing in a familiar context; it also made the resources of a major city available to him as he recovered and began to build a new life and reputation as the "good gray poet," for whom maintaining the appearance of a working-class identity was essential for his literary project of celebrating the common American citizen.

In his poem, "Prayer of Columbus," composed in 1874 and published in *Harper's Magazine*, Whitman seems to draw a parallel with the beleaguered explorer and his own state in Camden: "A BATTER'D, wreck'd old man, / Thrown on this savage shore, far, far from home."[2] But, as Whitman recovered from the physical and emotional trials of recent years, he began to make acquaintances in the nearby factories and railyards and on the ferries. Sometimes he would ride across the Delaware as entertainment: "I love to hear the ice craunch [*sic*]," he is reported to have said.[3] "The life of the streets and of the people was so near, so dear," writes Edward Carpenter of his visit in 1877: "The men on the ferry were evidently old friends; and when we landed on the Philadelphia side we were before long quite besieged."[4] With his shaggy white beard and casual gray suit, Whitman became a recognizable figure in the streets of Philadelphia. He often would sit at the foot of Market Street, near the fruit stalls, striking up conversations, and Philadelphians of that era remember him riding the horsecars, sauntering along Walnut and Chestnut Streets, and reading newspapers in the Mercantile Library on 10th Street. Whitman "was so unexpected in Philadelphia," writes Elizabeth Robins Pennell, "I could almost have imagined that it was for the humour of the thing he came to settle where his very appearance was an offence to the proprieties." According to Pennell, Whitman enjoyed creating a spectacle: "Walt Whitman, from top to toe, proclaimed the man who did not bother to think of the conventions, much less respect them." She remembered the conductors shouting "Walt" as they passed him in the streets.[5] Others were less charmed. The literary historian Ellis Paxon Oberholzer (who was not an admirer) notes that Whitman was "regarded as an 'odd stick,' even by those that he assumed most fully to represent." Describing a walk with the humorist Charles Godfrey Leland, Oberholtzer writes, "Walt took him into a squalid little bar-room and introduced him to a number of tramps."[6] The physician and editor Reynell Coates also complained, "I do not object to his [Whitman's] going to public houses and getting his tipple upon my credit, but when he impersonates me and does it, it is too much, and I will not stand it."[7] "Whitman was, from first to last, a boorish, awkward *poseur*," writes Rebecca Harding Davis, author of the novella *Life in the Iron Mills* (1861). "He sang of the workingman as of a god, but he never did an hour's work himself if he could live by alms."[8] Whitman eventually made many allies, even among the social elites of the city, but he never would be fully embraced as a person or as a poet; his reputation would remain tinged with scandal well into the next century.

As a poet who identified himself with the nation – who gravitated to historic scenes such as Washington during the Civil War – Whitman arrived in Camden at a seemingly well-timed moment: Philadelphia was preparing to become the site of the 1876 Centennial Exposition. As the city made plans for a complex of buildings and exhibitions in Fairmount Park, Whitman prepared a "Centennial Edition" of *Leaves of Grass* and *Two Rivulets* as a matched set of volumes, as well as *Memoranda During the War*, a collection of his journal writings from the Civil War. Whitman also changed the title of his poem "After All, Not to Create Only," which he had read at 40th annual exhibition of the American Institute in New York in 1871, to "Song of the Exposition," with prefatory remarks about the Centennial, and tried to publish it in several magazines, apparently with the expectation that he would be included in the event. Whitman's *Leaves of Grass* had been for sale in Philadelphia as early as the 1856 edition, sold by an outlet of the phrenological publishers, Fowler and Wells, at their agency on 231 Arch Street. Much had been done since then to moderate Whitman's reputation: his *Drum-Taps* and *Sequel to Drum-Taps* (1865–66) included the relatively conventional poem, "O Captain!

My Captain!" His character had been defended in *The Good Gray Poet: A Vindication* (1866) by William D. O'Connor and in *Notes on Walt Whitman as Poet and Person* (1867) by John Burroughs. Also an expurgated collection of his poems, edited by William Michael Rossetti, was published in London in 1868, helping to establish the poet's reputation in England. Nevertheless, Whitman remained too controversial, and socially unconnected, even to be considered for the various ceremonies associated with the Centennial Exposition. Three other poets were included: Sidney Lanier, John Greenleaf Whittier, and, most prominently, Bayard Taylor – a regional native who once had satirized Whitman's "Song of the Exposition" – delivered the ode at the celebration on the Fourth of July. Whitman visited the Exposition, but it seems not to have left a significant impression upon him though it was a landmark event in the history of the city and the nation.

Whitman's invisibility at the Centennial Exposition must have confirmed populist grievances that he had been nurturing from the beginning of his career as a poet, if not earlier. In January 1876, he had published an anonymous article in the *West Jersey Press*, "Walt Whitman's Actual American Position." It was an exposé of how he supposedly had been neglected and abused by his fellow Americans: "Whitman's poems in their public reception have fallen still-born in their country. They have been met, and are met to-day, with the determined denial disgust and scorn of orthodox American authors, publishers and editors, and, in a pecuniary and worldly sense, have certainly wrecked the life of their author" (quoted in Reynolds, 516). The poet arranged for the article to be reprinted in London, resulting in a heated transatlantic dialogue in the press about the poet's reception and circumstances. Whitman published a second anonymous essay in the *West Jersey Press* that further presented him as "a continuous target for slang, slur, insults, gas-promises, disappointments, caricature – without a publisher, without a public" (quoted in Reynolds, 520). Though Whitman had faced criticism and was not wealthy, such exaggerations made him even less likely to be embraced by the leading citizens of Philadelphia. The "Genteel Tradition" was especially strong at that time, and most of the elite institutions of that city – the literary societies, libraries, and gentleman's clubs – had a reputation for being inbred, conventional in taste, and ostentatiously concerned about social respectability.

Nevertheless, partly because of the *West Jersey Press* affair Whitman attracted more admirers outside of the United States, especially in England, where collections were organized to support him. Edward

Carpenter, later known as the "English Whitman" for poetic works such as *Towards Democracy* (1883), came to Camden in 1877. In the same year a Canadian physician, Richard Maurice Bucke, called upon Whitman: Bucke would write his biography in 1883, with substantial collaboration by the poet himself, and would became one of his closest friends and a literary executor. The already famous Irish dramatist Oscar Wilde came to Camden in January 1882 and returned for a second visit in May: "I have an admiration for that man which I can hardly express," he wrote. Whitman found Wilde "genuine, honest and manly."[9] Anne Gilchrist, a scholar of the poet and artist William Blake and a friend of Rossetti's, had published an adulatory essay, "An Englishwoman's Estimate of Walt Whitman," in 1870 and struck up a correspondence with Whitman that proclaimed her love but eventually settled into a mutually respectful friendship. In September 1876, she arrived in Philadelphia with her children: Beatrice, who became a student at Philadelphia's Woman's Medical College; Herbert, a painter whose subject became Whitman; and Grace, who was a teenager interested in music. The Gilchrist family settled at 1929 North 22nd Street and remained there until April 1879, when they returned to England after brief periods in Boston and New York. Whitman was a regular guest at the Gilchrists' house, which had a room always prepared for him. Gilchrist and Whitman enjoyed many conversations and entertained prominent visitors; the poet became personally devoted to her children, and their correspondence continued until Anne's death in 1885. He wrote the poem "'Going Somewhere'" about Anne, describing her as "my noblest woman-friend."[10]

Admiration from abroad helped to encourage more local support for Whitman, and, by the end of the 1870s, he had several new patrons among the eminent Victorians of Philadelphia. George W. Childs, publisher of the city's leading paper, the *Public Ledger*, accompanied Henry Wadsworth Longfellow, then the nation's most famous poet and a resident of Cambridge, Massachusetts, on a visit to Camden in 1876 in the wake of the *West Jersey Press* affair. After that, Whitman would become an occasional overnight guest at Childs' mansion at 2118 Walnut Street. Childs even offered to publish an edited version of *Leaves of Grass* in 1878 and helped Whitman buy the house on Mickle Street in 1884. John W. Forney, owner of the Philadelphia *Progress*, helped to sponsor the poet's trip to the American West in 1879 for a lecture to a large audience honoring the twenty-fifth anniversary of the formation of the Kansas territory. Such activities reflected a poet who had been leavening his rebellious stance with more conventional pieties, particularly as a public performer. Whitman gave a lecture in Philadelphia focusing on the noble principles and character of Thomas Paine in 1877, and on the "Death of Abraham Lincoln" at Association Hall in 1880, the Chestnut Street Opera House in 1886, and, for the last time, at the Philadelphia Art Gallery in 1890, always concluding with a moving recitation of his most popular – but also most uncharacteristic – poem, "O Captain! My Captain!" Often recalling his service in the hospitals of Washington, Whitman made a competitive bid to become the poet laureate of the Civil War in a city that prominently commemorated its role in the preservation of the Union. As the 1880s proceeded, it might have been difficult for some Philadelphians to recall what had once made Whitman so controversial: he had become "the good gray poet."

When the 1881–82 edition of *Leaves*, published in Boston by James R. Osgood, was charged with obscenity by the Boston district attorney, it seems to have confirmed the belief among Whitman's allies in Philadelphia that Whitman was being unfairly targeted based on old-fashioned, moralistic standards of poetry, overly beholden to European traditions, and at odds with the values of the emerging Progressive Era. Using the plates of the Osgood edition, which had been given to Whitman, a small Philadelphia bookseller and publisher, Rees Welsh and Company, managed by David McKay, at 23 South Ninth Street, risked prosecution by printing a new edition of *Leaves of Grass* in 1882. Partly because of the publicity of the Boston banning, the book of poetry went through five printings and sold about six thousand copies, which was the greatest success of Whitman's career as a poet up to that time. McKay bought out Rees Welsh and became Whitman's American publisher for the remainder of his life, though Whitman retained the right to sell copies himself from his residence in Camden. McKay also immediately published a collection of prose writings, *Specimen Days and Collect* (1882), Bucke's biography (1883), and later brought out Whitman's shorter collections, *November Boughs* (1888), *Good-Bye My Fancy* (1891), and, finally, the so-called "Deathbed Edition" of *Leaves* coupled with *Complete Prose Works* (1892).

During the mid-1880s, Whitman, though still considered disreputable by some, was becoming one of the grand, old men of Philadelphia in ways that increasingly complicated his identification with the common American and standing as a literary outsider. Talcott Williams, a journalist for the *Philadelphia Press* who had managed to get the prohibition of *Leaves* from the federal mail revoked, introduced Whitman to Philadelphia's progressive Contemporary Club, where the poet was one of its first speakers in 1886. Agnes Repplier, the Club's first president and

later the doyenne of Philadelphia literary society, remembered liking
Whitman, despite his plain clothes, far better than the critic and novelist
Henry James; Whitman, she said, spoke "beautifully, well within bounds,
and with a charming grace and manner."[11] Robert Pearsall Smith, a glass
manufacturer of prominent Quaker descent as well as a leader of the
Holiness Movement, visited Whitman in Camden at the encouragement
of his daughter, Mary Whitall Smith, and the poet soon became a guest at
their house in Germantown. Whitman would later describe Mary as his
"staunchest living woman friend."[12] Her brother, the writer Logan Pearsall
Smith, dedicated an entire chapter of his autobiography, *Unforgotten Years*
(1939), to the family's relationship with Whitman, writing that *Leaves of
Grass* "revealed to us the miracle of our own existence."[13] Whitman also
became a frequent guest of Thomas Donaldson, a Philadelphia lawyer who
provided the poet with free ferry passes and organized a collection to buy
him a horse and buggy in 1885. Whitman found other influential allies in
Philadelphia, including two on the faculty the University of Pennsylvania:
Horace Howard Furness, a Shakespeare scholar and brother of the
Philadelphia architect Frank Furness, and Daniel Garrison Brinton,
a professor of linguistics and archaeology. Other new friends included
George Henry Boker, a wealthy diplomat, poet, and dramatist who
wrote *Francesca da Rimini* (1853); Leland, mentioned earlier, a local journalist and folklorist, as well as the first director of Philadelphia's Public
School of Industrial Art (also the uncle of Elizabeth Robbins Pennell); and,
most notably of all, the American realist painter Thomas Eakins, director
of the Pennsylvania Academy of Fine Arts from 1882 to 1886.

In the 1890s, Eakins and his friends, such as Williams, referred to
themselves as "all us Whitman fellows."[14] Eakins painted Whitman in
1887, and both possessed a literary and artistic commitment to frankness
and open sexuality that eventually would make them inspirations for
succeeding generations of progressives and modernists. Both had prepared
major works for the Centennial Exposition and faced rejection; Eakins's
masterpiece, *The Gross Clinic* (1875), was considered a mere occupational
portrait and displayed with surgical instruments. In addition to being
banned in Boston, Whitman had lost his job at the Department of the
Interior in 1865 for being the author of *Leaves of Grass*, and Eakins was
forced to resign his teaching position in 1886 for removing the loincloth
from a male model to explain the structure of the pelvis to a class of female
students. Whitman shared Eakins's interest in medicine; they had a mutual
friend in the writer and physician Silas Weir Mitchell who developed the
"rest cure," memorably described by Charlotte Perkins Gilman in her short

story "The Yellow Wallpaper" (1892). Whitman also knew one of the most influential physicians of the nineteenth century, Sir William Osler, who lived in Philadelphia from 1884 to 1889 and provided care for Whitman at the request of Bucke, who himself became the first president of the American Medico-Psychological Association. Indeed, it seems that physicians were as fascinated by Whitman as the artists with whom they were often friends. Philadelphia's Wistar Institute obtained the poet's brain for the collections of the American Anthropometric Society, though it was accidentally destroyed later.[15]

Whitman's most devoted local disciple was Horace Traubel, a child of Jewish immigrants from Germany, who grew up in Camden, trained as a printer, worked initially at the *Camden Evening Visitor*, and then as a clerk at the Philadelphia Farmers and Mechanics' Bank, a job he eventually lost for being a socialist. Traubel visited Whitman almost daily from the mid-1880s until his death in 1892. From their conversations, Traubel published three volumes of *With Walt Whitman in Camden* between 1906 and 1914; six more would be published later from his notes. Whitman wrote a will in 1888 that named Traubel, Bucke, and Thomas Harned (Traubel's brother-in-law) as his literary executors. The following year, on May 31, they organized the first public birthday celebration for Whitman – his seventieth – and the testimonials of the evening were published by McKay in 1889 as *Camden's Compliment to Walt Whitman*. The birthday celebrations became a tradition: after the poet's death in 1892 Traubel and his comrades gathered in Philadelphia and named themselves the "Walt Whitman Reunion Association."[16] A jeweler, John H. Johnston, served as chairman. The group met again in New York in 1893 and then in Philadelphia in 1894, renaming themselves the "Walt Whitman Fellowship: International" with Brinton as President. From 1895 to 1900, the Fellowship alternated meetings between Boston and Philadelphia. The Fellowship eventually had more than 200 members, including artists such as Marsden Hartley and Alfred Stieglitz and writers such as Max Eastman and John Erskine. By the time of Traubel's death in 1919, when the group ceased meeting, they had published 123 "Walt Whitman Fellowship Papers" and became the parent organization for several other Whitman-related literary groups.[17]

Whitman's health had been precarious since his stroke in 1873, but he persisted for nearly two decades, until his final decline began in the early 1890s. In 1892, a farewell volume of retrospections and poems, *Good-Bye My Fancy*, and the "Deathbed Edition" of *Leaves of Grass* were published by McKay, marking what the poet rightly expected would be his final attempt at a work he claimed to have written with future generations in mind. Whitman died of pneumonia on March 26, 1892, attended by Daniel Longaker, a local physician who was also a member of Philadelphia's Society for Ethical Culture of which Traubel was a leading member. In addition to many old friends, more than a thousand local citizens, most of them working-class, passed by Whitman's coffin in the parlor at Mickle Street. Haddonfield Pike was lined with people watching the hearse pass, and the slopes of Harleigh Cemetery were crowded during the speeches given by Harned and Bucke, among others, though not by Traubel, Whitman's self-proclaimed "spirit child," who may have been too choked up with grief.[18] In 1893, Traubel, Bucke, and Harned, with McKay, would publish *In Re Walt Whitman*, which includes accounts of the poet's last days and funeral; all three would present themselves as disciples for the remainder of their lives. In many respects, Whitman's legacy took on the trappings of an emerging religion.

Born initially of personal tragedy and necessity, residency in Camden, even when he could have lived elsewhere, enabled Whitman to rebuild a life that was familiar to him. More than that, his life in Camden allowed him to sustain an image consistent with his idealized self-conception, even as he was giving high-profile speeches, being lionized at testimonial dinners, accepting contributions from "Robber Barons" such as Andrew Carnegie, encouraging cult-like devotion and donations from ordinary readers, allowing his work to be expurgated after all – such as in *Gems from Walt Whitman* (1889) – and building a tomb that cost more than his house. But it was, arguably, because of those seemingly contradictory actions that *Leaves of Grass* became established, in the final decades of Whitman's life, as a work of national and global significance.

Notes

1. Russell F. Weigley, et al., *Philadelphia: A 300-Year History* (New York, NY: Norton, 1982), 488.
2. Walt Whitman, "Prayer of Columbus," *Harper's New Monthly Magazine* 48 (March 1874), 524.
3. Ellis Paxson Oberholtzer, *The Literary History of Philadelphia* (Philadelphia, PA: George W. Jacobs, 1906), 413.
4. Edward Carpenter, *Days with Walt Whitman* (London: George Allen, 1906), 8.
5. Elizabeth Robins Pennell, *Our Philadelphia* (Philadelphia, PA, and London: J. B. Lippincott Company, 1914), 324–26.
6. Paxson Oberholtzer, *The Literary History of Philadelphia*, 413.
7. Ibid., 413–14.

8. Ibid., 414.

9. Gay Wilson Allen, *The Solitary Singer: A Critical Biography of Walt Whitman* (New York, NY: New York University Press, 1967), 502.

10. Walt Whitman, "'Going Somewhere,'" *Lippincott's Magazine*, November 1887, 722.

11. George Stewart Stokes, *Agnes Repplier: Lady of Letters* (Philadelphia, PA: University of Pennsylvania Press, 1949), 102.

12. Henry Bryan Binns, *A Life of Walt Whitman* (London: Methuen, 1905), 303.

13. Logan Pearsall Smith, *Unforgotten Years* (Boston, MA: Little, Brown and Company, 1939), 108.

14. Kathleen A. Foster and Cheryl Leibold, *Writing about Eakins: The Manuscripts in Charles Bregler's Thomas Eakins Collection* (Philadelphia, PA: University of Pennsylvania Press, 1989), 179.

15. Brian Burrell, "The Strange Fate of Whitman's Brain," *Walt Whitman Quarterly Review* 20 (Winter/Spring 2003), 107–33.

16. William A. Pannapacker, "Associations, Clubs, Fellowships, Foundations, and Societies," in *Walt Whitman: An Encyclopedia*, eds. J. R. LeMaster and Donald D. Kummings (New York, NY: Garland Publishing, 1998), 37.

17. Ibid., 38.

18. Ed Folsom, "Traubel, Horace L. [1858–1919]," in *Walt Whitman: An Encyclopedia*, 740.

CHAPTER 4

Washington, DC

Kenneth M. Price

Washington, DC, is the location of the crucial mid-stage of Walt Whitman's career, 1863–73. The start and end of his career have attracted the most attention from scholars and biographers, however, with the former featuring his groundbreaking early work and the latter featuring his most comprehensive collections of poetry and prose – the so-called "deathbed edition" of *Leaves of Grass* (1891–92) and the *Complete Prose Works* (1892). Yet Whitman's remarkable mid-career accomplishments are ripe for reassessment, and they can be better understood when they are situated both temporally and geographically in the nation's capital during the 1860s and 1870s. Doing so clarifies how both Whitman and Washington experienced crises, tried on new identities, and went through interrelated transformations.

During the war years Washington tripled in size and metamorphosed from a sleepy Southern town with a busy political season, to a crowded city notable for its increased federal power and bureaucratic control. The city, a prized target of the Confederate Army, went from being undefended to the most fortified city in the world. In his decade there Whitman similarly changed in profound ways. He visited thousands of soldiers in Washington's many Civil War hospitals, became a clerk in an expanding federal bureaucracy, developed a new personal and intellectual network, and deepened and enriched his writings, producing some of his most compelling journalism, notebooks, poetry, and personal narratives. Not surprisingly, he also altered his persona from a New York "rough" to the nation's "good gray poet."

Washington in the 1860s also gave rise to a new book of Whitman poems, *Drum-Taps* (1865). Eventually absorbed into the 1867 and later editions of *Leaves of Grass*, these war poems signaled a shift from the enthusiastic nation-building of Whitman's antebellum poetry. Here the poems are less optimistic, occasionally even brooding, as Whitman shifts to conflict, suffering, and mourning. To help families cope with the loss of loved ones, Whitman de-particularizes as he depicts soldiers. That is, as Adam Bradford notes, the Civil War soldiers in *Drum-Taps* are stripped of the "identities that marked them as unique, irreplaceable human beings." Lacking markers of identity, Bradford continues, "the poetic soldiers become reflections of a reader's mind – constructions that were at the very least intimate projections from the reader's own consciousness, and likely corresponded to actual individuals in the material world with whom the reader could now imaginatively connect."[1] Yet in this same decade Whitman drafted *Memoranda During the War* (1875–76), his prose account of the "convulsion" that changed the country, with its micro-level specificity about individuals and distinctive urban settings, especially the hospital wards. Pairing *Drum-Taps* with *Memoranda* reveals how Whitman's relationship to poetry and prose had changed: in 1855, poetry and prose partook of the same characteristics; by the time of the Civil War, however, Whitman's poetry and prose had distinctly different purposes and characteristics.

In Washington, then, Whitman's poetic style changed at a time when he combined seemingly incongruous roles: functionary and visionary, government clerk and the poet of democracy. He was employed as a scribe in government offices – initially in the Army Paymaster's Office, then in the Bureau of Indian Affairs (Department of the Interior), and later in the Attorney General's Office. As a scribe he also wrote on behalf of wounded soldiers. Relatedly, he increasingly experimented with developing additional personae in his poetry. In this decade of national crisis Whitman sought ways to revitalize his poetic project, one so closely tied to his hopes for his country and to visions of unity and wholeness, even as he had to come to terms with division, catastrophic destruction, and mass death.

Seeing Washington City in a decade of crisis and change

With habits shaped by earlier decades as a New York-area journalist, Whitman appreciated Washington as a spectacle: this was a city of vistas, a city designed to be seen, a city of symbols. In Washington City, as it was often called in the nineteenth century, avenues were built to produce "reciprocity of sight," in the words of planner Pierre Charles L'Enfant.[2] Yet even though the capital was designed to celebrate the nation's and specifically the federal government's greatness, its grand aims could also highlight present shortcomings as well.[3] The aspirations of Washington City were visible everywhere, but equally apparent, especially during the war years, was its half-built, underdeveloped state. Pigs were the main source of refuse removal; only Pennsylvania Avenue was paved, making the city famous for its mud; and the City Canal, connecting the Potomac and the Eastern Branch (now called the Anacostia), was dank, malodorous, and dangerous. The city was overrun with new arrivals who had come to support, aid, and sometimes fleece the soldiers who passed through or defended the city. Washington was a place of potential power interlaced with gritty problems.

In the first of Whitman's government jobs, in the Army Paymaster's Office, he was located on the fifth floor with a "noble and broad view" from his window that encompassed the Washington monument. From the beginning of Whitman's time in Washington, this monument and its broader setting was on his mind as a letter to two of his bohemian friends in New York makes clear:

> I take a pause, look up a couple of minutes from my pen and paper – see spread, off there, the Potomac, [. . . and] the Washington monument, not half finished – the public grounds around it filled with ten thousand beeves, on the hoof – to the left the Smithsonian with its brown turrets – to the right, far across, Arlington Heights, the forts, eight or ten of them – then the long bridge, and down a ways, but quite plain, the shipping of Alexandria. (Corr., 1:84)

The glimpse of 10,000 cattle grazing on the mall is a reminder of what a massive undertaking – requiring an expanded bureaucracy – it was to feed the thousands of troops who passed through Washington. The eight to ten fortresses seen in the distance were a sobering reminder that the city – wedged between a slaveholding state in rebellion (Virginia, with its shipping at Alexandria) and a slaveholding border state of doubtful loyalty (Maryland) – was in fact so vulnerable to attack that it became necessary to build a ring of forts around it and create a vast citizen army to defend it. Most striking of all, perhaps, was the half-completed shaft of a monument to the nation's founding father. Left in a stunted state, it provided silent but telling commentary on the ideological divisions that had kept it from being completed and on a national experiment gone awry. Was this stump a mockery, a symbol of vast ambition and blighted achievement, as Whitman's bitterest comments in *Democratic Vistas* (1871) seem to suggest? What did Washington the city, named of course for the nation's first president, represent during the Civil War and later Reconstruction when that nation's founding principles were violently contested?

As a symbol, George Washington was implicated both in the rebellion and in the Union defense. Fittingly, his image adorned both the

Confederate seal and the federal dollar. Propagandists of both North and
South claimed him: for the North he was a "defender of union and critic of
slavery and [for the South] a slaveholding planter and leader of rebellion."[4]
In fact, starting at age eleven, Washington was a slaveholder and remained
one for more than fifty years. A wealthy man, he possessed more than 300
slaves at his death.[5] His misgivings about the institution were deep, however, and he freed his slaves in his will, alone amongst slaveholding
founding fathers. Whitman, like many others, typically repressed the
Washington of slave ownership. Yet the legacy of slavery haunted the
capital city bearing his name. Arlington House, part of Whitman's prospect from his federal window, on a hillside rising above the Potomac
served as the home of Confederate General Robert E. Lee and his wife,
a granddaughter of George Washington's wife. Once the war began, the
Union Army seized this land as a graveyard that ultimately became
Arlington National Cemetery. Both house and cemetery underlined the
death-sowing paradox of slavery within an American system ostensibly
devoted to liberty and democracy.

Washington City as a whole, however, possessed a Southern tone and
atmosphere. It had itself been a slaveholding locale until April 1862,
shortly before Whitman arrived. He found the city both fascinating and
disturbing, just as he had been intrigued by New Orleans earlier in life.
He noted the presence of "contrabands," ex-slaves who had made it to
the Union lines and whose legal status remained ambiguous even after
the Emancipation Proclamation, since fugitive slaves from loyal border
states remained subject to the fugitive slave law. He also observed
young black girls in the capital and wondered about the "prospect"
before them in a new era of freedom (NUPM, 2:622–23). In his prose
jottings and notebooks especially, Whitman often gives specific locations for his encounters with African Americans as he did for white
soldiers. Some of these reports can make modern readers cringe, as
when he notes encountering contrabands, itself a dehumanizing term,
on 15th Street on February 16, 1863, who had "physiognomies of hogs or
chimpanzees" (NUPM, 2:557). It is regrettable, given Whitman's fascination with blacks amid urban life in these years, that he did not do
more to help imagine a new vibrant, multiracial society. Whitman
leaves us only with the riddle of how to balance his private writings
(displaying a full range of comments from derogatory to admiring) with
his nearly complete silence on blacks in *Drum-Taps* and his most
important prose writings, including *Democratic Vistas*. He saw blacks
in the streets, in the boarding houses where he lived, and in his office in

the Treasury building, but he struggled to translate what he saw everywhere about him to a revised mental map of what the country could or should look like. His goal of adhesiveness, his imagining of an egalitarian brotherhood, foundered on the color line.

Hospital visitor

Yet the goal of adhesiveness was also realized in remarkable ways in these years, particularly in his devoted work in the hospitals. At the beginning of the war the city had a single hospital, which was soon lost in a fire. Because of the proximity of major battles Washington received more wounded soldiers than any other city and responded by converting an array of buildings – from the capitol itself to churches to a blacksmith shop – into temporary hospitals. (Nearly one quarter – eighteen out of seventy-nine – of the churches in Washington, Georgetown, and Alexandria were turned into hospitals.) Roughly two-thirds of the patients were in make-shift rather than purpose-built hospitals.[6] Whitman's work in the Washington hospitals prompted him to write the most powerful and moving letters of his life. Whitman had few reasons to write letters prior to the war when he had family and friends close at hand. His letters datelined Washington, however, construct his new locale for friends elsewhere, describing the city and its ways even as he gradually redefines himself in relation to a time and place very different from the New York he had left not long before.

Whitman's letters to the families of soldiers are famous, and he reproduced a memorable one himself in *Memoranda*. His letter to the mother of Frank Irwin is a model of specificity, directness, and sensitivity.

> Your son, Corporal Frank H. Irwin, was wounded near Fort Fisher, Virginia, March 25th, 1865 – the wound was in the left knee, pretty bad. He was sent up to Washington, was receiv'd in Ward C, Armory Square Hospital, March 28th – the wound became worse, and on the 4th of April the leg was amputated a little above the knee – the operation was perform'd by Dr. Bliss, one of the best surgeons in the army – he did the whole operation himself – there was a good deal of bad matter gather'd – the bullet was found in the knee. [. . .] He died first of May.

In this letter, Whitman referred to himself mostly to emphasize to the family that their son did not die alone, that he had an affectionate companion.

> I was in the habit of coming in afternoons and sitting by him, and soothing him, and he liked to have me – liked to put his arm out and lay his hand on my knee – would keep it so a long while. [. . .] All the time he was out of his head not one single bad word or thought or idea escaped him. It was remark'd that many a man's conversation in his senses was not half as good as Frank's delirium.[7]

These letters are key illustrations of the positive effect of Whitmanian comradeship. What the poet in 1860 could best imagine by the pond side away from scrutiny found a consequential testing ground in the semi-public space of the hospitals where its positive effect on soldiers was undeniable.

His letter written as a proxy for Robert Nelson Jabo, an illiterate soldier, is different in that it is a touching effort to enter into the mind of another to convey his thoughts and yearnings to loved ones.[8] *Memoranda* attests that Whitman did this frequently for those unable to write themselves because of lack of education, injury, or exhaustion: "When eligible, I encourage the men to write, and myself, when call'd upon, write all sorts of letters for them, (including love letters, very tender ones)."[9] Whitman later explained to his friend and biographer Horace Traubel that he "wrote hundreds of such, similar, letters for the boys: letters for their friends – for their folks: fathers, mothers, sweethearts: they were too sick to write, or not sure of themselves, or something" (WWC, 3:578). Only a handful of these letters have been identified thus far, though many more may remain to be discovered. The letter for Jabo illustrates that Whitman's wish articulated in the 1855 Preface to "go freely with powerful uneducated persons" was not a mere idealized fantasy but something he experienced directly in a heartfelt performance of this role (LG55, vi).

The hospital work helped him usher in the new genre of war reporting. Essays such as "The Great Army of the Sick," "Letter from Washington," and "Fifty-first New-York City Veterans," are often praised in biographies and critical studies, but his Civil War journalism as a whole has not received thorough treatment in part because these items have only recently become easily available. It is an overstatement to claim that the war – or the boys – "gave" Whitman *Leaves of Grass*, as he once asserted, but these experiences helped make Washington, DC, the birthplace of his correspondence and the high-water mark of his journalism (WWC, 3:581–82).

The Blue Book and *Drum-Taps*

The Blue Book was a copy of the third edition of *Leaves of Grass* (1860) in blue paper covers that Whitman heavily revised as he planned a never-realized future edition. The book, found at Whitman's desk by an over-zealous supervisor, James Harlan, famously led to Whitman's firing from the Bureau of Indian Affairs, part of the Department of the Interior. The book can be regarded as a ghost edition since it was never published as such, and it shows the imprint of Washington itself. Whitman was rethinking *Leaves of Grass* at a time when war threatened not only the existence and future of American democracy, but also the place he lived and the federal government he himself represented. Intriguingly, at this fraught moment, Whitman marked eleven of the "Calamus" poems for deletion. In some ways, this seems inexplicable: Why would Whitman retreat from his long-held devotion to comradeship and same-sex affection, which is most explicitly expressed in the "Calamus" poems? His war experience in the hospitals had if anything powerfully affirmed his vision.

At a personal level, of course, Whitman was not renouncing "manly love." His most intense and gratifying personal interactions were with a former confederate soldier and Washington horsecar conductor, Peter Doyle, one of the great loves of his life. Doyle spoke to that side of Whitman attracted to working men, often uneducated, and typically much younger than himself. But many of the "Calamus" poems may have just seemed ill-fitting to a war-torn country. Whitman also may have been rethinking how the personal and the political would be welded together in the new nation.

The firing of Whitman led to a wide-ranging, extravagant defense of him by critic, fiction writer, and fellow government clerk William Douglas O'Connor, who penned *The Good Gray Poet* (1866). O'Connor, a Washington friend whose strong attachment to Whitman like that of his wife Nelly was tinged with eroticism, credited Whitman with saintly status to counter the charges of obscenity that had been levelled against the poet for years, not just by his former boss. More importantly, perhaps, Whitman himself came to embrace the new persona outlined in O'Connor's pamphlet. The grandfatherly, caring, Christ-like figure devoted to hospital work gradually replaced the bohemian persona, "one of the roughs," that characterized the antebellum poet.

Whitman and Washington bureaucracies

In Washington, Whitman was not only subject to the government, he ultimately became a functionary of it. The change required the first in a long series of negotiations between what he characterized as his "old pirate" ways and "vagabond life" and the decorousness, tedium, and formal requirements of bureaucratic enterprises, negotiations that no doubt contributed in subtle but important ways to his changing poetic style (Corr., 1:90–93). Whitman ultimately embraced his work in the Attorney General's Office, a result that could not have been foreseen in light of his earlier comments. In 1856, in "Broadway," an article published in *Life Illustrated*, he spoke disparagingly about clerks, holding in contempt foppish ones befouled in perfume and hair oils.[10] At the time of the third edition of *Leaves of Grass* (1860) he remained dismissive of clerks, associating one of their tasks, copying, with cowardice. In number 13 of "Chants Democratic" he declared: "There shall be no subject but it shall be treated with reference to the ensemble of the world, and the compact truth of the world – And no coward or copyist shall be allowed" (LG60, 185).

On January 20, 1863, Whitman signed papers to become a delegate of the Christian Commission, thus beginning the first of his affiliations with governmental or quasi-governmental bureaucracies. Neither at this time nor in his subsequent Washington jobs did Whitman conform perfectly to rule following. Typically, he gained acceptance and was granted remarkable amounts of flexibility to chart his own way. What he reported to John Addington Symonds was generally true of all of his interactions with Washington bureaucracies: "I [. . .] continue to work here in Washington in a government office, finding it not unpleasant – finding, in it, indeed sufficient and free margin" (Corr., 2:159). He used the same language of "free margin" in another letter to William Michael Rossetti, implying that he adhered to typical practices while also seeking and receiving some tolerance for unconventional ways.[11] On balance, then, he found both governmental institutions and non-governmental bureaucracies accommodating and more to his liking than he ever expected.

Whitman worked longest in the Attorney General's Office, and that phase of his government work is by far the best documented thanks to the recent discovery of approximately 3,000 government documents he inscribed.[12] Located in the Treasury Building, Whitman interacted with a small group of clerks and a series of attorney generals and their assistants. In the office of the attorney general he had an up-close look at key events as they played out, including the expansion of the railroad into the West, plural marriage in Mormon communities, battles with Native Americans, and the rise of the Ku Klux Klan. Whitman also developed important new networks in Washington with the soldiers and, to a lesser extent, the caregivers in the hospitals. He also developed a network with fellow clerks who tended to be educated, interesting people, often writers themselves. William O'Connor and John Burroughs, authors respectively of *The Good Gray Poet* and *Notes on*

Walt Whitman as Poet and Person (1867), were the most famous of this set though there were many others including Charles Eldridge, who had helped publish the third edition of *Leaves of Grass* and was now in the Internal Revenue Bureau; John Binckley, a Washington lawyer associated with the *National Intelligencer* and who was in the Attorney General's Office for several years; and Joseph B. Marvin, a clerk in the Treasury Department. Marvin was a friend and admirer of Whitman's poetry, who was from 1866 to 1867 the coeditor of the *Radical*.[13]

Did Whitman the clerk in some sense become "owned" by the government, with the self-described poet of egalitarian democracy kneeling, paradoxically, within a hierarchical order? A great number of the documents Whitman inscribed as a clerk close with a formulaic declaration of subservience: "your obedient servant." This is the voice of the speaker or drafter, not the inscriber, and is of course a conventional sign-off. Yet inscribing such a closing dozens if not hundreds of times no doubt had some effect on the inscriber. Even if Whitman told himself he was not speaking in his own voice, the compartmentalization of a mind is rarely so complete as to prevent seepage. It is by no means certain that he was always the passive copyist rather than creator of these documents since the question of authorship is vexed, and there is evidence that the attorney general occasionally called on Whitman to complete partially drafted material of consequence, including a speech about Abraham Lincoln (James Speed wished to dedicate a bust of Lincoln in Speed's home town of Louisville, Kentucky and as attorney general was too busy to complete the speech himself).[14] A revealing language of decorum certainly appears in Whitman's letter to John Binckley, assistant attorney general, when the poet declined to seek the position of pardon clerk. Here as his own person, as an employee, rather than as a ventriloquist or copyist, Whitman writes:

> In reference to the brief conversation between us a few days since, allow me in candor to say, that I should decidedly prefer to retain my present post as Record Clerk, the duties of which I feel that I can fulfil properly – & that I would therefore, as far as my personal choice is concerned, wish to be not thought of in view of the pardon clerkship.
>
> Only in case of urgent wish on your or [the attorney general's] part, would I deem it my duty to waive the preference mentioned, & obey your commands.[15]

At one level, this is routine employee-employer correspondence. Yet it is also fascinating as written by a poet who once claimed "I cock my hat as I please indoors or out" and asked (with the obvious answer being "no"): "Shall I venerate and be ceremonious?" (LG55, 25). The contextual situation of these varying utterances is entirely different, of course, and that is part of the point. Did a poet, especially an unconventional one like Whitman, risk being lulled and dulled by a stultifying bureaucracy? An unpublished pair of poetic lines, probably drafted around 1860 when he experimented with aphoristic poems called "Thoughts," illustrates again that even before he began his government work he was concerned with the interplay of public and private roles:

> What would it bring you to be elected and take your place in the capitol?
> I elect you to understand yourself; that is what all the offices in the republic could not do.[16]

Here "offices" do not advance and may actually undermine self-understanding.

As scholarship goes forward, a better comprehension of how Whitman negotiated the demands of these years will emerge. How did it change him not just to speak within the government but to speak as the government, to embody the government, to enact policy and law through his fingertips, to witness the less romantic but increasingly powerful effects of federal legal interventions?

Notes

1. Adam Bradford, "Re-Collecting Soldiers: Walt Whitman and the Appreciation of Human Value," *Walt Whitman Quarterly Review* 27 (Winter 2010), 139.
2. Letter from Pierre Charles L'Enfant to George Washington, June 22, 1791, *Founders Online at the National Archives,* National Historical Publications and Records Commission, https://founders.archives.gov/.
3. Sarah Luria, "Designing Washington, D.C.: 'The City of Magnificent Intentions,'" *American Association of Geographers Newsletter* 44 (2009), 7.
4. Kirk Savage, "The Self-Made Monument: George Washington and the Fight to Erect a National Memorial," *Winterthur Portfolio* 22.4 (1987), 231.
5. Willard Sterne Randall, *George Washington: A Life* (New York, NY: Henry Holt, 1997), 500.
6. Susan C. Lawrence, "Military Hospitals in the Department of Washington," in *Civil War Washington: History, Place, and Digital Scholarship,* ed. Susan C. Lawrence (Lincoln, NE: University of Nebraska Press, 2015), 107.
7. Walt Whitman, *Memoranda During the War* (Camden, NJ: 1875–76), 50–51, WWA.
8. The letter Whitman inscribed for Jabo is reproduced in Kenneth M. Price and Jacqueline M. Budell, "'Written by Walt Whitman, a friend': Three Letters from Soldiers," *Prologue* 48 (2016), 36–45.
9. Whitman, *Memoranda During the War,* 9.

10. Walt Whitman, "New York Dissected, Part IV. Broadway," *Life Illustrated*, August 9, 1856, 116, WWA.

11. With Rossetti he again conveyed his feelings through a double negative: "I still remain here as clerk in a government department – find it not unpleasant – find it allows quite a free margin – working hours from 9 to 3 – work at present easy – my pay $1600 a year (paper)" (Corr., 2:159).

12. See the "In Whitman's Hand" section of WWA.

13. For Marvin, see Corr., 2:317–18.

14. Margaret B. Collins, "Walt Whitman: Ghost Writer for James Speed? or 'None Goes His Way Alone,'" *Filson Club History Quarterly* 37 (October 1963), 305–24.

15. Walt Whitman to John M. Binckley, March 24, 1868, the Charles E. Feinberg Collection of the Papers of Walt Whitman, 1839–1919, Library of Congress, WWA.

16. Walt Whitman, "[To pass existence]," Integrated Catalog of Walt Whitman's Literary Manuscripts, WWA.

CHAPTER 5

The American South

Matt Cohen

Walt Whitman's writing was shaped profoundly by the American South as both idea and reality. He lived and worked there – in New Orleans for a few months in 1848, more famously in Washington, DC, from late 1862 to 1873 – and planned more Southern travel, "among the rest Tennessee and Alabama," he wrote in 1879 to 1880.[1] The national controversy over the expansion of the slave economy into the new territories that defined the antebellum period also shaped Whitman's journalism and his early editions of *Leaves of Grass*. The horrors of the Civil War and the anxieties of national unity during Reconstruction shifted the course of Whitman's poetry and brought some of his most famous works into being. One of his most passionate relationships was with a Southerner, Peter Doyle. And perhaps most importantly, Whitman's ambition to represent the United States as its bard required him not just to embrace a range of Southern identities but to embody them poetically.

This attempt to be the poetic representative of the entire country set Whitman on a course of robust, difficult, and evolving engagement with the South. Inasmuch as the South might be considered both a political entity and an emotional one – a projection as well as a project – Whitman's many representations of it, experiences of it, and links to its people offer multiple ways of regarding the South as context. The relationship continues to represent a challenge and a provocation to researchers both because Whitman's views on race were problematic, changeable, and hard to track and because of the material circumstances of print in the South, which make it difficult to know in depth what uses were made of his writing in that region. But we know enough to suggest that if Whitman was conflicted about – and because of – the South, the South was also conflicted about Whitman.

Whitman's publishing career began in the late 1830s in New York, at a time when the journalistic world was still intensely local. As the 1840s progressed, Whitman began working for papers with larger circulations and extensive exchange relationships with other papers across the United States. Whitman was a Free Soil advocate and opponent of the 1850 Fugitive Slave Act – the federal mandate to return runaway slaves to their owners. His early representations of the South in editorials and in poems like "A Boston Ballad" (1854), about the Northern reaction to the Anthony Burns case, associate the region with slavery and with a corrupting influence on national politics. Burns, an escaped slave living in Boston, was captured under the power of the act, tried amidst mass protest, and returned by force to the South. In "A Boston Ballad," Northerners dependent upon the cotton economy are figured – against their self-depiction as captains of modern, moral industry – as the puppets of a deathly regime. But to oppose slavery was not necessarily to imagine social equality for the races. His 1842 novel *Franklin Evans* witnesses Whitman's more or less conventional Northern attitudes about race, with its sexualization of black bodies, sympathetic portrait of a slaveholder, and linking of miscegenation with intemperance and social collapse. Ironically enough, *Franklin Evans* first appeared in the number of *The New World* immediately following Charles Dickens's *American Notes for General Circulation* (1842), which featured a scathing indictment of slavery and the South.[2]

Whitman's stay in New Orleans with his brother Jeff doubtless opened the young New Yorker's eyes to some of the realities of life under a slaveholding regime. Though he was only in residence for three months in 1848, working for the New Orleans *Crescent*, the impact of his experience of the city would be lasting. There Whitman saw slave auctions first-hand. And there he witnessed not just the extremes of dispossession and wealth customary from critical depictions of the South, but a social order of a degree of complexity and cosmopolitanism comparable to that of his beloved New York City. New Orleans was and remains a hub of the global South linking Indigenous, Hispanophone, and Afro-Caribbean cultures of the Gulf to the USA, by way of both overland trade and Mississippi River shipping. Whitman would write journalism and poems inspired by this sojourn, including "The Mississippi at Midnight" (first published in the *Crescent* in 1848 and later revised for *Specimen Days and Collect* in 1882) and the "Calamus" poems spawned from his manuscript "Live Oak with Moss," as well as the 1887 prose essay "New Orleans in 1848," published in the New Orleans *Picayune*.

The literary industry of New Orleans was only one of Whitman's engagements with Southern writing and thought. The poet had met Edgar Allan Poe and read his works – Whitman would famously be one

of the few literati in attendance at the unveiling of a memorial for Poe in
Baltimore in 1875. As a participant in the bohemian circles of Pfaff's beer
cellar in New York City, Whitman enjoyed the company of Southerner
Ada Clare. Clare, born Ada Agnes Jane McElhenney, came from a wealthy
slaveowning family in Charleston, South Carolina, and along with fellow
Charlestonite Edward Howland revolted against the slave order by using
her money to support New York's bohemia.[3] And Whitman read with care
the literary-critical essays and historical speculations of South Carolina's
William Gilmore Simms, marking enthusiastically the margins of his copy
of Simms' *Views and Reviews in American Literature, History and Fiction*
(1845). The poet's ideas about Native Americans never strayed far from
those expressed by Simms.

Whitman's lifelong doubts about social equality among races and black
suffrage were commonly held by Northern whites, but they also put him
on a sympathetic footing with white Southerners. A heavily edited manuscript, probably from late in his life, suggests how Whitman's conceptions
of racial difference and affiliation were woven into his conceptions of
region, axial to his definition of politics, and deeply challenging to express
in writing:

> ~~Emotional & personal relations are deeper than political ones~~
> – I know not how others may feel but to me the South – the *true* old true
> South, & its succession & presentation ~~to-day~~ the New true South after all
> of today Virginia the Carolinas, Georgia – is yet inexpressibly dear. – ~~Its~~
> ~~The wh~~ To ~~day~~ night I would say ~~a~~ one word for ~~the~~ that South – the whites.
> I do not wish to say one word and will not say one word against the
> blacks – * ~~th~~ but the ~~whites of the South are~~ *my brothers* ~~I love them yet.~~
> ~~Others The~~ blacks can never be to me what ~~they are they are~~ the whites are
> Below all political relations, even the deepest, are still deeper, personal,
> physiological and *emotional* ~~relations~~ ones, the whites are my brothers
> ~~coming down for me common revolutionary ancestry~~ & I love them.
> ~~In the name of [?] the [?] much of the hearts-blood of the north, I say At the~~[4]

If Whitman vacillates here between loving Southern whites "yet" and
loving them unqualifiedly, or between basing that friendship in
a "revolutionary" ancestry (one of course shared by many black and
Indigenous people) or the "hearts blood," one thing is clear: political
difference with the South is not as important as same-race love.[5]

In *Leaves of Grass*, Whitman began to take a more complex approach to
the South than in his journalism and fiction. "I am the poet of slaves and of
the masters of slaves," an early notebook draft of one of his most famous
poetic declarations reads (NUPM, 1:67). The cocky Yankee rough of the

frontispiece of the first edition of *Leaves of Grass* was paired with an enthusiastic embrace of Southern landscapes and denizens, "The blue breadth over the inland sea of Virginia and Maryland" and the "Mississippi with annual freshets and changing chutes" (LG55, iv). By the 1860 edition of *Leaves*, Whitman had not only generated deeply sympathetic portraits of slaves and masters but strident denunciations of slavery itself. That edition, significantly, was issued by the radical abolitionist press of Thayer and Eldridge in Boston, which published James Redpath's biography of John Brown and his *Echoes of Harper's Ferry* (1860) the same year, and which had contracted to publish Harriet Jacobs's *Incidents in the Life of a Slave Girl* (1861). Whitman asks his readers to imagine idyllic scenes "in Virginia, the planter's son returning after a long absence, joyfully welcom'd and kiss'd by the aged mulatto nurse," even as he demands "Freedom to every slave on the face of the earth" (LG60, 162, 194).

Whitman's time in Washington may have been transformative for his perspective on the South and not just because of the trauma of the secession and war. In the city's hospitals he spent time with Confederate soldiers; on its streets, he interacted with its African American residents and refugees and befriended men like Confederate veteran Peter Doyle; and eventually, as a government employee, he participated in the workings of national power in the throes of early Reconstruction. As a clerk for the US Attorney General's Office, Whitman took down many letters dealing with Southern matters, including attempts to fight the Ku Klux Klan, and prepared lists of Alabamans petitioning for pardons. He spent time there with fans like Elizabeth Paschal, a Texas debutante working as a journalist in the capitol. "He made us fragrant Virginia coffee," Paschal reported in her memoir *I Myself* (1910), "and brought out some old-fashioned Southern gingerbread for me, and then he read for quite an hour, with an occasional glance at me."[6] Written during this time, the poems of *Drum-Taps* (1865) bear the marks of a stern confrontation with the realities of war and of the South, even as, in "To the Leaven'd Soil They Trod," Whitman claims a central role for "the hot sun of the South" in maturing his poems.[7] If one thread running through Whitman's postbellum poetry attempts to re-knit North and South, another, particularly in his reflections on Abraham Lincoln, asks readers to hold secession in their minds as the root cause of the tensions reverberating through Reconstruction and beyond.

The South was a crucial context for Whitman's writing – but did his writing matter to the South? During his lifetime, we have tended to think, the poet of masters and of slaves was read by neither. Before the war, prohibitions on the circulation of abolitionist literature dampened the spread of poetry like Whitman's, and anti-literacy laws restricted black reading. The South's literary industry was crippled by the Civil War, and the increasingly violent regime of Jim Crow in the wake of Reconstruction was not a catalyst for democratic experiments in poetry. In his early work, Whitman's political opposition to slavery's expansion put him at odds with dominant positions among white Southerners. For all its claims to represent the masters, *Leaves of Grass* spends more time sympathizing with slaves and laborers than with their overseers:

> I will not have a single person slighted or left away,
> The kept-woman, sponger, thief, are hereby invited – the
>   heavy-lipped slave is invited, the venerealee is invited,
> There shall be no difference between them and the rest.   (LG56, 32)

This was not the white South's vision of democracy – and to top it off, the poem that perhaps did the most to make Whitman famous in the United States, "O Captain! My Captain!" celebrated Abraham Lincoln.

As it turns out, however, Whitman in the postbellum period was fast becoming something of a household name in the South, as he was elsewhere in the United States. Even during the war, the poet had been followed: the Memphis *Daily Appeal* reported in June 1863 that

> Walt Whitman is now in Washington making gruel for the wounded soldiers. The *Saturday Evening Gazette* says: "We dare say his gruel is better than his poetry:" and we may add, if it is "warmer" than "Leaves of Grass," there must be some scalded throats in the Washington hospitals.[8]

In 1881, the *Appeal* reprinted the *New York Tribune*'s review of that year's edition of *Leaves of Grass* with a short introduction. "Some years ago," the anonymous writer declares, "when these 'Leaves' were first given to the public as the result of private publication by the author, the Appeal expressed its views of the poet and his work – filthy beyond words to tell, with only the one redeeming trait of unusual poetic power in treatment and expression."[9] Readers in Wheeling, West Virginia had heard about Whitman's global fame in a similar tone of disdain in 1875:

> Walt Whitman, the eccentric poet, now a resident of Camden, enjoys the honor of having his productions translated into the German, Danish, Hungarian, and French languages. [...] Yes, and strange to say the English reader can be about as much edified by them in either of those languages as if they appeared in his native Anglo-Saxon.[10]

Still, the Wheeling papers tracked the poet steadily until his passing in 1892.[11] Of course, as has always been true, negative press from critics hardly means a work was not read. Nothing attracts readers quite like critical conviction of filthiness "beyond words."

Even at the most esoteric levels of Southern literary writing, both before and after the war, Whitman took his lumps. Poems like "Longings for Home" opened themselves to ridicule with their attempts to identify with the South: "O to be a Virginian, where I grew up! O to be a Carolinian! / O longings irrepressible! O I will go back to old Tennessee, and never wander more!" (LG60, 390). This poem was reprinted in the *Southern Literary Messenger*, the region's leading, nationally read literary journal. There the Secessionist George Bagby framed the poem as an example of Emersonian "pantheism" and as an aesthetic catastrophe, "obnubilate, incoherent, convulsive flub-drub."[12] Northern victory did nothing to change Southern literary critics' assessments of the good gray poet.

In most cases of sustained attention to Whitman's writing in the South, it was not his political orientation that rankled but what critics perceived as his atheism and his aesthetic violations. Flaunting formal literary conventions was, for a region steeped in rank and honor-based patriarchal sociality, tantamount to assaulting hierarchies essential to maintaining white racial superiority and the dominance of the plantation elite.

But what of readers in the rural South, with access to papers but few bookstores or libraries? Whitman, in fact, had a long-term friendship with one: John Newton Johnson, a former slaveowner and Confederate veteran who farmed in Mid, Alabama. Johnson, who was an avid, largely self-educated reader, encountered Whitman's poetry in 1874, and was inspired to write to the poet. Having "this summer learned in my backwoods hermit home that Walt's Poems were in books, and that 'English critics consider him the greatest Poet of America,'" Johnson had acquired *Leaves of Grass* and *As a Strong Bird on Pinions Free* (1872) from a New York bookseller. "I think your works are not known here," Newton lamented, signing his letter, "John Newton Johnson / The Hermit, eccentric farmer / and self-styled 'Philosopher and Poet.'"[13] Whitman answered, and the two struck up a correspondence. Johnson explained to the poet that, in the wake of the war, he felt depressed and isolated, and Whitman's work had energized him. Though he had, like many slaveholders, lost almost two-thirds of his net worth and the status of master as a result of the war and emancipation, equally depressing for Johnson were what he regarded as outdated forms of religion, an underappreciation of the arts, and petty jealousies among his fellow small landholders in northern Alabama. "Lack of culture and the *love of the ideal* in any sense other than the *old* and *barbarous* is the main defect," Johnson wrote, "*Orthodoxy* flourishes with the usual *lack* of *flowers* or *fruit*."[14]

Early in their correspondence, Johnson raised the matter of their having been on opposite sides of the Civil War and the slavery question. Whitman's replies are not known to have survived, but the conversation seems to have turned to the question of the definition of freedom. "While *you* show us that Universal Suffrage is certain to not give us the very worst of characters for rulers," Johnson writes, "may it ∧ ^not^ be inferred that the White ascendancy here again will hardly produce any intolerable event."[15] The negative construction of Johnson's claim about Whitman's arguments in *Democratic Vistas* (1871) suggests the way in which the complex hedges in Whitman's essay open the potential for dialogue between Northern and Southern views. Whitman's *Two Rivulets* (1876), with its extended discussions of democracy and the nation, became central to Johnson's discussions with Whitman. Johnson more than once made reference to the concluding footnote titled "Freedom" in *Two Rivulets*, regarding it as ambiguous on the question of the relationship between personal freedom and that of the mass, but agreeing with its spirit. Johnson asserts that he first struggled with Whitman's assertion there (and, he suggested, that resonated in "Children of Adam") that, as the poet put it,

> More precious than all worldly riches, is Freedom – freedom from the painful constipation and poor narrowness of ecclesiasticism – freedom in manners, habiliments, furniture, from the silliness and tyranny of local fashions – entire freedom from party rings and mere conventions in Politics – and better than all, a general freedom of One's-Self from the tyrranic domination of vices, habits, appetites, under which nearly every man of us, (often the greatest bawler for freedom,) is enslaved.[16]

While Johnson regards Whitman here as having "only formulated what I was conscious of, preaching, and living," his rebellion against the notion that one must become a "eunuch for the Commonwealth of Man's sake!!!!!!!" seems to persist in passionate punctuation no less than its inversion of scripture.[17] But at a broader level, Whitman's use of the metaphor of slavery here and his assertion that universal law forces a reconsideration of the politics of personal freedom create a tension from the standpoint of a reader like Johnson, for whom the philosophy of self-control and management of free will implied here registers more powerfully than Whitman's versions of national unity.

Johnson named one of his children after the poet and in 1879 visited Whitman in Camden, causing a stir among Whitman's disciples and in the press. Whitman maintained his ties with Johnson down to the final days of his life, against the derision of those around him, even as Johnson braved the disdain of a locale that tended to make fun of Whitman at best and regard him as a moral poison at worst. The long conversation between the two men illustrates the presence of Whitman's work in the South and the poet's personal engagement with one of its denizens. Moreover, it suggests the rich and contradictory ways that region could be related to nation, but at the same time, the ways by which Whitman and his work fueled a thinking about the self beyond geographic definitions.

"I have really called Two Rivulets *our* book," Johnson wrote, and in many ways, thinking of Whitman's works as products of a dialogue among regions can be illuminating.[18] Whitman's influence in the South has grown since his death, and the complex relationship between his message of liberation and his writings' racial politics persists. In a 2001 essay about being a queer Southerner, Laura Milner describes Whitman as having been pivotal for her attempt to overcome the internalization of patriarchal, Christian gender norms. Reading "Whitman's 'Song of Myself,' which insists 'it is as great to be a woman as to be a man,'" Milner writes, "I cracked open the door and found myself there, waiting." Yet the Mississippi-born African American writer Natasha Trethewey reminds us that Whitman's writing foreshadows "the narratives of blacks relegated to the margins of public memory." The fragility of civic memory is witnessed in Whitman's fear that "the real war will never get in the books" (PW, 1:115), and in the fact that his message of loving democracy must be serially recovered during waves of divisive patriotism. As yet we know so little about black Southern readers of Whitman during his lifetime, or about how the Indigenous people marching the Trail of Tears, which ran right through John Newton Johnson's small Alabama town, read Whitman's work. To a region still struggling with racism, homophobia, and xenophobia, America's bard holds out both warnings about representation's failures and a salutary demand to see a world both "nigher and farther" than any region. "Whitman's take on the South is much like my own," Trethewey writes, "it is a love/hate relationship."[19]

Notes

1. Quoted in Walter Eitner, *Walt Whitman's Western Jaunt* (Lawrence, KS: University Press of Kansas, 1982), 65.
2. For an argument that Whitman's more complex navigation of the South begins with his revisions of *Franklin Evans* into 1846's "Fortunes of a Country-Boy; Incidents in Town – and his Adventure at the South," see Stephanie Blalock and Nicole Gray, "Introduction to *Franklin Evans* and 'Fortunes of a Country-Boy,'" WWA.

3. Edward Whitley, "The Southern Origins of Bohemian New York: Edward Howland, Ada Clare, and Edgar Allan Poe," in *The Bohemian South: Creating Countercultures, from Poe to Punk*, eds. Shawn Bingham and Lindsey Freeman (Chapel Hill, NC: University of North Carolina Press, 2017).

4. "Emotional and personal relations are deeper," manuscript held at the Harry Ransom Center, University of Texas–Austin, Walt Whitman Collection, container 1.4. Versions are published in NUPM, 6:2160, and Emory Holloway, "Notes from a Whitman Student's Scrapbook," *American Scholar* (May 1933), 273.

5. See Ed Folsom's discussion in "Lucifer and Ethiopia: Whitman, Race, and Poetics before the Civil War and After," in *A Historical Guide to Walt Whitman*, ed. David Reynolds (New York, NY: Oxford University Press, 2000), 45–96.

6. Elizabeth Paschal O'Connor, *I Myself* (London: Methuen, 1910), 82.

7. Walt Whitman, *Leaves of Grass* (Washington, DC, 1871–72), 298, WWA.

8. *Daily Appeal* (Memphis, TN), June 17, 1863, 1.

9. "Walt Whitman's 'Leaves of Grass,'" *Daily Appeal* (Memphis, TN), November 23, 1881, 2.

10. "General Notes," *Daily Register* (Wheeling, WV), July 30, 1875, 1.

11. After his death, the poet's work continued to be reprinted and discussed in papers across the South, and he began to be referenced more and more frequently in the works of Southern writers, including Rebecca Harding Davis, Belle Kearney, John McIntosh Kell, and John G. Paxton.

12. George William Bagby, "Editor's Table," *Southern Literary Messenger* 31 (July 1860), 74.

13. John Newton Johnson to Walt Whitman, August 13, 1874, Charles E. Feinberg Collection of the Papers of Walt Whitman, Library of Congress.

14. Johnson to Whitman, October 7, 1874, Charles E. Feinberg Collection of the Papers of Walt Whitman, Library of Congress.

15. Johnson to Whitman, undated letter, Charles E. Feinberg Collection of the Papers of Walt Whitman, Library of Congress.

16. Walt Whitman, *Two Rivulets: Including Democratic Vistas, Centennial Songs, and Passage to India* (Camden, NJ, 1876), 31–32.

17. Johnson to Whitman, undated letter, Charles E. Feinberg Collection of the Papers of Walt Whitman, Library of Congress. Johnson also mentions the "Freedom" footnote in his letter of May 20, 1877.

18. Johnson to Whitman, February 8, 1878, Charles E. Feinberg Collection of the Papers of Walt Whitman, Library of Congress.

19. Laura Milner, "From Southern Baptist Belle to Butch (and Beyond)," in *Out in the South*, eds. Carlos L. Dews and Carolyn Leste Law (Philadelphia, PA: Temple University Press, 2001), 189. Natasha Trethewey, "On Whitman, Civil War Memory, and My South," *Virginia Quarterly Review* 81.2 (2005), 50.

PART II

Literary and Artistic Contexts

CHAPTER 6

Verse Forms

Michael C. Cohen

The continuity of American poetry, according to Roy Harvey Pearce's once-famous series of formulations, was

> that of the antinomian, Adamic impulse, as it thrusts against a culture made by Americans who come more and more to be frightened by it [. . .]. The American poet, in his dedication to the idea of the dignity of man, has had as his abiding task the reconciliation of the impulse to freedom with the impulse to community, as the use of language in poetry may help bring it about.[1]

Though Pearce tracked a long poetic arc, from the Puritans to Wallace Stevens, it is likely not surprising that Whitman served a transitional role in his story. "Song of Myself" needed to be situated within a tradition of American epic-writing, for instance, but once "we look at *Song of Myself* as an exemplar of a further stage in the development of an American epic, we may see how it was necessary for the success of the poem that it be in no way externally or generically structured."[2] The critical desire to "find in it some firm structural principle" was misguided, Pearce felt, for "there is a movement here, but not a form."[3]

Perhaps also unsurprisingly, Longfellow, with his commitments to European verse forms, served as foil to Whitman's expansiveness: "Longfellow's world was closed," Pearce noted in a terse, four-page judgment on the best-selling poet of the century. "As a kind of liaison-man between older cultures and the new, he [. . .] succeeded only in cutting down that literature to his readers' size."[4] Yet despite the apparent finality of this dismissal, Pearce acknowledged Longfellow's far stronger grasp on the imaginations of readers:

> Recalling such poems [. . .], remembering how many of them there are, letting ourselves be inveigled into staying with them by the sheer dexterity of their formal handling and by the ease with which their maker glosses over hard fact and harder motivation – recalling such poems, we recall an age's

hopes to understand itself in the very terms which gives the poems such
staying power as they have.[5]

The language of memory and recall is important: though Pearce wrote at
the nadir of Longfellow's critical reputation, the poet's place in a scholastic
curriculum of popular, pedagogic verse had remained unchallenged for
almost a century, and thus his work exerted a heavy gravitational pull on
the minds of four generations of students. "The sheer dexterity of their
formal handling" was perhaps meant as a putdown of Longfellow's poems,
but it also named the source of their astonishing "staying power." Whether
he called it "structural principal" or "formal handling," Pearce recognized
verse form as an inchoate force that could inveigle readers "into staying
with it," bringing an age to an understanding of itself and thereby reconcil-
ing "the impulse to freedom with the impulse to community."

It is tempting to dismiss Pearce's work – especially its over-determined
opposition between open and closed systems – as another "Cold War
reading" of American literature, but it is not my intention to argue against
his notions of Whitman's poetic mobility or Longfellow's formal con-
straint, nor am I interested simply in reversing their positions.[6] I cite Pearce
because, going against his own argument, I believe his terms offer a point of
entry to explore Whitman's deep investment in questions of verse form.
The goal of this brief essay is not to locate the "structural principal" of
Leaves of Grass, nor to catalog the variety of genres Whitman adapted
throughout his career. Rather, I hope to glimpse the utopian horizon that
Whitman's understanding of "form" makes visible in his poetics.
My examples will be the Preface and untitled first poem – later called
"Song of Myself" – of the 1855 edition of *Leaves of Grass*.

Comparing Whitman and Longfellow is a hoary tradition in American
literary studies, going back to the nineteenth century, and it has almost
always worked in Whitman's favor, even when critics seek to complicate
the terms of reception. Angus Fletcher, for instance, in a sympathetic
reading that argues for Longfellow as an "extraordinarily original" author,
writes that:

> One might call Whitman "original" and Longfellow "derivative," but only if
> one took a rather narrow view of what constitutes originality. [. . .]
> On a more technical level one might claim that Whitman was a poetic
> innovator of entirely new verse-forms (free verse), while Longfellow
> observed the traditional patterns of English poetry, but this too would be
> misleading, since although Whitman's verse inventions are indeed remark-
> able, Longfellow's metrical art [. . .] shows once again the typically American
> passion for engineering things in a new way.[7]

This account of "verse formalism," though it seeks to revise mid-century oppositions between freedom and formality (such as that presented in F. O. Matthiessen's *American Renaissance* [1941]), still coordinates metrical artistry and poetic originality in ways that maintain a critical fiction about nineteenth-century poetics, for the belief that Whitman had broken with traditions of formal versification was not widely held before the twentieth century.[8] Edmund Clarence Stedman, one of the most influential critics of the late nineteenth century and, like Whitman, an habitué of Pfaff's in the late 1850s, offered a very different take, characterizing *Leaves of Grass* as "formalism of a pronounced kind" while identifying Whitman as "the poet of the over-refined and the doctrinaires."[9] Longfellow's *Hiawatha* (1855), in contrast, "[reminds] us that poetry is the natural speech of primitive races; the 'song' of Hiawatha has the epic quality that pertains to early ballads, the highest enjoyment of which belongs to later ages and to the creature that Whitman terms the civilizee."[10] Longfellow's innovations – such as "the novelty of the rhymeless trochaic dimeter" that is the most striking feature of *Hiawatha* – were evidence of the "nicest skill" necessary to render the poem natural-sounding ("primitive") and thus protect it from "an effect of burlesque or commonplace" that would otherwise have sunk it.[11] In comparison, Whitman's "irregular, manneristic chant is *at the other extreme of artificiality*" because it avowed itself so openly.[12]

Stedman's point is that both poets practiced an adventurous formalism, using ostentatious experiments in versification to render "primitive" or ordinary content enjoyable to sophisticated readers, but they did so in different directions, with Longfellow obscuring his virtuosic style in the service of a fictive naturalism, and Whitman foregrounding his synthetic aestheticism to render "poetic" the everyday materials in his text. These strategies speak to the larger expectations of each author's mid-century project. The precision of Longfellow's concept of form in *Hiawatha* generates a series of translations – these songs were the land's, then they were the natives', now they are mine, and soon they will be yours – that inculcate the pedagogy of an imperial poetics.[13] In contrast, the looseness of the term "form" in Whitman's vocabulary allows him to toggle between ideals of perfect poems and ideals of beautiful bodies in ways that enable the larger ethical aims of his work. This intention becomes clear early in the Preface, in a passage that begins with a negative definition of aesthetics before reversing into an exposition of organic wholeness:

> The poetic quality is not marshalled in rhyme or uniformity or abstract addresses to things nor in melancholy complaints or good precepts, but is

the life of these and much else and is in the soul. The profit of rhyme is that it drops seeds of a sweeter and more luxuriant rhyme, and of uniformity that it conveys itself into its own roots in the ground out of sight. The rhyme and uniformity of perfect poems show the free growth of metrical laws and bud from them as unerringly and loosely as lilacs or roses on a bush, and take shapes as compact as the shapes of chestnuts and oranges and melons and pears, and shed the perfume impalpable to form. (LG55, v)

Like many innovators before him, Whitman seeks to reinvigorate poetry by reinvesting in the natural principles ("metrical laws") inherent in the language, with poems analogically imagined as a series of botanical figures – buds, flowers, and fruits. Make poems as you would grow oranges or melons or pears; all are the products of cultivation and therefore require the maker or grower to follow rules. Whitman is not advocating a "free" verse, therefore, but the "free growth" of verse. Perfect poems are the subjects of metrical laws, but formal rules imposed or pursued without the principle of "free growth" create mere "gaggery," since "the fluency and ornaments of the finest poems [. . .] are not independent but dependent" on the first principles of natural metrical laws (LG55, v). You will know the finest poems by the "perfume impalpable" that they circulate, a sensory awareness repeated in an enigmatic early passage of "Song of Myself": "Houses and rooms are full of perfumes . . . . the shelves are covered with perfumes, / I breathe the fragrance myself, and know it and like it, / The distillation would intoxicate me also, but I shall not let it" (LG55, 13). Smell, among the most physically embodied senses, is second in importance only to touch in Whitman's poetics:

> The atmosphere is not a perfume . . . . it has no taste of the distillation
> . . . . it is odorless,
> It is for my mouth forever . . . . I am in love with it,
> I will go to the bank by the wood and become undisguised and naked,
> I am mad for it to be in contact with me.   (LG55, 13)

Whitman evokes here a relation to the universe predicated on neither self-dissolution nor self-mastery but instead on an "undisguised and naked" contact with the "atmosphere." Such joyous embodiment comes through the multi-sensory perceptions of the "perfume impalpable," which is opened up by – but is not reducible to – the free-growing laws of poetic form.

It is customary at this point to situate Whitman's argument about form in relation to Emerson's famous statement in "The Poet" that "it is not metres, but a metre-making argument, that makes a poem."[14] Circumstantial evidence suggests that Whitman may have attended and reviewed Emerson's lecture on "Nature and the Powers of the Poet," so there are reasons to think he had Emerson's ideas in mind while composing the first edition (Loving, 43).[15] However, it is also easy to overstate the relation between the two. Jay Grossman has demonstrated the underlying conflict between each author's notions of what a poem is. As Grossman brilliantly observes, Emerson's famous letter to Whitman, which praised *Leaves of Grass* as the "most extraordinary piece of wit and wisdom that America has yet contributed," never refers to the book (even once) as poetry, poetic, or a poem.[16] Perhaps in response, Whitman included the word "Poem" in the title of every text in the 1856 second edition. And there are other ways to see the non-Emersonian implications of Whitman's poetics, for as I have already indicated, Whitman's formalism is about bodily and social as well as ideal (poetic) form. Interestingly, and in a manner unlike Emerson, Whitman's credo in the Preface quickly shifts from a statement about aesthetic principles into an ethical imperative, before heralding a vision of something like secular embodiment. "Who troubles himself about his ornaments or fluency is lost," Whitman states, because "all beauty comes from beautiful blood and a beautiful brain" (LG55, v). Having loosely correlated aesthetic beauty and bodily expression, he then turns to his reader:

> This is what you shall do: Love the earth and sun and the animals, despise riches, give alms to every one that asks, stand up for the stupid and crazy, devote your income and labor to others, hate tyrants, argue not concerning God, have patience and indulgence toward people, take off your hat to nothing known or unknown or to any man or number of men, go freely with powerful uneducated persons and with the young and with the mothers of families, read these leaves in the open air every season of every year of your life, re examine all you have been told at school or church or in any book, dismiss whatever insults your own soul, and your very flesh shall be a great poem and have the richest fluency not only in its words but in the silent lines of its lips and face and between the lashes of your eyes and in every motion and joint of your body. (LG55, v–vi)

In the space of a few sentences Whitman travels from a discussion of what a poem should be, to an exhortation about what a person should be. The form of the first – again, not "rhyme or uniformity or abstract addresses to things" but "the free growth of metrical laws" – bears a rooted relation ("in the ground out of sight") to the form of the second – "your very flesh shall be a great poem" – and the poem *Leaves of Grass* is the medium of transfer between the two. "Read these leaves in the open air every season of every year of your life," he urges, in a particularly evangelical appeal that is also, to my knowledge, the only moment in the Preface that refers to the actual book that will follow. The aesthetic practice and the ethical practice unify in the scene of reading, and what results will be an enlightened but non-transcendent mode of embodied life: "your very flesh shall be a great poem" expressed bodily, "in the silent lines of its lips and face and between the lashes of your eyes and in every motion and joint of your body."

Michael Robertson has argued that critics must take seriously the tradition of the "Whitmaniacs," Whitman's most devoted readers, who have used *Leaves of Grass* as a secular bible and guide for living in an alienated age.[17] Far from being naïve or mistaken, Robertson explains, such readers put into practice the book's most far-reaching ambitions, and recovering their experiences can make sense of the ways in which the formal innovations of Whitman's poetry were meant to awaken readers into a more fundamental and worldly embodiment. "Long enough have you dreamed contemptible dreams," he writes late in "Song of Myself." "Now I wash the gum from your eyes, / You must habit yourself to the dazzle of the light and of every moment of your life" (LG55, 52). Throughout the poem Whitman transforms aesthetic or literary considerations back into physical, social, and erotic relations. As he pronounces in an early moment:

Have you reckoned a thousand acres much? Have you reckoned the earth much?
Have you practiced so long to learn to read?
Have you felt so proud to get at the meaning of poems?
Stop this day and night with me and you shall possess the origin of all poems,
You shall possess the good of the earth and sun .... there are millions of suns left,
You shall no longer take things at second or third hand .... nor look through the
    eyes of the dead .... nor feed on the spectres in books,
You shall not look through my eyes either, nor take things from me,
You shall listen to all sides and filter them from yourself.   (LG55, 14)

Practicing to read and getting at the meaning of poems are decidedly not the point of *Leaves of Grass* but instead are achievements as spurious as the accumulation of wealth dismissed in the opening line – even the earth falls short of the kind of knowledge, "the origin of all poems," that comes from "[stopping] this day and night with me," and this knowledge gained in intimate proximity to another is ultimately a clarified mode of being in the world. The poem opens into its reader, but this opening in requires the reader's own opening out to others. Later, near the midpoint of the poem, Whitman claims:

To be in any form, what is that?
If nothing lay more developed the quahaug and its callous shell were enough.

Mine is no callous shell,
I have instant conductors all over me whether I pass or stop,
They seize every object and lead it harmlessly through me.

I merely stir, press, feel with my fingers, and am happy,
To touch my person to some one else's is about as much as I can stand.

(LG55, 32)

To be in form is not to be walled off like a clam in its shell, isolated and enclosed. Form is not the tactile limits of something, but is rather the capacity to imagine one's own unfolding connectivity with the world. Here again *Leaves of Grass* figures its formal ambitions, "to seize every object and lead it harmlessly through me." What might remain a strictly aesthetic abstraction of form in the Emersonian tradition is rerouted into a mode of sociality that is also a self-relation, which generates well-being at a primary level – "I merely stir, press, feel with my fingers, and am happy." This ideal of the good is the poem's point, reiterated near its end:

There is that in me .... I do not know what it is .... but I know it is in me.

Wrenched and sweaty .... calm and cool then my body becomes;
I sleep .... I sleep long.

I do not know it .... it is without name .... it is a word unsaid,
It is not in any dictionary or utterance or symbol.

Something it swings on more than the earth I swing on,
To it the creation is the friend whose embracing awakens me.

Perhaps I might tell more .... Outlines! I plead for my brothers and sisters.

Do you see O my brothers and sisters?
It is not chaos or death .... it is form and union and plan .... it is eternal
   life .... it is happiness.

(LG55, 55)

The capacity to remain in uncertainty about one's self ("I do not know what it is .... but I know it is in me") and the willingness to be available to others ("the friend whose embracing awakens me") without dissolving either state into the other – maintaining both a self-relation and a social relation – is the way of being the poem ultimately seeks to bring about. The open-endedness that *Leaves of Grass* promulgates as its desired condition is "radical" in the sense of being "from the root" – "it swings on more than the earth I swing on." But open-endedness is a principle of Whitman's verse only to the extent that his poetry seeks to reintegrate aesthetic and ethical practice. The poem has "form and union and plan," in other words, but the free growth of its formalism seeks as its end worldly, which is to say bodily, happiness.

Notes

1. Roy Harvey Pearce, *The Continuity of American Poetry* (Princeton, NJ: Princeton University Press, 1961), 5–6.
2. Ibid., 73.
3. Ibid., 72, 73.
4. Ibid., 210.
5. Ibid., 212.
6. Cf. Donald E. Pease, "*Moby Dick* and the Cold War," in *The American Renaissance Reconsidered*, eds. Walter Benn Michaels and Donald E. Pease (Baltimore, MD: The Johns Hopkins University Press, 1985), 113–55.
7. Angus Fletcher, "Whitman and Longfellow: Two Types of the American Poet," *Raritan* 10.4 (1991), 131–45.
8. Recent work that situates Whitman's poetics in nineteenth-century contexts includes: Edward Whitley, *American Bards: Walt Whitman and Other Unlikely Candidates for National Poet* (Chapel Hill, NC: The University of North Carolina Press, 2010); David Haven Blake, *Walt Whitman and the Culture of American Celebrity* (New Haven, CT: Yale University Press, 2006); Michael Warner, "Whitman Drunk," in *Breaking Bounds: Whitman and American Cultural Studies*, eds. Betsy Erkkila and Jay Grossman (New York, NY: Oxford University Press, 1996), 30–43; and Christine Stansell, "Whitman at Pfaff's: Commercial Culture, Literary Life, and New York Bohemia at Mid-Century," *Walt Whitman Quarterly Review* 10.3 (1993), 107–26.
9. Edmund Clarence Stedman, *Poets of America* (Boston, MA: Houghton, 1885), 387, 386. The essays in this volume first appeared in *Scribner's Monthly* in 1880. While Stedman's critique of Whitman may seem surprising to readers today, the unexpected element for readers of the 1880s was his willingness to treat Whitman on an equal footing with Longfellow, Whittier, Bryant, and other fireside poets. As Mary Loeffelholz argues, Stedman's work pushed Whitman into an emerging canon of American poets; see "Stedman, Whitman, and the Transatlantic Canonization of American Poetry," in *Whitman among the Bohemians*, eds. Joanna Levin and Edward Whitley (Iowa City, IA: University of Iowa Press, 2014), 213–30.
10. Stedman, *Poets of America*, 202–03.
11. Ibid., 201, 202.
12. Ibid., 387; italics in the original.
13. For an extended elaboration of this argument, see Virginia Jackson, "Longfellow's Tradition; or, Picture-Writing a Nation," *Modern Language Quarterly* 59.4 (1998), 471–96.
14. Ralph Waldo Emerson, "The Poet," *The Essential Writings of Ralph Waldo Emerson* (New York, NY: Modern Library, 2000), 290.
15. Loving is more definite than others that Whitman attended Emerson's March 1842 presentation in Manhattan and wrote an anonymous review of it for the *New York Aurora*. Much of Whitman's commentary

linking *Leaves of Grass* to Emerson came after the publication of the first edition.

16. Ralph Waldo Emerson, "Letter to Walt Whitman," *Walt Whitman: The Contemporary Reviews*, ed. Kenneth M. Price (New York, NY: Cambridge University Press, 1996), 87; Jay Grossman, *Reconstituting the American Renaissance: Emerson, Whitman, and the Politics of Representation* (Durham, NC: Duke University Press, 2003), 93.

17. Michael Robertson, *Worshipping Walt: The Whitman Disciples* (Princeton, NJ: Princeton University Press, 2008), esp. 1–13. On the topic of Whitman's devoted readers, see also Max Cavitch, "Audience Terminable and Interminable: Anne Gilchrist, Walt Whitman, and the Achievement of Disinhibited Reading," *Victorian Poetry* 43.2 (2005), 249–61. On a somewhat different note, Michael Moon considers in relation to Whitman's poetics the political consequences of antebellum male embodiment, especially in the context of emerging queer and homophobic cultures; see Michael Moon, *Disseminating Whitman: Revision and Corporeality in Leaves of Grass* (Cambridge, MA: Harvard University Press, 1991), esp. 1–25.

CHAPTER 7

Periodical Poetry

Ingrid I. Satelmajer

Walt Whitman published more than 150 poems in periodicals throughout the span of his adult life, working actively in the greater New York City area at a time when the region was becoming the publishing capital of the world.[1] As a laborer in the periodical industry before the Civil War, Whitman's efforts at times were a symbiotic merger between his will and the mechanics of the industry. Periodicals also represented a site of resistance to the hands-on author, however, and, especially when framed as functional gatekeepers in the postbellum period, they occupied a heightened role in the narratives of access and ego so central to Whitman's project. Characterizations of Whitman in his final years at Camden depict the poet nearly buried as he read the tide of newspapers and magazines regularly delivered to him. Whitman, we are told, shrugged off some of the medium's essential qualities in this process: "Avoiding discussions of religion and politics he seeks those items which out of the daily history of a time are its contributions to the permanent."[2] Even so, it was in fact the complexly cluttered nature of the periodical network – its apparent impermanence; its partisan, regional, and personal concerns; and its compartmentalized nature – that shaped the contours of Whitman's publishing life and likely helped form his relationship to the ideologies of his day, both within and without *Leaves of Grass*.

***

Whitman's early poetry is unremarkable. Derivative and imitative, with genteel, light, occasional, and political subjects, it functions as the kind of space-filling verse often associated in an insulting way with the medium. As periodicals in some senses were offering a new model for poets to reach the public, Whitman drew an almost absolute line between his early publications and the premiere of his poetic self with the 1855 *Leaves of Grass*. Even so, Whitman's periodical work was, as Susan Belasco argues, the "foreground" that Ralph Waldo

Emerson saw behind the poet's remarkable 1855 book.[3] In addition, critics argue, some of Whitman's journalism demonstrates the poet's distinct voice and techniques, as well as select themes and subjects, and the jobs he held at a wide variety of publications led him to read and cover material that may have been transformative as he developed his extraordinary poetic voice.[4]

Even the most derivative of Whitman's poems, moreover, are revealing of the relationship between his writing and the publishing industry. Whitman started working as a laborer in the publishing industry when he was eleven years old, and his earliest poems came out in publications that he ran, at which he worked, or for which he wrote. Descriptions of the industry reveal the physical, hands-on nature of the jobs. As Shelly Fisher Fishkin notes, Whitman was "taught how to sort fonts, dampen paper, ink type, and pull impressions" at the *Long Island Patriot*, and his writing experience accorded with the local nature of the industry;[5] further, Whitman's first known published poem came when he "bought a used hand press and case of types for fifty dollars" and started the *Long-Islander*, the first paper he ran, and his early published poems continued to be published largely because the poet revised and republished them himself, often in places where he worked, and, at least in one instance, in the same publication where the poem originally had appeared.[6] One of the few outliers of his largely New York-based publications in the antebellum period, "The Mississippi at Midnight," was placed in the *New Orleans Daily Crescent* when Whitman was working on the paper.[7] The circulation of Whitman's original poems, especially in the years before the late 1850s, thus largely came from very real hands-on efforts by the poet as printer and self-publisher.

As Whitman's work experience presumably made him alert to opportunities, however, he became part of the developing publishing exchange dominated by the less material connections of imitation, friendship, and political sympathies – a circulation process scholars of nineteenth-century American poetry increasingly have emphasized as an important part of the genre's circulation and reception.[8] Whitman's friendship with William Cullen Bryant stands as the most famous example of his early relationship with the discourse (and people) associated with America's schoolroom poets; it also highlights Whitman's early political allegiances. As Wendy J. Katz argues, Whitman "was embedded in and even at times resistant to prevailing Democratic aesthetics" with his early poems that simultaneously upheld the pursuit of singular achievement and fame even as they envisioned democratic communities or rewards.[9]

Still, several years before Whitman fully severed his ties with Democratic publications and founded the short-lived *Brooklyn Freeman*, his poetry began to circulate through the developing antislavery movement's network of publications. Whitman's early prose writings had directly addressed temperance and other reform efforts of the 1830s, as David Reynolds notes, but the earliest dissemination I have identified of Whitman's poetry through the antislavery network may have been inadvertent and without the poet's knowledge (Reynolds, 61). In 1842, after Whitman published "No Turning Back" in the *Sunday Times*, William Lloyd Garrison's *Liberator* published a poem with the same title and final stanza, claiming the text was a reprint from the *Limerick Morning Star*, another abolitionist paper. Signed "D M L R," the poem suggests Whitman's entrance into the abolitionist network may have been through another writer's plagiarism, but the movement of Whitman's words from New York to Maine to Massachusetts without additional presswork by the poet nonetheless illustrates how the early formation of specialized networks could take Whitman's work beyond its immediate physical location. And as Whitman transformed in the antebellum period from a pro-Jacksonian Democrat to a Free Soiler opposed to the extension of slavery, he received more direct experiences with the antislavery network when he published four "angry, agitated poems" protesting the Compromise of 1850: "Song for Certain Congressmen" in Bryant's *New York Evening Post* and "Blood-Money," "House of Friends," and "Resurgemus" in Horace Greeley's abolitionist and otherwise pro-reform *New York Daily Tribune* (Reynolds, 127). All four were reprinted within a relatively short time, one in the *Post* and the other three in the *Liberator*, with "Resurgemus" also appearing in the *Portland Transcript*.[10]

Whitman's link to Greeley's publication stands out in the context of antebellum New York, a city increasingly dominated by the relatively young penny press tradition that mixed sensationalist content with news in an attempt to reach the masses. Much of Whitman's presswork had been, and would continue to be, about developing and participating in linked exchanges – a process, argues Meredith McGill, reflected in Whitman's poetics and vision for a national literature.[11] But Whitman's strategic creation of divisions also matters in understanding his publishing record. In the pages of the *Aurora*, Whitman had denounced James Gordon Bennett, founder of the *New York Herald*, a pro-Southern publication that was the most popular newspaper in the country, and although he continued to take news from the paper, the line Whitman drew between himself and Bennett seems important. Greeley, Bennett's most visible competitor, reportedly liked Whitman's journalism and published three of Whitman's four poems that responded to the 1850 Compromise, and those poems proved significant for Whitman's groundbreaking 1855 *Leaves*. "Resurgemus" was the only published poem that Whitman included in the book, but the whole group became part of Whitman's continuing process of reinvention; "Blood-Money," claims an unsigned *Every Saturday* article in 1866, was "a declaration of independence," and "the first [poem] he ever wrote."[12]

It also was one of the last poems Whitman published in periodicals for almost a decade. Much of the 1850s was taken up with the preparation and promotion of the 1855 and 1856 *Leaves* – which included Greeley's *Tribune* publishing the congratulatory letter Emerson wrote to Whitman about the 1855 *Leaves*. But then, in 1858, Whitman started spending time at Pfaff's, a Manhattan beer cellar that was a social center for many writers and printers, including Henry Clapp, editor of the *Saturday Press*, and the bohemian writers similarly associated with the publication. The Pfaffians' connections to the abolitionist network, however soft and casual, placed Whitman in a community simultaneously separate from pro-slavery positions and tolerant of the poet's well-documented ambivalence toward abolitionist activism. Clapp had edited *The Pioneer*, a protemperance, antislavery weekly in Lynn, Massachusetts, in the 1840s; his advocacy of "Free Speech" in his earlier writings had upheld an imagined communication network where one voice could spread among many – a clear template for the social atmosphere of Pfaff's, which offered a meeting place for the loosely associated network that already had reprinted Whitman's poetry in the 1840s and 1850s.[13] In *The Pioneer* Clapp had written about the history and purpose of *The Liberator*, and at Pfaff's Whitman had spent time with William Law Symonds, a writer associated with the same *Portland Transcript* that had republished "Resurgemus" and that later would reprint two of Whitman's most popular poems, both associated with the Civil War: "Beat! Beat! Drums!" and "O Captain! My Captain!"[14]

When the *Saturday Press* introduced the poet on December 24, 1859, with "A Child's Reminiscence" – later, "Out of the Cradle, Endlessly Rocking" – Whitman broke an almost nine-year silence of placing original poetry in periodicals. "A Child's Reminiscence," presented as a gift to readers, was a distinctly consequential poem in what could be a field of ephemeral productions. But Whitman's time with Clapp and the bohemians also marked a new relationship for the author that solidified connections between his periodical publications and his books. Clapp, in addition to publishing Whitman's poetry, had manufactured an associated campaign to bring Whitman out onto a performative, collaborative stage that emphasized contests and controversies. Combining self-righteous proclamations about the quality of his publication even as he refused to play by his own rules, Clapp might only have reinforced rather than taught Whitman his showmanship; the editor, after all, had his own literary aspirations, and Whitman long had demonstrated a taste for the kind of theater and compartmentalized performance spaces that Clapp so effectively created in the *Press*. Still, Whitman's time with the publication signaled a new relationship with a publisher and a new approach to the relationship between periodicals and his books. Whitman's publication of poems in the *Saturday Press*, Amanda Gailey has argued, likely was an important precedent to Whitman's being contacted by Thayer & Eldridge, the antislavery publisher of his 1860 *Leaves*.[15] And the book, which included poems already published in the *Saturday Press*, *Atlantic Monthly*, and *New York Times*, established a new pattern in which the periodicals became a staging ground for subsequent book publication.[16] That pattern largely held until Whitman's death in 1892, even as the poet increasingly laid claim almost entirely to the individualist tradition of antebellum New York and established distance between the socially conscious network that had most effectively conveyed his poetry in the antebellum period.

***

Whitman's move to Washington, DC, during the Civil War placed the poet in a dramatically different American subculture. His time spent on the battlefield and in DC tending to wounded soldiers – "his more direct participation," as Eliza Richards frames it – has given his wartime writings unusual credence.[17] But in Washington City, where Whitman primarily stayed until 1873, his publishing strategies moved away from hands-on creation and close participation and toward greater detachment. In his later years, a period marked by Whitman's stroke in 1873 and the time he spent in Camden, New Jersey, in ill health until his death in 1891, Whitman's writing devolved, many have argued, into an inferior byproduct of his compromised existence. The author published prolifically, releasing far more original poems in periodicals than he had in earlier years, but he also, during this period, regarded elite periodicals as stubborn gatekeepers that treated him unfairly. Nonetheless, while Whitman cast his struggle as part of a personal literary project, his later-year publications in periodicals were part of a complex communications system that emerged after the bloody, fractious war.[18]

As Whitman applauded postbellum technological developments, including the completion in 1869 of the transcontinental railroad, he also voiced concern about the collective American voice and literature and upheld a "tolerant regionalism" that allowed him to push back at "the cultural supremacy of New England."[19] Although he and his writing both received significant coverage in Washington, DC, papers, we have record of only one original poem in a DC publication during this time. Whitman otherwise cultivated his standing connections – the *Atlantic Monthly* and the *New York Evening Post*, for example – and followed new outlets made available through his Free Soil network.

Whitman's relationship with William Douglas O'Connor, an abolitionist who had worked at the Boston-based Thayer & Eldridge, led to new publishing opportunities; O'Connor recommended the poet to the New York-based *Galaxy*, which published several poems and prose pieces by Whitman into the early 1870s, as well as a promotional piece by John Burroughs.[20] Whitman also established ties with the short-lived Republican-oriented *Kansas Magazine*, which was edited by Henry King and incorporated by several prominent Republicans from the "Bloody Kansas" period, including the state's postbellum Surveyor General. The opening issue, published in January 1872, established solid antislavery credentials for the paper during this post-war period, with publications by William Ellery Channing, John Hay, James Redpath, and F. B. Sanborn; a few months before the incorporation of the magazine, King, the paper's editor, had emphasized his connection to Hay, Lincoln's secretary: "Col. Hay and Capt. King were brought up together in Hancock County, Illinois, where the parents of both still reside."[21]

Whitman had written with anger in 1856 about the election in the Kansas territory of a proslavery legislature.[22] Now, in the postbellum period, Whitman's poems in the magazine played to the zeitgeist of post-war Kansas, dominated as it was by Republicans. In "The Mystic Trumpeter" especially, published in the magazine's second issue, Whitman offered a self-affirming portrait of the kind of "electric" communication system that both he and Clapp had advocated for in the 1840s and that Greeley and other antebellum publishers had facilitated. The trumpeter calls one to a crusade, to war; the speaker himself becomes the instrument, taking in "the enslaved, the overthrown, the hurt, the opprest of the whole earth" until, with "War, sorrow, suffering gone," he is left only with "Joy!"[23]

Highlighting the paper's literary credentials, Whitman cast it as a "Western" *Atlantic*. Certainly, the paper placed Whitman in company that otherwise supported him, as both Redpath and Sanborn were important publishing connections for the author.[24] Still, Whitman's publishing landscape continued to change as magazines proliferated and closed in great numbers after the war and with the deaths in 1872 of two of the most prominent personalities associated with the penny press tradition: Bennett, of the *Herald*, and Greeley, of the *Tribune*.[25] Whitman's own personal circumstances were changing at the same time. His publication in *Kansas Magazine* took place in the context of his recitation of poems by invitation at the American Institute exhibition in New York City (September 1871) and two college graduation ceremonies, but after he suffered a severe stroke and then the death of his mother in 1873, the June 1874 Tufts College Commencement poem was delivered in absentia. The poems from all three of these events were published as original texts in periodicals and in the climate of nineteenth-century poets as icons, where advancing printing technologies allowed local performances to be conveyed as "events" to increasingly national audiences and poets' images to be transmitted through developing illustration practices.

Still, whether from the breakdown of Whitman's health or his perceived neglect, his continued participation in the Republican post-war culture came while he also forged an entirely new path for his writings, with several important disruptive events especially framing his publishing activities in 1876.[26] The year is most commonly known in Whitman scholarship for the author's famous placement of an anonymous complaint in the *West Jersey Press* about supposed ill treatment; the subsequent rallying of forces from as far as England was part of the poet's attempt to gain more attention from the elite cultural vanguards of the day. Even as he complained about perceived exclusion, however, Whitman concurrently developed a new sustaining contractual relationship in a publishing network he once had shunned.[27] After publishing his final poem in the *Tribune* – "A Death Sonnet for Custer" – Whitman reached out to his old sometimes antagonist, the *New York Herald*, and developed a relationship with the *New York Daily Graphic*, a new publication created by David Goodman Croly (who stands out as one of the unnamed authors of a hoax pamphlet that coined the word "miscegenation" and attempted to derail the Republican Party in the 1864 election).[28]

The *Herald* eventually published more Whitman poems than any other periodical, and Whitman's relatively tame writings in the paper, Elizabeth Lorang argues, show him "crafting short poems that could be understood by a mass readership and that participated in the public discourse of the community in which they were published."[29] Even so, Whitman's work in the *Herald* came as the newspaper was losing ground in circulation and reach to Pulitzer's *World* and as magazines arguably were becoming the more effective vehicles of mass communication. Horace Traubel's accounts of Whitman near the end of the poet's life reveal the poet simultaneously engaged with and dismissive of the tide of publications that entered his home. These publications failed to offer Whitman perfect mechanisms for projecting his voice and at times resisted including him; however, they also represented a larger field of shifting terrains and compartmentalized spaces for his theatrical performances – spaces where the author of Free Soil protest poems could erase the earlier Jacksonian Democrat, and where the later poet who pushed back against the Fifteenth Amendment in the streets of Washington, DC, could nevertheless continue to participate in the Republican publishing network. Receiving late in life the *Long Islander*, the first paper he had created, and the first that we know of to contain one of his poems, as well as papers from Camden, Philadelphia, New York, and Boston, and "foreign papers," Whitman still valued localized identities in this era of a dawning national print network.[30]

Notes

1. On the numbers, see Elizabeth Lorang, "Editing Whitman's Poems in Periodicals," WWA. The archive of Whitman's periodical publications, edited by Susan Belasco with assistance from Lorang, has been a valuable resource for this essay.
2. Horace L. Traubel, "Walt Whitman at Date," in *In Re Walt Whitman*, eds. Horace L. Traubel, Richard Maurice Bucke, and Thomas B. Harned (Philadelphia, PA: David McKay, 1893), 137.
3. Susan Belasco, "Introduction to Walt Whitman's Poetry in Periodicals," WWA.
4. See Shelley Fisher Fishkin, *From Fact to Fiction: Journalism and Imaginative Writing in America* (Baltimore, MD: Johns Hopkins University Press, 1985), 15–18; and Reynolds, 41.
5. Fishkin, *From Fact to Fiction*, 14.
6. Ibid. One possible new exception to Whitman's direct participation that I have identified is the reprinting of the July 14, 1840 "We All Shall Rest at Last" (*Long Island Democrat*) in an August 1840 issue of the *American Masonic Register and Literary Companion*.
7. Whitman was hired by the *New Orleans Daily Crescent* for several months in 1848 "to help create connections with northeastern newspapers in order to exchange news and information" (Belasco, "Introduction").
8. See, e.g., Meredith L. McGill, *American Literature and the Culture of Reprinting, 1834–1853* (Philadelphia, PA: University of Pennsylvania Press, 2003).

9. Wendy J. Katz, "A Newly Discovered Whitman Poem about William Cullen Bryant," *Walt Whitman Quarterly Review* 32 (2014), 69–76, 69.

10. The *Walt Whitman Archive* identifies the *Evening Post* reprint; the *Liberator* reprints are my own identification.

11. Meredith L. McGill, "Walt Whitman and the Poetics of Reprinting," in *Walt Whitman, Where the Future Becomes Present*, eds. David Haven Blake and Michael Robertson (Iowa City, IA: University of Iowa Press, 2010), 37–58.

12. See *Every Saturday: A Journal of Choice Reading*, November 17, 1866, 580. Whitman also included in the 1855 *Leaves* "Poem of Apparitions in Boston," an 1854 poem, but I can find no record of its earlier publication.

13. See Ingrid Satelmajer, "Publishing Pfaff's: Henry Clapp and Poetry in the *Saturday Press*," in *Whitman among the Bohemians*, eds. Joanna Levin and Edward Whitley (Iowa City, IA: University of Iowa Press, 2014), 40–41.

14. Henry Clapp Jr., *The Pioneer: Or, Leaves from an Editor's Portfolio* (Lynn, MA: J. B. Tolman, 1846), 112–15, 187. On Whitman's association with Symonds, see William Winter, *Old Friends: Being Literary Recollections of Other Days* (New York, NY: Moffat, Yard, 1909), 89. The *Transcript* reprinted the former on October 5, 1861 and the latter on March 10, 1866.

15. Amanda Gailey, "Walt Whitman and the King of Bohemia: The Poet in the *Saturday Press*," in *Whitman among the Bohemians*, 23.

16. Gailey emphasizes Whitman's desire for distribution when she argues that this new pattern "fit squarely within the same attitudes toward publishing that [Whitman] demonstrated throughout his six editions of his book." See Amanda Gailey, "The Publishing History of *Leaves of Grass*," in *A Companion to Walt Whitman*, ed. Donald D. Kummings (Malden, MA: Blackwell, 2006), 409–38, 417.

17. Eliza Richards, "Correspondent Lines: Poetry, Journalism, and the U.S. Civil War," *ESQ: A Journal of the American Renaissance* 54.1–4 (2008), 145–70.

18. On the "realities" of disruptions in printing and personnel in the press that helped shape Whitman's supposed silence during the early 1860s, see Ted Genoways, *Walt Whitman and the Civil War: America's Poet during the Lost Years of 1860–1862* (Berkeley, CA: University of California Press, 2009), 11.

19. Robert Scholnick, "*The Galaxy* and American Democratic Culture, 1866–1878," *American Studies* 16.1 (April 1982), 69–80.

20. Susan Belasco, "*The Galaxy*," WWA.

21. "Col. John Hay – A Sketch of His Life," *White Cloud Kansas Chief* (White Cloud, KS), May 25, 1871. On Redpath and Sanborn, see Reynolds, 453.

22. See his unprinted 1856 pamphlet "The Eighteenth Presidency!"

23. Walt Whitman, "The Mystic Trumpeter," *Kansas Magazine*, February 1, 1872, 113–14.

24. Susan Belasco, "*Kansas Magazine*," WWA.

25. On magazines, see Frank Luther Mott, *A History of American Magazines: 1865–1885*, vol. 3 (Cambridge, MA: Harvard University Press, 1938–68), 5.

26. See, for one negative review, the potentially biased "Management at the American Institute Fair," *New York Herald* (New York, NY), September 10, 1871, 6. For Whitman's connection to a Republican-based network, see Susan Belasco, "*The Philadelphia Press*", WWA.

27. Robert Scholnick, "Whitman and the Magazines: Some Documentary Evidence," *American Literature* 44.2 (May 1972), 222–46.

28. David Goodman Croly, *Miscegenation: The Theory of the Blending of the Races, Applied to the American White Man and Negro* (New York, NY: B. Dexter Hamilton and Co., 1864).

29. Elizabeth Lorang, "'Two More Throws against Oblivion': Walt Whitman and the *New York Herald* in 1888," *Walt Whitman Quarterly Review* 25.4 (Spring 2008), 167–91, 168.

30. Traubel, "Walt Whitman at Date," 137.

CHAPTER 8

Periodical Fiction

Stephanie M. Blalock

In the "Pieces in Early Youth" section of *Collect* (1882), Walt Whitman published revised versions of short stories he had composed when he was in his twenties in order, he claimed, to avoid their "surreptitious issue."[1] In an introductory note to *Collect*, Whitman summed up his feelings about his fiction, writing, "My serious wish were to have all those crude and boyish pieces quietly dropp'd in oblivion."[2] Nine years later, in 1891, the aging poet told his biographer and disciple Horace Traubel that he wrote the stories "to fill in corners, gaps in the magazines" and that the tales were "of no importance to anybody but me, and of no importance to me, but for the fact that they supplied me with necessaries" (WWC, 8:410). Just as Whitman longed for his short fiction to disappear from view in his final years, he similarly wished to distance himself from his novels.[3] In 1888, Whitman explained to Traubel that he had composed his bestselling temperance novel *Franklin Evans, or the Inebriate: A Tale of the Times* (1842) for financial reasons, completing it at the request of Park Benjamin, the editor of *The New World* newspaper.[4] Whitman then described the narrative as "damned rot," insisting that he had written it in three days, "with the help of a bottle of port" (WWC, 1:93).

Whitman adopted a different set of strategies to separate himself from his second novel: *Life and Adventures of Jack Engle: An Auto-Biography* (1852).[5] He published *Jack Engle* anonymously as a work of serial fiction in six installments from March 14 to April 18, 1852, in the *Sunday Dispatch*, a New York weekly newspaper edited by Amor J. Williamson and William Burns. Without a byline to attribute the novella to the author of the immensely popular *Franklin Evans* and with little publicity to herald its publication, *Jack Engle* remained unremarked for nearly 165 years, until Zachary Turpin discovered it in 2016. Yet, with the exception of a plot outline Whitman wrote in his "Schoolmaster" notebook that would lead Turpin to the novella, he seems to have remained uncharacteristically silent about the tale.[6] No self-promotional reviews of the novella and no explicit mentions of it by Whitman have come to light.[7]

It is not surprising that Whitman had moved beyond his fiction by the 1880s since the novels and short stories reflected his early political beliefs and youthful affinity for social reform movements. But his efforts to deflect attention away from the fiction late in his life contributed to a devaluing of the role that the periodical fiction played in establishing his literary reputation before he became known as America's poet.[8] Whitman's biographer Henry Seidel Canby saw Whitman's attempts at periodical fiction as "pretty terrible," declaring him "a bad hack writer even according to the low standards of really popular writing at the time."[9] Paul Zweig characterized Whitman's fiction as "magazine filler" not unlike the poetry, temperance tales, and other miscellaneous items – much of the material anonymously authored – that made up the content of some antebellum periodicals.[10] In the introduction to his edited collection of *The Early Poems and the Fiction* (1963), a volume of the *Collected Writings of Walt Whitman*, Thomas Brasher asserted, "The plain fact is that Whitman had no talent for fiction."[11]

In the twentieth and twenty-first centuries literary scholars have begun to reexamine Whitman's fiction, locating within it considerations of race, class, sexuality, and male camaraderie, themes that reemerge in his poetry.[12] Vivian Pollak reads in Whitman's fiction a resistance to traditional plots and family structures, as well as a need to explore homosocial and homoerotic bonds – relations that would significantly shape his poetic vision of comradeship.[13] In the short fiction and *Franklin Evans*, for example, barrooms become sites of male–male affection; in *Jack Engle*, the friendship between Engle and Tom Peterson lingers long after Engle's marriage. At the same time, the recovery of *Jack Engle* shows that Whitman persisted in writing and publishing fiction for more than a decade, and the discovery of numerous reprints of his stories in nineteenth-century newspapers and magazines suggests that his fiction was more popular among readers than was previously imagined. Reconsidering the publication history of Whitman's fiction offers evidence of the wide circulation of some of his stories in the United States and signals the emergence of an international readership that encountered Whitman's prose in periodicals at least nine years before the first edition of *Leaves of Grass* (1855) was published.[14] Whitman's periodical fiction showcases his ability to utilize popular nineteenth-century fiction genres while wrestling with social reforms and cultural issues of his time. His revision and republication practices highlight the interconnectedness of his short stories with his novels and foreshadow his perpetual editing and rearranging of his poetry. This essay positions Whitman's fiction-writing career as a vital chapter in his development as a writer of national and international note. In doing so, it reveals the place of the fiction in his literary life and the new life that his fiction took on in the myriad periodical contexts in which it was published.

In the 1840s, Whitman began building his literary reputation by writing periodical fiction. He spent eleven years – from 1841 to 1852 – and possibly more, composing at least twenty-six short stories and two novels, *Franklin Evans* and *Jack Engle,* all of which were first published in New York newspapers and magazines.[15] Whitman's fiction draws on or incorporates his personal experience, historical events, reform literature, religious narratives, ghost stories, and crime and detective fiction. His stories are set in barrooms, schoolrooms, boarding houses, and law offices, with feature characters ranging from widows and war heroes to law clerks and a "dancing girl."[16] He writes in support of temperance reform (*Franklin Evans,* "Reuben's Last Wish") and in opposition to corporal punishment in schools ("Death in the School-Room"). He illuminates the lives of writers and impoverished, yet ambitious young men ("Lingave's Temptation," "The Shadow and the Light of a Young Man's Soul") and relates frightening accounts of unyielding fathers ("Bervance: or, Father and Son," "The Death of Wind-Foot"). He characterizes a widow as a model of unwavering loyalty ("The Tomb-Blossoms"), highlights male homosocial bonds ("The Love of the Four Students," "The Child's Champion"), and criticizes corrupt lawyers and shady business dealings ("Revenge and Requital," *Jack Engle*). His tales were published first in approximately twelve different New York periodicals, including the prestigious *Democratic Review,* which published nine of his stories; *The Columbian Lady's and Gentleman's Magazine,* which published four; and the *Aristidean,* which also published four.[17]

The periodical short fiction and the culture of reprinting

As a journalist, newspaper editor, and writer of fiction and poetry for a variety of serial publications, Whitman was deeply involved in periodical culture. Throughout his fiction-writing career, Whitman served as the editor of a number of newspapers, including the *Aurora* (1842), the *Brooklyn Daily Eagle* (1846–48), and the *New Orleans Crescent* (1848).[18] While editing the *Eagle,* Whitman published numerous items about fiction in addition to revising and reprinting many of his own short stories and his temperance novel, dividing most of these works into serial installments and printing them over multiple issues of the paper. Of his position as an exchange editor at the *Crescent*, Whitman wrote that his time was spent "overhauling the papers rec'd by mail, and 'making up the news,' as it is called, both with pen and scissors," which suggests he mined much of the *Crescent*'s content from that already published in other newspapers (NUPM, 1:87). As a result of these experiences as an editor, he was familiar with the process of choosing pieces that were to be printed or reprinted in the newspapers under his charge, with recirculating his own writings, and with a literary marketplace significantly shaped by periodical publications.[19]

Meredith McGill describes the literary marketplace of the period from 1834 to at least 1853, when Whitman was editing newspapers and writing periodical fiction, as "built and sustained" by a "culture of reprinting" in which material published in uncopyrighted newspapers and magazines was "freely excerpted by other periodicals."[20] Whitman was aware of the circulation of his fiction within this "culture of reprinting," and both his later denials regarding his fiction and his anxieties about "surreptitious issue" stand in stark contrast to the pride he took in his fiction and the reprints of it at the time of its initial publication. Whereas, in 1891, Whitman told Traubel that he "should almost be tempted to shoot" an editor rumored to be gathering the fiction for publication (WWC, 8:551), when he was twenty-two he wrote a letter to Nathan Hale Jr., editor of the *Boston Miscellany*, proudly proclaiming, "My stories, I believe, have been pretty popular, and extracted liberally" (Corr., 1:26). Whitman was justi-fied in suggesting that his fiction was widely reprinted, reaching periodical readers across the nation. His first short story, "Death in the School-Room" (1841), an anti-corporal punishment tale in which a teacher flogs the already lifeless body of a student for a crime the child did not commit, was reprinted more than 135 times in the nineteenth century.[21] "A Legend of Life and Love," a moral story intended to explain that achieving happiness in life requires risking great pain, was reprinted more than a hundred times, while "The Tomb-Blossoms," the tale of a widow bringing flowers for her hus-band's grave, was reprinted at least forty-two times.[22] Each of these three most often-reprinted tales was published first in John O'Sullivan and Samuel Langtree's *Democratic Review*, a respected journal known for publishing literature by prominent American authors like Nathaniel Hawthorne and William Cullen Bryant. Editors of local and regional newspapers in New York and the Northeast, in turn, reprinted Whitman's fiction from the *Democratic Review*, often running the stories on the front page of their papers.[23]

As more periodicals reprinted Whitman's fiction, its reach expanded beyond his native New York and even New England. Whitman's short stories were reprinted in seventeen US states in 1841, the year he began publishing periodical fiction, and they were reprinted in thirty-one states and Washington, DC, during his lifetime. Significantly, Whitman's fiction had likely garnered an international readership by 1846. Some of the earliest international readers of any writing by Whitman were those in Canada, England, and Tasmania who encountered his fiction in periodicals. In 1842, Whitman's "A Legend of Life and Love" was reprinted in the *Chronicle & Gazette and Kingston Commercial Advertiser* (Kingston, Canada), and "The Tomb-Blossoms" was published in London's *The Great Western Magazine and Anglo-American Journal*.[24] In April 1846, Whitman's "The Death of Wind-Foot," the story of a Native American chief whose son dies as a result of a long-standing feud between neighboring tribes, was reprinted in the *Colonial Times and Tasmanian*, a paper published in what is now known as Hobart, Tasmania.[25] Periodical readers in the United States and abroad – whether knowingly, or unknowingly in the absence of attribution – likely encountered Whitman's fiction before seeing the poetry he would be known for in the decades that followed.

Whitman's novels in newspapers: *Franklin Evans* (1842) and *Jack Engle* (1852)

Although Whitman's novels were published in New York newspapers a decade apart, they were both influenced by nineteenth-century popular fiction genres. Yet, they are strikingly different in terms of publicity and reception in periodicals. *Franklin Evans* praises the Washingtonian Temperance societies and (arguably) forwards the temperance cause by presenting Evans's account of his journey to sobriety. But the novel's sensational plot hinges not simply on temperance but also on Evans's trips to the barrooms, his failed first marriage, a murder, an interracial marriage, and a suicide.[26] The week before *Franklin Evans* was published as an extra edition of *The New World*, readers of the *New York Sun* and the *Evening Post* were given a glimpse of the forthcoming novel. An excerpt – the conversion narrative of Evans's benefactor Mike Marchion upon the death of his sister – was extracted from *Franklin Evans*, titled "The Reformed," and printed as a preview of and a successful advertisement for the novel.[27] *Franklin Evans* went on to sell 20,000 copies, which is more than any other work Whitman published in his lifetime.[28]

Following the novel's publication, notices and reviews in periodicals hailed its success. Writers for *The New Bedford Mercury* "inclined to augur for the novel a great career," while those at *The American Traveller* encouraged readers to follow those literary trendsetters who had "laid [the novel] by for a second and third perusal."[29]

Whitman took a similar approach to writing *Jack Engle* since he employed elements of popular fiction genres – including sentimentalism, adventure fiction, and detective fiction – to relate the tale of the orphaned Jack Engle, who is adopted by a butcher and his wife, foils the schemes of a corrupt lawyer, and marries a young Quaker woman.[30] Readers of *Jack Engle* accompany the hero on his adventures in a law office, in a cemetery, and on a river boat, while navigating a series of documents – namely a letter, tombstone inscriptions, and a prisoner's manuscript – reminiscent of the tradition of the epistolary novel. Although *Jack Engle*, with its cast of eccentric characters, is Whitman's best novel there are no known announcements for it beyond a literary notice that called it "a rich revelation" and promised some "familiar cases and characters."[31] This notice appeared in three New York papers – the *Tribune*, the *Herald*, and the *Daily Times* – one day before the publication of the first installment was printed in the *Dispatch*, but no subsequent articles about or reviews of *Jack Engle* have yet been located.[32]

Despite the disparities in the response of the periodical press to Whitman's novels, both works are inextricably connected to his short fiction. In the case of *Franklin Evans*, Whitman included within the narrative two embedded stories, "The Reformed" and the Native American tale that would later be published with the title "The Death of Wind-Foot."[33] Whitman also altered parts of "The Last of the Sacred Army," a short story he published in the *Democratic Review* in March 1842, for reuse in *Franklin Evans*.[34] In the case of *Jack Engle*, Whitman reintroduced some familiar characters. Zachary Turpin has pointed out that Mr. Covert, the corrupt lawyer Engle must outwit, is certainly a different character than the lawyer Adam Covert, who appears in Whitman's earlier story "Revenge and Requital" (1845).[35] But the repetition of the telling surname and the association of both lawyers with deception and unethical practices suggest that the earlier tale was on Whitman's mind as he crafted the plot of *Jack Engle*. A definitive link between the novella and Whitman's early fiction is the character of Violet Foster, Ephraim's wife. The description of Violet in the novella, particularly her large, masculine features and her cheerfulness are based on and, at times, borrowed from Whitman's depiction of "Violet Boanes" in his unfinished novel

"The Fireman's Dream" (1844).[36] *Jack Engle* was also not the first work in which Whitman represented the life of a young man training to become a lawyer. Jack Engle himself is reminiscent of the students learning from a legal professional in "The Love of the Four Students" (1843), the earliest known title of the story later called "The Boy-Lover." The reuse of these characters and characterizations suggests that, as Whitman completed his second novel, he was returning to fiction he had composed in the 1840s – mining it for characters and plots, and transforming old tales into new ones – just as he would revise lines and rearrange entire poems when he prepared new editions of *Leaves of Grass*.

The persistence and contexts of Whitman's periodical fiction

A reconsideration of the publication history of Whitman's short fiction and the extent of its circulation within the periodical press offers new insight into the poet's fiction career. It has long been accepted among biographers and literary critics that Whitman's fiction-writing career began with the publication of "Death in the School-Room" in the *Democratic Review* in 1841 and ended with the printing of "The Shadow and the Light of a Young Man's Soul" in the *Union Magazine* in 1848. Turpin's unearthing of Whitman's 1852 novella *Jack Engle* has significantly altered this timeline, as well as the linear, sequential narrative of Whitman as fiction writer and, later, an author of radical poetry by offering definitive proof that Whitman was writing and publishing fiction while deciding what form *Leaves of Grass* would take – poetry, a play, or something else entirely.[37] The persistence of Whitman's fiction – its circulation within the culture of reprinting – also complicates easy divisions between poet and periodical fiction writer. For example, in 1856, the year that the Brooklyn firm of Fowler and Wells published Whitman's second edition of *Leaves of Grass*, his story "Death in the School-Room" resurfaced in newspapers in Wisconsin. During the Civil War, while Whitman was volunteering in the hospitals of Washington, DC, "Death in the School-Room" and his second short story, "Wild Frank's Return," were republished in several Pennsylvania newspapers. In fact, "Death in the School-Room" was still being reprinted in Maryland in 1875.

The longevity of Whitman's fiction in periodicals may be attributed to the aforementioned resurfacing of the stories and to the unique periodical contexts in which the fiction was published. Whitman, for instance, is rarely imagined as a children's author, but two nineteenth-century periodical editors placed his fiction in this context. The editor of *The Universalist*

Union reprinted Whitman's story "Little Jane" in the section designated "Youth's Department" in 1846.[38] In 1881, the editor of *Our Boys and Girls*, a London children's magazine, renamed Whitman's "The Tomb-Blossoms" as "The Tomb Flowers" and condensed the story, retaining only the major plot events when it printed the tale, thus repackaging Whitman's fiction for an audience of younger readers.[39]

Conclusion

If Whitman was known among national and international readers in the 1840s and early 1850s, it was likely as a writer of periodical fiction. His "serious wish" that his fiction might disappear has and has not been realized. In the months following his death on March 26, 1892, the fiction persisted; newspapers across the country reprinted two stories Whitman had written fifty years earlier, "The Tomb-Blossoms" and "The Last of the Sacred Army," as a tribute to America's poet.[40] Such reappearances of Whitman's stories serve as reminders of the importance of his fiction in his life and writing career. Yet, one piece of his fiction, *Jack Engle*, did disappear for nearly 165 years, and the novella may not be the only work of fiction by Whitman waiting to be discovered in periodicals. After all, he authored various prose fragments that have yet to be definitively linked to any published work of fiction (NUPM, 1:46–52).[41] Whitman's practice of revising and reusing his fiction – and the extent to which he may have borrowed material from other authors to compose his tales – merits further exploration. In future studies of Whitman's periodical fiction, it will also be necessary to ask why his stories were reprinted during the Civil War and just after his death, and it will be essential to determine if additional pieces of his fiction can be recovered even if they have, as Whitman put it, "quietly dropp'd in oblivion."

Notes

1. Walt Whitman, *Specimen Days and Collect* (Philadelphia, PA: Rees Welsh & Co., 1882–83), 202.
2. Ibid.; Stephanie M. Blalock, "Walt Whitman's Early Fiction in Periodicals: Over 250 Newly Discovered Reprints," *Walt Whitman Quarterly Review* 30.4 (2013), 171.
3. Blalock, "Walt Whitman's Early Fiction," 171.
4. Stephanie M. Blalock and Nicole Gray, "Introduction to *Franklin Evans* and 'Fortunes of a Country-Boy,'" WWA.

5. [Walt Whitman], *Life and Adventures of Jack Engle: An Auto-Biography*, ed. Zachary Turpin, *Walt Whitman Quarterly Review* 34.3–4 (2017), 262–357.

6. Turpin followed evidence from digitized images of Whitman's "Schoolmaster" notebook, which includes character names and a plot outline, to newspaper databases, where he found an announcement for a forthcoming novella that promised an autobiographical tale of "Jack Engle." Turpin matched the character names and plot events in Whitman's notebook to those of the full novella, which allowed him to attribute it to Whitman for the first time since 1852. See Whitman, "A Schoolmaster" (Notebook LC #82), WWA.

7. Zachary Turpin, "Introduction to Walt Whitman's 'Life and Adventures of Jack Engle,'" *Walt Whitman Quarterly Review* 34.4 (2017), 231.

8. Blalock, "Walt Whitman's Early Fiction," 172.

9. Henry Seidel Canby, *Walt Whitman: An American* (Boston, MA: Houghton Mifflin Company, 1943), 41.

10. Paul Zweig, *The Making of the Poet* (New York, NY: Basic Books, 1984), 115.

11. Thomas Brasher, "Introduction," in *The Early Poems and the Fiction*, ed. Thomas Brasher (New York, NY: New York University Press, 1963), 18.

12. Stephanie M. Blalock and Nicole Gray, "Introduction to Walt Whitman's Short Fiction," WWA.

13. Ibid.; Vivian R. Pollak, *The Erotic Whitman* (Berkeley, CA: University of California Press, 2000), 54–55.

14. Blalock and Gray, "Introduction to Walt Whitman's Short Fiction," WWA.

15. Ibid. For digital editions of the short fiction and *Franklin Evans*, see Stephanie M. Blalock and Nicole Gray, eds., "Whitman's Fiction," WWA.

16. [Whitman], *Life and Adventures of Jack Engle*, 278.

17. Blalock and Gray, "Introduction to Walt Whitman's Short Fiction," WWA.

18. Meredith L. McGill, "Walt Whitman and the Poetics of Reprinting," in *Walt Whitman, Where the Future Becomes Present*, eds. David Haven Blake and Michael Robertson (Iowa City, IA: University of Iowa Press, 2008), 39–40.

19. Ibid.

20. Meredith L. McGill, *American Literature and the Culture of Reprinting, 1834–1853* (Philadelphia, PA: University of Pennsylvania, 2003), 1–2.

21. Stephanie M. Blalock, "About 'Death in the School-Room.' A Fact," WWA.

22. Blalock, "About 'A Legend of Life'"; "About 'The Tomb-Blossoms,'" WWA.

23. Susan Belasco Smith, *"Democratic Review"* in *Walt Whitman: An Encyclopedia*, eds. J. R. LeMaster and Donald D. Kummings (New York, NY: Garland Publishing, 1998), WWA.

24. Blalock and Gray, "Introduction to Walt Whitman's Short Fiction," WWA. For citations for these and all known reprints of Whitman's fiction in periodicals, see Stephanie M. Blalock, "Whitman's Fiction: A Bibliography," WWA.

25. Ibid.

26. Blalock and Gray, "Introduction to *Franklin Evans*," WWA.

27. Ibid.; Walter Whitman, "The Reformed," *New York Sun* (New York, NY), November 17, 1842, 4; Walter Whitman, "The Reformed," *Evening Post* (New York, NY), November 19, 1842, 1.

28. Ed Folsom and Kenneth M. Price, "Biography," WWA.

29. Blalock and Gray, "Introduction to *Franklin Evans*," WWA; "Original Temperance Novel," *New Bedford Mercury* (New Bedford, MA), December 2, 1842, 1; "Original Temperance Novel," *American Traveller* (Boston, MA), November 29, 1842, 2.

30. Turpin, "Introduction," 242.

31. Ibid., 232; "A Rich Revelation," *New York Daily Times* (New York, NY), March 13, 1852, 3.

32. Turpin, "Introduction," 230.

33. Blalock and Gray, "Introduction to *Franklin Evans*," WWA.

34. Ibid.

35. Turpin, "Introduction," 238–39.

36. Two chapters of "The Fireman's Dream" were printed in the *New York Sunday Times and Noah's Weekly Messenger* on March 31, 1844; no additional installments have been located.

37. Turpin, "Introduction," 226–27.

38. "Little Jane," *Universalist Union* (New York, NY), December 19, 1846, 95–96. Whitman revised "The Reformed" and gave it the new title of "Little Jane" before publishing it in the *Brooklyn Daily Eagle* on December 7, 1846.

39. Blalock and Gray, "Introduction to Walt Whitman's Short Fiction," WWA; "The Tomb Flowers," *Our Boys and Girls: A Monthly Magazine*, July 1881, 51. WWA.

40. Ibid. For full citations, see Blalock, "Whitman's Fiction: A Bibliography," WWA.

41. Turpin, "Introduction," 227–28.

CHAPTER 9

Journalism

Jason Stacy

Fire and paper

The fire that destroyed New York's printing district on August 12, 1835, came almost two years after the first successful penny newspaper was published in the United States. Of the five people killed, including two printers and a bookbinder, one jumped from a fourth-story window to escape the flames, two burned to death, and two were buried under collapsing buildings.[1] Though a more devastating fire swept through New York City that December, the printing district fire that August proved life-changing for the journeyman printer Walt Whitman.[2]

Whitman was on his way to becoming a skilled printer that summer. After ending school at age eleven, he worked for a short time in a lawyer's office before entering a printing apprenticeship in Brooklyn with Samuel E. Clements, editor of the *Long Island Patriot*, and, later, with Alden Spooner at the *Long Island Star*.[3] As a "printer's devil," so called because of the ink that turned the apprentices' skin black, Whitman learned the trade from a position "very little above [. . .] errand-boy."[4] By the summer of 1835, the future poet worked as a compositor, where he honed his technique at carefully arranging type on the compositor's stick for the press (Reynolds, 46).

Whitman traced his passion for "crowded and mixed humanity" to this period (PW, 1:16–17). He saw some of his earliest pieces published and recalled sixty years later, "it made my heart double-beat to see *my* piece on the pretty white paper."[5] Along Broadway, he encountered politicians like Henry Clay and Andrew Jackson, and, later, members of the transatlantic literati like Charles Dickens and James Fennimore Cooper (PW, 1:17). By 1835, young Whitman was a pedestrian on the crossroads of literary celebrity, political democracy, and industrial production, all of which came together in the printing offices of the penny press.

Pennies on the street

At about the time young Whitman became an apprentice printer, the *New York Sun*'s twenty-year-old founder, Benjamin Day, was building his newspaper in opposition to the subscription periodicals of the period. While other editors had attempted the penny format before the *Sun*, Day united low-cost production, topics of everyday interest, and advertising revenue into a profitable combination. The *Sun*'s first issue on September 3, 1833, was printed on four small pages of about eight and a half by eleven inches, as opposed to the "blanket sheets" of the commercial press, so named because they were large enough to cover a dozing reader.[6] Whereas most newspapers were sold by subscription for six cents per copy, paperboys hawked the *Sun* on the street for a penny.[7] In his first issue, Day offered "all the news of the day" rather than the exclusive mercantile news of the more well-heeled newspapers like the *Journal of Commerce*.[8]

Day's *Sun* combined entertaining anecdotes and salacious stories alongside copious advertising to supplant the subscription funds that supported the commercial press. By late 1835 it claimed a circulation of 10,000 readers daily and owed its reach to technological changes in printing.[9] Jonas Booth introduced New York's first steam-driven printing press in 1823,[10] and by 1835 Richard Hoe perfected the single small and large cylinder presses, which made the production of print possible on an industrial scale.[11] That same year, the *Sun* imagined its impact in ambitious terms, "diffusing knowledge among the operative classes of society, [to] effect [. . .] the march of independence to a greater degree than any other mode of instruction."[12] Ten years later, Whitman described the power of the penny press in similar terms, "the cheap papers have influence with th[e] mass, they can [. . .] afford to let their inflated neighbors parade their [. . .] claims to exclusiveness."[13]

But it was James Gordon Bennett, founder of the *New York Herald*, who perfected Day's formula of cheap and engaging news. The *Herald* mixed moralism and salacious topics with a boisterous claim to represent the common man against corrupt power. Within a year of its founding in 1835, the *Herald*'s extended coverage of the murder of a New York prostitute, Helen Jewett, swelled the newspaper's readership to a daily circulation of 20,000.[14] This popularity allowed Bennett to establish a template for the city's penny press, which fed a daily dose of raucous print journalism to the masses, an audience Whitman eventually sought for his own journalism and, later, for his poetic "word En-Masse" (LG, 1).

Long Island exile

When seventeen-year-old Whitman left New York City for rural Long Island in the aftermath of the printing district fire, he left behind a skilled craft on the cusp of industrial transformation. During the 1840s, the roles of the printer-journalist became increasingly distinct, but Whitman largely underwent this transformation away from the action. Starting in 1838, he composed, edited, and published the *Long-Islander* in Huntington, working the press himself. Here appeared his first published poem, "Our Future Lot," and local stories of sensational interest like the drowning of two boys, the mangling of another in a cotton factory, and the unfortunate results of a famer carrying a pitchfork in a thunderstorm (Loving, 43–44; Reynolds, 60; Journ., 1:6–7).

But after 1840, Whitman was largely finished with his work as a printer-journalist. That year, he began to publish "Sun-Down Papers – From the Desk of a Schoolmaster," which ranged topically from the immanency of death, the pitfalls of consumerism, the nobility of unaffected etiquette, the folly of holding grudges, and the joys of clam hunting. One essay contained Whitman's earliest celebration of loafing, "How I do love a loafer! [...] Give me your calm, steady, philosophick son of indolence."[15] In this fashion, Whitman took the professional title of "schoolmaster" and built around it a rhetorical identity, much like in the first edition of *Leaves of Grass*, where he inhabited the well-known occupation of "poet" and used it to craft a new poetic persona. By using the identity of a schoolmaster at his desk at the end of the day, Whitman turned his ambivalence about school teaching into his first print identity that surveyed the world both in and out of the game.

New York return

Whitman returned to New York in 1841 with the portfolio of a journalist. After some freelance work, he began to steadily publish in the *New York Aurora*, a mid-sized paper started the year before by Anson Herrick and John F. Ropes, which like many small papers during this era, courted controversy to sell papers. The editor of the *Aurora*, Thomas Low Nichols, a former reporter from Bennett's *Herald*, raised the *Aurora*'s weekly circulation to about 5,000 by providing accounts of soirees of New York's upper ten thousand and a steady flow of exposés, crime stories, trial reportage, and replays of prize fights and lectures of general interest, all in the penny press's tone of familiarity with the reader.[16] When Nichols was fired from the *Aurora* in February for publishing a libelous story, Whitman became editor of the growing paper. On March 28, 1842, Herrick and Ropes introduced Whitman as a "bold, energetic and original writer."[17]

Though he only lasted about a month at the *Aurora*, Whitman's editorials for the paper exhibited some of the earliest examples of inviting the reader along for saunters through the city, observing passing humanity along the way, "You may meet a sleepy looking boy, neatly dressed, and swinging a large brass key as he goes along. He is an under clerk in some store, and on his way to open the establishment, sweep it out, and, if need may be, kindle the fire."[18] Whitman also wrote reviews of drama and lectures, including one where he lauded Ralph Waldo Emerson but mocked the pretense of Emerson's sympathetic audience.[19]

Despite these wide-ranging topics, the *Aurora* editorial pages were increasingly swamped in the spring of 1842 with the latest news on the Maclay bill, a proposal to fund Catholic schools with public money initiated by Albany Whigs to attract Irish Catholic votes. On this subject, Whitman struggled with his own ambivalence toward state funding for sectarian education and his antipathy toward the nativist sentiments of the *Aurora*'s publishers. Through March and early April, Whitman's editorials swung from liberal tolerance ("Our love is capacious enough [...] to encircle all men") to anti-Catholic diatribe ("What American blood does not burn [...] at the gross [...] impudence of these creatures?") and back again ("it is [...] unnecessary that we should draw the line of exclusiveness").[20]

It is not entirely clear why Whitman left the *Aurora*. On May 3, Herrick and Ropes described Whitman as the "laziest fellow who ever undertook to edit a city paper," and considering that Whitman's lead editorial less than a month before described a day where he "pottered" the morning away, arrived at the *Aurora* at two, and, soon after, "sauntered forth to have a stroll down Broadway," the owners of the paper may have had a real grievance.[21] After his departure, Whitman described Herrick and Ropes as "ill bred vagabonds" incapable of "constructing two lines of grammar or meaning."[22] Whatever the reason for his departure, Whitman's career as a journalist continued; by summer, he was publishing in the *Evening Tattler* and the *Sunday Times*.

National news and local reporting

Between 1833 and 1846, celebrity editors like Day of the *Sun* and Bennett of the *Herald* dominated the press. By the mid-1840s, technological changes fostered a hierarchy of print where access to information through the telegraph offered the latest news to a few large newspapers and left smaller papers to report local news and provide commentary. The *Sun* pioneered the acceleration of news early in the decade with the chartering of express locomotives and the use of carrier pigeons, but Morse's invention and the beginning of the Mexican-American War in 1846 compelled the five largest New York newspapers to agree to share telegraphic news from the front.[23] This conglomerate, later named the Associated Press, shut out many of the smaller, local papers from timely reporting on national events.

Whitman worked on small to mid-sized papers during the mid-1840s and his journalism therefore remained largely local and reactive. After short stints as editor of small papers and extensive writing for the *Brooklyn Evening Star* (which brought him back into contact with his old employer, Alden Spooner), Whitman landed a position in 1846 at the *Brooklyn Daily Eagle*, a local Democratic paper aligned with New York's Tammany Hall (Journ., 1:xxxiv). During the mid-1840s, Whitman honed his democratic inclinations into an aesthetic ethos. Beginning with "Heart-Music and Art Music" for the *Evening Star*, he began an extended meditation on the merits of unaffected art where actors and singers best expressed emotions when they "feel them" and "throw the feeling [...] into the [...] act" (Journ., 2:24). For Whitman, singers like the Cheneys and actors like Charlotte Cushman presented a democratic alternative to the aristocratic arbiters of taste on both sides of the Atlantic. Whitman's disdain for the influence of Europe on American art reflected a broader nativist and working-class antipathy toward the confluence of upper-class tastes and European critics, which, for example, inspired the Astor Place Riot of May 10, 1849.[24] This aesthetic nativism foreshadowed the democratic bard of *Leaves of Grass*, who, as "referee" of the people, captured their true nature in verse (LG55, iv).

Isaac Van Anden hired Whitman in 1846 as editor of the *Brooklyn Daily Eagle* in an attempt to transform the newspaper from political sheet to a journal of commentary on news and culture. A "Hunker" Democrat – so named for their ability to "hunker down" and maintain party unity – Van Anden defended Tammany Hall interests and national party cohesion. In 1846, this meant that Whitman had to support the policies of President Polk: a lower tariff, westward expansion, and the extension of slavery to the West. Whitman readily supported the first, served as a booster for the second, but ultimately lost his job over the third. After Representative David Wilmot, Democrat of Pennsylvania, proposed in 1846 that the territory gained in the Mexican-American War be closed to slavery for the sake of American farmers and workingmen, Whitman increasingly became a proponent of a "free-soil" platform contrary to the position of the Democratic Party (Journ., 2:349). In November, he blamed the defeat of the Democrats on the party's rejection of the Wilmot Proviso (Journ., 2: 318–20, 349). In January 1848, he published his last editorial in the *Eagle*.

A personified voice

Though Whitman was once again out of steady work he continued to publish, first as an editor for the New Orleans *Daily Crescent*, then as an editor of a small free-soil publication, the *Brooklyn Freeman*, and as a freelance journalist for the *Daily Advertiser*, the *National Era*, and the *Evening Post*. More importantly during this period, Whitman began to refine his authorial voice into a persona that united the newspaper's eye-witness purview of the street, the reader, and a poet's interest in more timeless themes. Whitman had published his poetry in newspapers since the late 1830s, and by 1855 he had seen over two dozen of his poems published in newsprint, most of them on conventional topics, but a few approaching themes that he worked into *Leaves of Grass*.[25] "The Play-Ground" offered an early example of the poet's admiration for unaffected childhood, while "Resurgemus" (1850) recounted the revolutions of 1848 in a poem that later appeared in *Leaves of Grass*.[26]

Whitman also continued to cultivate the journalistic voice of familiar confidant. This style had been popular with editors since the earliest days of the penny press: the *Herald's* James Gordon Bennett took readers along to view in intricate detail the body of the murder victim Helen Jewett[27] and Thomas Low Nichols guided readers through upper-crust New York soirees. In "Letters from a Traveling Bachelor" (1849–50) and "Letters from Paumanok" (1851), Whitman emulated this style, "I went down to Montauk Point a day ago [. . .] and we came among a band of such amphibious men, – great unshaved, gigantic-chested beings, with eyes as clear as coals, and flesh whose freedom from the gross humors of artificial life told its tale in the dark and unpimpled brown of their faces and necks."[28] In another example from this period, Whitman employed rhetorical questions to establish intimacy with the reader in a manner similar to *Leaves of Grass*,

> Have not you, too [. . .] known this thirst of the eye? Have you not, in like manner, while listening to the well-played music [. . .] felt an overwhelming desire for measureless sound – a sublime orchestra of a myriad orchestras –

a colossal volume of harmony, in which the thunder might roll in its proper place; and above it, the vast, pure Tenor, – identity of the Creative Power itself?[29]

In this way, the bard of *Leaves of Grass* owed some debt to the journalist of the penny papers.[30]

Starting in the late 1850s Whitman began to edit the *Brooklyn Daily Times*, which positively reviewed both editions of *Leaves of Grass*, though Whitman himself composed one of these reviews.[31] At the *Times*, Whitman wrote news and commentary while revising *Leaves of Grass* for a third edition, composing a poem for "Calamus" on the reverse side of a draft editorial on water sanitation.[32] Some of his editorials in the *Times* appear to contradict earlier arguments regarding women's rights, the death penalty, and African American rights, and some scholars have questioned the extent to which Whitman even wrote for the *Times* (Loving, 228–32). However, while George Bennett, the publisher, played a strong role in the tone and composition of the paper, it is increasingly evident that Whitman edited the *Times* between 1857 and 1859 alongside Bennett.[33]

But one can imagine that during the 1850s journalism increasingly became a grind for Walt Whitman. Paeans to the democratic power of the press largely disappeared from the *Times* editorials,[34] and while he was writing editorials on public schools, yellow fever, water works, and ferries, Whitman also patronized the bohemian scene around Pfaff's beer cellar and befriended Henry Clapp, editor of the *Saturday Press* and booster for the third edition of *Leaves of Grass*.[35] Karen Karbiener describes Whitman during this period as "a man with two faces: a hack thinking about word count, and a poet thinking about words."[36] While at the *Times*, Whitman published an extensive series called "Manly Health and Training" for the *New York Atlas* under the pseudonym "Mose Velsor," a name he had used occasionally since 1848.[37] Though Whitman's interest in the male physique and natural health in this series also found its way into the "Calamus" cluster in the 1860 edition of *Leaves of Grass*, "Manly Health and Training" represented the end of an era for Whitman. While journalism continued to provide steady work for him in the late 1850s, the medium proved constraining. After 1860, he increasingly published under his own name and reputation as a New York poet. In this regard, Walt Whitman's poetry owed a debt to his journalism as an incubator of its style and, ultimately, an inhibitor of its actualization. The third edition of *Leaves of Grass* was the greatest commercial success to date for Walt Whitman. Afterward, his youthful journalism became the long foreground at the beginning of a great career.

Notes

1. Philip Hone, *The Diary of Philip Hone: 1828–1851*, 2 vols., ed. Bayard Tuckerman (New York, NY: Dodd, Meade and Company, 1889), 1:154–55.

2. Edwin G. Burrows and Mike Wallace, *Gotham: A History of New York City to 1898* (New York, NY: Oxford University Press, 1999), 598.

3. Walt Whitman, "*Brooklyn Daily Times*, June 3, 1857," in *The Uncollected Poetry and Prose of Walt Whitman, Vol. II*, ed. Emory Holloway (Gloucester, MA: Peter Smith, 1921), 3–4; Loving, 35–6; PW, 1:14; Reynolds, 46.

4. Douglas Jerrold, *Punch's Letters to his Son, Punch's Complete Letter Writer, and Sketches of the English* (London: Bradbury and Evans, 1853), 301.

5. Walt Whitman, *Autobiographia: or the Story of a Life* (New York, NY: Charles L. Webster, 1892), WWA.

6. James Gordon Bennett, editor of the *New York Herald*, coined the term "blanket sheets" as a term of derision for the eleven-column, 58-inch-wide *Journal of Commerce*, William E. Huntzicker, *The Popular Press: 1833–1865* (Westport, CT: Greenwood Press, 1999), 11.

7. Huntzicker, *The Popular Press*, 1.

8. Ibid.

9. Ibid., 11.

10. Wesley Washington Pasko, *American Dictionary of Printing and Bookmaking* (New York, NY: Howard Lockwood & Co., 1894), 63.

11. John Hruschka, "Order Books: The Development of a Modern American Book Trade," unpublished diss., Pennsylvania State University, 2008, 97.

12. *New York Sun*, September 3, 1833, quoted in Huntzicker, *The Popular Press*, 2.

13. "Newspaperial Etiquette," *New York Aurora* (New York, NY), April 18, 1842, WWA.

14. "New York Herald is Eighty-One," *Fourth Estate* (New York, NY), May 13, 1916.

15. "Sun-Down Papers No. 9," *Long-Island Democrat* (Long Island, NY) November 24, 1840, WWA.

16. See the following *Aurora* articles on WWA: "Ball of the Erina Benevolent Society," February 4, 1842; "Mr. Abbott's Lecture"; "Capture of a Bowery Boy"; "In the Midst of Life We are in Death," February 8, 1842; "The Great Boz Ball," February 16, 1842.

17. "Announcement," *New York Aurora* (New York, NY), March 28, 1842, WWA.

18. "Life in New York," *New York Aurora* (New York, NY), March 14, 1842; also see "An Hour in a Balcony," *New York Aurora* (New York, NY), March 23, 1842; "A Peep at the Israelites," *New York Aurora* (New York, NY), March 28, 1842, WWA.

19. "Mr. Emerson's Lecture," *New York Aurora* (New York, NY), March 7, 1842, WWA.

20. Editorial, *New York Aurora* (New York, NY), April 18, 1842, WWA.

21. April 6, 1842, WWA. Herrick and Ropes quoted in Joseph Jay Rubin, *The Historic Whitman* (University Park, PA: Pennsylvania State University Press, 1973), 83.

22. Rubin, *The Historic Whitman*, 83.

23. The five original papers in the agreement were the *Sun, Herald, Journal of Commerce, Courier and Enquirer*, and *Express*. The *New York Tribune* joined the cooperative in 1849, the *New York Times* in 1851. See Menahem Blondheim, *News Over the Wires: The Telegraph and the Flow of Public Information in America, 1844–1897* (Cambridge, MA: Harvard University Press, 1994), 49–57.

24. Edwin Burrows and Mike Wallace, *Gotham: A History of New York to 1898* (New York, NY: Oxford University Press, 1990), 763. See also Lawrence W. Levine, *Highbrow/Lowbrow: The Emergence of Cultural Hierarchy in America* (Cambridge, MA: Harvard University Press, 1988).

25. "Walt Whitman's Poems in Periodicals: A Bibliography," WWA.

26. Walt Whitman, "The Play-Ground," *Brooklyn Daily Eagle* (Brooklyn, NY), June 1, 1846, and "Resurgemus," *New York Daily Tribune* (New York, NY), June 21, 1850, WWA.

27. *New York Herald*, April 11, 1836, reprinted in Patricia Cline Cohen, *The Murder of Helen Jewett: Life and Death of a Prostitute in Nineteenth-Century New York* (New York, NY: Vintage Books, 1999), 16.

28. Walt Whitman, "Letters from a Travelling Bachelor," *New York Sunday Dispatch* (New York, NY), October 14, 1849, WWA.

29. Walt Whitman, "Letters from Paumanok," *New York Evening Post* (New York, NY), August 14, 1851, WWA.

30. For connections between Whitman's journalism and his poetry see Shelley Fisher Fishkin, *From Fact to Fiction: Journalism and Imaginative Writing in America* (Baltimore, MD: Johns Hopkins University Press, 1985); C. Carroll Hollis, *Language and Style in Leaves of Grass* (Baton Rouge, LA: Louisiana State University Press, 1983); Rubin, *The Historic Whitman*; Jason Stacy, *Walt Whitman's Multitudes: Labor Reform and Persona in Whitman's Journalism and the First Leaves of Grass, 1840–1855* (New York, NY: Peter Lang, 2008).

31. Karen Karbiener, "Reconstructing Whitman's Desk at the *Brooklyn Daily Times*," *Walt Whitman Quarterly Review* 33.1 (2015), 24.

32. Ibid., 28.

33. See Karbiener, "Reconstructing."

34. An article from July 21, 1858, "The Press – Its Future," is a half-hearted exception.

35. Joanna Levin and Edward Whitley, eds., *Whitman among the Bohemians* (Iowa City, IA: University of Iowa Press, 2014), especially Amanda Gailey, "Walt Whitman and the King of Bohemia: The Poet in the *Saturday Press*," and Karen Karbiener, "Bridging Brooklyn and Bohemia: How the *Brooklyn Daily Times* Brought Whitman Closer to Pfaff's."

36. Karbiener, "Reconstructing," 39.

37. See Zachary Turpin, "Introduction to Walt Whitman's 'Manly Health and Training,'" *Walt Whitman Quarterly Review* 33.3 (2016), 147–83. Stephanie Blalock notes that Whitman was inspired by *Fistiana; or The Oracle of the Ring* (1841) by Pierce Egan, which was reprinted in the *New York Clipper* in 1857 and perhaps borrowed from *Onanism, Spermatorrhoea: Porneiokalgynomia-Pathology: Boyhood's Perils and Manhood's Curse* (1858) by Seth Pancoast, email to author, August 16, 2016.

CHAPTER 10

Oratory

Leslie Elizabeth Eckel

Walt Whitman's devotion to oratory might come as a surprise to readers most familiar with the figure of the American poet he describes and celebrates in his Preface to the 1855 edition of *Leaves of Grass*. In this introduction to his first edition, Whitman places the poet at the very center of his theory of democracy, which unspools itself in generous, diverse lines of "unrhymed poetry" (LG55, iii). What makes the United States unique, he argues, is its natural propensity for poetic thought and action: "Of all nations the United States with veins full of poetical stuff most need poets and will doubtless have the greatest and use them the greatest. Their Presidents shall not be their common referee so much as their poets shall" (LG55, iv). In this statement, Whitman appears to be minimizing the public role of politicians, for whom he shows distrust elsewhere in the Preface, and elevating instead the more private figure of the self-authorizing literary creator as national leader. If we take Whitman at his word here, we might follow the trajectory of his print production – likely through the multiple editions of *Leaves of Grass* – to understand how he strived to become the poet capable of fulfilling his vision in that early Preface.

Instead of treading that more familiar path, this chapter considers the counter-narrative of Whitman's development as an orator. Rooted in the 1850s, much like his poetic ambitions, this counter-narrative reaches its high point in the series of lectures on "The Death of Abraham Lincoln" that Whitman performed at the end of his career from 1879 to 1890. Thinking about Whitman first and foremost as an orator and then as a poet, as he himself suggested in his manuscript notes of the 1850s, generates a different story about his development as a cultural figure. In this light, Whitman's poems could be read as a written record that he felt was complementary or even secondary to the live presence he intended to maintain before an eager American audience. Even before Whitman printed the first edition of *Leaves of Grass*, James Perrin Warren notes, he "considered pursuing a career on the lecture circuit."[1] Whitman was raised in "the Golden Age of Oratory": those decades between the American Revolution and the Civil War in which local lyceums flourished and political speech from various parties and their representatives animated the landscape of daily life. According to David S. Reynolds, Whitman followed the orations of politicians and preachers such as Daniel Webster, Edward Everett, Cassius Clay, and Henry Ward Beecher with particular interest (Reynolds, 45). As Ralph Waldo Emerson made his name on the lyceum and lecture circuit at home and abroad, he hailed Whitman's 1855 *Leaves of Grass* as "the beginning of a great career," and Whitman responded by seeding his own self-promotional campaigns with that phrase (LG56, 345).[2] While many readers imagine Whitman answering Emerson's call in his essay "The Poet" (1844) for a writer who could evoke the "ample geography" of the US that "dazzles the imagination," envisioning Whitman as an orator means reconsidering the degree to which he might have been inspired by Emerson's public persona to take the stage himself.[3]

On his thirty-ninth birthday in 1858, Whitman set the lofty goal of bringing about "a revolution in American oratory." He mapped out this revolution in his plans for a series he called "Walt Whitman's Lectures."[4] These lectures, which he also evokes as "American Lectures / New sermons / America-Readings – Voices Walt Whitman's Voices," would be given in state capitals with what Warren explains as the intent of "teaching the American people his 'grand ideas' of American democracy."[5] Each lecture was to be accompanied by a printed program so that audience members could absorb Whitman's ideas by listening, reading, and reflecting at a later date. Although "Walt Whitman's Lectures" never actually came to fruition, his vision of himself as a "wander-speaker" energizes his poems and prose writings, and these imagined oratorical performances place his words within a lively, expansive theatrical context.[6] In "A Song of Joys," which first appeared in 1860 as "Poem of Joys," Whitman proclaims:

> O the orator's joys!
> To inflate the chest – to roll the thunder of the voice out
>   from the ribs and throat,
> To make the people rage, weep, hate, desire, with yourself,
> To lead America – to quell America with a great tongue.   (LG60, 268)

These lines celebrate the physical power of the orator, who harnesses breath and voice to draw out wild emotions from an audience, even as he presumably participates in the great catharsis; he is there "with yourself." Yet there is a strange element of mastery in Whitman's portrait of the orator who "quell[s]" as he "lead[s]," bringing American listeners under control by force, mesmerizing them with his presence onstage. In our era of the public reading and the poetry slam, it has become increasingly common for writers to perform their work as they become physically involved in the machinery of literary promotion, from book tours to YouTube channels. Whitman imagines for the poet-orator, his "wander-speaker," a now familiar and arresting magnetism that was understandably hard to achieve in his own time.

Instead, as scholars such as C. Carroll Hollis have noted, Whitman channeled his oratorical energies into his poems, turning them into "illocutionary acts": works that "carry out what they are saying as they are being said."[7] These poems incorporate Whitman's physical presence as they describe the poet's body in detailed terms, making him visible, palpable, and even companionable to the reader. Reynolds observes that Whitman most emulated orators for their "direct contact with the people," so he cultivated that direct relationship in his writing, using "oratorical devices such as exclamations, rhetorical questions, negations, parallelism, invocations to a 'you,'" his imagined reader/listener (Reynolds, 47–48). In "Crossing Brooklyn Ferry," the speaker advances on the reader as deliberately as he can, stopping just short of walking through the page:

> Closer yet I approach you,
> What thought you have of me now, I had as much of you –
> I laid in my stores in advance,
> I consider'd long and seriously of you before you were born.   (LG, 163)

Many of Whitman's poems suggest intimacy with the reader, but this moment reveals just how complex this connection is: he has built this relationship over a "long" period of time, taken it "seriously," and readied his "approach" in order to have a particular impact on his audience.[8] This is not just a piece of writing, but a carefully rehearsed performance.

Whitman's dream of oratorical success was realized neither in "Walt Whitman's Lectures" nor in subsequent plans during the Civil War and the years that followed, which consisted of his remembrances of "The Dead in This War" and reflections on "German transcendental philosophy" in "Sunday Evening Lectures."[9] It was his lectures on "The Death of Abraham Lincoln," given nineteen times in different cities from 1879 to 1890, that allowed him to master the art of performing before the captive audience of which he had always dreamed. Although Whitman may have been trapped to a certain extent by what William Pannapacker calls the "unalterable public ritual" these lectures represented, in which he paired

his reflections on Lincoln with a recitation of "O Captain! My Captain!"
a poem that reliably thrilled audiences, they nonetheless constituted one of
his greatest triumphs.[10] That peculiarly Whitmanian drama –
a combination of poetry, politics, and popular culture, all magnetically
centered on the figure of the ethereally aging poet – enabled him to write
himself into a narrative of national identity that remains with us today.

Whitman had a long history of showmanship in print. For him, poetry
writing alone was never enough to satisfy his urge to make the newest and
boldest cultural statement possible. In a self-authored review of the first
edition of *Leaves of Grass*, he asked, "where in American literature is the
first show of America?"[11] In his detailed catalogs, Whitman would introduce as many players to the national stage as he could, but he always
insisted on exerting full creative control over that "show." Whitman made
it clear that he was the star performer, boasting, "He proceeds himself to
exemplify this new school, and set models for their expression and range of
subjects. He makes audacious and native use of his own body and soul."[12]
Whitman's grandiose critical rhetoric has its roots in his early work as
a journalist and, as Reynolds has observed, in his fascination with the
New York theater world of the 1830s and 1840s (Reynolds, 154–93).
The combination of Whitman's professional training and his personal
interest in drama produced a creative mind that could report on its own
"new school" of poetic thought and its "audacious[ly]" exhibitionist techniques to what he imagined was an eager public. David Haven Blake's
work on Whitman's rise to celebrity status encourages us to see Whitman's
career as a series of publicity "campaigns" that established his position at
the center of the national imaginary.[13] What these campaigns have in
common is Whitman's insistence on his ability to constitute the nation
both in person and in print and a paradoxical combination of the threat of
damning neglect and the assurance of lasting literary fame.

It was from this position of simultaneous marginality and confirmed
cultural significance that Whitman rose to the challenge of giving his
first Lincoln lecture in 1879. In his wartime memoranda on Lincoln,
Whitman had observed that the president put on "no great show" in
Washington (PW, 1:60), but in the lecture itself he would call Lincoln
"the leading actor in the stormiest drama known to real history's stage
through centuries" (PW, 2:504). An intermediary entry in Whitman's
prose journal *Specimen Days* (1882) helps explain what was at stake for
Whitman in elevating Lincoln to the dramatic heights he may have
shunned during his lifetime. Written on the day of Lincoln's death, this
piece begins to draw a portrait of the president that Whitman asserted

had not yet been accurately composed by any other artist. Lincoln appears in this journal entry with a halo that looks familiar to those who recall Whitman's image of himself crowned with "spokes of light" in "Crossing Brooklyn Ferry" (LG, 161). In *Specimen Days*, Whitman writes, "The tragic splendor of [Lincoln's] death, purging, illuminating all, throws round his form, his head, an aureole that will remain and will grow brighter through time, while history lives, and love of country lasts" (PW, 1:98). As Whitman transfers his gesture of self-apotheosis to Lincoln, he grants Lincoln the cultural divinity that he seeks for himself. Whitman's Lincoln is a champion of "UNIONISM" whose sacrificial death renders the nation itself "immortal" (PW, 1:98–99). While Whitman appears to have let go of his national ambition to "illuminate all" in the floodlights of his poetic vision, it is precisely the performative aspect of the event's "tragic splendor" and the theatrical way in which Whitman bestows it upon Lincoln that keeps him onstage alongside the great "leading actor" he sought to praise.

Whitman usually began his Lincoln lectures by downplaying his ability to handle the emotionally challenging task that lay before him. Confronting the anniversary of Lincoln's death, he claimed, left him at a loss for words. He admitted to his audience, "Yet now the sought-for opportunity offers, I find my notes incompetent, (why, for truly profound themes, is statement so idle? why does the right phrase never offer?) and the fit tribute I dream'd of, waits unprepared as ever" (PW, 2:497). The "barbaric yawp" of "Song of Myself" has been replaced by halting, self-conscious phrases, and this seemingly "incompetent" public speaker is no longer the Whitman we think we know. When Whitman gave the lecture for the last time in 1890, he warned his listeners, "I am not going to tell you anything new" (PW, 2:685). If the poet had indeed given up his familiar persona – the bold provocateur who sought to innovate and to startle by "Unscrew[ing] the locks from the doors! / Unscrew[ing] the doors themselves from their jambs!" – then who exactly was this humble, staid old man who had taken his place? (LG, 52). This Whitman walked his audience through a summary of the turbulent Civil War years and then arrived at what appeared to be the main event: an account of the actual assassination of Lincoln. Drawing on his journalistic background, Whitman persuaded his audience that he was "reporting live" from Ford's Theater, thereby plunging his listeners into a trance-like state in which they were convinced they were reliving the terrible event itself. One audience member, the poet Stuart Merrill, said afterwards: "I was there, the very thing happened to me. And this recital was as gripping as the messengers' reports in Aeschylus."[14]

The man who had succeeded in generating this deep impression was himself a far more professional actor than he had initially let on.

Whitman's ability to recreate the drama of "that chilly April day" in 1865 was not his most significant achievement in the Lincoln lectures, however (PW, 2:497). He may have skillfully directed the three layers of drama involved in the lecture – the actual performance of *Our American Cousin* (1858), the high tragedy of the assassination, and the spectacle of his own presence onstage, which a *New York Times* critic called "impressive in the extreme" – but what truly mattered was the cultural drama going on behind the immediately visible scenes.[15] In that drama, Whitman cast himself as the arbiter of "the immeasurable value and meaning of that whole tragedy" (PW, 2:507). In *Specimen Days*, Whitman argued that Lincoln's death rendered the "Nation [. . .] immortal," and in the lecture, he returned to that theme with even greater gusto (PW, 1:99). Assuming a mantle of moral authority, he concluded:

> The final use of a heroic-eminent life – especially of a heroic-eminent death – is its indirect filtering into the nation and the race, and to give, often at many removes, but unerringly, age after age, color and fibre to the personalism of the youth and maturity of that age, and of mankind. Then there is a cement to the whole people, subtler, more underlying, than any thing in written constitution, or courts or armies – namely, the cement of a death identified thoroughly with that people, at its head, and for its sake. Strange, (is it not?) that battles, martyrs, agonies, blood, even assassination, should so condense – perhaps only really, lastingly condense – a Nationality. (PW, 2:508)

By "identif[ying]" Lincoln's death as the force that "condense[s] – a Nationality," Whitman places both that event and his representation of it at the center of the nation's imagination of itself. He suggests that Lincoln will "filter into the nation," adding "color and fibre" to the character of its citizens, which transfers the textual influence wielded by the speaker of "Song of Myself" – who promises to "filter and fibre" the "blood" of the reader – into the script of Whitman's later performance (LG, 89). The poet moves to dismiss that which is "written" in favor of something he claims is even more permanent, "more underlying" than words alone can be.

In this complex moment, the full historical power of Whitman's Lincoln drama becomes evident to us. Diana Taylor has distinguished between what she calls the "repertoire" of performance and the "archive" of written texts.[16] Taylor elevates the alternative history that political and theatrical events often represent, as they challenge the written records of a culture in significant ways. In his Lincoln lectures, Whitman draws on both the power of performance and the weight of writing as he incorporates previously written material into the script of his lecture. By performing the words that previously existed only in the two-dimensional world of the text, Whitman works to ensure that they will come to rest in the permanent archive of American history. He fully intends to make his version of "Nationality" "a cement to the whole people" and to imply that the nation itself could not exist without him (PW, 2:508). Whitman was barely strong enough to take the stage for his final Lincoln lecture in 1890, but he insisted on making one last stand, explaining to Horace Traubel, "I hope to be identified with the man Lincoln, with his crowded, eventful years – with America as shadowed forth into those abysms of circumstance."[17] By aligning himself with – and to borrow Joseph Roach's term, acting as a dramatic "surrogate" for – Lincoln, Whitman seeks to irrefutably embody his own concept of "America."[18]

"O Captain! My Captain!" the poem that Whitman habitually recited at the end of his Lincoln lectures, also capitalized on the popular repertoire's capacity to shape the textual content of the archive. The poem is highly unusual in the Whitman canon, for it constrains its lines to fairly strict metrical regularity and it seems to have been written for performance. It combines images of a ship of state, on whose "deck my Captain lies / Fallen cold and dead," with intimations of the stage itself, whose boards the Whitmanian speaker "mournful[ly] tread[s]" as the poet did in his own lectures (LG, 338). In this ritualized utterance, there is little of the spontaneous Whitman that we expect. Instead, the speaker focuses his attention on the audience that awaits the ship – "the swaying mass, their eager faces turning" – who "call" for the fallen captain, thereby completing a vision of national mourning for the President and a fantasy of ultimate cultural acceptance for the poet himself.

When Whitman concluded his 1879 Lincoln lecture in New York's Madison Square Theater with this poem, both he and his audience were moved to tears. As he struggled with the verses, a young girl walked onstage with a basket of lilacs, reciting the line, "I've brought you some lilacs that in our door yard bloomed."[19] At this moment, even in the midst of an emotional breakdown, Whitman was in full command. His elegy for Lincoln, "When Lilacs Last in the Dooryard Bloom'd," had been hovering in the wings, relinquishing the stage to the poet himself and to the explicit assessment of Lincoln's cultural significance that he sought to dramatize. When the lilacs themselves were offered, they were the only conceivable tribute to Whitman, for they were the products of the symbolic imaginary that he had created. Whitman lived almost to the turn of the twentieth century: long enough to witness and to study the afterlives of characters and stories invented by such antebellum peers as Henry Wadsworth Longfellow and Harriet Beecher Stowe. These afterlives almost always played themselves out in theatrical performances that offered endless versions and corruptions of the original narratives of Hiawatha and Uncle Tom, among other characters. Kerry Larson has perceived a "decline into mental and creative lethargy" in Whitman's final years that he contends is signaled by the "hackneyed sentiments" in which Whitman indulged in his Lincoln lectures.[20] I would argue that Whitman's engagement with the sentimentalist strategies that had proven so effective for Stowe demonstrates not a failure of imagination, but rather a flexibility of professional approach that enabled him to grow into the national fame that other writers enjoyed much earlier in their careers.

As Whitman suggests in "O Captain! My Captain!," it is the "eager faces" of the audience that matter most to the performer onstage. On this particular evening in New York, those faces were familiar both to Whitman and to us, for he had drawn a crowd that included such luminaries as Mark Twain, Boston intellectuals James Russell Lowell and Charles Eliot Norton, sculptor Augustus St. Gaudens, and Cuban poet José Martí. Andrew Carnegie, who, according to Daniel Mark Epstein, "considered Whitman the greatest poet in America," paid for box seats but did not attend.[21] In the presence of these figures and through the means of oratory, Whitman enjoyed the feeling of immediate cultural acceptance he had craved his entire writing life, and as he gained the admiration and sympathy of those such as Lowell and Carnegie, who were leaders and founders of academic institutions, he secured his place as an American institution in his own right. While it was crucial for Whitman to win the approval of those who represented the national establishment, his greatest influence in fact may have been wielded through the work of Martí and others who attempted to define American culture from their vantage points abroad. Martí's response to the lecture, published in the Argentinian newspaper *La Nación*, hails Whitman as a divinity, or at least a high priest in a new, secular American religion. Martí writes, "All literate New York attended that luminous speech in religious silence, for its sudden grace notes, vibrant tones, hymnlike fugues, and Olympian familiarity seemed at times the whispering of stars."[22] As Martí shares this mystical experience with readers elsewhere in the Americas, he urges them to "Hark to what this industrious, satisfied people is singing; hark to Walt Whitman. His exercise of himself raises him into majesty, his tolerance into justice, his sense of order into happiness." In order to hear the true voice of the United States, Martí asserts, one must listen reverently to Whitman's "majestic" song. As news of Whitman's performative "exercise" travels abroad, this time taking a different route than the familiar Anglo-American trajectory of Victorian letters, we can see the beginnings of the global network of literary imagination that binds us to Whitman today.

Notes

1. James Perrin Warren, *Culture of Eloquence: Oratory and Reform in Antebellum America* (University Park, PA: The Pennsylvania State University Press, 1999), 169.
2. Whitman cited this acclamation on the spine of the 1856 edition of *Leaves of Grass* and reprinted Emerson's congratulatory letter in the collection of reviews he called "Leaves-Droppings" at the end of the book.
3. Ralph Waldo Emerson, *The Collected Works of Ralph Waldo Emerson*, 10 vols., eds. Robert E. Spiller et al. (Cambridge, MA: Belknap Press of Harvard University Press, 1971–2013), 3:22.
4. Warren, *Culture of Eloquence*, 169, 171.
5. Whitman quoted in Reynolds, 168; Warren, *Culture of Eloquence*, 170.
6. Warren, *Culture of Eloquence*, 174.
7. C. Carroll Hollis, *Language and Style in Leaves of Grass* (Baton Rouge, LA: Louisiana State University Press, 1983), 66. See also Mark Bauerlein, "The Written Orator of 'Song of Myself': A Recent Trend in Whitman Criticism," *Walt Whitman Review* 3.3 (1986), 1–14.
8. For a more extensive treatment of "Crossing Brooklyn Ferry" as an oratorical poem, see Jake Adam York, *The Architecture of Address: The Monument and Public Speech in American Poetry* (New York, NY: Routledge, 2005), 19–95.
9. Warren, *Culture of Eloquence*, 183.
10. William Pannapacker, *Revised Lives: Walt Whitman and Nineteenth-Century Authorship* (New York, NY: Routledge, 2004), 23.
11. [Walt Whitman], "Walt Whitman and His Poems," *The United States Review*, September 1855, WWA.
12. Ibid., 2:12.
13. David Haven Blake, *Walt Whitman and the Culture of American Celebrity* (New Haven, CT: Yale University Press, 2006), 174–215.
14. Justin Kaplan, *Walt Whitman: A Life* (New York, NY: Simon and Schuster, 1980), 30.
15. Daniel Mark Epstein, *Lincoln and Whitman: Parallel Lives in Civil War Washington* (New York, NY: Ballantine, 2004), 330.
16. Diana Taylor, *The Archive and the Repertoire: Performing Cultural Memory in the Americas* (Durham, NC: Duke University Press, 2003).
17. Blake, *Walt Whitman*, 194.

18. Joseph Roach, *Cities of the Dead: Circum-Atlantic Performance* (New York, NY: Columbia University Press, 1996), 2.

19. Epstein, *Lincoln and Whitman*, 339; Blake, *Walt Whitman*, 192.

20. Kerry C. Larson, *Whitman's Drama of Consensus* (Chicago, IL: University of Chicago Press, 1988), 232.

21. Epstein, *Lincoln and Whitman*, 327.

22. José Martí, "The Poet Walt Whitman," in *Walt Whitman and the World*, eds. Gay Wilson Allen and Ed Folsom (Iowa City, IA: University of Iowa Press, 1995), 98–100. Originally published in *La Nación* (April 19, 1887).

CHAPTER 11

Opera

Carmen Trammell Skaggs

> We invite you to spend an evening with us at the opera, and listen to
> the music, and look at the place and people. [. . .] You need not travel
> hither; [. . .] we will bring the opera to you – even Italian opera – in
> full bloom.[1]

Although scholars broadly acknowledge opera as an important influence
on Walt Whitman's *Leaves of Grass*, they also differ significantly in how
they define that influence. Because Whitman refers to specific opera
performances, venues, performers, instruments, and vocal techniques in
both his poetry and prose, he ensures that any thorough assessment of his
work must take seriously his recollection about opera's influence on his
composition during the decade preceding the publication of the first
edition: "Oh! those great days! great, great days! Alboni, Badiali, in particular: no one can tell, know, even suspect, how much they had to do with
the making of *Leaves of Grass*" (WWC, 2:173). Alternately identified as his
inspiration, his subject, and his method, opera infuses not only the poet's
imagination but also his artistic palette of diction and metaphor. Creating
what Whitman describes as "a new world – a liquid world,"[2] opera offers
a fluid, authentic voice for describing the new nation, its people, and its
landscape. Opera's socio-economic connotations were also fluid. Opera
might seem out of character for the poet self-described in the 1855 version
of "Song of Myself" as "an American, one of the roughs" (LG55, 29), but it
was, as Lawrence W. Levine reminds us, both "popular and elite," enjoyed
by a wide segment of the population in mid-nineteenth-century America
even as "smaller socially and economically elite groups" began to garner
"social confirmation from it."[3] While other American writers would find
the spectacle and spaces of opera well-suited for illustrating the young
democracy's class-based and commodity-driven aspirations, Whitman
would instead discover in the hybrid art a metaphor for the artist's
embodied voice.[4] Through the lens and language of opera, Whitman
celebrates the heroism, nobility, beauty, and equality of America. In the

process of translating this foreign art form in his poetry, he simultaneously democratizes opera and transcends the limits of written language, offering the sounds, emotions, and messages to all who will listen.

Before immersing himself in Italian opera, Whitman echoed familiar sentiments that disparaged the art form as another "stale, second-hand, foreign method, with its flourishes, its ridiculous sentimentality, its anti-republican sentiment, and its sycophantic tainting [of] the young taste of the nation."[5] In a very brief time, however, the editor of the *Brooklyn Daily Eagle* would find himself praising not only the typical elements reviewed – the players, the singers, the setting, and the audience – but also the vocal technique. As Robert Faner observes, Whitman's "journalistic days in Brooklyn and New York coincided with one of the golden moments in the history of opera in this country, a moment when the musical fashion insisted upon a type of opera in which the voices of singers were displayed as never before or since, and a moment when singers of heroic stature had miraculously appeared to perform."[6] In addition to the opera exposure his press pass allowed in New York, Whitman most likely experienced the opera in New Orleans – which, along with New York, was one of the cultural centers for opera in the United States – during the late 1840s when he worked on the editorial staff of the *Daily Crescent* newspaper.[7] Prior to the Civil War, New Orleans hosted the only continuously performing opera company, including tours of the Eastern seaboard from 1827 to 1833.[8]

Providing New York its first taste of *bel canto*, Rossini's *Il Barbiere di Siviglia* was performed at the Park Theatre on November 29, 1825. Characteristic of Italian *bel canto* operas, the ornamental vocal flourishes allowed the performers to astound audiences with the versatility of the human voice. Julia Spiegelman argues that "it was at the opera that Whitman first conceived the free rhythmical style of his verse."[9] More precisely stated, the free form of the *bel canto* provided a model for the experimental form of free verse that Whitman would select for celebrating the commonplace. Further, Whitman acknowledges the "emotional rapture"[10] of opera, highlighting not only the sounds and arrangement of the musical notes but also the human instrument: the singer's voice. Whitman catalogs his exposure to the *bel canto* style of operatic performance in an excerpt from *Specimen Days* (1882):

> All through these years, off and on, I frequented [. . .] the Italian operas at Chambers-street, Astor Place or the Battery – many seasons was on the free list, writing for papers even as quite a youth. [. . .] I heard, these years, well render'd, all the Italian and other operas in vogue, "Sonnambula," "the Puritans," "Der Freischutz," "Hugenots," "Fille du Regiment," "Faust,"

"Étoile du Nord," "Poliuto," and others. Verdi's "Ernani," "Rigoletto," and "Trovatore," with Donizetti's "Lucia" or "Favorita" or "Lucrezia," and Auber's "Massaniello," or Rossini's "William Tell" and "Gazza Ladra," were among my special enjoyments. I heard Alboni every time she sang in New York and vicinity – also Grisi, the tenor Mario, and the baritone Badiali, the finest in the world. (PW, 1:19)

Although not a trained musician, Whitman observed and admired the physical power, stamina, and control opera singers exerted over their bodies. Linda and Michael Hutcheon describe the "physically embodied instrument" of an opera singer as being "like a wind instrument: it has a bellows (the lungs), a windpipe (the bronchi and trachea), a reed (the vocal cords), resonators (the closed cavities in the cranium and face), and a speaking trumpet (the mouth)."[11] From this embodied art, he drew inspiration. Exploring "The Perfect Human Voice," Whitman concludes, "beyond all other power and beauty, there is something in the quality and power of the right voice (*timbre* the schools call it) that touches the soul, the abysms." Indeed, in the voice of the opera singer, Whitman identified the touchstone for his poetic perception, musing, "the best philosophy and poetry, or something like the best, after all these centuries, perhaps waits to be rous'd out yet, or suggested, by the perfect physiological human voice" (PW, 2:495).[12]

Throughout the body of his work, Whitman returns to the metaphor of singing to describe not only the voices of America that speak to him, as in "I hear America singing," but also the poems that have yet to be created. In "A Backward Glance O'er Traveled Roads," Whitman explains: "Plenty of songs had been sung – beautiful, matchless songs – adjusted to other lands than these – another spirit and stage of evolution; but I would sing, and leave out or put in, quite solely with reference to America and to-day" (LG, 563–64). By using references to the poet's and the singer's voices so interchangeably, Whitman creates a common vocabulary for describing poetic transcendence. In the celebrated opera singers of his age – Brignole, Bettini, Badiali, and Alboni – Whitman discovers embodied examples of the vocal power he admired. Whitman compares the voice of a "vast, pure Tenor" to "the identity of the Creative Power itself – rising through the universe, until the boundless and unspeakable capacities of that mystery, the human soul, should be filled to the uttermost, and the problem of human cravingness be satisfied and destroyed."[13] As Whitman's description suggests, the singer's voice transcends the limits of human expression, transporting the listener. An innovative poet-critic, Whitman's willingness to embrace physicality allowed him to recognize the embodied nature of opera well before the scholarly work of such twentieth-century critics as Michel Poizat, who also underscores the significance of this vocal cry, tracing the progression of opera as "begin[ning] with speech, sung as closely as possible to the phrasing of spoken language; cover[ing] a trajectory in which singing grows more and more detached from speech and tends more and more toward the high notes; and culminat[ing] in the pure cry."[14]

Considering the poet's power in "Vocalism," Whitman muses on "the practis'd and perfect organ" and "develop'd soul" that belong to singers (LG, 384). Notably, Whitman found both male and female opera singers capable of achieving this transcendence and acknowledged attending all ten of the operas Madame Marietta Alboni appeared in during the 1852–53 season in New York, observing, "I heard Alboni every time she sang in New York and vicinity" (PW, 1:19). In his tribute to Signor Pasquale Brignole, "The Dead Tenor," Whitman discovers the "perfect singing voice," allowing the poet to "fold thenceforth, or seek to fold, within [his] chants transmuting, / Freedom's and Love's and Faith's unloos'd cantabile" (LG, 523). In "Song of Myself," Whitman proclaims that the voices of the "tenor large and fresh as the creation" and "the train'd soprano" provoke a powerful and erotic physical response, "convuls[ing] me like the climax of my lovegrip" (LG55, 32). Whitman thus anticipates Samuel Abel's claim that "at opera's moments of intense erotic fulfillment, the singer becomes pure voice; the body, the scenery, everything other than the voice of the singer disappears from consciousness; and we in the audience become one with the ecstatic cry of the unmediated voice."[15]

For Whitman, opera not only provides the inspiration and the subject for poetry but also his method. In "Out of the Cradle Endlessly Rocking," the poet observes "two feather'd guests from Alabama" while "cautiously peering, absorbing, translating" (LG, 248). Later in the poem, he describes the he-bird's song as an "aria" (LG, 251), revealing opera's structure as a method for reading the poem. Operas are composed of a variety of musical numbers, ranging from an aria – a solo that suspends the action of the drama and extends a single emotion – to recitative – semi-sung dialogue designed to propel the action. By allowing the he-bird in his poem to sing an aria, Whitman reveals his intimate familiarity with opera's methods and also focuses the reader's attention on the solitary sorrow of the bird. Differentiating the poet's and the bird's thoughts, Whitman italicizes the bird's mournful aria. Even in his prose writings, Whitman compared the technical prowess of an opera singer to a bird. Recalling Anna Bishop's vocal performance in Gaetano Donizetti's *Linda di*

Chamounix, Whitman likened the "silvery clearness" and "flexibility" of her tones to "gyrations of a bird in the air."[16] Whitman's young, awakening poet, however, translates the he-bird's sorrow into an intelligible – although inescapable – cry. As the young boy listens to the aria, he recognizes that not only does he react to the physical sounds of the song, but he also understands their message, articulating this language foreign to human ears:

> O you singer solitary, singing by yourself projecting me,
> O solitary me listening, never more shall I cease perpetuating you,
> Never more shall I escape, never more the reverberations,
> Never more the cries of unsatisfied love be absent from me,
> Never again leave me to be the peaceful child I was before what
>   there in the night,
> By the sea under the yellow and sagging moon,
> The messenger there arous'd, the fire, the sweet hell within,
> The unknown want, the destiny of me.　　　　　　　　(LG, 252)

Acknowledging in that moment his own poetic identity, the boy recognizes the mystery of life and death: "Now in a moment I know what I am for, I awake" (LG, 252).

In the months following the poem's initial publication in the *Saturday Press* as "A Child's Reminiscence," theater critic Edward G. P. "Ned" Wilkins – one of Whitman's fellow Pfaff's bohemians – casually linked Whitman, opera, and artistic innovation:

> The only thing worth mentioning in the Operatic way, – because the only thing that could claim the merit of novelty (a great merit in these latter days, when everybody is continually doing the same thing over and over again, except Walt Whitman, who does nothing as nobody ever did it before), – is the presentation of *Der Frieschutz*, Opera by Carl Von Weber.

As Edward Whitley has argued, "it is not entirely clear why Wilkins would cite Whitman's poetry as an example of creative innovation in the context of New York opera," since "writing a poem made up of arias and recitatives hardly seems enough to qualify someone as an innovator in the performing arts."[17] Instead, Whitley notes that Wilkins and the other Pfaff's bohemians sought to build "an image of Whitman as both a critical authority and creative force" in an effort to bolster their own authority as "tastemakers of American judgment against the democratic judgment of the theatergoers."[18] Interestingly enough, however, Whitman's real innovation in the context of opera was a democratic one, consisting of his ability to relocate and to transpose staged art and its voices – particularly operatic ones – in nature, speaking in the language of the common man. In his role as poet-performer, he expands the stage, bringing the players and sounds of opera beyond the performance hall.

While his early exposure to opera in the 1840s began as a vocational necessity, he eventually found himself seeking out performances of his own accord, noting in an 1863 letter written after attending a performance of *Lucrezia Borgia* that "such singing and strong music always give me the greatest pleasure – and so the opera is the only amusement I have gone to, for my own satisfaction, for the last ten years" (WWC, 3:104). During these pivotal decades, Whitman not only discovers in opera a vehicle for transcendence but also an expression of American spirit:

> You listen to this music, and the songs, and choruses – all of the highest range of composition known to the world of melody. [. . .] If you have the true musical feeling in you, from this night you date a new era in your development, and, for the first time, receive your ideas of what the divine art of music really is. [. . .] This is science! This is art! You envy Italy, and almost become an enthusiast; you wish an equal art here, and an equal science and style, underlain by a perfect understanding of American realities, and the appropriateness of our national spirit and body also.[19]

By moving opera out of the confines of the performance halls – where a showdown between America's aristocracy and plutocracy played itself out in a battle for social status and prestige among the young nation's elites,[20] Whitman simultaneously celebrated opera's voices and America's diverse landscape of people and places.

In an August 1851 account of his visit to Castle Garden to see *La Favorita*, Whitman distinguishes himself from the New York socialites: "Come, I will not talk to you as one of the superficial crowd who saunter here because it is a fashion; who take opera glasses with them, and who make you sick with shallow words, upon the sublimest and most spiritual of the arts."[21] The years that Whitman worked on the various editions of *Leaves of Grass* correspond roughly with the building of New York's main opera houses. Although numerous theaters hosted opera performances, the decade after Italian opera's introduction to New York initiated growing interest in building a venue exclusively for opera. The noted librettist Lorenzo Da Ponte, living in New York at the time, declared: "Italian opera presupposed an Italian opera house."[22] With his leadership, a group of subscribers raised the funds to support the New York Italian Opera House in 1833. In the years following, several other opera houses opened, including Palmo's (1844) and Astor Place (1847). The patrons that most visibly embodied Whitman's "superficial crowd," however, were the

social elites who patronized the Academy of Music (1854). Emphasizing
that the Academy provided New York's aristocracy opportunities for both
diversion and public display, Lloyd Morris notes, "Opera was essential to
the fashionable, the socially elect. For where else but in the Academy's
boxes – fortunately so limited in number – could you perform the obliga-
tory rituals of public display? Was not society morally bound to show itself
to the people in full regalia of ball dresses and jewels?"[23] When the nouveau
riche asserted their prominence over the old guard of the academy by
building the Metropolitan Opera House in 1883, they hoped to establish
wealth, not ancestry, as the measure of social status in New York.[24]
By choosing to move the voices of Italian opera outside of the traditional
opera venues, however, Whitman allowed opera to express democratic
values. Instead of becoming embroiled in opera as another form of cultural
consumption, he focuses on the "honied perfection of the human voice,"
noting that "never before [listening to Bettini's singing] did I realize what
an indescribable volume of delight the recesses of the soul can bear from
the sound."[25] As Whitman's "That Music Always Round Me" (1860)
illustrates, he expands the landscapes these operatic voices inhabit: "That
music always round me, unceasing, unbeginning, yet long untaught I did
not hear, / But now the chorus I hear and I am elated, / A tenor, strong,
ascending with power and health, with glad notes of daybreak I hear, /
A soprano at intervals sailing buoyantly over the tops of immense waves"
(LG, 449). As their sounds bounce across waves and sky, the poet acknowledges his ability to translate these notes: "I hear not the volumes of sound
merely, I am moved by the exquisite meanings" (LG, 449). Like an
immigrant assimilated into the new world, Italian opera – through
Whitman's poetry – finds a home in America. No boundaries – whether
time, geography, or space – are sufficient to suppress the transcendent
energy and passion of operatic expression.

Describing himself in "Proud Music of the Storm" (1869) as "a new bard
caroling in the West" (LG, 409), Whitman acknowledges his "obesisan[ce],"
send[ing] his love" to the "Composers! mighty maestros! / And you, sweet
singers of old lands, soprani, tenori, bassi!" (LG, 409). As the poem continues,
the poet explains the process of absorbing the sounds of the opera singers,
allowing himself to serve as the vehicle of transferring and then translating
these sounds into poems for the American people and its diverse landscapes:

> Give me to hold all sounds, (I madly struggling cry,)
> Fill me with all the voices of the universe,
> Endow me with their throbbings, Nature's also,

> The tempests, waters, winds, operas and chants, marches and dances,
> Utter, pour in, for I would take them all! (LG, 409)

At the conclusion of "Proud Music of the Storm," Whitman explains that in searching for "a new rhythmus fitted" for the new nation, he would strive to create "poems bridging the way from Life to Death" (LG, 410), a fitting pursuit for the self-proclaimed "poet of the Body" and "poet of the Soul" (LG, 48). The hybrid art of opera offered Whitman the framework for moving from an embodied voice to a transcendent one – capable of overcoming the limitations of time, space, gender, and class. An operatic voice has "breathing blood within it; the living soul."[26] As the poet-performer, Whitman translates these voices, allowing Americans "of every hue and caste" and "every rank and religion" (LG, 45) to be transported by their sounds.

Notes

1. Walt Whitman, *New York Dissected*, eds. Emory Holloway and Ralph Adimari (New York, NY: Rufus Rockwell Wilson, 1936), 19.
2. Ibid., 22.
3. Lawrence W. Levine, *Highbrow/Lowbrow: The Emergence of Cultural Hierarchy in America* (Cambridge, MA: Harvard University Press, 1988), 86.
4. Carmen Trammell Skaggs, *Overtones of Opera in American Literature from Whitman to Wharton* (Baton Rouge, LA: Louisiana State University Press, 2010), 12.
5. Walt Whitman, *The Gathering of the Forces*, eds. Cleveland Rodgers and John Black, 2 vols. (New York, NY: G. P. Putman's Sons, 1920), 2:347–48.
6. Robert Faner, *Walt Whitman and Opera* (Carbondale, IL: Southern Illinois University Press, 1972), 228.
7. Louise Pound, "Walt Whitman and Italian Music," *American Mercury* 6.21 (1925), 58.
8. Henry A. Kmen, *Music in New Orleans: The Formative Years, 1791–1841* (Baton Rouge, LA: Louisiana State University Press, 1966), vii, 125.
9. Julia Spiegelman, "Walt Whitman and Music," *South Atlantic Quarterly* 41.2 (1942), 171.
10. Ibid., 707.
11. Linda Hutcheon and Michael Hutcheon, *Bodily Charm: Living Opera* (Lincoln, NE: University of Nebraska Press, 2000), 125.
12. Skaggs, *Overtones of Opera*, 18.
13. Walt Whitman, *The Uncollected Poetry and Prose of Walt Whitman*. 2 vols., ed. Emory Holloway (Gloucester, MA: Peter Smith, 1972), 1:256.
14. Michel Poizat, *The Angel's Cry: Beyond the Pleasure Principle in Opera* (Ithaca, NY: Cornell University Press, 1992), 40.

15. Samuel D. Abel, *Opera in the Flesh: Sexuality in Operatic Performance* (Boulder, CO: Westview, 1996), 46.

16. Whitman, *Gathering of the Forces*, 2:352.

17. Edward Whitley, "Whitman, the Antebellum Theater, and the Cultural Authority of the Bohemian Critic," in *Whitman among the Bohemians*, eds. Joanna Levin and Edward Whitley (Iowa City, IA: University of Iowa Press, 2014), 106. Wilkins quoted in Whitley, 106.

18. Ibid., 98–99.

19. Whitman, *New York Dissected*, 22.

20. Allen Churchill, *The Upper Crust: An Informal History of New York's Highest Society* (New Jersey, NJ: Prentice Hall, 1970), 136.

21. Whitman, *Uncollected Poetry and Prose*, 1:256.

22. John Dizikes, *Opera in America: A Cultural History* (New Haven, CT: Yale University Press, 1993), 75.

23. Lloyd Morris, *Incredible New York: High Life and Low Life of the Last Hundred Years* (New York, NY: Random House, 1951), 69.

24. Skaggs, *Overtones of Opera*, 6.

25. Ibid., 257.

26. Whitman, *Uncollected Poetry and Prose*, 1:257.

CHAPTER 12

Performance and Celebrity

David Haven Blake

People commonly think of celebrity as a sign of distinction that sets men and women apart from the crowd. From this perspective, celebrity is a form of exalted individualism, one that signifies self-determination and the prominence that comes from talent, accomplishment, and will. When we think of celebrity as performance, however, we put forward a different set of assumptions and values. Celebrity becomes less an act of self-creation than a set of roles and conventions that individuals and audiences perform. The famous may appear brilliantly self-reliant, but, more than their anonymous counterparts, they collaborate with others in determining who or what they are. In ironic, surprising ways, celebrity intersects with one of the most challenging ideals of American life: how the many can be represented in the one.

Walt Whitman understood the performative aspects of celebrity, and he championed the role that readers played in deciding what was important in their world. "The sum of all known value and respect," he wrote in the poem that he eventually titled "A Song for Occupations," "I add up in you whoever you are." "All doctrines, all politics and civilization exurge from you, / All sculpture and monuments and anything inscribed anywhere are tallied in you" (LG55, 60). Whitman's regard for public approval, a regard that was rooted in the notion of popular sovereignty, led him to tell readers that, without them, "The most renowned poems would be ashes" and "orations and plays would be vacuums" (LG55, 60). But this was not only a constitutional principle to Whitman: it signaled a radically new aesthetic in which the people ratified their cultural representatives in a deeply collaborative relationship. He announced this reasoning in the Preface to the 1855 edition of *Leaves of Grass*: "The proof of a poet is that his country absorbs him as affectionately as he has absorbed it" (LG55, xii). Whitman soon distanced himself from this standard, but the principle behind it would remain: an audience's communion with the artist was central to his performance.

Whitman liked to invoke the concept of sympathy to express the state of being absorbed in another's world. "I am he attesting sympathy," he says in "Song of Myself," one of the many times he uses the word to characterize the poet of *Leaves of Grass* (LG55, 27).[1] The importance of sympathy is a persistent theme in nineteenth-century literature, but even when he was working as a journalist from 1838 to 1849, Whitman put great emphasis on the word. As the editor of the Democratic Party newspaper the *Brooklyn Daily Eagle*, he praised the "curious kind of sympathy" that ties an editor with his readers, suggesting that their "daily communion creates a sort of brotherhood and sisterhood between the two parties."[2] Just as editors adopted the plural pronoun "we" to acknowledge their institutional voice, Whitman later wrote that the exchange between reader and writer depended on "giving up one's attention to another's thoughts."[3] The practice of writing for a regular group of readers filtered into *Leaves of Grass*, helping Whitman think about his individual voice as a communal performance.

Working as a reporter also gave Whitman a remarkable view into the popular culture of his time and its growing emphasis on celebrity as an expression of American democracy. Whitman interviewed the showman P. T. Barnum, admired the theatrical presentation of Brooklyn minister Henry Ward Beecher, and reviewed Dan Rice's circus.[4] With a reporter's access, he saw the ways that artists could become cultural heroes and emblems not simply of individual talent but of democratic pride. He praised the outspoken republican values of the Hutchinson Family Singers when they performed in New York, touting the warm reception of the thirteen brothers and sisters as "the musical embodiment of the American character."[5] According to Bonnie Carr O'Neill, he understood, as a reporter and editor, how newspapers invested "personal feelings in the representation of public figures."[6]

The question for Whitman was how to translate the bustling energy of American popular culture into a new kind of poetry. In the years before *Leaves of Grass*, Whitman had published verse, short stories, and two novels, *Franklin Evans* (1842) and the recently discovered *Life and Adventures of Jack Engle* (1852). None of these works suggested the kind of personal and literary transformation that produced *Leaves of Grass*. Whitman's book existed in a category by itself, and in 1855 many reviewers wondered whether it even qualified as poetry. (Ralph Waldo Emerson reportedly referred to *Leaves of Grass* as a "combination of the *Bhagavad-Gita* and the New York *Herald*."[7]) While Whitman hoped to be affectionately absorbed by the nation, his book plainly announced that he would not follow the "rhymesters" of the period in bowing to popular taste (PW, 2:412). Whitman's aesthetic innovations made his quest for an audience difficult, for he was neither satisfied with the support of the avant-garde nor eager to bend his talents toward a mass audience.[8] As the poet later suggested, the proof of a poet would be "sternly deferr'd" until the public was ready for his work (LG, 351).

The antebellum United States provided many examples of how artistic celebrity could work. Whitman's frequent trips to lower Manhattan theaters brought him in contact with nationally celebrated actors such as Junius Brutus Booth and Edwin Forrest, and as he recounted in *November Boughs* (1888), he had vivid memories of the crowds that thunderously greeted these populist heroes (PW, 2:595). Whitman also encountered numerous plays about the Bowery b'hoys who inhabited lower Manhattan – young, urban rowdies whose tough, carefree attitude appealed to him as a distinctly American type. These young men helped shape Whitman's appearance in the 1855 edition of *Leaves of Grass* as a swaggering, working-class hero. Though Whitman himself did not adopt the b'hoys' highly stylized appearance (his author portrait portrays a self-assured common laborer), he announces his name in "Song of Myself" as "Walt Whitman, an American, one of the roughs" (LG55, 29).

Like many antebellum men and women, Whitman was also attracted to oratory as a democratic art, and he admired the power and grace of speakers such as New Hampshire senator Daniel Webster and abolitionist Lucretia Mott. Whitman himself had once hoped to join the flourishing lyceum circuit and become a nationally recognized lecturer but, as C. Carroll Hollis has shown, he instead incorporated the scene and style of nineteenth-century oratory into his poems.[9] The early editions of *Leaves of Grass* are filled with moments in which the poet addresses his audience as if they were assembled before him. "A call in the midst of the crowd," he announces in "Song of Myself," "My own voice, orotund sweeping and final" (LG55, 46). In "I Sing the Body Electric," he takes over for a slave auctioneer to declaim the beautiful humanity of the African American bodies before him. In "Song of the Open Road," he announces "Allons!" or "Let us go!" to the army of travellers following him (LG, 154). With tremendous skill, Whitman balances these scenes of public address with the highly personalized, seemingly intimate address that pervaded the works of antebellum celebrity authors such as Fanny Fern. "Are you the new person drawn toward me?" he asks in an 1860 "Calamus" poem. As if readers should regard the illusions of fame with skepticism, he cautions,

"To begin with, take warning, I am surely far different from what you suppose" (LG, 123).

For Whitman, the purest form of oratory was song, a form of expression he praised in "I Hear America Singing" as being as varied as it was unifying to the nation. But Whitman was also attracted to virtuosic performances. He regularly attended the opera and lovingly admired the Italian singer Marietta Alboni whom he praised in "Proud Music of the Storm" as "The lustrious orb, Venus contralto," and "Sister of loftiest gods" (LG, 407). Opera, as numerous scholars have demonstrated, had a tremendous impact on Whitman's work.[10] In "Out of the Cradle Endlessly Rocking," the poet recounts a boyhood experience of hearing a mockingbird's aria-like laments for its lost love which effectively turn the boy into a singer himself:

> O you singer solitary, singing by yourself, projecting me,
> O solitary me listening, never more shall I cease perpetuating you,
> Never more shall I escape, never more the reverberations,
> Never more the cries of unsatisfied love be absent from me,
> Never again leave me to be the peaceful child I was before what
>   there in the night,
> By the sea under the yellow and sagging moon,
> The messenger there arous'd, the fire, the sweet hell within,
> The unknown want, the destiny of me.   (LG, 252)

With its extraordinary musicality, the poem helped identify *Leaves of Grass* with the transformative power of song.

The emerging art of photography played the most significant role in Whitman's conception of celebrity. Even as a young reporter, Whitman understood the daguerreotype's ability to capture the true essence of individuals, while also allowing them to create and promote new personas. The portraits – some of which Whitman included in *Leaves of Grass* – are among the most iconic images in US literature. From the author portraits Mathew Brady took in Washington, DC, to the exquisite, old-age studies taken in Camden, New Jersey, these images conveyed the message of Whitman's "So Long!" that what readers held in their hands was a man, not a book.[11] Photography provided a visual complement to Whitman's claim in "To a Historian" to be the "Chanter of Personality," one of the cornerstones of American democracy (LG, 4).

It makes sense that photography and popular music would be vehicles of fame in the nineteenth-century United States. What may surprise some readers, however, is how deeply enmeshed poetry was in this emergent culture of celebrity. Although Whitman himself struggled to find an audience, some of his contemporaries experienced the public embrace that *Leaves of Grass* vividly imagined. His performance of celebrity is best understood alongside the passion many nineteenth-century Americans had for poetry. Poems appeared in magazines, newspapers, and trade journals. Advertisers used verse to attract customers, sometimes reprinting the work of famous authors and, other times, composing their own rhymes. Readers copied out passages from their favorite poems in diaries, letters, and commonplace books. They exchanged handwritten poems as gifts and tokens of affection, as Emily Dickinson did. For many of Whitman's contemporaries, the circulation of poetry was a hallmark of both public and private life.

The most famous poet of Whitman's era was Henry Wadsworth Longfellow, who sold over 285,000 books of lyric, ballad, and narrative poetry between 1839 and 1858.[12] A professor of languages at Harvard University, Longfellow moved with ease among American and European cultural elites who praised his erudition, character, and sentiment. Longfellow's personal stature appealed to middle-class Americans who saw in his poems the kind of uplifting spiritual message they associated with self-improvement. Images of Longfellow and his family circulated around the nation, leading many readers to think they knew him personally. According to Christoph Irmscher, the poet received over 1,300 written requests for autographs and letters from over 6,200 correspondents.[13] Longfellow's home, Craigie House, had been the Boston headquarters of General George Washington during the Revolutionary War and was widely showcased in books and magazines. The poet found so many visitors on his doorstep that he began to keep a box of pre-signed autographs on the mantelpiece.

In old age, Whitman criticized Longfellow for writing "the little songs of the masses." Longfellow was "no revolutionaire," he complained, and he "never broke new paths" (WWC, 3:24). The comments capture the complexity of Whitman's aspirations, for, as a great paean to American democracy, *Leaves of Grass* challenged popular thinking in a way that *The Song of Hiawatha* (1855) or *The Seaside and the Fireside* (1849–50) did not. Faced with a relatively indifferent public, Whitman turned to numerous acts of self-advertisement. He anonymously reviewed his own work; he exaggerated details about his book sales; he created scandals to get his name in the newspapers. "The public is a thick-skinned beast," he once told William Roscoe Thayer, "and you have to keep whacking away at its hide to let it know you're there."[14] While Longfellow silently wearied of his followers, Whitman tried to create them.

Longfellow, however, was not alone in attracting readers from around the country. Research into nineteenth-century celebrity culture has shown that many poets inspired what we might now call fan communities.[15] Like Longfellow, for example, Lydia Sigourney received several thousand letters from readers who associated her fame not with detachment but intimacy. To men and women alike, her regular appearance in the newspapers and the beloved quality of her verse turned her into a public figure whom they might approach with a request for a personal poem or letter.[16] Edgar Allan Poe's "The Raven" received extraordinary popular and critical attention. (Whitman met Poe in the mid-1840s, and, as editor of the *Daily Eagle*, he published an unsigned parody of "The Raven.")[17] Poe attracted a coterie of admirers who claimed to communicate with his spirit after his death in 1849. As Eliza Richards has explained, the group's mesmeric contact with Poe helped them form a "mystic kinship system" that stretched up and down the Atlantic seaboard.[18] In poems and letters to each other, the women conveyed the messages Poe seemingly sent them from the spirit world, often incorporating key symbols and techniques from his work into their own poems.

The Quaker poet John Greenleaf Whittier inspired his own group of readers. Michael C. Cohen has described a community of Pennsylvania abolitionists who painstakingly created two handwritten volumes containing poems that they had written, shared, copied, parodied, clipped from newspapers, and altered as if they were "fragments from the unpublished writings" of Whittier, their friend and fellow resident.[19] These volumes suggest a peculiarly collaborative approach to literary fame, as they use the author's works as a frame for the community's own creative endeavors. Borrowing a term from the media theorist Henry Jenkins, we might see the Poe and Whittier fans as engaging in forms of "textual poaching" in that they appropriate the work of the famous author for their own purposes.[20] Another term comes from Ellen Gruber Garvey, who describes this practice as "textual gleaning," thus implying that these reader-fans were harvesting the surplus meaning of the original works.[21]

The greatest influence on Whitman's conception of literary celebrity was Ralph Waldo Emerson, the poet, lecturer, and essayist whom Whitman addressed as "Dear Master" in the letter he appended to the 1856 edition of *Leaves of Grass*. Emerson achieved considerable fame during his lifetime, and, although he was a shy and uncharismatic presence at the podium, his lecture tours were highly successful public events that brought reviews, interviews, features, and discussion in the local newspapers. As Mary Kupiec Cayton has demonstrated, audiences were especially interested in Emerson's personality, and reporters happily obliged their readers with descriptions of his awkward appearance. "He was by turns bashful, ungraceful, embarrassed, and half-apologetic, but each designation only added to his mystique as an uncalculating soul of pure wisdom and character."[22] Emerson inhabited a peculiar role on the lyceum circuit in that his discomfort with performance became a sign of both his renown and integrity.

Bonnie Carr O'Neill has argued that the experience of celebrity deeply challenged Emerson's belief in self-reliance, noting that there is a significant tension between the culture's "interest in persons, particularly celebrities, and the social conformity that Emerson consistently urges his readers to shun."[23] Emerson found the collaborative aspects of celebrity troubling. As O'Neill explains, Emerson's work "consistently upholds the ideal of a self forged in and refreshed by privacy through solitary reflection and study," and thus he "rejects the idea that effective self-making can occur in public."[24] Celebrity for Emerson posed the intellectual problem of how to maintain one's independence from the crowd, even as that crowd was engaged in a constant "negotiation over the meaning of the [celebrity] persona."[25]

There is considerable evidence that Whitman personally felt the need for public affirmation in a way that Emerson did not. As he labored over the first edition of *Leaves of Grass*, he recorded in a notebook his profound dependence on public affirmations of his personality:

> I should think poorly of myself if I should be even a few days with any community either of sane or insane people, and not make them convinced, whether they acknowledged it or not, of my truth, my sympathy, and my dignity. – I should be certain enough that those attributes were not in me.[26]

Whereas the famous Emerson distrusted public affirmations of self, Whitman periodically questioned whether the self could exist outside its communal display. Haunted by feelings of loneliness and inadequacy, the poet populated the early editions of *Leaves of Grass* with images of eager readers and ecstatic crowds. With tremendous skill, he cultivated an imagined public of readers even as he endeavored to make his name better known.

In his last decades, Whitman mounted a series of publicity stunts that exaggerated the antagonism *Leaves of Grass* had received from critics, the press, and government officials.[27] Rather than boast of his popularity, he tried to attract audiences by depicting himself as a pioneer who had overcome extraordinary hostility in his quest for a democratic art. The change in tactics served the poet well, as readers on both sides of the Atlantic Ocean came to his defense. Played out in the international press, the controversies about Whitman's poverty and neglect inspired groups of admirers in both England and the United States, and visitors from around the world came to his home in Camden, New Jersey. Like many nineteenth-century celebrities, Whitman was soon hounded by what he called the "Autograph Monster," and, as Eric Conrad has shown, he cleverly promoted *Leaves of Grass* by selling signed photographs of himself to support a local orphanage.[28] Whitman's long-time interest in becoming a lecturer came to fruition when he began offering a series of lectures on the anniversary of Abraham Lincoln's death. While American audiences failed to respond to the swaggering populist of 1855, they warmly gathered around Whitman as a smiling patriarch, the good gray poet who had nursed Union soldiers in the Civil War and then elegized the fallen president.

Whitman took this sense of controversy and grievance into his final years, incorporating it into the story of *Leaves of Grass* in the way that he had regularly overstated the book's success in the 1850s. Four years before his death in 1892, he seemed satisfied with the results. "In spite of the howl and slander of the opposition," he told his friend Horace Traubel, "the *Leaves* got out after all" and "once out went along – stormily, fiercely, rocked and shaken" until, as if recognized by an old friend, the book was "within hail" of the audience it had been waiting for all along (WWC, 1:6).

Notes

1. Jane Bennett, "Whitman's Sympathies," *Political Research Quarterly* 69.3 (2016), 607–20. A good history of sympathy in relation to nineteenth-century celebrity is Thomas N. Baker, *Sentiment and Celebrity: Nathaniel Parker Willis and the Trials of Literary Fame* (New York, NY: Oxford University Press, 1998).

2. "Ourselves and the 'Eagle,'" *Brooklyn Daily Eagle* (Brooklyn, NY), June 1, 1846, in Journ., 1:391.

3. "A Merry Christmas," *Brooklyn Daily Eagle* (Brooklyn, NY), December 24, 1847, 2.

4. On P. T. Barnum, see Loving, 165. On Henry Ward Beecher, see Reynolds, 39–40. On Whitman and Dan Rice, see David Carlyon, *Dan Rice: The Most Famous Man You've Never Heard Of* (New York, NY: Public Affairs, 2001), 204–05.

5. "The Hutchinson Family," *Daily Plebeian* (New York, NY), December 4, 1843, in Journ. 1:176.

6. Bonnie Carr O'Neill, "The Personal Public Sphere of Whitman's 1840s Journalism," *PMLA* 126.4 (October 2011), 984.

7. The anecdote comes from Bliss Perry, *Walt Whitman* (New York, NY: Houghton-Mifflin, 1904), 276.

8. On Whitman's relation to the bohemian writers and artists who gathered at Pfaff's beer cellar see Joanna Levin and Edward Whitley, eds., *Whitman among the Bohemians* (Iowa City, IA: University of Iowa Press, 2014).

9. C. Carroll Hollis, *Language and Style in Leaves of Grass* (Baton Rouge, LA: Louisiana State University Press, 1983), 94–95.

10. On Whitman and opera, see Carmen Trammell Skaggs, *Overtones of Opera in American Literature from Whitman to Wharton* (Baton Rouge, LA: Louisiana State University Press, 2010), 13–33; and Lawrence Kramer, *After the Lovedeath: Sexual Violence and the Making of Culture* (Berkeley, CA: University of California Press, 1997), 55–61.

11. "This is no book, / Who touches this, touches a man," Whitman wrote in the 1860 version of "So long!" (LG60, 455).

12. Charles C. Calhoun, *Longfellow: A Rediscovered Life* (Boston, MA: Beacon, 2004), 198–99.

13. Christoph Irmscher, *Longfellow Redux* (Urbana and Chicago, IL: University of Illinois Press, 2006), 24.

14. William Roscoe Thayer, "Personal Recollections of Walt Whitman," in *Whitman in His Own Time*, ed. Joel Myerson (Detroit, MI: Omnigraphics, 1991), 304.

15. David Haven Blake, "When Readers Become Fans: Nineteenth-Century American Poetry as a Fan Activity," *American Studies* 52.1 (2012), 99–122.

16. Lydia Howard Sigourney, *Letters of Life* (New York, NY: D. Appleton, 1868), 369–77.

17. Whitman describes meeting Poe in the *Specimen Days* essay "Broadway Sights" (PW, 2:17). The Poe parody "A Jig in Prose" can be found in the *Brooklyn Daily Eagle* (Brooklyn, NY), January 11, 1848, 1.

18. Eliza Richards, *Gender and the Poetics of Reception in Poe's Circle* (New York, NY: Cambridge University Press, 2004), 130–31.

19. Michael C. Cohen, *The Social Lives of Poems in Nineteenth-Century America* (Philadelphia, PA: University of Pennsylvania Press, 2015), 80–88.

20. Henry Jenkins, *Textual Poachers: Television Fans and Participatory Culture* (New York, NY: Routledge, 1992).

21. Ellen Gruber Garvey, "Scizzoring and Scrapbooks: Nineteenth-Century Reading, Remaking, and Recirculating" in *New Media, 1740–1915*, eds. Lisa Gitleman and Geoffrey B. Pingree (Cambridge, MA: MIT Press, 2004), 207–08.

22. Mary Kupiec Cayton, "The Making of an American Prophet: Emerson, His Audiences, and the Rise of the Culture Industry in Nineteenth-Century America," *American Historical Review* 92.3 (June 1987), 616. See also Joel Myerson and Ronald A. Bosco, eds., *Emerson in His Own Time* (Iowa City, IA: University of Iowa Press, 2003), xvii.

23. Bonnie Carr O'Neill, "'The Best of Me is There': Emerson as Lecturer and Celebrity," *American Literature* 80.4 (December 2008), 741.

24. Bonnie Carr O'Neill, "Fame," in *Ralph Waldo Emerson in Context*, ed. Wesley T. Mott (New York, NY: Cambridge University Press, 2014), 252.

25. O'Neill, "The Personal Public Sphere," 991.

26. See David Haven Blake, *Walt Whitman and the Culture of American Celebrity* (New Haven, CT: Yale University Press, 2006), 68.

27. See Robert Scholnick, "The Selling of the 'Author's Edition': Whitman, O'Connor, and the *West Jersey Press* Affair," *Walt Whitman Review* 23 (March 1977), 3–23.

28. Eric Conrad, "'Anything honest to sell books': Walt Whitman and the Autograph Monster," *Walt Whitman Quarterly Review* 32.4 (2015), 193–94.

CHAPTER 13

Visual Arts and Photography

Ruth L. Bohan

As an amalgam of the human and the technological, photography has occupied a central position in investigations into the life and poetry of Walt Whitman. Scholars, detecting a creative synergy between the modern poet and the modern medium of photography, have long seized on photography as the visual medium most closely allied with the poet and his verse. Significantly slower to attract scholarly attention has been the poet's relationships with and passion for the more traditional arts of painting, sculpture, and printmaking. Whitman's many friendships with artists and his scrutiny of a broad range of visual modes of representation, including book and magazine illustration and the exhibition format itself, are providing fruitful new avenues of investigation into the visual contexts of Whitman's life and verse. So, too, are studies of Whitman's presence among a diverse group of modernist artists active internationally after the poet's death.

Whitman's rise as a poet paralleled the rise of photography in America. Ed Folsom, the foremost investigator of Whitman's longstanding association with the medium, writes persuasively that "the key to Whitman's unwavering devotion to photography" stemmed from the medium's faithful representation of the material world in all its confusion and clutter. For Whitman, Folsom argues, "photography was the harbinger of a new democratic art, an art that would not exclude on the basis of preconceived notions of what was vital."[1] Whitman was particularly attracted by photography's potential as a viable and affordable means of representing one's likeness and exploring issues of identity, the hallmark of his verse. Beginning in the 1840s and continuing up to his death in 1892, Whitman sat for some 130 photographic portraits. In doing so he availed himself of the knowledge and friendship of many of this country's leading professional photographers. One of his favorites was Gabriel Harrison, the Brooklyn daguerreotypist who took the unorthodox representation with which Whitman introduced himself to his readers in the 1855 *Leaves of*

Grass. Reams have been written about this provocative portrait, which defied the traditional portrayal of authors as noble and refined members of the nation's intellectual elite. Whitman instead cast himself as "one of the roughs" (LG55, 29), a working-class loafer who wears his hat "as I please indoors or out" (LG, 47). Several reviewers, including the poet himself in a number of unsigned reviews, offered their assessment of the image's multiple unorthodoxies. One found the image, like the book, "rough, uncouth, vulgar"; another likened the pose to "an all-pervading atmosphere of Yankee-doodle." Whitman likened the book to "a reproduction of the author," noting, "His name is not on the frontispiece, but his portrait, half length, is."[2]

Over the years Whitman would deploy a range of multiple and competing representations of himself on the pages of *Leaves of Grass.* These images not only mapped his changing appearance over time, but visually acknowledged the multiple selves that populated the text.[3] For Folsom, the images constituted part of the poet's democratic poetics in allowing him "to conceive of his own life as a kind of democratic crowd, a contradictory series of separate selves joined mysteriously into an overarching unity."[4] All but one of the images derived from photographs; the one outlier was an engraving based on a painting by his friend Charles Hine chosen for the much-heralded 1860 edition. Later editions, beginning with the 1876 *Leaves,* expanded the visual offerings beyond the frontispiece, with select images functioning in visual dialogue with individual poems. One such image (based on a photograph by George C. Potter) was the wood engraving by Whitman's friend, the acclaimed British wood engraver, William J. Linton, which appeared opposite "The Wound-Dresser" in the "Drum-Taps" sequence where it personalized the poem's opening lines: "An old man bending I come among new faces, / [...] / Now [to] be witness again" (LG, 308–9).

Mathew Brady and Alexander Gardner made numerous bust and half-length photographs of the poet during his extended residency in the nation's capital. In New York, Boston, and Philadelphia Whitman sat for an array of photographers, including such well-known celebrity photographers as G. Frank Pearsall, William Kurtz, Napoleon Sarony, and George C. Cox, among others. Cox's "Laughing Philosopher" image, taken following the poet's 1887 New York Lincoln Lecture, was one of several autographed images sold to relieve Whitman's dire financial straits late in life. Although Whitman was rarely photographed with others, several of these, none of which were published during the poet's lifetime, show him in the company of his young male friends. Folsom has provocatively labeled these "Whitman's Calamus Photographs" and proposes that they construct the "hieroglyphs of an emerging sign system of male-male desire."[5] Toward the end of his life, as he contemplated the piles of photographs littering the floor of his Camden home, Whitman expressed concern that he had been "photographed to confusion" (WWC, 2:454). "I meet new Walt Whitmans every day," he lamented. "There are a dozen of me afloat. I don't know which Walt Whitman I am" (WWC, 1:108). An unrealized project inaugurated by Whitman and his friends toward the end of his life was to compile a volume of his most significant photographs. That project, in greatly expanded form, has finally been realized by the annotated display of all the known Whitman photographs on the *Walt Whitman Archive*.

The critical focus on Whitman and photography has often obscured the poet's interest in the more traditional arts of painting and sculpture. Throughout his life and especially during the very years he was composing the first edition of *Leaves of Grass* Whitman associated with all manner of artists, not just photographers. Two of his closest associates during these years were genre painter William Sidney Mount and sculptor Henry Kirke Brown, in whose studio Whitman fondly declared himself "one among the wellbeloved stonecutters" (LG, 714). Much like his friend, poet, editor, and art patron William Cullen Bryant, Whitman regularly visited artists in their studios, studied their works at the galleries of the National Academy of Design and the American Art Union, wrote thoughtful reviews in the local press, and was invited to give the opening address at the artist-run Brooklyn Art Union.

In his early writings on art, Whitman allied himself with mainstream reformers who sought to stimulate a native art tradition independent of Europe. He favored paintings that approached their subjects with little or no flourish and dismissed the "coldly correct" paintings of the conservative artists of his day.[6] He wrote of spending "long half hours" gazing into the face of Christ in Ary Sheffer's *The Dead Christ*,[7] and proclaimed himself so taken with the "rich and electric" portraits of Charles Elliott, who would later paint his portrait, that he "then dreamed of them at night."[8] Whitman was also swayed by the landscapes of his friend Jesse Talbot and by the Indian collection of George Catlin, which he urged the government to purchase. He advocated strongly for the spread of free art exhibitions and for the moral and aesthetic benefits of having art in the home, whether "tasty prints [or] cheap casts of statuary" (Journ., 1:279). One of Whitman's favorite artists was the French Barbizon painter Jean-François Millet, whose sympathetic paintings of French peasants achieved widespread acclaim and popularity, especially in Boston following the Civil War. "The Leaves are really only Millet in another form," Whitman asserted, "they are the Millet that Walt Whitman has succeeded in putting into words" (WWC, 1:7).

Whitman moved easily between discussions of painting and photography in his journalistic writings, not favoring one over the other but valuing each for their attention to detail and commitment to portraiture. An 1846 review of an exhibition of portraits at Plumbe's daguerreotype gallery that is frequently cited as supporting Whitman's preference for photography actually praises both painting and photography. After describing his fascination with the "thousand human histories, involved in those daguerreotypes" displayed in the gallery, he shifts the discussion to the "peculiar influence [. . .] possessed by the *eye* of a wellpainted miniature or portrait," detecting in such works "a sort of magnetism." Claiming to have miniatures "in our possession, which we have often held, and gazed upon the eyes in [. . .] for the half-hour!" Whitman concludes with the assertion that "An electric chain seems to vibrate, as it were, between our brain and him or her preserved there so well by the limner's cunning" (Journ., 1:449).

Whitman's interest in the visual arts extended well beyond his enthusiasm for the fine arts and photography to include the popular arts and especially the art of book and magazine illustration. He noted in particular "The popular tastes and employments taking precedence in poems or anywhere" (LG, 218). Whitman strengthened his commitment to the popular arts during his association with the bohemian community at Pfaff's beer cellar, which counted among its regulars some of the leading comic illustrators of the period, including Thomas Nast, Frank Henry Temple Bellew, and Edward Mullen. In such a community Whitman himself became the focus of the artists' pen, including in a number of unsigned and seemingly impromptu sketches inscribed directly on the pages of his notebook. A major aspect of his appeal was that Whitman projected in his person and his verse the qualities, confusions, and ambiguities of the bohemian assault on bourgeois values. At the hands of his bohemian colleagues Whitman figured prominently in a series of verbal and visual assaults on the marginalized and sexually ambivalent figure of the counter jumper. One of the drawings, attributed to Mullen, framed the caricature of the poet with the distinctive leaf of the calamus plant. The visual appearance of Whitman's coded symbol of "manly attachment" (LG, 113) strongly implies that Whitman shared his sexualized use of the term with his Pfaffian friends a full two months prior to its introduction in the 1860 *Leaves*.[9]

Scholars have attributed the striking visual character of Whitman's verse in no small measure to his familiarity with the visual arts and photography. Miles Orvell, who aptly characterized Whitman as an "enormous cultural sponge" and declared the 1855 frontispiece "symptomatic of the visual orientation of *Leaves of Grass*," stressed the significance of the camera's "concrete picturing of reality" on Whitman's visualist poetics.[10] Ed Folsom has effectively argued that one of the original poems in the 1855 *Leaves*, later called "Faces," "may well derive from Whitman's frequent tours of New York daguerreotype galleries."[11] The poem, which chronicles the democratic spectacle of faces Whitman encountered on his daily strolls through the streets of New York, reenacts in the out of doors the "legion of human faces" Whitman admired on the walls of Plumbe's daguerreotype gallery (Journ., 1:449). Folsom also makes a strong case for the importance of the Civil War photographs of Mathew Brady and Alexander Gardner in shaping Whitman's understanding and portrayal of the war and its aftermath in both *Leaves of Grass* and *Specimen Days* (1882).

F. O. Matthiessen in *American Renaissance* (1941) was the first critic to articulate a connection between Whitman's verse and the realist tendencies of mid-nineteenth-century American painting. Whitman shared with the rising number of genre and portrait painters whose works filled the New York galleries an abiding commitment to recording with precision and immediacy the textures, events, and look of everyday American life. Scholars have long acknowledged striking similarities between the passage in "Song of Myself" about the marriage of the trapper and his Indian bride (LG, 37) and one of several versions of Baltimore artist Alfred Jacob Miller's painting, "The Trapper's Bride." Scholars have also identified passages which recall specific scenes in the paintings of Missouri artist George Caleb Bingham and Whitman's friend, the landscape artist Jesse Talbot. Whitman gained valuable knowledge about Indians through his study of George Catlin's Indian Gallery and in the late poem "Yonnondio" asserted the belief, which he shared with Catlin, that "unlimn'd they disappear" (LG, 524).

Whitman's language reveals and reinforces his absorption in the visual arts culture of nineteenth-century America. In one of his unsigned reviews of the 1855 *Leaves* he graphically declared the "contents of the book [...] a daguerreotype of his inner being"[12] and later hailed the volume as "my definitive *carte de visite* to the coming generations of the New World" (LG, 562). He literally becomes the artist in a section of "Song of Myself," employing the technical language of art to emphasize his role as artistic creator over that of passive observer. Thus he speaks of "Lithographing

Kronos," of "driving the mallet and chisel," and "In my portfolio placing
Manito loose, Allah on a leaf, the crucifix engraved" (LG, 75). In "Out
from behind This Mask" he acknowledges the engraver's skill with his
specialized tool to construct "These burin'd eyes, flashing to you to pass to
future time" (LG, 382). In his prose writing Whitman entitled a series of
articles in the *New York Leader* "City Photographs," then broadened the
media reference by signing them Velsor Brush. The name's painterly
implications recall Washington Irving's earlier trans-genre invention,
Geoffrey Crayon, a connection overlooked by scholars focused primarily
on identifying its connection to Whitman's ancestors, Louisa Van Velsor
and Hannah Brush.

Whitman's catalogs have long impressed scholars with their striking
visuality. Graham Clarke describes Whitman as assuming the role of
"photographer/poet," with *Leaves* becoming "an album (a catalogue) of
photographic images held together through his compulsive presence."[13]
For Orvell the catalogs represent "the literary equivalent of the quick
sketch." He also finds a constructive analogy between the catalogs and
the exhibition practices of the day. If "the camera provided the foundation
for Whitman's way of looking at the world," he writes, "the exhibition hall,
in all of its various forms, provided a model for the structure of the long
poem Whitman never stopped writing."[14] Works in nineteenth-century
exhibitions were hung not in a single horizontal line as today but were
dispersed liberally across the wall's entire surface, considerably thickening
the experience and creating a sense of being immersed in art from all sides.
"What a spectacle!" Whitman exclaimed in the thrall of Plumbe's daguerreotype gallery. "In whatever direction you turn your peering gaze, you see
naught but human faces! There they stretch, from floor to ceiling –
hundreds of them" (Journ., 1:449). Whitman's first excursion into the
gallery trope was the poem "Pictures," which adopted the then-popular
conceit of representing the imagination as a picture gallery of the mind.
Here and in the catalogs in *Leaves of Grass* the range and type of images,
with their broad focus on genre, historical, imaginary, and mythological
subjects, approach the range of works common in the fine arts exhibitions
of Whitman's day. In recognition of this similarity, Whitman's friend the
naturalist John Burroughs termed the catalogs "one line genre word
paintings" and judged "every line [. . .] a picture."[15]

During the last decade of his life Whitman attracted a steady stream
of artists intent on painting, sculpting, and photographing his
likeness. The artists included the noted academic painter John White
Alexander, Herbert Gilchrist (the son of British writer Anne Gilchrist),

Figure 13.1 Thomas Eakins, *Walt Whitman* (1887–88). Courtesy of the Pennsylvania
Academy of the Fine Arts.

the minister-turned-sculptor Sidney Morse, and the Philadelphia portrai-
tist Thomas Eakins. Alexander's idealized rendering of the poet
(Metropolitan Museum of Art) corroborated the mythologizing attempts
of Richard Maurice Bucke and others to cast the poet as an aging
prophet.[16] Far more anchored in the everyday realities of Whitman's life
were Gilchrist's several oil portraits of the poet. But Gilchrist's deep-seated
commitment to the conservative ranks of his profession denied him the
support of Whitman and his friends. "Herbert is determined to make me
the conventional, proper old man," Whitman intoned: "his picture is very
benevolent, to be sure: but the Walt Whitman of that picture lacks guts"
(WWC, 1:153–54). Not so with the little known Sidney Morse, whose naïve
and crudely finished sculptures struck Whitman as evocative visual tropes
for his own rough edges and unconventionality. As he noted: "I am not
looking for art: I am after spiritual expression" (WWC, 2:460).

Whitman expressed mixed feelings about Thomas Eakins' seated portrait (Figure 13.1, Pennsylvania Academy of the Fine Arts) which Horace

Traubel likened to "a rubicund sailor [...] about to tell a story" (WWC, 7:42). "Of all the portraits of me made by artists I like Eakins's best," Whitman noted. "It is not perfect but it comes nearest being me" (WWC, 1:131). Eakins went on to produce portraits of several of Whitman's friends and to paint *The Concert Singer* (Philadelphia Museum of Art), formerly known as *The Singer*, which weaves a potent tribute to Whitman through the person of Weda Cook, a young Camden singer who often sang for Whitman. Together with his colleague, the sculptor Samuel Murray, who assisted him in the making of Whitman's death mask, Eakins also produced some of the most poignant photographic portraits of the aging poet in the months before his death. In his late years in conversations with Horace Traubel Whitman often expressed greater sympathy for photography than for painting, noting, "I'd rather have a good photo than a bad oil: I am getting more and more in spirit with the best photographs, which are in fact works of art" (WWC, 4:434).

Eakins shared Whitman's interest in the body, particularly the nude body, and both men recorded in their respective arts their personal encounters with nature in the nude. The painting *Swimming*, 1885 (Amon Carter Museum), Eakins' highly regarded tribute to the male body and comradeship, derives from just such experience. Scholars have long proposed that Eakins filtered the scene through the enlarging lens of Whitman's poetry. In "Whitman's Calamus Photographs" Folsom further posits that, sometime before Whitman posed for his own portrait, he posed in the nude as part of Eakins's "naked series" of photographs. Eakins' posthumous inclusion of Whitman seated in the all-male arena immediately above the nearly nude male boxer in *Between Rounds*, 1899 (Philadelphia Museum of Art) seems an artful reenactment of the painter's inclusion of himself surrounded by a similarly all-male audience and peering down on the nearly nude body of the male patient in *The Gross Clinic* some twenty years before. Whitman displayed a print of *The Gross Clinic*, given to him by Eakins, in the parlor in his Camden home.

Whitman's appeal among artists continued to resonate long after the poet's death. As I argued in *Looking into Walt Whitman: American Art 1850–1920*, the multifaceted nature of Whitman's verse and especially the pervasiveness of its emphasis on self-discovery galvanized the attention of a broad range of early twentieth-century modernist artists. Whitman nurtured and encouraged artists internationally to move beyond the long-held conventions of their profession and to experiment instead with new ways of seeing and experiencing the world. Across a range of modernist practices, extending from the vibrant, expressionist landscape paintings of

Marsden Hartley to Italian immigrant artist Joseph Stella's mystical-technological representations of the Brooklyn Bridge, artists absorbed the poet into the form and fiber of their art.[17] In doing so their art significantly expands the visual contexts of Whitman's verse.

Notes

1. Ed Folsom, *Walt Whitman's Native Representations* (New York, NY: Cambridge University Press, 1994), 102.
2. Kenneth M. Price, ed., *Walt Whitman: The Contemporary Reviews* (New York, NY: Cambridge University Press, 1996), 43, 49, 18.
3. Ruth L. Bohan, *Looking into Walt Whitman: American Art, 1850–1920* (University Park, PA: The Pennsylvania State University Press, 2006), 31.
4. Folsom, *Walt Whitman's Native Representations*, 172.
5. Folsom, "Whitman's Calamus Photographs," in *Breaking Bounds: Whitman and American Cultural Studies*, eds. Betsy Erkkila and Jay Grossman (New York, NY: Oxford University Press, 1996), 206.
6. W[alt] W[hitman], "An Hour at the Academy of Design," *Sunday Dispatch* (New York, NY), April 25, 1852, in Wendy J. Katz, "Previously Undocumented Art Criticism by Walt Whitman," *Walt Whitman Quarterly Review* 32.4 (Spring 2015), 224.
7. Paumanok, "About Some Matters Nearer Home," in *The Historic Whitman*, ed. James Rubin (University Park, PA: The Pennsylvania University Press, 1973), 339.
8. W[alt] W[hitman], "An Hour Among the Portraits," *Evening Star* (Brooklyn, NY), June 7, 1853, 2:2.
9. Ruth L. Bohan, "Whitman and the 'Picture-Makers,'" in *Whitman among the Bohemians*, eds. Joanna Levin and Edward Whitley (Iowa City, IA: University of Iowa Press, 2014), 136.
10. Miles Orvell, *The Real Thing: Imitation and Authenticity in American Culture, 1880–1940* (Chapel Hill, NC: The University of North Carolina Press, 1989), 4, 9, 6.
11. Folsom, *Walt Whitman's Native Representations*, 136.
12. Price, *Walt Whitman: The Contemporary Reviews*, 18.
13. Graham Clarke, "'To emanate a look': Whitman, Photography and the Spectacle of Self," in *American Literary Landscapes: The Fiction and the Fact*, eds. Ian F. A. Bell and D. K. Adams (London: Vision Press; New York, NY: St. Martin's Press, 1989), 82.
14. Orvell, *The Real Thing*, 20, 5.
15. John Burroughs, *The Writings of John Burroughs, vol. 10, Whitman: A Study* (Boston, MA: Houghton Mifflin, 1904), 143, 139.
16. Bohan, *Looking into Walt Whitman*, 94.
17. Bohan, *Looking into Walt Whitman*, 8.

CHAPTER 14

Erotica

Paul Erickson

William Sanger's *History of Prostitution* (1858) gives one of the clearest descriptions available of how sexually explicit printed materials were sold on the streets of antebellum New York: "Boys and young men may be found loitering at all hours round hotels, steam-boat docks, rail-road depots, and other public places, ostensibly selling newspapers or pamphlets, but secretly offering vile, lecherous publications."[1] This passage also highlights a belief that was common among urban observers of the time: public spaces in the city, especially hotel lobbies and ferry landings, were the primary sites of the retail smut trade.

Sanger's study of prostitution in New York appeared midway between the publication of the second and third editions of Walt Whitman's *Leaves of Grass* in 1856 and 1860, a period when he would change a piece called "Sun-Down Poem" into "Crossing Brooklyn Ferry," which became one of his best-known poems. This poem describes a ferry trip from Brooklyn to the Fulton Street landing in Manhattan, examining the urban crowds who joined Whitman in his commute. Yet in this poem, and in many others that index the antebellum city, Whitman ignores the easy availability of sexually explicit print on New York's streets, much less its particular presence at the ferry's landing. Prostitutes, dancers, model artistes, and other figures from the blurry worlds of sex-related work in 1850s Manhattan appear in *Leaves*, yet printed erotica is conspicuously absent, particularly in light of the attacks on Whitman's book as being indecent.

Late in life, Whitman famously described to his friend Horace Traubel his motivations for writing: "sex, sex, sex: sex is the root of it all: sex" (WWC, 3:452–53). But what sorts of books about sex were available at the time that Whitman was writing and publishing? And what legal frameworks governed their sale? This chapter focuses on sexually explicit printed material that was available in antebellum American cities. A note on terms is probably necessary. The books and prints discussed here are not finely bound collections of recherché imagery – most of them are not "erotica," with its implications of connoisseurship and its privileging of literary ambition over commercial success. While expensive editions of works like Boccaccio's *Decameron* were available from high-end bookstores, most of the erotic printed materials available in antebellum New York were inexpensive books and images produced quickly for sale to a mass market. The word *pornography* did not come into use until the 1860s, so it is slightly anachronistic for this period. Yet it has two virtues: it is shorter than "sexually explicit printed matter" and it is generic rather than evaluative, unlike the term *obscene*, which is a legal rather than an artistic category. When discussing prosecutions involving these materials, I will use "obscene" and "obscenity," but these terms did not have set legal definitions in the nineteenth century. The standard language in obscenity indictments in antebellum New York charged sellers of such books with "creating inordinate and lustful desires," making the defining characteristic of obscene literature the response of its readers rather than any specific content. So even though "pornography" was not a term that Whitman and his contemporaries would have used – and even though this chapter is titled "Erotica" – "pornography" comes closest to describing the materials considered here.

Pornographic materials were widely available in antebellum cities, either through the mail or at retail outlets. Novelty items constituted a significant segment of this market – things like watch cases and snuff boxes with explicit images painted inside, transparencies for magic lanterns, playing cards, aphrodisiacs, sexual aids, and contraceptives. Many merchants who sold printed pornography also sold these other items, but not all. And risqué performances were also common in most large cities, including *tableaux vivants*, where performers on stage would reenact famous paintings or historic scenes, and model artiste shows, where thinly veiled (or entirely nude) women would strike poses in a precursor to later burlesque shows (this is to say nothing of commercial sex itself). Along with the traffic in novelty items emerged a trade in pornographic daguerreotypes, which became much more affordable as daguerreotype galleries proliferated through the 1840s and 1850s. Frederic Lane writes that, in the late 1840s, daguerreotypes of scantily clad or nude women could be bought from stationery stores and pushcart vendors in New York.[2] While Whitman would likely have been familiar with all of these types of goods, this chapter's focus will be on the print context for Whitman's published work. This world of print ranged from newspapers to novels, from single cheaply made illustrations to expensive sets of engravings. It included sensational fiction that verged on obscenity and texts from the genres of medical education and moral reform, from the centuries-old compendium *Aristotle's Master-piece* (first published in 1684) to progressive works of physiology that attempted to demystify human sexuality. While scholars traditionally exclude these physiological texts from the realm of matter that was designed to arouse, antebellum "lectures to young men" warn of the dangers of reading such books, and several sensational novels from the period depict young men buying physiologies and then masturbating while they read them. The same text, whether a novel or a work of physiology, could be published with varying sets of images; the number and content of the illustrations featured in a book often played a larger role in determining whether a book was obscene, and also played the largest role in setting the book's price.

Walt Whitman spent virtually his entire career in New York's world of print and knew it intimately. He is well known for having been a printer and a newspaper editor and columnist in the 1840s and 1850s; indeed, "There was not a single kind of popular periodical he did not serve as either an editor or a contributor" (Reynolds, 82). His forays as a novelist are also fairly familiar. Less well known is that he operated a bookshop in Brooklyn for several years, starting in 1849, where he sold pens, stationery, musical instruments, and all types of books (Reynolds, 126–27). He worked for years in the neighborhood around Nassau and Fulton Streets in Lower Manhattan, which held the densest concentration of printers and publishers in the city, and thus the largest number of pornographers. There is no question that Whitman knew that this business existed and understood how it worked.

The trade in pornography

The streets of antebellum New York posed countless menaces to the innocent, honest, and witless. Runaway omnibuses hurtled down Broadway, pickpockets lurked in the crowds, strolling prostitutes marketed their charms, con men offered fake goods for sale, and feckless young men peddled indecent books on public sidewalks in broad daylight. An 1855 article in the *New York Times*, entitled "A Flagrant Nuisance," provides a tidy sketch of how the retail trade in pornography worked:

> There are few of our male readers who [. . .] have not been accosted by a hang-dog looking boy of fifteen or thereabouts, with a stealthy, lowered eye, an unwholesome skin, and a brown paper parcel under his arm. This fellow, if you look at him with any earnestness, will sidle up to you, and opening his brown paper parcel, disclose a number of books: *The Dey-street*

Cellar, or the Chameleon of the Swamp; Cabbage for the Contemplative; The Sisters of the Cemetery, or the Death-kiss of the Aqueduct. On your refusing to purchase either of these [. . .], the boy comes closer, glances mysteriously around, and slyly opens an inner fold of the paper, wherein lies *perdue* an obscene book, with a tawdrily indecent drawing, colored like a sixpenny cotton, stuck in as a frontispiece. "Something nice, Sir," says the boy, with a meaning wink and a gross intonation in his voice that makes you shudder.[3]

Antebellum newspapers and popular fiction warned of the dangers of consuming pornography. These books and images were part of the wave of print that flooded the United States in the 1830s to 1850s. Many of the affidavits presented in antebellum New York obscenity prosecutions testified to the easy availability of obscene materials on the city's streets. In his 1842 testimony against the lithographer Henry R. Robinson, the printer James Craft claimed that he paid Robinson $3.50 for obscene prints at his store "in a room partitioned off for that purpose [. . .] though clearly so publicly exposed in his principal store room where persons were continually passing in and out."[4] Edward Scofield, a newsboy, was apprehended in 1842 selling obscene books that he had received from Cornelius Ryan, a book dealer with a sidewalk stall on Wall Street. Scofield testified that "said books are kept by Ryan in a Tin Box under his stand."[5]

Scofield's arrest was part of a larger crackdown on New York's pornography dealers by George Matsell, the chief of police, the first of a series of waves of suppression of obscenity in antebellum New York. (While Scofield avoided incarceration in 1842, he was arrested again for selling obscene books in 1847 and was sentenced to six months in jail, which Donna Dennis notes was "the heaviest penalty imposed for an obscenity offense in antebellum New York.")[6] The affidavits from these prosecutions outline a two-tiered structure in the pornography trade; some dealers acted as wholesalers, selling small quantities of material (typically individual prints or books) to boys working as sidewalk vendors. Other booksellers conducted a retail trade out of their own bookshops, stalls, or carts. Some dealers – like Cornelius Ryan – probably did both, acting as a supplier to street peddlers while also selling retail from the "tin box" under the counter.

A customer of a street vendor could expect to receive a short novel and several explicit images depicting scenes of naked women, masturbation, or heterosexual sex of all kinds for anywhere from fifty cents to one dollar. For example, in September of 1857, an Officer Beany of the Second Precinct arrested a lame bookseller in Lovejoy's Hotel from whom he bought a novel and "some very scandalous prints" for forty-five cents.[7] At these prices, pornographic texts would have been affordable to most employed New Yorkers, and there is evidence that their sale crossed economic, class, and educational boundaries. These vendors likely sold editions of some of the steady sellers of the genre, including *The Lustful Turk* (1828), *Fanny Hill* (1748), and *Mysteries of Venus, or the Amatory Life* (1830).

The abolitionist clergyman Moncure Conway wrote in 1866 of having visited Whitman in New York in the late 1850s, riding the ferries and walking the streets with the poet. Conway wrote:

> "Look at that face!" he exclaimed once as we paused near the office of the Herald. I looked and beheld a boy of perhaps fifteen years, with certainly a hideous countenance, the face one-sided, and one eye almost hanging out of a villainous low forehead. He had a bundle under his arm. "There," said Walt, "is a New York reptile. There's poison about his fangs I think." We watched him as he looked furtively about, and presently he seemed to see that we had our eyes on him, and was skulking off. At that my companion beckoned him, and after a little succeeded in bringing him to us, when we found that he was selling obscene books.[8]

While Whitman was obviously familiar with the street trade in pornography, more was likely sold via mail order, promoted by ads in the popular press. Booksellers employed certain terms in their advertisements that would have told knowing consumers what was on offer. Books advertised as "Rich, Rare, and Racy" typically went just up to the line of obscenity but did not cross it. Anything advertised as being French – novelties, engravings, transparencies – was likely to be sexually explicit in nature, as were "Books of Love" and any goods described as "sporting" or "fancy."

The street-level retailers purchased their stock from larger producers who incurred much more risk, and who made large investments in their businesses. In response to an 1842 federal law prohibiting the importation of "indecent and obscene pictures," the USA developed a domestic pornography industry, and men like William Haines, George Akarman, and Jeremiah Farrell became kingpins of the business. When Akarman was arrested in 1857 for publishing *Venus's Miscellany*, a pornographic weekly newspaper targeted at a national, middle-class audience, he was doing business under four different names, and was generating annual profits of around $12,000 (nearly $250,000 today).[9] The discovery of his storeroom, which reportedly contained over six cartloads of explicit books and pictures, as well as his print shop, where he employed young women to color engravings, caused a furor in the press and raised awareness that pornography was big business. There is no question that someone as deeply embedded in New York's world of print as Whitman would have heard of both Akarman's arrest and the scale of his profits.

Prosecuting obscenity

Obscenity was prosecuted fitfully in the antebellum decades in the USA. Until the mid-1830s, most states did not have any laws against obscenity on the books; New York did not pass one until 1868. Thus almost all obscenity prosecutions took place on the local level. Before the passage of specific obscenity statutes, local jurisdictions relied on the unwritten English common law tradition, prosecuting the sale of pornography either as "criminal nuisance" or "obscene libel." Legal scholar Donna Dennis discovered only three obscenity prosecutions before the city's first major crackdown on pornography dealers, starting in late 1841.[10] The suppression of the trade in the mid-1850s was the result of Fernando Wood's election as mayor of New York (Wood had run on a law-and-order platform). In the periods between these bursts of prosecution, "most people did not seem to view sexually explicit publications as a major social problem or public concern."[11]

When people were prosecuted for selling obscene materials, the charges were rooted in one primary question: Were the books or prints they sold likely to deprave or corrupt the minds of people who read them? Between 1840 and 1860, Manhattan grand juries identified twenty separate books as obscene – all of them described sex acts, and many of them contained explicit illustrations.[12] Several affidavits contain passages from the books included in the indictment as evidence of their indecent nature. Those passages were recycled in future prosecutions; if a person was arrested for selling *Fanny Hill*, there were passages from the novel that had been cited in previous cases that proved the book's obscenity, which were simply copied. Typically, these passages described sex acts in fairly specific detail, and they often included descriptions of characters experiencing orgasms, given that the description of sexual pleasure was thought to be particularly indecent.

When the first edition of *Leaves of Grass* appeared in 1855, many critics urged criminal prosecution of its publishers. A representative criticism in this vein appeared in the *Criterion*: "Thus, then, we leave this gathering of muck to the laws which, certainly, if they fulfil their intent, must have power to suppress such gross obscenity."[13] Such comments make clear that reviewers understood certain texts to be "obscene" rather than merely erotic, and that the government had the power to suppress their sale.

Sympathetic critics knew about this response to Whitman's poetry, and offered their own defenses against the charge. In her 1856 review of *Leaves* in the *New York Ledger*, the hugely popular columnist Fanny Fern wrote "I am not unaware that the charge of coarseness and sensuality has been affixed to [Whitman's poems]. My moral constitution may be hopelessly tainted – or too sound to be tainted, as the critic wills – but I confess that I extract no poison from these 'Leaves.'"[14]

Accusations that *Leaves* was obscene would escalate with future editions, particularly after the 1860 edition, the first to include the "Enfans d'Adam" section, which contains the book's most sexual poems (poems that Emerson famously tried to dissuade Whitman from including). Calvin Beach wrote a savage review in the *New York Saturday Press* that not only denounced the poems as obscene, but also situated Whitman's work within the context of pornography available at the time. Beach wrote:

> I write simply to express my unqualified disgust with the portions I have read. Whether those portions are the best, or the worst, or an average, I do not know nor care to know. [. . .]
>
> I make no quotations from those pages. I would offer neither to The Press, nor its readers, the offence of spreading before them even the daintiest lines those pages of filth contain. Until such time as the novels of de Kock find place upon parlor tables, and the obscene pictures, which boys in your city slily offer for sale upon the wharves, are admitted to albums, or grace drawing-room walls, quotations from *Enfans d'Adam* would be an offence against decency too gross to be tolerated.
>
> I am not at all squeamish. [. . .] Amorous poetry, so far from being to me offensive, is delightful, and the soft, liquid lines of tender love, and the deep strains of a burning passion, seem to me alike fit hymns for man to offer up. But Walt Whitman's poems are not amorous; they are only beastly.[15]

Beach not only compares Whitman's poems to the racy novels of the French author Charles Paul de Kock (and the American writers who issued their own lubricious books under the name), he equates the "Enfans d'Adam" poems with the pornography being sold by Manhattan street vendors. He also draws the distinction that was still being worked out in nineteenth-century legal discourse between "amorous poetry" and the merely "beastly," or between the erotic and the obscene (a distinction to which Whitman was acutely sensitive). William O'Connor, Whitman's most enthusiastic contemporary defender, also compared *Leaves of Grass* to the mass-market erotic material of the period, arguing that *Leaves* did not deserve being classed with "the anonymous lascivious trash spawned in holes and sold in corners, too witless and disgusting for any notice but that of the police."[16] Readers in Whitman's time were clearly aware of the range of pornography available in the marketplace. The debate was over whether *Leaves of Grass* belonged in that category or not.

Given that obscenity is a category that is geographically and temporally contingent, the question remains: Were Whitman's poems obscene? Which is to say, even though Whitman's publishers would not face legal challenges until the 1880s, could his poems have been classified as obscene by prevailing standards at the time? An 1842 New York indictment against a book vendor named Richard Hobbes includes a passage from the pornographic novel *The Curtain Drawn Up, or The Education of Laura* (1818). Depicting a threesome, the cited passage reads:

> His instrument had now recovered its first magnitude, and as Justine with her face upon the bed could see nothing, he began to introduce it into the slit of Isabella when Justine turning her head, got off the bed [...] and pulled him off her [...]. Then taking hold of his pego, "Come my dear Courbelon," says she, "put it into mine, it will content it, and you will risk nothing with me." She then gave it two or three shakes, but in doing so she deprived him of the power of complying with her wishes, for Courbelon taking hold of her breast with one hand and sucking the nipple of the other, jetted out of his pego a white liquid, that convinced me, by the convulsions and signs it made him use, gave him great pleasure.[17]

The detailed (if blunt) descriptions of genitalia – Isabella's "slit," Courbelon's "instrument" – and of ejaculation are likely what qualified this passage as obscene in 1842. There are some notable similarities between that passage and one from Section V of "I Sing the Body Electric":

> Hair, bosom, hips, bend of legs, negligent falling hands all diffused, mine too diffused,
> Ebb stung by the flow and flow stung by the ebb, love-flesh swelling and deliciously aching,
> Limitless limpid jets of love hot and enormous, quivering jelly of love, white-blow and delirious juice,
> Bridegroom-night of love, working surely and softly into the prostrate dawn,
> Undulating into the willing and yielding day,
> Lost in the cleave of the clasping and sweet-flesh'd day.   (LG, 96)

Although it uses more metaphoric language, the poem's delineation of an erect penis ("love-flesh swelling"), female genitalia ("the cleave of the clasping and sweet-fleshed day") and its graphic celebration of ejaculation treads the same ground as the passage from *The Curtain Drawn Up*. Thus it would appear that critics who called for *Leaves* to be prosecuted as obscene had a point, at least according to the standards that prevailed in antebellum New York.

Yet it would not be until 1882, well after the passage of the 1873 Post Office Act – still referred to as the "Comstock Act" – that *Leaves of Grass* would encounter legal difficulties. Named after Anthony Comstock, a mercantile clerk who made a career as a crusader against obscenity, this law changed the practices of all nineteenth-century publishers who produced sexually explicit materials, prohibiting the distribution through the mails of any items related to contraception and abortion as well as obscene books and prints. The Act did not provide a specific definition of obscenity, so the 1882 suppression in Boston of the James Osgood edition of *Leaves* that was conducted by the New England branch of Comstock's Society for the Suppression of Vice still relied on local definitions of obscenity. This action against Whitman's poems on the basis of their sexual content took place only after the rich local context of sexually explicit printed materials in which Whitman's early career took shape had been completely altered by the rise of Comstock's national authority.

Notes

1. William W. Sanger, *The History of Prostitution: Its Extent, Causes, and Effects throughout the World* (New York, NY: Harper and Brothers, 1858), 521–22.
2. Frederick S. Lane III, *Obscene Profits: The Entrepreneurs of Pornography in the Cyber Age* (New York, NY: Routledge, 2000).
3. "A Flagrant Nuisance," *New York Daily Times* (New York, NY), November 10, 1855, 4.
4. People v. Henry R. Robinson; District Attorney Indictment Papers, Court of General Sessions, 1790–1879, Reel 212, Box 413 (September 28, 1842), New York City Municipal Archives and Records Center.
5. Helen Horowitz, *Rereading Sex: Battles over Sexual Knowledge and Suppression in Nineteenth-Century America* (New York, NY: Alfred A. Knopf, 2002), 211.
6. Donna Dennis, *Licentious Gotham: Erotic Publishing and its Prosecution in Nineteenth-Century New York* (Cambridge, MA: Harvard University Press, 2009), 146.
7. "Another Alleged Obscene Publisher Arrested," *New York Times* (New York, NY), September 29, 1857.
8. Moncure Conway, "Walt Whitman," *The Fortnightly Review* 6 (October 15, 1866), 545–46.
9. "Great Seizure of Obscene Literature," *New York Herald* (New York, NY), September 16, 1857; "A Publishing Establishment Broken Up," *New York Tribune* (New York, NY), September 16, 1857.
10. Dennis, *Licentious Gotham*, 37.
11. Ibid., 39.
12. Ibid., 94–96.

13. [Rufus W. Griswold], "Walt Whitman's *Leaves of Grass*," *Criterion: Art, Science, and Literature* 1 (November 10, 1855), 24, WWA.

14. Fanny Fern, "Leaves of Grass," *New York Ledger* (New York, NY), May 10, 1856, 4, WWA.

15. Calvin Beach, "Leaves of Grass," *New York Saturday Press* (New York, NY), June 2, 1860, WWA.

16. William Douglas O'Connor, *The Good Gray Poet* (New York, NY: Bunce and Huntington, 1866), WWA.

17. People v. Richard Hobbes, September 28, 1842, New York City Municipal Archives.

CHAPTER 15

Notebooks and Manuscripts

Matt Miller

Despite the thousands of notebook and manuscript pages left after his death, until recently Whitman has generally been seen as a "poet of print," often in contradistinction to his nineteenth-century counterpart, Emily Dickinson, whose handwritten and, during her lifetime, unpublished writings resulted in her conception as a poet of script. Whitman's intense interest and personal involvement in printing, print technology, and bookmaking, as well as his incessant revision and refashioning of *Leaves of Grass*, for decades led scholars to focus almost solely on his publications, while his notebooks and manuscript fragments received scarce attention. When scholars did consider Whitman's script writings, their complex nature, flawed documentation, and limited accessibility often resulted in misunderstandings, some quite consequential, from which we are still disentangling Whitman and his poetry. Over the last two decades, the *Walt Whitman Archive* has greatly facilitated the study of Whitman's notebooks and manuscripts, leading to some spectacular discoveries and critical revisions to our understanding of the poet's life and work.

The perception of Whitman as a "poet of print" has been shaped by a series of critical decisions by Whitman, his literary executors, and his posthumous editors. After suffering a series of strokes in 1888, Whitman composed a will that bequeathed his literary estate, including his voluminous collection of notebooks, manuscripts, notes, and fragments to his three literary executors: Richard Maurice Bucke, Thomas B. Harned, and Horace L. Traubel.[1] He had already lost many notebooks and manuscripts and given others away as gifts, and he continued to until his death in 1892. One especially large and important collection of manuscripts had apparently been given to the Rome Brothers, Whitman's first publisher, in 1859, to create a printer's copy of poems to be included in the third edition of *Leaves of Grass*.[2] Thus the notebook and manuscript collection was already incomplete and scattered when his executors inherited what remained. Bucke, Harned, and Traubel did not settle upon a systematic method for preserving these literary treasures, although Harned did organize and catalog his portion and donated it to the Library of Congress in 1918.[3] Much of what remained was gradually donated and distributed to over seventy other archival repositories, with the largest collections today at the Library of Congress, Duke University, the University of Virginia, and the New York Public Library.[4] Each of these archives employed their own system of organization and notation, and this, combined with their scattered (and often disassembled) status, rendered it prohibitively expensive and difficult for scholars to explore and integrate Whitman's manuscript writings in coherent interpretations.

In part because of these challenges, until recently Whitman's posthumous editors have not attempted any kind of systematic presentation of his manuscripts. Aside from an early 1896 article,[5] the first publication of Whitman's manuscripts was a small, "apparently random gathering of manuscript fragments" that appeared as part of *The Complete Writings of Walt Whitman* in 1902.[6] This was followed by a more generous (but still woefully incomplete) selection by Clifton Joseph Furness in 1928, which was the first book-length collection published.[7] Some of Whitman's Civil War-era manuscripts and notebook fragments were published in 1933, and most of the collection inherited by the Rome Brothers in 1859 was published in 1955.[8] This represented only a fraction of Whitman's extant notebooks and manuscripts, and the first attempt at any kind of comprehensive publication came with New York University Press's monumental *The Collected Writings of Walt Whitman*. Originally slated for twenty-two volumes (later supplemented to twenty-five), the editors made the unusual decision not to include poetry manuscripts in the nine volumes designated for script writings, instead reserving them for a three-volume Variorum edition of *Leaves of Grass*. In the end, the Variorum edition was published without reference to these manuscripts, leaving the nine volumes of published notebook material bereft of Whitman's most important poetry manuscripts. Scholars wishing to explore Whitman's notebooks were further hindered by the decision to divide these nine volumes between two editors, William White, who edited the six-volume *Notebooks and Unpublished Prose Manuscripts*, and Edward F. Grier, who employed completely different editorial conventions in his three-volume *Daybooks and Notebooks*. Critically important, though flawed and incomplete, these were for decades the most-cited sources for Whitman's notebooks and other script writings.

Scholars subsequently attempted to amend and improve the record with major efforts such as Joel Myerson's three-volume *The Walt Whitman*

Archive (1993, not to be confused with the online *Walt Whitman Archive*), as well as a CD-ROM edition of *The Collected Writings* (1997), which expedited research by allowing digital searches in the volumes edited by Grier and White. Yet even as these and other editions were published with many of the poet's known manuscript and notebook writings, new manuscripts and related writings rapidly appeared, leaving any print edition incomplete, even as it first appeared on bookshelves. The vast paper trail Whitman left his readers continues to grow, subverting the value of any kind of "complete" published edition and demanding new editorial practices if we are to keep up with the discoveries. Over the last two decades, the online *Walt Whitman Archive* has worked to address these problems, going beyond the idea of static editions in an effort to present a continually updated and searchable archive of Whitman's writings. At present, users can already search the majority of Whitman's scattered archival materials and view digital page images of most of them. Searchable typographic transcriptions are available in many cases, and recently the *Archive* has made considerable progress presenting transcriptions of the major notebooks as well, all of which are accompanied by links to high-quality digital scans of the original materials. Edited by Ed Folsom and Kenneth M. Price, the *Whitman Archive* has revolutionized our understanding of Whitman's writing, providing the foundation for transformative studies of the poet's biography, politics, and writing process, as well as facilitating critical reinterpretations of his most important poetry and prose.

It is easier to delineate Whitman's script writings chronologically than it is based on their material nature. The materials range from a word or two scribbled on tiny loose scraps of paper to voluminous, multi-use notebooks containing several years of related (and sometimes unrelated) efforts. There are notebooks containing shopping lists, lists which became poetry, and lists of wounded soldiers and the humble gifts they craved on their deathbeds. Essential first drafts of Whitman's most famous lines are found alongside mundane ephemera, and sometimes the most seemingly prosaic and quotidian material is itself transformed into poetry. Recent scholarship has focused on the poet's marginalia, often to his own writing, as well as what might be described as scrapbooks or commonplace books containing fragments of texts cut from a variety of sources and pasted together on his notebooks' leaves. Scholars have long struggled to describe and categorize these writings according to editorial conventions. While the phrase "notebooks" has endured as a persistent category, a variety of other descriptions have also been employed, leading to confusion about these writings' material nature, especially when the original source was no longer available. Even within what was ostensibly a single edition, editors have employed contradictory naming conventions. Editing *The Collected Writings*, White was content describing a variety of bound or once-bound materials as "notebooks," while Grier insisted on dividing them into "daybooks and notebooks." Both scholars labored to separate his poetry from his prose manuscripts, a dubious distinction given how so many of Whitman's poems, especially his early ones, were originally composed in prose and later given line breaks. The online *Walt Whitman Archive* employs four categories for writing "In Whitman's Hand": "manuscripts," "scribal documents," "marginalia and annotations," and "notebooks." These categories are sensible, though by necessity they obviate how these categories overlap and complicate each other in attempting to organize such a heterogeneous mass of writing.

Chronologically, Whitman's notebooks and manuscripts can be divided into four periods: his early notebooks mostly composed prior to the 1855 publication of the first edition of *Leaves of Grass*, the mostly manuscript notebooks composed mainly during his prolific phase between 1855 and the Civil War, the Civil War notebooks, and his late career notebooks. The early notebooks are remarkable not only for what they contain but for what they lack. While there is a good deal of various forms of prose writing that the poet much later revised into lines, in these early notebooks, it is important to note that Whitman drafted very little in verse until a year or two prior to the publication of the first edition of *Leaves of Grass*. During this period, Whitman seldom considered his work in terms of poetry, focusing instead on unrealized projects including a dictionary focusing on American use of English, a variety of public lectures, and other creative endeavors which never came to fruition. On a pair of large leaves crammed with various notes that seem to have once been part of a larger notebook (known to scholars as the "Med *Cophósis*" notebook, based on the first legible text), Whitman even seems to have considered a career as a novelist or playwright. Fascinatingly, just a few lines down Whitman drafts in prose text what later came to be known as "There Was a Child Went Forth." This document can be dated to 1853 or 1854,[9] suggesting just how malleable his concept of his own creative life's work was, even with *Leaves of Grass* less than two years away from publication.

Perhaps Whitman's most famous single notebook, the "Talbot Wilson" notebook, dates from this early period and has been the source of considerable controversy and critical interest.[10] Part of the Harned Collection at the Library of Congress, the notebook was packed and stored for safe-keeping during World War II along with many other precious documents. When the container it was stored in was returned, this notebook, along with nine others, was discovered missing, and it remained so until 1995, when the notebook appeared for auction and was eventually returned. Lacking the actual document, for over fifty years scholars were dependent upon a flawed transcription and low-quality microfilm that was itself missing until 1967. These copies suggested that Whitman began composing trial lines for *Leaves of Grass* during 1847 (or even earlier); however, access to the actual notebook revealed this dating to be flawed, because it was based on a section of the notebook Whitman had used several years earlier for bookkeeping purposes. Only by examining the actual artifact was it apparent that Whitman had recycled an old notebook, cutting out most of the old material but leaving the 1847 date on a mostly blank page that he repurposed for literary notes and drafts. This mistaken dating led Whitman scholars to believe that Whitman conceived of *Leaves of Grass* as early as 1847, while the "Med *Cophósis*" notebook shows that he did not even conceive of himself primarily as a poet until at least 1853. The effects of this mistaken dating haunt Whitman scholarship to this day, and many of the most frequently cited biographical accounts continue to repeat erroneous assertions about the origins of *Leaves of Grass*.[11] The story of the "Talbot Wilson" notebook clearly reveals the limitations of print transcriptions and the importance of being able to study the actual notebooks, whether in person or through high-quality digital images.

Once it became clear to Whitman just how important poetry would be to him as a creative vehicle, he naturally began to write more often in lines and with poetry specifically in mind. Thus the notebooks he used primarily between 1855 and the beginning of the Civil War are significantly different from the earlier notebooks due their extensive use as intentional manuscript drafts for future poems. In notebooks dated to 1854 and 1855 – after Whitman had conceived of *Leaves of Grass* but before it was published – he often abstractly contemplates what it could mean to be a poet in America or theorizes about the underlying nature of poetry. Many of these ideas were reworked in the Preface to the first edition, and after its publication Whitman seems to have moved on toward a phase of prolific composition, often facilitated by the poet ransacking his old, pre-poetry notebooks for material suitable for his lines. Whitman was ferocious and omnivorous in his recycling of old material, culling lines from notes on human anatomy, drafts of aborted plans for speeches, phrenological commentary, a speech on the "uses of iron" by the iron magnate and future New York mayor Abram S. Hewitt, and even passages from self-written reviews of the first edition of *Leaves of Grass*.[12] Many of the most important and revealing notebooks date from this period, including a small notebook containing the now-infamous "Live Oak, with Moss" sequence, which was never published or even, so far as we know, mentioned by Whitman. Originally conceived in separate fragments, Whitman later took particular care in assembling the poems as a twelve-part sequence narrating the speaker's passionate affair with a man. Whitman later disassembled the sequence and republished each section as a separate poem in the "Calamus" cluster of the 1860 edition of *Leaves*. Published separately, the poems are still provocative, but in their sequential form they reveal what seems clear evidence of a substantial long-term love affair, most likely with Fred Vaughan, a young man who lived with Whitman for a period during the late 1850s.[13] The collected sequence was originally discovered in manuscript form by Fredson Bowers, who first described it in a 1953 article, but despite the obvious importance of the sequence it was neglected for decades until more recently becoming a focal point of critical interest and controversy.

There are many other important notebooks from this period, several of which include intriguing drafts of poems for the second edition, such as "Broad-Axe Poem," "Poem of the Road," and "Sun-Down Poem,"[14] but some of the most interesting examples of Whitman's script writing are found on fragments that were either never a part of a notebook or which were separated and cannot be reassembled. Even some rather slight, ambiguous notes from this period have taken on considerable importance, such as this one, brief enough to quote in its entirety:

> *The Great Construction* – of the *New Bible*
> Not to be diverted from the principal object – the main life work – the three Hundred & sixty-five – it ought to be ready in 1859. – (June [?] '57)[15]

The phrase "New Bible" is perhaps the single most frequently cited short passage in all of Whitman's unpublished script writing. The poet's words here (and his convenient self-dating) have been used by nearly all major Whitman scholars to describe his poems. Understanding *Leaves of Grass*, especially the third edition, as Whitman's "New Bible" is such a truism in Whitman studies that scholars now cite the notion as fact without seeing the need for substantiation, and yet this tiny scrap of paper is the only place in all of his writing where Whitman himself uses the phrase. Considered in context, it is not at all apparent he was describing *Leaves of Grass* at all. Whitman was prolific in the late 1850s, but not so prolific that he could expect to roughly quadruple his output and complete "the three Hundred & sixty-five" poems suggested here within two years, an absurd overestimate. Disappointed by the sales of the first two editions, Whitman considered many other projects during this period, including a book of "lessons" and "*Religious Canticles*."[16] Perhaps he was discussing one of these ideas in this fragment, or perhaps he was considering a work patterned after the calendar, with a brief poem for each day, a structure echoing lectionary prayer books such as the popular Elizabethan *Book of Common Prayer*. In the 1855 Preface and elsewhere, Whitman did occasionally describe *Leaves* in biblical terms, but the idea of *Leaves*-as-Bible seems to articulate a broad conception of how he hoped his audience would receive his work, as opposed to a specific, formal conception or creatively generative idea. The uncertainty surrounding the "New Bible" fragment shows there remains a vital need to reexamine our assumptions about Whitman in light of the actual extant evidence.

Whitman continued his practice of keeping notebooks during his Civil War years, but the way he used his notebooks changed. After Whitman relocated to Washington, DC, and began regularly visiting Civil War hospital tents and tending to wounded soldiers, dealing with the immediate traumas of war took priority over drafting lines. Whitman returned to using his notebooks mainly for prose notations that do not seem to have been originally composed with literary purposes in mind. As with the early notebooks these contain little actual poetry, but their prose content, again much like in the early notebooks, often later became fodder for later published writing, some poetry (mostly poems eventually assembled in *Drum-Taps*), and some prose (mostly notes and sketches eventually gathered in *Specimen Days and Collect*).[17] Whitman accurately characterized the content of the notebooks in a lengthy footnote at the beginning of *Specimen Days*, describing "cases, persons, sights, occurrences in camp, by the bed-side, and not seldom by the corpses of the dead." These were "scratch'd down from narratives [. . .] heard and itemized while watching, or waiting, or tending somebody amid those scenes." He described the notebooks as "soil'd and creas'd livraisons," and the record shows it is true that some were "composed of a sheet or two of paper, folded small to carry in the pocket, and fasten'd with a pin [. . .] blotch'd here and there with more than one blood-stain, hurriedly written" (PW, 1:7). Whitman's depictions of the suffering and endurance of the men he loved and cared for during the Civil War, along with his own reactions – variously shocked, heart-broken, and inspired – make for dramatic reading, especially in their original form, and some of the most important of these notebooks are now available at the *Walt Whitman Archive*, where they can be read alongside page images of the originals. A good deal of commentary has been based on these writings, and they remain a vital source for historical information about the war, biographical information about Whitman, and the later published writings the poet made of these astonishing notebooks.[18]

Less work has been done on Whitman's late notebooks. Whitman returned to working extensively on his poetry, and the later notebooks, like the ones from 1855 until 1861, contain extensive drafts and revisions. Many of these notebooks show Whitman committed to revision and formal re-conception of his poetry, as he arranged and rearranged his lines in various formations before publishing them, occasionally editing or removing critical passages.[19] He returned to his habit of taking notes for speeches; however, unlike many of his pre-1855 drafts, Whitman actually delivered many of them. Some notebooks reveal Whitman self-conscious of his place in history, recording events such as New York City's reaction to the assassination of President Lincoln. In one particularly important notebook from 1870, Whitman used a numerical code to refer to his lover, Peter Doyle, describing the trauma he experienced trying to separate himself from the relationship.[20] Perhaps because most of his last poems were relatively brief, toward the end of his life, Whitman often seems to have composed on loose leaves and scraps of paper, as opposed to in notebooks. He did still use some notebooks, and many, especially the very late ones, remain unexplored.

New manuscripts in the poet's hand continue to appear, and it is likely that even more notebooks will be discovered. While work at the *Walt Whitman Archive* has made many of these notebooks and manuscripts more accessible, with such access comes challenges. With so much script writing available the extant record can seem comprehensive, when we know this is far from true. Such an enormous and relatively well-preserved paper trail as Whitman left has tempted some to cherry-pick from the notebooks, leading to one-sided, presumptuous, and sometimes flatly incorrect portrayals. Using Whitman's notebooks and manuscripts responsibly requires patience, diligence, and skepticism, but faced with such an embarrassment of riches, prospects are ripe for new discoveries and revolutionary rereadings of America's most essential poet.

Notes

1. Artem Lozynsky, "'Us Three Meaning America': Whitman's Literary Executors," *The Papers of the Bibliographical Society of America* 68.4 (1974), 442–44.

2. Fredson Bowers, "Introduction," in *Whitman's Manuscripts: Leaves of Grass (1860), A Parallel Text*, ed. Fredson Bowers (Chicago, IL: University of Chicago Press, 1955), xxiii–xxxi. This collection of manuscripts was resold a number of times and was eventually inherited by Clifton Waller Barrett, becoming known as "The Valentine-Barrett Manuscripts." Today this collection is held in Albert and Shirley Small Special Collections Library at the University of Virginia. Digital page images of these notebooks and manuscripts, like most others, can be accessed at the online *Walt Whitman Archive*.

3. Anon., "Collection: Thomas Biggs Harned Collection of Whitman Papers (About This Collection)," *Library of Congress*, www.loc.gov.

4. Ed Folsom and Kenneth M. Price, *Re-Scripting Walt Whitman: An Introduction to His Life and Work* (Malden, MA: Blackwell, 2005), 135.

5. William Sloane Kennedy, "A Peep into Walt Whitman's Manuscripts," *Conservator* 7 (1896), 53–55.

6. Folsom and Price, *Re-Scripting Walt Whitman*, 130.

7. Clifton Joseph Furness, ed., *Introduction to Walt Whitman's Workshop: A Collection of Unpublished Manuscripts* (New York, NY: Russell & Russell, [1928] 1964), 1–24.

8. Charles I. Glicksberg, ed., *Walt Whitman and the Civil War: A Collection of Original Articles and Manuscripts* (Philadelphia, PA: University of Pennsylvania Press, 1933).

9. Matt Miller, *Collage of Myself: Walt Whitman and the Making of Leaves of Grass* (Lincoln, NE: University of Nebraska Press, 2010), 14–15.

10. Andrew C. Higgins, "Wage Slavery and the Composition of *Leaves of Grass*: The 'Talbot Wilson' Notebook," *Walt Whitman Quarterly Review* 20.2 (Fall 2002), 53–77.

11. Ibid., 6–7.

12. For details on these examples as well as many others, see Miller, *Collage of Myself*, especially chapters 2–4.

13. Charley Shively, *Calamus Lovers: Walt Whitman's Working-Class Camerados* (San Francisco, CA: Gay Sunshine Press, 1987).

14. These poems are better known by their final titles, "Song of the Broad-Axe," "Song of the Open Road," and "Crossing Brooklyn Ferry," respectively.

15. Transcription mine.

16. Walt Whitman, c. late 1850s to 1860, Literary Manuscripts in the Trent Collection of Whitmaniana, Duke University, Durham, North Carolina, MS 4 to 31, available online via the WWA, *Whitman Archive* ID: duk.00282.

17. It took many years for Whitman's Civil War prose writings to be published and even more before they were available to many of his readers. Some of these Civil War prose writings were first published in six articles for the *New York Weekly Graphic* (1874). These articles were later gathered and published in *Memoranda During the War* (1875–76), which was printed privately in a small batch of less than a hundred copies. *Memoranda During the War* was later republished as a section of *Two Rivulets* (1876), and these writings are best known to most of Whitman's readers today by their

inclusion in *Specimen Days and Collect* (1882), where they are joined by other prose writing including biographical commentary and some previously unpublished Civil War notes.

18. According to the online bibliography of the *Walt Whitman Archive,* dozens of articles – far too many to cite individually – have been published in the twentieth-first century alone that depend upon these Civil War writings. In addition there have been major scholarly books published that have recently put these notebooks to substantial use, including Ted Genoways, *Walt Whitman and the Civil War: America's Poet During the Lost Years of 1860–1862* (Berkeley, CA: University of California Press, 2009); Robert Roper, *Now the Drum of War: Walt Whitman and His Brothers in the Civil War* (New York, NY: Walker, 2008); and Roy Morris Jr., *The Better Angel: Walt Whitman in the Civil War* (New York, NY: Oxford University Press, 2000).

19. For example, Ed Folsom has explored how Whitman's late revision to "The Sleepers" for the 1871–72 edition of *Leaves* undercut the poet's previous interest in race and racial concerns. See Folsom and Price, *Re-Scripting Walt Whitman,* 49–55.

20. This simple numeric code, "16.4," was eventually cracked by Robert K. Martin, who used the notebook to convincingly demonstrate Whitman's passionate, sexual love for other men at a time when some scholars still regarded such love as controversial or even questionable, despite the extensive evidence in his published and unpublished writing. The numbers correspond to the sequential position of Peter Doyle's initials in the alphabet. See Robert K. Martin, *The Homosexual Tradition in American Poetry* (Austin, TX: University of Texas Press, 1979).

CHAPTER 16

Bookmaking

Nicole Gray

Long largely ignored by critics, Walt Whitman's involvement in the making of his books has become a focal point in scholarship in the past decade. Scholars have argued convincingly that reading Whitman's poetry often entails examining the books themselves. The material characteristics of Whitman's books have been discussed within a range of analytical approaches, from ecocriticism to transatlantic publication and distribution.[1]

Whitman's books were the products of his determination – driven, in some cases, by necessity – to work directly with printers, binders, and tradesmen. The form of his volumes was never disconnected from their content and the author never too far removed from the production or the producers.[2] Often distinctive and idiosyncratic, the books helped to enforce the intimacy between reader and author sought by the poetry even as they reflected the industrialization of bookmaking in the nineteenth-century USA. Produced over almost a forty-year period, Whitman's books manifest several of the trends and technological improvements in book manufacturing in the last half of the nineteenth century. All of the editions of Whitman's books were produced on machine-made paper and profited from the nineteenth-century introduction of binder's cloth and die-stamped decoration on book covers. Editions after 1855 were printed from plates. Many editions included a frontispiece and other illustrations and showcased a variety of type designs.[3] As Michael Winship has pointed out, "the benefits of industrial ways were an article of faith" in society more broadly, a fact that Whitman himself expressed in his poems. His books, however, were examples not just of the impersonal machinery of mechanical reproduction but also of the persistence of human interaction and textual variation.[4]

The narrative that has emerged about Whitman as bookmaker casts him as a controlling force in the making of his books, involved at every point in the process, from design to printing, binding, and distribution. The first edition of *Leaves of Grass* was self-published, and it is possible that, having had more or less free rein over book decisions at the beginning, he got into the habit. Twice he traveled to Boston to oversee the publication of his books in that city. Over the course of his life he made hundreds of decisions about type, spacing, layout, organization, binders' cloth, and stamping. It may well be that "no other American author was more involved in the publication process than was Whitman," as Joel Myerson writes.[5] One factor that made Whitman's involvement possible was his familiarity with some of the industries related to book production. In his early years he had worked as a printer's apprentice, journeyman printer, journalist, newspaper editor, and bookseller. Such work meant he had connections in the printing industry, people like Andrew Rome in whose shop on Fulton Street Whitman printed the first edition of *Leaves*.

Whitman's attentiveness to the details of the physical book combined with external factors like sales and financial constraints to produce a surprising variety of books, even sometimes within single issues and editions. Both Myerson's descriptive bibliography and Winship's Whitman section of the *Bibliography of American Literature* bear witness to the dizzying complexity of Whitman's assembly and reassembly of the various texts he published into different book formations, creating more than one "bibliographical tangle," as Myerson puts it.[6] Occasionally such productions were the result of new printings, but often they were reuses of already printed pages, rebound for later distribution or sewn into other volumes. These actions suggest that the raw materials of books, from unbound sheets that sat around until he could afford to bind them, to the stereotype or electrotype plates that he sometimes purchased, reused, and revised, constituted for Whitman not just the vestigial stuff of publishers and printers but rather fertile ground for ongoing book-construction.[7] Whitman was a designer of books, deeply interested in typography, white space, and bindings, but he was also a *builder* of books, both his own and others'. In the curious case of Henry David Thoreau's *A Week on the Concord and Merrimack Rivers* (1849), Whitman cut out several pages and sewed them back together, effectively creating a new book out of the old, editing and reconstructing even as he read.[8]

In his later years, when he was largely immobile, Whitman asked his young friend and devotee Horace Traubel to act as his go-between in the production of several books, starting with *November Boughs* (1888). This collaboration made it possible for Whitman to continue publishing until the end of his life. In *With Walt Whitman in Camden*, the many conversations between Whitman and Traubel about binding, type, proofs, and other bookmaking matters demonstrate the level of detail that the process of book production involved for Whitman. Whitman insisted several times on Traubel working directly with the printers, as Whitman himself had done for previous editions of *Leaves*. Traubel's notes show Whitman constantly proofing, selecting, looking at samples, complaining about inking, negotiating prices, changing his mind, autographing, tipping in, and taking out.

A study of Whitman's bookmaking suggests that Whitman never saw one of his books – any more than the nation he associated *Leaves of Grass* with – as "finished." He several times revised the poems or the structure of a volume while it was coming off the press, or in response to conditions like the size or expense of paper. He made stop-press changes to and had notices and reviews bound in some copies of the 1855 edition of *Leaves*.[9] After Abraham Lincoln's assassination, Whitman quickly added a sequel to *Drum-Taps*, the structure of which had already been adjusted because of the high war-time cost of paper. During production of the 1867 edition of *Leaves*, Whitman considered how to add the Civil War into the book, and he had some copies of that edition issued with unsold sheets of *Drum-Taps* and the sequel bound in.[10] Where some might have despaired about things wrong or incomplete, he simply changed course mid-production, or updated later.[11] He was gleeful as a child when the proof sheets or the first bound copies came in. Of one book Traubel wrote: "He pushed the roll of proofs into a side pocket. 'It's more precious than gold,' he exclaimed to some one who came and remarked what he was doing, 'it's my baby book just born today – don't you see?'" (WWC, 1:240).

The first edition of *Leaves* in 1855 was an intimate affair, printed with hand-set type in Rome's small printing shop. Whitman later said he had set some of the type himself (Figure 16.1).[12] By the time he got to the 1860 edition of *Leaves*, published in Boston and printed from plates, Whitman had landed a publisher and could draw on the increased availability of type and variety of typefaces in the nineteenth century. He made the most of the opportunity. Barbara Henry has argued that the display types used for poem titles in that edition would have been unusual in the world of book printing, which tended to be less typographically adventurous than commercial printing. Ed Folsom has suggested that the type selection for the 1860 edition also speaks to a revision in the way Whitman was imagining the poems.[13] Instead of the vegetative design on earlier bindings, Whitman in 1860 selected a spermatoid design for the cover, title page text, and ornaments (Figure 16.2). In this case, as for many of his other books, he both designed the cover and selected several of the typefaces from a

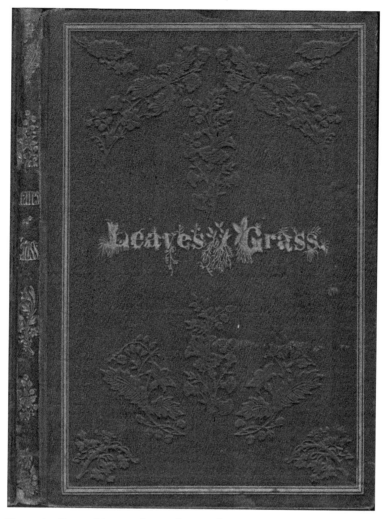

Figure 16.1 Cover of the 1855 edition of *Leaves of Grass*. Courtesy of the University of Iowa Libraries, Special Collections & University Archives and the *Walt Whitman Archive* (whitmanarchive.org).

type-specimen catalog, working with the printers to ensure his instructions were followed.

Whitman devoted careful attention to the binding of all of the editions of his books. The variety of bindings made possible by emerging technologies is apparent in the range of cloth colors and grains and the gold and

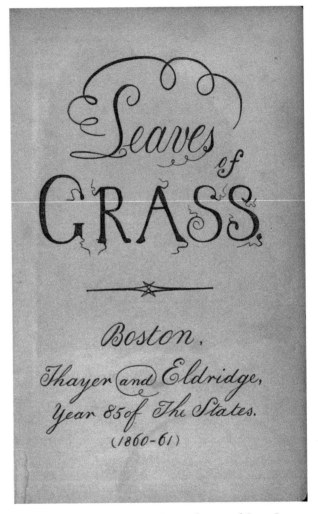

Figure 16.2 Title page of the 1860 edition of *Leaves of Grass*. Courtesy of Kenneth M. Price and the *Walt Whitman Archive* (whitmanarchive.org).

blind-stamped decorations across issues and editions of *Leaves*. In 1856, Whitman made the extraordinary move of having a quote from Ralph Waldo Emerson's letter praising the previous edition of *Leaves* gold-stamped on the spines of the books without Emerson's authorization. In other editions the binding resonates with the poetry. The leaf design and the green color of the most elaborate cloth binding of the 1855 edition matched the organic metaphor of the title. Continuities across the editions are visible in the bindings. Two different gold-stamped or embossed finger-holding-a-butterfly designs appear on the spines of some bindings of the 1860 and 1881 editions. The bindings also speak to the author's positioning of his books in national time. Folsom has associated the blindstamped images of sun and globe and the colors of the binders' cloth selected for the 1860 edition – which was bound in orange and purple, as well as the green of earlier editions – with the situation of the nation on the eve of war.[14] With the publication of different editions of *Leaves*, Whitman set himself in dialogue with the nation's history, with nature, and with other literary figures, and readers could have gleaned these associations from the covers before they ever encountered the content of his books.

Even as Whitman's books illustrated some of the larger trends in nineteenth-century bookmaking, they departed from others. Whitman's relationship to the publishing industry distinguished him from prominent US authors. Whitman did not have a recurring publisher who was involved with his books more than nominally until late in his life, and he had a series of mishaps with publishers before then.[15] His publishers Thayer and Eldridge went out of business shortly after the production of the 1860 edition of *Leaves*. James R. Osgood and Company, who signed on for the 1881 edition, withdrew the book from circulation after printing 2,000 copies.[16] After Osgood dropped the book, Whitman bound the remaining 225 sets of sheets, obtained the plates, and contracted with Rees Welsh and Company to print more copies. David McKay, who was affiliated with Rees Welsh, went on to buy the company and thereafter became Whitman's regular book publisher. Whitman would work with him on *Specimen Days and Collect* (1882–83), *November Boughs* (1888), *Complete Poems and Prose* (1888), *Good-Bye My Fancy* (1891), and several of the versions of *Leaves* issued after 1881.[17]

Based on the stop-press changes to the 1855 *Leaves* and the different signature combinations in different copies, Folsom has speculated that "*every copy* of the first edition may be unique."[18] It may be going too far to extend this claim to all of Whitman's books, but it is certain that the radical variation of that edition did not evolve into standardization or uniformity in later editions. Whitman's recycling of plates and printed sheets produced objects that often defy the logic of reproducibility that underwrote industrial printing. Editions went through multiple issues, multiple states, and multiple stages of binding, sometimes with different binders. Many copies were autographed; some included intercalations. Reprints of older texts were bound into new books, at times producing a patchwork of pagination and multiple or cancelled title pages. In some cases, text was

removed from the title pages of earlier sheets by scraping it away.[19]
Complete Poems and Prose, published in Camden with Traubel's help in
1888, was printed from the altered 1881 plates of *Leaves of Grass*, the altered
1882 plates of *Specimen Days and Collect*, and the 1888 plates of *November
Boughs*, and included new material at front and back. The edition was
limited to 600 copies, in three different bindings, all signed by Whitman
on the title page. The first issue of *Two Rivulets*, published in 1876, was
bound to match the 1876 edition of *Leaves* (together the volumes were
called the "Centennial Edition"). The volumes of *Two Rivulets* included
reissues of earlier sheets of *Democratic Vistas* (1871) and *As a Strong Bird on
Pinions Free* (1872), and first issue sheets of *Memoranda During the War*
(1875–76), all bound together but with original pagination and separate
title pages. A second issue of *Two Rivulets* made up of newly printed sheets
with revisions and alterations made to the plates for the entire volume
(with the exception of *Memoranda*, which continued to be supplied by
earlier sheets) was issued later the same year. The first issue of the 1876
edition of *Leaves* had printed slips pasted in; a later printing, issued the
same year, featured new sheets printed with the text on these intercalations
added to the printing plates. Coordinating the work of multiple printers
and binders, cutting, pasting, signing, editing, and recycling, Whitman
made small batches of singular books throughout his life. Consciously or
unconsciously, it seems almost as if he wanted to create for each individual
reader his or her own individual book.

   In part because he began making books comparatively late in life (he was
thirty-six when the first edition of *Leaves* was published), Whitman's
bookmaking offers a useful way to think about Whitman in context. His
efforts reveal the influence of the many nineteenth-century industries with
which he had been involved. The way he approached bookmaking over-
lapped with his approaches to carpentry, real estate, editorial work, and
newspaper printing. Before the Civil War, his books were produced by
companies that handled a range of non-literary printed materials. His first
volume was printed by a job printer who typically produced pamphlets and
legal forms (Rome); his second was produced by a publishing firm known
for phrenological texts (Fowler and Wells). His third book was published
by Thayer and Eldridge, a firm that specialized in abolitionist and reform
publications. Even as late as 1876, Whitman was printing segments of his
books in a newspaper printing shop.[20]

   In his poems Whitman speaks many times against books, rhapsodizing
about things that cannot be put into print. Alternatives to print are cast as
nature, mystery, and the intimate connection between author and reader.

But bookmaking *was* an intimate affair for Whitman, in practice, and he worked hard to keep it that way. His insistence on working directly with printers, his admonition to Traubel that "you come into personal, direct contact with the printers – their shops – know what is there, what can be done," to "stay close to the printers: you will understand each other," all point to the ways that he resisted the alienation of the medium in the making of his books, much as he did in the poetry (WWC, 2:514, 3:86). If anyone could make the book an intimate affair, it was Walt Whitman, and he did it at every point from production to poem.

Whitman often complained about the vagaries of bookmaking, but mostly he made his peace with the product. Traubel describes one case: "Instead of a paper binder had put on a board back: but on the edge and at the corners the book was finished with green cloth and marbleized paper to represent leafage. W. accepted the errors as 'inspiration'" (WWC, 3:212). Bookmaking was both a cooperative and an agonistic process for Whitman, not just in his interactions with the people who printed, proofed, bound, and illustrated his books but also in the appearance of the books themselves, which helped to determine how (and by whom) they would be read. Even at the end of his life, against the arguments of friends like Richard Maurice Bucke, Whitman resisted the pressure to create overly ornate or elaborate books, preferring instead "simple things made by simple people for simple people" (WWC, 4:20). A close look at Whitman making books suggests that the struggle with the materials and the production may have been part of the creative process for this inveterate reviser. "I always have great faith in *ends*," Whitman would tell Traubel in 1888, as they discussed the edition of *Complete Poems*. "We miss a lot as we go along – mix up bad and good and indifferent – but the end is sure – the right end" (WWC, 2:215).

Books also sometimes meet their ends. Today a copy of Walt Whitman's 1860 edition of *Leaves of Grass*, owned by Ken Price, sits unbound and looking forlorn in the offices of the *Walt Whitman Archive* at the University of Nebraska–Lincoln. The copy is now in pieces, front and back boards still cloth-covered but no longer attached, punctures in the signatures showing where they had been sewn together. Fragments of print are now visible, glued to the binders' cloth that once covered the spine. These printed fragments offer another way to think about Whitman in context: they are bits from waste sheets of Harriet Beecher Stowe's *First Geography for Children* (1855), used by the binder to constitute part of this copy of Whitman's 1860 *Leaves*. Such clues to the way the raw materials of nineteenth-century literary production were recycled and bound into each other suggest the many configurations of context. Literature is made out of literature, and not just in the more intangible ways – like influence – that literary critics have discussed. What other connections lie hidden in the physical objects that Whitman's bookmaking produced?

Whitman of course made many books other than the ones that were printed. Like many people in the nineteenth century, he wrote in notebooks, pasted together scrapbooks, and kept account books. In the remarkable case of the 1860 Blue Book, he created a book that was meant to serve as the working draft for an edition of *Leaves* that was never printed.[21] As he would say to Traubel:

> "What a sweat I used to be in all the time [. . .] over getting my damned books published! When I look back at it I wonder I didn't somewhere or other on the road chuck the whole business into oblivion. Editions! Editions! Editions! like the last extra of a newspaper: an extra after an extra: one issue after another: fifty-five, fifty-six, sixty-one, sixty-seven – oh! edition after edition. Yes, I wonder I never did anything violent with the book, it has so victimized me!" I broke out into a broad "Ha! ha!" He lifted his head – leaned on his elbow. "What the hell! What are you breaking loose about now?" "Oh! I was only thinking how the poor victim is still making edition after edition: now, even, in eighty-eight – thirty-three years after fifty-five." W. chuckled over this too. "It does seem rather laughable, don't it? But the fact is, the bug bites: we can't help ourselves: we are in a web – we are moths in flames: all of us: you, too, damn you! you'll have your bug some day: then maybe you'll have some sympathy for me!" (WWC, 3:561–62)

Whitman's web is a complex phenomenon, not least because it stretches so far forward and backward in time. Today a new generation of Whitman scholars and fans has been bitten by the bug and is busily producing a whole new set of editions, remaking Whitman's books and his poems both digitally and in print.[22] The work of "this preposterous printer-poet," the making, unmaking, and remaking of books, goes on.[23]

Notes

Thanks to Michael Winship, Matt Cohen, Ken Price, and Ed Folsom for their comments on drafts of this chapter.
  1. See Christine Gerhardt, "'Earth adhering to their roots': Dickinson, Whitman, and the Ecology of Bookmaking," in *American Studies as Media Studies*, eds. Frank Kelleter and Daniel Stein (Heidelberg: Winter, 2008), 37–46; Jessica DeSpain, *Nineteenth-Century Transatlantic Reprinting and the Embodied Book* (London: Routledge, 2014); Matt Cohen, *Whitman's Drift: Imagining Literary Distribution* (Iowa City, IA: University of Iowa Press, 2017).

2. Whitman wrote in a December 4, 1864 letter to Ellen M. O'Connor: "I feel that it is best for me to print my books myself, (notwithstanding some very good objections to that course, but the reasons in favor are far stronger)" (WWA).

3. For further discussion of these and other trends in bookmaking, see Michael Winship, "Manufacturing and Book Production," *A History of the Book in America*, vol. 3, eds. Scott E. Casper, et al. (Chapel Hill, NC: University of North Carolina Press, 2007), 40–69.

4. Ibid., 40.

5. Joel Myerson, "Folsom, Ed. *Whitman Making Books / Books Making Whitman: A Catalog and Commentary* [review]," *Walt Whitman Quarterly Review* 24.2 (2006), 41.

6. Joel Myerson, *Walt Whitman: A Descriptive Bibliography* (Pittsburgh, PA: University of Pittsburgh Press, 1993); Michael Winship, "Walt Whitman," in *Bibliography of American Literature*, vol. 9 (New Haven, CT: Yale University Press, 1991), 28–103; Myerson, "Folsom, Ed," 42.

7. See Peter J. L. Riley, who compares Whitman's carpentry with his book-making and remarks on his reuse of raw materials in the 1856 *Leaves* ("*Leaves of Grass* and Real Estate," *Walt Whitman Quarterly Review* 28.4 [2011], 163–87).

8. This reconstructed "book" is held at Middlebury College Library, Special Collections. The original copy of *A Week* is part of the Charles E. Feinberg Collection at the Library of Congress. For images of marked pages and partial transcriptions, see WWA.

9. Gary Schmidgall, "1855: A Stop-Press Revision," *Walt Whitman Quarterly Review* 18 (2000), 74–76.

10. Eric Conrad, "Whitman's Earliest Attempt to Absorb the Civil War into *Leaves of Grass*," *Walt Whitman Quarterly Review* 28.4 (2011), 209–10.

11. This is not to say he did not complain when things went wrong: "I am sensitive to technical slips, errors – am as ready as anyone to have everything shipshape, or as nearly so as I can make them. I abhor slouchy workmen – always admonish them in offices doing my work: Don't put on a slouchy printer" (WWC, 2:237).

12. In a letter to unidentified correspondents on March 31, 1885, Whitman wrote, "copies were struck off on a hand press by Andrew Rome, in whose job office the work was all done – the author himself setting some of the type" (WWA). See also WWC, 2:471.

13. Ed Folsom, "'A spirt of my own seminal wet': Spermatoid Design in Walt Whitman's 1860 *Leaves Of Grass*," *Huntington Library Quarterly* 73.4 (2010), 585–600; Barbara Henry, "The Design and Typography of *Leaves of Grass* (1860)," *Huntington Library Quarterly* 73.4 (2010), 601–12.

14. For more, see Ed Folsom, *Whitman Making Books / Books Making Whitman* (Iowa City, IA: University of Iowa, 2005).

15. Whitman did publish three books in 1871 with J. S. Redfield, a New York publisher who probably had only nominal involvement with the books' production.

16. The withdrawal was ultimately a product of concerns expressed by the Boston district attorney about obscenity and followed some negotiation between Osgood and Whitman.

17. Charles Green, "David McKay: Whitman's Final Publisher," *Walt Whitman Quarterly Review* 24.2 (2006), 126–40.

18. Ed Folsom, "The Census of the 1855 *Leaves of Grass*: A Preliminary Report," *Walt Whitman Quarterly Review* 24.2 (2006), 80.

19. See for instance three of the title pages included in the first issue of *Two Rivulets*, described in Winship, "Walt Whitman," 39–40.

20. The pages of *Two Rivulets* were printed in the office of the Camden, New Jersey, *New Republic*.

21. Kenneth M. Price, "Love, War, and Revision in Whitman's Blue Book," *Huntington Library Quarterly* 73.4 (2010), 679–92.

22. For recent examples of printed interpretations of Whitman's work, see Barbara Henry, *Walt Whitman's Faces: A Typographic Reading* (Jersey City, NJ: Harsimus Press, 2012), and Allen Crawford, *Whitman Illuminated: Song of Myself* (Portland, OR : Tin House Books, 2014).

23. Folsom, "Census," 83.

CHAPTER 17

The Literary Marketplace

David O. Dowling

Walt Whitman's nuanced appreciation of publicity and promotion informed both his literary art and conception of himself as a professional author. Not only did he draw on a diverse blend of popular trends in the publishing industry to market his work, he tenaciously pursued patronage and endorsements from the era's most influential authors and editors. Whitman vigorously adapted to the increasingly commercial terrain of the antebellum literary marketplace that transformed authorship into a competitive free market scramble. In the prior era, writers enjoyed the economic security of patrician patronage if they were not engaged in literary production as a private amateur pastime with no intent to publish. During Whitman's era, authors responded to vulnerability and risk in the highly volatile climate by forming literary circles that functioned as protective enclaves offering vital aesthetic and professional support. Although he never gained the privileges on the inner circles of Young America in New York City or the transcendentalists in Concord, Whitman won the favor – however short-lived – of several powerful patrons during his career. Any economic risk in pursuing a literary career was offset by the promise of the expanding publishing industry's power to generate unprecedented revenue, as evidenced by the lucrative income of Henry Wadsworth Longfellow, Charles Dickens, and Harriet Beecher Stowe. This chapter provides an overview of the literary marketplace Whitman encountered during his career, followed by a case study of his adaptation to it through his personal and professional relationship with Fanny Fern, the famous columnist for the nation's most popular weekly at the time, the *New York Ledger*.

William Charvat's early research on the profession of authorship identified a linear progression from amateur writer to professional literary practice during the antebellum period. Charvat's thesis has since been revised to reflect a more complex context for literary production during the antebellum era. Ronald J. Zboray and Mary Saracino Zboray, for example, have argued that most writers during this period considered themselves "social" rather than professional authors since the vast majority of literary production was practiced by amateurs. After the Civil War, they contend, authorship became "reprivatized."[1] Leon Jackson has forwarded a more thorough revision of Charvat, pointing out that amateur and professional authorship developed in tandem through a variety of "embedded economies" of exchange in complex networks of production for nonmonetary favors and gifts.[2] This form of exchange generated cultural prestige, which in turn provided social advantages of the sort described in Pierre Bourdieu's field theory of symbolic capital. Michael Everton also makes use of Bourdieu's apt observation that publishers were "cultural bankers" invested in maintaining and developing various forms of capital.[3] Whitman's eclectic literary practice during the antebellum period reflects aspects of each approach, especially in his dual roles of Walter Whitman, professional journalist, and Walt Whitman, the artisanal craftsman of *Leaves of Grass*.

Surges in the development of print media production, including ever-more efficient technologies such as the double-cylinder printing press, combined with the expansion of the railroad transformed literature into business. As literacy rates soared, production and distribution hit a fever pitch to meet rising demand. The industry attracted more start-up publishers than it could accommodate, however, as most only stayed in business an average of sixteen months during the antebellum era.[4] In the absence of copyright law, pressure mounted on the unwritten code of trade courtesy (also known as prior claim) regulating the publishing industry, an agreement that publishers would refrain from luring authors away from each other in order to prevent bidding wars that might increase authors' wages. The business culture of retribution in the absence of codified law prevailed as publishers began to recognize the power of celebrity writers in the periodical press to attract readers.

Whitman operated both as a professional insider via his early journalism, and as an amateur outsider through his self-publishing of the 1855 edition of *Leaves of Grass*. Along with monthly magazines, the rising number of daily and weekly newspapers at the time increased opportunities for publishing poetry. Thus a shift from manuscript to print led to the broad readership of amateur literary efforts previously restricted to small groups of close friends. Print elevated the status and prestige of verse text, advancing it toward professional modes of production and publication. Whitman typifies the era's fluidity between amateur and professional literary practice, as the two roles of professional journalist and amateur/artisanal poet frequently bled into each other. His now famous "Crossing Brooklyn Ferry," for example, had its first iteration in prose as an editorial for the *Brooklyn Daily Eagle*. Indeed, he cultivated his appreciation for the aesthetic spectacle of the urban masses through his first-person narrative voice in "The Philosophy of Ferries" and other newspaper writings.[5] Unlike his relatively secure economic situation as journalist, Whitman's role as poet became an independent enterprise after his first attempt to place *Leaves* with a commercial publisher failed. Undeterred, he sought the help of his printer friends, who were responsible for setting most of the type. He hired jobbers to set the binding and assemble the book and actively sought opportunities with commercial publishers for future editions, as evidenced by the advantages that accrued from his long relationship with the mass-market publisher David McKay.

Whitman's ambition, however, was not to remain an outsider to the literary marketplace, nobly and diligently pursuing his own publicity and distribution through the sort of autonomous renunciation of the free market economy associated with his figure of the poet in *Leaves*. To the contrary, he eagerly accepted any signs of attention from commercial publishers.[6] Even "a pair of upstart publishers with abolitionist sympathies," William R. Thayer and Charles W. Eldridge, were irresistible to Whitman. "We want to be publishers of Walt Whitman's Poems," they wrote in direct and unadorned prose, signaling their allegiance with the urban working class. Voicing their admiration for his first edition in which "a man dares to speak his thought in this day of refinement – so called," they sympathized about how difficult it is "to find his mates to act amen to it." Not to be mistaken with a vanity press for amateurs, they go on to describe their intention to produce a competitive product for a market already dominated by the tailored lines and well-mannered meter – free verse's opposite – of Henry Wadsworth Longfellow. They proposed to "put your books into good form and style attractive to the eye; we can and will sell a large number of copies; we have great facilities by and through numberless Agents in selling," concluding the letter with a proposition Whitman could not refuse: "We 'celebrate' ourselves by acts. Try us. You can do us good. We can do you good – pecuniarily."[7] This fraternal bond of plain-dealing artisanal comradeship with Whitman does not elide their intention to leverage the latest technologies to reach the widest audience possible. Whitman accepted their offer to publish the 1860 edition of *Leaves* at a tiny ten percent of net sales, only to watch Thayer and Eldridge go bankrupt during the Civil War.

To recover production costs from the 1855 edition, Whitman self-fashioned reviews and blurbs, often appropriating such popular trends as phrenology in the process. Whitman recognized that the best blurbs served the dual purpose of certifying the work's quality while also instructing readers on the nature of its content. At that time he won the backing of Fanny Fern, the popular columnist for the *New York Ledger*. He identified with Fern's aesthetics, advocacy of women and the working class, and aggressive tactics in the market. Both suffered galling rejections from powerful patrons at moments when they were most vulnerable. Emerson distanced himself from Whitman after expressing his initial support; Fern's own brother, N. P. Willis, refused her request of support for her fledgling writing career. As editor of *The Home Journal* and widely respected arbiter of moral values and aesthetic taste from home décor to fashion and literature, Willis was one of the most influential literary figures in antebellum America. He had left a lasting sting with the comment that "you overstrain the pathetic and your humor runs into dreadful vulgarity sometimes." (Critics assailing Whitman's *Leave of Grass* similarly cited vulgarity as his chief sin.) Worse still was Willis's sense that she would sully his professional reputation. "I am sorry that any editor knows that a sister of mine wrote some of these which you sent me," he sniffed.[8] Fern's retaliation in an 1853 column titled "Apollo Hyacinth" provided the impetus for her more fully realized diagnosis of the flaws in the publishing industry she elaborated two years later in *Ruth Hall* (1855), especially with respect to the aforementioned gentleman publisher's code of prior claim that prevented authors from accepting higher wages from publishers with competitive bids. She indicts precisely the solicitous patronage that rankled Whitman. "Should you die tomorrow," Fern wrote, "Apollo would write a poetical obituary notice of you, which would raise the price of pocket handkerchiefs; but should your widow call on him in the course of a month, to solicit his patronage to open a school, she would be told 'he was out of town.'"[9]

Like Fern, Whitman defined his literary identity against the aesthetics of the conservative sentimental elite associated with Willis and Lewis Gaylord Clark, editor of the Whiggish *Knickerbocker Magazine*. Their clubbish exclusivity systematically denied authors without insider connections access to the rich advantages of their inner circle. Editor Evert Duyckinck's *Literary World* and Young America, the Democratic literary circle that once included Herman Melville and Cornelius Mathews, rebuffed Whitman. "Yes, I was left out," he recalled decades later. "Why not? It was not surprising: I am not even today accepted in New York by the great bogums – much less then." As with Fern, he used that outsidership as an emblem of his allegiance to the masses, one set in sharp contrast to Young America's gatekeeper Duyckinck, the most influential editor in New York during the 1850s, and his brother who assisted him. Whitman recalled how he "met these brothers: they were both 'gentlemanly men' – and by the way I don't know any description it would have pleased them better to hear: both very clerical looking – thin – wanting in body: men of truly proper style, God help 'em!" (WWC, 1:139). Melville also casts Duyckinck as an anemic prig in his 1852 novel *Pierre*, where he appears as the dandy editor Glen Stanly. Melville's "Young America in Literature" chapter in the novel that followed the disastrous reception of *Moby-Dick* (1851) aligns with Whitman's bitterness toward the Duyckinck group in the wake of his own critical abuse at their hands.

Fern, however, pledged her devotion to Whitman the moment she encountered the 1855 edition of *Leaves of Grass*. Sensing he was a kindred spirit aligned against the genteel snobbery of literary New York, she wrote him an adoring letter. "Leaves of Grass," she addressed him, "you are *delicious*! May my might right hand wither if I do not tell the world before another week, what *one* woman thinks of you," she gushed, promising to puff his book in her weekly *New York Ledger* column. By the letter's date of April 21, 1856, her column held considerable influence since her bestselling autobiographical novel *Ruth Hall* had been in circulation for a year. "Walt," she calls him alluding to the grandiose poet figure on *Leaves of Grass* as distinct from the Walter of his daily identity, "what *I* assume, *you* shall assume! Some one evening this week, you are to spend with Jemmy [James Parton] & me – Wednesday? – say."[10] James Parton, who had introduced Whitman to Fern soon after their marriage, was Fern's fellow staff writer at the *New York Ledger*. Parton's lucrative popular biographies of *Tribune* editor Horace Greeley and Fern herself supplemented Fern's outlandish salary of $100 per column and royalties from Mason Brothers for *Ruth Hall*. Their combined income enabled them to provide financial assistance to Whitman, who was notoriously frank about soliciting it.[11]

Fern appreciated Whitman's unpretentious manner and attire. In a series of sketches for the *Ledger* profiling the New York literati, she extolled the bohemian portrait on the frontispiece of *Leaves of Grass*. She took his open "shirt collar turned off from his muscular throat" as welcome relief from the fashionable "smirking fops and brainless belles" filling the pages of popular journals such as *Godey's Lady's Book*. Refusing to isolate his charisma to his superficial image, she locates his magnetic – and indeed erotic – appeal in his voice. She describes how "his shoulders are thrown back as if even in that fine, ample chest of his, his lungs had not sufficient play-room," urging readers to "Mark his voice!"[12] Whitman responded by proclaiming he "liked her better than any woman," and began to keep company regularly with her and her husband in Manhattan.[13] Since Whitman was under pressure to generate his own publicity, he was acutely aware that Fern's platform and reach could be instrumental to expanding his audience. Whitman thus wrote a flattering sketch of *Ledger* publisher Robert Bonner in the same spirit as Fern's heroic portrait of him. In it, he celebrated Bonner as a "hero of unheard-of and tremendous advertising" with ballyhoo worthy of Bonner himself, calling his journal a "gorgeous and unprecedented sheet."[14]

Fern's widely read *Ledger* column was only the beginning of Whitman's publicity campaign. He also leveraged Fern's circle of literary friends through social gatherings held at her home. There he met Thomas Butler Gunn, whom he convinced to "put him in pen and ink" in a published portrait. Gunn's diary reveals that Whitman actively worked himself into the good graces of Fern, turning his visits into something of a performance. Whitman stood out as the most garrulous of her guests. Gunn noted that "Walt talks *well* – but occasionally too much, being led by the interest with which his remarks are received into monopolizing the converse." He also distinguished himself for his parting ritual of dramatically kissing Fern. Her husband Parton, however, "isn't jealous of Walt's kissing her, which he always does on quitting."[15]

Fern's affinity for Whitman appears in her glowing review of *Leaves of Grass*. In it, she lauds the volume, whose title was inspired by Grace Greenwood's *Greenwood Leaves* (1850) and her own popular 1853 *Fern Leaves from Fanny Fern's Portfolio*. By situating himself with these works he reached out to middle-class women readers, whom he also courted in gift-book editions of his poetry such as the 1889 volume *Gems from Walt Whitman*. Fern admired how Whitman's pen could "paint not nude Nature, but stealing Virtue's veil, with artful artlessness now conceal, now exposes, the ripe and swelling proportions." Whitman's revolutionary approach to poetry was also couched in commercial rhetoric designed for publicity in the literary market much like Fern's own writings. Her review was particularly daring since the overwhelming majority of the critical community had condemned the volume for being vulgar, a term Willis had used against her. Fern and Whitman suffered similar unjust treatment at the hands of critics and potential patrons. She thus found *Leaves of Grass* "unspeakably delicious" in contrast to "the forced, stiff, Parnassian exotics" like Willis and Emerson "for whom our admiration has been vainly challenged." She appreciated his willingness to dignify the everyday lives of mothers, daughters, and sisters, figures otherwise solicited as objects of sentimentality in Henry Wadsworth Longfellow's widely read verse. Given that achievement, Fern acknowledged, "the effeminate world needed thee."[16] But Whitman and Fern's relationship ended as quickly as it began. Just one year later, Whitman refused to repay a loan he had taken from Fern's husband, James Parton. Making matters worse, the funds were drawn from the couple's income from their *Ledger* contributions; Whitman had effectively stolen the fruits of their literary labor in search of his own.[17] Two years later, she admitted the charismatic voice she had praised in her 1856 column was that of a charlatan, lamenting "The dollars that fellow has borrowed on that voice, the drinks he has swallowed on the strength of it, not to mention the strength of the drinks." She vowed, "No, I believe no more in voices."[18] Although Parton and Fern severed ties with the poet in a ritual burning of *Leaves of Grass* in their fireplace, almost a decade later Fern softened her stance, allowing that "He really did not *mean* to incur debts he could not pay." She nonetheless continued to vent her frustration that "he never could keep a cent of money."[19]

In "To Rich Givers," Whitman dignifies the solicitation for patronage of the sort he won from Fern. The poem is his brazen justification of his open solicitations for "A little sustenance, a hut and garden" along with "a little money." He asks, "Why should I be ashamed of such gifts?" His justification? "I myself am not one who bestows nothing upon man and woman, / For I know that what I bestow upon any man or woman is no less than the entrance to all the gifts of the universe." The poem reflects more than his characteristic boldness. It also seeks to shock and destabilize conventional values with his confident swagger, in the process providing a key to Whitman's economy. He drops the mask of anti-commercialism of the poet figure in *Leaves of Grass*, one averse to the dehumanizing and reifying effects of industrial labor and market transactions. He enters into that market here, exposing his desires plainly. The good he produces is spiritual, and thus unlocks the key to unlimited gifts for which he is more than deserving of financial compensation. He is aware of the culture's disapproval of a poet approaching his craft with such entrepreneurial self-promotion, asking why he "should be ashamed to own such gifts" from wealthy patrons, "or to advertise for them." He seeks the privilege of authorship as the primary vocation and demands enough food and shelter to enable him to "rendezvous with my poems" (LG60, 399).

As "To Rich Givers" attests, craft and self-promotion were openly connected in his poetry. Indeed, in this poem the justification of such a link provides the material for his art. His open desire for money enables the creative process not through extravagances that might distract him from it. Patronage, like the kind he solicited from Emerson, is a priority to him, and he finds the exchange not an unsightly necessity of the romantic poet's trade to be discreetly hidden from view. To the contrary, he highlights it and considers such a transaction a rich and telling subject of poetry, as "To Rich Givers" sounds both a note of gratitude and a barbaric yawp of self-aggrandizement testifying to his own powers. The poem is not so much a gesture of shameful self-indulgence as a frank and upright embrace of being paid for one's work that offers a valid and valuable product in return. That literary product, like all other art objects, indeed provides entrance "to all the gifts of the universe" (LG60, 399).

Authors such as Harriet Beecher Stowe, Fanny Fern, and Sylvanus Cobb leveraged serialized publication in journals for later publication in book form. Whitman's prolific journalism career that prefaced his turn to poetry in 1855 did not cease with his focus on verse. Instead, his journalism intensified in 1858 with his *Atlas* "Manly Health and Training" series. The series departs from his journalism and even his more lyrical editorials, as in the previously mentioned "The Philosophy of Ferries" in the *Brooklyn Daily Eagle* that provided the basis for "Crossing Brooklyn Ferry." He did not intend the *Atlas* series to be a one-off project, as he had of *Franklin Evans* (1842). "Manly Health" has fascinating implications for the literary marketplace, particularly as his attempt to tap into the popularity of the health movement among literary authors. Thoreau was among the many writers of the period to take physical health as a metaphor for the nation's moral well being and cultural vitality. "Only while we are in action is the circulation perfect," he observed, registering his astonishment at the sedentary habits of his fellow citizens of Concord. "The writing which consists with habitual sitting is mechanical, wooden, dull to read."[20] Thoreau covered roughly twenty miles per day on foot as he estimated in his lecture on "Walking." Catharine Beecher's wildly popular *Treatise on Domestic Economy* (1841) provided girls with health and nutrition advice as the foundation of the nation's development. Whitman similarly saw the healthy body as the basis for democracy, and the mechanisms of journalism and the literary market the means through which to inspire health and vigor. Thirteen installments of 47,000 words amount to a project opposite of *Franklin Evans* – journalism that reads like literature, intended not as ephemeral diversion (or lowly lurid fascination) but as reading to be done by "three-fourths of the young and middle-aged men" up to "once or twice a year, during the remainder of their lives," enduring literature for the sustenance of the nation's democratic future.[21] Emerson's original description of *Leaves of Grass* might equally apply to "Manly Health and Training": "It has the best merits, namely, of fortifying and encouraging."[22] Whitman never abandoned his belief that the periodical press could carry the message of his broader democratic vision.

Notes

1. Ronald J. Zboray and Mary Saracino Zboray, *Literary Dollars and Social Sense: A People's History of the Mass Market Book* (New York, NY: Routledge, 2005), 12.
2. Leon Jackson, *The Business of Letters: Authorial Economies in Antebellum America* (Stanford, CA: Stanford University Press, 2008), 2–4.
3. Michael Everton, *The Grand Chorus of Complaint: Authors and the Business Ethics of American Publishing* (New York, NY: Oxford University Press, 2011), 15.
4. Everton, *Grand Chorus*, 17.
5. Walter Whitman, "The Philosophy of Ferries," *The Brooklyn Daily Eagle* (Brooklyn, NY), August 13, 1847.
6. David Dowling, *Capital Letters: Authorship in the Antebellum Literary Market* (Iowa City, IA: University of Iowa Press, 2009), 92.
7. Thayer & Eldridge to Walt Whitman, February 10, 1860. WWA. See also Andrew Lawson, *Walt Whitman and the Class Struggle* (Iowa City, IA: University of Iowa Press, 2006), 28.
8. Thomas N. Baker, *Sentiment and Celebrity: Nathaniel Parker Willis and the Trials of Literary Fame* (New York, NY: Oxford University Press, 2005), 163.
9. Fanny Fern, *Ruth Hall and Other Writings*, ed. Joyce W. Warren (New Brunswick, NJ: Rutgers University Press, 1986), 163.
10. Joyce W. Warren, *Fanny Fern: An Independent Woman* (New Brunswick, NJ: Rutgers University Press, 1992), 164.
11. David Dowling, *The Business of Literary Circles in Nineteenth-Century America* (New York, NY: Palgrave, 2011), 250.
12. Fanny Fern, "Peeps from Under a Parasol," *New York Ledger* (New York, NY), April 19, 1856.
13. Quoted in Warren, *Fanny Fern*, 162.
14. Ibid., 163.
15. Ibid., 164.
16. Fern, *Ruth Hall*, 274–76.
17. Joyce W. Warren, "Subversion versus Celebration: The Aborted Friendship of Fanny Fern and Walt Whitman," in *Patrons and Protégées: Gender, Friendship, and Writing in Nineteenth-Century America*, ed. Shirley Marchalonis (New Brunswick, NJ: Rutgers University Press, 1988), 59–93.
18. Fanny Fern, "On Voices and Beards," *New York Ledger* (New York, NY), April 3, 1858.

19. Fanny Fern, "Unprincipled Talent," *New York Ledger* (New York, NY), October 28, 1865.

20. Henry David Thoreau, *The Writings of Henry David Thoreau: Journal,* 14 vols., ed. Bradford Torrey (Boston, MA: Houghton Mifflin, 1906), 2:405.

21. Mose Velsor [Walt Whitman], "Manly Health and Training," *New York Atlas,* September 12, 1858. Reprinted in *Walt Whitman Quarterly Review* 33.3 (2016), 184–310.

22. Ralph Waldo Emerson, *The Letters of Ralph Waldo Emerson, Vol. 8,* eds. Ralph L. Rusk and Elanor M. Tilton (New York, NY: Columbia University Press, 1939), 446.

CHAPTER 18

Transatlantic Book Distribution

Jessica DeSpain

A longstanding myth surrounds the British distribution of the 1855 edition of *Leaves of Grass*. William Michael Rossetti, the editor of the first British publication of Whitman's poems, received his copy as a Christmas gift from the Pre-Raphaelite painter William Bell Scott. Scott explains that he picked up the book from cork-cutter Thomas Dixon, who himself purchased the book illegally in Sunderland from an indigent peddler. These stories of a folksy underground in which Whitman's book was passed from hand-to-hand by a working-class readership efface his intentional work to cultivate a transatlantic reputation.[1] In fact, Whitman's bookseller Fowler and Wells sent copies to their British representative William Horsell. Some versions of the 1855 *Leaves of Grass* have a four-leaf gathering sewn into the front with reviews and Emerson's letter.[2] Many of the eight British reviews mention that their offices received this version, suggesting that Whitman directly courted British attention.

Yet, unlike in the United States where Whitman maintained control over almost all aspects of book design, editions of his works printed in Britain during the nineteenth century were projects of compromise, expurgation, and editorial framing. Studying Whitman's relationships with publishers and editors illuminates how he operated in a literary marketplace where he had little power. When remembering his British editors, Whitman told Horace Traubel, "Damn the expurgated books! I say damn 'em! The dirtiest book in all the world is the expurgated book!" (WWC, 1:124). Despite his distaste for these editions, examining Whitman's reception from the 1855 *Leaves of Grass* to the final 1891–92 edition reveals a positive shift in British perception of the poet because of editorial interventions. British reviews of the 1855 *Leaves of Grass* describe Whitman's poetry as exotic and obscene, but by century's end Whitman becomes representative of democracy itself among working-class audiences.

Whitman began *Leaves of Grass* during a significant period in the development of the transatlantic book trade. Because there was no international copyright law, American publishers produced a bulk of cheap British literature by remunerating authors only a little or not at all. In her book *American Literature and the Culture of Reprinting, 1834–1853*, Meredith McGill explores how authors framed their works within a system that privileged cheap literature as a republican right.[3] The first edition of *Leaves of Grass* postdates the limits of McGill's study during a period when British publishers began to reprint an equally impressive and inexpensive multitude of American works. British trade practices and copyright laws shifted frequently, and British publishers tried any number of things to secure exclusive rights to American works. By 1854 legal precedent required American authors to reside on British soil on the date their work was published, a luxury that few could afford. Instead, they sought out reputable publishers hoping that trade courtesy – wherein competitors would uphold the exclusive rights of an authorized publisher – would protect their literary property.[4] Yet, by the 1850s, the growth of reprinting as a lucrative market meant that few followed these rules.

The significant rise in American reprints during the 1850s was primarily due to a growth in British reading audiences as women, children, and the working classes had the ability and the leisure to read in increasing numbers. Still, a typical British worker had approximately three shillings of disposable income per week – not much for purchasing books.[5] By mid-century changing technologies and marketing strategies made one shilling cardboard-covered pocket volumes, or "yellow backs," a common offering at railway stands.[6] American fiction sold especially well in this format. Harriet Beecher Stowe's *Uncle Tom's Cabin* (1852) and Susan Warner's *The Wide, Wide World* (1850) were reprinted in a variety of cheap formats and reached unprecedented sales figures abroad.[7]

Poetry, however, experienced a transatlantic fate that was tied to critical as well as readerly reception. As Meredith McGill explains in her introduction to *The Traffic in Poems: Nineteenth-Century Poetry and Transatlantic Exchange*, "American poets, relying on the British periodical press to recognize and ratify their emergent literary tradition, eagerly reprinted even slender evidence of British approbation."[8] In this way, Britain retained control over poetic acclaim in both nations. Even so, American poetry was much cheaper for British audiences than their native Tennyson. From 1801 to 1862, according to Simon Eliot's work on the pricing of nineteenth-century poetry in Britain, Tennyson had twenty-four items published before his works passed out of copyright, only three of which were two shillings or less, with most of his titles selling for five shillings. The American poet Henry Wadsworth Longfellow, by contrast, had seventy-one items published during the same period, twenty-three of which were two shillings or less, making the poet much more accessible to British audiences and perhaps explaining the author's British canonization as a featured bust in Westminster Abbey's Poet's Corner.[9]

The effects of British influence on American poetry may also clarify Whitman's paradoxical anger toward and courting of British reception. Whitman opens the Preface to the 1855 *Leaves of Grass*, his manifesto for a new global poetics, with a metaphor in which the European past is a "corpse" that is being "slowly borne from the eating and sleeping rooms of the house" as a new "heir" approaches who is "stalwart and wellshaped" (LG55, iii). Yet, the poet was systematic in his sharing of both the laudatory and the defamatory reviews from the British Isles with his readers. In the 1856 edition, he ended the book with an advertising section called "Leaves-Droppings" wherein he lists Horsell as his British distributor and reprints Emerson's letter along with eight reviews, over half of which are British. Similarly, Thayer and Eldridge's promotional "Imprints" pamphlet for the 1860 edition is subtitled "American and European Criticisms of *Leaves of Grass*." Just as he did with Emerson's letter, Whitman capitalized upon his British reception as another means to expand notice of his work; the negative reviews stirred literary nationalism whereas the positive reviews gave him literary caché both at home and abroad.

Examining Whitman's reception among other popular transatlantic poets reveals that he received substantial notice (or at least notoriety). Longfellow's *Hiawatha*, which was also published in 1855 without the benefit of a British copyright, serves as an ideal comparison. According to Kate Flint, "Three editions of *Hiawatha* were released by prominent reprint publishers in 1855, eleven other editions appeared by 1900, the collection was extensively reviewed, and *Hiawatha* inspired several musical spin-offs."[10] Though *Leaves of Grass* did not initially tempt reprinters, booksellers distributed the 1855, 1860, 1876, and 1881 American editions.[11] The first British publication came in 1868 when James Camden Hotten printed 1,500 copies of a selected edition titled *Poems of Walt Whitman* (*Hiawatha* sold 17,250 copies in its first year).[12] Hotten later printed 500 copies of a forged version of the 1872 *Leaves of Grass* (the only complete British edition published during Whitman's lifetime). In addition, the scholarly publisher Trübner's released a version of the 1855 Preface in 1881. In 1871, Sampson Low distributed copies of *Democratic Vistas*. By the 1880s, Whitman's works became standard in the reprint series of Walter Scott Publishing Company. They released a selection in 1886 titled *Leaves of Grass: The Poems of Walt Whitman* in the Canterbury Poets series that sold 8,000 copies in two months. The company's Camelot series issued *Specimen Days in America* in 1887 and *Democratic Vistas and Other Papers* in 1888. British publications reviewed Whitman's works at least sixty-five times. And Whitman, like Longfellow, was a musical inspiration; in 1884 British composer C. Villiers Stanford released choral music to accompany "When Lilacs Last on the Dooryard Bloom'd." Yet Longfellow, especially early in the century, was seen by critics as the quintessential American bard.

Most British reviews pronounced Whitman as an American exotic: a "Caliban," a "madman," a "monster." In George Eliot's 1856 more measured, positive review for *The Leader*, she explains that Whitman had been "received by a section of his countrymen as a sort of prophet, and by Englishmen as a kind of fool."[13] Rather than understanding Whitman's use of common language as intentional, critics charged him with dissembling toward a higher art. *The Critic*'s reviewer compared Whitman's poems to "the war-cry of the Red Indians" and argued that Whitman was like "Caliban flinging down his logs, and setting himself to write a poem." How, asked the reviewer, could "this man with the 'barbaric yawp' [. . .] push Longfellow into the shade?"[14] As Caliban, *The Critic*'s Whitman is the native incapable of eloquent speech who seeks to usurp Longfellow's prominence as the American poet.

Foregrounding Whitman's Americanness positions him more as spectacle than respectable. "We had ceased to be surprised at anything that America could produce," grieves *The Critic*'s reviewer. "We had become stoically indifferent to her Woolly Horses, her Mermaids, her Sea Serpents, her Barnums, and her Fanny Ferns; but the last monstrous importation from Brooklyn, New York, has scattered our indifference to the winds." This list of oddities is mythological, sensational, and sordid, as in the case of Fanny Fern, whose 1854 novel *Ruth Hall* was a thinly veiled autobiography that appalled critics by revealing domestic dramas. Like Fern, Whitman is criticized for speaking the unspoken, a tendency that some reviewers label as obscenity. These concerns were acute in Britain because the Obscene Publications Act of 1857 gave police the power to forcibly seize printed materials at their own discretion.

When James Camden Hotten decided to release a selection of Whitman's poems in 1868, he had to proceed with caution. Moncure D. Conway, then visiting England, was tasked with helping Whitman find a British publisher. In a letter dated December 5, 1866, William O'Connor encouraged Conway to seek out Hotten, the publisher of Swinburne's *Poems and Ballads* (1866), which had themes of lesbianism and sadomasochism. Hotten was renowned for publishing American literature as well as erotica and the avant-garde.[15] However, in a letter dated April 30, 1867, Conway told O'Connor he had been in discussions with Swinburne, William Michael Rossetti, and Hotten, and that some passages in Whitman's poems would "bring a legal prosecution on any publisher."[16]

Despite the April 1867 correspondence, Whitman sent Conway a letter on July 24, along with the most recent edition of *Leaves of Grass* and an introduction for English audiences, hoping his friend would find a publisher for the complete *Leaves* (Corr., 1:332–33). It was not to be; Conway soon discovered Hotten had commissioned Rossetti that September to edit only a selection. It was not uncommon for American books to be introduced to British audiences with editorial framing of this type. Rossetti, brother to poets Christina and Dante Gabriel, had authored a favorable review of Whitman earlier that year. Conway notified Whitman on October 12 and assured him Rossetti was a good choice (letter copied in WWC, 3:297). The selection would include half of the 1867 edition, and Rossetti wanted to print the 1855 Preface with changes to the phrases "father-stuff," "venereal sores or discolorations," "onanist," and "any depravity of young men." In a November 1 letter, Whitman acknowledged he could do little else than accept Rossetti's edition and grant permission to change the Preface's wording (Corr., 1: 346–47). Whitman wrote further letters asking for clarifications to Rossetti's introduction, for a title page of his own devising, and for a title change from "When Lilacs Last in the Dooryard Bloom'd" to "President Lincoln's Funeral Hymn" (Corr., 1:347–51). Rossetti could honor only Whitman's poem title request because the edition was already underway. The editorial back-and-forth that Whitman experienced in his correspondence with Hotten and Rossetti was not unusual. Clarence Gohdes's work on Longfellow's relationship with his authorized British publishers is a litany of similar stories. Like Whitman, Longfellow received little remuneration, and his requests were rarely heeded. In one instance, W. Kent and Co. hatched a later-abandoned scheme to print unidentified poems from a British author intermixed with Longfellow's so poachers of the text would be in violation of British copyright.[17]

Most critics now conclude that Rossetti's edition was meant to sanitize Whitman for elite audiences. It sold for six shillings, or two weeks of a British workman's disposable income. Rossetti rationalizes his selections by explaining that he wants readers to take Whitman seriously, so he has removed poems that might be "deemed offensive to the feelings of morals or propriety in this peculiarly nervous age."[18] Rossetti made no changes to the poems themselves, but he reordered them into four sections taken from Whitman's own writings: "Chants Democratic," "Drum Taps," "Walt Whitman," and "Leaves of Grass." He also retitled poems that had previously been listed by first line. Rossetti did not include "Song of Myself." Not surprisingly, he cut the "Children of Adam" cluster. He also trimmed "Calamus" from forty-four poems to seventeen and distributed the poems to new sections, taking away their combined emphasis on comradeship and homosexual love.

In 1867 concerns about equality and suffrage, at the forefront of debate in both nations, reshaped Whitman from spectacle into political critic. Whitman had just published the first post-war version of *Leaves of Grass*, which contained four separately paginated books hastily stitched together like the American Union itself: a substantially edited *Leaves of Grass* and the Civil War and Reconstruction collections *Drum-Taps*, *Sequel to Drum-Taps*, and *Songs Before Parting*. Britain was undergoing its own social upheaval because of Benjamin Disraeli's Reform Act of 1867, which "raised the total number of voters from 1,358,000 to 2,477,000."[19] In "Shooting Niagara: and After?" Thomas Carlyle argued the Reform Act would destroy Britain, using the enfranchisement of African Americans in the United States as illustration. That year, Whitman issued a response to Carlyle in three essays that would later become *Democratic Vistas*.

In his edition, Rossetti solidifies Whitman's importance as an ambassador for democracy by ending his introduction with a quote from Shelley – "Poets are the unacknowledged legislators of the world." Of Whitman, Rossetti adds "the uttermost avatars of democracy will confess him not more their announcer than their inspirer."[20] He shapes Whitman's persona by talking about the poet's work in Civil War hospitals and the philosophical importance of the tension in the poems between "One's-Self" and "En Masse." Rossetti's emphasis on the Civil War continued in the book itself wherein he distributed the poems from *Drum-Taps* and *Sequel to Drum-Taps* into their own section, resituating into other sections those poems not directly applicable to the war. Thus, he accomplished the act of reconstruction that neither Whitman nor the American Union had successfully completed. Julianne Ramsay argues that, despite Whitman's later critiques, Rossetti's "Drum Taps" section was roughly the same as that Whitman would reproduce in later editions of *Leaves of Grass*.[21] These subtle reworkings had the effect of changing Whitman's critical reception and ultimately the breadth of his British distribution.

The resulting book was reviewed eleven times. Many of the earlier threads continued, with some reviewers too distracted by what the missing poems contained to give Whitman a fair reading; however, the emphasis that Rossetti placed on the Civil War mitigated the criticism. By 1871, Edward Dowden writes in *The Westminster Review*: "These are the poems which naturally arise when a man of imaginative genius stands face to face with a great democratic world [. . .]. He is the first representative democrat in art of the American Continent."[22] Even *The Critic*, a publication that had issued Whitman's harshest reviews, owns by 1881 that Whitman "represents [. . .] the struggling, blundering, sound-hearted, somewhat coarse, but still magnificent vanguard of Western civilization that is encamped in the United States of America."[23] By the time Ernest Rhys became passionate about workingman's editions of Whitman in the 1880s, the groundwork was laid for understanding Whitman's representative value for universal democracy.

Rhys, the Welsh son of a wine-shop manager, who became a mining engineer and later moved to London to establish himself as a literary man, understood Whitman's desire to reach working-class audiences. His life's work would be devoted to providing canonical literature at a cheap price. Rhys was invested in cultivating readers with enough education and agency to alter political systems. In his Preface to *Leaves of Grass: Poems of Walt Whitman* (1886), he writes, "We want now a poetry that shall be masterfully contemporary, of irresistible appeal to the hearts of the people; and this we certainly have not in England to-day."[24] Whitman saw Rhys as a specimen of this democratizing work, telling Traubel, "Rhys is the type of [. . .] young men who will rightly perceive, measure us, and then go back and democratize Great Britain" (WWC, 1:221). But Rhys was also invested in his Welsh heritage and did not espouse the same anti-traditionalist strain in poetic form as Whitman. In one conversation with Traubel, Whitman says of Rhys, "having dug so deep into the old English balladry he becomes convinced of the necessity of the lilt, the regular flow, the notation, [. . .] hence his lingering distrust of the *Leaves*" (WWC, 1:124). This tension between old world poetics and new world democracy would frequently characterize Whitman's concerns about his British editors and readers.

The Walter Scott Publishing Company, for whom Rhys worked, created a business by organizing uniform series. These books, selling at approximately one shilling in uniform bindings advertised alongside their siblings in the series, had a tendency of removing the individualism of authors represented. Within the full body of works that comprised the Canterbury Poets and the Camelot Series, Whitman's manifesto of American democracy became one voice among many in an English tradition leading toward a British version of democracy. Though Rhys only slightly reordered the poems (just a few in "Inscriptions"), like Rossetti, he omitted one hundred poems, including "Song of Myself" and the "Children of Adam" cluster. Rhys kept most of "Calamus," though he cut poems tied closely to sexuality, including "Trickle Drops," "City of Orgies," "Behold This Swarthy Face," "I Saw in Louisiana a Live-Oak Growing," and "We Two Boys Together Clinging." Still, the edition became a touchstone for the working-class audiences whom Whitman had hoped to reach.

By the end of his life, Whitman's home was a common stop on American tours for members of the elite audience that first learned of his poems from Rossetti. After a visit to the poet, Oscar Wilde said, "The people in England, for whose opinion he would care, read him, and wonder at him."[25] It is hard to know whether Wilde was referring to working-class audiences or to poets and thinkers like Edward Carpenter and John Addington Symonds, who actively debated Whitman's politics and his sexuality. Whitman, though, had reached both audiences in equal measure. His working-class readers used the poet to create their own distinctive blends of protest. James Clunie, for instance, a Marxist housepainter, claimed that he was "inspired to rebel against the factory system by the 'stimulating anarchism of Walt Whitman and the prophetic works of Robert Burns.'"[26] The poet was delighted by letters and visits of members of the Whitman Fellowship, a group of mill workers in Bolton, Lancashire, who met regularly to discuss Whitman's poetry.

That Whitman finally reached these diverse British audiences was no accident but the result of his own work to see the books distributed and reviewed abroad. Though he may have lamented the compromises he had to make to see the Rossetti and Rhys selections take shape, these editorial interventions were part and parcel of the formation of the British Whitman, who morphed from an obscene oddity into a respected representative for democracy itself.

Notes

1. William Michael Rossetti, "Dedication," in *Poems by Walt Whitman*, ed. William Michael Rossetti (London: James Camden Hotten, 1868), viii, WWA. Also see John T. Winterich, *The Romance of Great Books and Their Authors* (New York, NY: Halcyon House, 1929), 17.
2. Joel Myerson, *Walt Whitman: A Descriptive Bibliography* (Pittsburg, PA: University of Pittsburg Press, 1993), 19.

3. Meredith L. McGill, *American Literature and the Culture of Reprinting, 1834–1853* (Philadelphia, PA: University of Pennsylvania Press, 2003), 1–4.

4. See Melissa Homestead, "American Novelist Catharine Maria Sedgwick Negotiated British Copyright, 1822–1857," *The Yearbook of English Studies* 45 (2015), 196–215.

5. Simon Eliot, "What Price Poetry?" *The Papers of the Bibliographical Society of America* 100.4 (2006), 427.

6. For accounts of shifting technological and trade strategies, see Richard Altick, *The English Common Reader: A Social History of the Mass Reading Public, 1800–1900*, 2nd edn. (Columbus, OH: Ohio State University Press, 1998), 300, 392–93; and William St. Clair, *The Reading Nation in the Romantic Period* (New York, NY: Cambridge University Press, 2004), 300.

7. Sales figures are difficult to track, but newspapers boasted *Uncle Tom's Cabin* sold more than 1.5 million British copies in its first year (Altick, *English Common Reader*, 384).

8. Meredith L. McGill, "Introduction: The Traffic in Poems," in *The Traffic in Poems: Nineteenth-Century Poetry and Transatlantic Exchange*, ed. Meredith L. McGill (New Brunswick, NJ: Rutgers University Press, 2008), 5.

9. Eliot, "What Price Poetry?" 430–31.

10. Kate Flint, "Is the Native an American? National Identity and the British Reception of *Hiawatha*," in *The Traffic in Poems*, 71.

11. See Edward Whitley, "Introduction to the British Editions of *Leaves of Grass*," WWA.

12. Clarence Gohdes, "Longfellow and His British Publishers," *PMLA* 55.4 (1940), 1172.

13. [George Eliot], "Transatlantic Latter-Day Poetry," *The Leader* (London), June 7, 1856, 547–54, WWA.

14. "Leaves of Grass (1855), by Walt Whitman [review]," *The Critic*, April 1, 1856, 170–71, WWA.

15. Morton D. Paley, "John Camden Hotten and the First British Editions of Walt Whitman – 'A Nice Milky Cocoa-nut,'" *Publishing History* 6.1 (1979), 6–7.

16. Moncure D. Conway to William O'Connor, April 30, 1867, Beinecke Rare Book and Manuscript Library, Yale University, quoted in Paley, "John Camden Hotten," 6.

17. Gohdes, "Longfellow and His British Publishers," 1173.

18. William Michael Rossetti, "Prefatory Notice," in *Poems*, 20.

19. J. B. Conacher, ed., *The Emergence of British Parliamentary Democracy in the Nineteenth Century: The Passing of the Reform Acts of 1832, 1867, and 1884–1885* (New York, NY: John Wiley and Sons, 1971), 73.

20. Rossetti, "Prefatory Notice," 27.

21. Julianne Ramsay, "A British View to an American War: Whitman's 'Drum Taps' Cluster and the Editorial Influence of William Michael Rossetti," *Walt Whitman Quarterly Review* 14.4 (1997), 166–75.

22. [Edward Dowden], "The Poetry of Democracy: Walt Whitman," *The Westminster Review* (London), July 1871, 33–68, WWA.

23. "Whitman's 'Leaves of Grass,'" *The Critic*, November 5, 1881, 302–3, WWA.

24. Ernest Rhys, "Introduction," in *Leaves of Grass: The Poems of Walt Whitman* (London: Walter Scott, 1886), xxvii, WWA.

25. "Mr. Oscar Wilde," *Evening Star* (Washington, DC), January 21, 1882, WWA.

26. Jonathan Rose, *The Intellectual Life of the British Working Classes* (New Haven, CT: Yale University Press, 2002), 51.

PART III

Cultural and Political Contexts

CHAPTER 19

Transcendentalism

Regina Schober

During his time as a journalist for various newspapers in the 1840s and before the publication of *Leaves of Grass*, Walt Whitman was already familiar with the flowering movement of American transcendentalism. In a favorable review for the *Brooklyn Daily Eagle*, he welcomed Margaret Fuller's *Papers on Literature and Art* (1846) "right heartily" and saved the pages on American literature for the rest of his life.[1] Four years earlier he had reviewed Emerson's lecture on "Nature and the Powers of the Poet," writing that he considered it "one of the richest and most beautiful compositions, both for its matter and style, we have ever heard, anywhere, at any time."[2] Yet, Whitman's background as a New York journalist and the intellectual culture of the New England literary establishment may seem an unlikely match. It is not surprising that Charles Eliot Norton famously characterized *Leaves* as "a compound of New England transcendentalist and New York rowdy" (quoted in Reynolds, 106). Recent scholarship has reviewed the image of Whitman as a transcendentalist poet personified. Critics have increasingly drawn attention to his complex relationship with Emerson, and the aesthetic as well as cultural complexity of his poetry that cannot singularly be classified as transcendentalist. Nevertheless, it proves fruitful to regard transcendentalism as an important, if not exclusive, part of what Emerson had called the "long foreground" to Whitman's work in his famous 1855 letter to the poet (LG56, 345). This essay will trace points of contact between transcendentalist thought and Whitman's poetry, especially as manifest in their notion of interconnectedness. At the same time, it will be shown how Whitman, in his own idiosyncratic style, transformed transcendentalist philosophy.

In his all-encompassing approach, Walt Whitman did not subscribe to any particular philosophical school or religion but forged what David Reynolds calls "a broadly ecumenical outlook that embraced all religions" (Reynolds, 76). "I adopt each theory, myth, god, and demi-god," he wrote in the 1867 poem "With Antecedents." "I see that the old accounts, bibles, genealogies, are true, without exception" (LG, 241). The diverse spiritual influences on Whitman's poetry, however, correspond with the eclectic nature of the transcendentalist movement itself. Lacking a uniform programmatic profile, American transcendentalism is largely associated with the intellectual circle around Ralph Waldo Emerson, including Bronson Alcott, Margaret Fuller, and Henry David Thoreau, centered in Emerson's New England home of Concord from the 1830s to 1860s. Emerging from New England Unitarianism and connecting with nineteenth-century social reform movements, transcendentalists believed in the liberating potential of the individual in opposition to the constraints of systems and institutions. In his lecture "The Transcendentalist," Emerson elaborates on the idealist belief in the metaphysical appearance of the world through subjective consciousness. Accordingly, "mind is the only reality" and "his thought, that is the Universe" calls for the primacy of individualism. From the assumption that what we call the world is rooted in our experience and our mind, Emerson deducts the transcendentalist ethics of self-reliance: "It is simpler to be self-dependent. The height, the deity of man is, to be self-sustained, to need no gift, no foreign force. Society is good when it does not violate me, but best when it is likest to solitude. Everything real is self-existent."[3] This demand for seclusion was most effectively put into practice by Henry David Thoreau, who wrote about his experiment of staying in a cabin on the shore of Walden Pond in *Walden* (1854).

Following German idealism and in particular Immanuel Kant's insistence on an intuitive or *a priori* knowledge, American transcendentalists fostered a notion of understanding (spiritual) truth without the mediating authority of God. Moreover, they believed in the concept of truth as transcending rational and material empiricism. Instead, the spiritual was believed to be present within everything and everyone, like a "spiritual ether that flows through all creation."[4] According to transcendentalist belief, the divine formed an intricate web between self, nature, and what Emerson calls Over-Soul, "the great nature within which every man's particular being is contained and made one with all other."[5] Like a divine network, the Over-Soul connects self and environment in a constant process of mutual reciprocity, yet without making them indistinguishable. According to transcendentalists, individualism and spiritual interdependence are not considered as contradictory. Rather, as Ed Folsom has noted, "Transcendentalism valued self-reliance and independent action, but it valued these qualities, paradoxically, as existing under a kind of amorphous central control, the Over-Soul."[6] Spiritual truth was primarily considered to be accessed through nature, as the privileged form of divine creation. By means of this, the spiritual was simultaneously connected with the Over-Soul through an organic universe. Nature, according to Emerson, is symbolically related to the divine, thus requiring the mediating capacity of language to "re-attach [. . .] things to nature and the Whole."[7] The poet, as the ideal translator of nature, the divine, and the self, is described as the person "who sees and handles that which others dream of, traverses the whole scale of experience, and is representative of man, in virtue of being the largest power to receive and to impart."[8]

Despite the prominence of language in transcendentalist thought, transcendentalism was not primarily a literary movement. Major importance has not been credited to the poetry created by Emerson, Fuller, and Thoreau, but to their essays and nonfictional work. Emerson's famous contention that America had not yet produced a poet with the outstanding perception and transformative capacity to restore organic unity left him to assert that "I look in vain for the poet whom I describe."[9] So, was Whitman the poet Emerson had envisaged? When Emerson's lecture on "The Poet" was published in 1844, Walt Whitman had not yet published *Leaves of Grass* but had attended a precursory lecture to this essay, entitled "Nature and the Powers of the Poet" in New York City in 1842. It can be assumed that he was familiar with the majority of Emerson's essays by then, since he increasingly incorporated transcendentalist ideas in his own writing.[10] It was not until Whitman sent his first edition of *Leaves of Grass* to Emerson in 1855, however, that the relationship between Whitman and Emerson advanced into a legendary construction of Whitman as *the* Emersonian poet.[11]

Fascinated by the freshness of *Leaves of Grass*, Emerson immediately wrote a letter to Whitman, stating that "I find incomparable things said incomparably well." He then added that "I greet you at the beginning of a great career." Emerson's praise was utilized by Whitman in an act of "shameless self-promotion" (Reynolds, 12), as Whitman reprinted the letter in the *New York Tribune* as well as in the 1856 edition of *Leaves of Grass* without Emerson's permission. He self-assuredly fashioned himself as the "bard of the future" who would rejuvenate American poetry through a liberal, original, and democratic perceptiveness (LG60, 186). In a statement to J. T. Trowbridge in 1860, Whitman declared, "I was simmering, simmering, simmering; Emerson brought me to a boil" (quoted in Reynolds, 82). Emerson, who had been patron to numerous other promising intellectuals, was no less interested in incorporating Whitman's poetry for his own purposes.[12] As Folsom argues, transcendentalists made as much a claim for *Leaves of Grass* in their promotion of the collection under their own label as Whitman utilized Emerson's praise for endorsing his poetry.[13] That Whitman (not unlike Emily Dickinson) has become canonized as a transcendentalist poet was thus also due to a mutually effective marketing strategy from the beginning onward.

No doubt, the poems met many of the claims Emerson had made in "The Poet." This was due to the metaphorical title of the collection alluding to the divine energy that arises from the individual self in constant and organic metamorphosis. Emerson's transcendental subject, as captured in the image of the "transparent eyeball; I am nothing; I see all; the currents of the Universal Being circulate through me," is an intersection of spiritual, subjective, and material flows, transcending subject-object dualisms in the process of divine recognition and "pure" experience.[14] In "Song of Myself," Whitman draws on this transcendental image when he alleges: "I know that the hand of God is the promise of my own, / And I know that the spirit of God is the brother of my own" (LG, 33). The speaker affirms a pantheistic world view fundamental to transcendentalism: "I hear and behold God in every object, yet understand God not in the least" (LG, 86). He thus admits the rational unattainability of the divine quality that can only be reached intuitively. Reminiscent of Emerson's call for "a poetry and philosophy of insight and not of tradition," freed from "the sepulchers of the fathers,"[15] Whitman similarly demands the need for original expression:

> You shall no longer take things at second or third hand, nor look
>   through the eyes of the dead, nor feed on the spectres in books,
> You shall not look through my eyes either, nor take things from me,
> You shall listen to all sides and filter them from your self.   (LG, 30)

The horizontal aesthetics of Whitman's catalog verse are consistent with the transcendentalist values of democracy, equality, and freedom, which informed transcendentalist investments in reform movements and also featured in their writing on an aesthetic level. The writing of Whitman and Emerson, and to a lesser degree also of Fuller, displays what Jonathan Levin has called the "poetics of transition," a style that is expansive, eclectic, pluralist, and decidedly contradictory.[16] "Do I contradict myself?" the speaker asks in "Song of Myself," conciliating "Very well then I contradict myself, / (I am large, I contain multitudes)" (LG, 88). Emerson's prose writing similarly displays an evolutionary and recursive style that embraces incongruity as a key to original expression. "Suppose you should contradict yourself; what then?" Emerson asks. "A foolish consistency is the hobgoblin of little minds [...]. With consistency a great soul has simply nothing to do. [...] To be great is to be misunderstood."[17]

Whitman's transcendentalist aesthetics parallel the frequent theme of interconnectedness addressed in his poems, rendering the concept of the network a fruitful figure of thought both as an idea and as a mode of writing. His aesthetics reflect the emergence of the network model in nineteenth-century epistemology (long before the digital revolution), and are influenced by a growing prevalence of network infrastructure (such as the railroad and the telegraph) but also, metaphorically, a sense of (spiritual) interconnectivity as well as notions of community and national unity, Whitman's poetry can be viewed as constituting part of an emerging *network aesthetic*, with transcendentalist belief in organicism, as a common principle of natural growth, reverberating in Whitman's style and subject matter. Accordingly, Eric Wilson has called Whitman's atomistic lists of diverse and highly fluid elements "a rhizomatic, nomadic field of grass, a sprawling, evolving ecosystem in which parts and whole enter into perpetual and unpredictable conversation."[18] Whitman's organic "chaos" is an infinitely horizontal network, a radically heterogeneous multiplicity. Emerson postulates the idea of universal relationality in "Worship," claiming that "relation and connection are not somewhere and sometimes, but everywhere and always; no miscellany, no exemption, no anomaly, – but method, and an even web; and what comes out, that was put in."[19]

It is especially in the process of writing, Emerson believes, that the material and the spiritual world interconnect in an ideal of unity in diversity. In the transcendental process of re-connecting individual entities to the Over-Soul, Emerson trusts the poet to "see [...] them fall within the great Order not less than the bee-hive, or the spider's geometrical web."[20] Whitman takes up the metaphor of the spider web most overtly in his poem "A Noiseless Patient Spider," a poem that ponders on the individual's position in the creative process. The spider, a metaphor for the isolated poet, remains "noiseless" and "patient," self-sufficient and unobtrusive, yet receptive to whatever may come (LG, 450). Although it looks like it stands "isolated," it is in constant exchange with its environment, "explor[ing] the vacant vast surrounding." The spider, in the center of the surrounding web, does no more than to create connections. Despite continuous action, it does not move nor tire but remains completely at ease with its seemingly simple action. "It launch'd forth filament, filament, filament, out of itself." The second half of the poem relates the experience of a spider weaving a web to the soul which is, similarly, "Surrounded, detached, in measureless oceans of space, / Ceaselessly musing, venturing, throwing, seeking the spheres to connect them" (LG, 450).

Like the spider, the speaker's soul is simultaneously "surrounded" and "detached, in measureless oceans of space," bridging the dichotomy between the external, material world and an endless, spiritual space within which the soul is embedded. The metaphor of a fragile spider web with its delicate threads suggests that the quality of individual links is frail, ephemeral, and only perceivable under careful attentiveness. The spider represents a transcendentalist symbol which, in line with Emerson's concept of nature, corresponds to a spiritual and thus universal truth. Through the act of looking at the spider, the speaker evokes a hitherto hidden link, enacting the union between subject and object. The speaker virtually connects with the spider and thus transforms the feeling of isolation into one of alliance and self-empowerment. Whitman's "A Noiseless Patient Spider" portrays the contemplation of nature as a transcendental act, one which connects the individual to nature and, simultaneously, to universal human experience. At the same time, the web as fabric conjures up notions of material texture. In fact, the poem itself, which James P. Warren has called "a web of description and analogy," represents a linguistic network of connotations, references, and allusions.[21] The web suggests coherence within the often unstable and fragmented process of writing, publishing, and revising.

Whitman's longer poem "Starting from Paumanok" also reflects transcendentalist notions of interconnectedness, while extending the implications of these notions to personal, social, and (trans)national phenomena. The US is conceptualized as a geographical and organic network, as "Interlink'd, food-yielding lands!" (LG, 24). The individual impressions of the speaker, who travels through the US, are metaphysically linked with the history of both natural and technological transformations. Geological images of rupture are evoked to describe and justify US expansionism. Through continuous unraveling, as Walter Grünzweig has noted, these ruptures lead to "victory, union, faith, identity, time," rendering America's "eternal progress" with its "many throes" a natural, and therefore inevitable process. Thus, the poem reflects Whitman's imperialist attitude grounded in a naïve belief in US exceptionalism.[22] According to Whitman's optimistically imperialist vision, the US is evolving as a natural network in the self-organizational logic of spread, driven by the dynamics of the multitude. In "Starting from Paumanok," Whitman translates transcendentalist notions of organic growth into national expansion, framing them as a necessary counterpart to spiritual and cultural evolution. For Whitman, the natural progression of the US facilitates not only prosperity and growth but is first and foremost imbued with the democratic vision of peaceful unity in diversity.

Despite the unmistakable transcendentalist influence on Whitman's poetry and notwithstanding Whitman's address to Emerson as "Master" in his letter reprinted in the 1856 edition of *Leaves of Grass*, there are also major points of divergence between Whitman's aesthetics and transcendentalist thought. The most obvious discrepancy concerns the treatment of the body. As Kenneth M. Price holds, "Emerson laments the custody of the flesh; Whitman celebrates the body and in particular sexual arousal."[23] "I am the poet of the Body and I am the poet of the Soul" (LG, 48), his speaker declares, extending Emerson's call for self-reliance with a decidedly physical connotation and demanding that "your very flesh shall be a great poem" (LG55, vi). In Whitman's poems, nuanced accounts of sensual perceptions, desires, and experiences share the same ontological status as do spiritual and material phenomena. Whitman's liberal treatment of sexuality, particularly in the context of the third edition of *Leaves of Grass*, irritated Emerson. Upon Whitman's visit in Boston in 1860, Emerson tried to convince him to cut out the poem "Enfans d'Adam" ("Children of Adam") because of its explicit erotic imagery – whether because he felt that such allusions would not fit the intellectual program of the transcendentalists, or for purposes of improving the edition's salability. In a true act of self-reliance, Whitman did not concede to this suggestion, noting that "I felt down in my soul the clear and unmistakable conviction to disobey all, and pursue my own way."[24]

Whitman's direct treatment of the body was only one instance in which he transformed transcendentalist thought. Given his strong investment in Jacksonian democracy it is not surprising that political matters figure frequently in his poetry, above all slavery and the fragile state of the union. As Ezra Greenspan notes, "where Emerson tended to mean by this the poet's metaphysical relationship with the universe, Whitman would naturally also have stressed the social component, the poet's relation to his time and community."[25] While Emerson believed in the transformative potential of solitude, Whitman, as a New Yorker, was rather a man of the masses.[26] Whitman's political involvement thus aligns him more with the practical reform efforts at the time than with Emerson's intellectual endeavors. As both a journalist and a poet, he was an eager commentator on educational reform, the slave question, and, in his earlier writing, on the temperance movement. For Whitman, reform was largely connected to individual engagement.

"The greater the reform needed," he notes in his poem "To a Pupil," "the greater the PERSONALITY you need to accomplish it" (LG60, 400). Social reform, to Whitman, was a matter of individual responsibility, yet he did not commit himself fully to one particular reform project and mocked those who would lose themselves in fighting for social change. Shortly before his death, he confessed, "I don't worry myself about doing things – doing philanthropies, good deeds, as people call them. My business is to be – the rest will come as a matter of course, a necessary incident!" (WWC, 8:330).

Opinions differ as to whether Whitman was the transcendental poet Emerson had called for, whether transcendentalism was only one of many pieces in the mosaic of influences on his diverse writing, whether he put transcendentalist thought into practice, or whether he actively transformed transcendentalist thought. As Jay Grossman asserts, we should be careful not to exaggerate the relationship between the personal figures of Emerson and Whitman, traditionally conceived of in terms of a master–disciple dualism.[27] Rather, we should aim at regarding "Whitman's work (and Emerson's, for that matter) as originating in, and reflective of, a much more capacious discursive context than the singularity of an author-driven canonical history permits."[28] That means to view Whitman in the larger context of a fundamentally incongruous movement categorized as transcendentalism, as well as accounting for the incommensurability of Whitman's poetry to any particular movement, school, or belief. Transcendentalism clearly seeps through Whitman's writing, yet the most transcendentalist aspect of Whitman's poetry may be the organicist belief that ideas cannot be fixed but may take up a life of their own, developing freely into unexpected shapes. As he writes in "Song of the Universal," "The blossoms, fruits of ages, orchards divine and certain, / Forms, objects, growths, humanities, to spiritual images ripening." However, the fruits that grow are ultimately diverse and unique: "Embracing carrying welcoming all, thou too by pathways broad and new" (LG, 228).

Notes

1. Quoted in Julian Mason, "Margaret Fuller," in *Walt Whitman: An Encyclopedia*, eds. J. R. LeMaster and Donald D. Kummings (New York, NY: Garland, 1998), 243.
2. Quoted in Jerome Loving, *Emerson, Whitman, and the American Muse* (Chapel Hill, NC: University of North Carolina Press, 1982), 10.

3. Ralph Waldo Emerson, *The Essential Writings of Ralph Waldo Emerson*, ed. Brooks Atkinson (Random House Publishing Group, 2009), 83.

4. Philip Gura, *American Transcendentalism: A History* (New York, NY: Hill and Wang, 2008), 94.

5. Ralph Waldo Emerson, *Ralph Waldo Emerson: Selected Essays, Lectures, and Poems*, ed. Robert D. Richardson (New York, NY: Bantam Classic, 1990), 176.

6. Ed Folsom, "Transcendental Poetics: Emerson, Higginson, and the Rise of Whitman and Dickinson," in *The Oxford Handbook of Transcendentalism*, eds. Joel Myerson, Sandra Harbert Petrulionis, and Laura Dassow Walls (New York, NY: Oxford University Press, 2010), 266.

7. Emerson, "The Poet," in *Selected Essays, Lectures, and Poems*, 216.

8. Ibid., 209.

9. Ibid., 225.

10. Loving, *Emerson*, 65.

11. Kenneth M. Price, *Whitman and Tradition* (New Haven, CT: Yale University Press, 1990), 35.

12. Loving, *Emerson*, 5–6.

13. Folsom, "Transcendental Poetics," 266.

14. Emerson, "Nature," in *Selected Essays, Lectures, and Poems*, 18.

15. Ibid., 15.

16. Jonathan Levin, *The Poetics of Transition* (Durham, NC, and London: Duke University Press, 1999).

17. Ralph Waldo Emerson, "Self-Reliance," in *Selected Essays, Lectures, and Poems*, 157.

18. Eric Wilson, *Romantic Turbulence: Chaos, Ecology, and American Space* (New York, NY: St. Martin's Press, 2000), 119.

19. Ralph Waldo Emerson, "Worship," in *The Collected Works of Ralph Waldo Emerson* vol. 6, eds. Barbara L. Packer, Joseph Slater, and Douglas Emory Wilson (Cambridge, MA: Harvard University Press, 2003), 117.

20. Emerson, "The Poet," 216.

21. James Perrin Warren, "Style," in *A Companion to Walt Whitman*, ed. Donald D. Kummings (Malden, MA: Blackwell Publishing, 2006), 388.

22. Walter Grünzweig, "Imperialism," in LeMaster and Kummings, *Walt Whitman*, 305.

23. Price, *Whitman and Tradition*, 47.

24. Quoted in Folsom, "Transcendental Poetics," 275.

25. Ezra Greenspan, *Walt Whitman and the American Reader* (New York, NY: Cambridge University Press, 1990), 95.

26. Roger Asselineau, "Transcendentalism," in LeMaster and Kummings, *Walt Whitman*, 739.

27. Jay Grossman, *Reconstituting the American Renaissance: Emerson, Whitman, and the Politics of Representation* (Durham, NC: Duke University Press, 2003), 76.

28. Ibid., 115.

CHAPTER 20

Philosophy

Stephen John Mack

In 1955, the centennial year of the publication of *Leaves of Grass*, the Library of Congress marked the occasion by inviting three noted scholars to lecture on what would have seemed the three most obvious dimensions of the author's life and work: Gay Wilson Allen, arguably Whitman's most important biographer, spoke on Walt Whitman "The Man"; Mark Van Doren, poet, novelist, critic, and one-time Pulitzer Prize winner, discussed Whitman "The Poet"; and David Daiches, a world-class literary historian and critic whose work and reputation spanned two continents, examined Whitman "The Philosopher." Man, poet, philosopher. All three designations were, and continue to be, sources of controversy. Whitman's biography, especially the relationship between his sexual identity and his homoerotic verse, prompted speculation and anxiety within "polite" society early in his career; likewise, his designation as a poet – especially considering the deliberately unconventional nature of his verse – became a subject of critical scorn within days of the *Leaves of Grass'* initial publication. But it is the claim that he was a philosopher – and not simply a writer who had a philosophy or thought abstractly – that seems to have generated the most persistent doubt, even among those otherwise sympathetic to Whitman's project. Indeed, it is a claim that is rarely, if ever, made without substantial qualification. As David Daiches himself put it more than six decades ago:

> Poets are rarely systematic philosophers. Their vision of life is embodied in their poetry, with all the rich overtones of symbolic meaning which poetic statement can provide; to paraphrase their ideas in prose generalizations is to risk losing all that is most valuable in the original. [. . .] [T]o treat Whitman as a systematic philosopher is an unrealistic and unprofitable procedure.[1]

A reasonable enough point, perhaps, that might have been a little more persuasive had Daiches not then proceeded to lay out the contours of a rather coherent and systematic Whitman philosophy.

Whitman's "disciples," of course – the men who surrounded and often cared for him in his declining years – were generally much more eager to bestow the title philosopher (even "mystic") on him. But if we are tempted to write off such inclinations as the exuberance of literary idolaters and side instead with David Daiches's more "sensible" view, we might consider the degree to which Daiches's understanding of philosophy – and indeed, that of most observers born in the twentieth century – will have been colored by the transformation of philosophy into a more or less exclusively academic discipline. The advent of analytic philosophy that began to take root in European and American universities in the early twentieth century not only stressed scientific-like precision in language, but also a positivistic interrogation of language itself as the terminological gateway to stable, timeless truths. Whitman, by contrast, was less concerned with viewing a reality that *is*, through the prism of inherited forms of expression, than inventing new expressive forms capable of revealing the world that *could be*, through a view of the promises and possibilities that remained latent in the world he found. From this vantage point, Whitman certainly did not fit the crimped notion of a philosopher that Daiches and others likely held. But he does have a "system" that is both coherent and comprehensive. He was, by nearly any standard outside the disciplinary prejudice of analytic philosophy, a philosopher. Specifically, Whitman was a philosopher of democracy. And to the extent that his chosen mode of expression, poetry, can be considered relevant at all, it supports more than undermines the value of that democratic philosophy: Poetry (particularly, Whitman's innovations in verse form) permitted him to imagine a more extensive range of connections than would have been possible with a more restrictive form of language. Whitman's achievement is that he systematizes democracy, contextualizing its essential but narrowly scoped political arrangements within a broader, *organic* system of interlocking psychological, cultural, economic, and spiritual prescriptions – imperatives that he views as the logical and *natural* extrapolations of democratic political practices. Descriptively, Whitman grounds his philosophy of *organic democracy* in a materialist metaphysics; but the pragmatic import of that philosophy is ethical in that it strives to temper the often illiberal impulses latent in both raw populism and unrestrained capitalism by subordinating them to the critical pressures of a utopian democratic tradition.

To appreciate that organic democratic system it is useful to sketch the contrasting influences that helped shape it and the philosophical and social tensions they helped him resolve. Indeed, Whitman drew on a wide range of sources, many of which he would have become familiar with in the course of writing book reviews for the various newspapers he edited in the 1840s.[2] In addition to the host of religious and utopian ideas swirling about in antebellum America, we can point to two primary streams of philosophical influence: The first of these was the rationalist "Enlightenment" ideals that shaped the Jeffersonian tradition. The second would be various forms of British and German romanticism that he encountered both directly, and as redefined through American transcendentalism. Still, it would not be fair to situate him squarely within either – or any – European philosophical tradition. Whitman essentially appropriated elements of other traditions, reinterpreted them as he saw fit, and synthesized them into something wholly different: Whitman's own complex vision of American democracy, the vast social, political, and deeply human network of realities that he regarded as a multifaceted but logically coherent *natural* force. America, *American democracy*, as he imagined it, was in one sense a metaphor for the entire cosmos, and in another, a manifestation of the natural laws by which it governed itself. The America he intuited, then, was his touchstone, both his primary influence and the existential authority that not only informed his poetry but guided his appraisal of the many literary and philosophical materials he read. At the same time – and somewhat conversely – America was also his subject. Whitman assumed the role of the nation's bard, a role he believed required him to theorize democratic America. "I speak the pass-word primeval, I give the sign of democracy," he announces in "Song of Myself" (LG, 52). And in *Democratic Vistas* he writes that he uses "the words America and democracy as convertible terms" (PW, 363).

Whitman's Jeffersonian influences came initially through his father, Walter Whitman Sr., who was himself deeply influenced by republican politics and ideas. The elder Whitman had even been an acquaintance of Thomas Paine in New York just after the latter's return from Europe.[3] But Whitman also participated in his era's veneration of the Founding Fathers which, as filtered through Jacksonian democratic politics and culture, spawned a wide range of working-class sympathies and individualist values. Whitman's democratic allegiances were doubtless a source of poetic insight. That is, republican thought – especially the more radical anti-government, anti-elitist formulations of Paine – likely grounded his deep affinity for the noisy, infinite variety of real individuals he stuffed into his many catalogs. But more to the point, they also informed his understanding of how the seemingly isolated, atomistic people and things represented in those catalogs could organize themselves, without external governance, into a single, coordinated whole. Thomas Paine had claimed that were we to consider "what the principles are that first condense men into society," and the motives that "regulate their mutual intercourse afterwards," we would discover government itself to be irrelevant because "nearly the whole of the business is performed by their operation of the parts upon each other."[4] It is that same principle, elevated to the cosmic level, that Whitman affirms at the end of section 50 of "Song of Myself" when he writes,

> Do you see O my brothers and sisters?
> It is not chaos or death – it is form, union,
>   plan – it is eternal life – it is Happiness.　　　(LG, 88)

Still, there is nothing in Enlightenment thinking that Whitman might have used to illuminate the America he envisions in his mature philosophy. While the *political* arrangements of American democracy were, of course, a product of eighteenth-century notions of individual liberty and autonomy, the only conception of a nation that might be derived from them was contractual. And nothing in Whitman's vision – not his cosmos, not his emblematic catalogs, not his America – is held together by contract. For Whitman, American democracy was an organic, interdependent reality. In section 5 of "Song of Myself," he depicts the processes of social (and cosmic) interrelation in terms of an autoerotic fantasy, a tryst between the poet and his own soul, the full spiritual meaning of which comes at the moment of orgasm. He summarizes the key insight as the sudden awareness that "all the men ever born are also my brothers, and the women my sisters and lovers, / And that a kelson of the creation is love" (LG, 33). To assert that love is the existential binding force of all creation is to repudiate the notion that it is conditional and crudely transactional, the function of a social contract. This was, to be sure, an intuition of Whitman's, gained from his own impressions of American society; it was also, of course, a deep desire fueled by the increasingly acrimonious sectionalism that characterized the United States before the Civil War. In order to formulate the ideas he needed to reach beyond the republican tradition he drew on British and German romanticism, both indirectly, as these ideas came to him through the prism of American transcendentalism, and, more or less directly, through his desultory reading of original sources or commentaries on them. Taken together, the effect of these influences was not to provide Whitman with precise theoretical formulations to counter contractualism; rather, they conditioned a particular romantic sensibility that individuals were not really isolated beings but people bound together in an interpenetrating, trans-historical community.

This sensibility is ubiquitous throughout Whitman's work, but it is movingly expressed in "Crossing Brooklyn Ferry." Here, while crossing on the ferry, the poet launches an extended mediation triggered by the realization that he shares the same sensory experiences of people who made the trip before him, or will make the trip after him. And common experience erases the boundaries erected by time. Addressing his future readers:

> It avails not, time nor place – distance avails not,
> I am with you, you men and women of a generation, or ever so
>   many generations hence.
> Just as you feel when you look on the river and sky, so I felt,
> Just as any of you is one of a living crowd, I was one of a crowd,
> Just as you are refresh'd by the gladness of the river and the
>   bright flow, I was refresh'd.   (LG, 160)

Eventually he directly challenges the notion that he and his readers are separate, asking "What is it then between us?" He answers his own question a stanza later: "Whatever it is, it avails not – distance avails not, and place avails not" (LG, 162). Shared sensory – and material – experience becomes both the vehicle for and validation of individual transcendence. And through the agency of poetry, it becomes the basis of a common consciousness. As he looks upon the Manhattan sights as the ferry nears the shore, he wonders what could be more admirable than that "Which fuses me into you now, and pours my meaning into you?" (LG, 164). It is, as he observes earlier in the poem, "The simple, compact, well-join'd scheme, myself disintegrated, everyone disintegrated yet part of the scheme" (LG, 160). That is, the boundaries that would insulate the atomistic self "disintegrate" as separate individuals "fuse," in time and through time, into a single timeless community.

But just as romanticism contravenes the atomism implicit in rationalist philosophy, it also undermines the concepts of justice that have been rationalism's great achievement. Indeed, it has long been a critical commonplace that romantic ontology lends itself to political passivity. After all, it is hard to rationalize engagement in civil conflict if we are all expressions of the same civil body. Emerson, for instance, was famously criticized for coming too late or too timidly to the abolitionist cause. Similarly, Whitman's romanticism seemed to leave him ill-disposed to criticize the social body – at least as a strictly theoretical matter. In the 1855 Preface to *Leaves of Grass*, he asserted that, "The greatest poet does not moralize or make applications of morals"; rather, he simply "knows the soul" (LG55, vi). To know, and especially to represent, the soul seemed to demand a kind of descriptive objectivity and factional neutrality. Hence, being the poet who contained multitudes and represented all of creation within his own metaphoric self meant being the poet who took seriously the obligation to embrace both good and evil without prejudice. Still, such a morally disinterested position was not entirely compatible with the more combative dimension of Whitman's sensibilities; the poet who enfolded all within himself was also a partisan street fighter with some very definite moralistic instincts. In section 10 of "Song of Myself," for instance, he dramatizes a scene in which he nurses back to health a runaway slave he is hiding in his home. "He staid with me a week before he was recuperated and pass'd north," he writes, then concludes the section with an assertion of political values in the form of an egalitarian gesture of trust: "I had him sit next to me at table, my fire-lock lean'd in the corner" (LG, 38).

Whitman hardly needed the permission of a literary or philosophical authority to fashion a critical edge within a philosophy that remained essentially romantic. The seeds of such criticism were already deeply planted in a vision in which personal liberty was a necessary pre-condition for the kind of vigorous self-regulation that Thomas Paine viewed as the natural alternative to tyranny. And indeed, Whitman tended to regard all socially imposed chains on the human body, mind, or spirit as abhorrent corruptions of nature; and emancipation, whether political, cultural, or psychological, a moral imperative. From this perspective, slavery was not only an existential evil, it was also an expression of a broader set of institutional impulses toward authoritarianism, social control, entrenched power, and cultural traditionalism – impulses that manifested themselves in a multitude of other ways. Of course, not the least of these for Whitman was sexual repression. Here he might well have found some encouragement in the political criticism implicit in the work of German poet Heinrich Heine, friend and distant relative of Karl Marx. Whitman apparently became familiar with Heine through translations of his work, around the time of the German poet's death in 1856.[5] And while he seemed to be attracted to his sarcasm and wit – commenting to Traubel in 1888 that his poetry was "rather ironical and melancholy, with a dash of the poetical craziness" – Whitman was, doubtlessly, more deeply drawn to Heine's notion that liberation was in one sense personal, a function of sensual and erotic emancipation. This idea is given an especially poignant expression in section 11 of "Song of Myself," immediately following, fittingly enough, his depiction of the runaway slave. As if written to be a companion to the runaway slave vignette, the poet here represents the impulse for personal liberation as a desire to escape from conventional sexual mores. In this scene, a richly dressed but lonesome twenty-eight-year-old woman secretly spies, from the safety of her own home, twenty-eight young men bathing down by the shore. Soon, her voyeurism turns to sexual fantasy as she imagines herself running along the beach to join them, her "unseen hand" passing over their bodies:

> The young men float on their backs, their white bellies bulge
>   to the sun, they do not ask who seizes fast to them.
> They do not know who puffs and declines with pendant and
>   bending arch,
> They do not think whom they souse with spray.   (LG, 39)

Whitman affirms the woman's instinctive drive for erotic liberation, a drive that is fundamentally personal. At the same time, however, he is also mindful of the fact that constraints placed on sexual expression have their origins in society and, hence, require social criticism. Whitman's concern with the social oppression of sexual behavior is briefly featured in section 15, for example, where he introduces a prostitute in one of his catalogs, a woman whose identity is cast as a function of sexual conduct:

> The prostitute draggles her shawl, her bonnet bobs on her tipsy
>   and pimpled neck,
> The crowd laugh at her blackguard oaths, the men jeer and wink
>   to each other,
> (Miserable! I do not laugh at your oaths nor jeer you;).   (LG, 43)

Whitman depicts the woman as a drunken, angry, and humiliated soul. But rather than constructing that condition as the natural consequence of her choice to be a prostitute – as though degradation was the appropriate price for sexual transgression in the moral economy – he treats her instead as a victim of a social injustice: the laughing, jeering crowd's effort to ostracize her from the social body. That is, while Whitman is performing the unromantic role of social critic, he does so, ironically, to preserve that same romantic conception of an inclusive, integrated, organic society.

Whitman's willingness to include moments of social criticism within his representation of ideal democracy – a practice that became even more pronounced in his post-Civil War work – offers a glimpse into how Whitman understood democracy to evolve. Implicitly, criticism functions as one of many forces animating the process of continual change. But, more abstractly, Whitman simply presents continuous change as an existential fact of the democratic organism, a kind of forward propulsion fueled by a cocktail of natural, social, and spiritual forces. He neither describes nor differentiates these forces, but in at least two senses Whitman's treatment of democratic evolution resonates with Darwinian processes: first, *material* change is foundational in his vision and often functions as its central metaphor; second, all change, whether physical, intellectual, moral, spiritual, technological, or cosmological, is essentially *developmental*, moving from some lower antecedent form to a higher one. But a more direct influence is probably Hegel. Whitman writes that Hegel "most fully and definitely illustrates Democracy by carrying it into the highest regions" (NUPM, 6:2017). What Whitman would have meant by "highest regions," and the way he employed Hegelian notions of historical change to frame them, is suggested by such poems as "Passage to India." Here, Whitman imagines the ultimate human (and democratic) journey as defined by the synthesis of two, dialectically opposed, "passages": the historical process of Western technological development that brings people physically together (symbolized by three great nineteenth-century achievements: the transcontinental railroad, the Suez Canal, and the transatlantic cable), and the history of spiritual achievement, the "myths and fables of eld, Asia's, Africa's fables, / The far-darting beams of the spirit" that mark Eastern societies. Once these passages come together, "Nature and Man shall be disjoin'd and difussed no more, / The true son of God shall absolutely fuse them" (LG, 416). Ultimately, for Whitman, historical change is teleological, as natural, social, political, and technological movements join in a spiritual unity – the "highest regions" of an existentially democratic cosmos.

Whitman cobbled together his organic democracy by drawing on an eclectic mix of sources that not only included philosophical statements but an extraordinary range of other materials gathered from religion, popular culture, science, imaginative literature, and politics as well. Still, those sources, when they can be identified in his work, exist primarily as appropriations or interpretations. His complete philosophy must be regarded as wholly his own. By the late 1860s, his mature philosophy of organic democracy began to stabilize with the publication of *Democratic Vistas* (1871). The essay was prompted by Thomas Carlyle's polemic against democratic reforms in England and the United States, which struck him as reckless as "shooting Niagara in a barrel."[6] Carlyle railed against a system that he believed elevated the rampant greed, hypocrisy, and mendacity he saw permeating social life in the latter part of the nineteenth century. Whitman saw the same evils but did not see them as the result of too much democracy, but too little. That is, he regarded mere political democracy as a necessary but not sufficient condition for successful associated human life. In *Democratic Vistas* he asks, "Did you, too, O friend, suppose democracy was only for elections, for politics, and for a party name?"

No, he answers, "I say democracy is only of use there that it may pass on and come to its flower and fruits in manners, in the highest forms of interaction between men and their beliefs" (PW, 2:389). Whitman argued for an enlightened awareness of the way all aspects of the natural and social world are actually of manifestations of a transcendent democratic reality; hence, each informs a unique expression of democratic values. To illustrate, in abbreviated form, a crude statement of Whitman's philosophy of organic democracy might read as follows: The franchise clearly expresses the individual right to self-government; but democratically considered, the fact of self-government is, in turn, an expression of the values that underlay acts of communication, deliberation, and cooperation. But, to communicate, deliberate, and cooperate *in good faith* requires the cultivation of certain ideas about democratic individuality – a conception of people who are morally and intellectually strong enough to make meaningful contributions to the collective effort of governing. Yet to even begin the arduous process of cultivating such a democratic people requires a deeper, *spiritual* recognition of the existential connectedness of all people, a spiritual fact that makes failure to cooperate inconsistent with the fundamental nature of being – that is, a democratic religion. But if the fundamental interconnectedness of humanity is an existential spiritual fact and humans are also material beings, then it must also be existentially true that human beings are *materially* one. And if human beings are a single (albeit, complex) material being, composed of the same substance that constitutes the rest of the material world, our very existence is wholly controlled by the same laws and principles by which the universe governs itself. This is to say, democracy is the central fact of all existence.

The logical train above, of course, does considerable injustice to Whitman's democratic philosophy. It is only intended as an illustration of the way Whitman interrelates the many dimensions of a world he views as essentially democratic in character. It does not capture the complexity, nuance, or force of his vision. It especially does not capture the depths he is able to achieve by using a form of poetic language built for suggestive power. And the uncertainty entailed in suggestion is key to Whitman's language because it is the only language appropriate to envision a democratic future that is, at best, no more than possible. Of course, the kind of descriptive precision privileged in analytic philosophy is, presumably, a paramount virtue in any attempt to faithfully represent the world as it is. But Whitman's world is constantly in motion. It is fundamentally democratic, which means – among a multitude of other things – it is constantly changing. As he saw it, the responsibility of a democratic poet is to reveal the democratic physics that shape the world's social terrain, then point the way forward. "We presume to write, as it were, upon things that exist not, and travel by maps yet unmade and a blank" (PW, 2:391). The ultimate defining fact of Whitman's philosophy of organic democracy is the imperative to navigate an always uncertain future, the inescapable obligation of self-government.

Notes

1. David Daiches, "Whitman the Philosopher," in *Lectures on Whitman by Gay Wilson Allen, Mark Van Doren, and David Daiches* (Washington, DC: Library of Congress, 1955), 35.
2. Floyd Stovall, *The Foreground of Leaves of Grass* (Charlottesville, VA: University Press of Virginia, 1974), 101–51.
3. Gay Wilson Allen, *The Solitary Singer: A Critical Biography of Walt Whitman* (New York, NY: Macmillan, 1955), 7.
4. Thomas Paine, "Rights of Man, Part II," in *Paine: Political Writings*, ed. Bruce Kuklick (New York, NY: Cambridge University Press, 1989), 167.
5. Stovall, *Foreground*, 222–30.
6. Thomas Carlyle, "Shooting Niagara: And After?" in *Prose Works of the Victorian Period*, ed. William Buckler (Boston, MA: Houghton, 1958), 170.

CHAPTER 21

Bohemianism

Joanna Levin and Edward Whitley

On December 24, 1859, the *New York Saturday Press* – known as "the independent organ of Bohemia"[1] – presented its readers with the Walt Whitman poem "A Child's Reminiscence" (which Whitman later titled "Out of the Cradle Endlessly Rocking"). Published at a time when the writers and editors of the periodical were themselves engaged in the process of defining an emerging urban type – the American bohemian – Whitman's new poetry provided an auspicious occasion for self-reflection and discovery. Indeed, in the months leading up to and following the publication of the 1860 *Leaves of Grass*, the fortunes of the bohemian *Saturday Press* and Whitman's poetry became inextricably linked. From 1859 to 1861, Henry Clapp Jr., editor of the *Saturday Press*, published no fewer than forty-six poems, parodies, reviews, and notices by or about Whitman and thirty-five advertisements for the 1860 edition.[2] Of Clapp, Whitman later told biographer Horace Traubel, "I have often said to you that my own history could not be written with Henry left out: I mean it – that is not an extravagant statement" (WWC, 4:195). Widely recognized as the "King of Bohemia," Clapp set the stage for the enduring cultural romance of *la vie bohème*, transposing the French prototype into an American phenomenon. To this end, Whitman, the poet whom Clapp heralded as "ardent and fierce" and "free as the sunshine," proved indispensable.[3] For his part, Whitman affiliated himself with the bohemians from 1859 to 1862, embracing their milieu – especially their nightly haunt, Pfaff's basement beer cellar at 647 Broadway – as a vital new context in which to reshape his ever-evolving persona and expanding *Leaves of Grass*.

Clapp had returned to the US in 1853 after a three-year sojourn in Paris, hoping to recreate *la vie bohème*, a heady new way of conceptualizing the artist as a cultural outsider. As Jerrold Seigel has argued, "from the start, Bohemianism took shape by contrast with the image with which it was commonly paired: bourgeois life."[4] By the late 1850s, Clapp had already had a varied history within antebellum reform movements (abolitionism, temperance, Fourierism, free love), but bohemianism granted him, in Christine Stansell's words, "a more protean oppositional identity than radical reform offered."[5] The underground Pfaff's – a lager beer saloon situated beneath the fashionable Colman House hotel, in the midst of Broadway's thriving shopping and theater district, a mere ten-minute walk from newspaper row – offered an ideal base of operation for the first self-declared American bohemia. At once within and without the commercial marketplace, Pfaff's was, like bohemia itself, both foreign and domestic: "The mild potations of beer and the dreamy breath of cigars," poet Bayard Taylor remembered, "delayed the nervous, fidgety, clattering-footed American hours."[6] Clapp quickly began to gather such kindred spirits as Ada Clare (a former Southern belle, unwed mother, actress, novelist, and witty essayist who became known as the "Queen of Bohemia") and Fitz-James O'Brien (whose reported "gypsy-like wildness of temperament" made him a likely denizen of bohemia).[7] These same qualities animated the *Saturday Press*, the weekly paper devoted to the arts that Clapp started in 1858, and that folded in 1860 (save for a brief reemergence in 1865). Though always on the verge of financial collapse (in true bohemian fashion), the *Saturday Press*, Whitman later recollected, "cut a significant figure in the periodical literature of the time," and no less a cultural gate-keeper than William Dean Howells stated, "It is not too much to say that it was very nearly as well for one to be accepted by the *Press* as to be accepted by the *Atlantic* [*Monthly*], and for the time there was no other literary comparison."[8] The *Saturday Press* was eager to promote this comparison, not only as a way of signaling its cultural prestige but also as a means of establishing itself as the rebellious New York "bohemian" in relation to the Boston *Atlantic*'s more established "bourgeois."[9]

Almost as soon as the bohemians began to congregate at Pfaff's, bohemianism became a flash point in contemporary cultural wars. The *New York Times*, for example, editorialized in 1858, "It would be better to cultivate a familiarity with any kind of coarse or honest art, or any sort of regular employment, than to become refined and artistic only to fall into the company of the Bohemians."[10] A few months later on September 8, 1858, from his seat at the *Brooklyn Daily Times*, Whitman himself piled on further warnings, insisting, "We suspect that the reason why so many literary men make bad husbands, and do not properly appreciate the softer sex, arises from the infection of 'Bohemianism' by which most authors become tainted in their introduction into the literary guild; and which creates a restless craving for mental excitement unsuiting them to breathe the clear and tranquil atmosphere of home enjoyment."[11] Whitman published these words shortly before, or soon after, he had begun to interact with the bohemians at Pfaff's. Whether borne of a need to generate copy (which could have led to a rote recapitulation of mainstream critiques) or as a defensive reaction to his own "restless craving[s]" and aversion to heterosexual domesticity, Whitman first entered the fray on the side of the very bourgeois norms that bohemia seemed to imperil. And yet, at some point in 1859, after the first two self-published editions of *Leaves of Grass* had failed to generate any widespread public acclaim, and most likely around the time he lost his job at the *Brooklyn Daily Times*, Whitman began to make a daily six-mile trip back and forth from his home in Brooklyn to Pfaff's.[12] He had fallen into the company of the bohemians.

"What wit, humor, repartee, word wars and sometimes bad blood!" Whitman later recollected of his time at "Pfaff's 'Bohemia'."[13] Whitman had had his share of "word wars" with some of the Pfaffians (notably with William Winter, whom he had derisively referred to as a "young Longfellow" and who later, in turn, described him as "commonplace" and "uncouth"[14]), but he recognized that he had been "accepted" by the majority of the bohemians and awarded "full membership" in their coterie. Membership had its privileges, and one of the benefits of being part of the bohemian "cabal" included a receptive audience that was willing to champion his work. "Queen of Bohemia" Ada Clare, for instance, used her regular column in the *Saturday Press* to defend "A Child's Reminiscence" against detractors ("Whitman's 'A Child's Reminiscence' could only have been written by a poet, and versifying would not help it. I love the poem").[15] Her wide-ranging column carved out a space of bohemian freedom, creating an implicit analogy between Whitman's free verse and the controversial feminist costume, "the Bloomer": just as Whitman's poetry eschewed cumbersome "versifying" in favor of a more unmediated utterance, so would "the Bloomer" circumvent the restrictive "hoop-skirt" and allow for natural movement.[16] Other bohemians embraced this understanding of Whitman, and he quickly became a touchstone for the essential freedom from stultifying conventions that the Pfaffians associated with *la vie bohème*. The artist A. L. Rawson observed, "It was the general conviction of the coterie that Whitman had torn off the conventional gewgaws from human nature and glorified man."[17]

For the Pfaffians, Whitman's independence from bourgeois convention was bound up in his ongoing status as "one of the roughs" (LG55, 29). In their effort to defy bourgeois "respectability," the bohemians made a virtue of their own liminal class positions, of their refusal – or inability – to settle into stable middle-class existences.[18] As Winter noted, "a harder time for writers has not been known in our country than the time that immediately preceded the outbreak of the Civil War," and most of the bohemians were "poor, and they were poorly paid" (at the time he was frequenting Pfaff's, Whitman was living in Brooklyn in a small basement apartment with his mother and three of his brothers).[19] Such economic difficulties inspired the legendary bohemian camaraderie and "careless mirth";[20] it also encouraged a strong skepticism regarding – in Ada Clare's words – "all social distinctions of rank and wealth."[21] Whether condemning police raids against the poor and homeless; satirizing the contemporary lexicon of class-based distinctions; railing against "those peculiar and distinct Wall Street operations by which money is, more or less honestly, made"; or puncturing the "inflated bladders" of Bostonian elites, the bohemians cast a critical eye on the social and economic hierarchies that, in their view, betrayed the nation's democratic promise.[22]

Yet in promoting Whitman as a working-class hero, the Pfaffians recognized that they risked betraying the very authenticity that they claimed Whitman exemplified. Clapp addressed the criticism that Whitman, his would-be bohemian original, was simply an affected poseur head-on:

> In determination to keep his personality against pretension and exclusive-ness of the literary and conventional classes, he has perhaps fallen [into] a pretension of his own. The reaction appears to the best readers a little exaggerated. Whitman is no such braggadocio, no such "rough." [But] [w]e allow for a little extravagant self-assertion in a man who goes for the first time among authors and the "cultivated," and is jealous lest he should discredit his class by stooping and compliance.

For Clapp, Whitman's "immense sincerity" ultimately trumped his "little affectation."[23]

On the other hand, this emphasis on Whitman's (relatively unvarn-ished) sincerity as the embodiment of bohemianism might seem to conflict with the Pfaffians' Francophilism, their interest in cultivating artistic sophistication by importing the foreign property, *la bohème*. In his anon-ymous self-review of the 1860 edition in the *Saturday Press*, for example, Whitman highlighted his own patriotic rejection of foreign precedents, writing that "bold Americans, can surely never live, for instance, entirely satisfied and grow to your full stature on what the importations hither of foreign bards, dead or alive, provide."[24] Despite having become a nightly fixture at Pfaff's, Whitman retained his nationalist bona fides. Thus, when the *New York Illustrated News* denounced those "flippant young gentlemen of the French school who do the brilliant for Bohemian clubs and newspapers," that paper hastened to distinguish Whitman: "True as the needle to the North is he true to his country."[25] For his part, Clapp gamely republished these words in the *Saturday Press*, no doubt eager to promote Whitman, bask in bohemian notoriety, and raise ongoing questions about the position of bohemia within American culture. For Clapp, Whitman represented the sort of "distinct national character" – one rooted in romantic conceptions of "Nature" – that could become the basis for a vibrant American bohemianism. In his own review of the 1860 *Leaves of Grass*, Clapp said of Whitman, "He has made the first extended picture of our life as we live it in America, where thought is not scholastic, where the influence of books is very little, of Nature very great."[26]

Perhaps in deference to his fellow Pfaffians and their Francophilic sensibilities, Whitman used a French phrase in the title of one of the new poetic clusters of the 1860 edition, "Enfans d'Adam" (later "Children of Adam"). As Betsy Erkkila has observed, Whitman's use of the French language in this context "was itself a means of defying the sensibilities of Puritan America by connecting the amative theme of the poems with the sexual freedom and libertarian traditions associated in the popular mind with France."[27] This controversial cluster, Ralph Waldo Emerson feared, would limit the sales of the new edition, and he counseled Whitman to remove it. (Emerson reportedly told a later confidant, "I had great hopes of Whitman until he became Bohemian."[28]) Nevertheless, in writing the "Enfans D'Adam" cluster, Whitman remained true to the vision of his work that he had shared in an open letter to Emerson as early as 1856, in which he insisted, "Of women just as much as men, it is the interest that there should not be infidelism about sex, but perfect faith. Women in These States approach the day of that organic equality with men, without which, I see, men cannot have organic equality among themselves." To achieve these political aims, Whitman resolved to blast "this tepid wash, this diluted deferential love" that reinforced patriarchal social hierarchies. Instead, he insisted, "the body is to be expressed, and sex is" (LG56, 356). With its emphatic "poems of eyes, hands, lips, hips, and bosoms" – along with "man-balls, man-root, / [. . .] / The womb, the teats, nipples, breast-milk" – "Enfans d'Adam" sought to realize this imperative, and, in the larger context of the 1860 edition and its reception, these new poems reinforced the alliance between Whitman, free-love radicals, and the bohemians at Pfaff's (LG60, 290, 300–01).

In the physical space of the beer cellar, and on the pages of the *Saturday Press*, Whitman joined forces with the bohemians, male and female alike, who were creating a new heterosocial culture, promoting women's rights, critiquing double standards of sexual morality, and challenging the ideology of separate spheres. The *Saturday Press* explicitly declared, "Our notion is that woman's peculiar sphere of action is whatever she finds herself best adapted to, and in which she can maintain herself, if need be, in entire independence of man."[29] Whitman's rejection of the binary logic of separate public and private spheres extended to the remarkable "Calamus" cluster, also published for the first time in 1860. This homoerotic cluster – which he significantly revised and expanded during the period in which he frequented Pfaff's – was based on a series of twelve sonnet-like love poems that Whitman copied into a notebook, most likely in the spring of 1859. Titled "Live Oak, with Moss," the original series charts the dissolution of a relationship, perhaps the ending of Whitman's relationship with the young stage driver, Fred Vaughan.[30] Vaughan had likely spent time with Whitman at Pfaff's; from surviving letters, we know that Vaughan "called in at Pfaffs [*sic*] two evenings in succession" in the hope of seeing Whitman before the poet left for Boston to oversee the production of the third edition of *Leaves of Grass* in March 1860.[31] Vaughan's letters to Whitman also reveal a potential source of tension between the two men. Vaughan reported that he had attended one of Emerson's lectures in New York, and that Emerson had affirmed the importance of "strong friendships," stating, "a man whose heart was filled with a warm, ever enduring not to be shaken by anything Friendship was one to be set on one side apart from other men, and almost to be worshipped as a saint." Vaughan balked at this notion, however, and, in a series of rhetorical questions, he suggested that such publicity would result in ridicule rather than worship: "There Walt, how do you like that? What do you think of them setting you & myself, and one or two others we know up in some public place, with an immense placard on our breasts, reading Sincere Freinds!!! [*sic*]."[32] At the very moment when Whitman was preparing to publish the homoerotic poems that would "tell the secret of my nights and days" and "celebrate the need for comrades" (LG60, 342), Vaughan recoiled from such public display.

In what may have been based on an experience at Pfaff's, and on a happy memory of Vaughan, "Calamus 29" offers a liminal, interstitial space between the public and the private:

One flitting glimpse, caught through an interstice,
Of a crowd of workmen and drivers in a bar-room, around the stove, late
    of a winter night – And I unremarked, seated in a corner;
Of a youth who loves me, and whom I love, silently approaching, and
    seating himself near, that he may hold me by the hand;
A long while, amid the noises of coming and going – of drinking and
    oath and smutty jest,
There we two, content, happy in being together, speaking little, perhaps
    not a word.   (LG60, 371)

Vaughan may have been able to sustain such a "flitting glimpse" into his intimacy with Whitman, but his letter suggests that he shied away from a more protracted, potentially judgmental public gaze. In the new cluster, however, Whitman extends this glimpse of affectionate comradeship, and the semi-public handholding that occurs in "Calamus 29" becomes a template for a more openly homoerotic future, one capable of providing the affective basis for a national and even global democratic brotherhood: "You twain! And all processions moving along the streets! / I wish to infuse myself among you till I see it common for you to walk hand in hand!" (LG60, 375).

For Whitman, a more complete realization of collective "Calamus" bonds would await his experience with the Fred Grey Association (which, as Stephanie Blalock has demonstrated, most likely began meeting at Pfaff's sometime between December 1861 and the spring of 1862) and his time as a regular hospital visitor during the Civil War.[33] Nonetheless, despite some in-fighting, Whitman found a supportive community among the bohemians at Pfaff's. In "Calamus 4," Whitman declared that the calamus-root "shall henceforth be the token of comrades" (LG60, 348), and, while he was in Boston preparing the 1860 edition, his bohemian friends revealed their familiarity with this "token" on the pages of *Vanity Fair*, a literary weekly that, like the *Saturday Press*, was born around the tables at Pfaff's. A full two months before the publication of the new edition, the illustrator Edward Mullen published a drawing of a Whitman, standing large and tall, surrounded by the distinctive long, leafy stalk of the phallic calamus plant; further, on May 19, the publication date of the third edition, *Vanity Fair* published a humorous "Agricultural Column" that predicted "an unusually active market for Calamus" and forecasted "a heavy crop of this health-giving root."[34] Evidence of the playful, collaborative relationship between Whitman and the bohemians can also be found in the twenty-four drawings that are scattered throughout the notebook that he used during his years at Pfaff's. As Ruth Bohan has argued, these drawings illustrate that "the question of bohemian identity and its pictorial manifestations was a recurring focus of the nightly discussions at Pfaff's."[35]

Oscillating between margin and center, public and private, the real and the phantasmagoric, and life and death, the "Calamus" poems resonate with the imagery of an unfinished poem that Whitman wrote about Pfaff's and titled, "The Two Vaults." In "Calamus 2," for example, Whitman uses death tropes to imagine an alternative realm,

> Give me your tone therefore, O Death, that I may accord with it,
> Give me yourself – for I see that you belong to me now above all, and
> are folded together above all – you Love and Death are,
> Nor will I allow you to balk me any more with what I was calling life,
> For now it is conveyed to me that you are the purports essential,
> That you hide in these shifting forms of life, for reasons – and that
> they are mainly for you. (LG60, 344)

Similarly, in "The Two Vaults," Whitman represents the entombed, underground world of Pfaff's – situated below the sidewalk of Broadway, underneath a double-vaulted ceiling – as a spirited antithesis to the commercial marketplace above: "The vault at Pfaffs where the drinkers and laughers meet to eat and drink and carouse / While on the walk immediately overhead, pass the myriad feet of Broadway / As the dead in their graves, are underfoot hidden / And the living pass over them, recking not of them." Paradoxically enough, within the sepulchral "vault" at Pfaff's, the bohemians "bandy the jests! Toss the theme from one to another!" and the "bright eyes of beautiful young men" illuminate the scene. Always in search of new lovers and readers, Whitman speaks of his "yearning, to arrest some one of you!" (NUPM 1:454–55) on the sidewalks above (and, in their effort to market the 1860 edition, the bohemians had plotted with him over how best to do just that), but the poem focuses on the exuberance of the underground bohemia, the place where Whitman later recalled, "there was as good talk [. . .] as took place anywhere in the world."[36] Nevertheless, written in the midst of the Civil War, Whitman left the poem unfinished, cutting it off just at the moment when he began to describe the inner recesses of a mysterious second vault, one that remained "entirely dark."

Whitman's bohemian days occurred during a liminal moment in his career, bridging the gap between the poet as "one of the roughs" and his later, post-war persona, "the good gray poet." And yet, as Henry Clapp intuited, it may well be that no identity more fully suited the poet of *Leaves of Grass* than that of the "bohemian" – especially as that concept was enlarged and redefined, with Whitman as its American exemplar, on the pages of *Vanity Fair* and the *Saturday Press*.

Notes

1. Getty Gay, "The Royal Bohemian Supper," *New York Saturday Press* (New York, NY), September 31, 1859, 2.
2. Amanda Gailey, "Walt Whitman and the King of Bohemia: The Poet in the *Saturday Press*," in *Whitman among the Bohemians*, eds. Joanna Levin and Edward Whitley (Iowa City, IA: University of Iowa Press, 2014), 20, 24.
3. Henry Clapp, "Walt Whitman: Leaves of Grass," *New York Saturday Press* (New York, NY), May 19, 1860, 2, WWA.
4. Jerrold Seigel, *Bohemian Paris: Culture, Politics, and the Boundaries of Bourgeois Life, 1830–1930* (New York, NY: Penguin Books, 1986), 5.
5. Christine Stansell, "Whitman at Pfaff's: Commercial Culture, Literary Life and New York Bohemia at Mid-Century," *Walt Whitman Quarterly Review* 10.3 (1993), 120.
6. Bayard Taylor, *The Echo Club and Other Literary Diversions* (Boston, MA: James R. Osgood and Company, 1876), 15.
7. William Winter, *Old Friends: Being Literary Recollections of Other Days* (New York, NY: Moffat, Yard and Company, 1909), 99.
8. William Dean Howells, *Literary Friends and Acquaintance: A Personal Retrospect of American Authorship* (Bloomington, IN: Indiana University Press, [1900] 1968), 64.
9. Winter, *Old Friends*, 92.
10. "Bohemia in New York," *New York Times* (New York, NY), January 6, 1858, 4.
11. Walt Whitman, *The Brooklyn Daily Times* (Brooklyn, NY), September 8, 1858, in *I Sit and Look Out: Editorials from the Brooklyn Daily Times by Walt Whitman*, eds. Emory Holloway and Vernolian Schwarz (New York, NY: AMS Press, 1966), 67.
12. Karen Kabriener, "Bridging Brooklyn and Bohemia: How the *Brooklyn Daily Times* Brought Whitman Closer to Pfaff's," in Levin and Whitley, *Whitman among the Bohemians*, 2.
13. Thomas Donaldson, *Walt Whitman the Man* (New York, NY: Frances P. Harper, 1896), 208–09.
14. Winter, *Old Friends*, 140.
15. Ada Clare, "Thoughts and Things," *New York Saturday Press* (New York, NY), January 14, 1860, 2.
16. Ibid.
17. A. L. Rawson, "A Bygone Bohemia," *Frank Leslie's Popular Monthly* 41 (January 1896), 106. For more on how the bohemians defined the

"cosmopolite," see Joanna Levin, *Bohemia in America, 1858–1920* (Stanford, CA: Stanford University Press, 2010), 38–49.

18. On the class connotations associated with the term "respectability," see Levin, *Bohemia in America*, 61.

19. Winter, *Old Friends*, 82, 92.

20. Ibid., 82.

21. Ada Clare, "Thoughts and Things," *New York Saturday Press* (New York, NY), February 11, 1860, 2.

22. See Levin, *Bohemia in America*, 34–35; 40–41; "The Twaddle of Business," *New York Saturday Press* (New York, NY), August 16, 1859, 1; "Edward Everett and His Critics," *New York Saturday Press* (New York, NY), August 11, 1860, 1.

23. Henry Clapp, "Walt Whitman and American Art," *New York Saturday Press* (New York, NY), June 30, 1860, 2.

24. Walt Whitman, "All About a Mocking-Bird," *New York Saturday Press* (New York, NY), January 17, 1860, 3.

25. "Books, Etc.," *New York Saturday Press* (New York, NY), July 7, 1860, 3.

26. Clapp, "Walt Whitman and American Art," 2.

27. Betsy Erkkila, *Whitman the Political Poet* (New York, NY: Oxford University Press, 1989), 177.

28. Charles J. Woodbury, *Talks with Ralph Waldo Emerson* (New York, NY: The Baker and Taylor Co., 1890), 62.

29. "Woman in the Kitchen," *New York Saturday Press* (New York, NY), July 21, 1860, 2.

30. Betsy Erkkila, "Afterword," in *Walt Whitman's Songs of Male Intimacy and Love*, ed. Betsy Erkkila (Iowa City, IA: University of Iowa Press, 2011), 111–13.

31. Fred Vaughan to Walt Whitman, March 19, 1860, WWA.

32. Fred Vaughan to Walt Whitman, March 27, 1860, WWA.

33. Stephanie M. Blalock, "'Tell what I meant by Calamus': Walt Whitman's Vision of Comradeship from Fred Vaughan to the Fred Gray Association," in Levin and Whitley, *Whitman among the Bohemians*, 178.

34. "Agricultural Column," *Vanity Fair*, March 17, 1860, 183; "Our Agricultural Column: Crop Prospects for 1860," *Vanity Fair*, May 19, 1860, 326.

35. Ruth Bohan, "Whitman and the 'Picture-Makers,'" in Levin and Whitley, *Whitman among the Bohemians*, 141.

36. "A Visit to Walt Whitman," *Brooklyn Daily Eagle* (Brooklyn, NY), July 11, 1886, https://www.bklynlibrary.org/.

CHAPTER 22

Gender

Maire Mullins

In both subtle and dramatic ways, Walt Whitman infused *Leaves of Grass* with portrayals of femininity and masculinity, crafting gender constructions that both reinforced and undercut the mid-nineteenth-century cultural mainstream. Whitman anticipated the work of historians, sociologists, psychologists, and literary theorists in the field of gender studies. While Whitman employed language to capture the social construction of gender in his poetry and prose, he also used his body as a template upon which nineteenth-century photographers, daguerreotypists, and artists could record the male body as it aged: beard, graying and white hair, hat, coat, posture, gaze. Whitman offered versions of the construction of masculinity in his many poses, images which accompanied the editions of *Leaves of Grass* beginning in 1855. His relationships with women, beginning with his mother Louisa Van Velsor Whitman and his sisters Mary Elizabeth Whitman Van Nostrand and Hannah Whitman Heyde, and continuing in his friendships with Abby Hills Price, Paulina Wright Davis, Ernestine L. Rose, and Ellen O'Connor (among many others), had a formative, ongoing influence on the construction of femininity in his writing.[1] A social institution comprised of norms, expectations, responsibilities, and behaviors, gender is expressed by individuals through a "sense of gendered self" and through "internalized patterns of socially normative emotions,"[2] but also in social institutions that regulate normativity. Judith Butler writes that "gender is culturally constructed, hence gender is neither the causal result of sex nor as seemingly fixed as sex."[3] Sex is tied to biology, but gender is taught, learned, and absorbed through culturally established norms. Comprised of socially constructed identities caught in time, gender possesses fluidity and is entangled in other ways of understanding identity – class, race, age, ability, religion, roles. These identities, too, are inherently present in the way Whitman frames his poems and his portraits, weaving in details that embody the complexity of identity. Whitman's is no static vision: ever-changing, flexible, and curious, in the editions of *Leaves of*

Grass Whitman attempted to capture "this *Time and Land we swim in*," as he noted in an 1865 letter to his friend William D. O'Connor (Corr., 1:246). Whitman observed and recorded normative gendered behavior in his poetry and prose, but he also questioned it, turning the questions back on entrenched social institutions and gender norms of mid-nineteenth-century America.

In his 1855 Preface to *Leaves of Grass*, Whitman states, "The Americans of all nations at any time upon the earth have probably the fullest poetical nature" (LG55, iii). This "poetical nature" can be found, he writes, in the "common people" (LG55, iii), thus locating the subject matter of his poems in his understanding of the everyday citizen: female, male, old, middle-aged, young, ethnic, enslaved, temperate, drunk, even-tempered. Cataloging the "common people," Whitman shows the collective gender practices of slices of urban New York city and rural Long Island in the mid-nineteenth century as well as imagined gender practices from "east to west" (LG55, iv). Recognizing that gender is a fluid construct, in section 15 of "Song of Myself" Whitman offers a nonstop catalog of women, men, and children at various instants in their everyday lives, instants that reveal the many ways that gender is constructed and performed. Whitman's large canvas encompasses Americans at work, but he also folds in images that undercut normativity: "The lunatic is carried at last to the asylum a confirm'd case, / (He will never sleep any more as he did in the cot in his mother's bed-room;)" (LG, 41). The removal of the "lunatic" takes place at the institutional level: he does not go to the "asylum" of his own accord; he is "carried," which suggests either coercion or, at the very least, a lack of agency. The next line provides a glimpse into the "lunatic's" domestic life: he will no longer sleep with those who love him and who have cared for him, particularly his mother. In this small vignette, the gender norm of the mother whose role is to care for her vulnerable, mentally ill son is reinforced, and the empty cot signifies the nature of their prosaic domestic arrangement. The empty cot further signifies the way in which the mother has been dispossessed of her gender role, a role disrupted by removal. Moments of quiet questioning in this section of "Song of Myself" are followed by larger rhetorical moments, a move that Whitman employs again and again: "The malform'd limbs are tied to the surgeon's table, / What is removed drops horribly in a pail; / The quadroon girl is sold at the auction-stand, the drunkard nods by the bar-room stove" (LG, 42). Gender is not a fixed concept: each movement, emotion, reaction, and interaction changes the composition. The "malformed limbs," the "quadroon girl," and the "drunkard" reinforce brokenness and loss: the loss of "limbs" needed for livelihood and mobility; the probable sexual assault and ongoing dehumanization of the young woman sold as a slave; the loss of family and social ties that the "drunkard" experiences.

Gender roles and gender identity are learned: humans are educated as children into accepted modes of performing gender. In order to do gender properly as an adult, one must witness the ways gender is enacted. The family is the first teacher of gender norms and roles, and the first enforcer through parenting and interactions with siblings. In "There Was a Child Went Forth," Whitman describes the formation of a child's consciousness as he absorbs his environment. The poem begins with a straightforward description of how the child goes "forth," repeating the word "object" to emphasize its importance in the child's developing consciousness (LG55, 90). The first section of the poem focuses on the natural world: plants, animals, the change of seasons. The poem captures the dynamic between the peaceful coexistence evident in the natural world and the differing levels of violence in the human world. The "old drunkard," whose story is not fully presented in the poem, signifies the transition to the world of humans. Having spent the night in an "outhouse," the drunkard staggers home. The school environment is then presented, but here too differing levels of violence are evident. Some of the boys are "friendly," others are "quarrelsome"; while the girls are "tidy and fresh-cheeked," the "negro boy and girl" are "barefoot" (LG55, 91). Undercurrents of the larger violence in society are present in this small vignette: "quarrelsome" suggests a habit of behavior that is truculent, angry, rooted in discord. The "barefoot" "negro" boy and girl suggest class/racial difference. Since slavery was legal at the time Whitman wrote this poem, it is possible that these children are slaves. Only the "schoolmistress" and the "girls" are presented in a hopeful light. In these opening scenes, Whitman is "doing gender" as part of "doing difference." This dynamic occurs, as Anne Fausto-Sterling notes, when we "establish identities that include race and class as well as gender, and we do gender differently depending upon our location in racial and class hierarchies,"[4] as well as our age, which impacts our gender roles. The speaker of "There Was a Child Went Forth" is both an adult remembering and a child experiencing. Whitman engages the romantic rubric for point of view and theme, but also includes scenes that suggest the violence of everyday living for the man/boy as he navigates his "place and time," caught in the present and the past that shaped him.

Perhaps the disrupted nature of daily violence ushers in the boy's hyperawareness of gender roles:

The mother at home quietly placing the dishes on the suppertable,
The mother with mild words .... clean her cap and gown .... a wholesome
   odor falling off her person and clothes as she walks by:
The father, strong, selfsufficient, manly, mean, angered, unjust,
The blow, the quick loud word, the tight bargain, the crafty lure.   (LG55, 91)

The father's violent behavior more than likely is directed toward the
mother as well as the boy. Witnessing the father's anger and juxtaposing
it with the mother's "mild" and "wholesome" ways, the boy experiences
both dislocation/insecurity *and* connection/security, a conflicted position
that provides him with a more nuanced understanding of the forces that
swirl around him and shape him. This swirling perspective is one that
Whitman captures often in his verse. Moving among a crowd of people,
the speaker notes what he is experiencing:

The sense of what is real .... the thought if after all it should prove unreal,
The doubts of daytime and the doubts of nighttime .... the curious whether
   and how,
Whether that which appears so is so .... Or is it all flashes and specks?
Men and women crowding fast in the streets .... if they are not flashes and
   specks what are they?   (LG55, 91)

The doubts swarm in upon him but also provide him with a vantage point
that allows him to see the "objects" differently as the poem ends.
The universe that surrounds the child is "solitary," "motionless," yet always
in motion, uncontained. The mother represents certainty, the father,
uncertainty. Both of these elements are now part of the child as he goes
forth. The gendered marital pattern that the boy absorbs helps to shape his
sensibility, his attitude toward justice, and his nascent questioning of
gender roles.

From the questioning of gender roles in the 1855 and 1856 editions of
Leaves of Grass, Whitman turns to the affirmation of same-sex relationships
in the 1860 edition. In the "Calamus" poems Whitman captures the effects
of the presence of male lovers, extending and developing a theme he had
introduced in the 1855 and 1856 editions but giving it space within
a reconfigured and expanded *Leaves of Grass*:

I heard the hissing rustle of the liquid and sands as directed to me whispering
   to congratulate me,
For the one I love most lay sleeping by me under the same cover in the cool
   night,
In the stillness in the autumn moonbeams his face was inclined toward me,
And his arm lay lightly around my breast – and that night I was happy.
                                                                      (LG, 123)

In the late 1850s, heteronormativity was enforced not just by cultural norms but also by the legal system and by religious institutions. As Glen H. Elder Jr. points out, "Human lives are socially embedded in specific historical times and places that shape their content, pattern, and direction. [...] Types of historical change are experienced differentially by people of different ages and roles."[5] Whitman understood clearly the gender role he was expected to perform as a white, working-class male. He chose a profession that enhanced his outsider status: journalist. As a journalist he could mask his gaze. He could exchange ideas with radical women who flouted gender normativity, like Mary Chilton.[6] He could cultivate relationships with women whose work was on the edge of gender norms, in the name of journalism. These relationships did not have to tip into heteronormative cultural patterns because of the veil of professionalism.

From 1855 until his death in 1892, Whitman faced tremendous cultural, social, religious, and political resistance to the subject matter of *Leaves of Grass*. In 1882, Boston's district attorney, Oliver Stevens, concluded that a proposed edition of *Leaves of Grass* (to be published by James R. Osgood & Co.) had to be withdrawn unless Whitman would consent to excise whole poems and passages from the edition. Whitman refused. In an effort to elucidate his project, however, Whitman wrote and published "A Memorandum at a Venture," in which he describes two contemporary points of view toward sexuality and gender. The first point of view is repression and censorship:

> The conventional one of good folks and good print everywhere, repressing any direct statement of them, and making allusions only at second or third hand. [...] In the civilization of today, this condition [...] has led to states of ignorance, repressal, and cover'd over disease and depletion, forming certainly a main factor in the world's woe. (PW, 2:492)

Whitman notes that this point of view may be found in most "modern literature," and possesses a "scent, as of something sneaking, furtive, mephitic" (PW, 2:492). The second point of view is "one of common life," and is located in "masculine circles, and in erotic stories and talk, to excite, express, and dwell on, that merely sensual voluptuousness which [...] is the most universal trait of all ages, all lands" (PW, 2:492). This point of view Whitman compares to "a disease which comes to the surface, and therefore less dangerous than a conceal'd one" (PW, 2:493). Against the formidable cultural forces of repression, concealment, and aberrant sexual behavior, Whitman proposes a "a third point of view" that will redeem "this subject from its hitherto relegation to the tongues and pens of blackguards, and boldly putting it for once at least, if no more, in the demesne of poetry and sanity" (PW, 2:493–94). If this could be accomplished, Whitman writes, then the resistance to women's equality in the public sphere would be removed: "To the movement for the eligibility and entrance of women amid new spheres of business, politics, and suffrage, the current prurient, conventional treatment of sex is the main formidable obstacle" (PW, 2:494). The question is both an "ethic" and an "aesthetic" one, Whitman concludes (PW, 2:494–95). Whitman wanted the reading public to know that *Leaves of Grass* did not belong to either of the two sociocultural contemporary approaches to gender and sexuality he describes, despite the repeated attempts of censors and some critics to place *Leaves of Grass* in these categories. He particularly objected to his work being placed in the second category.[7] *Leaves of Grass* celebrates the human body and includes many explicit passages about the naked body, but its approach is not pornographic or sexually deviant. Whitman argues that unveiling the body is the first step toward a new understanding of the relation between the sexes: "The rising tide of 'woman's rights,' swelling and every year advancing farther and farther, recoils from it [prurient conventional treatment of sex] with dismay. There will in my opinion be no general progress in such eligibility till a sensible, philosophic, democratic method is substituted" (PW, 2:494). Whitman was convinced that *Leaves of Grass* was both harbinger and hallmark of this new approach.

In some poems Whitman captures moments when women elude heteronormativity. In "The Sleepers" Whitman includes a vignette about his mother's memory of an incident from her girlhood. Louisa invites the woman inside the house; as she does so she dwells on the woman's physical appearance, minutely describing the overwhelming physical attraction she feels for her:

> My mother looked in delight and amazement at the stranger,
> She looked at the beauty of her tallborne face and full and pliant limbs,
> The more she looked upon her she loved her,
> Never before had she seen such wonderful beauty and purity. (LG55, 74)

As she cooks a meal for her and admires her physical beauty, Louisa offers the woman temporary shelter. In its portrayal of same-sex love between two women, between two races, between differing classes, and perhaps between an older woman (the Native American) and a younger woman (Louisa), the passage demonstrates intersectionality. The Native American woman's age is not indicated, but she is referred to as "tallborne," and as "full and pliant": the implication is that she is older than Louisa. Louisa confides in Walt, who serves as the story's first auditor and whose role is to listen. In Louisa's story, the woman does not just leave – she goes "away." The word "away" echoes an earlier passage in "The Sleepers" that focuses on women's desire: "I hear the heart-beat ... I follow ... I fade away" (LG55, 72). By telling her story to Walt, Louisa gains access to the public sphere. As Robert Asen notes, "Participation in public discussions does not proceed only through voice and body; inclusions and exclusions also occur in the perceptions of others – the imaginings of others. Sometimes, individual and groups 'appear' in debates from which they are physically absent as images (linguistic and/or visual representations) circulate in public discourse."[8]

A gifted oral storyteller, it is likely that Louisa never learned to write. So Louisa impresses upon her son the significance, for her, of the Native American woman's visit: she learned to love, and she learned that love at times entails loss. Doubly absent from discourse, silenced, and all-but-eradicated, the image of the Native American woman is included as part of a larger text about sleep and dreams, portraying a cross-cultural racial encounter between a Euro-American adolescent and a native woman. The genre of the poem simultaneously undercuts and reinforces what has happened. Woman's same-sex desire is located in "The Sleepers" perhaps because the dream vision could serve as the least threatening mode of poetic discourse. Alan Trachtenberg describes "The Sleepers" as "a story of the experience of night, especially the loss of demarcation between oneself and others caused by darkness and its oneiric reflexes. Making the dreams of others one's own dream is to fulfil the most errant promise of night."[9] Sinking Louisa's story into "The Sleepers" gives it a mildly unreal effect, even though it is based on an incident from Louisa's adolescence. The story is told at twilight, dinnertime, when daylight is receding and the night advances. The speaker of the poem, a non-participant, becomes implicated in the scene, both "speaking for" them and "speaking about" them. Louisa and Walt fade to the background as the "red squaw" becomes the object of dual desire – Louisa's, then Walt's through Louisa. This triangulated method of portraying women's sexual desire is a technique that Whitman also uses in section 11 of "Song of Myself" when the speaker/Whitman latches on to the twenty-ninth bather's point of view.

Section 11 of "Song of Myself" tells the story of a twenty-eight-year-old woman who looks out from the window of her house upon twenty-eight young men who are bathing in the water below her "fine house by the rise of the bank" (LG, 38). They do not know that she watches them; she "hides handsome and richly drest aft the blinds of the window." Age, class, and gender normativity are set aside; the woman caresses the men as they bathe, emerging from her house in her imagination and passing her hand "over their bodies." The poet, who sees the woman, speaks to her directly, "Where are you off to, lady? for I see you, / You splash in the water there, yet stay stock still in your room" (LG, 38). In a flash the speaker comprehends her loneliness, her isolation, and her unbounded, transgressive desire. Yet, there is nothing "sneaking" or "furtive" about this scene, qualities that Whitman criticizes as part of contemporary discourse in "A Memorandum at a Venture." The act of leaving her house is portrayed as both escape *and* fulfillment. The woman leaves behind the trappings of class, the accoutrements of containment, the adornments and dress of gender display that are allied with conformity. Instead she finds joy as, "Dancing and laughing," she moves along the beach and toward the young men. Her exhilaration increases as she is released from the "fine house," the house of behavioral, linguistic, and physical gender status that obscures, hides, and ultimately dehumanizes her. No longer confined, she becomes the water which glistens through the beards of the "young men," then through "their long hair," then, in "little streams [...] all over their bodies." Her sexual desires are no longer contained within socially and individually patterned gender norms:

> An unseen hand also pass'd over their bodies,
> It descended tremblingly from their temples and ribs.
> The young men float on their backs, their white bellies bulge to the sun, they
>   do not ask who seizes fast to them,
> They do not know who puffs and declines with pendant and bending arch,
> They do not think whom they souse with spray. (LG, 39)

In "A Memorandum at a Venture" Whitman writes, "In the present memorandum I only venture to indicate that plan and view – decided upon more than twenty years ago, for my own literary action, and formulated tangibly in my printed poems [...] that the sexual passion in itself, while normal and unperverted, is inherently legitimate, creditable, not necessarily an improper theme for a poet" (PW, 2:493). The woman in section 11 of "Song of Myself" explores her sexual passion alone and abandons gendered behavioral norms in her imagination. The percipient speaker understands her initial isolation and entrapment, and the ways in which she gives expression to her desire by overturning entrenched gender systems.

Whitman wanted his readers to understand that his project in *Leaves of Grass* and in his prose writings was to indicate the ways in which a "new departure – a third point of view" (PW, 2:493) could displace the diseased, malformed, and sexually violent publications that had taken hold of nine-teenth-century discourse, publications which in turn shaped societal gender norms and limited women's capacity for participation in the Republic as fully formed citizens. David S. Reynolds calls Whitman's technique of fusing "sexual and nature images" in a purifying manner *"cleansing rhetoric –* that is, the yoking together of refreshing nature images and sensational ones in an effort to overcome prurient sexuality."[10] Whitman's project included this impulse but its scope was far larger: he hoped to transform the societal and cultural understanding of gender. *Leaves of Grass*, combined with his voluminous prose writings, supported this effort.

Notes

1. See Sherry Ceniza, *Walt Whitman and Nineteenth-Century Women Reformers* (Tuscaloosa, AL: University of Alabama Press, 1998) for an extended analysis of the formative relationships Whitman had with Abby Hills Price, Paulina Wright Davis, and Ernestine L. Rose.

2. Anne Fausto-Sterling, *Sexing the Body: Gender Politics and the Construction of Sexuality* (New York, NY: Basic Books, 2000), 251.

3. Judith Butler, *Gender Trouble: Feminism and the Subversion of Identity* (New York, NY: Routledge, 1990), 6.

4. Fausto-Sterling, *Sexing the Body*, 244.

5. Glen H. Elder Jr., "The Life Course and Human Development," in *Handbook of Child Psychology, Vol. I: Theoretical Models of Human Development*, ed. Richard M. Lerner (New York, NY: Wiley, 1998), 969.

6. See Ceniza, *Walt Whitman*, 192, for further exploration of this topic.

7. See David S. Reynolds, "Whitman and Nineteenth-Century Views of Gender and Sexuality," in *Walt Whitman of Mickle Street: A Centennial Collection*, ed. Geoffrey M. Sill (Knoxville, TN: University of Tennessee Press, 1994), 38–45. Reynolds notes that in "A Memorandum at a Venture" Whitman describes the writers in this second category as "subversive" because they wanted to demonstrate that the "upper classes were rotten to the core"; thus portraying the rich in particular as engaging in sexually deviant behaviors, a "twisted world" of "violence, entrapment, and manipulation" (39).

8. Robert Asen, "Imagining in the Public Sphere," *Philosophy and Rhetoric* 35.4 (2002), 347.

9. Alan Trachtenberg, "Whitman at Night: 'The Sleepers' in 1855," in *Leaves of Grass: The Sesquicentennial Essays*, eds. Susan Belasco, Ed Folsom, and Kenneth M. Price (Lincoln, NE: University of Nebraska Press, 2007), 125.

10. Reynolds, "Whitman and Nineteenth-Century Views," 43.

CHAPTER 23

Sexuality

Jay Grossman

During his long life that extended virtually from one end of the nineteenth century to the other, Walt Whitman lived, worked, and wrote in the endless, sustaining company of other men. He built his life upon the foundation of these emotional, affectionate, and sexual bonds, which are the central facts of both his biography and his poetry, as well as the necessary starting place for any exploration of Whitman and sexuality. Moreover, Whitman placed the body, sex, desire, and love at the very center of his poetic and prophetic mission. As he insisted in his 1856 public letter to Ralph Waldo Emerson: "I say that the body of a man or woman, the main matter, is so far quite unexpressed in poems; but that the body is to be expressed, and sex is" (LG56, 356). Other lines from the first edition of *Leaves of Grass* further clarify this mission:

> Through me forbidden voices,
> Voices of sexes and lusts . . . . voices veiled, and I remove the veil,
> Voices indecent by me clarified and transfigured.   (LG55, 29)

Whitman shifted the landscape of what it is possible to express in poetic language by insisting upon the poetic value and validity of the sexual and embodied aspects of the American experience not previously treated in verse. This is one of the reasons gay men and other sexual minorities, progressives of all kinds, and an entire line of American poets, have long been drawn to celebrate his writing and the example of his life.

At the same time, Whitman's life coincides with the century that saw significant changes in the ways sex, desire, and sexuality were understood, conceptualized, and lived. Within a range of cultural discourses, including medicine, the law, and literature, people living in the nineteenth century began to understand sexual desires differently. Gradually, and likely unevenly, over the course of decades people came to believe and to experience their lives as if they "had" a "sexuality" that made them a particular kind of person. Prior to this gradual, but hugely consequential shift, people likely thought of their sexual desires and erotic urges not as expressive of who they were – of their "identities" – but rather as kinds of behaviors in which they preferred to engage; indeed, there is evidence into the twentieth century of people still conceiving their desires this way, as tendencies and acts, rather than identities and selves.[1] Still, by sometime near the end of both the nineteenth century and Whitman's life, it came to seem that one was (born) a "homosexual" or a "heterosexual" (new medical terms at the time) in just the way one was (born) a male or a female, and the choices within this novel system were not equivalent ones: clearly the pressure to be heterosexual, for women and especially for men, was urgent and ubiquitous. Whitman's life and writings, as well as their reception by readers over the last 150 years, are an exquisitely precise barometer for reckoning changes in the ways in which sex and this new category of sexual identity have been understood, and with what interpretive and cultural consequences. This essay will necessarily take account of not only the meanings attached to Whitman's writings during his life, but also the ways in which these texts look different, but no less relevant for us now, as we read them in the twenty-first century.[2]

***

I begin with a photograph, taken near the end of the Civil War, that shows Whitman and "his rebel soldier friend Pete Doyle" (Figure 23.1). The photograph appears even more intimate than standard nineteenth-century images of husband and wife. Indeed, it looks as if the camera has caught the two men unawares; they are not only gazing and smiling at each other, but Doyle's left arm is touching Whitman's left leg and hidden from view by it. This is not simply emotional intimacy but physical intimacy as well, and it takes place between two men from different regions – Whitman a Northerner from New York and Doyle his Ireland-born, Confederate-army friend. The war is one important context for reading the photo, as Whitman's handwritten caption emphasizes, and one to which we will return.

Within a few decades of its creation, this intimate photo caused distress for some of its viewers, even among Whitman's closest friends. On Wednesday, January 16, 1889, the photograph entered a conversation between the poet, Thomas Harned, and Horace Traubel, who recorded what transpired:

> I picked up a picture from the box by the fire: a Washington picture: Whitman and Peter Doyle photoed together: a rather remarkable composition: Doyle with a sickly smile on his face: W. lovingly serene: the two

Figure 23.1 M. P. Rice, *Washington D.C. 1865 – Walt Whitman & his rebel soldier friend Pete Doyle* (c. 1868). Courtesy of the Library of Congress, Prints and Photographs Division, Washington, DC, and the *Walt Whitman Archive* (whitmanarchive.org).

looking at each other rather stagily, almost sheepishly. [...] Whitman laughed heartily the instant I put my hands on it (I had seen it often before) – Harned mimicked Doyle, Whitman retorting: "Never mind, the expression on my face atones for all that is lacking in his. What do I look like there? Is it seriosity?" Harned suggested: "Fondness, and Doyle should be a girl" – but Whitman shook his head, laughing again: "No – don't be too

hard on it: that is my rebel friend, you know," &c. Then again: "Tom, you
would like Pete – love him: and you too, Horace: you especially, Horace –
you and Pete would get to be great chums."³ (WWC, 3:542–43)

Thomas Harned's insistence that "Doyle should be a girl" makes his
anxiety perfectly clear: approximately twenty-five years after the photo
was taken, intimate, loving gazes are acceptable, according to Harned,
only between members of the (so-called) opposite sex. Harned's response
shows us that a broader heteronormativity is taking hold: "fondness"
between men has become suspect. Which is to say that not the least of
what Harned reveals about himself here is how unsuited he is to serve as an
executor for Whitman's writings, since same-sex affections are crucial to
virtually everything Whitman wrote. The conversation suggests that the
normative is beginning to shift and around the turn of the century it will
land squarely on the side of the heterosexual, and reactions like Harned's
will become more commonplace. For example, in 1913, W. C. Rivers uses
this same photograph as the frontispiece for a book in which he declares
that Whitman paid "a strange and fearful price" – that is, his homosexuality – for his genius, which he compares to the insanity of lunatics and
criminals.⁴ As if to signal just how out of line Harned's comment is,
Whitman in his response doubles down by insisting that everyone in the
room, including Harned, would come to "like Pete – love him" just as he
himself does. That is, Whitman implicates Harned into precisely the realm
of same-sex affection that so discomforts him. Let us call this whole
exchange "Exhibit B."

"Exhibit A" occurred a few years earlier. In 1882, the Boston district
attorney, egged on by the New England Society for the Suppression of
Vice, informed Whitman and his publisher that certain "obscene"
passages in the latest edition of *Leaves of Grass* needed to be removed
or else the book would be banned in Boston.⁵ Whitman refused to
make any of the cuts: "The list whole & several is rejected by me, &
will not be thought of under any circumstances."⁶ The incident is
important, though, not only because of Whitman's unyielding defense
of First Amendment principles but also because, in the list of passages
to be excised, the DA entirely ignored any lines or poems from
Whitman's most explicitly same-sex poems, the homoerotic
"Calamus" cluster first published in the 1860 edition of *Leaves of
Grass* that describe relationships like the one in the photograph that
made Harned so uncomfortable: "In the stillness, in the autumn
moonbeams, his face was inclined toward me, / And his arm lay lightly

around my breast – And that night I was happy" (LG60, 358). Instead the DA's attention is wholly directed toward passages that depict explicit cross-sex sexual activity, especially poems showing active female erotic desire.[7] What worried Harned – the obvious affection between Doyle and Whitman – is not even noticed by the Boston DA, which gives us a sense of how uneven and unclear the boundaries and the meanings attached to same-sex male affection at the end of the nineteenth century could be. And yet variability or unevenness is not the same thing as innocuousness, as the conviction of Oscar Wilde, in 1895, on charges of "gross indecency" (that is, sex with other men) makes perfectly clear. The incoherence of these Anglo-American proscriptions does not necessarily make them any less lethal, especially when we take into account in the case of Wilde his conviction for particular allegedly indecent *acts* even in the context of the incipient model of "identities."

Despite what we now recognize as the centrality of same-sex male affection in *Leaves of Grass*, the DA's concern with women's bodies and women's sexual desire is by no means ancillary to the story of Whitman and sexuality. "*Leaves of Grass* is essentially a woman's book" (WWC, 2:331), Whitman is known to have said, and while the comment is ambiguous (does it mean the book was written for women, or with women in mind, or from the perspective of a "woman"?) we know that women reacted powerfully to many of the poems in it. And for good reason. An episode like that of the twenty-eight young male bathers (eventually section 11 in "Song of Myself") has something for every seeming erotic interest: not only the homoerotic energies of the naked men frolicking in the water, but the woman who voyeuristically watches them and whose desirous gaze replicates that of the presumably male speaker. That is, Whitman provided an opportunity for women to share in the spectacle, and part of its erotic charge depends on gender ambiguity: "The young men float on their backs, their white bellies swell to the sun" as if they are pregnant, even as the woman joins the men, "dancing and laughing" – in her mind's eye, at least – as "the twenty-ninth bather" (LG55, 19).

As a second example of explicit female desire in *Leaves*, consider "A Woman Waits for Me," one of three complete poems the Boston DA insisted had to be deleted in full. "Without shame the man I like knows and avows the deliciousness of his sex, / Without shame the woman I like knows and avows hers," proclaims the speaker (LG56, 240). No wonder the DA was nervous. For one thing, the speaker here openly announces that he "likes" both men and women, and the balanced syntax of the lines make his desires both proximate and equivalent. At the same time, women readers appreciated the straightforward insistence that they also possess erotic desires that should be recognized and celebrated. Indeed, to thank him, some women wrote to Whitman asking whether they could have his baby.

"A Woman Waits for Me" is also worth pausing over, however, because it is an excellent example of a text that has changed with the times. When it first appeared women were attracted to the poem's expansive catalog of women's capabilities: "They know how to swim, row, ride, wrestle, shoot, run, strike, retreat, advance, resist, defend themselves" (LG56, 241). But for modern readers it has become difficult to read past the way the speaker's own desires fully circumscribe those of the women who "wait": "It is I, you women – I make my way, / [...] / I do not hurt you any more than is necessary for you, / [...] / I brace myself effectually – I listen to no entreaties" (LG56, 242). The power imbalance in a scene that reads like rape reminds us that neither writing nor reading occurs in a historical vacuum, and the changing contexts within which Whitman's sexual representations continue to take shape must also be at the center of any account of Whitman and sexuality.

***

Whitman revolutionized modern poetry in part through his invention of the poetic catalog as a mode of democratic inclusivity. His poetic lines give equal weight to every member of his poetic republic, from "the pure contralto" to "the carpenter" to "the quadroon girl," one after another, and one at a time, until a crucial juxtaposition is reached at the bottom of page 22 in the first edition:

> The prostitute draggles her shawl, her bonnet bobs on her tipsy and pimpled neck,
> The crowd laugh at her blackguard oaths, the men jeer and wink to each other,
> (Miserable! I do not laugh at your oaths nor jeer you,)
> The President holds a cabinet council, he is surrounded by the great secretaries.
> (LG55, 22)

Placing the prostitute next to the president, these lines exemplify the radical democratic impulse behind Whitman's poetic vision, as well as his full-frontal assault on polite literary values, sexual taboos, and bourgeois niceties. By restoring the sexual to pride of place – beside the president, and including the prostitutes – he insists on the poetic value and validity of the sexual and embodied aspects of American experience not previously treated in verse.

In his notebooks, Whitman collected and catalogued men in much the same way he assembled representative Americans in his poetry; he had a particular fondness for stage-coach drivers like Peter Doyle (Figure 23.2):

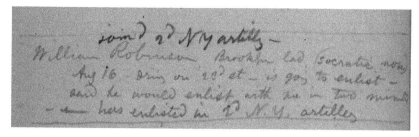

Figure 23.2 Excerpt from Walt Whitman Notebook 94. Courtesy of the
Library of Congress.

William Robinson [–] Brooklyn lad (socratic nose)
Aug 16 – driving on 23d st – is going to enlist –
said he would enlist with me in two minutes
– has enlisted in 2d N. Y. artillery[8]

Robinson's desire to enlist with Whitman serves as a kind of marriage
proposal and signals his urge to get to know Whitman more intimately.
The entry also shows the near instantaneity ("in two minutes") of the bond
between Robinson and Whitman, who was frequently described as posses-
sing an almost magnetic aura. During Whitman's service in the Civil War
hospitals in and around Washington, DC, his electric presence was both
much in evidence and much in demand among the soldiers he nursed and
comforted: "Many a soldier's loving arms about this neck have cross'd and
rested, / Many a soldier's kiss dwells on these bearded lips," he remembered
in "The Wound-Dresser."[9] These are bonds between men that the conclusion of the Civil War may have made less familiar. After all, the
comradeship of brothers-in-arms is a central aspect of the stories told
about warfare, but what happens once the war is over and domestic life
returns to "normal"? Is that part of what Harned is reacting to (whether he
knows it or not), a change in context that makes "normal" relations
between men look different by the late 1880s?[10]

And yet: to tell the story of Whitman's life in the closing decades of the
century is to tell a story of his ongoing intimate attachments to a range of
younger men. In 1876, the poet met Harry Stafford, who was thirty-nine
years his junior, in a print shop where the Centennial Edition of *Leaves of
Grass* was in production: "Dear Harry, not a day or night passes but I think
of you [. . .] Dear son, how I wish you could come in now, even if but for
an hour & take off your coat, & sit on my lap" (Corr. 3:86). As historian
Jonathan Ned Katz notes, "Kinship terms – father-son, uncle-nephew,

Figure 23.3 Augustus Morand, *Walt Whitman and Harry Stafford* (1878). Stafford
and Whitman appear in the "standard" marriage pose, with the "husband" seated.
Whitman recorded one of Harry's visits in February, 1878: "Monday – Harry here –
put r[ing] on his hand again – had picture taken at Morand's." Courtesy of the
Edward Carpenter Collection at the University of Sheffield and the *Walt Whitman
Archive* (whitmanarchive.org).

brother-brother – provided nineteenth-century males several ways to name
and define intimacies."[11] Years later, when Harry married and had a family
of his own, they became acquainted with Whitman as well, which reminds
us of the ways in which the boundaries between what looks to us like the
homosexual and the heterosexual – Harry's relation with Whitman, Harry's
relation with his wife – are not (yet) mutually exclusive (Figure 23.3).

Harry Stafford was followed in the 1880s by Bill Duckett, who served as Whitman's carriage driver and likely also sometimes lived with the poet. The two also shared one especially noteworthy acquaintance, the Philadelphia painter and photographer Thomas Eakins, who shared Whitman's belief in the liberatory possibilities of representing the naked body in art and who took a series of photographs of both Whitman and Duckett posing nude.[12] Finally, Warren Fritzinger, a one-time sailor, served as a nurse during Whitman's last illness and was at his side when he died: "Warrie and I come to understand each other pretty well–*very* well. I like his touch [...] – he has that wonderful indescribable combination [...] which, with great manly strength, unites sweet delicacy, soft as a woman's," explained Whitman (see WWC, 6:82–83). As the notebook lists of men suggest, these photographs and accounts of Whitman and his young men stand in for a wide range of unnamed, unphotographed others with whom he shared his love, his life, and his body as well.

***

Whitman's "Calamus" poems, named for the phallic-looking marsh grass, are the published versions of the relationships with men recorded in his notebooks and photographs. Among the most affectionately explicit male–male poems in English to this point in history, Whitman's same-sex proclamations have empowered generations of gay men and their allies, as well as inspired a tradition of gay male Anglo-American poets, from Edward Carpenter to Hart Crane to Allen Ginsberg and beyond. However, these poems also demonstrate differences from later understandings of gay sexuality that are equally crucial:

> There shall from me be a new friendship – It shall be called after my name,
> It shall circulate through The States, indifferent of place,
> It shall twist and intertwist them through and around each other –
>   Compact shall they be, showing new signs,
> Affection shall solve every one of the problems of freedom.
> [...]
> One from Massachusetts shall be comrade to a Missourian,
> One from Maine or Vermont, and a Carolinian and an Oregonese, shall be
>   friends triune, more precious to each other than all the riches of the
>   earth.
> [...]
> It shall be customary in all directions, in the houses and streets, to see
>   manly affection,
> [...]

> The most dauntless and rude shall touch face to face lightly,
> The dependence of Liberty shall be lovers,
> The continuance of Equality shall be comrades.   (LG60, 349–51)

This prophetic poem imagines "a new friendship" as the basis for restoring national, comradely unity at precisely the moment of national dissolution. Here, what we would recognize as a form of "homosexuality" is seen as central to state formation, not as a crime or in opposition to the stable structures of government and civic life.

This poem also, crucially, extends the perimeters of male friendship beyond the bounds of the couple. Whitman explicitly writes about "friends triune," a sexual-political three-way relationship between "One from Maine or Vermont, and a Carolinian and an Oregonese." A few years later he reiterated the model in a letter to one of his "soldier-boys," Lewis K. Brown:

> You speak of being here in Washington again about the last of August –
> O Lewy, how glad I should be to see you, to have you with me – I have
> thought if it could be so that you, & one other person & myself could be
> where we could work & live together, & have each other's society, we three,
> I should like it so much – but it is probably a dream.[13] (Corr., 1:121)

Pushing beyond the paradigm of the couple, Whitman's ideal is a *ménage à trois* rather than a simple pair. This, too, is an aspect of Whitman's difference from many, perhaps most, of his twenty-first-century heirs, for Whitman imagines a wider comradeship knitting together the nation and extending the reach of the sexual beyond the privacy of a couple living and loving apart. Whitman's conception of male relations is undoubtedly political, but it is not precisely the forerunner of the contemporary politics of marriage equality.

Thinking we know what a queer family looks like today may actually keep us from being able to see just how queer the notions of family, collectivity, and finally, politics, may have been for Whitman, for whom sexuality was not a secret private core inside but rather a public principle. He placed his sexual and affectionate attraction to men at the very center of his poetry and his political hopes for the nation. The resonance and the significance of the claims he made on behalf of this affection have lost very little of their power in the intervening 150 years. Indeed, there may be few moments as powerful as when it is made clear in a literature or a history classroom that America's great poet of democracy is also America's great gay poet. At the same time, we should remember that calling Whitman "gay" in our terms is a simplification, and that this is a case where the word "queer" can do some genuinely important work for us. After all, Whitman may not have been "a homosexual" as that identity category eventually takes hold, but he is the great poet of male affection and of cross-identification, as these brief, adjacent verse-paragraphs from "Song of Myself" demonstrate:

> I turn the bridegroom out of bed and stay with the bride myself,
> And tighten her all night to my thighs and lips.
>
> My voice is the wife's voice, the screech by the rail of the stairs,
> They fetch my man's body up dripping and drowned.   (LG55, 38)

Writing poetry that relentlessly shifts between voices and perspectives, and trying to bring into being a world that foregrounds affection and that recognizes the complex permeability of identities and desire, Whitman as much as any American poet would have understood the urgency around the prefix "trans" playing out on the national stage and in the lives of more and more individuals.

> You must be he I was seeking, or she I was seeking, (It comes to
>   me, as of a dream,)
> [. . .]
> You grew up with me, were a boy with me, or a girl with me,
> I ate with you, and slept with you – your body has become not
>   yours only, nor left my body mine only.   (LG60, 366)

Whitman would have understood the power of naming one's own desires and choosing one's own identifications, and he still challenges us to make possible in our own lives and in the lives of others a world he helps us to see and that he helped to shape.

Notes

1. For a discussion of the persistence of these older modes of sexual self-understanding, see Jay Grossman, "The Canon in the Closet: Matthiessen's Whitman, Whitman's Matthiessen," *American Literature* 70.4 (1998), 799–832.
2. This paragraph is a thumbnail redaction of the foundational work of two theorists of sexuality with whom any student of Whitman and sexuality must conscientiously engage: Eve Kosofsky Sedgwick, *Epistemology of the Closet* (Berkeley, CA: University of California Press, 1990); and David M. Halperin, "How to Do the History of Male Homosexuality," *GLQ: A Journal for Lesbian and Gay Studies* 6.1 (2000), 87–124, and *How to Do the History of Homosexuality* (Chicago, IL: University of Chicago Press, 2002).

3. I am indebted to Ed Folsom, "Whitman's Calamus Photographs," in *Breaking Bounds: Whitman and American Cultural Studies*, eds. Jay Grossman and Betsy Erkkila (New York, NY: Oxford University Press, 1996), 193–219.

4. W. C. Rivers, *Walt Whitman's Anomaly* (London: George Allen, 1913), 9.

5. See John Tessitore, "'Plainness is Purity': *Leaves of Grass*, Free Religion, and Boston's Morals Campaign," *Mickle Street Review* 19/20 (April 2008), http://micklestreet.rutgers.edu/.

6. Quoted in Justin Kaplan, *Walt Whitman: A Life* (New York, NY: Simon and Schuster, 1980), 20.

7. Richard Maurice Bucke, *Walt Whitman* (Philadelphia, PA: David McKay, 1883), 148–53, provides the complete list of lines to be excised.

8. Whitman's Civil War notebooks can be viewed through the Library of Congress website; to see this entry, search for "Whitman Notebook 94" at www.loc.gov, and then find image 13.

9. Walt Whitman, "The Dresser" [original title], *Walt Whitman's Drum-Taps* (New York, NY, 1865), 34, WWA.

10. For an exploration of male relations during the war, see Jay Grossman, "Brothers in Arms: Masculinity in Whitman's Civil War," *The Classroom Electric: Dickinson, Whitman, and American Culture*, 2001, www.classroomelectric.org.

11. Jonathan Ned Katz, *Love Stories: Sex between Men before Homosexuality* (Chicago, IL: University of Chicago Press, 2001), 170.

12. Eakins's series of photographs of a nude old man who may be Whitman is owned by the J. Paul Getty Museum: www.getty.edu; search for "Naked Series Old Man." His photographs of Bill Duckett can be viewed on the website of the Pennsylvania Academy of the Fine Arts: www.pafa.org; search for "Duckett."

13. Quoted in Charley Shively, ed., *Drum Beats: Walt Whitman's Civil War Boy Lovers* (San Francisco, CA: Gay Sunshine Press, 1989), 119, though Shively has "love" for Whitman's "live"; Corr. 1:121, also available WWA. Shively, along with Robert K. Martin in his groundbreaking *The Homosexual Tradition in American Poetry* (Austin, TX: University of Texas Press, 1979), foregrounded the significance of Whitman's sexuality long before it became more widely acceptable to acknowledge it.

CHAPTER 24

Politics

Kerry Larson

Although my topic is politics, I want to come at the subject indirectly by first noting the prevalence of praise in Whitman's poetry. What does not escape his admiring gaze? The seagulls at the ferry, the drunkard staggering from the outhouse, the president at a cabinet meeting, the lichen on the fence-post – there is seemingly no limit to Whitman's relentless magnanimity. "The greatest poet hardly knows pettiness or triviality," we are told in the Preface to the 1855 *Leaves of Grass*. "What balks or breaks others is fuel for his burning progress to contact and amorous joy" (LG55, v–vi). Writing and celebrating are conjoined activities for Whitman because the given world is already animated by an "amorous joy" that his poetry is meant to affirm, attend to, and honor in what he calls "its fit proportions" (LG55, vi, iv). He wishes primarily to call out and name, not transform and interpret. The purpose of the poem, that is to say, is not to take up the disparate particulars of experience and shape them into an ordered whole. A sense of harmony does resonate through this verse but it is one that preexists or stands outside the frame of representation, like the "hum" or "lull" of the soul's "valved voice" (LG, 33). Whitman thus says of the poet that "his thoughts are the hymns of the praise of things" (LG55, v).

Robert von Halberg suggests that modern readers are apt to struggle with praise poetry because it so strongly favors affirmation over argument. It is, in this respect, "unreasonable."[1] It is true that praise poetry may make room for skepticism and even despair, as von Halberg also points out in connection with devotional verse such as the Book of Psalms or the sonnets of Hopkins. From time to time, Whitman, too, is afflicted by what he called the terrible doubt of appearances, a metaphysical dread that objects of praise might not be real after all. But this is hardly a major strain in his writing. In 1854 Thoreau had complained that "there is nowhere recorded a simple and irrepressible satisfaction with the gift of life, any memorable praise of God,"[2] but I think most readers would agree that with the appearance of *Leaves of Grass* one year later, Thoreau's complaint would be answered. Indeed, measured against the authors discussed by von Halberg, Whitman's praise poetry takes unreasonableness to new extremes since it assumes that everything is conceivably a candidate for esteem. You need to be an aristocrat and win an athletic contest to be celebrated by Pindar, but Whitman, breaking the connection between praise and accomplishment, has no restrictions whatever. Mindful of von Halberg's more skeptical modern intellectual, we may ask whether esteem so liberally bestowed does not become empty. Is not the whole point of esteem that it be selective? What, after all, could be less praiseworthy than a drunkard staggering from an outhouse?

Here Thoreau can be of help when he goes on to note in *Walden* (1854) that "it is something to be able to paint a particular picture, or to carve a statue, and so to make a few objects beautiful; but it is far more glorious to carve and paint the very atmosphere and medium through which we look, which morally we can do."[3] The drunkard who appears in Whitman's beautiful poem "There Was a Child Went Forth" is not really singled out as an object of praise in any standard sense of the term; yet to the extent that he emerges alongside other sights that greet the child's wondering gaze – like the new-born calf in the barn or the goldfish in the pond – the drunkard, too, is an object of wonder and appreciation. Circulating freely, praise becomes the medium through which one sees. Or putting this another way, we can say that Whitman's interest is less in praise than in praiseworthiness, the susceptibility of scenes, gestures, actions, and behaviors to be lit up with a sense of grace and vitality that is not reducible to any one object since these qualities shine through all.

Once we recognize the primacy of praise as "the very atmosphere and medium through which we look," we can see why it is a mistake to think of politics in Whitman's poetry as a matter of taking positions or insinuating arguments. As a journalist in New York City during the 1840s and 1850s, Whitman was deeply involved in political debate and witnessed at first hand the splintering of both the Whig and Democratic Parties as war approached. But insofar as there is a difference between writing an editorial for the *Brooklyn Daily Eagle* and writing a poem, we should be on guard against assuming that we can extract a politics from *Leaves of Grass* in the way we might extract a thread from a tapestry. The religious, aesthetic, and political are so interwoven in its "hymns of the praise of things" that singling out any one of these three filaments independent of the others is likely to appear arbitrary (LG55, v). An ostensibly political concept like equality is to Whitman both holy and beautiful, both sacred and sublime. A reverential gratitude bordering on awe that so often informs Thoreau's experience of nature likewise informs Whitman's experience of the democratic, so enthralled is he with what he calls "the tremendous audacity of its crowds and groupings and the push of its perspective spreads with crampless and flowing breadth, and showers its prolific and splendid extravagance" (LG55, iii). Even in this brief quotation (from the Preface to the 1855 *Leaves of Grass*) we see how the outwardly political, manifest in the "audacity" and "push" of the people, invites and is accompanied by other registers as in the admiration of the easy, unforced grace of this audacity, beautiful in its "flowing breadth," or in the appreciation for the bounty of an "extravagance" bestowed as though from above, as if in divine benediction.

As important as this interpenetration of praise and the political is to Whitman, it does nevertheless pose a set of challenges for his interpreter. In the space remaining, I want to shift gears somewhat by first describing what I take these challenges to be and how commentators have attempted to meet them before venturing some remarks of my own about what it means to speak of a political vision in *Leaves of Grass*.

We can start by noting a familiar tension between celebrating things as they are and celebrating things as they might be. When Michael Moon writes that Whitman's "body-politics is designed to reconstitute the readers' very subjectivity in relation not only to the author's but their own and everyone's else bodily existence" and further asserts that "Whitman revises readerly subjectivity in the direction of a heightened, transforming sense of the constructedness and hence the dense politicality of all bodily experiences, erotic and otherwise," one takes his point even as one balks at formulations such as "is designed to reconstitute" or "revises [. . .] in the direction of."[4] Similarly, when Jason Frank tells us that "Whitman hoped to invigorate individual and political capacities, to further encourage and enhance the individual and collective self-enactments he thought exemplary of American democracy,"[5] there is a sense in which his statement is both plausible and off-kilter. To see what is at stake here, we may think back on von Halberg's point about the "unreasonableness" of praise poetry, a quality which, as I have suggested, Whitman magnifies. What is notable about the claims of Moon and Frank is their recuperation of the reasonable. Concepts of purpose, design, and desired ends restore what the idea of pure affirmation deliberately leaves out. Whitman's image of the people "shower[ing] its prolific and splendid extravagance" back on itself, in a kind of benign feedback loop, expressly brackets interest in aims and instrumentalities, while the assumption that Whitman writes in order to get us to "revise," "transform," or "enhance" something suggests that a consideration of aims and instrumentalities is crucial. In short, the impulse to view the phenomenal world as inherently praiseworthy and the imperative to reform would seem to be at odds. Praise abides in the fullness of the present; this is why it is apt to seem unreasonable. Dissatisfied with this present, reform looks to the future, which is nothing if not reasonable.

One way around this tension between praise and politics is to stress the importance of *potentiality* or possible effects. The present deserves our acclamation partly because of the future latent within it, ready to unfold. This is the logic of Frank's "encourage and enhance": by capturing in verse "the polyvocality of the vox populi" as it actually exists, *Leaves of Grass* "thereby offer[s] to the body politic an aesthetically transformed depiction of itself as sublime potentiality further enhancing its latent autopoetic power."[6] According to Frank, it is precisely because "quotidian democratic practices" are cherished in and of themselves, without apology and without recourse to abstractions such as justice or the law, that allows the people to move toward a fuller understanding of their power as "a collective reservoir of sublime potentiality."[7] This same identification of the political with the power of the poetry to unlock a hidden potential is central to George Kateb's influential understanding of Whitman as "a great philosopher of democracy." Kateb reads *Leaves of Grass* as an exercise in civic pedagogy, its most important lesson being that of "receptivity or responsiveness," which is "the most important component of democratic individuality, by far."[8] To grasp the true spirit of democratic connectedness is to perceive that "all the personalities I encounter, I already am." What this in turn implies, Kateb points out, is that "all of us are always indefinitely more than we actually are. I am potentially all personalities, and we equally are infinite potentialities."[9] The purpose of *Leaves of Grass* is to make vivid to its reader this infinite potential – to keep before him or her the fact that "one is an immense and largely untapped reservoir of potentiality."[10] Expressions such as "Whitman's teaching" or "thus the poem seeks to teach," or "Whitman wants to coax us into thinking" abound throughout Kateb's essay.[11] "Mutual recognition," "democratic acceptance," and "self-overcoming" are, for him, the keynotes of the poet's didacticism.[12]

Both Frank and Kateb write as though the effects they ascribe to the poetry are so obviously a part of the poetry itself that one follows naturally from the other. But do they? One might agree with Kateb that a work like "Song of Myself" displays "an amazing diversity of personalities" while also wondering what an ethic of "receptivity and responsiveness" can really mean when encountering "personalities" that are little more than mere notations on the page.[13] "The Wolverine [who] sets traps on the creek," "The squaw wrapt in her yellow-hemm'd cloth," or "The clean-hair'd Yankee girl [who] works with her sewing-machine": the references are so brief and fleeting that it seems unlikely that Whitman wanted us to channel our inner Wolverine, squaw, or Yankee girl (LG, 42). Even to speak of "acceptance," democratic or otherwise, seems misreading. For the notion of acceptance implies a process of deliberation and judgment, in this case set in motion by a wish to correct or overcome the limitations of one's identity. This underlying fear of the individual's proclivity toward narrowness and intolerance clearly aligns Kateb with the great philosophers of liberalism from Hobbes to Mill. Kateb simply assumes that Whitman shares this fear as an overriding concern, but in doing so he can sometimes lose track of the difference between interpreting a poem and re-writing it. Consider, for example, his commentary on the famous opening lines of "Song of Myself":

> Whitman says that "every atom belonging to me as good belongs to you." Let us emphasize the word "atom." What does it mean in this poem? An atom is a potentiality, I think. Every individual is composed of potentialities. Therefore, when I perceive or take in other human beings as they lead their lives or play their parts, I am only encountering external actualizations of some of the countless potentialities in me, in my soul. These atoms are in everyone; hence "every atom belonging to me as good belongs to you."[14]

On the face of it, the line quoted by Kateb is meant to explain why the poet confidently declares "what I assume you shall assume": his warrant for saying this is that "I" and "you" are composed of the same stuff, the same atoms (LG, 28). Materiality here licenses the claim to connectedness. Kateb, on the other hand, equates this materiality with potentiality ("An atom is a potentiality, I think"). This simple move is what enables him to extrapolate a politics for Whitman's poetry, one grounded in a reasonably clear and coherent set of principles. As sheer materiality, connectedness just is, something that can no more be accepted than rejected. As a potentiality it becomes a project, an idea whose meanings require understanding and acceptance and whose lessons it is for the poet to teach and impart. There is no denying that Kateb's extrapolation will be more attractive for many readers, not least because its commitment to diversity as a means of "self-overcoming" is so congenial to the liberal temperament. The question remains, however, whether this more attractive approach does not take up where Whitman leaves off by supplementing the poet's invocation of the basic equivalence of all things (everything

made of the same stuff) with a much more robust, principled "theory" of
political commitment.

Indeed, to press this last question a little further, it is remarkable how
discordant and starkly incompatible opinions about Whitman's politics
can be. Everyone agrees that "Whitman is a political poet, a poet who holds
that poetry has an essential role to play in the life of American
democracy,"[15] but after that the consensus quickly unravels. Wai Chee
Dimock, reading Whitman as if he were a precursor to John Rawls, claims
that he sacrifices the particular on the altar of an abstract universalism
favored by liberal ideology, while Angus Fletcher links the poet's rhetoric
to writers like John Clare who exhibit an ethics of "deep description" and
"diurnal knowledge" and whose attentiveness to lived experience sets it
against "myths of progress" and other totalizing systems of knowledge.[16]
Martha Nussbaum holds that, as "the equable man," Whitman's poet
subscribes to "a model of rational judgment that is required of
a democratic nation," one that is "flexible and context-specific" without
any "concession to the irrational," while Jane Bennett argues that
Whitman cultivates a non-judgmental mode of judging that "underplay[s]
the differences between human and nonhuman specimens [. . .] to stave off
the normal criteria of judgment" of the kind Nussbaum thinks that
Whitman follows.[17] Moon maintains that an essential feature of
Whitman's oppositional stance is its disruption of gender norms, while
Mark Maslan, pointing out that the terms of such disruption are in fact
indebted to definitions of sexual desire conventional at the time, believes
that Whitman's true radicalism consists in his understanding of homosexuality as foundational to popular authority, as distinct from being
subversive of it.[18] Finally, if, as we have seen, Kateb thinks that
Whitman's pedagogy is meant to awaken individuals to their full potentiality, Frank believes that Whitman's interest in individuals is subordinate
to his concern with activating a dormant collectivity.

Judgments so opposed, arrowing off in so many different directions,
may give rise to a feeling of being unanchored, as if each critic under
minimal guidance from the author were doing their best to fill in the
blanks. Of course, this work of creative inference is frequently held up as an
explicit goal in many of Whitman's texts, which call upon the reader to be
a collaborator or active participant in the construction of the poetry's "faint
clews and indirections." That said, something different is at stake here. It is
disarming to find a critic like Nussbaum catalog the salient features of
Whitman's democratic idealism only then to turn around and conclude
her essay by reviewing the various ways in which the poetry betrays,

disregards, or falls short of these ideals. Like Kateb, who objects to Whitman's nationalism, politicizing of comradeship, or war poetry because it unduly narrows his message of "receptivity and responsiveness," Nussbaum takes exception to the poet's coercive egotism, morbid worship of death, and mystical invocations of the fusion of body and soul because they run counter to the message of "a bold and defiant" eroticism free of shame and impatient of bourgeois hypocrisy.[19] Both Kateb and Nussbaum make clear that they consider these occasional lapses in judgment or execution which should not distract us from the core principles of his project, but one may wonder whether their essays, along with the welter of competing and often conflicting political agendas ascribed to *Leaves of Grass* by other critics, do not begin to imply, despite themselves, the *absence* of any such core principles. Nor is the situation changed when we redefine the content of these principles, as when Peter Coviello makes the case that the poet is intent upon releasing "intimacy from the constrictive teleologies of heterosexual reproduction that were increasingly taken to define the sexual as such."[20] Here again the implication is that it is only when we recognize the true significance of some regulative ideal – in this case, what Coviello calls "the world-making power of sex"[21] – that we can grasp the true import of Whitman's politics. But the question remains whether there is some such ideal or organizing principle to which Whitman's verse seeks to be true.

I realize the terms of my discussion may seem somewhat abstract, so it is worth noting that the issue I am raising can often confront us directly when negotiating Whitman's texts. Readers of "Song of Myself" who are touched by the bard's succor of the runaway slave or by his tender compassion for the twenty-ninth bather may find themselves confused by his amiable identification with "a Southerner [. . .] a planter nonchalant and hospitable" or his later mention of the "overseer" watching "from his saddle" slaves at work in the fields (LG, 37–39, 44, 42). Citing this last example in addition to others that jar us with their apparent inappropriateness, Theo Davis notes how Whitman's "disarticulation of praise from justice" can create an impression of a headlong willfulness that any thoughtful reader of *Leaves of Grass* cannot fail to miss.[22] The significance of this willfulness for Davis is that it underscores how deeply this poetry is fascinated by impositions of force and contingent arrangements of effects, as opposed to reflecting "an essential truth or underlying logic."[23] In effect, Davis takes as central what critics like Kateb or Nussbaum bracket as an indiscretion or lapse; as she notes, even when embracing equality (e.g., "I will accept nothing which all cannot have their counterpart of on the same terms" [LG, 52]), Whitman makes a point of having his affirmation come off as "a personal fiat or eccentric demand."[24] More generally, the poetry's obvious delight in the random, arbitrary, and even forced, evident in bestowing praise on objects that may strike us as disagreeable or undeserving, or in the lack of any apparent rationale for the length of his catalogs, suggests that the self-proclaimed "poet of democracy" may be better described as a poet of anarchy. Going against a long tradition in Whitman studies, Davis asserts that it is in fact "a lack of relation between the principle of equality and social being [that] animates Whitman's poetry."[25]

And yet it is possible that the "lack of relation" Davis speaks of here may also be bound up with a commitment to that mysterious and elusive concept, equality itself. After all, what makes Whitman's nod to the plantation owner or overseer troubling is not that it violates the principle of inclusiveness but that it insists on this principle. Conversely, but with a similar effect, Nussbaum lauds Whitman for "the overcoming of hatred with the attainment of inclusive and impartial love"[26] without pausing to ask whether such a thing is possible, much less desirable. What would "impartial love" look like? "The poet is no arguer, he is judgment," we are told in the 1855 Preface. "He judges not as the judge judges but as the sun falling around a helpless thing" (LG55, v). This impartial love radiates a heartless compassion: nonhuman, irresistible, and unanswerable. Recurring throughout the poetry, figures of an imperturbable, serene remoteness are the other side of the "impressed, contingent responses" entailed by "Whitman's bearing-down on the world"[27] that Davis emphasizes. They appear as the "Me Myself" that stands "Apart from the pulling and hauling" in "Song of Myself" or the woman "inviting none, denying none," who is entranced by her image in a mirror in "The Song of the Rolling Earth" or the Wound Dresser who ministers to the dead and dying with an "impassive hand," to name just a few examples (LG, 32, 222, 311). Detachment and connectedness are two sides of the same coin: to be receptive to all aspects of the given world is necessarily to be removed from them. Ultimately, this impersonality or abstraction from experience is what critics like Kateb and Nussbaum really value about reading Whitman, just as this same condition is what other critics (Dimock, for example) most distrust and fear. In contrast, I would suggest that the paradox of detachment and connectedness, like the tension between praise and politics, says more about the difficulties of conceiving equality as a truly relational value that is at home in our world. The strangely ungrounded, unanchored character of Whitman's politics – the sense in which its various and often conflicting pronouncements are pasted on and thus can just as easily be peeled off and expounded as "lessons" or "teachings" – is one indication of this difficulty. Absurd as it is to call Whitman's poetry apolitical, it is not entirely accurate, I think, to call it political either. This is not because it abjures the promise of democratic equality but, on the contrary, because it takes that promise so much to heart.

Notes

1. Robert von Halberg, *Lyric Powers* (Chicago, IL: University of Chicago Press, 2008), 44.
2. Henry D. Thoreau, *Walden, Civil Disobedience and Other Writings*, ed. William Rossi (New York, NY: Norton, [1854] 2008), 57.
3. Ibid., 65.
4. Michael Moon, *Disseminating Whitman: Revision and Corporeality in Leaves of Grass* (Cambridge, MA: Harvard University Press, 1990), 4.
5. Jason Frank, *Constituent Moments: Enacting the People in Postrevolutionary America* (Durham, NC: Duke University Press, 2010), 193.
6. Ibid., 208.
7. Ibid., 206.
8. George Kateb, "Walt Whitman and the Culture of Democracy," in *A Political Companion to Walt Whitman*, ed. John E. Seery (Lexington, KY: The University Press of Kentucky, 2011), 20.
9. Ibid., 25.
10. Ibid., 28.
11. Ibid., 25, 28, 29.
12. Ibid., 29, 32.
13. Ibid., 23.
14. Ibid.
15. Martha Nussbaum, *Upheavals of Thought: The Intelligence of Emotions* (New York, NY: Cambridge University Press, 2001), 645.
16. Wai Chee Dimock, *Residues of Justice: Literature, Law, Philosophy* (Berkeley, CA: University of California Press, 1996), 113–20; Angus Fletcher, *A New Theory for American Poetry: Democracy, the Environment, and the Future of Imagination* (Cambridge, MA: Harvard University Press, 2004), 93, 91.
17. Nussbaum, *Upheavals of Thought*, 658; Jane Bennett, "The Solar Judgment of Walt Whitman," in Seery, *A Political Companion to Walt Whitman*, 139.
18. Moon, *Disseminating Whitman*; Mark Maslan, *Whitman Possessed: Poetry, Sexuality, and Popular Authority* (Baltimore, MD: The Johns Hopkins University, 2001).
19. Nussbaum, *Upheavals of Thought*, 671–78; quotation at 646.
20. Peter Coviello, "Intimate Nationality: Anonymity and Attachment in Whitman," *American Literary History* 73.1 (2001), 100, 110.
21. Ibid., 109

22. Theo Davis, *Ornamental Aesthetics: The Poetry of Attending in Thoreau, Dickinson, and Whitman* (New York, NY: Oxford University Press, 2016), 177.
23. Ibid., 181.
24. Ibid.
25. Ibid., 179.
26. Nussbaum, *Upheavals of Thought*, 671.
27. Davis, *Ornamental Aesthetics*, 181.

CHAPTER 25

Imperialism and Globalization

Walter Grünzweig

Any discussion of Whitman in the context of imperialism, internationalism, and globalization changes with the state of international – and global – affairs, as my own decades-long inquiry on the topic reveals. Contemporary geopolitical realities have variously highlighted the dual meanings of Whitman's orientation toward the world, drawing critical attention both to his cosmopolitan, international inclusiveness and to his more troubling commitment to such ethnocentric ideologies as manifest destiny. My article with the paradoxical title "Noble Ethics and Loving Aggressiveness: The Imperialist Walt Whitman" appeared in 1990, when the bi-polar system of global dominance between the USA and the USSR was still in place, although Soviet power was eroding quickly.[1] At that time, imperialism as practiced by the two superpowers was something to be criticized – and Whitman with it. "In spite of the silence on the part of the Whitman community on the subject," I argued, "Whitman *was* an imperialist poet, as much as he was an expansionist poet."[2] By 1996, when my article on Whitman's internationalism was included in Betsy Erkkila and Jay Grossman's collection *Breaking Bounds: Whitman and American Cultural Studies*, the breakdown of the USSR had led to America becoming commonly known as the "sole remaining superpower."[3] Although this estimate always seemed a bit overrated, it was so much a part of the contemporary discourse that it prompted a second article from me only one year later, interpreting this "new empire grander than any before" as a version of "democratic imperialism."[4] This then led to my entry on imperialism in the Whitman *Encyclopedia* in 1998 and, eventually, in the post-9/11 world, to a longer article in the *Companion to Walt Whitman* in 2006.[5] For me, Whitman had remained an imperialist, but I exculpated him by noting that he "proceed[ed] from his idea of America as a 'composite' nation containing all elements of humanity."[6]

By the mid-2000s, the challenges to the United States' status as the "sole remaining superpower" had become ubiquitous, but the push for

US global leadership still remained and was characterized by both a willingness to use unilateral force on behalf of American interests and a multilateral approach to world order. Because of the latter, I came to view Whitman's imperialism in an even more positive, global light:

> Poems like "Salut au Mode!" have firmly established Whitman's status as an international poet – another iconic Whitman – and subsequently as a poet of the globalized world. From this perspective, Whitman's international iconography can be explained as a variant of the "Americanization" of world culture but also, and at the same time, of the specific, oftentimes anti-hegemonic uses of such American icons.[7]

Analyses of Whitman's notion(s) of imperialism cannot ignore the political conditions and climate of the United States. The present article, commissioned ten years after the *Companion* piece, must take into consideration a new imperial claim made at the outset of the Trump presidency, one that revives a venerable tradition in American political thinking, namely isolationism, in a modified, imperialist version. The attempt to "put America first" – vis-à-vis other nations or supra-national organizations – formulates a nationalist program in an international framework. By negative example, the ideology of "America First" provides a telling contrast, one that further highlights Whitman's own more open, cosmopolitan orientation to the world.

Years before I began to analyze Whitman in the contexts of internationalism, imperialism, and globalization, earlier critics had variously seen in Whitman an ally or foil for their own views on these topics. For example, parallel to his canonization as a major national American poet in the postwar period and especially during the Cold War, Whitman was on the internationalist agenda of the political and cultural Left. The members of the Walt Whitman Fellowship International around Horace Traubel represented anti-capitalist and "progressive" positions. Even a critic like Gay Wilson Allen, whose work stands at the beginning of mainstream Whitman scholarship, started out by calling Whitman "a link in the chain of proletarian writers – but a very important link, as it will be found when the history of the proletarian literature is finally written."[8] In both the nineteenth and twentieth centuries, Whitman's poetry inspired leftist anti-establishment forces in all camps, from the 1848ers to the anarchists, to social-democrats and the orthodox ("Stalinist") as well as anti-orthodox "New" Left.[9]

One of the key qualities, which these many different leftists admired in Whitman, was his Internationalism (with a capital I), foremost in "Salut au

Monde!," one of the most widely translated poems of Whitman's oeuvre. This benevolent internationalism was often set against an evil imperialism, which Whitman's poetry supposedly counteracted. Thus Georg Lukács considered Whitman to be part of an *anti-imperialist* canon in line with Ibsen, Shaw, Tolstoy, or Gorki.[10] When the World Peace Council, a "Communist Front Organization" by Western estimates, celebrated Whitman and *Leaves* as a major force of peace in the Cold War, an East German critic wrote that in *Democratic Vistas* (1871) Whitman had recognized that "the growing hyeana of monopolism and imperialism had almost completely destroyed democracy."[11]

However, other critics, such as Mauricio Gonzáles de la Garza in his 1971 study *Walt Whitman: Racista, Imperialista, Antimexicano*, felt that Whitman was an "hombre contradictorio" whose superficial "sentimiento del internacionalismo" in some of his poetry was invalidated by his adherence to a radical version of manifest destiny and imperial sentiments in his prose – from his journalism to *Democratic Vistas*.[12] He criticized the uncritical admiration shown by Latin American authors from José Martí to Pablo Neruda and the Russians who considered him a "Saint."[13] Gonzáles de la Garza's differentiation between an idealist-internationalist poetry and a materialist-imperialist prose, however, ignores the fact that Whitman's lyrical texts themselves display a strong imperialist tone.

For example, in "A Broadway Pageant" the speaker, reflecting the relationship between Asia and the "world on my Western Sea," ecstatically proclaims: "I chant America the mistress, I chant a greater supremacy" (LG, 244–45). While this "greater supremacy" is achieved by including Japan and other Asian countries into a more global picture, "sail-ships and steam-ships threading the archipelagoes" and the "stars and stripes fluttering in the wind" are expansionist images forcing Asia to become "renew'd as it must be" (LG, 245). The admonition to "Young Libertad" to be "considerate" with "venerable Asia" is almost more threatening than reassuring (LG, 245). The imperialist Whitman is also apparent in the "Song of the Exposition," a poem in which Whitman identifies the "great cathedral sacred industry" as foundation of America's new leadership (LG, 199). The poem, designed to "introduce the stranger, (what else indeed do I live to chant for?) to thee Columbia," places the US "cathedral" in a long line of dominant symbolic buildings from past empires (LG, 198). And this cathedral is, characteristically, "Mightier than Egypt's tombs, / Fairer than Grecia's, Roma's temples, / Prouder than Milan's statued, spired cathedral" (LG, 199). Further, in "The Return of the Heroes," a reconstruction poem that attempts to give meaning to the Civil War and ultimately rejects "the sad, unnatural shows of war" (LG, 360), "Fecund America" is placed into the center of the world: "Thou envy of the globe! thou miracle! / Thou, bathed, choked, swimming in plenty" (LG, 359). Even in the 1855 edition of *Leaves*, in the unnamed poem starting with the line "Great are the myths," the imperial discourse and tone are fully developed:

> Great is the English speech . . . . What speech is so great as the English?
> Great is the English brood . . . . What brood has so vast a destiny as the
>   English?
> It is the mother of the brood that must rule the earth with the new rule,
> The new rule shall rule as the soul rules, and as the love and justice and
>   equality that are in the soul rule.   (LG55, 94)

This is an imperial sentiment based on an uncomfortable ethnic argument highlighting Anglo-Saxon superiority. The British mother has provided a language, which will serve the American "brood" to rule the earth opening up a "vast" global destiny, possibly prefiguring the special transatlantic relationship between the United States and her former colonial owner.

In "By Blue Ontario's Shore," the voice repeating much of the Preface of 1855 in a lyrical format goes even further, connecting America "build[ing] for mankind" with a vague and highly problematic reference to a "native" national essence:

> Underneath all, Nativity,
> I swear I will stand by my own nativity, pious or impious so be it;
> I swear I am charm'd with nothing except nativity,
> Men, women, cities, nations, are only beautiful from nativity.
>   (LG, 352–53)

Is Gonzáles de la Garza then right in his criticism of Whitman's imperialist vision, and is the poet, unfortunately, only an ideological forerunner of a more fully developed political and military imperialism in the twentieth and twenty-first centuries? Or is there something that mitigates this "rule" of the earth, which is after all called a "*new* rule" characterized by "love and justice and equality"?

In 1907, Felix Schelling, professor of English at the University of Pennsylvania and Elizabethan scholar, wrote to the Whitmanites of his time:

> Of late I think we have laid especial stress on the fact that Mr. Kipling in his imperialism, his sense of expansion and his large treatment of large issues is,

when all has been said, a disciple of Walt Whitman. It was the contemporaneousness of Whitman that made him the man that he was and will long remain. It was a great truth to be told that in literature we must not dwell wholly in the past.[14]

The frank and unashamed celebration of Whitman's imperialism is surprising but makes sense in light of the exceptionalist language that frames it. The idea that America dispenses with the past and that the historian must learn to "project the history of the future," as Whitman says in "To a Historian," has been a standard part of the discourse of "manifest destiny" since the 1840s, if not earlier (LG, 4). Whitman, however, seems particularly interested in the past as he attempts to incorporate it into his American present and into the future of humankind. In "On the Beach at Night Alone," the speaker has a vision of "All nations, colors, barbarisms, civilizations, languages, / All identities that have existed or may exist on this globe, or any globe" and his understanding of the "similitude" of everybody and everything "shall forever span them and compactly hold and enclose them" (LG, 261). In "With Antecedents," the speaker assumes a dominant but also prophetic posture: "In the name of these States and in your name and my name, the Past, / And in the name of these States and in your name and my name, the Present time," he includes "Assyria, China, Teutonia, and the Hebrews" by bringing them into "this present day," obviously an American day which is the "centre of all days, all races" (LG, 241).

The argument made here, then, is at heart exceptionalist, meaning that America, in the history of the world, is a unique project. America's "greatness" is built on the idea that it is inclusive, both geographically and historically. In the 1855 poem that came to be known as "Great are the Myths" Whitman writes, "Great is the greatest nation ... the nation of clusters of equal nations" (LG55, 94), and therefore the United States has a mission that other nations cannot fulfill, namely, to speak for humanity at large and to spread the values of democratic America globally. In every period there is "one nation [that] must lead, / One land [that] must be the promise and reliance of the future" (LG, 343). He continues,

Others take finish, but the Republic is ever constructive and ever keeps vista,
Others adorn the past, but you O days of the present, I adorn you,
O days of the future I believe in you – I isolate myself for your sake,
O America because you build for mankind I build for you.   (LG, 346)

One may of course argue that the humanist argument is invalid because it is formulated in the interest of imperialism. But imperialism is a curious phenomenon that, while it is highly exploitative economically, also brings widespread social and political change (for better or for worse). None other than the author of the most influential analysis of imperialism, Vladimir Ilyich Lenin, saw not only the exploitative side of imperialism but also recognized it as an indicator of the bankruptcy of capitalism.[15] At the beginning of the twenty-first century, Michael Hardt and Antonio Negri proclaimed, "Imperialism actually creates a straitjacket for capital – or, more precisely, at a certain point the boundaries created by imperialist practices obstruct capitalist development and the full realization of its world market."[16]

"Empire," as defined by Hardt and Negri, represents a step beyond imperialism; it is "characterized fundamentally by a lack of boundaries: Empire's rule has no limits."[17] In this limitlessness, it has a "potential for liberation."[18] The differentiation between bordered "imperialism" and the borderless "empire" speaks to the difference between the propagators of free trade, who call for comprehensive international agreements such as NAFTA, TTIP, and TPP, and those who seek to renationalize the American (and world) economy. This renationalization often translates, on the ideological level, into a comprehensive xenophobic and racist orientation, which may destroy progress made in international integration the world over. In contrast to the new nationalist tendencies emerging in the United States and many other parts of the world, Whitman's poetry – and prose – (in spite of all the imperialist indicators mentioned above) actually reflects a globalist worldview. There is indeed a genuine global vision, which manifests itself in poems such as "Salut au Monde!" or "Song of the Exposition."

Of course, globalization comes at a price and has positive and negative implications. With surprising lack of passion, the speaker of "Salut au Monde!" looks at the world as a technological system:

> I see the tracks of the railroads of the earth,
> I see them in Great Britain, I see them in Europe,
> I see them in Asia and in Africa.
>
> I see the electric telegraphs of the earth,
> I see the filaments of the news of the wars,
>   deaths, losses, gains, passions, of my race.   (LG, 141)

There is a strange disconnect between the empathetic reference to "my race" and the casual reporting of human tragedies through electric telegraphs. There is no differentiation between the railroad tracks in Europe and in the colonial world, the "unexplored countries" as he says in rather blind colonialist language and certainly no reference to the human trage-dies connected with railroad construction (LG, 144).

Further, in "Song of Exposition," the global vision of the world is essentially technological and one-sidedly Western:

> With latest connections, works, the inter-transportation of the world,
> Steam-power, the great express lines, gas, petroleum,
> These triumphs of our time, the Atlantic's delicate cable,
> The Pacific railroad, the Suez canal, the Mont Cenis and Gothard and
>   Hoosac tunnels, the Brooklyn bridge,
> This earth all spann'd with iron rails, with lines of steamships thread-
>   ing every sea. (LG, 203)

This passage seems to confirm the negative judgments of the poem, namely that it is overly functional and thus fundamentally lacking in vision. The many deaths that occurred in the construction of the monumental tunnels are completely ignored, as is the colonial-imperialist venture of the Suez Canal. They are the "triumphs" of our time, which leave the victims of such triumphs unmentioned. The economic basis of these "latest con-nections" that manifest themselves in energy transportation at first do not leave much space for an interpretation beyond exploitative materialism.

In "Passage to India," the speaker's vision is again colonialist. The aggressive travels of explorations are downplayed ("Ah Genoese thy dream! thy dream!"), although the language of absence ("Doubts to be solv'd, the map incognita, blanks to be fill'd") is revealing enough (LG, 414, 417). The idea that "the poet worthy that name, / The true son of God shall come singing his songs" will arrive *after* "the seas are all cross'd," *after* "the great captains and engineers have accomplish'd their work," *after* "the noble inventors, after the scientists, the chemist, the geologist, ethnologist" indeed makes it appear as though the creative voice merely embellishes a reality dominated by profited-oriented technology (LG, 415).

Yet, there are two features of these poems that transcend this limited functional and reified perspective, and that lift Whitman beyond the imperial framework to that of a positive global vision. On the one hand, there is a strong *teleological* dimension, which amounts to a vision of a unified humanity living on a shared globe:

> Passage to India!
> Lo, soul, seest though not God's purpose from the first?
> The earth to be spann'd, connected by network,
> The races, neighbors, to marry and be given in marriage,

> The oceans to be cross'd, the distant brought near,
> The lands to be welded together.   (LG, 412)

The reference to "God's purpose" is not a naïve return to a theist world but signals a "purpose" which avoids a profit-driven motivation. This principle of human development is reminiscent of Emerson in its turn to a One and All, but Whitman imagines it unfolding through material changes, specifically through migration and technology. Welding, causing fusion between materials, is an adequate metaphor for an indissoluble connection of countries and continents. In the palaces devoted to industry in "Song of the Exposition," the final objective is not the commodity but the producer:

> Somewhere within their walls shall all that forwards perfect
>   human life be started,
> Tried, taught advanced, visibly exhibited.
>
> Not only all the world of works, trade, products,
> But all the workmen of the world here to be represented.   (LG, 200)

This vision of a community of workers as part of a utopian life also goes beyond the imperialist framework based on relentless competition.

Three lines at the beginning of "Song of the Exposition" connect this teleological moment to a second feature of Whitman's global poetry: the *ecocritical* image of the round earth itself: "Long and long has the grass been growing, / Long and long has the rain been falling, / Long has the globe been rolling round" (LG, 196). The long development of the planet is here connected to the image of the rotating globe, which appears strikingly on three other occasions, always evoked by the word "rondure." The aforementioned section that lists triumphs in engineering from the Pacific Railroad to the Hoosac Tunnel in Vermont ends with a very contrapuntal line: "This earth all spann'd with iron rails, with lines of steamships threading every sea, / Our own rondure, the current globe I bring" (LG, 203). The "networks" covering and structuring the earth are not alien to its original shape but actually emphasize it. The speaker brings – to the muse – the technical achievements confirming the roundness of the "current" globe.

In the 1844 Webster, the entry for the word "rondure" is as follows: "RON'DURE, n. [Fr. *rondeur*.] A round a circle. [Not in use.] – Shak."[19] It is identified as French in origin, brought into English by Shakespeare but no longer "in use." Whitman, however, does use it on two more occasions in "Passage to India":

Again Vasco de Gama sails forth,
Again the knowledge gain'd, the mariner's compass,
Lands found and nations born, thou born America,
For purpose vast, man's long probation fill'd,
Thou rondure of the world at last accomplish'd. (LG, 414)

Although placed in Christopher Columbus's colonialist, explorative context, America in "Passage" was born for "purpose vast," not for mere national(ist) reasons or material gain. Rather, humankind, before America, had been on "probation" (the metaphor here is not primarily legal), the completion of which has finally given the world its full "rondure." Finally, so the striking metaphor in the next line suggests, the globe has achieved its perfection not only morally but also aesthetically: "O vast Rondure, swimming in space, / Cover'd all over with visible power and beauty" (LG, 414). This image has a redeeming ecocritical quality that helps to transform exploitative imperialism into a global vision. In Christine Gerhardt's words, Whitman, by "creating a new global reality [. . .] gives space to the globe as a natural entity and cosmic body."[20] Whitman is "moving toward a nature-centered global vision."[21] Earth, swimming (not floating) in space, has become an autonomous agent. The image of a "Rondure," now capitalized, which is "cover'd all over" with the ultimate human qualities is fairly the opposite of the neo-imperialist vision of "America first." Rather, "America" has become the fulfillment of an age-old global idea. In spite of all the dystopian qualities of a digitalized, economically globalized, "networked," world, it is far more attractive than an existence where new walls, fences, and other boundaries keep "clusters" of population in and out.

Notes

1. Walter Grünzweig, "Noble Ethics and Loving Aggressiveness: The Imperialist Walt Whitman," in *An American Empire: Expansionist Cultures and Policies, 1881–1917*, ed. Serge Ricard (Aix-en-Provence: Université de Provence, 1990), 151–65.
2. Ibid., 163.
3. Walter Grünzweig, "'For America – For all the Earth': Walt Whitman as an International(ist) Poet," in *Breaking Bounds: Whitman and American Cultural Studies*, eds. Betsy Erkkila and Jay Grossman (New York, NY: Oxford University Press, 1996), 238–50.
4. Walter Grünzweig, "The New Empire Grander than Any Before: Nineteenth-Century American Versions of a Democratic Imperialism," in *Empire: American Studies*, eds. John G. Blair and Reinhold Wagnleitner (Tübingen: Narr, 1997), 243–50.

5. Walter Grünzweig, "Imperialism," in *A Companion to Walt Whitman*, ed. Donald D. Kummings (Malden, MA: Blackwell, 2006), 151–63; and Walter Grünzweig, "Imperialism," in *Walt Whitman: An Encyclopedia*, eds. J. R. LeMaster and Donald D. Kummings (New York, NY, and London: Garland, 1998), 304–05.

6. Ibid., 305.

7. Walter Grünzweig, "The Iconic Whitman: Americanness and the Global Culture," in *American Cultural Icons: The Production of Representative Lives*, eds. Günter Leypoldt and Bernd Engler (Würzburg: Könighausen & Neumann, 2010), 152f.

8. Gay Wilson Allen, "Walt Whitman – Nationalist or Proletarian?" *English Journal* 26 (1937), 52.

9. Cf. Walter Grünzweig, *Constructing the German Walt Whitman* (Iowa City, IA: University of Iowa Press, 1995), 151–60.

10. Georg Lukács, *Kurze Skizze einer Geschichte der neueren deutschen Literatur* (Darmstadt and Neuwied: Luchterhand, 1975), 140.

11. Helmut Findeisen, "Gedenktag der Weltfriedensbewegung: 'Grashalme' – der weltweite Siegeszug einer Dichtung. Zum 100. Jahrestag der Erstveröffentlichung von Walt Whitmans berühmten Gedichten," *Börsenblatt für den deutschen Buchhandel*, July 9, 1955, 504–05.

12. Mauricio González de la Garza, *Walt Whitman: Racista, Imperialista, Antimexicano* (Mexico: Colección Málaga, 1971), 9.

13. Ibid., 11.

14. Quoted in Grünzweig, "Noble Ethics," 155.

15. Vladimir I. Lenin, *Imperialism: The Highest Stage of Capitalism. A Popular Outline*, rev. trans. (New York, NY: International Publishers, 1939).

16. Michael Hardt and Antonio Negri, *Empire* (Cambridge, MA, and London: Harvard University Press, 2000), 234.

17. Ibid., xiv.

18. Ibid., 43.

19. Noah Webster, *American Dictionary of the English Language, 1844*, "RON'DURE," Cynthia L. Hallen, ed. Renovated Online Edition of Noah Webster's 1844 American Dictionary of the English Language, 2009, http://edl.byu.edu.

20. Christine Gerhardt, *A Place for Humility: Whitman, Dickinson, and the Natural World.* (Iowa City, IA: University of Iowa Press, 2014), 218.

21. Ibid., 220.

CHAPTER 26

Nineteenth-Century Religion

Brian Yothers

If Walt Whitman could "contain multitudes," as he wrote in a frequently quoted passage from the poem "Song of Myself," he resembled nineteenth-century American religious culture in this regard (LG, 88). The United States during Whitman's lifetime was at once heavily Protestant and stunningly diverse, both in the alternatives to Protestant religious belief ranging from religious alternatives like Catholicism and Mormonism to secular alternatives like deism and transcendentalism, and the many alternative forms of religious belief within the mainstream Protestant consensus. Beyond the variations on Christianity that were available to nineteenth-century Americans, Whitman's contemporaries in the United States were also increasingly engaged by religions closely linked to Christianity like Judaism and Islam and by more distant alternatives like Hinduism, Buddhism, Zoroastrianism, and the various indigenous faiths of the Americas, Africa, and the Pacific Islands.

Nineteenth-century American religious culture inherited considerable diversity from the colonial and early national periods in American history, as both Whitman's work and his life attest. New England, of course, had a longstanding association with religious modes that were Calvinist in theology and Congregationalist or Presbyterian in church government, going back to the Puritan seventeenth century. Within New England, Calvinism coexisted uncomfortably with Unitarianism, which shared Calvinism's devotion to logic and its distrust for ecclesiastical authority but had abandoned orthodox belief in such major doctrines as the Trinity and the fallen-ness of humanity. If we associate Calvinism most immediately with New England, the theological system reached well beyond areas settled by the English Puritans, as Scots-Irish Presbyterians on the frontier and Dutch Reformed burghers in New York State also fell within the Calvinist tradition. Quakers had been distinguished by religious enthusiasm and radical egalitarianism (which did not necessarily rule out slaveholding) in their earlier years, but had since become a sect renowned for sobriety, pacifism, and, almost uniquely among American religious groups, a steadfast opposition to slavery. Episcopalianism served as the faith of the elite in American society, particularly among the Virginia planters who formed the nation's first dominant political class, but in part as a result of its elite status, in part because of its association with the former British rulers in the colonial period, it struggled to find adherents among the masses. Catholics and Jews constituted modest minorities that were participants in the nation's life from the start but did not have the numbers to challenge Protestant cultural dominance in the early years of the nineteenth century, although by mid-century Catholics represented a substantial religious minority, and in the later years of Whitman's life Jewish immigration meant that New York also had a substantial Jewish minority.

Nor were Americans limited to branches of Christianity and Judaism: Islam has often been treated as nonexistent in the early years of the republic, but recent scholarship has made it increasingly clear that there were a number of Muslims among those enslaved in antebellum America. Religious orthodoxy of whatever kind, meanwhile, was far from the only game in town, and Whitman's own father seems to have fit in with the rising secularism in the United States as an admirer of the deist Thomas Paine (Loving, 31).[1] Increasingly, as a result of trade, of translations coming out of the British imperial confrontation with Indian cultures and religions, and of American missionary work in Asia, Americans were also becoming aware of Hinduism, Buddhism, and Sufi Islam, and thus were becoming engaged with questions that would resolve themselves into the field of comparative religion. This awareness of religious diversity extended to representations of indigenous faiths in the Americas, Africa, and the South Pacific, as both missionary writers and their ambivalent admirers and critics provided a sense of where faiths from the western frontier to Tahiti and the Marquesas might stand in relation to Christianity. We see Whitman's encounter with layers of religious diversity in such lines as

I do not despise you, priests;
My faith is the greatest of faiths and the least of faiths,
Enclosing all worship ancient and modern, and all between ancient and
    modern,
Believing I shall come again upon the earth after five thousand years,
Waiting responses from oracles . . . honoring the gods . . . saluting the sun,
Making a fetish of the first rock or stump . . . powwowing with sticks in the
    circle of obis,
Helping the lama or brahmin as he trims the lamps of the idols,

Dancing through the streets in a phallic procession . . . . rapt and austere in the
  woods, a gymnosophist,
Drinking mead from the skullcup . . . to shasta and vedas admirant . . . minding
  the koran,
Walking the teokallis, spotted with gore from the stone and knife – beating the
  serpent-skin drum;
Accepting the gospels, accepting him that was crucified, knowing assuredly that
  he is divine,
To the mass kneeling – to the puritan's prayer rising – sitting patiently in a pew.

(LG55, 48)

Whitman's catalog is stunning in its range, and it reflects the array of
religious possibilities that nineteenth-century Americans had available to
them as a result of the combination of missionary work, trade, and
Orientalist scholarship that had emerged in the past century.
Significantly, it also reflects one dimension of the Second Great
Awakening and popular Protestant religious culture, the importance of
a personal relationship to the divine, while rejecting the idea that the divine
could only be accessed through the Hebrew and Christian scriptures, and
indeed raising the possibility, which Whitman entertained in common
with various nineteenth-century authors, that new scriptures could be
written.[2] Whitman moves through a range of religious experiences, from
those that many nineteenth-century American Protestants would identify
as "heathen," including indigenous practices in North America, Mexico,
and Northern Europe and the religious practices of ancient Greece, along
with elements of contemporary world religions like Islam, Hinduism, and
Buddhism. When he reaches the end of the catalog, he is on more familiar
territory – the reference to the Crucifixion brings Christianity into the mix,
and Whitman incorporates three varieties of Christianity, defined by their
most characteristic bodily poses. He describes himself as kneeling to the
mass, and thus participating in the Catholic faith, which constituted both
America's largest (and for many Protestants, most feared) religious minority and its largest single denomination. Whitman's opening to the
extended catalog also indicates that he empathizes with those who have
no particular religious faith, and he consistently expresses the idea in early
editions of *Leaves of Grass* that he is at home with any variety of belief or
unbelief.

Of particular note in the passage quoted above is the relationship that it
bears to the Second Great Awakening, which constituted the central
religious event in America during Whitman's lifetime prior to the Civil
War. Whitman's speaker in 1855 was declaring a direct relation to the

divine that echoed not only Emerson's transcendental "original relation to the universe" but also Charles Grandison Finney's evangelical appeal for direct, felt experience of the divine, expressed in his *Memoirs* as "an impression, like a wave of electricity, going through and through me [. . .] in waves and waves of liquid love."[3] Like Emerson and Finney, Whitman embraces a faith that he can call his own, and he frequently calls upon the metaphor of electricity, as Finney does, as a means of defining it. This claiming of "my faith" had implications for institutional structures in the United States: as Nathan O. Hatch has pointed out, the denominations that were dominant in the decades leading up to Whitman's birth, from Presbyterianism to Episcopalianism, lost a great deal of their power as arbiters of American religious authority during the Second Great Awakening, and the Methodists and Baptists led a variety of religious upstarts that became the characteristic American Protestant faiths of much of the nineteenth century. At the same time, as Rodney Stark and Roger Finke have demonstrated, church attendance was up considerably during the first half of the nineteenth century, meaning that Whitman lived in a time that was both characterized by increasing religiosity and considerable religious turbulence.[4] Whitman's own tendency toward religious statements that were at once fervent and heterodox fit well with the times: one of the appeals of the Awakening, as Hatch has observed, was its empowerment of the individual religious seeker and its tweaking of received orthodoxies, notably Calvinism. That many of Whitman's contemporaries were devout did not mean they could not be ferociously skeptical of the certainties of other Protestants. Even as American Protestantism was experiencing its period of greatest vitality and expanding into the wider world, Protestantism was ceasing to be the default identity for Americans as a result of Catholic and Jewish immigration and of the rise of secular movements like deism and transcendentalism.

The religious impulses that fired the Second Great Awakening could also help to undermine as well as reinforce the Protestant consensus in the United States. Most notably, Joseph Smith followed what might initially seem to be a fairly standard trajectory from youthful confusion and doubt to certainty through a dramatic and intensely personal conversion, but he then moved on to proclaiming the rediscovery of lost scriptures under divine guidance and founding a faith distinct from any of the Protestant denominations associated with the Awakening. Several scholars have seen parallels between Whitman and the Mormon prophet; most recently, Michael Robertson has suggested that Whitman and Smith both function as disseminators of previously unknown scriptures in the middle of the nineteenth century, and that together they constitute models for broader cultural trends toward new religious visions.[5] Although Smith might be the most spectacular example of Protestant principles being employed in the service of a faith that renounced significant aspects of Protestantism itself, the substantial doctrinal divisions between earlier Calvinist orthodoxies and the religious instinct for a return to an earlier, simpler version of the faith that appeared in the various Baptist denominations and the Campbellite and Methodist movements suggested that the nature of Protestantism itself was changing. In relation to Protestant enthusiasm, Whitman can be read as an outsider despite his affinities: he does not record a dramatic conversion experience, he enunciates doctrines in "Song of Myself" and other poems that are wildly heterodox by the standards of American Protestantism, and he equates non-Christian scriptures with Christian ones and natural science with divine revelation.

When we turn from religion in practice to matters of theology, we see that the nineteenth century was characterized, as E. Brooks Holifield has argued, by both a continuation of the eighteenth-century quest for "evidences" of the truth of Christianity in the natural world and by a revolt against eighteenth-century rationalism in favor of intuition.[6] The Whitman who writes "a mouse is miracle enough to stagger sextillions of infidels" in "Song of Myself" bears the impress of both sides of this debate: Whitman presents the biology of the mouse as an evidence for meaning in the universe, but the faith suggested is indistinct, and the hyperbole, even humor, in the statement suggests that Whitman is not advocating the careful sifting of evidence so much as the intuitive leap to belief that comes from truly seeing the natural world (LG55, 34). Whitman finds his closest analogues on the American religious scene in the liberal theology of Horace Bushnell and the secularized religion of the New England transcendentalists.

The liberal theology that served as Whitman's most direct counterpart in mainstream religious culture wrestled with developments in the natural sciences that seemed to threaten the very foundations of Christian doctrine. Charles Darwin's *On the Origin of Species* (1859) offered the prospect of a world in which theological explanations no longer needed to undergird attempts to understand natural phenomena. For Whitman, Darwin's naturalistic explanations of human existence and development could complement Emerson's influence on his poetry and thought: Darwin, through his explanation of the role of natural processes in human development could offer, for Whitman as for other religious liberals, the prospect of an understanding of human nature and destiny "at one with the blowing clover and the falling rain."[7] Whitman could thus find that the emerging scientific consensus that would so trouble nineteenth-century evangelicals and twentieth-century fundamentalists and could work to reinforce a poetic religious voice that could find evidence of divinity in the humble mouse.

The ways in which transcendentalists, liberal religion and skepticism, and scientific developments contributed to Whitman's vision find parallels in much more orthodox Protestant venues. Americans were not only encountering world religions through the texts that transcendentalist intellectuals were reading in translation, however. A vigorous missionary movement in the nineteenth century meant that devout Christians in the United States could read about Islam, Hinduism, Buddhism, and the indigenous faiths of North America and the South Pacific without venturing beyond the productions of their own churches' presses. The American Board of Commissioners for Foreign Missions had missionaries in the Near East, West Africa, South Asia, and East Asia as well as the South Pacific by the time that Whitman was writing his major verse, and these missions were pumping out a vast amount of printed matter.[8] Even as Whitman was imagining the writing of a world-spanning poetry as the most heroic of enterprises, his contemporary Rufus Wilmot Griswold could describe American missionary women as the figures in nineteenth-century America who best captured the character of epic heroes; arguing that in missionary women, "the highest type of chivalric character has been abundantly illustrated in every year since the foundation of the Board, by deeds of daring and endurance for the love of God, from which the heroes of the Nibelungenlied, would have shrunk back appalled in their bravery for self."[9]

Griswold argued that female missionaries represented a continuation of a heroic ethos that his contemporaries might believe had vanished, and he saw the nineteenth century as a time of heroic Christian exertion, rather than as a time of declension. The efforts of the missionaries extended and intensified the individualistic religious energies of the Second Great Awakening and, indeed, they blended, in many cases, the fervor of the antebellum Awakeners with that of abolitionists and postbellum New England schoolmistresses who sought to spread both literacy and gospel knowledge among the African American population of the South, as illustrated in particular by the efforts of the Misses Leitch in Ceylon who seamlessly drew together their missionary work in the postbellum South, their temperance activism, and the overseas work in the north of Ceylon (present-day Sri Lanka).[10] The missionaries occupied a curious place in nineteenth-century American religious consciousness: revered as bringers of the light of the gospel to those in darkness and often enough as martyrs for their faith, they also could be seen as exploiters of indigenous people who mainly needed to be saved from the rapacity of Christian Europeans and North Americans. Herman Melville writing in *Typee* in the 1840s and Mark Twain writing in "To the Person Sitting in Darkness" in the 1890s could be equally scathing on the subject of Christian missions.

Whitman's understanding of the relationships among cultures provides signs of both analogies and resistances to the expansive missionary religious culture of his time. When, later in his career, Whitman described technology as the source of spiritual union in "Passage to India," he was expressing something quite similar to the evangelical belief that missionaries were moving the world toward a millennial era of peace and amity through their labors in increasingly remote "fields" around the world. At his most ebulliently millennial, Whitman writes:

> Passage to India!
> Lo, soul, seest thou not God's purpose from the first?
> The earth to be spann'd, connected by network,
> The races, neighbors, to marry and be given in marriage,
> The oceans to be cross'd, the distant brought near,
> The lands to be welded together.
>
> A worship new I sing,
> You captains, voyagers, explorers, yours,
> You engineers, you architects, machinists, yours,
> You, not for trade or transportation only,
> But in God's name, and for thy sake O soul.   (LG, 412)

We see in Whitman's vision of a world spiritually unified a secularized version of what his missionary contemporaries would have called the Great Commission that Jesus enunciated for his disciples in Matthew 28:16–20: Christian missionaries go into the world to preach the gospel, thus uniting disparate peoples in the bonds of a common faith; the technological civilization Whitman describes in "Passage to India" binds people together without the need for conversion from one religious tradition to another, as Whitman makes clear when he praises the "myths and fables of eld, Asia's, Africa's fables" (LG, 412).

As "Passage to India" shows, Whitman tapped into an increasing religious cosmopolitanism in the nineteenth-century United States. Especially within Unitarian and transcendentalist circles, Americans were becoming engaged with world religions that previous generations might

have grouped together loosely under a rubric like "paganism" or "idolatry."
Ralph Waldo Emerson, one of Whitman's central inspirations as he
reenvisioned what poetry might look like in the United States, was deeply
engaged by both Hinduism and Sufi Islam, and Henry David Thoreau
deepened and extended this interest. Whitman is not often read as a male
version of Lydia Maria Child, but in some ways his status as a religious
thinker would become clearer if he was. The same year Whitman published
the 1855 first edition of *Leaves of Grass*, Child published her monumental
work *The Progress of Religious Ideas*, which took in not only Judaism and
Christianity but also Islam, Hinduism, Buddhism, and Zoroastrianism.[11]
Although she certainly maintained the preeminence of a liberal variety of
Protestantism, Child sought to show the interrelationships among religious traditions from every part of the world. Whitman was not
a systematic thinker, and it is difficult to imagine his constructing the
sort of compendium that Child did, but the impulse to draw upon
religious traditions from around the world in a free spirit of inquiry is
common to both Whitman and Child. A similar impulse appears in the
work of another of Whitman's literary contemporaries, Herman Melville,
whose *Clarel, A Poem and Pilgrimage in the Holy Land* (1876) brings
together a stunning array of religious stances against the backdrop of
Ottoman Palestine.[12] By the last days of Whitman's life, Americans
could go so far as to convert to faiths outside of the monotheistic tradition.
In the 1880s, Henry Steel Olcott, an American who had been brought up as
a Presbyterian, declared his conversion to Buddhism and, like a proper
Presbyterian Buddhist, published *A Buddhist Catechism* in British-ruled
Ceylon.[13]

Charles Taylor's *A Secular Age* has mapped the ways in which
religious belief and doubt can be seen as feeding each other in the
nineteenth century: describing the "nova effect" ("a kind of galloping
pluralism on the spiritual plane"), he argues that secularism helped to
enable the explosion of religious options in the nineteenth century.[14]
Whitman can serve as perhaps the nova effect's most characteristic poet,
responding in his writing to the proliferation of religious possibility in
the nineteenth century even as he maintained his own independence
from a single religious tradition. Whitman responds to precisely those
features of secularization that are most amenable to the re-enchantment,
as well as the disenchantment, of the material world. For Whitman, the
accelerating diversity and complexity of religious impulses in the nineteenth century fed the internal diversity of his poetry and indeed of the

poetic self that gave form to his entire career, from 1855 to his death. In the Preface to the 1855 *Leaves of Grass*, Whitman wrote:

> There will soon be no more priests. Their work is done. They may wait a while … perhaps a generation or two … dropping off by degrees. A superior breed shall take their place … the gangs of kosmos and prophets en masse shall take their place. A new order shall arise and they shall be the priests of man, and every man shall be his own priest. The churches built under their umbrage shall be the churches of men and women. Through the divinity of themselves shall the kosmos and the new breed of poets be interpreters of men and women and of all events and things. (LG55, xi)

The religiously complex poetic persona that voices these words would not be possible were it not formed by a religious context in which American Protestant religious diversity, immigrant faiths, and world religions were in contact and dialogue. The rejection of priestcraft reflects a Protestant religious sensibility that defines its doctrinal diversity against Catholicism, while the embrace of a "new breed of poets" as the prophetic voice of a new faith is suggestive of how little control various Protestant orthodoxies were able to maintain during Whitman's life. That a prophet could be a "kosmos" indicated that Whitman had truly absorbed his country's growing fascination with world religions and with global currents of cultural exchange. Whitman's "multitudes" may be in part elements in the individual voice of an idiosyncratic prophet, but they also comprise the multitudinous voice of a religiously diverse, even dissonant, nation that saw itself as opening up into a new religious world.

Notes

1. On secularism and Protestantism as complementary and conflicting, see Tracy Fessenden, *Culture and Redemption: Religion, the Secular, and American Literature* (Princeton, NJ: Princeton University Press, 2007).
2. On "literary scripturism," see Lawrence Buell, *New England Literary Culture from Revolution to Renaissance* (New York, NY: Cambridge University Press, 1986). On the Second Great Awakening, perhaps the largest religious revival in American history, see Nathan O. Hatch, *The Democratization of American Christianity* (New Haven, CT: Yale University Press, 1989).
3. Charles Grandison Finney, *Memoirs of Rev. Charles G. Finney* (New York, NY: A. S. Barnes, 1876), 20.
4. See Hatch, *Democratization*; Roger Finke and Rodney Stark, *The Churching of America, 1776–2005*, rev. edn. (New Brunswick, NJ: Rutgers University Press, 2005).

5. See Michael Robertson, "The New American Bibles of Walt Whitman and Joseph Smith," in *Above the American Renaissance*, eds. Harold K. Bush and Brian Yothers (Amherst, MA: University of Massachusetts Press, 2018).

6. E. Brooks Holifield, *Theology in America: Christian Thought from the Age of the Puritans to the Civil War* (New Haven, CT: Yale University Press, 2003), 5–8.

7. Ralph Waldo Emerson, "The Divinity School Address," in *Essential Writings of Ralph Waldo Emerson*, ed. Brooks Atkinson (New York, NY: Random House, 2009), 68.

8. Michael Winship, "The Printing Press as an Agent of Change?" *Common-Place: The Journal of Early American Life* 8.2 (2008), http://commonplace.org.

9. Rufus Wilmot Griswold, "The Heroism of the Knights Errant and of the Female Missionaries of North America," *Godey's Magazine and Lady's Book*, August 1848, 61.

10. Mary Leitch and Margaret W. Leitch, *Seven Years in Ceylon: Stories of Mission Life* (New York, NY: American Tract Society, 1890).

11. Lydia Maria Child, *The Progress of Religious Ideas Through Successive Ages* (New York, NY: C. S. Francis, 1855).

12. Herman Melville, *Clarel, A Poem and Pilgrimage in the Holy Land* (Evanston and Chicago, IL: Northwestern University Press and The Newberry Library, [1876] 1993).

13. Henry Steel Olcott, *A Buddhist Catechism* (Boston, MA: Estes and Lariat, 1885).

14. Charles Taylor, *A Secular Age* (Cambridge, MA: Harvard University Press, 2007), 300.

CHAPTER 27

Civil War

Peter Coviello

"The war of attempted secession," Whitman would write, some years after its conclusion, "has, of course, been the distinguishing event of my time" (PW, 1:2). In this – as his *of course* seems to signal – the poet was hardly alone. The war itself was all unpredicted and, in many respects, unprecedented in its scale: a huge mobilization of bodies and materials; a tremendous displacement of persons across an immensity of territory; and, with it all, a catastrophic loss of life. "Never one more desperate in any age or land," the poet would write, and whatever Whitman's nationalist hyperbole it is the case that much of the staggering carnage of the war was a matter of cruel historical timing (PW, 1:47). As many historians have noted, the American Civil War transpired within an especially terrible in-between moment, both *after* the industrialization of technologies of harm (artillery, bullets) and slightly *before* the discoveries in medicine (antiseptics and antibiotics, say) that would do so much to revolutionize care. In the space of this hiccup in historical time, the bodily wreckage of the Civil War unfolded, where, gruesomely, the loss of life to infection and disease greatly exceeded battlefield deaths. Whitman, who famously spent several years of the war in and around the military hospitals of Washington, DC, knew of this first-hand.

But the war was momentous for reasons beyond its massiveness of scale and human carnage. Here again, Whitman offers us a singular angle of perception. We know, of course, that the war between the states rewrote, at least in the idioms of law and statecraft, the very definitions of freedom, of enslavement, and of state sovereignty, as they would come into force in the United States. Perhaps less famously, it rewrote as well the codes according to which the national public was to encounter scenes of de-individuated mass death. (As Max Cavitch notes, the war produced a crisis of *representation* in which statistics provided a new manner of massified accounting for death.[1]) But alongside these crises and transformations, and alongside so immense a mobilization – recall that very few of the participants in the war would have had reason or occasion to travel much beyond their hometowns – the war made for enormous alterations, too, in what we might think of as the intimate terrain of national life: in relations, that is, not merely between North and South, or between slave and freedman, but between women and women, and men and men, and women and men. Given the vast rescripting of all these possibilities for relations we might say that the war marked a kind of watershed moment in *another* strand of history, one in which Whitman's work and life have always been central: the history of sexuality.

In what follows I want to suggest that Whitman's writing in the Civil War shuttles between these two great crises: crises in how the nation came to represent itself, to itself, and crises in the meaning and parameters of gender and of sex. As we shall see, the war effectively destroys Whitman's early-career expressivist utopianism – his belief, that is, that it was the role of writing, indeed of *his* poetry, not merely to represent the nation but to *induce* nationness, to forge the very bonds of national attachment as it circulates reader-to-reader. The sectarian violence of the war and the uncountable number of dead bring this project to a crisis for Whitman. Over the course of his long postbellum career, it does not recover. And yet Whitman finds, too, in the teeth of all this wreckage and collapse a strange kind of replenishment along the way, a redoubling of certain of his initial commitments. These have to do with unexpended possibilities of sex. And it is the war – of all catastrophic and unlikely things – that brings them into focus for Whitman.

***

In the popular imagination Whitman appears as a nurse in the Civil War, tending to the wounded and infirm. This is not exactly right. But for a short-lived association with the Christian Commission, shortly after his arrival in Washington, DC, he was an unaffiliated visitor in the city's many hospitals, making tours on his own time and in his own order, speaking with the soldiers there, bringing them candy and drinks, writing on their behalf, and above all providing affectionate companionship for young men stranded desperately far from family and familiars. His was a role less medical or official than, fittingly, self-fashioned.[2]

Whitman had in fact come to the war somewhat late, departing to Washington after seeing his brother George's name in a casualty list in December of 1862. The years before he had spent in New York, and it was there that he had brought into its first and most vivid realization his career-defining expressivist project, what we might call his poetics of erotic nationalism. In later years, after the cataclysm of the war, he would in fact insist that it was in no one text so much as his "Calamus" cluster, those 1860 poems of "manly affection" and scenes of cruisy anonymous erotic solicitation, that his vision of national belonging had reached its "clearest expression." Looking back on the "Calamus" cluster in his Preface to the 1876 edition of *Leaves of Grass*, he would write,

> To this terrible, irrepressible yearning, this never-satisfied appetite for sympathy, and this boundless offering of sympathy – this universal democratic comradeship – this old, eternal, ever-new exchange of adhesiveness, so fitly emblematic of America – I have given in that book, undisguisedly, declaredly, the openest expression. Besides, important as they are in my purpose as emotional expressions for humanity, the special meaning of the "Calamus" cluster of "Leaves of Grass," (and more or less running through the book, and cropping out in "Drum-Taps,") mainly resides in its political significance. In my opinion, it is by a fervent, accepted development of comradeship, the beautiful and sane affection of man for man, latent in all young fellows [. . .] that the United States of the future, (I cannot too often repeat,) are to be most effectually welded together, intercalated, anneal'd into a living union. (PW, 2:471)

For Whitman, the appetite for contact and attachment that is anchored in sex is the very fiber of American national coherence. In the years before the war, Whitman had roamed the streets of his beloved Manhattan and there, in the erotic spark that kindled between strangers, had found a fit emblem for a kind of nationness made not of shared obedience or geographic happenstance – or, notably, bioracialized uniformity – but of *desire*: of sex, unloosed from its containment in marital coupledom, as the cohering element of civic belonging. And so, in "Calamus," Whitman portrays an America that looks like this: "Passing stranger! you do not know how longingly I look upon you, / [. . .] / You give me the pleasure of your eyes, face, flesh, as we pass, you take of my beard, breast, hands in return" (LG60, 366). Or like this:

> States!
> Were you looking to be held together by the lawyers?
> By an agreement on a paper? Or by arms?   (LG60, 349)

This is what it means to say that "America," in the senses he specifies for us in the 1876 Preface, is for Whitman at its base a scene of a sustained impassioned intimacy between strangers: an erotic sodality.

There was more than this. For as a poem like "Whoever You Are Holding Me Now in Hand" would demonstrate so beautifully, an ardent and desiring relation between strangers was precisely what the poem itself, in its print-circulation through the anonymous spaces of public life, sought not merely to represent but to *enact*, to kindle and prolong and extend. Speaking in the voice of his book, held in the hand of his reader, the poet marks the printed object as a prod, a solicitation, to the state of carnal relatedness that, for the poet, *is* citizenship:

> Or, if you will, thrusting me beneath your clothing,
> Where I may feel the throbs of your heart, or rest upon your hip,
> Carry me when you go forth over land or sea;
> For thus, merely touching you, is enough – is best.   (LG60, 346)

Whitman's is a vision of the printed poem circulating through the anonymous spaces of the print public sphere, igniting as it goes a binding, distance-traducing desire. In all, by the time of the war Whitman had crafted a vision of an erotically rooted national life, at the center of which was the cohering power of writing, of poetry, of *his* poetry. He sets about, as he says, planting "comradeship as thick as trees along all the rivers of America" (LG60, 351). To precisely this nationalist dream of sex – we might think too of the letter to Emerson he included at the end of the 1856 *Leaves of Grass*, in which he wrote, "The courageous soul, for a year or two to come, may be proved by faith in sex, and by disdaining concessions" (LG56, 356) – "Calamus," Whitman insists, had given the openest expression.[3]

For an expressivist-erotic utopianism such as this the war was, in virtually all the ways one can imagine, a catastrophic rebuke. A horrific spectacle of disunity, anatomization, and the indifference of citizen to distant citizen, the war put to rout not only Whitman's rosier vision of national cohesion but, quite as directly, his belief in the nearly limitless civic power of writing itself, of representation. We can feel this pained recalibration everywhere in Whitman's writing from the era. It is there, for instance, in the syntactic strain and excruciated delay of a war poem like "Vigil Strange I Kept on the Field One Night," which features lines such as, "And there and then and bathed by the rising sun, my son in his grave, in his rude-dug grave I deposited" (LG, 304). Where once was a poet who had claimed with supreme confidence "I am the man, I suffered, I was there," we now find a poet confronting scenes that are all unyielding recalcitrance, that seem to defy their translation into the very poetic idioms Whitman had brought to such polished articulacy in previous years.

Perhaps nowhere else is the need for a recalibration of writerly strategies expressed more directly, or with such plangency, than in Whitman's prose memoir of the era, his *Memoranda During the War* (1875–76). Consider the opening, where Whitman announces what his writing here will, but also will *not*, encompass. "I have perhaps forty such little note-books left," he says of the war writings around which *Memoranda* is based,

> forming a special history of those years, *for myself alone*, full of associations never to be possibly said or sung. I wish I could convey to the reader the associations that attach to these soil'd and creas'd little livraisons, each composed of a sheet or two of paper, folded small to carry in the pocket, and fasten'd with a pin. I leave them just as I threw them by during the War, blotch'd here and there with more than one blood-stain.[4]

If the blood-stains noted here work as a kind of badge of authenticity for Whitman and the document that follows from them – he was, as *Leaves* has it, *there* – they mark too a limit, a residue of what Timothy Sweet calls "the unrepresentable traces of war."[5] When Whitman confides that he wishes he could convey the war, that his experiences are for himself alone, and are never to be sung, he is reminding us how thoroughly the war had devastated his ideal of an American unity and coherence made up of a vast network of "beautiful and sane affection" (as he puts it in the 1876 Preface), of which the printed poet is both source and cynosure.[6] For *Memoranda During the War*, Whitman will venture no such claims.

And yet, despite all this – despite Whitman's mournful, dirge-like insistence that "the real war will never get in the books" (PW, 2:116) – this is not the whole of the story of Whitman at war. Nested inside these multiplying forms of resignation is a notably different strain. For even as Whitman's faith in writing buckles, his belief in the fantastic power of *sex* not only sustains itself; it solidifies and, in strange ways, expands. In the "Calamus" poems, Whitman had professed an unchecked ardor for the strangers who, in their promiscuous circulation, made up the national public. He had sought, indeed, to kindle that erotic charge, to *make nationness happen*, through the print-circulation of his poetry. In the war, Whitman himself circulates not in the form of his printed book but *in person*, bed by bed by bed, offering an affection to the ranks of wounded soldiers he finds in the hospitals that, if it is marked by an avuncular and paternal and at moments explicitly maternal mode of care, does not at any time forswear the desire that invests it. This is the counterstory of Whitman's war, and we see it throughout his work from and about the traumas of the era. We see it in his loving attentiveness to soldiers like

Oscar Wilbur or Erastus Haskell or the many, many who remain unnamed. We see it, too, with uncanny vividness, in the piquant, splendidly cruisy encounters he stages between himself and none other than President Abraham Lincoln. "I see very plainly ABRAHAM LINCOLN'S dark brown face," he writes in *Memoranda*, "with the deep-cut lines, the eyes, always to me with a deep latent sadness in the expression. We have got so that we exchange bows, and very cordial ones." And above all we see it in his tender bed-by-bed ministrations, as he extends an affection to men whose broken bodies in no way diminish his erotic investment in them. As he writes of Thomas Haley, by whose bedside he finds himself,

> Poor youth, so handsome, athletic, with profuse shining hair. One time as I sat looking at him while he lay asleep, he suddenly, without the least start, awaken'd, open'd his eyes, gave me a long, long steady look, turning his face very slightly to gaze easier – one long, clear silent look – a slight sigh – then turn'd back and went into his doze again. Little he knew, poor death-stricken boy, the heart of the stranger that hover'd near.[7]

Precisely these scenes – of an unchastened carnal investedness in the bodies of men no matter how broken or wounded or near to death – repeat across the range of Whitman's writings, as vivid there as the passages of anonymous intimacy in "Calamus." In these respects we might say that the war in fact *replenishes* Whitman's sense of desire as the cohering element of national life and his vision of sex itself – sex set loose from its confinement in matrimonial intimacy – as the great force capable of forging a public, a citizenship, a nation. It is the unforesworn ideal that draws even his writing about bloodletting, horror, and loss toward a strange, sometimes eerie kind of utopianism, a straining belief in the war as a kind of *blessing*, a gift to the greater cause of the Union. To read Whitman's war writing is to watch him laboring to nourish this countervision, this claim for the ampler possibilities of an erotic sodality, in the teeth of fantastic devastation and grief; and it is just this doubleness, what Robert Leigh Davis elegantly describes as a kind of oscillation in Whitman, that makes for much of the sorrowful, stinging poignancy of the work.[8]

There are, of course, grievous limits to such a vision. Whitman's postwar accounts were not free of the notes of nostalgic heroization that were to be so much a part of the postbellum apologetics around the *failure* of Reconstruction (and, with it, by some measures, the failure of the war itself): the failure, that is, to establish a just and lasting peace not just between North and South but for the African American populations given a nominal freedom, which soon proved a freedom to be exploited and brutalized in the expanding machinery of industrial capitalism. That the war itself might in these terms be understood to have been both a cataclysm *and* a catastrophic failure – a colossal expenditure of blood and treasure, issuing in no genuine expansion of liberty – is not a possibility that flickers into steady visibility in Whitman's corpus. What Michael Warner, in a powerful reading of Melville's Civil War poetry, describes as a "delegitimating perception of the war" fractures Whitman's own work very little.[9] It is, in truth, nearer to unthinkable in the most of it.

But if the labor to hold to some portion of a badly damaged ideal makes for a kind of blindness in Whitman, it enables, too, some of his most powerful, mournful, indelibly beautiful work. Here we need only think of a poem like "When Lilacs Last in the Dooryard Bloom'd," Whitman's threnody on the death of Lincoln and the enormity of the war, which manages at once to inhabit the long vibrant tradition of the pastoral elegy and to make it speak, as it were, in new tongues. As an extended reading like Max Cavitch's demonstrates with painstaking precision, the poem moves through a series of meditations on the interlacing of death, violence, mourning, and the occulted possibilities for replenishment found not in the refusal of devastation but in the path through it. Or, as Cavitch puts it, "the elegy involves both a submission of grief to a transformation by decorum and an apprehension of grief as an incentive to promiscuous achievements of combination."[10] Here is how Whitman ends the poem:

> Yet each to keep and all, retrievements out of the night,
> The song, the wondrous chant of the gray-brown bird,
> And the tallying chant, the echo arous'd in my soul,
> With the lustrous and drooping star with the countenance full of woe,
> With the holders holding my hand nearing the call of the bird,
> Comrades mine and I in the midst, and their memory ever to keep,
>   for the dead I loved so well,
> For the sweetest, wisest soul of all my days and lands – and this for his
>   dear sake,
> Lilac and star and bird twined with the chant of my soul,
> There in the fragrant pines and the cedars dusk and dim.   (LG, 337)

In such "achievements of combination" as these we find what is perhaps Whitman's most wrought and precise balancing of devastation against replenishment, of devouring grief against the eroticized possibilities of futures still calling, cracked open, unpredetermined. So it is that Virginia Jackson describes "Lilacs" as "the most beautiful lines ever written on the relation between seasonal redemption, Christian myths of resurrection, and cultural reformation."[11] They are, in all events, the place where the tumult we have been tracking – of ideals for writing, as well as for civic life, shattered and renewed – finds voice for Whitman as funereal incantation, mournful song, the chant of the war.

Notes

1. Max Cavitch, *American Elegy: The Poetry of Mourning from the Puritans to Whitman* (Minneapolis, MN: University of Minnesota Press, 2007).
2. On Whitman's life before and during the war, see Roy Morris Jr., *The Better Angel: Walt Whitman in the Civil War* (New York, NY: Oxford University Press, 2000).
3. He writes also in the 1856 "Letter to Ralph Waldo Emerson," "Of bards for These States, if it come to a question, it is whether they shall celebrate in poems the eternal decency of the amativeness of Nature, the motherhood of all, or whether they shall be the bards of the fashionable delusion of the inherent nastiness of sex, and of the feeble and querulous modesty of deprivation" (LG56, 356).
4. Walt Whitman, *Memoranda During the War*, ed. Peter Coviello (New York, NY: Oxford University Press, 2004), 3–4, emphasis added.
5. Timothy Sweet, *Traces of War: Poetry, Photography, and the Crisis of the Union* (Baltimore, MD: Johns Hopkins University Press, 1990), 48. Sweet's is a strong account of "the acknowledged impossibility of full representation" in the war, of how "the lived experience of war will always exceed the representational capacity of any medium" (48).
6. On this ideal and its expression in the "Calamus" poems, see Peter Coviello, *Intimacy in America: Dreams of Affiliation in Antebellum Literature* (Minneapolis, MN: University of Minnesota Press, 2005), 143–55. Those disclaimers, and the move away from the national representativeness of poems into the avowed quasi-privacy of prose, mark some of Whitman's distance from the post-war triumphalism sometimes ascribed to him. See especially in this respect John P. McWilliams Jr., "'Drum-Taps' and *Battle-Pieces*: The Blossom of War," *American Quarterly* 23.2 (1971), 181–201.
7. Whitman, *Memoranda*, 40–41, 28. For a splendid account of the erotics of Whitman's silences read in relation to "Whitman's practice of the free-love technique known in the nineteenth century as 'Karezza' – a form of coitus reservatus, or the practice of the male repeatedly halting his own sexual exertions just short of ejaculation," see Michael Moon, "Solitude, Singularity, Solidarity: Whitman vis-à-vis Fourier," *ELH* 73.2 (2006), 311.
8. My work here follows the lead of a number of fine critics doing work on Whitman, sex, and the war. These include: Betsy Erkkila, *Whitman the Politcal Poet* (New York, NY: Oxford, 1989); Charlie Shively, *Drum Beats: Walt Whitman's Civil War Boy Lovers* (San Francisco, CA: Gay Sunshine Press, 1987); Robert Leigh Davis, *Whitman and the Romance of Medicine* (Berkeley, CA: University of California Press, 1997); Max Cavitch, *American Elegy;*

Michael Warner, "Civil War Religion and Whitman's *Drum-Taps*," in *Walt Whitman, Where the Future Becomes Present*, eds. David Haven Blake and Michael Robertson (Iowa City, IA: University of Iowa Press, 2008), 81–90. My sense here of what we might call Whitman's erotic nationalism is informed by other readings as well: Eve Kosofsky Sedgwick, *Between Men: English Literature and Male Homosocial Desire* (New York, NY: Columbia University Press, 1985); Michael Moon, *Disseminating Whitman: Revision and Corporeality in Leaves of Grass* (Cambridge, MA: Harvard University Press, 1990); Vivian R. Pollack, *The Erotic Whitman* (Berkeley, CA: University of California Press, 2000); and Mark Maslan *Whitman Possessed: Poetry, Sexuality, and Popular Authority* (Baltimore, MD: Johns Hopkins University Press, 2001).

9. Michael Warner, "'What Like a Bullet Can Undeceive?'" *Public Culture* 15.1 (2003), 50. For edifying meditations on the larger conceptual problems raised here with respect to Whitman and the raced United States, see the excellent volume Ivy G. Wilson, ed., *Whitman Noir: Black America and the Good Gray Poet* (Iowa City, IA: University of Iowa Press, 2014).

10. Cavich, *American Elegy*, 258.

11. Virginia Jackson, *Dickinson's Misery: A Theory of Lyric Reading* (Princeton, NJ: Princeton University Press, 2005), 77.

CHAPTER 28

Reconstruction

Martin T. Buinicki

Walt Whitman's popular 1865 elegy for Abraham Lincoln, "O Captain! My Captain!" employs an extended metaphor to convey the tragedy and triumph that marked the end of the Civil War:

> But the ship, the ship is anchor'd safe, its voyage closed and done;
> From fearful trip, the victor ship, comes in with object won;
> Exult, O shores, and ring, O bells!
> But I, with silent tread,
> Walk the spot my captain lies,
> Fallen cold and dead.[1]

With ink scarcely dry on headlines reporting Richmond's fall, followed quickly by Lee's surrender at Appomattox, the nation reeled at news of Lincoln's death on April 15, 1865. The poem's image of a captain perishing at the moment of his victorious return captures the terrible juxtaposition of these momentous events. At the same time, however, it also sounds a note of optimism. The captain – President Lincoln – has successfully navigated the ship of state to safe harbor, even if fate denies him the opportunity to enjoy his success. The "object" – a reunified nation – has been won.

While the poem did not appear until November 1865, it expresses the hope that marked the early days of the end of the war. In fact, Whitman's metaphor is similar to one Horace Greeley employed in his editorial "The Dawn of Peace," published the day of Lincoln's shooting. Greeley writes,

> There are ships that will encounter the toughest storms and rot to pieces in the calms that succeed them. But ours is not one of these. The storm caught us with our rigging unbraced, our sails flapping, our decks in disorder, our yards unmanned, our rudder unshipped. A ship put in order to encounter peril amid such multiplied danger, and that then rode out the tempest is too staunch and too well-conditioned to fear any wind that blows or any swell it can upheave. With flag and pennant streaming gaily out upon the breeze, she takes a new departure upon a smiling sea.[2]

After four years of bloodshed, the idea that the worst was over must have been appealing. The reality was far different, however. As Mark Summers notes, fear and dread were all too common during the post-Civil War years: "phantasms of conspiracy, dreads and hopes of renewed civil war, and a widespread sense that four years of war had thrown the normal constitutional process dangerously out of kilter" haunted the public and politicians.[3] Such fears were hardly ungrounded: continued racial violence in the South, congressional turmoil in Washington, and the tumultuous presidencies of Andrew Johnson and Ulysses S. Grant proved the storm was far from over.

As he had throughout the war, Walt Whitman watched events unfold, his employment in Washington, DC, providing a unique vantage point from which to observe the nation grappling with the difficult work of reconstruction. Through it all, he continued writing; indeed, his pace of publication in the decade following Appomattox verged on the frenetic. His book of war poetry, *Drum-Taps*, which he hurriedly revised in a fruitless attempt to capture the unfolding sequence of events of the spring of 1865, was closely followed by the *Sequel to Drum-Taps* – so closely, in fact, that new material was literally stitched into existing copies of the former work, with a separate title page and pagination. He produced two more editions of *Leaves of Grass*, one in 1867 and another in 1871, each startlingly different from the one preceding it; *Democratic Vistas* (1871), his most extensive statement on the political situation in the United States; and *Memoranda During the War* (1875–76), the "special history" of his war experiences he composed in the notebooks he carried with him through the hospitals. At nearly the same time, he published *Two Rivulets* (1876), a collection of poetry and prose that coincided with his release of an "Author's edition" of *Leaves of Grass*.

Each of these texts offers a particular response to the events of Reconstruction, a period scholars generally recognize as spanning from the end of the war to Rutherford B. Hayes's disputed rise to the presidency in 1877. Taken collectively, Whitman's dizzying catalog of volumes reflects a poet striving to represent – or, to use one of his favorite terms, "absorb" – the tumultuous post-war years, and to come to terms with his own wartime experiences. This extensive body of work also reflects the new reality of American publishing. The Civil War created a voracious demand for news that fueled advances in printing and an unprecedented expansion in the periodical press. Military necessity also provided the infrastructure that allowed publishers to reach a larger audience than ever before: "All told, the federal government handed rail corporations 158 million acres of public lands and more than $64 million in federal bonds to underwrite construction. By the 1870s, one-third of all the iron being manufactured in the United States went into rails."[4] This remarkable growth opened a market for Whitman's writing vastly different from the one that existed prior to the war, and he did everything he could to take advantage of it.

Whitman was visiting his family in New York the night Lincoln was shot, but he returned to Washington promptly, in time to see the Grand Review of the Union army in a city already being transformed by the new post-war reality. In a letter to his mother, Louisa Van Velsor Whitman, the poet described not only the spectacle of the returning soldiers but also the large number of freed slaves, his language emphasizing their racial and regional difference: "great battalions of blacks, with axes and shovels and pick axes, (real southern darkies, black as tar)" (Corr., 1:261). Watching from the platform was Andrew Johnson, the new president, as yet untouched by the battles over Reconstruction that would lead to his impeachment. For Whitman, his presence highlighted the genius of democracy: "it seemed wonderful that just that plain middling-sized ordinary man, dressed in black, without the least badge or ornament, should be the master of all these myriads of soldiers."[5] The poet also saw Ulysses S. Grant, noting, "He looks like a good man – (and I believe there is much in looks)."[6] Caught up in the spectacle, the poet did not reflect on how the Grand Review served as much as a preamble for the political struggles to come as it did a symbolic end to the military conflict. How the freed slaves would be integrated into society, how Johnson would take up the work of Reconstruction in place of the fallen Lincoln, the role the immensely popular Grant would play – these were all questions whose answers would affect both the poet and the nation in the months and years to come.

As a bureaucrat in Washington, DC, Whitman played a material role in the implementation of Reconstruction policy. Shortly after assuming the presidency, for example, Johnson issued his Amnesty Proclamation; in it, the president "restored all property rights (except for slaves) to most Confederates who would take a loyalty oath" while "wealthy slaveholders and those who held high offices in the Confederate government or army [...] were required to apply for pardons directly from the president."[7] Viewed as magnanimous by some and dangerously naïve by others, this proclamation became one of many points of contention between Johnson and Republicans in Congress.

Working as a clerk in the US Attorney General's Office, Whitman was tasked with helping fulfill the terms of the proclamation. In two "Small

Memoranda," written in August and September of 1865 but first published many years later in *November Boughs* (1888), the poet describes the scene in Washington as Southerners sought the presidential pardons. On August 22, he wrote,

> The suite of rooms here is fill'd with southerners, standing in squads, or streaming in and out. [...] All are mainly anxious about their pardons. [...] They are from Virginia, Georgia, Alabama, Mississippi, North and South Carolina, and every Southern State. Some of their written petitions are very abject. [...] I see streams of the $20,000 men, (and some women,) every day. I talk now and then with them, and learn much that is interesting and significant.
>
> [...] The crowds that come here make a curious study for me. I get along very sociably, with any of them – as I let them do all the talking; only now and then I have a long confab, or ask a suggestive question or two. (PW, 2:610)

Whitman's remarks suggest his work allowed him to see the economic and emotional effects of the war on the South, and his attitude is strikingly free of rancor.[8] In emphasizing how much he can learn from the Southern petitioners, and the "curious study" they make for him, Whitman echoes earlier descriptions of his time in the hospitals, where wounded soldiers served as "specimens." If the hospital provided his view of Civil War America, his post-war view was informed by his vantage point in the offices of Washington, DC.[9]

In observations less than a month later, Whitman considered the pardon process in the larger context of Johnson's approach to Reconstruction:

> The arrivals, swarms, &c., of the $20,000 men seeking pardons, still continue with increas'd numbers and pertinacity. I yesterday [...] made out a long list from Alabama, nearly 200, recommended for pardon by the Provisional Governor. [...] The President, indeed, as at present appears, has fix'd his mind on a very generous and forgiving course toward the return'd secessionists. He will not countenance at all the demand of the extreme Philo-African element of the North, to make the right of negro voting at elections a condition and *sine qua non* of the reconstruction of the United States south, and their resumption of co-equality in the Union. (PW, 2:611)

Whitman's comment regarding Johnson's attitude toward the franchise anticipates the significant criticism the president faced regarding his approach to Reconstruction. Following the passage of harsh "Black Codes" in the South, and as word of violence against freed slaves spread, the call for increased military protection in the former Confederate states and for giving African American men the right to vote grew louder in

Northern papers and among Republicans in Congress. This lay the groundwork for the Civil Rights Act of 1866, which Johnson vetoed, and eventually the Fourteenth Amendment in 1868, providing equal protection of the rights of citizens.

Whitman's reference to "extreme" supporters of the franchise, along with his apparent sympathy for the Southerners flooding his office and for Johnson's "generous and forgiving course," places him rather far from the Republican Party in the immediate aftermath of the war. Following Johnson's veto of the Civil Rights Act in the spring of 1866, Whitman wrote to his mother in July,

> It is generally expected Congress will adjourn the last of this month, & then there will be some high old times in politics & the Departments – most of us think that A[ndrew] J[ohnson] is only waiting for that, to lay around him & kick up his heels at a great rate. Well, we shall see what comes to pass – but I guess the Republicans are just every bit as ferocious as he is – they won't back down an inch. (Corr. 1:280–81)

In spite of his earlier support for Johnson, Whitman's views on the conflict over African American rights are more difficult to discern here, beyond the fact that he presents himself more as an observer than a partisan.

Observing the arguments from abroad, Scottish philosopher and writer Thomas Carlyle, on the other hand, excoriated the push for civil rights in the United States. In his essay "Shooting Niagara: And After?" he writes,

> Singular, in the case of human swarms, with what perfection of unanimity and quasi-religious conviction the stupidest absurdities can be received as axioms of Euclid, nay as articles of faith [. . .] . Divine commandment *to vote* ("Manhood Suffrage," – Horsehood, Doghood ditto not yet treated of); universal "glorious Liberty" (to Sons of the Devil in overwhelming majority, as would appear); count of Heads the God-appointed way in this Universe, all other ways Devil-appointed.[10]

In strikingly racist language, Carlyle goes on to decry the cost paid by Americans during the Civil War in order that "three million absurd Blacks [. . .] are completely 'emancipated'; launched into a career of improvement, – likely to be 'improved off the face of the earth' in a generation or two!"[11]

Given Whitman's ambivalence regarding developments in Congress supporting equal rights for African Americans, the fact that Carlyle's text was a catalyst for the poet's most sustained discussion of democracy, two essays he would eventually expand and publish as the small book *Democratic Vistas* in 1871, is surprising. However, as Ed Folsom notes, in a project he initially conceived of as a response to Thomas Carlyle's racist diatribe [. . .]. Whitman set out to address the burning issue in America of black suffrage, but by the time the essay was published [. . .] African Americans were absent, and the issue of suffrage was reduced to a whisper in an after-note, where race was perhaps implicit but not explicitly mentioned.[12]

As Folsom explains, this was not an isolated incident: Whitman's public silence on issues of race and equality continued, although one of his closest friendships ended in 1872, apparently over a disagreement regarding Whitman's opposition to equal rights.[13] In examining the poet's writings on race, Folsom argues that Whitman's practice of keeping his most offensive statements out of his prominent public works effectively safeguarded his reputation as a champion of democracy.[14]

In spite of Whitman's efforts, the shadow of the debate over suffrage and fair treatment of African Americans looms over *Democratic Vistas*. For the poet who in the Preface to the 1855 edition of *Leaves of Grass* wrote that the "genius of the United States" was found in "the terrible significance of their elections" (LG55, iii), Whitman's general dismissal of the importance of voting is striking. The poet promises that he "will not gloss over the appalling dangers of universal suffrage in the United States,"[15] but, as Folsom notes, this is exactly what he does. Whitman writes, "Admitting all this, with the priceless value of our political institutions, general suffrage, (and fully acknowledging the latest, widest opening of the doors,) I say that, far deeper than these, what finally and only is to make of our western world a nationality superior to any hitherto known, and outtopping the past, must be vigorous, yet unsuspected Literatures" (PW, 2:364). He writes that developing American authors is the "fundamental want" in the United States, "affecting politics far more than the popular superficial suffrage, with results inside and underneath the elections of President or Congresses" (PW, 2:365).

This Reconstruction-era shift away from the importance of elections is evident once again in a poem Whitman wrote in 1874 on the occasion of the opening of a new school in Camden, New Jersey. In "An Old Man's Thought of School," the speaker reflects on his own experiences and then asks,

And you, America,
Cast you the real reckoning for your present?
The lights and shadows of your future – good or evil?
This Union multiform, with all its dazzling hopes and terrible fears?
Look deeper, nearer, earlier far – provide ahead – counsel in time;
Not to your verdicts of election days – not to your voters look,
To girlhood, boyhood look – the teacher and the school.[16]

The turn away from the "verdicts of election days" in the post-Civil War period suggests the poet's disillusionment with either voting specifically or politics in general. Certainly, the controversies continued. While the Fifteenth Amendment, which passed in 1869, guaranteed the rights of African Americans to vote, it was repeatedly challenged, and the US Supreme Court ruled in 1876 that the power to decide who voted and under what conditioned rested with the states: "The court's decisions emasculated the Fifteenth Amendment and made it increasingly difficult to prosecute for racial violence, intimidation, and election frauds."[17]

Events surrounding Grant's administration may also have fed the poet's turn away from politics. While Whitman had long admired Grant, he was dismayed by public corruption; Jerome Loving argues that "Nay, Tell Me Not To-Day the Publish'd Shame," published in 1873, was a response to the Crédit-Mobilier scandal (Loving, 353), which implicated Grant's vice president, Schuyler Colfax. The poem's military diction in the first stanza, when the speaker laments "The merciless reports verbatim, still branding forehead after forehead, / The guilty column following guilty column,"[18] certainly suggests "unconditional surrender," Grant's former military glory replaced now by "merciless reports" and "columns" of scandal.[19]

Regardless of the poet's political views, this period also saw Whitman produce his fullest poetic representation of race and Reconstruction in "Ethiopia Saluting the Colors." Completed in 1867 with the title "Ethiopia Commenting," it was not published until its inclusion in the 1871 *Leaves of Grass*. The poem's speaker is a soldier in Sherman's army who encounters an elderly African American woman who, "rising by the roadside," "greets" the flags of the passing soldiers. In answer to the speaker's questions she gives a short answer, one of the rare moments in Whitman's poetry where a voice *other* than the speaker's is included: "*Me, master, years a hundred, since from my parents sunder'd, / A little child, they caught me as the savage beast is caught; / Then hither me, across the sea, the cruel slaver brought.*"[20]

The manuscript shows Whitman describing the woman as "towering" several times and in several different places, including the line when first the soldier spies her "towering by the roadside,"[21] and then striking the word out. Whitman's revisions minimize the woman's prominence in the poem, and Ivy G. Wilson argues that the speaker's description emphasizes racial and national difference: "the dusky woman's turban [...] is meant to differentiate and Orientalize her as an exotic. Accentuated by the contrast of colors upon the white palette of hair, the yellow, red, and green tones are meant to evince her affinity with Ethiopia. Her insignia as a foreign national is set against the designation of the guidon of the military uniform."[22] While the woman's statement addresses the years and miles separating her from the site of her initial enslavement, the soldier's reply, with its persistent questioning, suggests an inability to understand her perspective.

At the same time, however, the woman's gesture of respect in "greeting" the Union flag represents her recognition of a relationship to it, even if the speaker in the poem cannot comprehend her response. His dismissive descriptions of her, "so blear, hardly human," do not address her persistence, "lingering all the day."[23] His inability to imagine "the things so strange and marvellous" she could "see or have seen" does not negate her vision, even if his language prevents the reader from sharing in it.[24]

Much the same might be said of Whitman's writing during Reconstruction. As George Hutchinson notes, "The whole epic story of black American experience of the conflict [the Civil War] lies outside Whitman's reach."[25] Nevertheless, the Reconstruction-era struggle for civil rights profoundly influenced the poet's life and work, and its traces remain visible not only in Whitman's numerous texts but also in the poet's troubling revisions and erasures.

Notes

1. Whitman revised this poem several times. The text here is from the poem's first appearance in the *New York Saturday Press*, November 4, 1865, WWA.
2. Horace Greeley, "The Dawn of Peace," *New York Tribune* (New York, NY), April 14, 1865, reprinted in *The Reconstruction Era: Primary Documents on Events from 1865 to 1877*, ed. Donna L. Dickerson (Westport, CT: Greenwood Press, 2003), 5.
3. Mark Wahlgren Summers, *A Dangerous Stir: Fear, Paranoia, and the Making of Reconstruction*, Civil War America Series, ed. Gary W. Gallagher (Chapel Hill, NC: University of North Carolina Press, 2014), 2.
4. Allen C. Guelzo, *Fateful Lightning: A New History of the Civil War and Reconstruction* (New York, NY: Oxford University Press, 2012), 518.
5. Ibid.
6. Ibid., 262.
7. Donna L. Dickerson, "Johnson's Presidential Reconstruction Plan, 1865–66," in *The Reconstruction Era*, 15.
8. Whitman made similar comments in a letter to a Union soldier dated August 26, 1865, noting of those seeking pardons, "I talk with them often, & find it very interesting to listen to their descriptions of things that have happened down south, & to how things are there now, &c." (Corr., 1:265). In that same letter, the poet observes, "What I hear & see about Andrew Johnson, I think he is a *good man*." While radical Republicans were already growing angry at the president during the summer of 1865, Whitman's views remained positive.

9. In the recently discovered trove of writings indicating some of the work Whitman did as a clerk, Kenneth M. Price discovered a letter to President Johnson that Whitman copied, wrote, or took dictation for in 1866 on behalf of the attorney general. It addresses the imprisonment of former Confederate president Jefferson Davis and reads, "Representations having been made to me from reliable persons that the confinement of Mr. Davis at Fortress Monroe is more onerous & severe than his safe custody requires, I beg to suggest that you cause an order to be issued to the commandant of the fortress to relax the rigor of the prisoner's confinement so far as may be compatible with his safe custody" (Henry Stanberry to Andrew Johnson, October 30, 1866, WWA). Whitman's involvement in writing this letter and its consideration of the fair treatment of one of the most high-profile figures in the Confederacy, indicates the degree to which his employment in the capitol provided him with a unique perspective on the issues tied to Reconstruction.

10. Thomas Carlyle, *Shooting Niagara: And After?* (London: Chapman and Hall, 1867), 4.

11. Ibid., 7–8.

12. Ed Folsom, "The Vistas of *Democratic Vistas*: An Introduction," in Walt Whitman, *Democratic Vistas: The Original Edition in Facsimile*, ed. Ed Folsom (Iowa City, IA: University of Iowa Press, 2010), xxx–xxxi.

13. Ibid., xlvii.

14. Ibid., xlviii–xlix.

15. Quoted in Folsom, "The Vistas," xlii.

16. Walt Whitman, "An Old Man's Thought of School," *New York Daily Graphic* (New York, NY), November 3, 1874, 11, WWA.

17. Donna L. Dickerson, "Black Suffrage: The Fifteenth Amendment and Beyond, 1869–77," in *The Reconstruction Era*, 293.

18. Walt Whitman, "Nay, Tell Me Not To-Day the Publish'd Shame," *New York Daily Graphic* (New York, NY), March 5, 1873, 2, WWA.

19. For a full discussion of Whitman's attitudes towards Grant, see Martin T. Buinicki, "'Average-Representing Grant': Whitman's General," *Walt Whitman Quarterly Review* 26.2 (2008), 69–91.

20. Walt Whitman, "Ethiopia Saluting the Colors (A Reminiscence of 1864)," in *Leaves of Grass* (New York, NY: J. S. Redfield, 1871), 357, WWA.

21. Walt Whitman, "Ethiopia saluting the colors," Catalog of the Walt Whitman Literary Manuscripts in the Pierpont Morgan Library, New York, NY, WWA.

22. Ivy G. Wilson, *Specters of Democracy: Blackness and the Aesthetics of Politics in the Antebellum U.S.* (New York, NY: Oxford University Press, 2011), 98–99.

23. Whitman, "Ethiopia Saluting the Colors," 358.

24. Ibid.

25. George Hutchinson, "The Civil War [1861–1865]," in *Walt Whitman: An Encylopedia*, eds. J. R. LeMaster and Donald D. Kummings (New York, NY: Garland Publishing, 1998), WWA.

CHAPTER 29

Death and Mourning

Adam Bradford

On December 24, 1889, an aged Walt Whitman rode through Camden's Harleigh Cemetery seeking a locale for his tomb. Ironically, he avoided the grassy lawns that stretched throughout the environs, choosing a wooded hillside instead. When complete, the tomb was an imposing monument – with roughly hewn granite walls and room for six hermetically sealed vaults within. Whitman's disciples were aghast at both the cost and at Whitman's bow to the contemporary convention surrounding death and mourning which the tomb represented. Nevertheless, Whitman defended it, saying, "It will justify itself – the tomb is one of the institutions of this earth: little by little the reason will eke out. Yes, it is 'for reasons'" (WWC, 8:428). While Whitman's tomb may have seemed problematic for disciples accustomed to the idea that Whitman would, in the words of his poetry, "bequeath myself to the dirt to grow from the grass I love," his comments nevertheless suggest that such conventions had a value that he appreciated (LG55, 56). In fact, the tomb served, and continues to serve, as a gathering spot for a community of individuals who seek to feel connected to Whitman. From his widely attended funeral to the present-day individuals who visit with *Leaves of Grass* in hand, Whitman's tomb has functioned as a valuable space in which individuals have sought an affective intimacy with the poet they admire. It is a space of communion – something Whitman seemingly understood.

Whitman's appreciation of the power of the conventions surrounding death and mourning extend well beyond the creation of his tomb. In fact, they were central to his corpus of poetry – from *Leaves of Grass*, to *Drum-Taps*, and beyond. In order to gain the purchase necessary to understand how the conventions surrounding death, grief, and mourning impacted the production of Whitman's oeuvre, it is necessary to comprehend both the psychology and social rituals of mourning during the period. Modern psychological theories of mourning, despite their permutations, are largely derived from the work of Sigmund Freud. In works like *Mourning and*

Melancholia (1917), Freud describes grief as the psychic pain experienced when one suffers the loss of a loved one and mourning as the process by which that pain is ameliorated. The mourning process begins only when we come to accept that "the loved object no longer exists," and on the heels of this undeniable truth, "carried out bit by bit, at great expense of time and cathectic energy," we work to "detach [. . .] the libido" from the absent loved one such that "the ego becomes free and uninhibited again" – ready to claim a new and viable love object.[1] Central to Freud's conceptualization are two fundamental ideas. First, that loss was irrevocable, and second, that psychic stability in the wake of loss depends on abandoning that which was lost in favor of a suitable replacement. Failure to do either of these things was seen by Freud as "pathological," capable of engendering a "hallucinatory, wishful psychosis" marked by a continued investment in an object that no longer existed. It was a pathology that delayed indefinitely one's return to a balanced, healthy psychosocial life.[2] The dead, Freud was essentially arguing, belonged to the dead, the living to the living.

Freud's belief in the need to detach from a lost loved one would have been met with deep resistance by most nineteenth-century Americans. For them, mourning was the antithesis of detachment; it was the means by which affective bonds between the dead and the bereaved were restored. This restoration, by which the "bereaved [were able to] remain involved and connected to the deceased," was considered a much-needed aspect of the "normal grieving process," and central to recovering psychological health.[3] This, as psychologists Dennis Klass, Phyllis R. Silverman, and Steven L. Nickman have shown, was because the subjectivity of the nineteenth-century mourner was cultivated prior to the rise of the type of modernist sensibility that Freud works within, a sensibility that prizes "autonomy" and "independence," rather than the "interdependence" that marked most nineteenth-century understandings of the self. For individuals within such societies, the complete loss of those that had been so integral to their understanding of self would seem unthinkable – given that the self was largely experienced as a web of ties existing between individuals. Restoring mental health in the wake of profound loss required mourners to find a way to perpetuate these ties. Thus, mourners within such societies open us up to an "understanding of melancholic attachments" to the dead that ultimately "depathologize those attachments" and revise Freud's model in the process.[4] For these mourners, so it seems, the dead may be dead, but that did not mean that they should no longer play an integral role in the ongoing lives of the living.

In keeping with the idea of interdependency, mourners relied extensively on their local community (and sometimes broader society) to assist
them in reinscribing the bonds that death had severed. They did so by
participating in a variety of rituals and practices of mourning. Besides
witnessing and recounting the moment of death, preparing the body for
burial, arranging the funeral, and selecting a gravesite and monument,
successful mourning included the production of remarkable mourning
objects: post-mortem photographs, portraits, hair weavings, mourning
quilts, mourning poems, and even memorial jewelry. These objects were
not ordinary keepsakes; rather, they functioned as powerful talismans for
preserving the identity of the deceased so as to allow the mourner to call up
vivid recollections of the lost beloved. Since many of these objects required
the participation of more than one individual to be made, or, in the case of
mourning poetry, were written and circulated by or among sympathetic
friends, the process of overcoming grief was far more often than not
a communal one.

Such mourning objects worked to preserve the identity of the deceased,
forecast a continued association with the otherwise lost individual, and
testify to the bereaved that sympathetically minded loved ones were
anxious to assist; and of these objects, mourning poetry was arguably the
most ubiquitous. Penned by the bereaved or loved ones, exchanged
between friends and family members, preserved in volumes, inscribed
onto quilts, stitched onto samplers, and even published in periodicals
and books, the poetry that the mourning process called forth proliferated
across various media and circulated both privately and publically to help
mitigate the pain of loss. Whitman was no stranger to such poetry – in fact,
long before he wrote *Leaves of Grass*, Whitman produced literature that
made extensive use of its conventions – working in the same vein as writers
like Lydia Sigourney, Emma Embury, and Frances Sargent Osgood.[5] Chief
among these conventions were apostrophe, or the direct address of an
absent object, and collective pronouns (favoring use of the first person
plural, "we," over "I"). For such writers, apostrophe was a key literary
device because the "direct address of an absent, dead, or inanimate being by
a first person speaker" worked to make the "entity addressed" seem "present, animate, and anthropomorphic" – precisely the sense of ongoing
presence and association that writers of mourning poetry were after.[6]
Moreover, collective pronouns broadened the sense of connection between
the speaker and the absent addressee to include a community of readerly
mourners. It was an experience of communion, these pronouns asserted,
that "we" were seemingly blessed to be having together. Paired with one

another, apostrophe and collective pronouns worked to "produce [...] a fictive, discursive event" in which speaker, readers, and the deceased seemed able to commune with one another in an imagined literary space – one "in which the important utopian promise of sentimentality – of nonviolated community, of restored losses, of healed wounds" could be realized.[7]

Whitman's familiarity with these conventions is made obvious by even a cursory examination of his earliest work. Of the roughly fifty pieces of literature that Whitman published prior to *Leaves of Grass*, death or mourning figure prominently in at least half. In these pieces, apostrophes and collective pronouns are generously used in an attempt to broker a sense of connection between readers, Whitman, and otherwise absent individuals and entities. Prominent examples are poems like "Our Future Lot," "We All Shall Rest at Last," and "The Death and Burial of McDonald Clarke."[8] Whitman's writings on Clarke, a poetic eulogy and an elegy published in 1842, give evidence of how these conventions worked. The eulogy, published in the *New York Aurora*, actually included a mourning poem written by Clarke prior to his death, as well as an invitation to readers to join with Whitman in supporting a "proposed memorial" – a gravestone – for the indigent man. It was an endeavor, Whitman asserted in true collective fashion, that "We commend [...] as a deserving one" – wrapping readers sentimentally into the proposed project by virtue of the collective pronoun, "we," he employed. This eulogy also ended with a poetic benediction in which Whitman apostrophically addressed the dead poet. Using Clarke's well-known pen name, he exclaimed, "Peace to thy memory, Afara! In 'the sphere which keeps the disembodied spirits of the dead,' may the love of angels, and the ravishing splendor of the Country Beautiful, and the communion of gentle spirits, and sweet draughts from the Fountain of all Poetry, blot out every scar of what thou hast suffered here below!" Whitman's use of apostrophe in this moment is notable because, like all mourning poetry, it seeks to make Clarke into an active and reachable being, ensconced in the "ravishing splendor of the Country Beautiful," certainly, but also apparently capable of communing not only with the "gentle spirits" that seemingly inhabit such a country, but also, by virtue of this poem, with those "here below."[9] Calling on him in this way – hailing him with "peace" and well-wishes – makes Clarke into a vital being whose existence is ongoing despite death, and with whom, it appears, one might hold affective communion brokered through the poetic language itself.

It is perhaps no surprise, then, that when Whitman put pen to paper in 1855, he made use of the same conventions to produce *Leaves of Grass*. In fact, one has to look no further than the opening sentence of "Song of Myself" to see Whitman relying on them to create a sense of affective communion and ensure a sense of presence for an otherwise absent entity. When Whitman voices his now iconic declaration, "I celebrate myself, / And what I assume you shall assume. / For every atom belonging to me as good belongs to you," he once again relies upon apostrophic direct address in order to create a sense of presence capable of fostering a feeling of affective communion – although this time the individual whose presence he seeks to invoke is his own, and the bonds of affective communion he seeks to foster are directly with his reader (LG55, 13). Countless critics have written about Whitman's infamous "you," its remarkable ability to "convey [...] a presence," to free "the poet himself [...] from the [material] contingencies" of time and place so that he could provocatively seek out communion with readers reading decades or centuries later.[10] At times, his presence seems almost palpable, such as when Whitman pens a scene of orgasmic ecstasy that takes the reader as his partner.

> I mind how we lay in June, such a transparent, summer morning;
> You settled your head athwart my hips and gently turned over upon me,
> And parted the shirt from my bosom-bone, and plunged your tongue to
> my barestript heart,
> And reached till you felt my beard, and reached till you held my feet.
>
> (LG55, 15)

Through the use of his apostrophic direct address and collective pronouns, "we" – this time reader and Whitman – find ourselves bound in a fervid union; his body is palpable, his presence undeniable. We seemingly feel his "hips," we see ourselves draw apart his "shirt," and we taste the skin of his "bosom-bone." While the goal of mitigating grief and facilitating successful mourning may no longer be of concern, the conventions Whitman originally employed for such ends now serve as the foundation for a radically new poetry – one that nevertheless makes Whitman, regardless of his actual physical state, seem reachable, touchable, available for ongoing, intimate communion.

Whitman's reliance on mourning conventions in order to shape his texts would take a new, powerful form in the wake of the Civil War with his production of *Drum-Taps*. Because many of the mourning practices that were employed during the period required access to the body of the deceased and because death on the battlefield was frequently anonymous –

with body counts so high that many soldiers were interred in mass graves before being identified – mourning as they knew how was impossible for far too many. Loved ones could not secure a lock of hair to weave into a memorial piece, or procure scraps of clothing that could be used to make mourning quilts. Bodies could not be washed, laid out, and lovingly interred beneath a monument testifying to the worth of the loved one. Loss, it seemed, was total – something the populace found intolerable. Whitman's *Drum-Taps* sought to remedy this by returning the lost soldiers of the war to their families, both literarily and literally. He did so by depicting soldiers in terms that were so generic that they could stand for almost any soldier who went off to war, allowing readers to, in essence, gain imagined access to the deceased through the act of reading. A good example of this is "Vigil Strange I Kept on the Field One Night." In this poem, a father figure sees his "comrade," a "son of responding kisses," felled by a bullet. While the dying boy lies on the battlefield his companion hovers over him, viewing him with a "look" of apparent concern that "your dear eyes return'd with a look I shall never forget," holding "your hand to mine [. . .] as you lay on the ground." Called back to the fight by the "even-contested battle" that rages around him, the man nevertheless returns at its end to find the boy "in death so cold." Settling down next to the body, the speaker holds a "Vigil of silence, love and death [. . .] for you, my son and my soldier" that ends when the speaker "rose from the chill ground, and folded my soldier well in his blanket, / And buried him where he fell."[11] The anonymity of the figures in this poem is remarkable, especially when one considers that it is the story of the death of William Giggee, as told to Whitman personally by "Arthur" – most likely William's brother, and the man who performed the actions of the poem.[12] Nevertheless, when Whitman relates William and Arthur's experience in such anonymity, he erases all detail that might otherwise impede a reader's ability to assign an identity of their choosing to those the poem represents. As written, these men could be Union soldiers as easily as Confederate; they could be black, white, or Native American – all are possibilities. For anyone who can see in the fallen boy his or her own lost loved one, the circumstances narrated grant the reader access to a number of events that were thought to facilitate successful mourning. The reader is able to witness the dying's "last look," verify that he had died a "good death," see his body lovingly cared for after death, and be "present" for his burial.[13] In short, the important events which the violence of war had prevented readers from witnessing were now made accessible through the poem's images and the reader's willingness to identify the anonymized soldier of the poem as his or her own.

Whitman's attempts to ameliorate grief did not end there. He also sought to provide his reader with the all-important "trace" of the lost loved one – something to stand in place of the hair, the piece of clothing, the letter in the loved one's hand – something capable of brokering a sense of ongoing connection to the beloved deceased. This "trace" came in the form of the physical text itself. Whitman's *Drum-Taps*, in both the 1865 and the 1865–66 editions, were bound in covers which connote the color of blood. The typography in the text's interior initially resembles the chevrons and piping that were found on the soldier's uniforms, before becoming organic in nature in the *Sequel to Drum-Taps* section – twisting and curling, resembling emerging tendrils of plants just coming into being. It is a shift which mirrors the message of a poem like "Pensive on her Dead Gazing, I Heard the Mother of All" in which Whitman suggests that the Earth "absorb[s]" these "young men's beautiful bodies," in order to make them the "essences of soil and growth." Their "blood, trickling, redden'd" and soaked the Southern landscape – the "grass," the cotton fields, and the "trees, down in [the] roots." As such, the bodies had become the fertilizer nourishing the landscape, taken in by the plants, "Which holding in trust for me, faithfully back again give me, many a year hence" in the form of trees, cotton bushes, and grass – plants whose pulp may well have been used to form the very paper with which the volume they held in their hands was made.[14] Thus, with its cover the color of the blood their loved ones shed, and with the leaves of paper that constituted it potentially made from the plants such blood would have nourished, Whitman seems to suggest that not only through the imagery but through the very material of the volume itself, their lost soldiers had been returned to them.

Whitman hoped that fostering successful mourning for countless bereaved individuals would also help heal the ongoing division of the national social body. In poems like "Come Up From the Fields, Father" Whitman reminds readers, North and South, that we are now bound into what one contemporary dubbed a "republic of suffering" – a nation bound together, despite political differences, by deep, virtually universal grief.[15] In the poem, a family receives a letter from their wounded soldier; however, it is not written in his hand. Even though the letter asserts that he will "soon be better," the truth is quickly discerned, "the only son is dead." The devastating loss leaves the mother trapped in her grief, "drest in black":

> By day her meals untouch'd – then at night fitfully sleeping, often waking,
> In the midnight waking, weeping, longing with one deep longing,

> O that she might withdraw unnoticed – silent from life, escape and
>   withdraw,
> To follow, to seek, to be with her dear dead son.[16]

Such a poem, which rehearsed the state of countless mournful readers,
reminds them they are not alone in their grief and that others feel as they
do. Thus, by instantiating a community of the bereaved who can understand and empathize with one another's loss, Whitman works to bring
them to a realization that they stand on common affective ground –
ground that unites them across partisan lines, drawing them together
into a national body, a "republic of suffering," despite the political differences that had divided them.

As *Drum-Taps* and *Leaves of Grass* show, Whitman relied extensively on
poetic and social conventions of mourning to produce his literature –
something that other works, such as *Two Rivulets* (1876) and *Democratic
Vistas* (1871), also testify to. Awash in a world in which the poetry and
material objects of mourning sought to overcome the separations that
space, time, and mortality enforce, Whitman learned to treat such otherwise irremediable impediments to ongoing intimacy as nevertheless sur-
mountable. Taking a cue from this mourning culture, Whitman learned,
in his own words, that "It avails not, neither time or place – distance avails
not," that in spite of them, he could reach across "a generation, or ever so
many generations hence" to whisper, "I am with you" and be confident
that we would nod our heads in agreement, feeling his ethereal presence
materialize through the text in the very moment of reading (LG60, 380).
Whitman's use of these conventions was generally in service of a much
larger set of concerns than those that typically marked the kind of local
grief work that most mourning poetry was committed to. Seeking to raise
readers to a sense of their democratic subjectivity, to celebrate America's
unique political achievements, to heal the national body politic in the wake
of civil dis-union, to clear space to celebrate all types of human love – all of
these and more were crucial to Whitman's poetic project, and all were
voiced in the radically intimate address of a poet whose life and attitudes
were generally less than conventional. However, this was not to say that
conventions were of no use to him. Reconfigured, molded, shaped, and
given "new life" in "new forms," the conventions of mourning and mourning poetry served Whitman as powerful tools (LG55, iii). Like his tomb,
these conventions became a means for reaching out to his beloved readers,
forming the powerful connections with them that would foster the otherwise radical work he wished to do.

Notes

1. Sigmund Freud, *The Standard Edition of the Complete Psychological Works of Sigmund Freud: The Ego and the Id and Other Works*, vol. 19, ed. James Strachey (London: Hogarth Press, 1957), 244–45.
2. Ibid., 244.
3. Phyllis R. Silverman and Dennis Klass, "Introduction: What's the Problem?" in *Continuing Bonds: New Understandings of Grief*, eds. Dennis Klass, Phyllis R. Silverman, and Steve L. Nickman (New York, NY: Taylor and Francis, 1996), 16.
4. Ibid., 14.
5. This is one of the primary reasons that Whitman's pre-*Leaves of Grass* poetry was long derided by critics. In the words of Thomas Brasher, Whitman's pre-*Leaves of Grass* poetry resembles that of "the innumerable horde of fourth-rate and unoriginal versifiers who occasionally found, as did Mrs. Lydia Sigourney, a following." Ignoring Brasher's dismissive tone, his comparison is otherwise astute. Sigourney was a prolific writer of sentimental literature, including mourning poems. See Brasher's introduction to Walt Whitman, *Early Poems and Fiction, vol. 9 of Collected Writings of Walt Whitman* (New York, NY: New York University Press, 1963), xv–xvi.
6. Barbara Johnson, "Apostrophe, Animation, and Abortion," *Diacritics* 16.1 (1986), 30.
7. Jonathan Culler, *Pursuit of Signs: Semiotics, Literature, Deconstruction* (Ithaca, NY: Cornell University Press, 2002), 153. Mary Louise Kete, *Sentimental Collaborations: Mourning and Middle-Class Identity in Nineteenth-Century America* (Durham, NC: Duke University Press, 2000), 47.
8. Others include "The Inca's Daughter," "The Spanish Lady," "Sailing the Mississippi at Midnight," "Ambition," "Time to Come," "Death of a Nature Lover," "The Love that is Hereafter," "The Winding Up," and "Each Has His Grief."
9. Walt Whitman, "[Untitled]," *New York Aurora* (New York, NY), March 8, 1842, 2, WWA.
10. Tenney Nathanson, *Whitman's Presence: Body, Voice, and Writing in Leaves of Grass* (New York, NY: New York University Press, 1992), 114. For a more thorough description of the various critical interpretations of Whitman's "you" see Adam Bradford, *Communities of Death: Whitman, Poe and the American Culture of Mourning* (Columbia, MO: University of Missouri Press, 2014), 108–09, 215.
11. Walt Whitman, *Drum-Taps* (New York, NY, 1865), 43, WWA.
12. Bradford, *Communities of Death*, 138, 221.
13. The "last look" and the "good death" supposedly indexed the state of the dying's soul. If the look was sweet and death peaceful, this was a sign that the dying was entering a state of heavenly bliss. Curiously, the "look" in the poem is simply described as "a look I shall never forget" – which, again, serves as an invitation to the reader to imaginatively construct the "last look" of their

dying beloved, presumably in a way that offers comforts about the beloved's ultimate state. With this in mind, the fact that the boy dies without raging or undue pain suggests a "good death" and an entrance into a glorious afterlife (Whitman, *Drum-Taps*, 42).

14. Whitman, *Drum-Taps*, 71.
15. Frederick Law Olmsted, *Hospital Transports: A Memoir of the Embarkation of the Sick and Wounded from the Peninsula of Virginia in the Summer of 1862* (Boston, MA: Ticknor and Fields, 1863), 115.
16. Whitman, *Drum-Taps*, 40.

CHAPTER 30

Slavery and Abolition

Ivy G. Wilson

In an essay sketching Walt Whitman's "New World vision," the activist, essayist, and poet June Jordan outlines a genealogy of Whitman's twentieth-century descendants that includes herself, Pablo Neruda, Langston Hughes, and Aghostino Neto, among others. Jordan announces in "For the Sake of a People's Poetry: Walt Whitman and the Rest of Us" that these "traceable descendants" of Whitman have produced "New World forms of experience and art" inspired by his "democratic faith." Depicting Neruda as one of Whitman's progeny, Jordan cites lines by Neruda from his *The Heights of Macchu Picchu* (1944), "The Woes and the Furies," and "The Dictators" as well as those from Whitman's "Song of Myself," "There Was a Child Went Forth," "Crossing Brooklyn Ferry," and "A Song of the Rolling Earth" to illustrate their shared commitment and "self-conscious decision to write in a manner readily comprehensible to the masses of [their] countrymen."[1] Jordan summarizes her sentiment about the good gray poet, noting that "What Whitman envisioned, we, the people and the poets of the New World, embody."[2]

Inasmuch as Jordan limns a theory of New World poetics in "For the Sake of a People's Poetry," her essay also should be approached metacritically for what it can evince about how the topics of slavery and abolitionism necessitate a dynamic hermeneutics where the meanings of Whitman's poetry are better apprehended when read with the marginalia of his drafts, notes, and manuscripts. Commenting on her own relationship to New World poetics, Jordan notes that,

> Nevertheless, it is through the study of the poems and the ideas of this particular father that I have reached a tactical, if not strategic, understanding of the racist, sexist, and anti-American predicament that condemns most New World writing to peripheral and unpublished manuscript status.[3]

While Whitman's poetry has not been "condemned" to "peripheral and unpublished manuscript status," it is precisely the archives of his peripheral and unpublished manuscripts on slavery and abolitionism that yield a fuller understanding of his politics and poetics. Taking Jordan's notion of the "traceable" as a methodological cue, this essay examines how a critique of Whitman's poems about slavery and abolitionism reveal as much about his politics as they do the reading practices invited by his poetics.

***

Much of the criticism on Whitman, slavery, and abolitionism prefigures a distinction between his poetry and prose writings, acknowledging that, while certainly no abolitionist, his representations of slavery were decidedly complex. A common undercurrent in Whitman criticism is that his antebellum poetry is more nuanced, while his prose hewed closely to the Free Soil party line. Whitman was committed to the white working class and worried that slavery, as economic institution, could only compromise and further erode the sanctity of labor by permitting degraded slave labor to persist. "We wish not at all to sneer at the South," Whitman wrote in a September 1, 1847, *Brooklyn Daily Eagle* editorial, "but leaving out of view the educated and refined gentry, and coming to the 'common' people of the whites, everybody knows what a miserable, ignorant, and shiftless set of beings they are."[4] Whitman begins articulating his disdain for the institution of slavery in his journalism, especially after the collapse of the Wilmot Proviso. The proviso, which sought to exclude slavery from territory acquired by the USA after the Mexican–American War (1846–48), was eventually blocked by the Senate in 1847, helping to spur the formation of the Free Soil party a year later. Whitman was himself an ardent Free Soiler, and his editorials at the *Brooklyn Daily Eagle* reveal his championing of white labor as the principal *raison d'être* for his opposition to slavery.

Inasmuch as Whitman addressed slavery in the 1840s, notably in his editorials and temperance novel *Franklin Evans; or, the Inebriate* (1842), one of his earliest representations of the "peculiar institution" in verse form appears in the so-called "Talbot Wilson" notebook, written perhaps in the early 1850s.[5]

> I am the poet of slaves and of the masters of slaves
> I am the poet of the body
> And I am
> I am the poet of the body
> And I am the poet of the soul
> I go with the slaves of the earth equally with the masters

And I will stand between the masters and the slaves,
Entering into both so that both shall understand me alike.

(NUPM, 1:67)

In the passage, a number of features that will become signature registers of Whitman's poetics are resonant: the ubiquity of the first-person pronoun "I" at the level of grammar; the use of anaphora at the level of prosody; and the use of the word "am" to underscore ontological questions about being.

The passage has elicited no small amount of attention from Whitman scholars concerned with the textual history of *Leaves of Grass* as well as its thematic significance to Whitman's political positions. Martin Klammer, for example, sees in these manuscript lines Whitman's attempt to equalize "all social distinctions by including both slaves and masters in the same syntactic and spatial unit" and hence illustrates Whitman's ostensible investment "in a fully inclusive and multiracial democracy."[6] Andrew Higgins, by contrast, contends that, rather than chattel slavery compelling Whitman to write poetry, it "was his concern about class that propelled [him] towards poetry in the mid-1850s."[7] For Ed Folsom, this passage represents Whitman's attempt to identify "the poles of human possibility – the spectrum his capacious voice would have to cover – as they appeared to him at mid-nineteenth century" with the speaker insisting "on becoming the voice of both the master and slave."[8]

Such an insistence of becoming the voice of both the master and the slave, however, would make Whitman an outlier to both ends of the slavery debate, especially to abolitionists from William Lloyd Garrison to Harriet Beecher Stowe, Gerrit Smith to Frederick Douglass, who held that any concession to the maintenance of slavery disabled America from realizing its full democratic potential. The possibility of being able to inhabit both the master and slave, as Whitman had imagined in this manuscript, certainly seemed untenable to abolitionists after stark political lines were drawn in the wake of the Fugitive Slave Law and Missouri Compromise (both in 1850) as well as the Kansas–Nebraska Act of 1854. Ralph Waldo Emerson, for example, delivered an impassioned speech in March 1854, denouncing the Fugitive Slave Law and claiming that it was essentially impossible to occupy the two positions of the master and slave simultaneously, exhorting his audience to consider whether Daniel Webster, and, by extension, the audience itself, "was forced by the peremptory necessity of the closing armies to take a side, – did he take the part of great principles, the side of great principles, the side of humanity and justice, or the side of abuse and oppression and chaos?"[9] Emerson's language here about "closing armies" will find an echo in Jordan's later sentiments about "reach[ing] a tactical, if not strategic, understanding" of New World writing *after* having studied Whitman.[10]

The "chaos" that Emerson mentions to his New York City audience at Tabernacle Hall would erupt weeks later in Boston because of the protests and federal interventions surrounding the capture of the escaped slave Anthony Burns, an incident that Whitman himself would address in his poem "A Boston Ballad." The Burns affair – not so much the trial but the resistant confrontation before it – galvanized New Englanders against slavery, many of whom had quietly accepted its existence before. Originally from Richmond, Virginia, Burns had in 1853 escaped to Boston, where he found gainful employment but was arrested the following year after being discovered while walking on Court Street. On the day of the trial, outraged Bostonians and abolitionists stormed the courthouse to attempt to free Burns, wrestling with reinforcements sent by President Franklin Pierce to help US marshals enforce the Fugitive Slave Law.

When Whitman elliptically addresses the Fugitive Slave Law in "A Boston Ballad," his focus is much less on the violence that slavery had done to Burns himself than how it has ostensibly violated the democratic values symbolized by the ghosts of the colonial soldier. "A Boston Ballad" is something of an anomaly in the 1855 *Leaves*, inasmuch as it and "Europe, The 72nd and 73rd Years of These States" are expressly topical poems. For a writer who utterly self-identified with corporeality, plain and direct language, and everyday themes, Whitman here works in different, if not counterintuitive, registers that are elliptical, muted, and veiled. Refusing to mention the Fugitive Slave Law or Burns explicitly, Whitman presents the poem as a lament of the death of American democracy and the re-installation of King George III; that is, Whitman presents 1854 as a historical moment that threatens to politically re-inscribe America back to a mere colony of Britain.

> But there is one thing that belongs here – shall I tell you what it is, gentlemen of Boston?
> I will whisper it to the Mayor, he shall send a committee to England,
> They shall get a grant from the Parliament, go with a cart to the royal vault,
> Dig out King George's coffin, unwrap him quick from the grave-clothes, box up his bones for a journey,
> Find a swift Yankee clipper – here is freight for you, black-bellied clipper,
> Up with your anchor – shake out your sails – steer straight toward Boston bay.
> (LG, 265–66)

In a poem utterly marked by a sense of theatricality and spectacle, the figure of Burns is never rendered visible to the reader, remaining what I have elsewhere called a "specter of democracy," underscored by the aura of correlative words such as "apparitions," "phantoms," and the "dead."[11] Here, to my mind, is one of the teleological endgames of Whitman's writing practices relative to the topic of slavery specifically (with its relay or traffic between the notes, manuscripts, and published works) and what that practice might signify less in terms of the politico-economics of chattel slavery than for the socio-political ones of imagining an America capacious enough to enfold blacks into the body politic. The non-appearance of Burns in "A Boston Ballad," in this sense, tracks a wider literary practice of Whitman erasing the black presence in *Leaves of Grass*, whether in the example of the "Talbot Wilson" manuscript that informs "Song of Myself" or the "Lucifer" section of "The Sleepers."[12]

Inasmuch as Burns does not "figure" in "A Boston Ballad" – either in the artistic sense of figuration or the financial one of computation – Whitman does in fact represent the fugitive slave in the body of "Song of Myself" in the "runaway slave" and "hounded slave" passages. Both of the passages intimate a different valence of Whitman's antislavery position, markedly distinct from his prose on the Fugitive Slave Law that privileged states rights to other positions in his verse where emotion, affect, and sensation could underwrite the poetics and politics of his democratic project. More specifically, this antislavery undercurrent of Whitman's poetry depended upon a distinction between sympathy and empathy. Inasmuch as these two passages enable Whitman to articulate an antislavery position not necessarily foremost beholden to protecting the white working class as its governing reason but rather the moral suasion underpinnings of abolitionism, they offer his readers an occasion to rethink Whitman's understanding of black humanity and national citizenship.

> The runaway slave came to my house and stopped outside,
> I heard his motions crackling the twigs of the woodpile,
> Through the swung half-door of the kitchen I saw him limpsey and weak,
> And went where he sat on a log, and led him in and assured him,
> And brought water and filled a tub for his sweated body and bruised feet,
> And gave him a room that entered from my own, and gave him some coarse
>   clean clothes,
> And remember perfectly well his revolving eyes and his awkwardness,
> And remember putting plasters on the galls of his neck and ankles;
> He staid with me a week before he was recuperated and pass'd north,
> I had him set next me at table .... my firelock leaned in the corner. (LG55, 19)

The politics of the "runaway slave" scene of "Song of Myself" depends upon a logic of sympathy where the speaker acknowledges the pain of the fugitive, offering comfort, assurance, and assistance. By contrast, when Whitman, in the later "hounded slave" passage, has his speaker declare that he is the hounded slave, Whitman is attempting to actualize a logic of empathy based on an ostensible shared experience. In this regard, Whitman operationalizes his aesthetic practice of embodiment ("For every atom belonging to me as good belongs to you" [LG55, 13]) as one that reimagines a political sociality beyond proxy representation in favor of a more direct representational practice enabled by acts of transubstantiation whenever he announces moving from a "feeling" to a "becoming." Both instances contrast with Whitman's characterization of the Fugitive Slave Law in "The Eighteenth Presidency!" (1856), a long, unpublished political tract, where, in rhetorically asking "Must Runaway Slaves Be Turned Back?" he replied simply, "They must."[13]

If Whitman worried that degraded slave labor would only abase free labor, adversely affecting the white working class in particular, he was able nonetheless to depict the black body in the honorific position of dignified labor with the "drayman" scene of "Song of Myself." At a superficial level, Whitman accentuates the drayman's physical command, illustrated by his firmly holding the reins of four horses and the way his shirt seems unable to contain his robust torso, coupled with limbs that are "polish'd and perfect" – he is, in a word, "picturesque." At the psychoanalytic level, the drayman might also be a more idealized version of the self-representation that appears on the engraving of Whitman that adorns the frontispiece of the first edition; this interpolation would not only transpose black for white but literary portraiture for visual portraiture, the manual labor of pulling a wagon with the creative labor of writing. The "drayman" episode may not only mark a degree of (self-)idealization, but may also be tinged with a (homo)erotic charge.

Whereas scenes from "Song of Myself" and, in an oblique sense, "A Boston Ballad," address slavery and black fugitivity, "I Sing the Body Electric" frames the auction block not only as a moment that conscripts black bodies within the political economies of racialized chattel slavery but as the transactional site that violates the divinity of the human form – and, in this sense, it might be, somewhat counterintuitively, thought of as Whitman's closest enunciation of an abolitionist sentiment. Whitman did not veer from expressing his disdain for abolitionists, holding the view that their agitation would destroy the compact of the Union. Furthermore, the views of African Americans he expressed after the Civil War can scarcely be said to indicate that he thought of them as the equals of whites. And yet, in "I Sing the Body Electric" we find lines detailing the exquisite beauty of the slave body. It is important to note that Jordan herself would cite this same passage in her essay "For the Sake of a People's Poetry" to frame her genealogy of a New World poetics. In ruminating on Whitman as the "pre-eminently American white father of American poetry," Jordan turns to the oft-cited lines that the generations of black fathers will beget "populous states and rich republics" (LG55, 81). One of the most conspicuous aspects of Jordan's invocation is how she summons it not to articulate the horrors of chattel slavery per se but to evince a register of the poem's salvific possibilities. Here, Whitman's depiction of the humanity of the slave is rendered in such a way as to almost veil the fact that men and women are being inspected at auction. The mention of the word "limb" in describing the male slave here echoes that of the drayman, almost to signify that the slave from "I Sing the Body Electric" could become, or would have been, the drayman from "Song of Myself."

But perhaps the most salient undercurrent of a would-be abolitionist register in Whitman's poetry is not his depiction of their physicality but their interiority; that is, soul. In addition to words about flesh (tendons, nerves, muscles, etc.), Whitman's speaker takes note of the head as the site of cognition, thought, and creation – "In that head the allbaffling brain, / In it and below it the making of the attributes of heroes." Similarly, Whitman extols the virtues of the enslaved woman's body, accentuating her as having a religious interiority with a soul of "divine mystery" (LG55, 81). In a historical moment where the machinations of chattel slavery sought to reduce black "flesh" into a mere "body," in the vein that Hortense Spillers has theorized the distinction, any concession that black bodies had something like an interiority – whether psychological, emotional, spiritual, or otherwise – would have perhaps been received as a radical declaration of black humanism or equality.[14]

Everywhere throughout "I Sing the Body Electric," Whitman makes use of dialectics and catalogs to animate his democratic poetics. By yoking slaves and immigrants together at this historical moment, "I Sing the Body Electric" enables Whitman to position his poetry as a theory, if not model, for what Alan Trachtenberg would call, in a different context, the "incorporation of America."[15]

> The man's body is sacred and the woman's body is sacred . . . . it is no
>   matter who,
> Is it a slave? Is it one of the dullfaced immigrants just landed on the
>   wharf?
> Each belongs here or anywhere just as much as the welloff . . . . just as
>   much as you.
>
> (LG55, 80)

Although Whitman intimates that both the slave and immigrant belong "here" as much as they do "anywhere," it is the "here" of the US, the America of the New World, that his ideas about the "common aggregate," "en masse," and "divine average" could emanate. The most dangerous threat to these ideas in Whitman's estimation was the damage that the institution of slavery would do to the nation's white working class as well as to the very idea of "organic compact" as a concept of political organization.

It is also apparent that *Leaves of Grass*, from the 1855 edition to the death-bed edition of 1891–92, are not perfect examples of the "organic compact" in literary form; not only because each volume grew larger than the previous one but primarily because analyses of *Leaves of Grass* warrant a reading practice that engages the core and the periphery, the literary and extraliterary, the printed and the shadowline to glean new understandings and interpretations. In this sense, the poems discussed in this essay not only tell us something about the topic of Whitman, slavery, and abolitionism, but reveal ways for us to think about how the "discarded writings" illuminate the "collected writings," how representations of African Americans as figures of non-citizenship underwrite and further extend the political aesthetics of Whitman's project.

Notes

1. June Jordan, "For the Sake of a People's Poetry: Walt Whitman and the Rest of Us," in *Some of Us Did Not Die: New and Selected Essays* (New York, NY: Civitas Books, 2003), 245–47.
2. Ibid., 247.
3. Ibid.
4. Walt Whitman, "American Workingmen, Versus Slavery," in *The Gathering of the Forces*, eds. Cleveland Rogers and John Black (New York, NY: G. P. Putnam's Sons, 1920), 1:209.
5. Andrew C. Higgins, "Wage Slavery and the Composition of *Leaves of Grass*: The 'Talbot Wilson' Notebook," *Walt Whitman Quarterly Review* 20.2 (Fall 2002), 54.

6. Martin Klammer, *Whitman, Slavery, and the Emergence of Leaves of Grass* (University Park, PA: Pennsylvania State University Press, 1995), 50.

7. Higgins, "Wage Slavery," 53. Higgins extends his argument, noting that "slavery, in fact, plays a very minor role in the notebook, that Whitman is far more concerned with issues of ownership and the soul, and that discussions of slavery, when they do appear, seem to be as much connected to working-class wage-slavery rhetoric as to Free Soil anti-chattel-slavery rhetoric" (61).

8. Ed Folsom, "Lucifer and Ethiopia: Whitman, Race, and Poetics before the Civil War and After," in *A Historical Guide to Walt Whitman*, ed. David S. Reynolds (New York, NY: Oxford University Press, 2000), 50 and "Erasing Race: The Lost Black Presence in Whitman's Manuscripts," in *Whitman Noir: Essays on Black America and the Good Gray Poet*, ed. Ivy G. Wilson (Iowa City, IA: University of Iowa Press, 2014), 9.

9. Ralph Waldo Emerson, "The Fugitive Slave Law: Lecture at New York," in *The Complete Works of Ralph Waldo Emerson*, 12 vols. (Boston, MA: Houghton Mifflin, 1903–06), 11:226.

10. Jordan, "For the Sake of a People's Poetry," 247.

11. Ivy G. Wilson, *Specters of Democracy: Blackness and the Aesthetics of Politics in the Antebellum U.S.* (New York, NY: Oxford University Press, 2011).

12. As Folsom notes, "Whitman, in moving his poetry and prose from manuscript notes to the printed page, often erased the African Americans who were a key to the very inception of his ideas and images" ("Erasing Race," 4).

13. Walt Whitman, "The Eighteenth Presidency!" in *Walt Whitman: Poetry and Prose*, ed. Justin Kaplan (New York, NY: Library of America, 1996), 1344.

14. "But," writes Spillers, "I would make a distinction in this case between 'body' and 'flesh' and impose that distinction as the central one between captive and liberated subject-positions. In that sense, before the 'body' there is the 'flesh,' that zero degree of social conceptualization that does not escape concealment under the brush of discourse, or the reflexes of iconography" (Hortense Spillers, "Mama's Baby, Papa's Maybe: An America Grammar Book," *Diacritics* 17.2 [1987], 67).

15. Alan Trachtenberg, *The Incorporation of America: Culture and Society in the Gilded Age* (New York, NY: Hill and Wang, 1982).

CHAPTER 31

Native American and Immigrant Cultures

Rachel Rubinstein

The nineteenth century's developing discourse of the United States as what Whitman called a "teeming nation of nations" depended upon a coemergent belief in the inevitable vanishing of the continent's indigenous peoples (LG55, iii). At the same time, both discourses masked the violence of conquest, expansion, and the exploitation of immigrant labor. Whitman, who witnessed both the Great Removal in his youth and the Wounded Knee Massacre when he was seventy, continually grappled with the nineteenth century's "insoluble" Indian problem.[1] However, the nineteenth century's so-called Indian problem and "the perpetual coming of immigrants" were politically, imaginatively, and – in Whitman's poetics – constitutively yoked (LG55, iv). "See, steamers steaming through my poems," he wrote. "See, in my poems immigrants continually coming and landing; / See, in arriere, the wigwam, the trail, the hunter's hut, the flat-boat, the maize-leaf, the claim, the rude fence, and the backwoods village" (LG60, iv). Whitman's interest in Native histories and languages, and in diversity, multilingualism, and national identity writ large, was conditioned by his coming of age in a rapidly transforming and internationalizing city. "Mannahatta," Whitman's 1860 poem, identifies the "aboriginal name" that he called "specific and perfect for my city," with "immigrants arriving, fifteen or twenty thousand in a week" (LG60, 404–05). Foregrounding the entanglement of immigrant and Native America in both the larger culture and in Whitman's poetics thus reframes the context for understanding Whitman's simultaneous and often paradoxical embrace of diversity and nationalism, Native erasures and appropriations.

Between 1800 and 1850, the territory of the United States tripled in size, while its population grew from 5.3 million to more than 23.1 million.[2] Massive immigration from Ireland, Scandinavia, and Western Europe transformed urban populations, particularly in the East, while immigrants from China populated, built, and transformed the West – Whitman himself noted the arrival of a "Chinese Junk" on exhibition in New York in 1847.[3] As Alan Trachtenberg has argued, the arrival of millions of immigrants provoked continual crises in national identity even as assaults against indigenous sovereignty and cultures accumulated.[4] Ideas and images of Indians and of immigrants therefore interacted, affected the perceived meanings of the other, and figured together in a shared context of racism and imperial conquest in the imagining of a "new" American national identity.[5] While Whitman seems to advance a celebration of the nation as a pluralistic and democratic community, Ali Behdad argues that Whitman's imagining of the "red aborigines" making way for the "perpetual coming of immigrants" in fact "embodies a strange nexus of acknowledgment and denial."[6] Whitman could acknowledge that Indians had been wronged and dispossessed, but at the same time he subscribed to notions of progress and continental expansion; the eradication of Indians was in service to an inevitable national destiny.[7]

Whitman's earliest works, beginning with the 1839 poem "The Inca's Daughter," embodied the paradoxical stereotypes about Indians (noble and vanishing in the past; degraded and degenerate in the present) that were widely deployed throughout nineteenth-century American literary and popular culture; some of these texts – including the pre-*Leaves of Grass* novellas *Franklin Evans* (1842) and *The Half-Breed* (1845) – can also be read as a commentary on Whitman's immigrant-dominated New York. "The Death of Windfoot," a tale embedded within *Franklin Evans*, describes a revenge drama between two warring tribes that leaves no survivors. The tale reflects on the larger temperance themes of *Franklin Evans* as its teller – an "antiquarian" and "enthusiast" on the subject of Indians – observes that "rum" is the "greatest curse ever introduced among them."[8] But it is an immigrant character from a Manhattan-based section of the text, Dennis the "Irishman," who serves for the narrator as a more immediate cautionary tale on the dangers of drink, as Dennis is discharged from his job for "tippling," and goes from "bad to worse" until he is at the "very lowest stage of degradation."[9] He steals a loaf of bread in hunger and desperation and dies in prison. Similarly, *The Half-Breed: A Tale of the Western Frontier* explicitly stages a dialectic between noble and degenerate Indians, which is mediated by an Irish immigrant. Arrowtip, the noble, pureblooded, and doomed Native character, is framed for a murder he did not commit by Boddo, the titular "half-breed," who is the "hunchbacked," "half-idiot, half-devil" offspring of an Irish immigrant and an Indian girl.[10]

During the peak period of pre-Civil War immigration (1847–57), 3.3 million immigrants entered the USA, including 1.3 million Irish and

1.1 million Germans. In 1855, 52 percent of New York's 623,000 inhabitants were immigrants, 28 percent from Ireland and 16 percent from the German states.[11] Anti-immigrant and anti-Catholic sentiment interacted in widespread hostility toward Irish and other non-Protestant migrants. While Whitman's editorials often defended immigrants as ideal potential citizens, David Reynolds characterizes his writing on immigrants as a "strange dance on the nativist question," citing an early *Aurora* editorial that criticizes Tammany Hall's courting of the "coarse, unshaven, filthy, Irish rabble" (Reynolds, 99). But by 1846, Whitman defended the Irish, "who seem to be, by some, the especial point of scorn and attack," asserting that they "have every where infused into the elements of our national character singularly little bad, to counterbalance the acknowledged good they have done" (Journ., 2:72). In 1847, he defended immigration in general: "Then let them come and welcome! Say we; and the more the better. This republic – with its incalculable and inexhaustible resources, lying for thousands of miles back of us yet, and not possibly to be developed for ages and ages – *wants the wealth of stout poor men who will work*, more than any other kind of wealth!" (Journ., 2:173). This story of America that Whitman told in 1847 understood immigrants to be the "hardworking, industrious" labor pool who would populate the West and replace the "Great Aboriginal Race now passing slowly but surely away" (Journ., 2:73; 2:67).

A fascinating exception to Whitman's vision of futurity in which European immigrants became the new ideal western American citizens was New York's Jewish community, which he described in language analogous to the romance of the vanishing Indian. In 1842, Whitman's "A Peep at the Israelites" described a visit to the Crosby Street synagogue:

> And here was a remnant of the mighty nation, who routed the warlike dwellers in Canaan, and who received the Law from the great I Am upon the mountain of clouds – their ancient pride swept to the winds – their name a jeering and mark for contempt – their might humbled, their old homes taken by the hand of the spoiler [...]; – yet here, scoffed, scouted, and scorned, they came, to worship their God after the manner of their ancestors. The heart within us felt awed as in the presence of memorials from an age that had passed away centuries and centuries ago. (Journ., 1:77)

In attendance at the Crosby Street synagogue and recognized by Whitman was Mordechai Manuel Noah, a Jewish diplomat, playwright, and politician who in the 1820s had advocated for the creation of an autonomous Jewish nation in upstate New York. Noah had invited Indians, as the long-lost brethren of the Jews, to join his nation.[12] Perhaps Whitman had

Noah's Ten-Tribist theories in mind when he persisted in imagining for Jews and Indians a similarly noble, proud, and mystical past and yoked them discursively through their present "scorned" and humiliated condition.

Whitman's brief sojourn in New Orleans in 1848 brought him face to face with Indians in the context of a cosmopolitan, multilingual, and multiracial city. For the first time Whitman witnessed the slave auction block, met soldiers returning from the Mexican–American War, encountered "French and Spanish Creole New Orleans people," and wandered the French Market, where he noted its "Indian and Negro hucksters with their wares," the "fine specimens of Indians, both men and women, young and old," and drank coffee from the "immense shining copper kettle of a great Creole mulatto woman" (PW, 2:606). Reminiscing years later, Whitman writes: "No one who has never seen the society of a city under similar circumstances can understand what a strange vivacity and *rattle* were given throughout by such a situation" (PW, 2:605). In New Orleans, with its French and Spanish influence, Whitman writes, he was moved to consider "that there is much and of importance about the Latin race contributions to American nationality in the South and Southwest that will never be put with sympathetic understanding and tact on record" (PW, 2:606–07). Whitman's early encounters with Indians, in other words, took place in New Orleans' distinct urban, multiethnic, and multilingual milieu, thus cementing his imagined association of Indians with both Eastern urban immigrant "rattle" and Western conquest.

The publication of *Leaves of Grass* in 1855 marked the definitive entry of Indians into Whitman's lifelong poetic project.[13] While *Leaves of Grass* can be read as in many ways dedicated to the project of what Whitman imagined earlier as, in his own words, a "*poem of the aborigines*" that would contain "every principal aboriginal trait, and name" (NUPM, 1:275), Whitman also imagined his epic poem as incarnating "The United States themselves" as "essentially the greatest poem" (LG55, iii). This should come as no surprise. In one of Whitman's most extended early pieces on Native culture, "Indian Life and Customs – A True Subject for American Antiquarian Research," he posits that "the spectres of the Brown Men, with their stately forms, and their flashing eyes, and their calm demeanor" would constitute the "proper subjects for the bard or the novelist" (Journ., 2:109). Whitman participated in the common nineteenth-century stereotype that Native cultures were a feature of a distant past and not dynamic, living cultures in the present – a stereotype that, despite Whitman's periodic post-Civil War encounters with Native leaders and representatives, he continued to exercise in such late poems as "Red Jacket (from Aloft)" (1884), "Osceola" (1890), and "Yonnondio" (1887).

Given the strains inherent in Whitman's identification of immigrants and Indians with territorial expansion, it is not surprising that his famous catalogs, implicating Indians, slaves, immigrants, and workers of all kinds in his vision of an amalgamated America, have been celebrated as foundational for modern multiculturalism by some, and critiqued as "consonant with American imperialism" by others.[14] Even more than signifying Whitman's own ambivalence concerning Indians and the nation, Nicholas Soodik suggests that "the Indian in Whitman's texts emblematizes the ambivalence of the nation's figuration."[15] In the passage in "Song of Myself" often referred to as "The Trapper and the Red Girl," Whitman imagines a wedding on the frontier that illustrates such ambivalence:

> I saw the marriage of the trapper in the open air in the far-west . . . . the
> bride was a red girl,
> Her father and his friends sat near by crosslegged and dumbly smoking
> . . . . they had moccasins to their feet and large thick blankets hanging
> from their shoulders;
> On a bank lounged the trapper . . . . he was dressed mostly in skins . . . .
> his luxuriant beard and curls protected his neck,
> One hand rested on his rifle . . . . the other hand held firmly the wrist of
> the red girl,
> She had long eyelashes . . . . her head was bare . . . . her coarse straight
> locks descended upon her voluptuous limbs and reached to her feet.
>
> (LG55, 18–19)

Ed Folsom reads this scene as an intermarriage between "irreconcilable opposites": the East and the West, the civilized and the savage, set together in an attempt to resolve the paradox of celebrating both the American Indian and the expansion of the United States.[16] For Edward Whitley, Whitman here "allegorizes the fusion of white and Native cultures," as a way to introduce himself – the poet of America – as their "metaphoric offspring."[17] Karen Sanchez-Eppler, however, notes the violent implications of the trapper's rifle, intimating the "precariousness and explosiveness of interracial contact" captured in the scene.[18]

According to Reynolds, Whitman based this scene on *The Trapper's Bride*, an 1837 painting by Alfred Jacob Miller based on his travels in the West (Reynolds, 290). When Miller himself described the context of the image, he intimated that the scene depicts an exchange of goods rather than an exchange of vows, with negative implications for both the trapper and the Native woman:

The price of acquisition in this case was $600 paid for in the legal tender of the region: viz.: Guns, $100 each, Blankets $40 each, Red Flannel $20 pr. yard, Alcohol $64 pr. Gal., Tobacco, Beads etc. at corresponding rates. A Free Trapper (white [or] half-breed) [...] is a most desirable match, but it is conceded that he is a ruined man after such an investment.[19]

The ethnic specificity of the trapper, who could be Métis, French-Canadian, or Mexican-American (these were all likely origins for mid-nineteenth-century fur trappers), remains unspoken by Whitman and unnoticed by later commentators on this passage. These multiple meanings of "The Trapper and the Red Girl" scene – Folsom's tension between "irreconcilable opposites," Whitley's "fusion" of white and Native cultures, Sanchez-Eppler's "explosive" scene of "interracial contact," and Miller's own sense of a commercial contract between a Native woman and a trapper of uncertain ethnicity – also make visible the immigrant histories undergirding this nation-making amalgamation between what historians would come to call a "white ethnic" and a Native woman, subtended by suggestions of violence, exploitation, and commodification.[20]

Toward the end of his life, Whitman recalled his frequent encounters with Native delegations and visitors during his months of employment at the Bureau of Indian Affairs in Washington at the close of the Civil War:

> Along this time there came to see their Great Father an unusual number of aboriginal visitors, delegations for treaties, settlement of lands, &c [...] the most wonderful proofs of what Nature can produce. [...] There is something about these aboriginal Americans, in their highest characteristic representations, essential traits, and the ensemble of their physique and physiognomy – something very remote, lofty, arousing comparisons with our own civilized ideals – something that our literature, portrait painting, etc., have never caught, and that will almost certainly never be transmitted to the future, even as a reminiscence. (PW, 2:577)

Whitman's admiration for the "unique picturesqueness" of "those great aboriginal specimens," however, takes for granted their eventual disappearance, and elides completely – with his casual "&c" – the contexts for their visits to Washington in the first place (PW, 2:578–79).[21] The post-Civil War years saw not only the Indian Bureau's rededication to its policies of assimilation and the dismantling of tribal governments (which were pursued through the very treaties the Indian delegates had come to Washington to negotiate and sign) but also a dramatic rise in the immigration that the Civil War had temporarily disrupted. Between 1865 and 1873, three million immigrants entered the country.[22] After 1880, increasing millions of immigrants poured in from Southern and Eastern Europe,

Asia, and Latin America. These "new" immigrants provoked widespread racial panic. Concurrently, in 1871, congress ruled that indigenous peoples would no longer be recognized as nations eligible to make treaties with the United States but only as "wards" of the federal government. "Both Indians and immigrants," Trachtenberg writes, "were subjected to a process called 'Americanization,' a set of institutional devices and regimes that operated with [...] an essentialist idea of a presumed cultural nationality."[23]

Two of Whitman's poems from this period, "Pioneers! O Pioneers!" (1865) and "Song of the Redwood-Tree" (1874), allude to the continuing and escalating violence of western expansion. "Have you your pistols? Have you your sharp-edged axes?" Whitman asks.

> All the past we leave behind,
> We debouch upon a newer mightier world, varied world,
> Fresh and strong the world we seize, world of labor and the march,
> Pioneers! O pioneers!   (LG, 229)

Similar language reappears in "Song of the Redwood-Tree," which Whitman wrote just after the Modoc War in California had concluded, a conflict that had been covered actively in the press.[24] Ostensibly a paean to the loggers who had clear-cut redwood forests in an effort to provide farmland for immigrants to California, "Song of the Redwood-Tree" employs language that brings to mind the forced relocation and extermination of indigenous peoples such as the Modoc of northern California and southern Oregon: "Riven deep by the sharp tongues of the axes, there in the redwood forest dense, / I heard the mighty tree its death-chant chanting" (LG, 206). Both redwoods and, implicitly, Indians accede to their own sacrifice, as Whitman recasts a historic conflict in what Steven Blakemore and Jon Noble call a "mystical American body politic."[25]

In "Song of the Redwood-Tree," immigrants take over the space from which Native peoples have been forcibly removed, leaving Whitman to imagine a cosmopolitan California like the New York and New Orleans of his youth:

> At last the New arriving, assuming, taking possession,
> A swarming and busy race settling and organizing everywhere,
> Ships coming in from the whole round world, and going out to the
> whole world,
> To India and China and Australia and the thousand island paradises
> of the Pacific,

Populous cities, the latest inventions, the steamers on the rivers, the
  railroads, with many a thrifty farm, with machinery,
And wool and wheat and the grape, and diggings of yellow gold.

(LG, 209–10)

In his 1856 letter to Emerson, Whitman described an America that "cheer-
fully" welcomed "immigrants from Europe, Asia, Africa," an internationalist vision that he poetically realized in "Salut Au Monde!" also composed
in 1856 under the title "Poem of Salutation": "Within me latitude widens,
longitude lengthens, / Asia, Africa, Europe are to the east – America is
provided for in the west" (LG56, 357, 104).

Whitman continued to vigorously defend immigration, even as he freely
participated in the racial stereotypes and pseudoscience of the late nineteenth
century. By the 1870s and 1880s, animus toward Asian immigrants resulted
in the passage of the first racially exclusionary immigration law in the United
States, the Chinese Exclusion Act in 1882. The Scott Act, passed in 1888,
further limited Chinese immigration. Whitman condemned these acts and
the widespread anti-immigrant racism that had eased their passage:

> America must welcome all – Chinese, Irish, German, pauper or not,
> criminal or not – all, all, without exceptions: become an asylum for all
> who choose to come. [. . .] America is not for special types, for the castes,
> but for the great mass of people – the vast, surging, hopeful, army of
> workers. Dare we deny them a home – close the doors in their face – take
> possession of all and fence it in and then sit down satisfied with our
> system – convinced that we have solved our problem? I for my part refuse
> to connect America with such a failure – such a tragedy, for tragedy it
> would be. (WWC, 2:34–35)

And yet at the same time, as Xilao Li points out, Whitman's relationship
with a young Japanese–German–American immigrant student and protégé
Sadakichi Hartmann, revealed Whitman's "characteristic ambivalences
and contradictions."[26] Whitman told Horace Traubel in 1889: "It is in
him something basic – something that relates to origins [. . .]. Hartmann –
oh! have you never seen him? He is a biggish young fellow – has a Tartaric
face. He is the offspring of a match between a German – the father – and
a Japanese woman: has the Tartaric makeup [. . .] and the Asiatic craftiness,
too – all of it!" (WWC, 5:38).

Only a few years earlier, in 1883, Whitman was invited to attend the
anniversary of a Spanish settlement in Santa Fe, New Mexico. Unable to
attend, he instead wrote a letter urging the nation not to think of itself as
a "second England only." "Many leading traits for our future national

personality, and of the best ones, will certainly prove to have originated from other than British stock," he wrote.

> To that composite American identity of the future, Spanish character will supply some of the most needed parts. No stock shows a grander historic retrospect – grander in religiousness and loyalty, or for patriotism, courage, decorum, gravity and honor. [...] As to our aboriginal or Indian population – the Aztec in the South, and many a tribe in the North and West – I know it seems to be agreed that they must gradually dwindle as time rolls on, and in a few generations more leave only a reminiscence, a blank. But I am not at all clear about that. As America, from its many far-back sources and current supplies, develops, adapts, entwines, faithfully identifies its own – are we to see it cheerfully accepting, and using all the contributions of foreign lands from the whole outside globe – and then rejecting the only ones distinctively its own – the autochthonic ones? (PW, 2:552)

Whitman here seems to revisit and reconsider his old assumptions about the inevitability of the vanishing of Native Americans, and does so in the context of a reassertion of the value of both immigrant and "autochthonic" elements in creating the "composite American identity of the future." It is testament to the continuing relevance of Whitman that this letter was republished in the *New York Times* in 2013 under the headline: "As Immigration Takes Center Stage, Thoughts from Walt Whitman."[27] In 2017, as protests over the Dakota Access Pipeline thrust the Standing Rock Sioux into national attention even as a renewed and reenergized nativism permeates our political culture, more than ever does the fate of this "teeming nation of nations" depend on the intertwined futures of its indigenous and immigrant members.

Notes

1. Ed Folsom, *Walt Whitman's Native Representations* (New York, NY: Cambridge University Press, 1994), 57.
2. Mary Beth Norton, et al., *A People and a Nation: A History of the United States*, 8th edn. (Boston, MA: Wadsworth Publishing, 2007), 339–62.
3. Xilao Li, "Walt Whitman and Asian American Writers," *Walt Whitman Quarterly Review* 10.4 (1993), 179.
4. Alan Trachtenberg, *Shades of Hiawatha: Staging Indians, Making Americans, 1880–1930* (New York, NY: Hill & Wang, 2005), xii–xiii.
5. Ibid., xii–xiii, xx.
6. Ali Behdad, *A Forgetful Nation: On Immigration and Cultural Identity in the United States* (Durham, NC: Duke University Press, 2005), 85–6.
7. Folsom, *Walt Whitman's*, 57.

8. Walt Whitman, *The Early Poems and the Fiction*, ed. Thomas L. Brasher (New York, NY: New York University Press, 1963), 132.

9. Ibid., 160.

10. Ibid., 272.

11. Norton, et al., *A People and a Nation*, 312–13.

12. Jonathan Sarna, *Jacksonian Jew: The Two Worlds of Mordechai Noah* (New York, NY: Holmes and Meier, 1981).

13. Folsom, *Walt Whitman's*, 69.

14. Charles Molesworth, "Whitman's Political Vision," *Raritan* 12.1 (1992), 100.

15. Nicholas Soodik, "A Tribe Called Text: Whitman and Representing the American Indian Body," *Walt Whitman Quarterly Review* 22.2 (2004), 68.

16. Folsom, *Walt Whitman's*, 72.

17. Edward Whitley, "'The First White Aboriginal': Walt Whitman and John Rollin Ridge," *ESQ* 52.1–2 (2006), 109.

18. Karen Sanchez-Eppler, *Touching Liberty: Abolition, Feminism, and the Politics of the Body* (Berkeley, CA: University of California Press, 1993), 77.

19. Quoted in Marvin C. Ross, *The West of Alfred Jacob Miller (1837): From the Notes and Water Colors in The Walters Collection with an Account of the Artist* (Norman, OK: University of Oklahoma Press, 1951), 12.

20. See also Betsy Erkkila, "Whitman and American Empire," in *Walt Whitman of Mickle Street*, ed. Geoffrey M. Sill (Knoxville, TN: University of Tennessee Press, 1994), 63.

21. See Martin Murray, "The Poet-Chief Greets the Sioux," *Walt Whitman Quarterly Review* 17.1 (1999), 25–37.

22. Norton, et al., *A People and a Nation*, 473.

23. Trachtenberg, *Shades of Hiawatha*, 29; xxii.

24. Steven Blakemore and Jon Noble, "Whitman and 'The Indian Problem': The Texts and Contexts of 'Song of the Redwood-Tree,'" *Walt Whitman Quarterly Review* 22.2 (2004), 111–12.

25. Ibid., 112.

26. Li, "Walt Whitman and Asian American Writers," 183.

27. Walt Whitman, "As Immigration Takes Center Stage, Thoughts from Walt Whitman," *New York Times* (New York, NY), January 30, 2013.

CHAPTER 32

The Rank and File

Jerome Loving

The butcher-boy puts off his killing-clothes, or sharpens his knife at
  the stall in the market,
I loiter enjoying his repartee and his shuffle and break-down.
(LG, 39)

Much has been written about Walt Whitman and labor in the nineteenth century.[1] The consensus is that he was more enthusiastic about the American labor movement before the Civil War than he was afterward, especially in the 1870s and 1880s, when labor agitation culminated in the Haymarket Riots. This Chicago event essentially killed off the Knights of Labor, the union that attempted to represent artisans across the various skills. During the highly publicized trial of the Haymarket Eight in 1886, Alfred R. Parsons, one of the accused ultimately executed, made it clear that at heart the strikers wanted to get rid of the wage system altogether. Whereas the unionists sought to improve the wage system, he said in his defense, he and his compatriots fought to destroy it. He compared scabs (those who crossed picket lines) to the fleas on a dog. "The Unionist wants to kill the fleas, but the Socialists would kill the dog; that dog is the wage-system of slavery."[2]

Nowhere in Whitman's known writings can we find any mention of this trial that captured world-wide attention – either to condemn it or lament it. The American press, then regarded by labor as "the mouthpiece of monopoly," generally condemned strikes. Whitman may have been by the 1880s a long way from the artisan worker he had championed in his newspaper editorials of the 1840s, but he probably was not ready to submerge individual talent into a system in which workers were rewarded by how much they needed and not by how much their labor was worth. In fact, labor's socialist attachments worried Whitman, as he made clear to his disciple Horace Traubel, who unsuccessfully tried to get Whitman to embrace socialist tenets.

The Poet of Democracy even kept company with the strike-breaking, steel king Andrew Carnegie, although it was Carnegie who initiated the relationship, as he moved into his philanthropic stage, building community libraries in his name around the country and making sure his heirs were not "ruined" by his wealth, which he mostly gave away. Whitman wrote a paean to another gilded age millionaire, George Peabody (LG, 379–81), but Peabody was one of the "good" robber barons, his generosity making him the "Father of Modern Philanthropy." He set the example for American philanthropists from Carnegie to Bill Gates. Whitman credits Peabody indirectly for the scenes of worker tranquility he sketches on the walls of the subject's mausoleum. The poem resembles Whitman's greatest elegy, "When Lilacs Last in the Dooryard Bloom'd," where the poet imagines scenes of democracy painted on the walls of Lincoln's tomb.[3] Lincoln, the grass-roots kind of leader he called for in "The Eighteenth Presidency!" (1856), was also a political moderate who placed the integrity of the Union ahead of the abolition of slavery. When George Peabody died in England in 1869, it was a newsworthy event in both in the United States and in London, where the millionaire's body rested temporarily in Westminster Abbey. Whitman would have learned almost instantly of his death in England because of the newly laid transatlantic cable, which he would soon celebrate in "A Passage to India" (1871). Born into New England poverty, Peabody became an international financier who gave away more than two-thirds of his fortune, primarily to the poor and to art, founding Yale's Peabody Museum and Baltimore's first academy of music.[4]

Whitman's support of labor before the war was bound up with his anti-slavery ideas. He supported the Wilmot Proviso, which condemned the spread of slavery into the new territories. He was always opposed to slavery, not merely because of its inherent evil but because it negatively impacted white workmen. Their work, he believed, had to be respected in the new American order. It was undermined when the black slave did for free what the white worker did for remuneration. Indeed, he opposed anything that threatened the democratic image of such labor. With Lincoln, he advocated temperance, writing *Franklin Evans; or the Inebriate* in 1842. Only a sober worker could defend himself against an exploitative employer. Later in the first and second *Leaves of Grass*, published in 1855 and 1856, he stood up for the "occupations," signifying his support not only in words but in his image of himself as the worker-poet in each frontispiece, wearing his hat indoors or out and appearing without coat or tie. In the 1860 third edition, he replaced the workingman's image with a more Byron-like look,

Figure 32.1 Portrait of Walt Whitman from the 1855 edition of *Leaves of Grass*.
Courtesy of the University of Iowa Libraries, Special Collections & University
Archives and the *Walt Whitman Archive* (whitmanarchive.org).

this one presenting the gentleman-poet, who now merely spoke up for the
worker or artisanal class, one who admired the "butcher-boy" from the
vantage point of the journalist-poet (Figures 32.1 and 32.2). As the war
approached and the young worker took up the labor of war, Whitman no
longer pretended that he was actually one of their rank and file. Certainly,

Figure 32.2 Portrait of Walt Whitman from the 1860 edition of *Leaves of Grass.*
Courtesy of Kenneth M. Price and the *Walt Whitman Archive* (whitmanarchive.org).

he was no "carpenter," though George, one of his two soldier-brothers, was a cabinet-maker.

Although he came from a lower-middle-class family of house builders, Whitman probably never truly worked with his hands. At least one of his short stories in the 1840s suggests that it was because of Walt's lack of manual skills that his father favored his elder brother Jesse,[5] but whatever the case the future poet quickly got into the "professions," first as a printer, then as a school teacher, and finally as a journalist. It was as an editorialist, best shown in his *New York Aurora* essays of 1842, that he became a champion, not of labor exclusively, but of the American democracy in which it would flourish. In those early days of American journalism, the editorial page blended comfortably with the news of the day. And in his role as observer of the busiest and most vital city in America, one already becoming diverse in nationalities and invigorated by the latest trends, he celebrated the rank and file of what he came to call the "divine average" (LG, 21). In 1842 he heard Emerson deliver his lecture on "The Poet" in New York City, calling it "one of the richest and most beautiful compositions" he had ever heard "anywhere, at any time." That year he may have gotten the idea for what became his famous catalogs in *Leaves of Grass* as he strolled up and down Broadway in search of material for his daily editorials (Journ., 1:44). "Here," he wrote in the *Aurora*, two days after hearing the great Emerson speak of the transcendentalist power theretofore lacking in American poetry, "are people of all classes and stages and rank – from all countries on the globe – engaged in all the varieties of avocations – of every grade, every hue of ignorance and learning, morality and vice, wealth and want, fashion and coarseness, breeding and brutality, elevation and degradation, impudence and modesty" (Journ., 1:44). "Of every hue and caste am I," he announced in "Song of Myself," "of every rank and religion, / A farmer, mechanic, artist, gentleman, sailor, quaker, / Prisoner, fancyman, rowdy, lawyer, physician, priest" (LG, 45). Sampling the professions, trades, and occupations, Whitman merges the one with the many.

The original 1855 version of "A Song for Occupations" opened as something we might find in the 1860 "Calamus" poems:

> Come closer to me,
> Push close my lovers and take the best I possess,
> Yield closer and closer and give me the best you possess.   (LG55, 57)

These lines were dropped in 1881, but they should have remained because the 1881 version is a palimpsest of the actual way Whitman loved, or made love to, labor – intimately and immediately. The poem originally appeared in the first *Leaves of Grass* untitled, following what became "Song of Myself." In one sense, "Poem of the Daily Work of The Workmen and Workwomen of These States" (as it was titled in the second edition) was a cutting from the original "Song of Myself," literary run-off of his democratic apostrophe to the American of whatever calling or occupation. It continues the "I-you" structure of "Song of Myself," as he addresses every American, each one an artisan in this conception, about the possibilities of life seen through the lens of transcendentalism – where nothing is too small to be insignificant, where everything is a microcosm of God. Breaking through "the cold types and cylinder and wet paper between us," the printer-poet becomes representative of every worker in America, where democracy ought to permit unencumbered labor: "If you are a workman or

workwoman I stand as nigh as the nighest that works in the same shop"
(LG55, 57).

The poet's placement of this poem over the six definitive editions of
Leaves of Grass might suggest a cooling of his ardor toward labor. By 1881, it
had been moved away from "Song of Myself" and shaved from 178 lines to
151. Yet it is still prominently displayed, standing apart from his poetic
clusters, as one of his featured poems in *Leaves of Grass*, such as "Crossing
Brooklyn Ferry" and "Song of the Exposition" (another labor poem).
Whitman never got his arrangement of *Leaves of Grass* quite to his complete satisfaction, and after the controversial 1881 sixth edition (the first
book to be "banned in Boston") he ceased to tamper with the arrangement,
placing further poems in two annexes ("Sands at Seventy" and "Good-Bye
My Fancy"). These were mainly poems of occasion as he measured out the
sights and sounds of his last decade.

Whitman's attention to labor was strongest before the war possibly
because slavery, and its extension to the western states, threatened to turn
artisanal value into market value and wage-work into wage slavery. It was
only in the free air of democracy that the artisan or laborer could get the
opportunity to avoid the wage slavery common to Europe and its old
dynasties. Yet such freedom had its risks, and alcoholism was one of the
most threatening. Whitman probably knew this first-hand with his
father, who may have been a drunkard (his brother Andrew certainly
was), and he, too, as I have suggested in my biography of the poet, may
have had his own tug-of-war with the bottle around 1840 (Loving, 71).
By then there were more than 4,000 local temperance societies in
America, all formed as an effort to turn around the nation's dependence
on beer and alcohol in an age when drinking water in its cities was
considered unhealthy and when many workers turned to "safer" alcoholic
beverages to slake their thirst.

In an editorial entitled "Temperance among Firemen" published in the
New York Aurora for March 30, 1842, he spoke of New York's fondness for its
firefighters, comparing "the mostly fine, stalwart, handsome young men [. . .]
in their close fitting dresses and red shirts" with Roman gladiators. He
questioned whether any other city could "turn out a more manly set of
young fellows." The only thing lacking was their unanimous embrace of the
temperance movement then captivating America. (The movement culminated with the Maine Law of 1851, after which state after state became dry in
America's first experiment with Prohibition.) "Once make temperance
a favorite and fashionable custom among the young men of our city, and
the whole conquest is over, – the enemy is vanquished" (Journ., 1:87).

The subject of labor in the nineteenth century centered on male workers, not female ones, who before the invention of the typewriter in the 1870s worked mainly as seamstresses and hands in textile factories. Even Whitman, who declared he was the poet of the woman along with the man, focused on the male when it came to labor. Also something of a eugenicist, he declared: "On women fit for conception I start bigger and nimbler babes, / (This day I am jetting the stuff of far more arrogant republics)" (LG, 74). "Arrogant republics" hardly conveys the concept of a socialist state. Whitman's recently discovered series on "Manly Health and Training" in the *New York Atlas* in 1858 is strictly concerned with male health. This is confirmed not only by the adjective in his title but the use of the word "training," as in the care and feeding of an athlete (of which, it needs to be said, there were no females).

Boxing is discussed approvingly in the essay published in the *Atlas* on October 31, just days after the bare-fisted Morrissey–Henan prize fight, a brutal contest of eleven two-minute rounds in which both men were seriously bloodied. The fight had to be held in Canada because boxing without gloves was already illegal in the United States. For Whitman boxing was simply part of the Grecian program for athletic fitness, the best condition for the American worker. He believed in the necessity of pugilism in order to develop *"a hardy, robust and combative nation."* In one sense Whitman was reflecting the superiority of the Anglo-Saxon race over Europeans (e.g., French, Spanish, and Italians) who allegedly preferred a dagger to their bare fists in a "fair fight." Boxers were clearly more "manly." He also may have been drawn to the scenes of two men stripped down to the waist grappling with each other. "Do we then [...] openly countenance the training of men for prize-fighting. We answer, explicitly, *we do.* [...] We believe it would be first-rate if the science of fighting were made a regular branch of a young man's education."[6]

After the Civil War, the poet saw labor perhaps more in terms of its relationship to technology. If "A Song for Occupations" was his antebellum labor poem, celebrating artisans, Whitman's postbellum companion piece was "After All, Not to Create Only," which he presented at the fortieth annual exhibition of the American Institute of New York, an organization promoting technology in the city. The *Washington Chronicle* of September 11, 1871, reported that Whitman stood and delivered his high-tech poem "to an audience of perhaps two or three thousand people, [...] carpenters, machinists, and the like, with saws, wrenches, or hammers in their hands" (quoted in Loving, 337). Although Whitman may have planted that article in the *Chronicle* – the paper was always friendly to his songs of himself – it did not exaggerate the significantly wider audiences he began to enjoy after the war with his occasional public appearances either to read a poem or deliver his lecture on the "Death of Abraham Lincoln." "Song of the Exposition" (as "After All, Not to Create Only" was retitled in 1876) was reprinted in at least a dozen newspapers.

Unfortunately, it is not a very good poem. The editors of the *Leaves of Grass, Comprehensive Reader's Edition*, Harold W. Blodgett and Sculley Bradley, note that "it does not surmount its own rhetoric" (LG, 196). As in the case of other postwar poems, like "Passage to India," his desire to make a speech or lecture sometimes interfered with the poetic process of uplifting the commonplace with vivid imagery instead of clotted verbosity. The poet Bayard Taylor, who to Whitman's chagrin became America's centennial poet in 1876 instead of Whitman himself, publicly criticized "After All, Not to Create Only." Taylor, whose poem for that grand occasion is now completely forgotten, also wrote a parody of Whitman that began,

> Who was it sang the procreant urge, recounted sextillions of subjects?
> Who but myself, the Kosmos, yawping abroad, concerned not at all
>   about either the effect or the answer.

Whitman responded to the attacks in the press in anonymous articles in the *Chronicle* and the *Evening Star*, noting that "After All, Not to Create Only" would be published separately by the Roberts Brothers, one of the up-and-coming firms of the day, the same one that would later publish the earliest selected editions of poems by Emily Dickinson.[7]

The bigger problem with Whitman's poem, certainly in terms of the poet's vision of labor, was that while it glorified work, the defining mark of identity in the New World in contrast to social standing in the Old, he failed to see that the technology would lead to more severe labor problems as new inventions reduced the variety of employments (as technology continues to do today with its cultural elevation of people who work with their heads over those who work with hands – the artisans of the nineteenth century). Mark Twain in greedy anticipation of just how rich the Paige typesetter might make him imagined a printing industry devoid of labor problems (the machine would not get drunk or go on strike), though he would also shift his attention from slavery (in *Huckleberry Finn*) to wage slavery (in *A Connecticut Yankee in King Arthur's Court*).[8]

The problem is perhaps best dramatized by another American writer, one who admired, responded to, and frequently wrote about Whitman:

John Updike. His *In the Beauty of the Lilies* (1996), while it does not directly invoke Whitman, nonetheless, responds to the problems of labor that Whitman raised. It is the saga of four generations of Americans, beginning with Clarence Wilmot, Presbyterian clergyman in Paterson, New Jersey, who in 1910 loses his faith in the existence of God. During a meeting of a church committee dinner that includes a mill owner and a recently dismissed and radicalized employee, the labor question is broached. The problem technology poses in this case is that it overworks the workers (e.g., by doubling the number of looms a factory worker must control in order to increase production). Also, the more profitable industry gets, the worse off the workers become because they share less and less in the expanding profit. "And where is the benefit for those without capital," asks Mr. Kleist, a German immigrant recently fired from a silk-weaving mill. "What profits invention makes possible are gobbled up at the top, and squandered on yachts and mansions and marrying off their daughters to dukes and counts overseas!"[9]

This novel is relevant here not simply because it touches on the labor problem in America as it extended into the twentieth century, but because the clergyman involved loses his faith in God. Whitman lived and died in the age of essentialism. Darwin's law of survival by "Natural Selection" had not yet trickled down to snuff out the idealism of the individual by 1892, the year of Whitman's death. Theories of "evolution" had, of course, been "in the air" since before the Civil War, but the concept of free will had yet not been blown away, as it would be when the implications of Darwin's theory became clear. Logocentric to the end, indeed a believer in the transcendentalist doctrine that nature was a conduit to God and a divine mirror of the worth of the individual, the poet who sang out for the average person could still safely envision a world of work in which the democratic worker could not be crushed by the laws of the marketplace. For the world to be a "safe place," a state in which Darwin's determinism did not include, or condemn, the talented and virtuous, there had to be a benevolent God. Social Darwinism, or the idea that exceptions were made for those who were industrious and moral, would keep the wolf from the door only until Whitman's death. Then Stephen Crane, a minister's son, and Theodore Dreiser, a fanatical Catholic's son, would dramatize the new reality in *Maggie: A Girl of the Streets* (1893) and *Sister Carrie* (1900). By then Darwin's theory of natural selection had already ushered in a deterministic world in which neither Crane's Maggie nor Dreiser's Hurstwood would be "naturally" selected.

If Whitman had seen this bleak future, one reflected in the naturalistic literature of fin-de-siècle America, he would perhaps have become more of a socialist, certainly more of a friend to "organized" labor in the late nineteenth century. Along with the socialist Traubel, Whitman would have settled for a "unionized" workplace. For as a believer in a benevolent God, he could better imagine a more equitable universe and better deal for the rank and file. Otherwise, in the agnostic view of the world God simply had nothing to do. In the words of Updike in this novel, "'His' laws as elicited by the great naturalist's patient observation were so invariable, as well as so impersonal and cruel, as to need no executor."[10]

Interestingly in the context of Whitman's last days, Updike's minister loses his faith by reading Robert G. Ingersoll, or "Col. Bob," as Whitman called him. Ingersoll, author of *Some Mistakes of Moses* (1879) and similar arguments against organized religion, was the featured speaker at Whitman's seventy-first birthday party in New York City. He also delivered the eulogy at Whitman's funeral a year later in Camden, New Jersey. Whitman found something "spiritual" in the famous orator. For his part, Ingersoll found something "material" in *Leaves of Grass*. Whitman's faith, unlike Clarence Wilmot's in *In the Beauty of the Lilies*, could not be shaken, even by the "great agnostic." Like Ingersoll, Whitman disapproved of organized religion, finding it stifling to "Liberty in Literature" (the title of one of Ingersoll's lectures, which raised money for the good gray poet).

Whitman was a transcendentalist, whose first proof of God was nature, which, as Emerson had taught him, was the emblem of the spirit. The beauty and harmony of nature (e.g., the "beauty of the lilies") reflected the beauty and harmony of God. So he retained his faith not only in the worker but also in the industrialist who promised great technological and economic progress for the United States on the eve of the twentieth century. Just as before the Civil War he naïvely believed that the people of the United States would ultimately rise up and abolish slavery in the natural course of things, he believed after the war that men like Andrew Carnegie and his successors would not abuse their employees. He had *faith* in them. Thus, the poet's shift from "A Song for Occupations" to "Song of the Exposition" did not involve a change of attitude toward the threat of labor, only a growing regard for the captains of the emerging technologies that would change and devalue work in ways Whitman simply failed to imagine.

Notes

1. See, among others, Joseph Jay Rubin, *The Historic Whitman* (University Park, PA: Penn State University Press, 1973); M. Wynn Thomas, *The Lunar Light of Whitman's Poetry* (Cambridge, MA: Harvard University Press, 1987); Alan Trachtenberg, "The Politics of Labor and the Poet's Work: A Reading of 'A Song for Occupations,'" in *Walt Whitman: The Centennial Essays*, ed. Ed Folsom (Iowa City, IA: The University of Iowa Press, 1992); Andrew Lawson, *Walt Whitman and the Class Struggle* (Iowa City, IA: University of Iowa Press, 2006); and Margaret Ronda, "Georgic Disenchantment in American Poetry," *Genre* 46.1 (2013), 57–76.
2. Lucy E. Parsons, *Life of Albert R. Parsons* (Chicago, IL: Mrs. Lucy E. Parsons, 1903), 125–26.
3. See M. Wynn Thomas, "Labor and Laborers," in *A Companion to Walt Whitman*, ed. Donald D. Kummings (Malden, MA: Blackwell, 2006), 73.
4. Peter W. Bernstein and Annalyn Swan, *All the Money in the World* (New York, NY: Alfred A. Knopf, 2007), 280.
5. Walt Whitman, "Wild Frank's Return," in *The Early Poems and the Fiction*, ed. Thomas L. Brasher (New York, NY: New York University Press, 1963).
6. Mose Velsor [Walt Whitman], "Walt Whitman's 'Manly Health and Training,'" ed. Zachary Turpin, *Walt Whitman Quarterly Review* 33.3–4 (2016), 258.
7. Gay Wilson Allen, *The Solitary Singer: A Critical Biography of Walt Whitman* (New York, NY: Macmillan, 1955), 433–44. Allen cites the poem "Walt Whitman" by Bayard Taylor.
8. Jerome Loving, *Confederate Bushwhacker: Mark Twain in the Shadow of the Civil War* (Hanover, NH: University Press of New England, 2013), 197–218.
9. John Updike, *In the Beauty of the Lilies* (New York, NY: Knopf, 1996), 29–33.
10. Ibid., 17.

CHAPTER 33

Romanticism

Edward S. Cutler

Leaves of Grass appeared in the twilight of the romantic era. Walt Whitman did not describe his poetry as romantic, a term that was becoming a critical pejorative with the rise of realism in the latter half of the nineteenth century. Even so, thematic elements broadly associated with romanticism are certainly evident in Whitman's poetry, most notably an emphasis on individualism and organic development over poetic conventions and the authority of tradition. Romantic valences of this general sort informed the aesthetic of many predecessors and contemporaries to Whitman, in particular Ralph Waldo Emerson. But this is hardly unexpected. By the mid-nineteenth century, few English language poets on either side of the Atlantic adhered to the Latinate diction and metrical technicalities of neoclassical poetics. The *Lyrical Ballads* (1798) of William Wordsworth and Samuel Taylor Coleridge no longer alarmed the literary status quo; indeed, British romanticism had become so domesticated as to make an aged Wordsworth the pensioner poet laureate of England in the same year that *The Dial* (1840–44), flagship journal of New England transcendentalism, would shut down due to flagging subscriptions.

Yet the conceptual and aesthetic energies that gave rise to romanticism persist well beyond the era proper. *Leaves of Grass* – the first three editions of 1855, 1856, and 1860 in particular – exemplifies the spirit of a comparatively minor but radically innovative strain of romantic philosophy that flashed up in Jena, Germany, during the closing years of the eighteenth century. Steeped in the metaphysics of Immanuel Kant and Johann Gottlieb Fichte, the *Frühromatik*, or early German romantics, rejected the systemic, foundational aspirations of philosophical idealism in favor of an aesthetic mode that sought to fuse poetry and philosophy. Brash and provocative, the young Friedrich Schlegel and Georg Philipp Friedrich von Hardenberg (better known by his pseudonym Novalis) contributed aphoristic fragments on philosophy and essays on romantic poetry to their short-lived journal, *Athenaeum* (1798–1800). Coleridge and

Thomas Carlyle were among the first English admirers of early German romanticism, and Edgar Allan Poe would reference the fragments of Novalis in his short fiction, as would Emerson in his notebooks and correspondence with Carlyle. However, early German romanticism would find its fullest exemplar and a kindred spirit in Whitman, who late in life would even declare himself "the greatest *poetical* representative of German philosophy."[1]

Whitman had little ability to read German, although his surviving notebooks, lecture drafts, and later essays disclose a longstanding interest in post-Kantian idealism, a period stretching from Fichte to Georg Wilhelm Friedrich Hegel. Among translations important to him during the formative years of *Leaves of Grass* none is more consequential than Frederic Henry Hedge's *Prose Writers of Germany* (1848), a book he described to Horace Traubel as "one of my resources," a "necessity," and "indispensable": "I am personally greatly indebted to Hedge – have been for 40 years. He was the man opened German literature to me" (WWC, 7:76; 9:2). A founding member of the Transcendental Club in Boston (originally called "Hedge's Club"), Hedge had studied under Hegel in Germany, and his deep knowledge of German literature and philosophy would influence Emerson, Margaret Fuller, George Ripley, and others associated with American transcendentalism.[2] *Prose Writers of Germany* offers more than five-hundred pages of original translations from the German, where Whitman would have encountered the abstract terminology of idealist thought that permeates *Leaves of Grass* – "the Soul," "appearances," "identities," "likenesses" – indeed, the "Germanic systems" referenced in Whitman's poem, "The Base of All Metaphysics," which recounts "Kant having studied and stated, Fichte and Schelling and Hegel" (LG, 121).

Many nineteenth-century Americans who found inspiration in German thought shared Whitman's debt to Hedge. Yet the "Germanic systems" of the period from Kant to Hegel are not characteristic of the anti-foundationalist tenor of early German romanticism, and the successive idealist philosophical systems that vied to supplant Kantian metaphysics serve more as a foil than a model for the romantics. Early German romanticism is distinguished precisely by a subversion of grand systems and a playful, often mystifying preference for paradox and self-negating irony. Hence Friedrich Schlegel's oft-cited fragment: "It is equally fatal for the mind to have a system and to have none. It will simply have to decide to combine the two."[3] Self-contradiction as a means of indicating an elusive, unassimilable whole likewise characterizes the insouciance of Whitman's

"I" in the early editions of *Leaves of Grass*, large enough to absorb its own contradictions, confident that its speech is "unequal to measure itself," even that it is finally "untranslatable," despite all the "omnivorous words" (LG56, 45, 99, 82).

The transcendental I of "Song of Myself" shares an ostensible affinity with the first wave of American idealism in New England. Emerson's own ideas about the relation of self and world stray little from those associated with Fichte, the first architect of a post-Kantian turn toward an "unconditioned" idealism grounded in the primal fact of selfhood. Fichte's influential argument for an unconditioned intellectual intuition, evident in the immediate activity of reflective consciousness, served as the tap-root of the various systems of idealist thought that followed. These Germanic systems share the general aim of securing a rational basis for an unconditioned self that can first know and act freely upon the manifold objects of phenomenal experience, rather than be acted upon, and thus conditioned, by them. Fichte and his successors thus hoped to complete Kant's Copernican turn in philosophy precisely where the Sage of Königsberg had infamously hedged, in the ultimate unknowability of objects as things in themselves. In the primal immediacy of self-reflection Fichte finds the rational ground for an unconditioned intellectual intuition that subordinates – even generates – the possible objects of experience. In Fichte's famous shorthand formula, I = I.[4] All appearances and objects, all that is Not-I, are but secondary derivations, the reflections of this primal self.

Emerson's initial idealist statement, *Nature* (1836), derives its general contours from Fichte, dividing primary intellectual intuition, his own reflective consciousness, from "all that is separate from us, all which Philosophy distinguishes as the NOT ME, that is, both nature and art, all other men and my own body."[5] In broad measure *Leaves of Grass* might appear the fulfillment of just such an "egotism," the Fichte–Emerson security of self-positing, self-reliance. A London review of the 1860 edition of *Leaves of Grass* offers a critique along these lines:

> [Whitman] deals with the intellectual, rational, and moral powers; showing throughout his treatment an intimate acquaintance with Kant's transcendental method, and perhaps including in his development the whole of the German school, down to Hegel; at any rate as interpreted by Cousin and others in France, and Emerson in the United States. He certainly includes Fichte, for he mentions the Egotist as the only true philosopher; and consistently identifies himself not only with every man, but with the Universe and its Maker.[6]

Whitman never actually mentions the "Egotist" as the only true philosopher. And while this review perceptively sets *Leaves of Grass* within an
idealist philosophical frame, it fails to discern what had become increasingly evident by the 1860 edition, which is that Whitman's faith is not
answered in Emersonian consciousness but uncertain externalities: the
human body, the touch of lovers, his readers, and the intersubjective
mediation of his own book.

In contrast to Fichte and his transatlantic echo in Emerson, Whitman's
I is self-contradictory and polyvocal from the start, and by the 1860 edition
all but burlesques the supposed security of transcendental self-reliance.
Beginning with the lines, "Of the terrible question of appearances," poem
7 of the "Calamus" cycle openly ventures that "may-be reliance and hope
are but speculations after all / That may-be identity beyond the grave is
a beautiful fable only" (LG60, 352). Perhaps "colors, densities, forms" are
only "apparitions," and "May-be they only seem to me what they are, (as
doubtless they indeed but seem,) as from my present point of view – And
might prove, (as of course they would,) naught of what they appear, or
naught any how, from entirely changed points of view" (LG60, 353).
"What terrible questions we are learning to ask!" Emerson had earlier
written of the illusory character of phenomenal, intersubjective
experience.[7] And when confronting "this kingdom of illusions [where]
we grope eagerly for stays and foundations," he effectively doubles down
on a Fichtean foundation: "There is none [stay or foundation] but a strict
and faithful dealing at home, and a severe barring out of all illusion there.
Whatever games are played with us, we must play no games with ourselves,
but deal in our privacy with the last honesty and truth."[8] In marked
contrast, Whitman finds his doubts about identity and appearances
"curiously answered by my lovers, my dear friends" – with "he whom
I love [. . .] holding me by the hand," the poet becomes indifferent to the
unanswerable question of appearances, yet filled with "untold and untel-
lable wisdom" (LG60, 353).

Novalis had earlier pushed against Fichte's I = I with a simple revision,
"I = You," a change that underscores the difference between Whitman's
romanticism and Emerson's cautious idealism.[9] In his essay "Experience,"
Emerson maintains that, "Never can love make consciousness and ascription of equal force," that there "will be the same gulf between every me and
thee, as between the original and the picture."[10] Emerson's "great and
crescive self" preserves self-identity at the expense of phenomenal experience, even lovers: "Marriage (in what is called the spiritual world) is
impossible."[11] But in ways that presage Whitman's departure from

Emerson, Novalis argues that Fichte's I is itself already based upon what Emerson dismisses as secondary "ascription"; that is, I = I is hardly self-identical but a formulaic representation requiring an image or "picture" of oneself. "Has not Fichte too arbitrarily packed everything into the I?" Novalis asks: "Can an I posit itself as *I*, without another I or Not-I – How are I and Not-I opposable [?]"[12]

Whitman's answer is that the I and the Not-I are not opposable, but co-extensive and complementary aspects of an incommensurable, groundless absolute that offers no sure footing. Emerson's putative gulf between every me and thee is dissolved in *Leaves of Grass*. Whitman's poetry presents nominal oppositions, checks, and hierarchies only as opportunities to dismantle and resolve them into "the whole," the poet's term for what idealism generally calls the absolute. "If one becomes infatuated with the absolute and simply can't escape it," a fragment from Schlegel holds, "then the only way out is to contradict oneself continually and join opposite extremes together."[13] Whitman's free-wheeling aside – "Do I contradict myself? / Very well then . . . I contradict myself; / I am large . . . . I contain multitudes" – speaks in the spirit of Schlegel, as if from the impossible standpoint of the absolute itself (LG55, 55). Romantic poetry's ironic rejoinder to foundational aspirations of philosophy is to open every circuit, including the special case of transcendental self-identity, in favor of an infinite, free activity.

Walter Benjamin's influential thesis on early German romanticism observes that whereas in Fichte "the function of reflection [. . .] in intellectual intuition" is limited to a single, originary case that produces "the absolute 'I,'" with "romantic intuition an unbridled activity transforms the process by which the mind becomes the 'form of the form as its content' into an infinite form of reflection."[14] In early German romanticism, Fichte's "thinking of thinking," Benjamin argues, "turns into the thinking of thinking of thinking (and so forth)."[15] Romanticism "sublates being and positing in reflection [. . . and] expands without limit or check, and the thinking given form in reflection turns into formless thinking which directs itself upon the absolute."[16] The notion of art as subjectively "expressive" gives way in romantic reflection to the more modern notion of "art as a medium of reflection and of the work as a center of reflection."[17]

Leaves of Grass exemplifies the romantic notion of the work in its very self-concept, as an invitation to unchecked reflection above and before any philosophical ground it may hope to secure. It directs itself upon the whole as a vital activity, with no assurance of securing the subject against contradiction and illusion. "Whoever you are holding me now in hand," the poet warns, "The way is suspicious – the result slow, uncertain, may-be destructive; / You would have to give up all else – I alone would expect to be your God, sole and exclusive" (LG60, 345). Its very invitation an admonition to set the book down and depart, *Leaves of Grass* subordinates passive reading to the intersubjective, reflective activity of the work itself: "It is you talking just as much as myself . . . . I act as the tongue of you, / It was tied in your mouth . . . . in mine it begins to be loosened" (LG55, 53). From the perspective of theology or foundational philosophy such claims would be dogmatic, blasphemous, and authoritarian. But Whitman's provocations are not leads toward systemic or doctrinal certitude; they circle the paradox of the whole, which the I and you share on equal terms. Whitman's famous conceit, identifying his I with the manifold of possible experiences – "not a youngster is taken for larceny, but I go up too and am tried and sentenced" – is just as frequently modified by negative provocations toward further reflection: "You are also asking me questions, and I hear you; / I answer that I cannot answer . . . . you must find out for yourself" (LG55, 43, 52).

Beyond the mercurial persona of the early editions of *Leaves of Grass*, Whitman's unusual conception of his book as a new kind of bible illustrates the German romantics' idea of the work as a center of reflection upon the absolute. Among his surviving notebooks is an entry from 1857: "The Great Construction of the New Bible" (NUPM, 1:353). Presumed to be the poet's plan for the third edition of *Leaves of Grass*, this fragment and a related 1859 note, "'Leaves of Grass' – Bible of the New Religion"[18] echo a fragment from Novalis that Whitman would have encountered in Hedge's *Prose Writers of Germany*: "The history of every man should be a Bible."[19] The bible motif appeals to Novalis and Whitman in a decidedly undogmatic way, as an imagined redistribution of the absolute concept of *the* Bible – a book of books – upon *any* starting point, the life of any human being or any point within the whole, as a related note from Whitman indicates:

> There are that specialize a book, or some divine life, as the only revelation: – I too doubtless own it whatever it is to be a revelation, a part, but I see all else, all Nature, and each and all that to it appertains, the processes of time, all men, the universes, all likes and dislikes and developments, – a hundred, a thousand other Saviour[s?] and Mediators & Bibles – they too just as much revelations as any. (NUPM, 6:2085)

This sentiment would recur from the 1855 poem that becomes "A Song for Occupations" – "We consider the bibles and religions divine . . . . I do not say they are not divine, / I say they have all grown out of you and may grow out of you still, / It is not they who give the life .... it is you who give the life" (LG55, 60) – to the "realms of budding bibles" in "Passage to India" (LG, 418).

In pursuit of a form approaching the absolute vision of *Leaves of Grass*, Whitman had likewise intuited the broader conceptual energy of early German romanticism regarding a new, absolute genre. Novalis's notes for his "romantic encyclopedia" – a project cut short by his early death – point up the challenge of writing a synthetic, absolute book: "A Bible is the supreme task of writing."[20] Like Whitman afterward, Novalis would extend this task to his own project: "My book shall be a scientific Bible – a real and ideal model – and the seed of all books."[21] Schlegel had also arrived at this idea of writing a new bible: "Is there another word," he wonders, "to distinguish a common book from the idea of an infinite book as Bible, as a book per se, an absolute book?"[22] Just as all poems "are only one poem when correctly viewed," Schlegel suggests, "all books should be only one book."[23]

"Stop this day and night with me and you shall possess the origin of all poems," the poet announces early in "Song of Myself" (LG55, 14). The most arresting feature of the early editions of *Leaves of Grass* is a recurring, negative insistence that it is not simply another book of poems, nor even a book in the usual sense: "What you are holding is in reality no book, nor part of a book" (LG60, 242). Novalis observes that a "book can have very different sorts of interest. The author, the reader, a purpose, an incident, its mere individual existence can be the axis around which it turns."[24] That it presents itself alone is enough to "awaken activity," Novalis holds, modifying the language of Fichte to underscore the unbound representational character of self-positing in romanticism: "The I must posit itself as presenting. [. . .] There is a particular power of presenting – that merely presents for the sake of presenting – presenting in order to present is *free* presenting."[25] Anterior to its very contents, *Leaves of Grass* thus insists, "For it is not for what I have put into it that I have written this book, / Nor is it by reading it you will acquire it" (LG60, 346).

Whitman's ironical affirmation of his book against its merely discursive aspects extends to the very text and type of which it is comprised: "It is not what is printed or preached or discussed .... it eludes discussion and print, / It is not to be put in a book .... it is not in this book" (LG55, 59). In his meditations on early German romanticism, Maurice Blanchot foregrounds this conception of the book that presents only in order to present. The theory of the "absolute of the book" Blanchot attributes to the romantics, for whom the work isolates "a possibility that claims not to have originated in any other anteriority."[26] Whitman stages this possibility as an impossible subject – a physical book – awaiting the one who might take it up and thus activate it: "In libraries I lie as one dumb, a gawk, or unborn, or dead," he writes in the voice of the printed book. "But just possibly with you on a high hill," he invites the reader to "put your lips upon mine [... / ...] / Or, if you will, thrusting me beneath your clothing, / Where I may feel the throbs of your heart" (LG60, 345–46). The playful eroticism of this encounter, notably, does not even require reading; the mere existence of *Leaves of Grass*, anterior to its content, to author and reader, to I and you alike, is the sufficient axis upon which it turns: "these [leaves] seeking you [... / ...] realizing my poems, seeking me" (LG60, 378). The seeking alone, like the "perpetual transfers and promotions" that inhere in all materials, for reasons the poet can no more explain than can a reader, but only ever indicate, is the enigmatic activity of *Leaves of Grass* (LG55, 54).

"The Romantic genre of poetry is the only one which is more than a genre, and which is, as it were, poetry itself," Schlegel writes.[27] Its aim "is not merely to reunite all separate genres of poetry and to put poetry in touch with philosophy," but to "now mingle and now amalgamate poetry and prose."[28] Romantic poetry alone can "become a mirror of the entire surrounding world" and "soar, free from all real and ideal interests, on the wings of poetic reflection, midway between the work and the artist."[29] Finally, Schlegel contends, its "peculiar essence is that it is always becoming and that it can never be completed."[30] The Preface to the 1855 *Leaves of Grass* resonantly announces that the "greatest poem" is absolutely synthetic and infinite,

> for ages and ages in common and for all degrees and complexions and all departments and sects and for a woman as much as a man and a man as much as a woman. A great poem is no finish to a man or woman but rather a beginning. Has any one fancied he could sit at last under some due authority and rest satisfied with explanations and realize and be content and full? To no such terminus does the greatest poet bring ... he brings neither cessation or sheltered fatness and ease. (LG55, xi)

Notes

1. Walt Whitman, *Walt Whitman's Workshop: A Collection of Unpublished Manuscripts*, ed. Clifton Joseph Furness (New York, NY: Russell & Russell, 1964), 236.

2. Charles Wesley Grady, "A Conservative Transcendentalist: The Early Years (1805–1835) of Frederic Henry Hedge," *Studies in the American Renaissance* 7 (1983), 53, 61.

3. Friedrich Schlegel, *Philosophical Fragments*, trans. Peter Firchow (Minneapolis, MN: University of Minnesota Press, 1991), 24.

4. Johann Gottlieb Fichte, *Foundations of Transcendental Philosophy (Wissenschaftslehre) Nova Methodo (1796/99)*, trans. and ed. Daniel Breazeale (Ithaca, NY: Cornell University Press, 1992), 112.

5. Ralph Waldo Emerson, "Nature," in *The Collected Works of Ralph Waldo Emerson, Volume 1: Nature, Addresses, and Lectures*, ed. Robert E. Spiller (Cambridge, MA: The Belknap Press of Harvard University Press, 1971), 8.

6. "Walt Whitman and His Critics," *The Leader and Saturday Analyst*, June 30, 1860, 614–15, WWA.

7. Ralph Waldo Emerson, "Illusions," in *The Collected Works of Ralph Waldo Emerson: The Conduct of Life*, ed. Douglas Emory Wilson (Cambridge, MA: The Belknap Press of Harvard University Press, 2003), 170.

8. Ibid., 172.

9. Novalis, *Notes for a Romantic Encyclopedia*, trans. and ed. David W. Wood (Albany, NY: State University of New York Press, 2007), 151.

10. Ralph Waldo Emerson, "Experience," in *The Collected Works of Ralph Waldo Emerson: Essays: Second Series*, eds. Alfred R. Ferguson and Jean Ferguson Carr (Cambridge, MA: The Belknap Press of Harvard University Press, 1983), 44.

11. Ibid.

12. Novalis, *Fichte Studies*, ed. Jane Kneller (New York, NY: Cambridge University Press, 2003), 7.

13. Schlegel, *Philosophical Fragments*, 17.

14. Walter Benjamin, "The Concept of Criticism in German Romanticism," in *Walter Benjamin: Selected Writings, Volume 1: 1913–1926*, eds. Marcus Bullock and Michael W. Jennings (Cambridge, MA: The Belknap Press of Harvard University Press, 1996), 128–29.

15. Ibid.

16. Ibid.

17. Ibid., 156.

18. Walt Whitman, *Notes and Fragments Left by Walt Whitman*, ed. Richard Maurice Bucke (London, Ontario: A Talbot, 1899), 55.

19. Novalis, "From the Fragments," in *Prose Writers of Germany*, trans. Frederic H. Hedge (Philadelphia, PA: Carey and Hart, 1849), 496.

20. Novalis, *Notes for a Romantic Encyclopedia*, 67.

21. Ibid., 99.

22. Friedrich Schlegel, *Dialogue on Poetry and Literary Aphorisms*, trans. and eds. Ernst Behler and Roman Struc (University Park, PA: The Pennsylvania State University Press, 1968), 156–57.

23. Ibid.

24. Novalis, *Fichte Studies*, 181.

25. Ibid.

26. Maurice Blanchot, "The Absence of the Book," in *The Infinite Conversation*, trans. Susan Hanson (Minneapolis, MN: University of Minnesota Press, 1993), 423.

27. Schlegel, *Dialogue on Poetry and Literary Aphorisms*, 141.

28. Ibid., 140.

29. Ibid.

30. Ibid., 141.

CHAPTER 34

The Natural World

Christine Gerhardt

The natural world provides one of the most multifaceted contexts of Whitman's work, both in terms of the rich symbolic resonances nature held for many contemporaries and regarding the massive changes that characterized people's actual, physical relationships to the nonhuman environment. In Whitman's time, romanticism and transcendentalism were interested in nature as a symbol of moral and philosophical truths, yet they also sought to grasp America's physical geography; natural theology and natural history understood the universe as proof of God's grace while fostering the newly empirical natural sciences; and the political doctrine of nature's nation connected ideas of social progress to a ruthless practice of "civilizing the wilderness." What makes Whitman's work so deeply resonant with these many, often contradictory ideas and practices is that from the 1855 cover of *Leaves of Grass* to his "nature-notes" in *Specimen Days* (1882), and in poems as different as "This Compost" and "Song of the Redwood Tree," he was as interested in exploring nature's symbolic dimensions as he was in its vivid physical presence. This chapter focuses on the ways in which Whitman's poetry embraced plants and animals, places and planets, and geographical and geological phenomena not only as tropes but also as parts of interconnected, living systems, and how in doing so it responded to a range of nineteenth-century environmental discourses that marked the beginning of a modern ecological consciousness in the US. It is to a large extent by engaging these discourses that Whitman pushed beyond "nature poetry" in the romantic tradition and anticipated a modern ecopoetics: he explored the possibilities and limits of language to express nature's materiality and the complex interactions between creatures and their organic and inorganic surroundings – and he did so without categorically separating the human from the nonhuman, natural from built environments, or nature from culture.

Such a discussion of Whitman's promise to "permit to speak at every hazard, / Nature without check with original energy" (LG, 29) in the context of nineteenth-century environmental discourses owes much to current developments in ecocriticism and the environmental humanities more broadly, yet it also takes up earlier strands in literary scholarship. Even before the advent of environmentally oriented literary and cultural studies, critics acknowledged the thick presence of "the visible and solid earth" in Whitman's work (LG, 96), with naturalist John Burroughs as an important early advocate of reading his poetry with an eye to nature's physical reality. Yet after several decades of mostly symbolic interpretations, it took critics until the 1970s and 1980s to link Whitman's views of the nonhuman world directly to ideas about environmental reform, pre-Darwinian science, and concern over the destruction of forests and buffalo. At that time, however, Whitman was not yet considered a "green" author. It was with the emergence of ecocriticism in the 1990s – and approaches to Whitman soon ranging from environmental rhetoric and eco-formalism to animal studies, postcolonial, and material ecocriticism – that such contextual approaches acquired a new edge, turning the analysis of Whitman's connections with nineteenth-century attitudes toward the natural world into an important vantage point for reading his poetry in explicitly environmental terms.[1] Such newer work investigates his poetry and prose in terms of its ties to early evolutionary theories, health and sanitary reforms, Humboldt and Burroughs, nature essays and the proto-ecological sciences.[2] Most recently, contextual ecocritics have also begun to explore intersections between nineteenth-century environmental and other cultural discourses, such as sexuality and mobility, in Whitman's work. These approaches may well point toward future explorations of Whitman's ecopoetics as engagement with the intersections between nineteenth-century environmental discourses and more wide-ranging views of history and progress, spirituality and personhood.

Regarding the environmental discourses of his time, three areas are particularly relevant for Whitman's ecopoetics: the proto-ecological sciences, emerging conservationist arguments, and popular nature essays.[3] The nineteenth century saw a shift from natural history, whose holistic views of a diverse, divinely ordered universe already contained certain ecological ideas, toward a range of increasingly specialized new sciences, many of which are now understood as direct precursors of ecology. The towering transitional figure was Alexander von Humboldt, whose "physical geography" focused on the empirical study of mutually dependent natural communities, developing an ecological epistemology *avant la lettre*. His best-selling *Kosmos* (1845–62) impressed Whitman so deeply that he copied excerpts to his notebooks, read *The Letters of*

Humboldt, and gave the word "kosmos" a prominent place in his 1855 Preface and "Song of Myself."[4] In the wake of Humboldt's ideas, several new sciences began to explore the interplay between biotic and abiotic factors, anticipating the concepts of ecosystems and plant communities. Chemistry, for instance, explored plants' intricate mineral needs; botany investigated the relationships between floral distribution and environmental factors; and biogeography linked these factors further to topographical boundaries and climatic zones. Whitman was aware of these debates as well, attending public lectures, following discussions of the latest science books in newspapers and journals, and even reviewing key proto-ecological studies such as Justus Liebig's *Organic Chemistry* (1840). Eventually, Charles Darwin's *On the Origin of Species* (1859), which foregrounded turbulence and change in organisms' interactions with their niches, paved the way for Ernst Häckel in 1866 to define "ecology" as "the whole science of the relations of the organism to the surrounding exterior world." Whitman, familiar with earlier developmental theories, soon declared that "Leaves of Grass is *evolution*," embracing the most foundational shift toward scientific ecology into his work (WWC, 6:129).

The nineteenth century also saw a turn toward perspectives that emphasized human responsibilities vis-à-vis the nonhuman world and even recognized nature's intrinsic value, anticipating the principles of nature conservation and preservation. In the face of deforestation, overfishing, and pollution, advocates of utilitarian environmental reform expressed increasing concern, and George Perkins Marsh's widely read *Man and Nature; or, Physical Geography as Modified by Human Action* (1864) warned against nature's indiscriminate exploitation and expressed alarm over species extinction. While Marsh favored wiser scientific management, others, including Henry David Thoreau and John Muir, emphasized nature's aesthetic and spiritual value. Such calls for restraint and care led to the protection of the Yosemite Valley in 1864, and the establishment of national parks later in the century. Whitman, also a poet of technology and progress, lived in close proximity to these debates and responded to them not only when he explicitly warned that "the tree question will soon become a grave one [because] often useless destruction has prevail'd," and that "the cultivation and spread of forests may well be press'd upon thinkers who look to the coming generations," but also in his recurrent celebration of plants and animals as autonomous agents, valuable in their own right (PW, 1:222).

Finally, the era's environmental discourses were also significantly shaped by the natural history essays, which mediated between specialized scientific nomenclature and the perspectives of amateur naturalists. These essays

combined detailed accounts of local landscapes with narratives of increasing environmental attentiveness and conventional moral instruction with
new eco-ethical arguments. Most popular journals of the day carried
examples, including chapters from Thoreau's *The Maine Woods* (*Union
Magazine*, 1848; *Atlantic Monthly*, 1858) and *Cape Cod* (*Putnam's Magazine*,
1855; *Atlantic Monthly*, 1864) as well as texts by immensely prolific writers
like Wilson Flagg and Celia Thaxter. As such, nature essays were a driving
force in America's increasing environmental awareness. For Whitman –
who published in the same journals ("As I Ebb'd with the Ocean of Life" in
the *Atlantic Monthly* in 1860, and "Song of the Redwood-Tree" in *Harper's
Magazine* in 1874), heavily annotated Thoreau's *A Week on the Concord and
Merrimack Rivers* (1849), and exchanged ideas about nature writing with
John Burroughs – they formed a vital part of the cultural conversations in
which he so enthusiastically participated.

   Throughout his work, Whitman referred to plants, animals, land- and
seascapes in ways that absorbed and responded to these environmental
discourses in multifaceted ways. His reference to grass as a central anchor
for his entire poetic project provides a suggestive starting point. Right on
the cover of the 1855 *Leaves*, where the grass serves as a symbol for
democracy and a new organic poetry grounded in the earth, Whitman's
use of "leaves" rather than "blades" clearly draws from the science of
botany, whose interest in plants' physical features in conjunction with
their habitat marked an important step in the development of proto-
ecological paradigms (Reynolds, 241). Moreover, the earthy gestures of
the letters' roots and leaves, together with the embossed floral ornaments,
link the cover to the time's popular amateur herbaria, which combined
Victorian notions of modesty with an ethics of detailed attention and
a literalized natural aesthetic; the 1855 and 1856 covers together further
resemble *Stray Leaves from the Book of Nature* (1855) by naturalist
Maximilian Schere De Vere.[5] As such, the cover anticipates a poetry that
takes up but also undermines the white middle-class "language of flowers,"
embraces the inherent mysticism of organicism as much as new scientific
models, and champions nature's materiality as much as its ineffability.

   In section 6 of "Song of Myself," the long answer to a child's question
"*What is the grass?*" carries similar eco-contextual reverberations (LG, 33).
The speaker looks at the grass as "flag" of his "disposition," which combines national allusions with a common botanical name for the calamus
grass, sweet flag. He then "guesses" that grass is "itself a child, the produced
babe of the vegetation," suggesting an ethics of care toward small life-forms
that resembles perspectives expressed in nature essays by Thoreau and

Susan Cooper. This guess also links vegetation to familial and "production" structures, echoing ideas about "nature's economy" that informed Haeckel's definition of ecology. Later, he ponders the grass's presence in "broad zones and narrow zones," evoking Humboldt's language of botanical geography, which studied climatic zones in relation to vegetation and human cultures; the section ends with a meditation on the grass "of graves" that links the ideal of organic language to mystical as well as chemical notions of decomposing (LG, 33–34). Yet instead of offering a definite answer, the list of potential answers, culminating in a scene of common death, undermines the notion of knowing nature and contributes to the section's overall stance of environmental humility, which already emerged from its passionate attention to a habitually overlooked plant.[6]

This nodal passage also points forward to "This Compost," another major moment in which Whitman's evocation of "the grass of spring," "herbs, roots, orchards, grain" crystallizes aspects of his contextual green poetics (LG, 368). Originally titled "Poem of Wonder at The Resurrection of The Wheat" (1856), it combines a religious sense of wonder vis-à-vis nature's annual rebirth with new ideas about the decomposition and recycling of organic matter. Indeed, the speaker not simply exclaims "What Chemistry!" but adopts the outlook of a science that was as crucial for the time's environmental reform as it was for the twentieth-century understanding of food chains and energy flows. Moreover, the poem is eco-ethically remarkable because, despite its enthusiastic response to recent scientific developments, it avoids gestures of epistemological control. Instead, its questions and tentative observations enact a sense of unassuming astonishment and awe. Along similar lines, its subtle echoes of environmental concern – especially in the observation that the Earth "gives such divine materials to men, and accepts such leavings from them at last" – take up some of the increasing moral urgency expressed in the nineteenth century's reform arguments without, however, formulating a prescriptive or normative stance (LG, 370). "This Compost" has also been linked to Thoreau's *Walden* (LG, 368–69n) and the negative environmental effects of New York's dense living conditions, which further highlights the poem's connections to contemporary environmental discourses, even as it ponders questions of mortality and regeneration, spirituality and cosmic purpose.[7] As such, Whitman's many reflections on the "grass and white and red morning-glories, and white and red clover" (LG, 364) combined suggest a scientifically grounded poetics of environmental attentiveness that sidesteps notions of human mastery, thus continually pushing against his poetry's parallel investment in viewing nature as a resource for individual and national growth. This ecologically resonant attentiveness to often-inconspicuous plants and vegetation is not in conflict but fully in tune with his equally powerful concern with human spiritual existence. When he writes in the "*What is the grass?*" section that "The smallest sprout shows there is really no death, / And if ever there was it led forward life, and does not wait at the end to arrest it / [. . .] / All goes onward and outward, nothing collapses" (LG, 34–35), or in "This Compost" that he is "terrified at the Earth, it is that calm and patient, / It grows such sweet things out of such corruptions, / It turns harmless and stainless on its axis, with such endless successions of diseas'd corpses" (LG, 369), the grander questions of life and death integrate such grassy moments into an eco-cultural imagination of ultimately cosmic proportions.

Whitman's references to animals similarly condense key aspects of his ecopoetics by way of their contextual resonances. Apart from enigmatic moments in which his speaker finds that "the cow crunching with depress'd head surpasses any statue, / And a mouse is miracle enough to stagger sextillions of infidels," or thinks he "could turn and live with animals, they are so placid and self-contain'd" (LG, 60), some of his most environmentally noteworthy evocations of animals revolve around birds. In particular, "Out of the Cradle Endlessly Rocking" (1859) has long been noted for its sensitivity to the birds' existence as birds, yet this quality attains fresh meaning when placed in the context of emerging environmental discourses.[8] The poem's keen attention to a pair of "dusky" birds "in some briers" on Long Island's "gray beach," to their movements, "their nest, and four light-green eggs spotted with brown" (LG, 248), combines ornithological and geographical detail in ways that resonate with contemporary efforts to study birds in direct relation to habitat conditions, as for example in Philip Lutley Sclater's ornithological publications or in popular amateur bird guides. Whitman's insistence that these mockingbirds are "guests from Alabama" is of particular ecological relevance because mockingbirds were once a Southern species whose range extension northward was discussed, precisely around mid-century, in terms of changing climatic conditions, agricultural practices, and an excessive songbird trade; at the same time, the attention to the fate of two stray birds also resonates with Darwin's (ornithology-based) theories of species' dynamic connections to place, published the same year as "Out of the Cradle." While Whitman's poem is far from expressing direct environmental concern here, it participates in these changing perceptions of nonhuman creatures in their fragile, often precarious conditions. The speaker's desire to understand birdsong also harks back to some of the modes used in popular nature essays, including their anthropomorphism, but eschews these essays' frequent didacticism and moral righteousness – also and especially because in the poem, "death" as nature's ultimate answer can only remain unfathomable, despite the boy-poet's repeated claims to exclusive understanding. As such, it is not only his careful attention to detail, and various gestures of minimizing actual and conceptual domination, but also the acknowledgement of death in nature, and the universe, that enables an ecopoetics that is informed by nineteenth-century environmental discourses while pointing far beyond them.

Another major Whitman poem, "When Lilacs Last in the Dooryard Bloom'd" (1865), further highlights these junctures between his animal imaginary and emerging green discourses. As it zooms in on a hermit thrush singing in a secluded realm among "fragrant cedars" and "ghostly pines" (LG, 334), the poem echoes the growing interest in wetlands as ecologically significant places expressed in Thoreau's 1862 essay "Walking" and Marsh's *Man and Nature* (1864).[9] Moreover, at a time when notions about animals as objects of ethical consideration were only just emerging, the focus on the bird's and poet's voices "tallying" one another takes the interest in such avian encounters further toward a moment of mutual creaturely empathy. Perhaps most importantly, the presence of death again intensifies these contextual environmentalist resonances. As a Lincoln elegy and post-Civil War poem, "Lilacs" deals with death on a much larger scale than "Cradle," and the bird's and speaker's acceptance of death, which does not lead to any sense of closure, further de-emphasizes potential notions of interpretive control.[10] It is this relative de-centering of human agency that turns such transformative interspecies encounters into crucial moments for the development of a new ecopoetics, whose eco-sensitivity is inseparable from its sensitivity to death and mortality.

Finally, Whitman's poetic commitment to actual places, to land- and seascapes as well as built environments, forms another axis of his multifaceted relationship with his culture's changing views of the non-human world. More than a poet of flora and fauna, Whitman was a poet of places – of Northeastern seashores and Manhattan, Western prairies, and the entire globe.[11] Among the many poems indicative of his intense, and intensely contextual, place imagination "As I Ebb'd with the Ocean of Life" (1860) holds a prominent position. Already its very turn to the sea, intent upon understanding the meaning of life, repeats a move performed by proto-ecological scientists of the day and indirectly echoes the impulse behind Darwin's voyage with the Beagle, Edward Forbes' research on oceanic fauna, and dozens of studies on marine geographies reviewed in contemporary journals. Moreover, Whitman's attention to topography and the ocean's autonomous agency mixes description, narration, and meditation much like numerous nature essays did, including Thoreau's *Cape Cod*, whose first chapters were published in *Putnam's Monthly* in 1855. Indeed, the poem's ending in which the speaker resigns himself to the waves, imagining his own death, is reminiscent of *Cape Cod*'s opening with its harrowing scene of a beach strewn with shipwrecked bodies. Yet in "Cradle," it is the poet's own death that marks both an end – after the sea has pushed him to identify himself with "a little wash'd-up drift," and to doubt his "arrogant poems" (LG, 254) – and the beginning of a transformed poetry that forever emerges from this intensely humbling experience.[12] Embracing death's continuing presence while being deeply concerned with the materiality of the body and the sources and direction of the soul, this poem of place constitutes one of Whitman's most remarkable expressions of an environmentally oriented ethics and poetics.

Yet Whitman's interest in place went beyond the intricate workings of local natural landscapes, and people's long-term ties to places of home. It encompasses urban realms, people's mobile relationships to place, as well as global place perspectives that include imperial gestures, making his work particularly relevant to current debates in the environmental humanities and beyond. For instance, "Crossing Brooklyn Ferry" (1856) is both an urban poem and a poem of mobility, and yet deeply resonant with an environmentally sensitive place imagination, which is again highlighted by its contextual references. Its meditation on the meanings of a tidal river crisscrossed by ferries, whose integrity is threatened but also defined by these interlocking dynamics, corresponds with contemporary tensions between utilitarian and preservationist environmental perspectives, between views of mobile human-nature relationships as part of the problem and part of the solution, and even between environmental and immigration politics. From a twenty-first-century ecocritical perspective, part of the poem's achievement lies in its evocation of mobility as integral to a modern sense of place, and in the suggestion that this may lie at the heart of how people are connected across history and place. In such a framework, even poems whose green undertones are genuinely complicated by Whitman's celebration of geographical movements that are linked to colonial power mechanisms, from "Passage to India" (1871) to "Song of the Redwood Tree" (1873), engage a range of geographically distinct places across the globe, in ways that absorb some of the time's conflicted attitudes vis-à-vis the earth and challenge them, if only by facing their excesses.

Overall, Whitman's commitment to the natural world was significantly informed by environmental discourses that were part of the culture he so fervently sought to absorb. Written at a decisive moment in the development of a modern ecological awareness, his poems responded to key ideas that were negotiated in the era's proto-ecological sciences, in debates about environmental reform and conservation, and popular nature writings. Yet whenever Whitman's poetry intersects with these discourses, it also clearly remains distinct from them. When he turned his attention to the flora, fauna, land- and seascapes that his contemporaries were beginning to understand as interdependent, fragile, and valuable in their own right, he did so by way of a differentiated ecopoetics of attentiveness, and even care, that sidesteps claims to nature's knowability and expressions of a normative ethics. Instead, he devised highly nuanced modes of expression that foreground experiential as well as relational aspects of human-nature interactions, decenter the human speaker, and face the alterity and ineffability of the non-human world – often by linking these concerns to meditations about death, mortality, language, and the meaning of (human) existence. From such a perspective, Whitman's own dictum that "The land and sea, the animals fishes and birds, the sky of heaven and the orbs, the forests mountains and rivers are not small themes . . . but folks expect of the poet to indicate more than the beauty and dignity which always attach to dumb real objects . . . . they expect him to indicate the path between reality and their souls" does not reject but fully embrace nature's materiality and its ethical dimensions, while integrating them in the largest possible individual and spiritual realms – which in itself constitutes a crucial eco-poetical move (LG55, v).

Notes

1. M. Jimmie Killingsworth, *Walt Whitman and the Earth: A Study in Ecopoetics* (Iowa City, IA: University of Iowa Press, 2004); Angus Fletcher, *A New Theory for American Poetry: Democracy, the Environment, and the Future of Imagination* (Cambridge, MA: Harvard University Press, 2004); M. Jimmie Killingsworth, "'As if the beasts spoke': The Animal/Animist/Animated Walt Whitman," *Walt Whitman Quarterly Review* 28 (Summer/Fall 2010), 19–35; Thomas C. Gannon, "Complaints from the Spotted Hawk: Flights and Feathers in Whitman's 1855 *Leaves of Grass*," in *Leaves of Grass: The Sesquicentennial Essays*, eds. Susan Belasco, Ed Folsom, and Kenneth M. Price (Lincoln, NE: University of Nebraska Press, 2007), 141–75; Aaron Moe, *Zoopoetics: Animals and the Making of Poetry* (Lanham, MD: Lexington, 2014); George Handley, *New World Poetics: Nature and the Adamic Imagination of Whitman, Neruda, and Walcott* (Athens, GA: University of Georgia Press, 2007); Jane Bennett, "Of Material Sympathies, Paracelsus, and Whitman," in *Material Ecocriticism*, eds. Serenella Iovino and Serpil Opperman (Bloomington, IN: Indiana University Press, 2014), 239–52.

2. For such contextual ecocritical readings, see Eric Wilson, *Romantic Turbulence: Chaos, Ecology, and American Space* (New York, NY: St. Martin's, 2000); Jim Warren, "Contexts for Reading 'Song of the Redwood-Tree,'" in *Reading under the Sign of Nature: New Essays in Ecocriticism*, eds. John Tallmadge and Henry Harrington (Salt Lake City, UT: University of Utah Press, 2000), 165–78; Daniel Philippon, "'I Only Seek to Put You in Rapport': Message and Method in Walt Whitman's *Specimen Days*," in *Reading the Earth: New Directions in the Study of Literature and Environment*, eds. Michael P. Branch et al. (Moscow, ID: University of Idaho Press, 1998), 179–93; Maria Farland, "Decomposing City: Walt Whitman's New York and the Science of Life and Death," *ELH* 74.4 (Winter 2007), 799–827; Laura Dassow Walls, *The Passage to Cosmos: Alexander Von Humboldt and the Shaping of America* (Chicago, IL: University of Chicago Press, 2009); Jim Warren, "Whitman Land: John Burroughs's Pastoral Criticism," *Isle* 8.1 (2001), 83–96; Christine Gerhardt, *A Place for Humility: Whitman, Dickinson, and the Natural World* (Iowa City, IA: University of Iowa Press, 2014).

3. For a more extended discussion of these nineteenth-century environmental discourses, see Gerhardt, *A Place for Humility*, esp. 27–29, 87–91, 144–49, 190–94.

4. Bruce Piasecki, "American Literary Environmentalism before Darwin," in *Teaching Environmental Literature: Materials, Methods, Resources*, ed. Frederick O. Waage (New York, NY: Modern Language Association of America, 1985), 13.

5. Cf. Christine Gerhardt, "'Earth Adhering to Their Roots': Dickinson, Whitman, and the Ecology of Bookmaking," in *American Studies as Media Studies*, eds. Frank Kelleter and Daniel Stein (Heidelberg: Winter, 2008), 37–46; Stefan Schöberlein, "The Ever-Changing Nature of the Sea: Whitman's Absorption of Maximilian Schele De Vere," *Walt Whitman Quarterly* 30.2 (2013), 55–77.

6. Gerhardt, *Place for Humility*, 61–66.

7. Farland, "Decomposing City," 803.

8. Cf. Christine Gerhardt, "'We must travel abreast with Nature, if we want to understand her': Place and Mobility in Dickinson's and Whitman's Environmental Poetry," in *Whitman and Dickinson: A Colloquy*, eds. Eric Athenot and Cristanne Miller (Iowa City, IA: University of Iowa Press, 2017), 111–28; Jonathan Rosen's *The Life of the Skies: Birding at the End of Nature* (New York, NY: Picador, 2008) also points in such a direction by linking the poem to John Audubon's paintings and Charles Darwin's evolutionary biology, and by discussing Burroughs's reading of the poem (58–70).

9. Killingsworth, *Walt Whitman and the Earth*, 116.

10. Gerhardt, *Place for Humility*, 130–35.

11. For Whitman as shore and island poet, see Killingsworth, *Whitman and the Earth*, esp. 98–131; for Whitman's place imagination from the micro to the global scale, see Gerhardt, *Place for Humility*.

12. Gerhardt, *Place for Humility*, 125–30.

CHAPTER 35

Science and Medicine

Lindsay Tuggle

In the Preface to the first edition of *Leaves of Grass*, Whitman cast scientists as "the lawgivers of poets" (LG55, vii). In tandem with his belief in the cellular unification of body and soul, Whitman saw science and poetry as symbiotically connected.[1] Toward the close of his life, Whitman reflected on his fascination with medicine, musing that he might have been a doctor had he not become a poet: "widely opposite as science and the emotional elements are, they might be joined in the medical profession, and there would be great opportunities for developing them. Nowhere is there such a call for them."[2] Despite seemingly oppositional forces, Whitman suggests that the medical field could advance "the emotional elements" alongside scientific objectivity. The aspiration to merge science and sensation influenced Whitman throughout his career. From the first to the final "deathbed" editions of *Leaves of Grass*, Whitman sought to unify scientific detachment and poetic empathy. During the Civil War, the "spiritual" yet "disinterested" specimen-soldier emerged as the embodiment of Whitman's union of science with spirit.[3]

Whitman's convalescent soldiers are often described as "specimens," a term that captures the poet's impulses toward scientific collection, erotic voyeurism, and reverential attachment. The Latin root, *specere*, means "to look or behold."[4] In *Specimen Days* (1882), Whitman charts the "eternal tendency" that swept through the century – an unrelenting drive to "preserve" that underlies "all Nature." In this "wayward, spontaneous, fragmentary book," the poet curates "specimen interiors" of a "strange, unloosen'd, wondrous" time (PW, 1:3). Specimen collection was more than a pastime in nineteenth-century America – it was a widespread cultural obsession. Amateur and professional naturalists and anatomists alike were possessed by the fervor.[5]

Writing from the vantage of a war that was both an unprecedented medical tragedy and a catalyst for numerous scientific discoveries, Whitman articulates the pre- and postmortem experiences of soldiers through a lens and a language that is reverential, rather than diagnostic. Whitman's "specimens cases" exist in a class distinct from their comrades. *Memoranda During the War* (1875–76) documents unique categories of "beings," influenced by Darwinian theories.[6] *On the Origin of Species* was published in 1859, one year prior to the third edition of *Leaves of Grass* (1860), in which the term "specimen" first appeared. Whitman had become intimately familiar with evolution by the time *Specimen Days* was published in 1882. He described Darwin and "the tenets of the evolutionists" as "unspeakably precious" (PW, 1:260). Whitman framed Darwin's significance to science in terms similar to his depiction of himself as the poetic incarnation of America: "Darwin is to me science incarnate" (WWC, 8:454). In *Specimen Days*, Whitman discussed the relationship between "Darwin's evolution" and "creation's incessant unrest," illuminating the cyclical and cellular correlations between "growth," "existence," and "decay" (PW, 1:289). Whitman's conception of his own infinite attachment to specimens foreshadows his enduring fidelity to Civil War soldiers, as much as it recalls the continuity of evolution: "Let others finish specimens – I never finish specimens, / I shower them by exhaustless laws, as nature does, fresh and modern continually" (LG60, 373). In his mind, evolution became synonymous with progress: democratic, ecological, and literary. Speaking to Horace Traubel in 1889, the poet described the morphology of his work as an embodiment of Darwin's theory: "Leaves of Grass is *evolution* – evolution in its most varied, freest, largest sense" (WWC, 6:129).

Whitman sought to salvage the Civil War's "human fragments" – to textually preserve the "animal purity" of their broken bodies. Volunteering in the hospitals, he began to document certain "unworldly" specimens, set apart by "a strange spiritual sweetness":

> Every now and then in Hospital or Camp, there are beings I meet – specimens of unworldliness, disinterestedness and animal purity and heroism – [. . . and] the power of a strange, spiritual sweetness, fibre and inward health have also attended.[7]

The poet appropriates medical rhetoric to catalog these "odd" specimens, but he employs these scientific tools to very different ends. Portraying dying soldiers as the Union's "blood" and "marrow," Whitman renders these men as corporeal matter trapped within a national wound.[8] The medical gaze and the mourner's last look merge in Whitman's eyes. The specimen-soldier inhabits the threshold between science and sentiment, the historical moment when the human cadaver was both lost love object and subject of anatomical violence.[9]

Throughout the nineteenth century, when anatomical specimens were in high demand but notoriously difficult to acquire, a black market trafficked in human remains. Expanding medical schools exhausted cadaver supplies, forcing anatomists to undertake drastic measures.[10] Body snatching, also known as medical resurrection, was rampant in antebellum America. While vehemently opposing body snatching, Whitman recognized the medical advancements that anatomy promised (NUPM, 6:2123). He was able to divorce resurrectionism from the science underpinning the market for stolen bodies. He included anatomists alongside astronomers, chemists, mathematicians, and phrenologists as forebears of "the sinewy races of bards" whose "construction underlies the structure of every perfect poem" (LG55, vii). In "I Sing the Body Electric," Whitman unites the "skin trades" of anatomy and slavery to catalog the evolutionary "wonders" of the human form:[11]

> Gentlemen look on this curious creature,
> Whatever the bids of the bidders they cannot be high enough for him,
> For him the globe lay preparing quintillions of years without one animal
> or plant,
> For him the revolving cycles truly and steadily rolled.
> [. . .]
> Examine these limbs, red black or white . . . . they are very cunning in
> tendon and nerve;
> They shall be script that you may see them.
> [. . .]
> Within there runs his blood . . . . the same old blood . . the same red
> running blood.
> (LG55, 80–81)

The slave's body is articulated to reveal "wonders within." The limbs are "stript" so that the reader can admire their "cunning tendons." Paradoxically, Whitman's poetic dissection seeks to restore human value by cataloging the inherent *sameness* of internal organs and "exquisite senses." Blood runs red beneath the skin of "red black or white" bodies. Yet this anatomical demonstration exists within a flawed economy of racial hierarchy. Whatever price is paid for this "curious creature" will never be "high enough" to compensate for the "revolving cycles" of evolutionary time that created him. At the poem's close, the structural hypocrisy of antebellum America's body-snatching phobia is rendered in black and white: juxtaposing the atrocities of slavery and the posthumous violence of dissection, Whitman insists that those who "degrade" "living human[s]" are as damned as those who "defile" the dead: "Who degrades or defiles the living human body is cursed, / Who degrades or defiles the body of the dead is not more cursed" (LG55, 82). Anatomical symmetry reveals our shared humanity. Regardless of race, all blood runs red, all organs are equally "lifelit."[12]

During the Civil War, the chronic shortage of cadavers available for dissection was suspended. Seemingly overnight, battlefield carnage transformed human bodies from rare commodities into abundant specimens. Army surgeons undertook the unprecedented, large-scale collection of bodies for medical instruction and public exhibition. Thousands flocked to view these human remnants, displayed at the new Army Medical Museum in Washington. In the aftermath of the Battle of Fredericksburg, as Whitman reunited with his soldier brother George, the museum's curator John H. Brinton scavenged the field hospital's medical waste in search of specimens. Whitman was immediately confronted by the medical detritus of war: "human fragments, cut, bloody, black and blue, swelled and sickening – in the garden near, a row of graves" (NUPM, 2:504–05). Surgeons operating inside the temporary hospital at Lacy House tossed severed limbs from windows bordering the makeshift operating tables. The "rejected members" landed at the base of a tree below. Brinton may have sifted through the same pile in his quest "to preserve for the Museum" the "mutilated limbs" that, without his intervention, "were usually buried in heaps."[13]

Despite his horror at the conditions inside Lacy House, Whitman resisted the temptation to sentimentalize what was in effect the necessary disposal of medical waste in a war triage setting: "The large mansion is quite crowded, upstairs and down, everything impromptu, no system, all bad enough, but I have no doubt the best that can be done; all the wounds pretty bad, some frightful, the men in their old clothes, unclean and bloody."[14] Brinton was far more scathing in his indictment of the unsanitary conditions in field hospitals: "I found bloodstained footmarks on the crooked stairs, and in the second story room [. . .] amputated arms and legs seemed almost to litter the floor; beneath the operating table was a pool of blood, the operator was smeared with it and the surroundings were ghastly beyond all limits of surgical propriety."[15] Medical practices that existed within the boundaries of "surgical propriety" were often equally "ghastly." Herein lies the catastrophic irony unique to the Civil War: this conflict was fought with new and lethally effective weapons such as the Minié ball, yet before the discovery of sepsis.[16] Soldiers suffered and died in unprecedented numbers because medical discoveries on how to heal the wounded body lagged behind technological innovations on how best to kill and maim. In the era prior to germ theory, the cure was often as deadly as the cause.

When he departed Falmouth on December 28, 1862, Whitman accompanied a convoy of wounded soldiers bound for Washington. While Brinton filled the Museum's cabinets with specimens collected from the Washington hospitals, Whitman established residency in the nation's capital as a "self-appointed Soldier's missionary," tending, by his own estimation, "80,000 to 100,000 of the wounded and sick, as sustainer of spirit and body."[17] Whitman constantly documented his hospital work: "I kept little note-books. [. . .] In these I brief'd cases, persons, sights, occurrences in camp, by the bedside, and not seldom by the corpses of the dead."[18] He revised the notebooks as *Memoranda During the War*, which was later absorbed, almost entirely, into *Specimen Days*. He hoped that *Memoranda* would "furnish a few stray glimpses into that life, and into those lurid interiors, never to be fully convey'd to the future."[19]

Elsewhere in Washington, another "lurid interior" was blooming. The Army Medical Museum's growing popularity echoed the unionist ideology that decay of the wounded democratic body could be arrested, that amputation of the secessionist states was not the only option. Skeletal remains from at least four soldiers featured in Whitman's *Memoranda* became artifacts in the Army Medical Museum: Oscar Cunningham, John Mahay, Oscar F. Wilber, and Frank H. Irwin.[20] As Brinton's specimens they are medical and military relics, reconfigured within the museum to demonstrate the enduring coherence of the Union. Whitman narrates his own unsevered attachments to the specimen-soldiers' absent bodies and abandoned parts.

In January 1864, Whitman witnessed the amputation of Lewis Brown's left leg. The young private was shot on August 21, 1862. The wound remained unhealed after sixteen months at Armory Square Hospital, where Brown and Whitman became intimate friends. Whitman watched from the doorway as Brown's leg was severed, recording the scene in his notebook: "Lewy came out of the influence of the ether," he wrote. "I could hear his cries sometimes quite loud, & half-coherent talk & cought [*sic*] glimpses of him through the open door. [. . .] His face was very pale, his eyes dull. [. . .] He remained very sick, opprest for breath, with deathly feeling" (NUPM, 2:669). In the following days, Whitman was never far from his bedside, sleeping on the adjoining cot, and documenting the neurological aftermath: "As usual in such cases [Lewy] could feel the lost foot & leg very plainly. The toes would get twisted, & not possible to disentangle them" (NUPM, 2:669). Whitman's characterization of Lewy's ghostly contractions as "usual" is a remarkable testament to his powers of observation. At the time of his writing, "phantom limb" did not yet exist as a medical phenomenon. The diagnostic term was coined by Whitman's friend and physician Silas Weir Mitchell, in an 1871 article detailing the first modern medical account of this "sensory ghost."[21] Whitman's hospital notebooks document the neural legacies of other amputations, such as the case history of "Thos. H. B. Geiger, co. B 53d Penn wounded at Fredericksburg – [...] young bright handsome Penn. boy – tells me that for some time after his hand was off – he could yet feel it – could feel the fingers open and shut" (NUPM, 2:606). In "The Wound-Dresser" Whitman describes the trauma of dismemberment:

> From the stump of the arm, the amputated hand,
> I undo the clotted lint, remove the slough, wash off the matter and blood,
> Back on his pillow the soldier bends with curv'd neck, and side-falling head,
> His eyes are closed, his face is pale, he dares not look on the bloody stump,
> And has not yet look'd on it. (LG, 310–11)

As the "dresser" removes his bandages, the soldier turns away, unable to look at what remains of his arm. The poet's gaze allows the reader to glimpse a wound so visceral that it remains unseen, foreshadowing Mitchell's description of amputees "haunted by a constant or inconstant fractional phantom of so much of himself as has been lopped away – an unseen ghost of the lost part."[22]

While the war shattered Whitman's beloved Union, its soldiers embodied his "Calamus" ideal of "the manly love of comrades" (LG, 117). The calamus plant was traditionally used as a naturopathic salve for "slowly healing wounds."[23] The poet applies his "reciprocal love" as an "adhesive" balm to soothe the burning pains of inflamed wounds (NUPM, 2:878). "The fractur'd thigh, the knee, the wound in the abdomen, / These and more I dress with impassive hand, (yet deep in my breast a fire, a burning flame" (LG, 311).

The "burning flame" in Whitman's breast recalls two other mysterious medical conditions that originated at Turner's Lane Hospital, where Mitchell first observed phantom limbs. Causalgia, also discovered by Mitchell, refers to a "burning pain" caused by a peripheral nerve injury. This pain was so severe that Mitchell recalled, "We have again and again been urged by patients to amputate the suffering limb."[24] The phenomenon known as "soldier's heart" was given its name by

Jacob Mendes Da Costa, who supervised the ward adjacent to Mitchell's, where he documented enigmatic cardiac disturbances.[25] Symptoms of "soldier's heart" included cardiac pain, palpitations, shortness of breath, sleep disruptions, and digestive complaints. Da Costa and his colleagues searched in vain for a physical cause that could explain their patients' suffering.[26] Whitman described the dichotomy between physical wounding and heartache in an earlier notebook: "You break your arm, and a good surgeon sets it and cures it complete; but no cure ever avails for an organic disease of the heart" (NUPM, 1:125). Reminiscent of the poet's incurable "burning heart," the phantom limb manifests as a physical presence felt most acutely in its absence. Like the ghostly pains of the amputee, Whitman inevitably returns, "in dreams' projections," to the hospital corridors (LG, 311). The presence of phantasmal soldiers throughout his postbellum poetry attests to the uncanny allure of the war's "rejected members" and their perpetually open wounds.[27]

In stark contrast to the fertile decay that characterizes antebellum editions, in the war's aftermath Whitman sought to preserve "all dead soldiers" within *Leaves of Grass*, "Embalm'd with love in this twilight song" (LG, 529, 549). In "Ashes of Soldiers," Whitman appropriates embalming technology to achieve what was formerly nature's sacred work: the "last chemistry" that banishes decomposition.

> Perfume therefore my chant, O love, immortal love,
> Give me to bathe the memories of all dead soldiers,
> Shroud them, embalm them, cover them all over with tender pride.
>
> (LG, 492)

Whitman's desire to "perfume" the dead echoes the era's medical fears of miasmatic contagion, a hygienic risk that embalmers endeavored to eradicate. In the years prior to Lincoln's assassination, embalmers claimed to have perfected the art of turning flesh to stone. Reminiscent of body snatchers, embalmers honed their skills on the corpses of soldiers stolen from battlefields.[28] Embalming appealed to sentimental as well as hygienic concerns, offering a practical method for the repatriation of fallen soldiers, and, eventually, for Abraham Lincoln.

Whitman's elegy for Lincoln, "When Lilacs Last in the Door-Yard Bloom'd," mourns a martyr unaltered by death. Although the funeral train passes through "endless grass," antebellum scenes of regenerative decay have vanished.[29] Lincoln's "sacred" body is not ecologically absorbed but encrypted within a "burial-house."[30] A practical explanation exists for this erasure of decomposition: the president's corpse was never meant to decay. Lincoln's embalmed corpse assumed what observers described as a "statuesque, marblelike appearance."[31] The "sacred preserv[ation]" of the presidential body symbolically erased the "lingering wounds" that troubled the post-war Union.[32] Blood relics saved by the surgeons who autopsied the president found their way to the Army Medical Museum, which was relocated to Ford's Theatre. Whitman predicted that the president's assassination would "incise" a lasting scar upon American history: "When, centuries hence, [. . .] the leading historians and dramatists seek for some personage, some special event, incisive enough to mark with deepest cut, and mnemonize this turbulent Nineteenth century [. . .], those historians will seek in vain for any point to serve more thoroughly their purpose, than Abraham Lincoln's death" (PW, 2:509). The cultural sensation of Lincoln's autopsy may have influenced Whitman's decision to allow his own cadaver to be dissected (WWC, 9:603–04). In the end, the "poet of the Body" chose to "bequeath" his corpse not to the grass he loved, but to science (LG, 48, 89).

Whitman died on March 26, 1892, less than a year after the final edition of *Leaves of Grass* was published. The cause of death was bronchial pneumonia, the final complication of tuberculosis contracted in the Civil War hospitals (Loving, 479). The *New York Mirror* memorialized the poet as a "magnificent specimen" whose "extraordinary vitality" was compromised by his war service:

> Whitman contracted hospital malaria and was never himself again. [. . .] Whitman was forty-two years old when he went into camp and hospital to nurse soldiers. He was a magnificent specimen of manhood physically, a perfect picture of strength and natural grace.[33]

This passage echoes Whitman's perception of the origins of his illness: "I suppose I should have been free of all of this today," he wrote, "if in those last years [I would have] avoided the hospitals [. . .]: but here I am, sick, nearly gone, and I do not regret what I did" (quoted in Loving, 461). Whitman considered his health a worthy sacrifice for the "noble specimens" who became integral to his life's work (WWC, 3:581–82).

During his twilight years, Whitman attracted a devoted cohort of disciples, enthralled by his famous "personal magnetism."[34] One man in particular was ever-present. Beginning in March 1888, Horace Traubel served as Whitman's constant companion, keeping meticulous records detailing the poet's life and letters. Traubel's account of Whitman's autopsy is a climactic moment in the collision of scientific and sentimental practices upon the body. The disciple elegiacally captures the convergence of mourning and medicine, as the scalpel opens Whitman's body to yield "unexpected fruits" (WWC, 9:604–05). Traubel's inventory of Whitman's organs bestows adoration on each part, recalling Whitman's empathic devotion to soldiers' severed limbs. Prior to the autopsy, Traubel marvels at the "strange beauty" of Whitman's corpse, "stretched out on god's own altar" (Corr., 1:127–29). This "anatomical benediction" does not end at the body's surface, the disciple's adoration pierces the skin to worship blood and bone.

The postmortem was conducted between 6:10 p.m. and 10:00 p.m. in the rear parlor of the poet's home. Whitman's physician, Alexander McAllister, and colleagues Daniel Longakre and Henry Cattell performed the autopsy, which had been postponed due to George Whitman's objections. In spite of the surgical violence inflicted upon the body that aroused in him so much devotion, Traubel was compelled to bear witness:

> To hear the claw and dip of the instruments – to see the skull broken and opened and the body given the ravening prey of the investigator had its horrors – then its compensations. I looked beyond and saw science, man, with benediction sweet. [. . .] Somehow I could not have gone home, leaving them at this work, or avoiding. I seemed to hear an injunction out of space, "Keep then close to the temple till the final toll is paid." And so I braved and threw that inner protest which so closely attended me throughout. To these men body and brain yielded unexpected fruits. (WWC, 9:604–05)

Whitman is a departed deity, his cadaver an abandoned "temple" housing sacred relics that multiply as each organ is removed: "The heart stood alone in its perfection and strength. Everything else was impaired." Whitman's brain was "extracted, and seemed without hurt"; the doctors remarked on the "magnificent symmetry of the skull" (WWC, 9:604–05).

Traubel almost certainly believed that Whitman's legacy would include an anatomical afterlife as a medical specimen alongside his literary celebrity. Brian Burrell and Sheldon Lee Gosline have illuminated "the strange fate of Whitman's brain," a century-old anatomical mystery.[35] Burrell makes a compelling case that Whitman was a member of the American Anthropometric Society. Founded in 1889 by prominent doctors interested in neurology, the society collected the brains of prominent men donated by premortem bequests.[36] Whitman's doctors William Osler and Silas Weir Mitchell were members and may have recruited the poet.[37] Whitman's brain was supposed to join those of other prominent intellectuals at the University of Pennsylvania's Wistar Institute. Yet, this cerebral fame was not to be, at least not in the manner that the society promised.

On December 5, 1908, the Philadelphia *North American* ran a story in which Anthopometric Society member Edward Spitzka claimed that the quality of the mind could be measured by the shape of the brain. The article included an offhand remark that Whitman's brain had been dropped by a laboratory assistant, sustained irreparable damage, and been discarded.[38] The poet's furious disciples demanded to know how the specimen came to such an end and why no one was notified.[39] In spite of the executors' outrage the ambiguity surrounding the destruction of Whitman's brain remained unresolved until 2014, when Gosline acquired the diary of Henry Cattell, the pathologist who took possession of Whitman's brain after it was extracted (WWC, 9:605). Cattell confessed in his diary to accidentally leaving the brain in an unsealed specimen jar overnight.[40] "Carelessness in handling" is the common thread that runs through Spitzka's published remarks and Cattell's private confession.[41] The poet's anatomical specimen was not given anything like the care that he lavished on his hospital cases, or the preservationist fame bestowed on their medical museum counterparts. The doctors who fought to obtain Whitman's brain despite his brother's objections treated it with negligence and discarded it as medical waste. No longer an object of "professional curiosity," the ruined brain was cast aside, reminiscent of the carelessness shown by antebellum anatomists toward the resurrection and disposal of dissected cadavers.[42] The cause of the brain's destruction – exposure in an unsealed specimen jar – eerily recalls the unburied war dead whose bodies were likewise uncovered and subjected to the elements.

If Whitman's brain had survived, it would have been examined, sketched, and moulded into a plaster cast, then languished in the basement of the Wistar Institute, largely forgotten alongside the other eminent brain specimens. As Burrell writes, "such has been the fate of almost all so-called 'elite' brains – oblivion."[43] Once reduced to anatomical material, the body – even the celebrated authorial body – is no longer seen as entirely human. The anatomical specimen donated by the "poet of the body" proved far more fragile and fleeting than his literary ghost, who would continue to haunt the American canon for centuries to come.

Notes

1. See Harold Aspiz, "Science and Pseudoscience," in *A Companion to Walt Whitman*, ed. Donald D. Kummings (Oxford: Blackwell, 2006), 216–33.
2. Quoted in Grace Gilchrist, "Chats with Walt Whitman," *Temple Bar* 113 (February 1898), 210, WWA.

3. Walt Whitman, *Memoranda During the War* (Camden, NJ: Author's publication, 1875–76), 27, WWA.

4. *Oxford English Dictionary.*

5. See Elizabeth B. Keeney, *The Botanizers: Amateur Scientists in Nineteenth-Century America* (Chapel Hill, NC: University of North Carolina Press, 2011).

6. On Whitman and Darwin see: Aspiz, "Science and Pseudoscience"; Joseph Beaver, *Walt Whitman: Poet of Science* (New York, NY: Octagon Books, 1974), 105–30; Reynolds, 246, 481–82.

7. Whitman, *Memoranda*, 27.

8. Walt Whitman to Ralph Waldo Emerson, January 17, 1863, WWA.

9. Lindsay Tuggle, "The Afterlives of Specimens: Walt Whitman and the Army Medical Museum," *Walt Whitman Quarterly Review* 32.1 (2014), 2.

10. See Michael Sappol, *A Traffic of Dead Bodies: Anatomy and Embodied Social Identity in Nineteenth-Century America* (Princeton, NJ: Princeton University Press, 2002).

11. On "skin trades" see ibid., 4.

12. Despite Whitman's sympathetic treatment of African Americans in his poetry, he did not advocate equal rights or citizenship for black Americans following the abolition of slavery. For further analysis of Whitman's ambivalent treatment of race, see Ed Folsom, "Lucifer and Ethiopia: Whitman, Race, and Poetics before the Civil War and After," in *A Historical Guide to Walt Whitman*, ed. David S. Reynolds (Oxford: Oxford University Press, 2000), 45–96; Isaac Gewirtz, "I am With [Some of] You," in *I am With You: Walt Whitman's Leaves of Grass 1855–2005* (New York, NY: New York Public Library, 2005), 10–46; David S. Reynolds, *Walt Whitman's America: A Cultural Biography* (New York, NY: Vintage, 1995), 471–72; Ivy G. Wilson, ed., *Whitman Noir: Black America and the Good Gray Poet* (Iowa City, IA: University of Iowa Press, 2014).

13. John H. Brinton, *The Personal Memoirs of John H. Brinton, Major and Surgeon, 1861–65* (New York, NY: Neale Publishing, 1914), 187.

14. Whitman, *Memoranda*, 6.

15. This quote is in relation to the field hospital at Fort Donelson. See Brinton, *Personal Memoirs*, 91.

16. Nancy Cervetti, *S. Weir Mitchell: Philadelphia's Literary Physician, 1829–1914* (University Park, PA: Pennsylvania State University Press, 2012), 82; Drew Gilpin Faust, *This Republic of Suffering: Death and the American Civil War* (New York, NY: Alfred A. Knopf, 2008), xi.

17. Whitman, *Memoranda*, 56.

18. Ibid., 3.

19. Ibid., 5.

20. Tuggle, "Afterlives," 21–26.

21. Silas Weir Mitchell, "Phantom Limbs," *Lippincott's Magazine of Popular Literature and Science* 8 (1871), 567, and *Injuries of Nerves and their Consequences* (Philadelphia, PA: Lippincott, 1872), 348. See also Cassandra S. Crawford, *Phantom Limb: Amputation, Embodiment and Prosthetic Technology* (New York, NY: New York University Press, 2014), 108–12.

22. Mitchell, "Phantom Limbs," 565.
23. Hans Fluck and Rita Jaspersen-Schib, *Medicinal Plants and their Uses*, trans. J. M. Rowson (London: W. Foulsham, 1976), 32.
24. Silas Weir Mitchell, George R. Morehouse, and William W. Keen, *Gunshot Wounds and Other Injuries of the Nerves* (Philadelphia, PA: Lippincott, 1864), 10.
25. Quoted in Jennifer Travis, *Wounded Hearts: Masculinity, Law, and Literature in American Culture* (Chapel Hill, NC: University of North Carolina Press, 2005), 23.
26. Ibid., 23.
27. Whitman, *Memoranda*, 15.
28. Faust, *Republic of Suffering*, 95.
29. Walt Whitman, *Leaves of Grass* (New York, NY: W. E. Chapin & Co., Printers, 1867), 4b, WWA.
30. Ibid., 7b.
31. Quoted by Gary Laderman, *The Sacred Remains: American Attitudes toward Death, 1799–1883* (New Haven, CT: Yale University Press, 1996), 159.
32. Ibid., 159.
33. "Walt Whitman," *New York Mirror* (New York, NY), April 1, 1892.
34. William Sloane Kennedy quoted in Michael Robertson, *Worshipping Walt: The Whitman Disciples* (Princeton, NJ: Princeton University Press, 2008), 6–7.
35. Brian Burrell, "The Strange Fate of Whitman's Brain," *Walt Whitman Quarterly Review* 20.3 (2003), 107–33; Sheldon Lee Gosline, "'I am a fool': Dr. Henry Cattell's Private Confession about What Happened to Whitman's Brain," *Walt Whitman Quarterly Review* 31.4 (2014), 158–62.
36. Burrell, "Strange Fate," 109; Gosline, "I am a fool," 159.
37. Burrell, "Strange Fate," 123.
38. Ibid., 110.
39. Ibid., 111.
40. Gosline, "I am a fool," 157–58.
41. Burrell, "Strange Fate," 123.
42. According to *The Philadelphia Press*, George Whitman did not issue an unqualified objection to the autopsy. He would only consent to the post-mortem "if he were satisfied that any scientific end was to be attained [. . .] but he felt that the only purpose of such a course of action on the part of the doctors was the satisfaction of professional curiosity," quoted in Burrell, "Strange Fate," 122.
43. Burrell, "Strange Fate," 110.

PART IV

Reception and Legacy

CHAPTER 36

Disciples

Michael Robertson

Near the beginning of *Walt Whitman: The Making of the Poet*, his superb study of Whitman's early career, Paul Zweig argues that the poet created a "puzzle" for his readers: "Do we respond to his poem as we might to a poem by a more conventional poet – Wordsworth, say, or Shelley – or as followers of an impassioned saint speaking radical new words?"[1] Since the early twentieth century, academic critics have generally opted for the former approach, analyzing Whitman's poetry with the same critical tools that they apply to his peers. During Whitman's lifetime, however, a significant number of readers believed that *Leaves of Grass* could not be approached like the work of other poets, that its author was as much prophet as poet, and that his work constituted a new bible.

The nature writer John Burroughs, for instance, who met Whitman during the Civil War and went on to produce two books and fifty articles about him, wrote that "*Leaves of Grass* is primarily a gospel and is only secondarily a poem." He scoffed at the notion of placing Whitman alongside "minstrels and edifiers"; the poet belonged among the "prophets and saviours."[2] "Do you suppose a thousand years from now people will be celebrating the birth of Walt Whitman as they are now the birth of Christ?" mused William Sloane Kennedy, journalist and Harvard Divinity School dropout, one December (WWC, 7:397). Burroughs and Kennedy, along with a substantial group of their peers, are now known as the Whitman disciples. During Whitman's lifetime, when his work was frequently ignored, ridiculed, or censured, they worked indefatigably to promote his books and polish his reputation. After his death, they were dismissed as "hot little prophets" – a wittily condescending epithet that was widely circulated throughout the twentieth century.[3]

Yet Whitman himself insisted on the religious dimensions of *Leaves of Grass*. "When I commenced, years ago, elaborating the plan of my poems," he wrote in 1872, "one deep purpose underlay the others, and has underlain it and its execution ever since – and that has been the religious purpose"

(PW, 2:461). In old age, he expressed surprise at the idea that some readers regarded him as irreligious – "as if I could have written a word of the Leaves without its religious root-ground," he exclaimed (WWC, 1:10). Planning the third edition of *Leaves of Grass* (1860), he wrote an emphatic note about the "*Great Construction* of the *New Bible*" (NUPM, 1:353) and called the book the "Bible of the New Religion."[4] As Brian Yothers explains in another essay in this volume, such pronouncements were not uncommon in antebellum America. The early nineteenth century was an era of religious fervor and creativity, a time when, as Richard Brodhead has noted, "the category of the prophetic was unusually accessible in America."[5] Composing his first three editions of *Leaves of Grass* during the 1850s, Whitman was not alone in his prophetic ambitions.

All of Whitman's nineteenth-century disciples responded passionately to the religious dimensions of *Leaves of Grass*, although each of them constructed a unique "Walt Whitman" in accord with his or her particular spiritual, affectional, and political needs. For some, he was a saintly figure of national unity, for others a celebrant of the natural world. He was seen as a liberator of women, a defender of same-sex passion, the forerunner of a new evolutionary spiritual consciousness, and the prophet of a libertarian socialism. Their writings on Whitman constituted an attempt to establish the poet as a world-changing prophet and *Leaves of Grass* as the bible of a democratic religion appropriate to the modern world. The disciples were a large, loosely affiliated, and international group. In what follows, I focus on the principal North American and British disciples, all of whom, with one exception, knew Whitman personally and experienced what William Sloane Kennedy described as the poet's "magnetic quality."[6]

Whitman gained his first two disciples, William O'Connor and John Burroughs, after he moved to Washington, DC, during the Civil War. O'Connor and Whitman had met before the war, while Burroughs left his position as a schoolteacher in New York State and relocated to Washington specifically in order to meet the man whom he later described as "the greatest personality [...] that has appeared in the world during the Christian era."[7] The two young men believed Whitman to be an inspired poet, and they were both infatuated with the man himself. Neither O'Connor nor Burroughs became Whitman's lovers, yet they, like all Whitman's disciples, demonstrated what Robert K. Nelson and Kenneth M. Price have called the "erotics of discipleship."[8] Whitman possessed a powerful charisma, and the disciples, prepared by their reading of the intensely personal poems, inevitably came to their first encounter with the poet prepared to be overwhelmed.

O'Connor was the least spiritually fervid of the disciples, with little interest in the religious themes within *Leaves of Grass* that attracted the others. His most famous publication is *The Good Gray Poet* (1866), a lengthy essay that O'Connor wrote in a furious white heat after Whitman was fired from his position as a government clerk for having authored an immoral book. The essay is an over-the-top defense of Whitman as a morally immaculate man and a poetic peer of Shakespeare, Aeschylus, Dante, and Homer. O'Connor placed great emphasis on Whitman's wartime work as a volunteer nurse, describing how he walked through the wards filled with wounded soldiers "in the spirit of Christ, soothing, healing, consoling, restoring."[9]

The next year O'Connor would expand on this description in "The Carpenter: A Christmas Story" (1867). The story is an exercise in high-Victorian sentiment, modeled on Dickens's *A Christmas Carol* (1843). It rolls together the spirits of Christmas Past, Present, and Yet to Come into the person of "the carpenter," a gray-bearded figure who spreads wealth, heals the lame, and reconciles father and son, husband and wife, Northerner and Southerner.[10] The carpenter is never named, but knowledgeable readers easily recognized the character as Walt Whitman. O'Connor insisted that his intention was not to identify Whitman as a Christ figure but to link him with the spirit of Christ – a fine distinction that some later disciples ignored. O'Connor's writings about Whitman publicized the poet's name, defended his stature as a major poet, and prepared the ground for future religiously charged interpretations.

Unlike O'Connor, John Burroughs was reluctant to compare Whitman to Shakespeare. Instead, he took the line that *Leaves of Grass* was "not poetry as the world uses that term" but instead was "an inspired utterance. [. . .] Lovers of Whitman no more go to him for poetry than they go to the ocean for the pretty shells and pebbles on the beach." Burroughs regarded *Leaves of Grass* as an oceanic force that connected readers to the salvific powers of nature. For fifty years Burroughs was America's most popular nature writer, and he enlisted Whitman's work in his campaign to replace "the religion of our fathers" – dominated by "sin, repentance, fear, Satan, hell" – with the progressive, nature-centered spirituality that he identified in *Leaves of Grass*. Whitman "sings a new [religious] song," he insisted, one that sanctifies the natural world and teaches that "the earth is as divine as heaven."[11]

Burroughs's religious appreciation of Whitman pales beside that of Richard Maurice Bucke, a Canadian psychiatrist who believed that the poet was "either actually a god or in some sense clearly and entirely preterhuman." Bucke was the most extreme religious enthusiast among the disciples, a true believer who regarded *Leaves of Grass* as the "bible of the future for the next thousand years."[12] Bucke discovered *Leaves of Grass* in 1868, when he was thirty-one. Four years later, having fed on a steady diet of Whitman, he experienced an overwhelming mystical "illumination." Bucke believed his illumination to be transcendent and transhistorical, identical to the mystical experience of sages from the Buddha to William Blake. However, his account of the experience borrows concepts and language from what Bucke believed to be the keystone passage in *Leaves of Grass*, the description of the poet's encounter with his soul in section 5 of "Song of Myself":

> Swiftly arose and spread around me the peace and knowledge
>   that pass all the argument of the earth,
> And I know that the hand of God is the promise of my own,
> And I know that the spirit of God is the brother of my own,
> And that all the men ever born are also my brothers, and the
>   women my sisters and lovers,
> And that a kelson of the creation is love.   (LG, 33)

Bucke was certain that his own illumination was essentially identical to Whitman's, and that he was thus uniquely qualified to preach the Whitmanite gospel to the awaiting world.[13]

Bucke met Whitman in 1877, an encounter that convinced him that the man Walt Whitman was identical with the superhuman persona of the poetry. Three years later he lured Whitman on a four-month visit to Canada, the better to observe him for a book Bucke was planning. Bucke's *Walt Whitman* (1883) is generally described as a biography, but it bears little resemblance to twenty-first-century conceptions of the genre. In essence, it is an extended exercise in hero-worship that depicts Whitman in Christological terms. Bucke's eccentric study did not have a major effect on Whitman's reputation; Burroughs's more temperate essays reached a much larger audience. After Whitman's death, however, Bucke published a volume that was equally eccentric but that became a worldwide bestseller. *Cosmic Consciousness* (1901), the culmination of Bucke's lifelong religious theorizing, has never been out of print and remains available in multiple editions. The book applies a progressive version of evolutionary theory to human consciousness, arguing that humankind, which originally shared the simple consciousness of animals, gradually developed self-consciousness. Bucke believed that the mystical experiences of religious geniuses – his roll call begins with the Buddha and Jesus and climaxes with

Walt Whitman – demonstrate the emergence of a new, higher consciousness. More than a century after the publication of *Cosmic Consciousness*, his
religiously charged interpretation of Whitman continues to influence the
poet's reception.[14]

Whitman's disciples formed a transatlantic community, with numerous
Britons prominent among them. Almost all of them came to Whitman
through William Michael Rossetti's edited volume *Poems by Walt
Whitman* (1868). Rossetti, brother of the poets Dante Gabriel and
Christina, issued his edition at a time when no British publisher would
touch *Leaves of Grass* because of the sexual frankness of parts of "Song of
Myself" and the poems in the "Children of Adam" cluster. Rossetti, an
admirer of Whitman's poetry but no disciple, responded with a selected
edition that avoided what he called the "gross" and "crude" qualities of the
verse.[15]

Two years later Rossetti, working in collaboration with O'Connor,
ushered into print "A Woman's Estimate of Walt Whitman," an essay
based on letters written to him by a friend. This eloquent, passionate, and
personal essay announced the arrival of Whitman's first English disciple,
declaring in its opening, "For me the reading of his poems is truly a new
birth of the soul." The writer connected her religious response to the
poems with the latest discoveries of nineteenth-century science, arguing
that Whitman was the first poet to reconcile faith in immortality with
a modern scientific worldview. In addition, she devoted much of her essay
to defending the sexual content of poems in the complete *Leaves of Grass*,
arguing that Whitman brought "grandeur and beauty" to sexual acts that
the broader culture regarded as shameful but that women, as wives and
mothers, instinctively understood to be beautiful.[16]

Rossetti did not fully agree with the writer's interpretation of Whitman,
but he wrote in his preface to the article that it was the most valuable
appraisal of the poet yet in existence because it was written by "*a woman.*"[17]
Rossetti sensed that this appreciation by a female intellectual could help to
dispel the scandal associated with Whitman's name, yet at the same time he
advised the author to publish her work anonymously. Immediately afterwards, she regretted taking Rossetti's advice. Anne Gilchrist was unafraid
to proclaim her admiration for Walt Whitman. This eminent woman of
letters, who was friends not only with the Rossettis but also with the
Carlyles and the Tennysons, is one of the most complex and fascinating
of the disciples. Dismissed by twentieth-century critics as a "pathetic
Victorian lady," more recently she has attracted attention as an original
and powerful reader of *Leaves of Grass* (Corr., 5:6).[18]

Gilchrist's twentieth-century notoriety came with the 1918 publication of her letters to Whitman. The letters reveal that Gilchrist fell in love with Whitman on the basis of his poetry and that the forty-three-year-old widow expected that they would marry. ("I am yet young enough to bear thee children, my darling," she wrote in her second letter.[19]) Readers at the time were astounded. Recent critics, Max Cavitch most prominently among them, have focused on the way that Gilchrist's letters reveal the paradoxical nature of Whitman's poetic project. On the one hand, Whitman sought an unprecedented intimacy with readers. "Camerado, this is no book, / Who touches this touches a man," he wrote in "So Long!" (LG, 505), and the 1867 edition of *Leaves of Grass* that Gilchrist read had more intimate and frankly erotic passages, such as the opening to "To Workingmen" (later "A Song for Occupations"):

> Come closer to me;
> Push close, my lovers, and take the best I possess;
> Yield closer and closer, and give me the best you possess.
> This is unfinished business with me – How is it with you?
> (I was chill'd with the cold types, cylinder, wet paper between us.)
> Male and Female!
> I pass so poorly with paper and types, I must pass with the contact of
>   bodies and souls.

Yet at the same time as Whitman invited readers' intimacy, he pushed them away:

> Are you the new person drawn toward me?
> To begin with, take warning – I am surely far different from what you
>   suppose;
> Do you suppose you will find in me your ideal?
> Do you think it so easy to have me become your lover?[20]

Ignoring Whitman's warnings, Gilchrist responded passionately to his provocative invitations. As Cavitch puts it, her "disinhibited" reading of *Leaves of Grass* "called the serious bluff of addressivity central to [Whitman's] eroticism."[21]

Gilchrist called the poet's bluff even more powerfully five years after her first letter to him, when she moved her entire household, including her three youngest children, to Philadelphia in order to marry Walt Whitman. No record exists of what passed between them at their first meeting in September, 1876. The testimony of contemporaries makes clear, however, that Gilchrist somehow managed to drop her romantic illusions and quickly established an easy, friendly relationship with Whitman. During the two years she and her family lived in Philadelphia, Whitman generally dined with them daily and frequently stayed at their house for days at a time. After she returned to England, she and Whitman maintained a cordial correspondence that lasted until her death in 1885. That year she published her second and final essay on Whitman, "A Confession of Faith." The essay concludes with an assertion that could serve as a creed for the Whitman disciples. Whitman's poems, she wrote, display "a resplendent faith in God and man which will kindle anew the faith of the world."[22]

It is likely that the young Irish poet Oscar Wilde was familiar with Gilchrist's "Confession"; he had loved Whitman's poetry, he told an interviewer, "from the cradle."[23] Wilde may have been sacrificing strict factual accuracy for dramatic effect; his mother evidently procured a copy of the Rossetti edition soon after it was published and read it aloud to her son, who was fourteen at the time. Wilde's sole publication on Whitman, "The Gospel According to Walt Whitman," parallels Gilchrist's in its attention to the poetry's prophetic qualities and its description of the poet as "a factor in the heroic and spiritual evolution of the human being."[24]

Few readers today are aware of Wilde's serious interest in Whitmanesque spirituality. Far better known is the statement he made later in his life: "The kiss of Walt Whitman is still on my lips."[25] The kiss was given on the second of two pilgrimages that Wilde made to Camden during his 1882 American lecture tour. This apostolic consecration remains a key moment in the construction of Whitman as a prophet not only of modern spirituality but also of modern homosexuality. In the years before the neologism *homosexual* entered English discourse in the 1890s, Wilde's contemporaries John Addington Symonds and Edward Carpenter promulgated a Whitmanesque gospel that mixed religious fervor and same-sex love.[26]

Symonds, an Oxford-educated poet and critic, was among the first people in England to read the 1860 *Leaves of Grass*, the first edition to contain the "Calamus" cluster celebrating love between men. He found the experience overwhelming. The brilliant, neurotic Symonds had recently married in a futile attempt to conquer his attraction to men. He gratefully embraced the "Calamus" poems' proud assertion that "the manly love of comrades," far from being degrading or shameful, was essential to the democratic body politic (LG, 117). Six years after this first reading, Symonds wrote Whitman an admiring and inquisitive letter, trying to find out if the poems' celebration of comradeship had a physical dimension. Whitman sent a friendly, evasive reply, thus initiating one of the most celebrated cat-and-mouse games in literary history. Symonds would repeatedly press Whitman on the hidden meanings of "Calamus"; Whitman would adroitly sidestep his questions. After two decades of this epistolary back-and-forth, Symonds, engaged in writing a book about Whitman, decided to be frank. "In your conception of Comradeship, do you contemplate the possible intrusion of those semi-sexual emotions and actions which no doubt do occur between men?"[27] It was the first direct mention of sexuality in his correspondence with Whitman, and the letter elicited a famous reply: any such "morbid inferences [. . .] are disavow'd by me & seem damnable" (Corr., 5:72).

Symonds rationalized away this discouraging response: "I do not think [Whitman] quite understood what I was driving at," he wrote to an American disciple. His book *Walt Whitman: A Study* (1892) devotes a chapter to "The Love of Comrades" and insists that there is "indeed a distinctly sensuous side" to adhesiveness. Yet Symonds also understood the political dimensions of Whitmanesque comradeship, and he linked male love, democracy, and spirituality in a mix that he called "cosmic enthusiasm" – his label for his own religious beliefs as well as Whitman's, and which he defined as the "recognition of divinity in all things."[28]

Symonds's project of using *Leaves of Grass* to advance progressive spirituality, democratic politics, and the acceptance of same-sex passion was supported and advanced by his acquaintance Edward Carpenter, a poet, essayist, and political activist who was known as the "English Walt Whitman." That label was applied to him on the publication of *Towards Democracy* (1883), a long free-verse poem reminiscent of "Song of Myself." M. Wynn Thomas has suggested that the poem can be seen as an instance of "intralingual translation," with Carpenter adapting Whitman's verse form to the political and cultural situation of late-Victorian England.[29]

Carpenter freely admitted his debt to Whitman. Reading *Leaves of Grass* contributed to his decision, at age thirty, to resign his position as an Anglican clergyman and Cambridge don and move to England's industrial north. That year he wrote his first letter to Whitman, thanking the poet for having given him "a ground for the love of men [. . .]. [Y]ou have made men to be not ashamed of the noblest instinct of their nature" (WWC, 1:160). Three years after writing this letter, Carpenter made the first of two pilgrimages to Camden. Throughout the rest of his long life, in a stream of poems and essays Carpenter promoted his Whitmanesque vision of same-sex lovers as the advance guard in the progress toward a utopian future. As Eve Kosofsky Sedgwick argues powerfully in *Between Men*, Carpenter used his reading of Whitman to advance an image of the male homosexual as a virile, idealistic, pro-feminist, and democratic socialist figure.[30]

Carpenter was in frequent contact with the group of disciples in Bolton, England, who became the center of British Whitmanism during the 1890s. The Bolton disciples had their origins in a weekly reading and discussion group led by J. W. Wallace, an architect's assistant. In 1886 this group of lower-middle-class men began an annual celebration of Walt Whitman's birthday and the next year started a correspondence with the poet. After Wallace and another member of the group made pilgrimages to Camden in 1890–91, *Leaves of Grass* became the focus of their attention. The Bolton disciples' reading of *Leaves* combined religious and political perspectives. They believed that the love of comrades led inevitably to socialist politics, and this view of Whitman spread widely in fin-de-siècle England, particularly in the industrial north, where a spiritualized socialism was widely popular. Readings from Whitman and Edward Carpenter were regular features of services in the Labour Church, which had fifty congregations at its height. Wallace wrote a profile of Whitman for the "Socialist Saints" feature of *Young Socialist* magazine and frequently spoke about the poet at socialist meetings.

For a few heady years during the 1890s, the Bolton disciples imagined that their spiritually infused interpretation of *Leaves of Grass* would become a crucial component of a millennial socialism destined to spread across Britain. Instead, after the turn of the century British socialists devoted their efforts to making links with trade unions and electing Labour representatives to Parliament, and the Bolton Whitmanites slipped into obscurity. Their reputation has been revived by writers interested in Whitman's transnational reception and in alternative histories of British socialism and homosociality.[31]

During his 1891 pilgrimage to Camden, Wallace became close to Horace Traubel, who, according to Wallace, was "the disciple Walt loved best."[32] As a teenaged printer's assistant in Camden, Traubel met Whitman in 1873, when the fifty-four-year-old poet moved to the city. Fifteen years later, while working as a bank clerk in Philadelphia, Traubel began visiting Whitman daily. He became Whitman's unpaid secretary, editorial factotum, and devoted conversational partner. Every evening he would transcribe their discussions, a project that lasted four years until the poet's death in 1892. The record reached almost two million words and was eventually published in nine volumes as *With Walt Whitman in Camden*

(1906–96). At the same time as he was compiling this voluminous record, Traubel served as unofficial coordinator of Whitmanite activities worldwide, writing twenty to forty letters each day to Whitman's disciples and admirers. A fervent religious cosmopolitan, he also cofounded the Philadelphia branch of the Ethical Culture Society and founded, edited, and published *The Conservator*, a monthly magazine promoting ethical culture and religious liberalism.

When Whitman died in March 1892, Traubel was the one holding his hand. At that moment, he wrote, his "new life" commenced, and "a luminous conviction lift[ed] me with [Whitman] into the eternal" (WWC, 9:600). Traubel's new life was devoted to what Bucke called "the Great Cause," which in Traubel's case involved a turn to writing free verse poetry and poetically charged prose, making over *The Conservator* into a Whitmanite journal, and founding the Walt Whitman Fellowship: International.[33] An informal group had been meeting annually in Camden or Philadelphia to celebrate Whitman's birthday, but Traubel imagined a much grander organization with branches across North America and Great Britain. For a brief period, it seemed as if his vision would be realized, but the Whitman Fellowship soon devolved into a loose confederation made up of *Conservator* subscribers and attendees at the annual Whitman birthday dinners held in New York.

The Fellowship became a meeting ground for middle-class bohemians and political radicals. In the 1850s, Walt Whitman had imagined becoming the poet of the American masses, but during the early twentieth century *Leaves of Grass* served as a sourcebook for a cultural avant-garde exploring new models of spirituality, politics, sexuality, and gender. Helen Keller and Charlotte Perkins Gilman attended the birthday dinners, and left-wing luminaries including Clarence Darrow, Jack London, Emma Goldman, and Eugene Debs regularly sent greetings. Whitman disciple Thomas Harned, who regarded Whitman as "a mighty spiritual force," complained that the Fellowship had become dominated by "socialists, anarchists, [and] cranks," but Traubel remained open to both political and spiritual perspectives on the poet.[34] The Fellowship's eclecticism is evident in the program for the 1911 birthday dinner, which included speeches on "What Walt Whitman Means to a Revolutionist" and "The Spiritual and Religious Significance of Whitman."

Both the Whitman Fellowship and *The Conservator* fell apart after Traubel's death in 1919. At the same time, *Leaves of Grass* became incorporated into the canon of the newly established academic field of American literary studies. By 1950 Brown University professor Charles Willard could note with satisfaction in his history of Whitman's reception that "the last of the band who knew [Whitman] personally, loved him, and believed him the founder of the religion of the future" was gone, and discussion of the poet was firmly established on the plane of "sane and traditional literary criticism."[35] Willard's history of Whitman's reception as an agon between crackpot disciples and rational academics has been challenged in recent years by numerous studies of the disciples and by writers both in and out of the academy who continue to find in *Leaves of Grass* an inclusive, democratic, and life-affirming spirituality.

Notes

1. Paul Zweig, *Walt Whitman: The Making of the Poet* (New York, NY: Basic Books, 1984), 15.
2. John Burroughs, "Walt Whitman and His Recent Critics," in *In Re Walt Whitman*, eds. Horace L. Traubel, Richard Maurice Bucke, and Thomas B. Harned (Philadelphia, PA: David McKay, 1893), 102; John Burroughs, *Whitman: A Study* (Boston, MA: Houghton Mifflin, [1896] 1904), 22.
3. Bliss Perry, *Walt Whitman* (Boston, MA: Houghton Mifflin, 1906), 286.
4. Richard Maurice Bucke, ed., *Notes and Fragments Left by Walt Whitman* (London, Ontario: A. Talbot, 1899), 55.
5. Richard Brodhead, "Prophets in America circa 1830: Ralph Waldo Emerson, Nat Turner, Joseph Smith," in *Joseph Smith Jr.: Reappraisals after Two Centuries*, eds. Reid L. Neilson and Terryl L. Givens (New York, NY: Oxford University Press, 2009), 20.
6. William Sloane Kennedy, *Reminiscences of Walt Whitman* (London: Alexander Gardner, 1896), 109.
7. John Burroughs, "The Poet of the Cosmos," in *Accepting the Universe* (New York, NY: Wm. H. Wise, [1920] 1924), 316.
8. Robert K. Nelson and Kenneth M. Price, "Debating Manliness: Thomas Wentworth Higginson, William Sloane Kennedy, and the Question of Whitman," *American Literature* 73.3 (2001), 498. On O'Connor and Burroughs, see Michael Robertson, *Worshipping Walt: The Whitman Disciples* (Princeton, NJ: Princeton University Press, 2008), 14–50.
9. William Douglas O'Connor, *The Good Gray Poet: A Vindication* (New York, NY: Bunce and Huntington, 1866), WWA. The major studies of O'Connor are Florence Bernstein Freedman, *William Douglas O'Connor: Walt Whitman's Chosen Knight* (Athens, OH: Ohio University Press, 1985) and Jerome Loving, *Walt Whitman's Champion: William Douglas O'Connor* (College Station, TX: Texas A&M University Press, 1978).
10. William O'Connor, "The Carpenter," *Putnam's Magazine*, January 1868, 55–90, WWA.

11. Burroughs, "Poet of the Cosmos," 317; Burroughs, *Whitman*, 290–91. The most important source on the Burroughs–Whitman relationship is Clara Barrus, *Whitman and Burroughs, Comrades* (Boston, MA: Houghton Mifflin, 1931). See also Edward J. Renehan, "Comrades: Scenes from the Friendship of John Burroughs and Walt Whitman," in *Sharp Eyes: John Burroughs and American Nature Writing*, ed. Charlotte Zoë Walker (Syracuse, NY: Syracuse University Press, 2000), 64–79; and James Perrin Warren, *John Burroughs and the Place of Nature* (Athens, GA: University of Georgia Press, 2006), 42–72.

12. Richard Maurice Bucke, "Memories of Walt Whitman," *Walt Whitman Fellowship Papers* 6 (September 1894), 38; Artem Lozynsky, *Richard Maurice Bucke, Medical Mystic: Letters of Dr. Bucke to Walt Whitman and His Friends* (Detroit, MI: Wayne State University Press, 1977), 119.

13. Bucke describes his mystical illumination in *Cosmic Consciousness: A Study in the Evolution of the Human Mind* (New York, NY: Penguin Arkana, [1901] 1991), 9–10.

14. On Bucke and Whitman, see Robertson, *Worshipping Walt*, 97–138.

15. William Michael Rossetti, ed., *Poems by Walt Whitman* (London: John Camden Hotten, 1868), 4, WWA. On Rossetti and Whitman's British reception, Harold Blodgett's *Walt Whitman in England* (Ithaca, NY: Cornell University Press, 1934) remains invaluable. See also M. Wynn Thomas, "Whitman in the British Isles," in *Walt Whitman and the World*, eds. Gay Wilson Allen and Ed Folsom (Iowa City, IA: University of Iowa Press, 1995), 11–70.

16. Anne Gilchrist, "A Woman's Estimate of Walt Whitman," reprinted in *Anne Gilchrist: Her Life and Writings*, ed. Herbert Harlakenden Gilchrist (London: T. Fisher Unwin, 1887), 288, 302.

17. Ibid., 288. Italics in the original.

18. More recent assessments of Gilchrist include Marion Walker Alcaro, *Walt Whitman's Mrs. G* (Cranbury, NJ: Associated University Press, 1991); Suzanne Ashworth, "Lover, Mother, Reader: The Epistolary Courtship of Walt Whitman," *Nineteenth-Century Contexts* 26.2 (2004), 173–97; Max Cavitch, "Audience Terminable and Interminable: Anne Gilchrist, Walt Whitman, and the Achievement of Disinhibited Reading," *Victorian Poetry* 43.2 (2005), 249–61; Steve Marsden, "'A Woman Waits for Me': Anne Gilchrist's Reading of *Leaves of Grass*," *Walt Whitman Quarterly Review* 23.3 (2006), 95–125; and Robertson, *Worshipping Walt*, 51–96.

19. Thomas B. Harned, ed., *The Letters of Anne Gilchrist and Walt Whitman* (New York, NY: Doubleday, Page, 1918), 66.

20. Walt Whitman, *Leaves of Grass* (New York, NY, 1867), 239, 129, WWA.

21. Cavitch, "Audience Terminable and Interminable," 249.

22. Gilchrist, "A Confession of Faith," in Harned, *Letters of Gilchrist and Whitman*, 54.

23. E. H. Mikhail, ed., *Oscar Wilde: Interviews and Recollections* (New York, NY: Barnes & Noble, 1979), 47.

24. Oscar Wilde, "The Gospel According to Walt Whitman," in *The Artist as Critic: Critical Writings of Oscar Wilde*, ed. Richard Ellmann (New York, NY: Random House, 1969), 125.

25. Oscar Wilde quoted in Richard Ellmann, *Oscar Wilde* (New York, NY: Knopf, 1988), 171.

26. On Whitman's contemporary British homosexual readers, see Jonathan Katz, *Gay American History* (New York, NY: Thomas Y. Crowell, 1976), 337–65; William Pannapacker, *Revised Lives: Walt Whitman and Nineteenth-Century Authorship* (New York, NY: Routledge, 2004), 105–27; Kenneth M. Price, *To Walt Whitman, America* (Chapel Hill, NC: University of North Carolina Press, 2004), 56–69; Robertson, *Worshipping Walt*, 139–97; Eve Kosofsky Sedgwick, *Between Men: English Literature and Male Homosocial Desire* (New York, NY: Columbia University Press, 1985), 201–17; and Gregory Woods, "'Still on My Lips': Walt Whitman in Britain," in *The Continuing Presence of Walt Whitman*, ed. Robert K. Martin (Iowa City, IA: University of Iowa Press, 1992), 129–40.

27. Herbert M. Schueller and Robert L. Peters, eds., *The Letters of John Addington Symonds*, vol. 3 (Detroit, MI: Wayne State University Press, 1969), 483.

28. Schueller and Peters, *Letters of John Addington Symonds*, 3:533; Symonds, *Walt Whitman: A Study* (London: John C. Nimmo, 1893), 157, 33.

29. Edward Aveling, "Towards Democracy [review]," in *Progress: A Monthly Magazine of Advanced Thought*, September 1883, 61; M. Wynn Thomas, *Transatlantic Connections: Whitman U.S., Whitman U.K.* (Iowa City, IA: University of Iowa Press, 2005), xvii.

30. Sedgwick, *Between Men*, 201–17.

31. See Harry Cocks, "*Calamus* in Bolton: Spirituality and Homosexual Desire in Late Victorian England," *Gender and History* 13.2 (2001), 191–223; Kirsten Harris, *Walt Whitman and British Socialism* (New York, NY: Routledge, 2016), 65–103; Joann P. Krieg, "Without Walt Whitman in Camden," *Walt Whitman Quarterly Review* 14.2 (1996), 85–112; Carolyn Masel, "Poet of Comrades: Walt Whitman and the Bolton Whitman Fellowship," in *Special Relationships: Anglo-American Affinities and Antagonisms*, eds. Janet Beer and Bridget Bennett (Manchester: Manchester University Press, 2002), 110–38; Robertson, *Worshipping Walt*, 198–231; and Paul Salveson, "Loving Comrades: Lancashire's Links to Walt Whitman," *Walt Whitman Quarterly Review* 14.2 (1996), 57–84.

32. J. W. Wallace to Horace Traubel, June 30, 1893, Horace and Anne Montgomerie Traubel Collection, Library of Congress. On Traubel, see Robertson, *Worshipping Walt*, 232–76.

33. Lozynsky, *Richard Maurice Bucke, Medical Mystic*, 185.

34. Thomas B. Harned, "Whitman and the Future," *The Conservator* (Philadelphia, PA), June 1895, 54; Harned to J. W. Wallace, n.d., Walt Whitman Collection, Bolton (England) Central Library.

35. Charles B. Willard, *Whitman's American Fame* (Providence, RI: Brown University, 1950), 32.

CHAPTER 37

Influence in the United States

Sascha Pöhlmann

In considering Walt Whitman's influence in the United States, it is crucial to note two interconnected aspects: the first is that Whitman defines poetic success from the very beginning of his career in terms of having as big an influence as possible, as the famous last sentence of the Preface to the first edition of *Leaves of Grass* (1855) shows: "The proof of a poet is that his country absorbs him as affectionately as he has absorbed it" (LG55, xii). The second is that Whitman has spent his entire career as a poet preparing his legacy, and both his poetry and prose are – with only few exceptions – overwhelmingly geared toward a future readership whose experience and judgment Whitman is trying to frame in his present. Perhaps no other American writer has worked so tirelessly and insistently on preparing his own reception and the poetic, social, and political influence he would have, and this self-reflexive, future-oriented framing is a central part of his aesthetics. This is not to say, of course, that Whitman's influence in the United States has been exactly how he wanted it to be – far from it – and that readers naïvely fell for his self-construction and simply repeated what he had prepared for them; in fact, Whitman the poet and Whitman's poetry have been read and (re)constructed in ways Whitman could neither have imagined nor prepared for.[1]

The reason why Whitman needed to keep working so hard on his legacy was that he could never be sure he would have one, given that his influence on the present United States (let alone a future one) was always doubtful. There is a profound insecurity behind Whitman's arrogance in proclaiming himself the beginner of American poetry, and every repetition of statements to that effect only highlights their underlying desire more, as well as their necessity: Whitman needed to tell everyone how important he was because hardly anybody thought so, and at the same time he had audience enough that at least someone would listen. Consider Ralph Waldo Emerson in contemporary comparison, who by "the mid-1850s [...] was dangerously famous"[2] and had to struggle with fame rather than seek it; or consider

Emily Dickinson, who "limited her self-promotional activities to a series of private letters."[3] The "proof of the poet" as he had described it in 1855 is appropriate in its ambiguity: it is anyone's guess what it means that a poet is "absorbed" affectionately by his country, and Whitman could not be sure of any variety of it. The failure of the first edition with many critics and especially a general public may have been indication enough of that perpetual uncertainty of "proof" and "absorption," and accordingly the Preface is not included in the second edition. In defining poetic success in such a vague yet ambitious way, Whitman has set the bar impossibly high, and as he kept failing to cross it, he more and more insistently needed to try to rationalize his failure into a postponement of success. The influence he sought was that of the poetic beginner who would be credited with inventing a truly American aesthetics but also that of a poet-prophet whose works would frame any development the democratic United States would undergo, and who would cultivate the openness of this culture without limiting its potential. The influence he had, however, was very different both in quality and degree, and while his "absorption" has certainly occurred, it was not necessarily affectionate.

This is especially true of the literary generation that rose to prominence only two decades after Whitman's death in 1892: the Anglo-American modernists, most notably Ezra Pound, T. S. Eliot, and William Carlos Williams. Following Pound's dictum to "make it new," the modernists' aesthetics were based on a radical desire to innovate and begin art itself again. For them, Whitman was as much a problem as a positive influence, since he had already embraced an aesthetics of beginnings, formal experiment, and openness that made him less a predecessor than a competitor. As Mark Morrison has it:

> Whitman's work and reputation caused an "anxiety of influence" (as Harold Bloom puts it) for the modernists, offering them an example of a distinctively modern American voice that could assault the genteel tradition of the later nineteenth century but also generate imitators who were already stultifying and sloppy, by the early twentieth century, and could potentially rob the modernists of their own originality.[4]

The modernists had to find ways of beginning again that would not seem like Whitman's beginnings, or else their desired innovation would really be a form of conservatism. T. S. Eliot's response to this dilemma is, somewhat ironically, closest to Whitman's own strategy in dealing with precursors and their influence: he simply ignored him, just as Whitman had decided to "Make no quotations, and no reference to any other writers" (NUPM,

1:159) in order to write as if he had invented writing itself. Eliot refused to acknowledge Whitman's formal achievements in creating a free verse that now seems proto-modernist, and he equally had no interest in Whitman's democratic aesthetics or his focus on American culture. One could construe the opening lines of Eliot's most famous poem "The Waste Land" (1922), "April is the cruellest month / breeding lilacs out of the dead land,"[5] as a reference to Whitman's elegy to Lincoln, "When Lilacs Last in the Dooryard Bloom'd," and yet this is as direct as it gets, and Eliot poignantly sought to avoid Whitman's influence rather than engage it.

Ezra Pound, perhaps the most influential figure in Anglo-American modernism, decided to pick a fight with Whitman rather than walk away, which is summarized most concisely in "A Pact" (1916):

> I make a pact with you, Walt Whitman –
> I have detested you long enough.
> I come to you as a grown child
> Who has had a pig-headed father;
> I am old enough now to make friends.
> It was you that broke the new wood,
> Now is a time for carving.
> We have one sap and one root –
> Let there be commerce between us.[6]

Pound cleverly deconstructs the usual hierarchies involved in the simplistic notion of chronological literary influence and places himself on the same level as his predecessor. He casts himself not as a passive recipient but rather as an active force who will finally refine the earlier blunt poetic attempts rather than imitate or continue them. The dynamic part is almost all Pound's here, and while he grudgingly acknowledges that Whitman's poetic achievement is too great to be ignored, he also addresses him in a patronizing way as a "pig-headed father" who will need to make way for the next generation and their own innovations. Accordingly, Pound's own poetry is not at all Whitmanian in form or content, except perhaps in a very abstract sense of openness, and so Whitman's influence is once more one to be actively overcome rather than to be fully embraced.

The modernist who decided most explicitly to build on Whitman rather than reject him is William Carlos Williams. He sought the raw material for renewal in US culture rather than in the high-cultural traditions of Europe or Asia, as the modernists in exile did. Yet Williams's acceptance of Whitman is far from uncritical, and it is perhaps even more dialectic than Pound's, whose "A Pact" remains a gesture that finds hardly an actual resonance in his poetics. In several essays on Whitman, Williams acknowledges his revolutionary achievement of breaking open the formal restrictions in poetry by creating free verse, yet he is quick to add that this is all Whitman was able to do and that he failed in adding a creative and controlling element to the liberating destruction he achieved. For Williams, Whitman's free verse is simply too free, lacking the measure and order the modernists sought to impose through art on a world they perceived to be increasingly chaotic and formless: "Free verse merely means verse whose proper structure escapes a man's efforts to control it."[7] Williams's paradoxically named "variable foot" is the most obvious result of his attempt to reign in Whitman's anarchic tendencies while not giving up on their freedoms either. All in all, then, Whitman's influence on the modernists remains an ambiguous affair to this generation: the exiles could reject him most easily along with anything else that seemed all too American for their projects, and the homegrown modernists needed to find ways of wresting the very notion of beginning from Whitman so they could begin again in America.

One particularly crucial and complex case in this regard is Langston Hughes, one of the most important poets associated with the Harlem Renaissance, an African American cultural movement that is affiliated but not identical with modernism. Hughes pursued a sociopolitical agenda that combined a struggle for equality of African Americans and the empowerment of the proletariat, as he considered the issues of race and class to be inseparable. At the same time, he pursued an aesthetic agenda in which poetry would often serve this political end but retain its autonomy in a temporary alliance. Hughes found an ally in Whitman with regard to both sides of the coin, and perhaps surprisingly so, since the material for his quest for African American cultural emancipation in the era of Jim Crow would hardly be the white American poetic tradition Whitman exemplified. And yet for Hughes "Whitman was the one white American writer who wrote the imaginary that continued to best sustain [...] African American writers in their American present."[8] This imaginary of inclusiveness and radical democracy provided a model for Hughes' own vision of America, although it must be noted that the issue of race is much more complex than that in Whitman's poetry, and a liberal reading will certainly find its counterpoint elsewhere. Nevertheless, Whitman's vision of America resonated with Hughes's, and it is mostly on that level Whitman's influence can be detected rather than on the level of form or content.

In his 1955 essay "Walt Whitman and the Negro," Hughes declared that *Leaves of Grass* is "as contemporary as tomorrow's newspaper,"[9] and he did write an affectionate poem on "Old Walt" that lacks any of Pound's harshness, and which imitates Whitman not by using long lines in free verse but rather by insistently employing his favorite tense of the present progressive:

> Old Walt Whitman
> Went finding and seeking,
> Finding less than sought
> Seeking more than found,
> Every detail minding
> Of the seeking or the finding.[10]

Hughes shared Whitman's strategy of holding the actual USA up to the standard of an ideal America, using the very ideology of Americanness against the USA as an effective means of critique, most notably in poems such as "Let America Be America Again." Yet while Whitman was usually quite happy to defer the actualization of America's promise into the future, the day-to-day realities of racial inequality that Hughes and other African American writers experienced resulted in greater urgency in both aesthetics and politics.

These cases mentioned so far show that Whitman's poetry is so all-encompassing and varied that potentially anyone could find their own Whitman to use as a role model, either in positively embracing or negatively rejecting that particular Whitman as an influence. This is possible because Whitman's aesthetics is so fundamentally built on contradiction and complexity: "Do I contradict myself? / Very well then .... I contradict myself; I am large .... I contain multitudes" (LG55, 55). Thus, Hughes could enlist Whitman in his liberal critique of racism even though Whitman's poetry and Whitman the poet are no less (or more) racist than their times. Similarly, Whitman's at times comically exaggerated masculinity, his arrogance and swagger, did not deter women and feminist writers from positively acknowledging his influence on their work – after all, Whitman may have been the first American poet to proudly announce "The Female equally with the Male I sing" (LG, 1).

Among the many American women poets of the twentieth century, it is Muriel Rukeyser who has drawn most explicitly on Whitman in her own poetics, and like Langston Hughes her aesthetic agenda is inextricably linked to a sociopolitical one as well, combining pacifism, socialism, and feminism. It may well be Rukeyser's Whitmanian touch that has caused her for a long time to fall through any of the meshes woven by academic critics of poetry. Louise Kertesz describes this succinctly:

A woman Whitman, a woman whose work recalls the boldness and scope of Whitman's, was offensive to critics of the forties and fifties. When one asks why Rukeyser has been given little attention in published scholarly discussions, the answer seems to be: she didn't fit. She didn't fit into critics' notions of what poetry should be, what poetry by a woman should be.[11]

Rukeyser's poetics is built on the notion of the poem as a meeting-place of communal action and interaction, as she outlines it in her poetological text *The Life of Poetry* (1949). This is related both to Whitman's poetics of many voices coming together in the poem and to its speaking persona, but differs precisely in the lack of this strong individual self incorporating and thus potentially subduing this multiplicity. Simply speaking, Rukeyser replaces the strong Whitmanian "I" with a "We," a first-person plural perspective that is no less complex than Whitman's singular one, although in a very different way. Like Hughes, she very explicitly draws on Whitman as a deliberately chosen tradition that is influential because it is welcomed as such in its particular construction by those who actively make their predecessors. Whereas the Anglo-American modernists may have felt a greater need to liberate themselves from the influence of an immediate predecessor, from his aesthetics and what he had come to symbolize, later writers outside of high modernism could take a step back from this first-generation rejection and more coolly utilize what they considered useful. Rukeyser is assuring her active and deliberate role in this in no uncertain terms: "If we are free, we are free to choose a tradition, and we find in the past as well as the present our poets of outrage – like Melville – and our poets of possibility – like Whitman."[12] She cherishes Whitman's poetry for its quality of "always making a meeting-place,"[13] and notably she adds a paragraph that summarizes concisely what it means to be influenced by Whitman to her and to the other poets discussed here:

> Whitman is a "bad influence"; that is, he cannot be imitated. He can, in hilarious or very dull burlesques, be parodied; but anyone who has come under his rhythms to the extent of trying to use them knows how great a folly is there. He cannot be extended; it is as if his own curse on "poems distill'd from poems" were still effective (as it forever is); but what is always possible is to go deeper into one's own sources, the body and the ancient religious poetry, and go on with the work he began.[14]

The poet who reveled in Whitman's bad influence – understood in those terms as an invitation to go deeper and further and to keep beginning without imitating – most eagerly and expansively in the twentieth century is Allen Ginsberg, the central figure of the Beat Generation in the 1950s. He is the one who built most directly and successfully on Whitman's poetics of long lines, anaphoric repetition, and free verse. As he states in "Notes Written on Finally Recording *Howl*":

> Whitman's form had rarely been further explored (improved on even) in the U.S. – Whitman always a mountain too vast to be seen. Everybody assumes (with Pound?) (except Jeffers) that his line is a big freakish uncontrollable necessary prosaic goof. No attempt's been made to use it in the light of early twentieth century organization of new speech-rhythm prosody to build up large organic structures.[15]

Ginsberg not only infused Whitman's lines with the bodily aspect of breath as the basic unit of measure in poetry, but he also made poetry even more of a vocal performance, building further on Whitman's oratory qualities and prefiguring the poetry slams of today. Especially Ginsberg's Beat phase – which is often overemphasized while his much more substantial later works are neglected – looks directly to Whitman as a prophet and aesthetic model of this contemporary counterculture, exemplified most obviously in poems such as "Howl" or "America." Whitman even makes a personal appearance in "A Supermarket in California" (1955), "childless, lonely old grubber, poking among the meats in the refrigerator and eyeing the grocery boys," who may still have some wisdom to share about the future but who is also perhaps outdated in a world that has changed so radically since his time: "Where are we going, Walt Whitman? The doors close in an hour. Which way does your beard point tonight? / (I touch your book and dream of our odyssey in the supermarket and feel absurd.)"[16] Ginsberg repeatedly invokes Whitman – along with William Blake – as a poet-prophet and a model for his own role as a poitically minded countercultural poet. In particular, in his constant critique of the USA he routinely cited Whitman's phrase in *Democratic Vistas* (1871) of the "fabled damned" (PW, 2:424) that describes a modern civilization that keeps materially progressing but spiritually deteriorating.

Ginsberg may be credited to no small extent with constructing Whitman as the "good gray poet" for the twentieth century after decades of critical engagement with Whitman's poetry and his poetic persona resulted in a much less celebratory (to say the least) perspective on him and his works. Perhaps Ginsberg is also partly responsible for the construction of Whitman as a gay poet, if not *the* gay American poet, which would occur as gay and lesbian studies began in the 1970s to reread and revise the canon of American literature. The story of Whitman's influence in the USA is thus one of different versions of Whitman that would be molded from the raw material provided by his poetry, whose complexity allows for any number of such constructions, none of which can claim to be singularly accurate or true. The latest instance of this invocation occurred after the terrorist attacks of September 11, 2001, when a considerable number of poems on 9/11 drew on Whitman and cast him once more in the idealized role of a good-natured advocate of universal love and democracy who could serve as a model of reconciliation and courage in trying times. Some poets unabashedly imitated Whitman's style and diction in usually failed attempts to transpose his nineteenth-century aesthetics and politics onto the twenty-first, while those were more successful who followed Rukeyser's lead and explored what might be salvaged from Whitmanian poetics to fit their own times and places (for example Robert Vas Dias's "Song of the Cities (After 9/11/01)").[17] Regardless of their very mixed quality these poems all testify to the persistence of Whitmanian influence in American poetry, as Whitman is the single most prominent canonical poet who is invoked in and by poems on 9/11, either in form or style or as a poetic persona.

This persistence manifests itself beyond the examples presented above, and they are merely selectively representing a much larger engagement with Whitman in American poetry that continues to this day. In 1981, Ed Folsom claimed in the highly recommendable introduction to the anthology *Walt Whitman: The Measure of His Song*, "So palpable is Whitman's presence that it's difficult for an American poet to define himself or herself without direct reference to him,"[18] and this statement still rings true today. However, one might qualify it by saying that, in the twenty-first century, this definition with Whitman may also occur more indirectly; if Pound thought he could still make a pact of "commerce" with Whitman, then later poets might find that their commerce needs to include Pound as well, and so Whitman may not necessarily be prominently visible as a node in this network of influence and connections, which does not detract from his structural relevance to it. Whitman's self-construction as *the* beginner of American poetry was partially successful in that he is considered *a* beginner of American poetry today, not the singular origin of any future American poetry but a strong beginning among only a few others of equal impact. Free verse is certainly Whitman's most lasting formal innovation, as it is arguably the standard poetic form today, but any exploration of its openness will now have to acknowledge Ginsberg's experiments as well as Whitman's. For this reason, Whitman's influence on American poetry remains processual, and if he has been "absorbed," then absorption means not disappearance but perpetual creative reengagement – which might be just the thing the author of the 1855 Preface was after in cultivating his legacy.

Notes

1. This indicates that the notion of influence can best be understood as a concise yet flawed metaphor for what is better described in terms of intertextuality, family resemblances, or continuities that are often in the eye of the beholder; I will use the term in this loose way here.
2. Robert D. Richardson, *Emerson: The Mind on Fire* (Berkeley, CA: University of California Press, 1995), 522.
3. David Haven Blake, *Walt Whitman and the Culture of American Celebrity* (New Haven, CT: Yale University Press, 2006), 52.
4. Mark Morrison, "Nationalism and the Modern American Canon," in *The Cambridge Companion to American Modernism*, ed. Walter Kalaidjian (New York, NY: Cambridge University Press, 2006), 15–16.
5. Thomas Stearns Eliot, "The Waste Land," in *The Waste Land and Other Poems* (New York, NY: Harcourt, 2014), 29.
6. Ezra Pound, "A Pact," in *Selected Poems 1908–1959* (London: Faber & Faber, 1975), 45.
7. William Carlos Williams, "America, Whitman, and the Art of Poetry," *Williams Carlos Williams Review* 13.1 (Spring 1987), 1.
8. Ed Folsom, "So Long, So Long! Walt Whitman, Langston Hughes and the Art of Longing," in *Walt Whitman, Where the Future Becomes Present*, eds. David Haven Blake and Michael Robertson (Iowa City, IA: University of Iowa Press, 2008), 129.
9. Langston Hughes, "Walt Whitman and the Negro," in *The Collected Works of Langston Hughes: Essays on Art, Race, Politics, and World Affairs*, ed. Christopher C. De Santis (Columbia, MO: University of Missouri Press, 2002), 348.
10. Langston Hughes, "Old Walt," in *The Collected Poems of Langston Hughes*, eds. Arnold Rampersad and David Roessel (New York, NY: Vintage, 1994), 446.
11. Louise Kertesz, *The Poetic Vision of Muriel Rukeyser* (Baton Rouge, LA: Louisiana State University Press, 1980), 43.
12. Muriel Rukeyser, *The Life of Poetry* (Ashfield, MA: Paris Press, [1949] 1996), x.
13. Ibid., 78.
14. Ibid., 79.
15. Allen Ginsberg, "Notes Written on Finally Recording *Howl*," in *Deliberate Prose: Selected Essays 1952–1995*, ed. Bill Morgan (New York, NY: Harper Perennial, 2000), 230.
16. Allen Ginsberg, "A Supermarket in California," in *Collected Poems 1947–1997*, (New York, NY: Harper Perennial, 2007), 144.
17. Robert Vas Dias, "Song of the Cities (After 9/11/01)," in *September 11, 2001: American Writers Respond*, ed. William Heyen (Silver Spring, MD: Etruscan Press, 2002), 385–86.
18. Ed Folsom, "Talking Back to Whitman: An Introduction," in *Walt Whitman: The Measure of His Song*, eds. Jim Perlman, Ed Folsom, and Dan Campion (Duluth, MN: Holy Cow! Press, 1998), 21. This is the revised second edition of the original book published in 1981.

CHAPTER 38

Impact on the World

Ed Folsom

Most students and scholars of Whitman in the United States read his work in a national context, hearing in it an attempt to articulate a democratic identity for the developing country, and finding in it responses to major American historical and cultural events, from the Revolutionary War through the Civil War, with commentary on the Constitution, US presidents, immigration, and an emerging urban sensibility. American poets from Whitman's time to the present – from Hart Crane to Langston Hughes, from Muriel Rukeyser to Robert Creeley, from William Carlos Williams to Allen Ginsberg, from June Jordan to Yusef Komunyakaa – have carried on a non-stop debate with him about his vision of the American nation, and they have viewed his radical poetics as essentially intertwined with the national character, a kind of distinct and distinctive American voice.

But another poetic dialogue has been taking place outside of the country's borders for the past 150 years, one that involves talking back to Whitman by an international group of poets – from Federico García Lorca to Pablo Neruda and Jorge Luis Borges, from Cesare Pavese to Czeslaw Milosz, from Fernando Pessoa to Artur Lundkvist, from Hermann Hesse to Thomas Mann, from Amin Rihani to Adonis, from Guo Moruo to Ai Qing, from D. H. Lawrence to Charles Tomlinson – as his influence has extended far and wide, not only across race and social class and ethnicity and poetic style but across nationalities, languages, and continents. The migration of Whitman from an American to an international context has been the result of many efforts on many fronts. Whitman himself, of course, imagined having an international reach, as he first made abundantly clear in his 1856 "Poem of Salutation." This is the Whitman poem that inevitably gets noticed and discussed in other countries but one that seldom gets examined in the USA, and, when it does, it is usually a source of some embarrassment. When he changed the poem's title, in a fumbling act of partial translation, to "Salut au Monde!"

in 1860, it was as if he were allowing the poem to slip off into another language even as it was being read. "What widens within you Walt Whitman?" the poet asks here, and answers, "Within me latitude widens, longitude lengthens," as he creates far-ranging catalogs that answer the questions "What do you hear Walt Whitman?" and "What do you see Walt Whitman?" (LG, 137–48). These catalogs extend around the globe.

Irene Ramalho Santos has read Whitman's "poetic effect" in this poem as "pretty much that of an unfolding of subjectivity [. . .] which ends up totally encompassing its object." "To be 'ready' for the Bard of America," Ramalho Santos concludes, "is to have been 'penetrated' (the phallic metaphor is Whitman's) by the 'divine rapport' of its all-encompassing, indeed, all-generating, spermatic imagination."[1] Walter Grünzweig, however, hears "Salut" in a very different way and has offered a bracing internationalist reading of the poem, which he calls "Whitman's most successful individual poem [. . .] from the point of view of the international reception to his work." Grünzweig views the poem as tied to Whitman's enthusiasm for "the mid-century revolutionary movements" in Europe, showing how Whitman's seemingly deadening catalogs in fact work to "render insignificant the 'official governmental map.' Oceans, mountains, rivers, and peoples form natural entities reaching beyond and thus ignoring political borders and institutions. Borders play no role whatsoever; the world in Whitman's poem is a liberated one."[2]

"Salut au Monde!" is the poem that Argentinian writer Jorge Luis Borges cited when he made his famous point about Whitman having created a singular fictional entity, a hero with a "threefold nature": one being Walt Whitman, the biographical entity living in the United States in the nineteenth century; the second being a projected shadow of that man, also named Walt Whitman, "magnified by hope, by joy, by exultation"; and, finally, "also the reader, any reader, any one of his present or future readers." "How this was done we shall never quite know," Borges continues; "He makes the reader speak to him: 'What do you hear Walt Whitman?'" Whitman's great feat, Borges says, was to make "the editor of the Brooklyn Daily Eagle into Walt Whitman, into America, into all of us," and Borges hears in the term "America" a broader projection, a desire that dissolves the United States into something larger, something beyond nationality, an idealized "America" that can speak for and as the world.[3]

Virtually everyone who has written on Whitman and imperialism or colonialism or expansionism or hegemonic discourse – and there have been numerous illuminating studies in the past three decades – comes up against some version of this unavoidable paradox: the poet who celebrates diversity, multiple identities, and democratic tolerance can sometimes seem dangerously and globally hegemonic. The democratic lover can be downright pushy: he is, as he says, "around, tenacious, acquisitive, tireless, and cannot be shaken away" (LG, 35). It is a negotiation that takes place on the dark borderland of America where Whitman's big, boisterous, generous democratic "I" meets the Other and decides, without asking, to make the Other a part of the I. There is a sexual valence to this dynamic and an imperialist one as well. Back in 1986, Doris Sommer examined the poet's "absorption of difference," identifying this as "the feature that appears to result in a political ambiguity between a democratic embrace through the leveling of relationships and an imperialist, centralizing thrust that denies difference and autonomy." Whitman, Sommer warns, "will love you, but he may love you to death."[4]

Betsy Erkkila has defined the problem elegantly: "The paradox of Whitman's poetic democracy is that, at the very moment when he seeks to be most inclusive, universal, and democratic, his poetry becomes most powerful – and most powerfully dangerous – in silencing and denying the rights, liberties, and differences of others." "We have not come fully to terms with the extent to which his bound-breaking work is simultaneously bound up with the paradoxical promise and limits, hope and blood violence that mark the history of American democracy," writes Erkkila.[5] Awareness of this paradox goes back a long way. Thomas Mann's son, Klaus Mann, wrote in 1941 about Whitman that "in many cases both elements – the spirit of nationalistic expansion and the spirit of universal solidarity – overlap and interfuse together."[6] Even Mauricio González de la Garza's 1971 book, aggressively entitled *Walt Whitman: Racista, Imperialista, Antimexicano*, puzzles over how this "hombre contradictorio" could write such internationally inflected poetry while holding such imperialistic attitudes in his journalism.[7] And Kerry Larson has written an entire book investigating one aspect of this paradox, what he calls Whitman's "conservative radicalism," exploring how this tension manifests itself in the very fabric of Whitman's poetry, in his familiar addresses to the reader that "simultaneously extend the promise of conversational intimacy at the same time they are driven to insist upon a textual authority that barricades itself against all scrutiny."[8] Here we have it: Whitman the cozy intimate, wanting to share your most inexpressible desires as he invites you to create *his* poem; and Whitman the tyrant, who tells you what you *must* do in order to even *begin* to understand him.

It should come as no surprise, then, that when we investigate Whitman's influence on and existence in other cultures, we find that

almost all countries have a dual tradition in absorbing Whitman. He enters
most cultures as both invader and immigrant, as the confident, pushy,
overwhelming representative of his nation, as the large and inscrutable
voice of the United States; *and* as the intimate, inviting, submissive,
endlessly malleable immigrant, whose work gets absorbed and rewritten
in always surprising ways. The Whitman who gets absorbed by other
countries is more of a *naturalized* figure, part of a popular tradition, who
takes up a new citizenship and gets read into various native cultural
traditions, often argued with or reinterpreted in ways that seem alien to
most American readers. So we get books in India that read *Leaves of Grass*
as a kind of Western yoga discipline, as in O. K. Nambiar's *Mahayogi Walt
Whitman*, or that see him as a Western inheritor of Vedantic tradition.[9]
In China, he often is read as a modern connection to Taoism, as someone
who reattached twentieth-century Chinese poets to the ancient texts of
Lao-Tzu and Chuang-tzu. He also has been read in detail in China and in
the former Soviet Union as a proto-socialist poet. What we see in the
varied national responses to Whitman is the cultural version of what
Whitman demanded of each of his readers: "the reader is to do something
for himself, must be on the alert, must himself or herself construct indeed
the poem, argument, history, metaphysical essay – the text furnishing the
hints, the clue, the start or frame-work" (PW, 2:425). So it is with each
country that translates the work (both literally and figuratively), as
Whitman knew – what would get translated would be something new,
something his text would furnish hints for while the original work itself
would remain inscrutable and untranslatable. *Leaves*, in good democratic
(and imperialistic) fashion, would eventually become something so vast
that it would incorporate all languages and traditions, altering them and
simultaneously changed by them.

This complex and conflicted international impact has only gradually
come into focus and gained as wide a lens as it has needed. Whitman's
supporters in Britain, like William Michael Rossetti and Anne Gilchrist,
were known during his lifetime as his English friends and offered testimony about his influence in and on British culture. It was perhaps
inevitable that the first extended study of Whitman's impact on and
absorption into another culture would be Harold Blodgett's 1934 *Walt
Whitman in England*,[10] which examined how Rossetti and Gilchrist, along
with other literary figures like Edward Dowden, John Addington
Symonds, Robert Buchanan, Algernon Charles Swinburne, and Edward
Carpenter, adapted and tempered and extended and responded to
Whitman's work during the last decades of the poet's life and the first

decades after his death. "How good that English crowd has always been to me," Whitman told Horace Traubel in 1888; "I want it to be forever recognized" (WWC, 1:281). Whitman experienced, with his British reception, the way his work – even when it stayed in the same language – could be heard in a very different way when it was read in another cultural context. Rossetti presented *Leaves of Grass* to British readers in 1868 in an expurgated form, leaving out poems (including "Song of Myself") that contained passages that he believed British readers would find offensive (his goal, he said, was "to omit entirely every poem which could with any tolerable fairness be deemed offensive to the feelings of morals or propriety in this peculiarly sensitive age").[11] As the century progressed, Whitman's work appeared in other British editions, including volumes in the popular and inexpensive Canterbury Poets and Scott Library series published by Walter Scott Publishing, works that made Whitman available to a wide working-class readership;[12] and then, under the guidance of Carpenter and the Bolton Eagle Street "college," British readers began to hear Whitman as a kind of socialist prophet with a liberating message of sexually charged comradeship.[13]

During Whitman's lifetime, writers from non-English speaking countries began to express an interest in getting *Leaves of Grass* translated into their languages. Whitman received overtures to translate his work into German and Russian, and he began to reconceive his purposes and goals in an international light. He wrote to T. W. H. Rolleston, an Irish writer who lived in Germany and who joined with the German translator Karl Knortz to produce the first booklength German translation of Whitman's poetry, about how he was rethinking the audience for his work: "It has not been for my own country alone – ambitious as the saying so may seem – that I have composed [*Leaves of Grass*]. It has been to practically start an internationality of poems" (Corr., 3:369). To a translator proposing a Russian edition of his work, Whitman wrote that his "dearest dream is for an internationality of poems and poets, binding the lands of the earth closer than all treaties and diplomacy," and he emphasized that his "purpose" was to create a "hearty comradeship [. . .] for all the nations of the earth."[14]

In 1946, Gay Wilson Allen concluded his influential *Walt Whitman Handbook* with a long chapter called "Walt Whitman and World Literature." It was the first piece to lay out the emerging awareness of just how widespread Whitman's influence had become in non-English-speaking countries.[15] Allen developed the implications of that chapter in his 1955 *Walt Whitman Abroad*, a revealing collection of essays on Whitman by writers from Germany, France, Scandinavia, Russia, Italy,

Spain and Latin America, Israel, Japan, and India.[16] Allen's book appeared just a year after Fernando Alegría had published the first book-length study of Whitman's influence in a non-Anglo literary culture by studying the poet's reception in Spanish-speaking Central and South America;[17] others have followed, each opening up a vast new area of study and each tracing an active creative and critical interplay with and response to Whitman in a foreign culture from the nineteenth century up to the time each book was published.

A number of the studies have focused on European and South American interactions with Whitman. Betsy Erkkila in 1980 examined Whitman's "strong political, social, and even temperamental affinity with France," and explored in detail his influence on French symbolist, postsymbolist, and *l'esprit nouveau* writers.[18] Maria Clara Paro has probed Portuguese and Brazilian responses, with a focus on the Brazilian writers Tasso da Silveira, Ronald de Carvalho, and Mário de Andrade.[19] Walter Grünzweig has offered "an intercultural textual study" of Whitman's widespread reception in German-speaking cultures and has examined the various translations of Whitman's work and the poet's influence on German writers, who constructed Whitman "as a cultural artifact."[20] Enrico Santí revisited and updated the Hispanoamerican influence, with a focus on the long and complex poetic conversations Pablo Neruda and Jorge Luis Borges engaged in with Whitman.[21] And Marta Skwara in 2005 offered the first full examination of "the reception of Walt Whitman in Poland from 1872 up to the present day," analyzing "the many ways Whitman was read, translated, and constructed in the Polish culture."[22]

In 1995, Allen and Ed Folsom updated Allen's *Walt Whitman Abroad* and published new overviews of Whitman's absorption into cultures around the world – the British Isles, Spain and Latin America, Brazil, Portugal, the German-speaking countries, the Netherlands, Belgium, Italy, the former Yugoslavia, Poland, Russia, Sweden, Denmark, Norway, Finland, Israel, India, China, and Japan. This book reprinted poems and essays by writers from the various countries, who all have talked back to Whitman across national and linguistic borders, and it listed translations of Whitman's work throughout the century following his death.[23] The volume significantly expanded the number and geographical range of countries that had lively, unique, and ongoing interactions with Whitman and his work. Since then, studies that go beyond Europe and Central and South America have proliferated. Guiyou Huang has explored the depth of the Chinese connections, analyzing Whitman's influence on modern Chinese poets, "his role in the new culture movement, and the general appropriation of Whitman by Chinese critics," "the relations between him and major Chinese intellectuals" (including Mao Zedong), and Whitman's "political ideology in the Chinese context."[24] Studies are also emerging about Whitman's associations with Mideastern cultures. J. R. LeMaster and Sabahat Jahan have recently tracked the similarities between Whitman's religious beliefs and those of two classical Persian poets, Hafez and Rumi, arguing that Whitman was a serious religious poet and that his religious ideas have a great deal in common with those of the Sufis;[25] and in 2012 Sholeh Wolpe and Mohsen Emadi translated the complete "Song of Myself" into Persian for the first time.[26] Jeffrey Einboden undertook the first extended comparison of Arabic and Hebrew translations of Whitman, exploring the choices and changes made by Middle Eastern translators and offering transnational readings of *Leaves of Grass*. Einboden's revealing analysis of how Iraqi poet Saadi Youssef's 1976 Arabic translation of *Leaves of Grass* displaces Whitman's work "from its American specificity" demonstrates some of the ways *Leaves of Grass* has begun to take on an "Arabic afterlife."[27]

At the same time as these book-length studies of Whitman in relation to specific foreign cultures have been appearing, another set of books and articles have focused on how specific poets in other nations have carried on career-long engagements with Whitman's work, often talking back directly to Whitman, as if his familiar address to "you" with its taunting request – "Listener up there! what have you to confide to me? / [. . .] / Will you speak before I am gone? will you prove already too late?" (LG, 89) – was to be taken literally, as poet after poet from other cultures has answered back in his or her native language, from another time and from another place, often arguing with or cajoling or affirming or denying Whitman in a direct address back to him. Lengthy studies of poets like Pablo Neruda (Chile), Pedro Mir (Dominica), Fernando Pessoa (Portugal), Federico García Lorca (Spain), Czeslaw Milosz (Poland), and Cesar Pavese (Italy) have been published in recent years, and more are on the way.[28]

Such work underscores the malleability of Whitman's work as it gets translated, responded to, interpreted, and absorbed by other cultures and languages, and this still emerging field is one of the most exciting, innovative, and demanding developments in Whitman scholarship. Even more studies are needed: detailed examinations of Whitman in Spain, Italy, Russia, and Japan are waiting to be written, and African writers' interactions with Whitman have yet to be examined fully.[29]

Every act of translation is, of course, an act of interpretation, and tracing the linguistic transformation of the work of the poet who bragged that

"I too am untranslatable" is particularly challenging, since Whitman built so much of his poetry on the endless interplay between two characters called "I" and "you" (LG, 89). Consider any translator's dilemma as he or she comes to the third line of "Song of Myself": "For every atom belonging to me as good belongs to you" (LG, 28). That "you" is one of the most difficult words in the poem to translate, because the second-person pronoun in modern English is quite promiscuous: "you" is the word we use to address our most intimate lover as well as a total stranger, a single person alone with us in a room or a vast crowd. Whitman teases out all the implications of this promiscuous English pronoun that signals at once only you, a "simple separate person," and also you, the "En-Masse," the world of potentially intimate strangers who always hover around us (LG, 1). Translators into most other languages must decide in each case whether the "you" is informal or formal, singular or plural, and in some cases masculine or feminine, and each time they make that decision, a bit of Whitman's wildly suggestive ambiguity disappears, and the poem begins to transmute into something uniquely different. In translation, Whitman alters the language that he disappears into at precisely the moment he magically appears anew in it; the new language alters Whitman as much as he alters it. It is that endless push/pull of imperialism and democratic affection, the insatiable desire to change what we encounter and, simultaneously, to be changed by it.

Notes

1. Irene Ramalho Santos, *Atlantic Poets: Fernando Pessoa's Turn in Anglo-American Modernism* (Lebanon, NH: University Press of New England, 2003), 89–90.
2. Walter Grünzweig, "'For America – For All the Earth': Walt Whitman as an International(ist) Poet," in *Breaking Bounds: Whitman and American Cultural Studies*, eds. Betsy Erkkila and Jay Grossman (New York, NY: Oxford University Press, 1996), 240, 242.
3. Jorge Luis Borges, "Foreword," in *Homenaje a Walt Whitman / Homage to Walt Whitman*, ed. Didier Tisdel Jaén (Tuscaloosa, AL: University of Alabama Press, 1969), xvi–xvii.
4. Doris Sommer, "Supplying Demand: Walt Whitman as the Liberal Self," in *Reinventing the Americas*, eds. Bell Gale Chevigny and Gari Laguardia (New York, NY: Cambridge University Press, 1986), 81.
5. Betsy Erkkila, "Whitman and American Empire," in *Walt Whitman of Mickle Street: A Centennial Collection*, ed. Geoffrey M. Sill (Knoxville, TN: University of Tennessee Press, 1994), 56–57.

6. Klaus Mann, "The Present Greatness of Walt Whitman," *Decision* 1 (April 1941), 27.

7. Mauricio González de la Garza, *Walt Whitman: Racista, Imperialista, Antimexicano* (Mexico: Coleccion Málaga, 1971), 9.

8. Kerry Larson, *Whitman's Drama of Consensus* (Chicago, IL: University of Chicago Press, 1988), 28, 23.

9. O. K. Nambiar, *Maha Yogi Walt Whitman: New Light on Yoga* (Bangalore: Jeevan Publications, 1978); see also V. K. Chari, *Whitman in the Light of Vedantic Mysticism: An Interpretation* (Lincoln, NE: University of Nebraska Press, 1964), and T. R. Rajasekharaiah, *The Roots of Whitman's Grass* (Rutherford, Madison, and Teaneck, NJ: Fairleigh Dickinson University Press, 1970).

10. Harold Blodgett, *Walt Whitman in England* (Ithaca, NY: Cornell University Press, 1934).

11. William Michael Rossetti, "Prefatory Notice," in *Poems of Walt Whitman* (London: John Camden Hotten, 1868), 20, WWA.

12. See Ernest Rhys, ed., *The Poems of Walt Whitman [Selected]* (London: Walter Scott, 1887), WWA; and *Democratic Vistas, and Other Papers* (London: Walter Scott, 1888); *Specimen Days in America* (London: Walter Scott, 1887).

13. For a recent extended investigation of this cultural translation of Whitman, see Kirsten Harris, *Walt Whitman and British Socialism: "The Love of Comrades"* (New York, NY: Routledge, 2016).

14. Walt Whitman to John Fitzgerald Lee, December 20, 1881. WWA.

15. Gay Wilson Allen, *Walt Whitman Handbook* (Chicago, IL: Packard and Company, 1946), 443–545.

16. Gay Wilson Allen, ed., *Walt Whitman Abroad* (Syracuse, NY: Syracuse University Press, 1955).

17. Fernando Alegría, *Walt Whitman en Hispanoamerica* (Mexico: Ediciones Studium, 1954).

18. Betsy Erkkila, *Walt Whitman among the French: Poet and Myth* (Princeton, NJ: Princeton University Press, 1980), 7.

19. Maria Clara Bonetti Paro, "Walt Whitman in Brazil," *Walt Whitman Quarterly Review* 11.2 (1993), 57–66; Bonetti Paro, "Leituras Brasileiras da Obra de Walt Whitman," unpublished PhD diss., University of São Paulo, 1995.

20. Walter Grünzweig, *Constructing the German Walt Whitman* (Iowa City, IA: University of Iowa Press, 1995), 3; this book is a condensed English version of Grünzweig's more extensive German study, *Walt Whitmann: Die deutsch-sprachige Rezeption als interkulturelles Phänomen* (Munich: Wilhelm Fink, 1991).

21. Enrico Santí, "This Land of Prophets: Walt Whitman in Spanish America," in *Ciphers of History: Latin American Readings for a Cultural Age* (New York, NY: Palgrave Macmillan, 2005).

22. Marta Skwara, *"Polski Whitman": O Funkcjonowaniu Poety Obcego w Kulturze Narodowej* (Kraków: Universitas, 2010), 455.

23. Gay Wilson Allen and Ed Folsom, eds., *Walt Whitman and the World* (Iowa City, IA: University of Iowa Press, 1995).

24. Guiyou Huang, *Whitman, Imagism, and Modernism in China and America* (Selinsgrove, PA: Susquehanna University Press, 1997), 37, 55, 73.

25. J. R. LeMaster and Sabahat Jahan, *Walt Whitman and the Persian Poets: A Study in Literature and Religion* (Bethesda, MD: Ibex, 2009).

26. "Song of Myself – Persian," trans. Sholeh Wolpe and Mohsen Emadi, *WhitmanWeb, University of Iowa International Writing Program*, 2012, https://iwp.uiowa.edu/.

27. Jeffrey Einboden, "'I too am untranslatable': Middle Eastern *Leaves*," in *Nineteenth-Century U.S. Literature in Middle Eastern Languages* (Edinburgh: Edinburgh University Press, 2013).

28. See, for example, James Nolan, *Poet-Chief: The Native American Poetics of Walt Whitman and Pablo Neruda* (Albuquerque, NM: University of New Mexico Press, 1994); George B. Handley, *New World Poetics: Nature and the Adamic Imagination of Whitman, Neruda, and Walcott* (Athens, GA: University of Georgia Press, 2007); Francesca Pasciolla, *Walt Whitman in Fernando Pessoa* (London: Critical, Cultural and Communications Press, 2016).

29. African writers strongly influenced by Whitman include South African author Alan Paton, Senegalese poet and politician Léopold Sédar Senghor, Sierra Leone poet Syl Cheney-Coker, Kenyan writer Ngũgĩ wa Thiong'o, Central African funk and groove musician Bibi Tanga, and Egyptian poet Abdel-Muneim Ramadan. South African prime minister Jan Smuts wrote one of the earliest book-length studies of Whitman's philosophy, *Walt Whitman: A Study in the Evolution of Personality* (Detroit, MI: Wayne State University Press, [1895] 1973).

Further Reading

1. Long Island

Genoways, Ted. "Notes on Whitman: 'Fish, Fishermen, and Fishing, on the East End of Long Island': An Excerpt from Walt Whitman's Uncollected Serial 'Letters from a Travelling Young Bachelor.'" *Shenandoah* 50 (2000), 49–56.

Harris, Walter E., III, and George Wallace, eds. *Primal Sanities!: A Tribute to Walt Whitman, An Anthology of Poems and Essays.* Selden, NY: Allbook, 2007.

Krieg, Joann P. *Long Island and Literature.* Interlaken, NY: Heart of the Lakes Publishing, 1989.

——. "Walt Whitman's Long Island Friend: Elisa Seaman Leggett." *Long Island Historical Journal* 9 (1997), 223–33.

Stacy, Jason. "Showing Their Condition: Walt Whitman and Ethical Aesthetics in 'The Sun-Down Papers.'" *Mickle Street Review* 19/20 (2008), http://mickle street.rutgers.edu.

Wheat, Maxwell Corydon, Jr. "Walt Whitman, Long Island and Sense of Place." *West Hills Review* 7 (1987), 76–80.

2. Brooklyn and Manhattan

Dunlap, William. *History of the New Netherlands, Province of New York, and State of New York.* 2 vols. New York, NY: Carter and Thorp, 1839. (Whitman's annotated copy is held by the Library of Congress Rare Books division.)

Krieg, Joann P. "Whitman and the City." *Mickle Street Review* 17/18 (2005). http://micklestreet.rutgers.edu.

Pannapacker, William. "The City." In *A Companion to Walt Whitman.* Edited by Donald D. Kummings, 42–59. West Sussex, UK: Wiley Blackwell, 2006.

Shaw, Lytle. "Whitman's Urbanism." In *The Cambridge Companion to the Literature of New York.* Edited by Cyrus R. K. Patell and Bryan Waterman, 76–89. New York, NY: Cambridge University Press, 2010.

Stiles, Henry R. *History of the City of Brooklyn, Including the Old Town and Village of Brooklyn, the Town of Bushwick, and The Village and City of Williamsburgh,* Vols. *1* and 2. Brooklyn, NY, 1867.

Thomas, M. Wynn. "Whitman's Tale of Two Cities." *American Literary History* 6.4 (1994), 633–57.
Trachtenberg, Alan. "Whitman's Lessons of the City." In *Breaking Bounds: Whitman and American Cultural Studies*. Edited by Betsy Erkkila and Jay Grossman, 163–73. New York, NY: Oxford University Press, 1996.
Whitman, Walt. *Walt Whitman's New York: From Manhattan to Montauk*. Edited by Henry Christman. New York, NY: New Amsterdam Books, 1989.

3. Camden and Philadelphia

Baltzell, E. Digby. *Puritan Boston and Quaker Philadelphia*. New York, NY: Free Press, 1979.
Davis, Robert Leigh. *Whitman and the Romance of Medicine*. Berkeley, CA: University of California Press, 1997.
Jackson, Joseph. *Literary Landmarks of Philadelphia*. Philadelphia, PA: David McKay, 1939.
Leon, Philip W. *Walt Whitman and Sir William Osler: A Poet and His Physician*. Toronto, Ontario: ECW Press, 1995.
Loving, Jerome. *Walt Whitman: The Song of Himself*. Berkeley, CA: University of California Press, 1999.
Perry, Bliss. *Walt Whitman: His Life and Work*. Boston, MA: Houghton Mifflin, 1906.
Price, Kenneth M. *Whitman and Tradition: The Poet in His Century*. New Haven, CT: Yale University Press, 1990.
Robertson, Michael. *Worshipping Walt: The Whitman Disciples*. Princeton, NJ: Princeton University Press, 2008.
Schmidgall, Gary, ed. *Conserving Walt Whitman's Fame: Selections from Horace Traubel's "Conservator," 1890–1919*. Iowa City, IA: University of Iowa Press, 2006.
Walker, Marion Alcaro. *Walt Whitman's Mrs. G: A Biography of Anne Gilchrist*. Madison, NJ: Fairleigh Dickinson University Press, 1991.
Weigley, Russel F., ed. *Philadelphia: A 300-Year History*. New York, NY: Norton, 1982.

4. Washington, DC

Epstein, Daniel Mark. *Lincoln and Whitman: Parallel Lives in Civil War Washington*. New York, NY: Random House, 2005.
Foner, Eric. *Reconstruction: America's Unfinished Revolution, 1863–1877*. New York, NY: Harper Collins, 2002.
Furgurson, Ernest B. *Freedom Rising: Washington in the Civil War*. New York, NY: Vintage, 2005.
Roper, Robert. *Now the Drum of War: Walt Whitman and His Brothers in the Civil War*. New York, NY: Walker, 2008.
Winkle, Kenneth J. *Lincoln's Citadel: The Civil War in Washington, DC*. New York, NY: Norton, 2014.

5. The American South

Bandy, W. T. "Whitman Viewed by Two Southern Gentlemen." *Walt Whitman Quarterly Review* 3.1 (1985), 16–22.

Krieg, Joann P. "Whitman and the City." *Mickle Street Review* 17/18 (2005), http://.micklestreet.rutgers.edu.

Moore, Rayburn S. "Literary World Gone Mad: Hayne on Whitman." *Southern Literary Journal* 10 (1977), 75–83.

Moss, William. "Walt Whitman in Dixie." *Southern Literary Journal* 22.2 (1990), 98–118.

Wilkenfeld, Jacob. "Re-Scripting Southern Poetic Discourse in Whitman's 'Longings for Home.'" *Walt Whitman Quarterly Review* 29.3 (2012), 47–65.

6. Verse Forms

Bradford, Adam C. *Communities of Death: Whitman, Poe, and the American Culture of Mourning.* Columbia, MO: University of Missouri Press, 2014.

Brooks, Van Wyck. *The Times of Melville and Whitman.* New York, NY: Dutton, 1947.

Cavitch, David. *My Soul and I: The Inner Life of Walt Whitman.* Boston, MA: Beacon Press, 1985.

Cavitch, Max. *American Elegy: The Poetry of Mourning from the Puritans to Whitman.* Minneapolis, MN: University of Minnesota Press, 2007.

Davis, Theo. *Ornamental Aesthetics: The Poetry of Attending in Thoreau, Dickinson, and Whitman.* New York, NY: Oxford University Press, 2016.

Matthiessen, F. O. *American Renaissance: Art and Expression in the Age of Emerson and Whitman.* New York, NY: Oxford University Press, 1941.

Noble, Mark. *American Poetic Materialism from Whitman to Stevens.* New York, NY: Cambridge University Press, 2015.

Pease, Donald E. *Visionary Compacts: American Renaissance Writings in Cultural Context.* Madison, WI: University of Wisconsin Press, 1987.

Reynolds, David S. *Beneath the American Renaissance: The Subversive Imagination in the Age of Emerson and Melville.* Cambridge, MA: Harvard University Press, 1988.

7. Periodical Poetry

Baker, Portia. "Walt Whitman and *The Atlantic Monthly.*" *American Literature* 6.3 (1934), 283–301.

Baker, Portia. "Walt Whitman's Relations with Some New York Magazines." *American Literature* 7.3 (1935), 274–301.

Cooper, Allene. "Science and the Reception of Poetry in Postbellum American Journals." *American Periodicals* 4 (1994), 24–46.

Eckstrom, Leif. "On Puffing: The *Saturday Press* and the Circulation of Symbolic Capital." In *Whitman among the Bohemians*. Edited by Joanna Levin and Edward Whitley, 53–74. Iowa City, IA: University of Iowa Press, 2014.

Karbiener, Karen. "Bridging Brooklyn and Bohemia: How the *Brooklyn Daily Times* Brought Whitman Closer to Pfaff's." In *Whitman among the Bohemians*. Edited by Joanna Levin and Edward Whitley, 1–18. Iowa City, IA: University of Iowa Press, 2014.

___."Whitman at Pfaff's: Personal Space, a Public Place, and the Boundary-Breaking Poems of *Leaves of Grass* (1860)." In *Literature of New York*. Edited by Sabrina Fuchs-Abrams, 1–38. Newcastle upon Tyne: Cambridge Scholars Publishing, 2009.

Lause, Mark. *The Antebellum Crisis and America's First Bohemians*. Kent, OH: Kent State University Press, 2009.

Levin, Joanna. *Bohemia in America, 1858–1920*. Stanford, CA: Stanford University Press, 2010.

Mabbott, Thomas Olive. "Walt Whitman Edits the *Sunday Times* July 1842–June 1843." *American Literature* 39.1 (1967), 99–102.

Stansell, Christine. "Whitman at Pfaff's: Commercial Culture, Literary Life and New York Bohemia at Mid-Century." *Walt Whitman Quarterly Review* 10.3 (1993), 107–26.

8. Periodical Fiction

Blalock, Stephanie M. "Bibliography of Walt Whitman's Short Fiction in Periodicals." *Walt Whitman Quarterly Review* 30.4 (2013), 181–250.

Castiglia, Christopher, and Glenn Hendler, "Introduction." In *Franklin Evans, or The Inebriate A Tale of the Times* by Walt Whitman. Edited by Christopher Castiglia and Glenn Hendler, ix-xxv. Durham, NC: Duke University Press, 2007.

Gannon, Thomas C. "Reading Boddo's Body: Crossing the Borders of Race and Sexuality in Whitman's 'Half-Breed.'" *Walt Whitman Quarterly Review* 22.2 (2004), 87–107.

Gautier, Amina. "The 'Creole' Episode: Slavery and Temperance in *Franklin Evans*." In *Whitman Noir: Black America and the Good Gray Poet*. Edited by Ivy G. Wilson, 32–53. Iowa City, IA: University of Iowa Press, 2014.

Grossman, Jay. "Representing Men." In *Reconstituting the American Renaissance: Emerson, Whitman, and the Politics of Representation*, 161–205. Durham, NC: Duke University Press, 2003.

Moon, Michael. *Disseminating Whitman: Revision and Corporeality in Leaves of Grass*. Cambridge, MA: Harvard University Press, 1991.

Warner, Michael. "Whitman Drunk." In *Breaking Bounds: Whitman and American Cultural Studies*. Edited by Betsy Erkkila and Jay Grossman, 30–43. New York, NY: Oxford University Press, 1996.

9. Journalism

Blondheim, Menahem. *News over the Wires: The Telegraph and the Flow of Public Information in America, 1844–1897*. Cambridge, MA: Harvard University Press, 1994.

Burrows, Edwin G., and Mike Wallace. *Gotham: A History of New York City to 1898*. New York, NY: Oxford University Press, 1999.

Cohen, Patricia Cline. *The Murder of Helen Jewett: Life and Death of a Prostitute in Nineteenth-Century New York*. New York, NY: Vintage Books, 1999.

Fishkin, Shelley Fisher. *From Fact to Fiction: Journalism and Imaginative Writing in America*. Baltimore, MD: Johns Hopkins University Press, 1985.

Hruschka, John. "Order Books: The Development of a Modern American Book Trade." Unpublished diss., The Pennsylvania State University, 2008.

Huntzicker, William E. *The Popular Press: 1833–1865*. Westport, CT: Greenwood Press, 1999.

Karbiener, Karen. "Reconstructing Whitman's Desk at the *Brooklyn Daily Times*." *Walt Whitman Quarterly Review* 33.1 (2015), 21–50.

Loving, Jerome. *Walt Whitman: The Song of Himself*. Berkeley, CA: University of California Press, 1999.

Reynolds, David. *Walt Whitman's America: A Cultural Biography*. New York, NY: Alfred A. Knopf, 1995.

Rubin, Joseph Jay. *The Historic Whitman*. University Park, PA: Pennsylvania State University Press, 1973.

Stacy, Jason. *Walt Whitman's Multitudes: Labor Reform and Persona in Whitman's Journalism and the First Leaves of Grass, 1840–1855*. New York, NY: Peter Lang, 2008.

Whitman, Walt. *The Journalism*, 2 vols. Edited by Herbert Bergman, Douglas A. Noverr, and Edward J. Recchia. New York, NY: Peter Lang, 1998–2003.

——. *Walt Whitman's Selected Journalism*, edited by Douglas Noverr and Jason Stacy. Iowa City, IA: University of Iowa Press, 2015.

10. Oratory

Carr O'Neill, Bonnie. "'The Best of Me Is There': Emerson as Lecturer and Celebrity." *American Literature* 80.4 (2008), 739–67.

Clark, Gregory, and S. Michael Halloran, eds. *Oratorical Culture in Nineteenth-Century America: Transformations in the Theory and Practice of Rhetoric*. Carbondale, IL: Southern Illinois University Press, 1993.

Erkkila, Betsy. *Whitman the Political Poet*. New York, NY: Oxford University Press, 1989.

Finkel, William L. "Walt Whitman's Manuscript Notes on Oratory." *American Literature* 22.1 (1950), 29–53.

LeMaster, J. R. "Oratory." In *A Companion to Walt Whitman*. Edited by Donald D. Kummings, 87–100. Malden, MA: Blackwell Publishing, 2006.

Pollak, Vivian R. "Whitman Unperturbed: The Civil War and After." In *Walt Whitman: The Centennial Essays*. Edited by Ed Folsom, 30–47. Iowa City: University of Iowa Press, 1994.

Vendler, Helen. "Poetry and the Mediation of Value: Whitman on Lincoln." *Michigan Quarterly Review* 39.1 (2000), 1–18.

York, Jake Adam. "When Time and Place Avail: Whitman's Written Orator Reconsidered." *Walt Whitman Quarterly Review* 19.2 (2001), 90–107.

11. Opera

Brasher, Thomas L. *Whitman as Editor of the Brooklyn Daily Eagle*. Detroit, MI: Wayne State University Press, 1970.

Cooke, Alice L. "Notes on Whitman's Musical Background." *The New England Quarterly* 19.2 (1946), 224–35.

Irwin, John T. "Self-Evidence and Self-Reference: Nietzsche and Tragedy, Whitman and Opera." *New Literary History* 11.1 (1979), 177–92.

Karbiener, Karen. "The Unexpress'd: Walt Whitman's Late Thoughts on Richard Wagner." In *Comparative Romanticisms: Power, Gender, Subjectivity*. Edited by Larry H. Peer and Diane Long Hoeveler, 81–99. Columbia, SC: Camden House, 1998.

Koestenbaum, Wayne. *The Queen's Throat: Opera, Homosexuality, and the Mystery of Desire*. New York, NY: Poseidon, 1993.

Kramer, Lawrence. *After the Lovedeath: Sexual Violence and the Making of Culture*. Berkeley, CA: University of California Press, 1997.

Rugoff, Kathy. "Opera and Other Kinds of Music." In *A Companion to Walt Whitman*. Edited by Donald D. Kummings, 257–71. Malden, MA: Blackwell Publishing, 2009.

12. Performance and Celebrity

Blake, David Haven. *Walt Whitman and the Culture of American Celebrity*. New Haven, CT: Yale University Press, 2006.

Braudy, Leo. *The Frenzy of Renown: Fame and Its History*. New York, NY: Vintage, 1997.

Dowling, David. *Capital Letters: Authorship in the Antebellum Literary Market*. Iowa City, IA: University of Iowa Press, 2009.

Folsom, Ed. *Walt Whitman's Native Representations*. New York, NY: Cambridge University Press, 1994.

Greenspan, Ezra. *Walt Whitman and the American Reader*. New York, NY: Cambridge University Press, 1990.

O'Neill, Bonnie Carr. "The Personal Public Sphere of Whitman's 1840s Journalism." *PMLA* 126.4 (2011), 983–98.

Reynolds, David S. *Walt Whitman's America: A Cultural Biography*. New York, NY: Alfred A. Knopf, 1995.

Robertson, Michael. *Worshipping Walt: The Whitman Disciples.* Princeton, NJ: Princeton University Press, 2008.

13. Visual Arts and Photography

Bohan, Ruth L. "Robert Henri, Walt Whitman and the American Artist," *Walt Whitman Quarterly Review* 29.4 (Spring 2012), 131–51.

Danly, Susan, and Cheryl Leibold. *Eakins and the Photograph.* Washington, DC, and London: Smithsonian Institution Press for the Pennsylvania Academy of the Fine Arts, 1994

Dinius, Marcy J. *The Camera and the Press: American Visual and Print Culture in the Age of the Daguerreotype.* Philadelphia, PA: University of Pennsylvania Press, 2012.

Dougherty, James. *Walt Whitman and the Citizen's Eye.* Baton Rouge, LA, and London: Louisiana State University Press, 1993.

Folsom, Ed. "'This heart's geography map': The Photographs of Walt Whitman." WWA.

Genoways, Ted. "'One goodshaped and wellhung man': Accentuated Sexuality and Uncertain Authorship of the Frontispiece to the 1855 Edition of *Leaves of Grass.*" In *Leaves of Grass: The Sesquicentennial Essays.* Edited by Susan Belasco, Ed Folsom, and Kenneth M. Price, 87–123. Lincoln, NE: University of Nebraska Press, 2007.

Miller, Edwin Haviland. *The Artistic Legacy of Walt Whitman.* New York, NY: New York University Press, 1970.

Reynolds, David S. *Walt Whitman's America: A Cultural Biography.* New York, NY: Alfred A. Knopf, 1995.

14. Erotica

Beisel, Nicola. *Imperiled Innocents: Anthony Comstock and Family Reproduction in Victorian America.* Princeton, NJ: Princeton University Press, 1998.

Cohen, Patricia Cline, Timothy J. Gilfoyle, and Helen Lefkowitz Horowitz, in association with the American Antiquarian Society. *The Flash Press: Sporting Male Weeklies in 1840s New York.* Chicago, IL: University of Chicago Press, 2008.

Comstock, Anthony. *Frauds Exposed; or, How the People are Deceived and Robbed, and Youth Corrupted.* New York, NY: J. Howard Brown, 1880.

Gilfoyle, Timothy J. *City of Eros: New York City, Prostitution, and the Commercialization of Sex, 1820–1920.* New York, NY: W. W. Norton, 1992.

Henkin, David. *City Reading: Written Words and Public Spaces in Antebellum New York.* New York, NY: Columbia University Press, 1998.

Luskey, Brian P., and Wendy A. Woloson, eds. *Capitalism by Gaslight: Illuminating the Economy of Nineteenth-Century America.* Philadelphia, PA: University of Pennsylvania Press, 2015.

Millner, Michael. *Fever Reading: Affect and Reading Badly in the Early American Public Sphere*. Durham, NH: University of New Hampshire Press, 2012.

15. Notebooks and Manuscripts

Bowers, Fredson, ed. *Whitman's Manuscripts: Leaves of Grass (1860), A Parallel Text*. Chicago, IL: University of Chicago Press, 1955.

Folsom, Ed. *Whitman Making Books/Books Making Whitman: A Catalog and Commentary*. Iowa City, IA: Obermann Center for Advanced Studies, 2005.

Folsom, Ed, and Kenneth M. Price. *Re-Scripting Walt Whitman: An Introduction to His Life and Work*. Malden, MA: Blackwell, 2005.

Genoways, Ted. *Walt Whitman and the Civil War: America's Poet during the Lost Years of 1860–1862*. Berkeley, CA: University of California Press, 2009.

Higgins, Andrew C. "Wage Slavery and the Composition of *Leaves of Grass*: The 'Talbot Wilson' Notebook." *Walt Whitman Quarterly Review* 20.2 (2002), 53–77.

Miller, Matt. *Collage of Myself: Walt Whitman and the Making of Leaves of Grass*. Lincoln, NE: University of Nebraska Press, 2010.

Stovall, Floyd. "Dating Whitman's Early Notebooks." *Studies in Bibliography* 24 (1971), 197–204.

Stovall, Floyd. *The Foreground of Leaves of Grass*. Charlottesville, VA: University Press of Virginia, 1974.

Zweig, Paul. *Walt Whitman: The Making of the Poet*. New York, NY: Basic Books, 1984.

16. Bookmaking

Bowers, Fredson. *Textual and Literary Criticism*. New York, NY: Cambridge University Press, 1966.

Cohen, Matt. "'To read the workmen direct': Horace Traubel and the Work of the 1855 Edition of *Leaves of Grass*." In *Leaves of Grass: The Sesquicentennial Essays*. Edited by Susan Belasco, Ed Folsom, and Kenneth M. Price, 299–320. Lincoln, NE: University of Nebraska Press, 2007.

Gailey, Amanda. "The Publishing History of *Leaves of Grass*." In *A Companion to Walt Whitman*. Edited by Donald D. Kummings, 409–38. Malden, MA: Blackwell Publishing, Ltd.

Genoways, Ted. "The Disorder of *Drum-Taps*." *Walt Whitman Quarterly Review* 24.2 (2006), 98–117.

Greenspan, Ezra. *Walt Whitman and the American Reader*. New York, NY: Cambridge University Press, 1990.

Miller, Matt. "The Cover of the First Edition of *Leaves of Grass*." *Walt Whitman Quarterly Review* 24.2 (2006), 85–97.

Moon, Michael. *Disseminating Whitman: Revision and Corporeality in Leaves of Grass.* Cambridge, MA: Harvard University Press, 1991.

Schmidgall, Gary. "'Damn 'em, God bless 'em!': Whitman and Traubel on the Makers of Books." *Walt Whitman Quarterly Review* 24.2 (2006), 141–57.

17. The Literary Marketplace

Blake, David Haven. *Walt Whitman and the Culture of American Celebrity.* New Haven, CT: Yale University Press, 2006.

Buinicki, Martin T. *Walt Whitman's Reconstruction: Poetry and Publishing between Memory and History.* Iowa City, IA: University of Iowa Press, 2011.

Dowling, David. *Capital Letters: Authorship in the Antebellum Literary Market.* Iowa City, IA: University of Iowa Press, 2009.

Everton, Michael. *The Grand Chorus of Complaint: Authors and the Business Ethics of American Publishing.* New York, NY: Oxford University Press, 2011.

Grossman, Jay. *Reconstituting the American Renaissance: Emerson, Whitman, and the Politics of Representation.* Durham, NC: Duke University Press, 2003.

Jackson, Leon. *The Business of Letters: Authorial Economies in Antebellum America.* Stanford, CA: Stanford University Press, 2008.

Whitley, Edward. *American Bards: Walt Whitman and Other Unlikely Candidates for National Poet.* Chapel Hill, NC: University of North Carolina Press, 2010.

18. Transatlantic Book Distribution

Blodgett, Harold. *With Walt Whitman in England.* New York, NY: Russell & Russell, 1939.

Buinicki, Martin T. "Walt Whitman and the Copyright Question." *American Literary History* 15 (2003), 248–75.

DeSpain, Jessica. *Nineteenth-Century Transatlantic Reprinting and the Embodied Book.* London: Routledge, 2014.

Folsom, Ed. "*Leaves of Grass, Junior*: Whitman's Compromise with Discriminating Tastes." *American Literature* 63.4 (1991), 641–63.

Gohdes, Clarence. *American Literature in Nineteenth-Century England.* Carbondale, IL: Southern Illinois University Press, 1944.

Grünzweig, Walter. "'For America – For All the Earth': Walt Whitman as an International(ist) Poet." In *Breaking Bounds: Whitman and American Cultural Studies.* Edited by Betsy Erkkila and Jay Grossman, 238–50. New York, NY: Oxford University Press, 1996.

Henkel, Scott. "Leaves of Grassroots Politics: Whitman, Carlyle, and the Imagination of *Democratic Vistas.*" *Walt Whitman Quarterly Review* 27.3 (2010), 101–26.

Price, Kenneth M., ed. *Walt Whitman: The Contemporary Reviews.* New York, NY: Cambridge University Press, 1996.

Thomas, M. Wynn. *Transatlantic Connections: Whitman U.S., Whitman U.K.* Iowa City, IA: University of Iowa Press, 2005.

19. Transcendentalism

Buell, Lawrence. *Literary Transcendentalism: Style and Vision in the American Renaissance.* Ithaca, NY: Cornell University Press, 1973.
Gura, Philip F. *American Transcendentalism. A History.* New York, NY: Hill & Wang, 2008.
Killingsworth, M. Jimmie. *The Growth of Leaves of Grass: The Organic Tradition in Whitman Studies.* Columbia, DC: Camden House, 1993.
Packer, Barbara. "The Transcendentalists." In *The Cambridge History of American Literature Vol. 2.* Edited by Sacvan Bercovitch, 329–604. New York, NY: Cambridge University Press, 1995.
Schober, Regina. "Transcending Boundaries: The Network Concept in Nineteenth-Century American Philosophy and Literature." *American Literature* 86.3 (2014), 493–521.

20. Philosophy

Erkkila, Betsy. *Whitman the Political Poet.* New York, NY: Oxford University Press, 1989.
Kateb, George. "Walt Whitman and the Culture of Democracy." *Political Theory* 18.4 (1990), 545–600.
Killingsworth, M. Jimmie. *Whitman's Poetry of the Body: Sexuality, Politics, and the Text.* Chapel Hill, NC: University of North Carolina Press, 1989.
Larson, Kerry C. *Whitman's Drama of Consensus.* Chicago, IL: University of Chicago Press, 1988.
Mack, Stephen John. *The Pragmatic Whitman: Reimagining American Democracy.* Iowa City, IA: University of Iowa Press, 2002.
Thomas, M. Wynn. "Whitman and the American Democratic Identity Before and During the Civil War." *Journal of American Studies* 15.1 (1981), 73–93.
Trachtenberg, Alan. "Whitman's Lesson of the City." In *Breaking Bounds: Whitman and American Cultural Studies.* Edited by Betsy Erkkila and Jay Grossman, 163–73. New York, NY: Oxford University Press, 1996.

21. Bohemianism

Cottom, Daniel. *International Bohemia: Scenes of Nineteenth-Century Life.* Philadelphia, PA: University of Pennsylvania Press, 2013.
Genoways, Ted. *Walt Whitman and the Civil War: America's Poet during the Lost Years of 1860–1862.* Berkeley, CA: University of California Press, 2009.
Karbiener, Karen. "Whitman at Pfaff's: Personal Space, a Public Place, and the Boundary-Breaking Poems of *Leaves of Grass* (1860)." In *Literature of*

New York. Edited by Sabrina Fuchs-Abrams, 1–38. Newcastle upon Tyne: Cambridge Scholars Publishing, 2009.

Lause, Mark. *The Antebellum Crisis and America's First Bohemians*. Kent, OH: Kent Sate University Press, 2009.

Levin, Joanna. *Bohemia in America, 1858–1920*. Stanford, CA: Stanford University Press, 2010.

Martin, Justin. *Rebel Souls: Walt Whitman and America's First Bohemians*. Boston, MA: Da Capo Press, 2014.

Whitley, Edward, and Robert Weidman, "The Vault at Pfaff's: An Archive of Art and Literature by the Bohemians of Antebellum New York." Lehigh University, http://lehigh.edu/pfaffs.

22. Gender

Aspiz, Harold. *Walt Whitman and the Body Beautiful*. Urbana, IL: University of Illinois, 1980.

Butler, Judith. *Undoing Gender*. New York, NY: Routledge, 2004.

—.*Bodies that Matter: On the Discursive Limits of Sex*. New York, NY: Routledge, 2011.

Foucault, Michel. *The History of Sexuality: Volume I: An Introduction*. New York, NY: Pantheon, 1978.

Killingsworth, M. Jimmie. *Whitman's Poetry of the Body: Sexuality, Politics, and the Text*. Chapel Hill, NC: University of North Carolina Press, 1989.

Moon, Michael. *Disseminating Whitman: Revision and Corporeality in Leaves of Grass*. Cambridge, MA: Harvard University Press, 1993.

Pollak, Vivian R. *The Erotic Whitman*. Berkeley, CA: University of California Press, 2000.

Reynolds, David S. *Walt Whitman's America: A Cultural Biography*. New York, NY: Knopf, 1995.

23. Sexuality

Chauncey, George. *Gay New York: Gender, Urban Culture, and the Making of the Gay Male World 1890–1940*. New York, NY: Basic, 1994.

Erkkila, Betsy, and Jay Grossman, eds. *Breaking Bounds: Whitman and American Cultural Studies*. New York, NY: Oxford University Press, 1996.

Folsom, Ed, and Ted Genoways. "'This Heart's Geography's Map': The Photographs of Walt Whitman." *Virginia Quarterly Review* 81.2 (2005), 6–15.

Garman, Bryan K. *A Race of Singers: Whitman's Working-Class Hero from Guthrie to Springsteen*. Chapel Hill, NC: University of North Carolina Press, 2000.

Looby, Christopher. "The Literariness of Sexuality: Or, How to Do the (Literary) History of (American) Sexuality." *American Literary History* 25.4 (2013), 841–54.

Marsden, Steve. "'A Woman Waits for Me': Anne Gilchrist's Reading of *Leaves of Grass.*" *Walt Whitman Quarterly Review* 23.3 (2006), 95–125.

Marsh, John. *In Walt We Trust: How a Queer Socialist Poet Can Save America from Itself.* New York, NY: Monthly Review Press, 2015.

Moon, Michael. *Disseminating Whitman: Revision and Corporeality in Leaves of Grass.* Cambridge, MA: Harvard University Press, 1991.

Whitely, Edward. "Elizabeth Porter Gould, Author of *Leaves of Grass*: Gender, Editing, and the Nineteenth-Century Literary Marketplace." *ELH* 75.2 (2008), 471–96.

24. Politics

Erkkila, Betsy. *Whitman the Political Poet.* New York, NY: Oxford University Press, 1989.

___, and Jay Grossman, eds. *Breaking Bounds: Whitman and American Cultural Studies.* New York, NY: Oxford University Press, 1996.

Grossman, Allen. "The Poetics of Union in Whitman and Lincoln: An Inquiry toward the Relationship Between Art and Policy," in *The American Renaissance Reconsidered.* Edited by Walter Benn Michaels and Donald E. Pease, 183–208. Baltimore, MD: The Johns Hopkins University Press, 1985.

Klammer, Martin. *Whitman, Slavery, and the Emergence of Leaves of Grass.* University Park, PA: Pennsylvania State University Press, 1995.

Larson, Kerry. *Whitman's Drama of Consensus.* Chicago, IL: University of Chicago Press, 1988.

Reynolds, David. *Walt Whitman's America: A Cultural Biography.* New York, NY: Knopf, 1995.

25. Imperialism and Globalization

Allen, Gay Wilson, and Ed Folsom, eds. *Walt Whitman and the World.* Iowa City, IA: University of Iowa Press, 1995.

Erkkila, Betsy. *Whitman the Political Poet.* New York, NY: Oxford University Press, 1989.

Mendelson, Maurice. *Life and Work of Walt Whitman: A Soviet View.* Moscow: Progress, 1976.

Rumyantseva, Nelly, ed. *Marx and Engels on the United States.* Moscow: Progress, 1979.

Schueller, Malini Johar. *U.S. Orientalisms: Race, Nation, and Gender in Literature, 1790–1890.* Ann Arbor, MI: University of Michigan Press, 1998.

26. Nineteenth-Century Religion

Bush, Harold K., and Brian Yothers, eds. *Above the American Renaissance: David S. Reynolds and the Spiritual Imagination in American Literary Studies.* Amherst, MA: University of Massachusetts Press, 2018.

Butler, Jon. *Awash in a Sea of Faith: Christianizing the American People.* Cambridge, MA: Harvard University Press, 1992.

Folsom, Ed. "That Towering Bulge of Pure White: Whitman, Melville, the Capitol Dome, and Black America." *Leviathan: A Journal of Melville Studies* 14.1 (2014), 87–120.

Modern, John Lardas. *Secularism in Antebellum America.* Chicago, IL: University of Chicago Press, 2011.

Spengemann, William C. *Three American Poets: Walt Whitman, Emily Dickinson, and Herman Melville.* South Bend, IN: University of Notre Dame Press, 2010.

Tyrell, Ian. *Reforming the World: The Creation of America's Moral Empire.* Princeton, NJ: Princeton University Press, 2010.

27. Civil War

Alcott, Louisa May. "*Hospital Sketches.*" In *Alternative Alcott.* Edited by Elaine Showalter. New Brunswick, NJ: Rutgers University Press, 1988.

Fenton, Elizabeth, and Valerie Rohy. "Whitman, Lincoln, and the Union of Men." *ESQ* 55.3–4 (2009), 237–67.

Hollis, C. Carroll. *Language and Style in Leaves of Grass.* Baton Rouge, LA: Louisiana State University Press, 1983.

McWilliams, John P., Jr. "'Drum-Taps' and *Battle-Pieces*: The Blossom of War." *American Quarterly* 23.2 (1971), 181–201.

Moon, Michael. "Solitude, Singularity, Solidarity: Whitman vis-à-vis Fourier." *ELH* 73.2 (2006), 303–23.

Nathanson, Tenney. *Whitman's Presence: Body, Voice, and Writing in Leaves of Grass.* New York, NY: New York University Press, 1992.

Roper, Robert. *Now the Drum of War: Walt Whitman and His Brothers in the Civil War.* New York, NY: Walker Books, 2008.

Shively, Charley, ed., *Calamus Lovers: Walt Whitman's Working-Class Camerados.* San Francisco, CA: Gay Sunshine Press, 1987.

28. Reconstruction

Blight, David W. *Race and Reunion: The Civil War in American Memory.* Cambridge, MA: Harvard University Press, 2001.

Buinicki, Martin T. *Walt Whitman's Reconstruction: Poetry and Publishing between Memory and History.* Iowa City, IA: University of Iowa Press, 2011.

Folsom, Ed. "Lucifer and Ethiopia: Whitman, Race, and Politics before the Civil War and After." In *A Historical Guide to Walt Whitman.* Edited by David S. Reynolds, 45–95. New York, NY: Oxford University Press, 2000.

Foner, Eric. *Reconstruction: America's Unfinished Revolution, 1863–1877.* New York, NY: Harper Perennial, 2014.

Gilette, William. *Retreat from Reconstruction, 1869–1879.* Baton Rouge, LA: Louisiana State University Press, 1979.

Mancuso, Luke. *The Strange Sad War Revolving: Walt Whitman, Reconstruction, and the Emergence of Black Citizenship, 1865–1876.* Columbia, SC: Camden House, 1997.

Murray, Martin. "Washington, D.C." In *Walt Whitman: An Encyclopedia.* Edited by J. R. LeMaster and Donald D. Kummings. New York, NY: Garland Publishing, 1998.

Richardson, Heather Cox. *The Death of Reconstruction: Race, Labor, and Politics in the Post-Civil War North, 1865–1901.* Cambridge, MA: Harvard University Press, 2001.

Thomas, M. Wynn. *The Lunar Light of Whitman's Poetry.* Cambridge, MA: Harvard University Press, 1987.

29. Death and Mourning

Aspiz, Harold. *So Long!: Walt Whitman's Poetry of Death.* Tuscaloosa, AL: Alabama University Press, 1996.

Breitweiser, Mitchell. *National Melancholy: Mourning and Opportunity in Classic American Literature.* Stanford, CA: Stanford University Press, 2007.

Cavitch, Max. *American Elegy: The Poetry of Mourning from the Puritans to Whitman.* Minneapolis, MN: University of Minnesota Press, 2007.

Farrell, James. *Inventing the American Way of Death.* Philadelphia, PA: Temple University Press, 1980.

Faust, Drew Gilpin. *This Republic of Suffering: Death and the American Civil War.* New York, NY: Knopf, 2008.

Henderson, Desiree. *Grief and Genre in American Literature, 1790–1870.* New York, NY: Routledge, 2011.

Laderman, Gary. *The Sacred Remains: American Attitudes Toward Death, 1799–1883.* New Haven, CT: Yale University Press, 1996.

Luciano, Dana. *Sacred Time and the Body in Nineteenth-Century American Literature.* New York, NY: New York University Press, 2007.

Pike, Martha, and Judith Armstrong, eds. *A Time to Mourn: Expressions of Grief in Nineteenth Century America.* Stony Brook, NY: Museums at Stony Brook, 1980.

Vendler, Helen. *Invisible Listeners: Lyric Intimacy in Herbert, Whitman, and Ashbery.* Princeton, PA: Princeton University Press, 2005.

30. Slavery and Abolition

Erkkila, Betsy. *Whitman the Political Poet.* New York, NY: Oxford University Press, 1989.

Folsom, Ed. "Lucifer and Ethiopia: Whitman, Race, and Poetics before the Civil War and After." In *A Historical Guide to Walt Whitman.* Edited by David S. Reynolds, 45–95. New York, NY: Oxford University Press, 2000.

Higgins, Andrew. "Wage Slavery and the Composition of *Leaves of Grass*: The 'Talbot Wilson' Notebook." *Walt Whitman Quarterly Review* 20.2 (2002), 53–77.

Klammer, Martin. *Whitman, Slavery, and the Emergence of Leaves of Grass.* University Park, PA: Pennsylvania State University Press, 1995.

Price, Kenneth M. "The Lost Negress of 'Song of Myself' and the Jolly Young Wenches of Civil War Washington." In *Leaves of Grass: The Sesquicentennial Essays.* Edited by Susan Belasco, Ed Folsom, and Kenneth M. Price, 224–43. Lincoln, NA: University of Nebraska Press, 2007.

Wilson, Ivy G., ed. *Whitman Noir: Black America and the Good Gray Poet.* Iowa City, IA: University of Iowa Press, 2014.

31. Native American and Immigrant Cultures

Berkhofer, Robert F. *The White Man's Indian: Images of the American Indian from Columbus to the Present.* New York, NY: Vintage, 1979.

Blackhawk, Ned. *Violence over the Land: Indians and Empires in the Early American West.* Cambridge, MA: Harvard University Press, 2008.

Burrows, Edwin G., and Mike Wallace. *Gotham: A History of New York City to 1898.* New York, NY: Oxford University Press, 2000.

Higham, John. *Strangers in the Land: Patterns of American Nativism 1860–1925,* rev. edn. New Brunswick, NJ: Rutgers University Press, 2002.

Krieg, Joann P. *Whitman and the Irish.* Iowa City, IA: University of Iowa Press, 2000.

32. The Rank and File

Bellot, Marc. "'The true America, heir of the past so grand. . .': Walt Whitman et l'épopée américaine." *Cercles: Revue Pluidisciplinaire du Monde Anglophone* 23 (2012), 4–14.

Cohen, Matt. "'To reach the workmen direct': Horace Traubel and the Work of the 1855 *Leaves of Grass.*" In *Leaves of Grass: The Sesquicentennial Essays.* Edited by Susan Belasco, Ed Folsom, and Kenneth M. Price, 299–320. Lincoln, NE: University of Nebraska Press, 2007.

Dow, William. "Whitman's 1855 *Leaves of Grass*: The Incarnational and 'Hard Work and Blood.'" In *American Poetry: Whitman to the Present.* Edited by Robert Rehder and Patrick Vincent, 35–52. Tübingen, Germany: Gunter Narr, 2006.

Erkkila, Betsy. "Melville, Whitman, and the Tribulations of Democracy." In *A Companion to American Literature and Culture.* Edited by Paul Lauter, 250 83. Hoboken, NJ: Wiley-Blackwell, 2010.

—. "Whitman, Marx, and the American 1848." In *Leaves of Grass: The Sesquicentennial Essays.* Edited by Susan Belasco, Ed Folsom, and Kenneth M. Price, 35–61. Lincoln, NE: University of Nebraska Press, 2007.

Hunnicutt, Benjamin Kline. "Walt Whitman's 'Higher Progress' and Shorter Work Hours." *Walt Whitman Quarterly Review* 26.2 (2008), 92–109.

Satelmajer, Ingrid. "Publishing Pfaff's: Henry Clapp and Poetry in the *Saturday Press.*" In *Whitman among the Bohemians.* Edited by Joanna Levin and Edward Whitley, 37–52. Iowa City, IA: University of Iowa Press, 2014.

Stacy, Jason. *Walt Whitman's Multitudes: Labor Reform and Persona in Whitman's Journalism and the First Leaves of Grass, 1840–1855.* New York, NY: Peter Lang, 2008.

33. Romanticism

Beiser, Frederick C. *German Idealism: The Struggle against Subjectivism, 1781–1801.* Cambridge, MA: Harvard University Press, 2002.

Day, Aidan. *Romanticism.* New York, NY: Routledge, 1996.

Eleanor, Sister Mary. "Hedge's *Prose Writers of Germany* as a Source of Whitman's Knowledge of German Philosophy." *Modern Language Notes* 61 (June 1946), 381–88.

Lacoue-Labarthe, Philippe, and Jean-Luc Nancy. *The Literary Absolute: The Theory of Literature in German Romanticism,* translated by Philip Barnard and Cheryl Lester. Albany, NY: State University of New York Press, 1988.

Whil, Gary. "The Manuscript of Walt Whitman's 'Sunday Evening Lectures.'" *Walt Whitman Quarterly Review* 18.3 (2001), 107–33.

34. The Natural World

Bennett, Jane. "Of Material Sympathies, Paracelsus, and Whitman." In *Material Ecocriticism.* Edited by Serenella Iovino and Serpil Opperman, 239–52. Bloomington, IN: Indiana University Press, 2014.

Fletcher, Angus. *A New Theory for American Poetry: Democracy, the Environment, and the Future of Imagination.* Cambridge, MA: Harvard University Press, 2004.

Gerhardt, Christine. *A Place for Humility: Whitman, Dickinson, and the Natural World.* Iowa City, IA: University of Iowa Press, 2014.

Handley, George. *New World Poetics: Nature and the Adamic Imagination of Whitman, Neruda, and Walcott.* Athens, GA: University of Georgia Press, 2007.

Killingsworth, M. Jimmie. "Nature." In *A Companion to Walt Whitman.* Edited by Donald D. Kummings, 311–24. Malden, MA: Blackwell, 2006.

Moe, Aaron. *Zoopoetics: Animals and the Making of Poetry.* Lanham, MD: Lexington, 2014.

Piasecki, Bruce. "American Literary Environmentalism before Darwin." In *Teaching Environmental Literature: Materials, Methods, Resources.* Edited by Frederick O. Waage, 9–18. New York, NY: Modern Language Association, 1985.

Tichi, Cecelia. *New World, New Earth: Environmental Reform in American Literature from the Puritans through Whitman.* New Haven, CT: Yale University Press, 1979.

Walls, Laura Dassow. *The Passage to Cosmos: Alexander Von Humboldt and the Shaping of America.* Chicago, IL: University of Chicago Press, 2009.

Warren, Jim. "Whitman Land: John Burroughs's Pastoral Criticism," *Isle* 8.1 (2001), 83–96.

35. Science and Medicine

Beaver, Joseph. *Walt Whitman: Poet of Science.* New York, NY: Octagon Books, 1974.

Davis, Robert Leigh. *Whitman and the Romance of Medicine.* Berkley, CA: University of California Press, 1997.

Hsu, David. "Walt Whitman: An American Civil War Nurse Who Witnessed the Advent of Modern American Medicine." *Archives of Environmental & Occupational Health* 65.4 (2010), 238–39.

Morris, Roy, Jr. *The Better Angel: Walt Whitman in the Civil War.* New York, NY: Oxford University Press, 2000.

Tuggle, Lindsay. *The Afterlives of Specimens: Medicine, Mourning, and Whitman's Civil War.* Iowa City, IA: University of Iowa Press, 2017.

36. Disciples

Kuebrich, David. *Minor Prophecy: Walt Whitman's New American Religion.* Bloomington, IN: Indiana University Press, 1989.

——. "Religion and the Poet-Prophet." In *A Companion to Walt Whitman.* Edited by Donald D. Kummings, 197–215. Oxford: Blackwell, 2006.

Robertson, Michael. *Worshipping Walt: The Whitman Disciples.* Princeton, NJ: Princeton University Press, 2008.

——. "Reading Poetry Religiously: The Walt Whitman Fellowship and Seeker Spirituality." In *American Religious Liberalism.* Edited by Leigh E. Schmidt and Sally M. Promey, 17–38. Bloomington, IN: Indiana University Press, 2012.

Schmidt, Leigh Eric. *Restless Souls: The Making of American Spirituality.* New York, NY: Harper Collins, 2005.

37. Influence in the United States

Cherkovski, Neeli. *Whitman's Wild Children.* Venice, CA: Lapis Press, 1988.

Martin, Robert K. *The Continuing Presence of Walt Whitman: The Life after the Life.* Iowa City, IA: University of Iowa Press, 1992.

Morris, Timothy. *Becoming Canonical in American Poetry.* Champaign, IL: University of Illinois Press, 1995.
Pöhlmann, Sascha. *Future-Founding Poetry: Topographies of Beginnings from Whitman to the Twenty-First Century.* Rochester, NY: Camden House, 2015.
Tapscott, Stephen. *American Beauty: William Carlos Williams and the Modernist Whitman.* New York, NY: Columbia University Press, 1984.

38. Impact on the World

Folsom, Ed, Éric Athenot, Blake Bronson-Bartlett, Walter Grünzweig, Vanessa Steinroetter, Marina Camboni, Marta Skwara, Matt Cohen, Nicole Gray, and Rey Rocha. "Translating 'Poets to Come' in Five Languages." 2012, WWA.
Franklin, Kelly Scott. "'Nicaraguan Words': José Coronel, the Vanguardia, and Whitman's 'Language Experiment.'" *Walt Whitman Quarterly Review* 34.1 (2016), 2–34.
Handley, George B. "On Reading South in the New World: Whitman, Martí, Glissant, and the Hegelian Dialectic." *Mississippi Quarterly* 56.4 (2003), 521–44.
Martin, Robert K. "Walt Whitman and Thomas Mann." *Walt Whitman Quarterly Review* 4.1 (1986), 1–6.
Rongqiang, Liu. "Whitman's Soul in China: Guo Moruo's Poetry in the New Culture Movement." In *Whitman East and West.* Edited by Ed Folsom, 172–86. Iowa City, IA: University of Iowa Press, 2002.
Rumeau, Delphine. "Federico García Lorca and Pablo Neruda's Odes to Walt Whitman: A Set of Choral Poetry." *Comparative Literature Studies* 51.3 (2014), 418–38.
Shusen, Liu. "Gu Cheng and Walt Whitman: In Search of New Poetics." In *Whitman East and West.* Edited by Ed Folsom, 208–20. Iowa City, IA: University of Iowa Press, 2002.
Sigurjonsdottir, Sigurbjorg. "Voices of Many Together in Two: Whitman's America and Ngũgĩ's Kenya." In *Critical Essays on Ngũgĩ wa Thiong'o.* Edited by Peter Nazareth, 93–122. New York, NY: Twayne, 2000.
Skwara, Marta. "The Poet of the Great Reality: Czeslaw Milosz's Readings of Walt Whitman." *Walt Whitman Quarterly Review* 26.1 (2008), 1–22.
Sommer, Doris. "José Martí, Author of Walt Whitman." In *José Martí's "Our America": From National to Hemispheric Cultural Studies.* Edited by Jeffrey Belnap and Raúl Fernández. (Durham, NC: Duke University Press, 1998), 77–90.

Index